The SECRET DOCTRINE *of the* KABBALAH

RECOVERING THE KEY TO HEBRAIC SACRED SCIENCE

LEONORA LEET

Inner Traditions
Rochester, Vermont

Inner Traditions International
One Park Street
Rochester, Vermont 05767
www.InnerTraditions.com

Library of Congress Cataloging-in-Publication Data

Leet, Leonora.
     The secret doctrine of the Kabbalah : recovering the key to Hebraic
sacred science / Leonora Leet.
        p.   cm.
     Includes bibliographical references and index.
     ISBN 0-89281-724-0
     1. Cabala—History. 2. Judaism and science. 3. Geometry—Miscellanea.
4. Physics—Miscellanea. I. Title.
BM526.L44   1999
296.1'6—dc21   99-24385
                                                  CIP

Printed and bound in the United States

10 9 8 7 6

Text design and layout by Crystal Roberts
This book was typeset in Goudy

The SECRET DOCTRINE *of the* KABBALAH

To my parents
Cecil Robert Leet and Tania Neznir Leet
in loving memory

Contents

Preface   x

PART 1: THEORETICAL FOUNDATIONS

1. **An Introduction to the Priestly Legacy**   2
   A Brief History of the Hebraic Priestly Tradition   2
   Kabbalistic Sacred Science:
     Gematria and the Tree of Life Diagram   11
   The Order and Implications of This Study   24
2. **The Hebraic Secret Doctrine of the Son**   30
   Texts of the Biblical Period   30
   The Merkabah Texts   46
   The Kabbalistic Texts   55
   Scholem and the Secret Doctrine   65
   The Esoteric Meaning of the Sh'ma   68
3. **Sacred Science: Modes and Meaning**   74
   The Pythagorean Mode   74
   The Kabbalistic Mode in the *Sefer Yetzirah*   87
   Meaning and the Complementarity of Shape and Sound   94
   Language and the Final Explanation   100

PART 2: THE KABBALISTIC SACRED SCIENCE OF LANGUAGE

4. **The Tetragrammaton and Hebraic Sacred Science**   117
   The Tetragrammaton and the Covenant of Number   117
   The Tetragrammaton Expansions   140
   The Tetragrammaton and the Vowel-Letters   148
   Pronunciation of the Tetragrammaton   158

5. **The Sacred Science of Sound and Spiritual Practice**   **165**
   The Vowel Sounds and the Body   165
   The Sefirot, the Chakras, and the Double Heart   169
   Introduction to the Practice of Vowel Intoning   175
   Vowel Intoning, the Harmonics, and the Sefirot   179
   Ish in Hebrew and Sanskrit   190

PART 3: THE KABBALISTIC SACRED SCIENCE OF GEOMETRY

6. **Kabbalistic Geometry and the Cosmic Genesis**   **202**
   The Science of Expressive Form   204
   The Hexagram and Hebraic Sacred Science   212
   Hexagram Construction and the Zoharic Account
       of Creation   218
   The Hexagram of Creation: Recovering the
       Esoteric Keys to Genesis   222
   Derivation of the Tree of Life Diagram   232
7. **Kabbalistic Geometry and the Genesis of the Son**   **252**
   Decoding the *Sefer Yetzirah* Diagram:
       The Sefirot and Meditation   252
   Solution to the Mystery of the *Sefer Yetzirah* Diagram   257
   The *Sefer Yetzirah* Diagram and the Lurianic Partzufim   270
   Final Implications of the *Sefer Yetzirah* Tree   288
8. **Kabbalistic Geometry and the Tree of Knowledge**   **295**
   The Sixfold Tree of Knowledge   295
   Relationship of the Sixfold and *Sefer Yetzirah* Trees   304
   Relationship of the Tree of Life Diagram to
       the *Sefer Yetzirah*   317

PART 4: SYNTHESES OF SACRED AND SECULAR SCIENCE

9. **A Synthesis of Sacred Science and Quantum Physics**   **332**
   The Matrix Model   332
   The Hadron Model   339
   The Hadron-Field Model   347
   The Lepton Model   356
   The Atomic Model   365
   Concluding Comments   369
   Epilogue on Probability   376

10. **A Synthesis of Kabbalistic and Quantum Cosmology**   380

     Tzimtzum vs. the Big Bang   380

     Dimensions of the Sabbatical Cosmos   390

     GUT Cosmology and the Four Cosmic Worlds   396

     Quantum Cosmology and the Future Worlds   403

Notes   413

Bibliography   442

Index of Persons   449

Index of Primary Sources   453

Index of Subjects   455

Preface

This is the second of what will finally be four books on the Kabbalah to result from a project begun in 1978 with the accidental discovery of what I have ever since believed to be the ultimate geometric source of the Kabbalistic Tree of Life Diagram, the major cosmological diagram of Western esoteric thought. Though this source diagram will only be a minor concern of the present book, the initial exploration of the Kabbalah undertaken from its perspective led in many unexpected but fruitful directions, the most theoretically significant of which have been gathered together in this volume and given the special focus of their shared subject matter, which can allow them to stand alone as a cohesive whole. Another major section of that project, concerned with Jewish spiritual practices, was published by Inner Traditions under the title *Renewing the Covenant: A Kabbalistic Guide to Jewish Spirituality*, a book that should complement the more theoretical emphases of the present volume. And as the remaining volumes appear, each will add new facets to the interpretation of the Jewish esoteric tradition being here developed that will both build on the foundations already presented and serve reciprocally to enlarge their implications.

The geometric discovery that was to initiate my serious study of the Kabbalah was partly the result of my initial exposure to Pythagorean geometry. In the fall of 1976 I took a course on such geometry with Robert Lawlor at a place called Lindisfarne, an institute founded by William Irwin Thompson that flourished for two and a half years in New York City and served me as something of a graduate school of esoteric learning at a time when I was undergoing a personal paradigm shift. Lawlor's explanations of the meaningfulness of geometric forms and processes gave a clarity to certain concepts that otherwise would not have been rationally acceptable to me, and my many quotations from his published works are a partial indication of my indebtedness to him.

By the time I made my initial geometric discovery in June of 1978, my exploration of various Western and Eastern esoteric traditions had finally brought me to the Kabbalah, with its strange, seemingly arbitrary diagram, and it was the convergence of these two streams of sacred geometry in my own awareness that enabled me to recognize both the fact and the importance of my chance discovery of a geometric key to the Tree of Life Diagram. Though I may not have been the scholar of the Kabbalah that I am of Renaissance English literature, my skills as a literary critic have proved to be just the hermeneutical tools needed to do the mode of modern Kabbalistic geometry I have called the Science of Expressive Form and which provided me with the new mode of access to the core of this ancient Hebraic tradition that was finally to reveal its most secret doctrine.

As I began the serious study of the Kabbalah, I sought a teacher, and I almost immediately found myself in the classes that Aryeh Kaplan was conducting in his Brooklyn home on the *Sefer Yetzirah*. The fifteen months we spent studying every word of this first extant and most geometric text of the Kabbalah laid a firm foundation for my later independent study of this tradition as well as the independent analyses of the geometry and meaning of this short but seminal text appearing in my book. Kaplan approached the Kabbalah not only as the scholar he assuredly was but as a Kabbalist, one who believes it to be an ancient though developing tradition that enshrines a coherent key to cosmic functioning, a sacred science whose rigor can be brought into coherence with modern secular science. And it is just such a Kabbalist that I became. Not only did Kaplan's sense of the meaningfulness of the Kabbalah have a profound influence upon me, but he was also of immense help to me both directly and indirectly, pointing me to the textual sources of certain materials that I needed and, in his works, providing me with a wealth of newly translated texts that, however differently I may have interpreted them from his own surrounding commentary, became the basis of much of my own analysis of this tradition. My indebtedness to Kaplan is apparent in the multitude of my quotations from his works, both those published and those still in manuscript. I am also very grateful to Seymour Applebaum, a psychiatrist, fellow student in Kaplan's classes, and editor of some of his posthumous papers, for having made certain of these manuscripts available to me, particularly Kaplan's unfinished translation of the first twelve chapters of the *Etz Chayyim* of Chayyim Vital, the most important text of the Lurianic Kabbalah.

Through all the long years that I have been engaged on this work, I have also been most beholden to my best friend, Esse Chasin, whose subtle knowledge of Hebrew was a treasure I could always call upon at need. All of my studies of biblical Hebrew are indebted to her to some extent. If these analyses make any contribution to biblical studies, it will be partially due to the timely and knowing aid she gave me. I am also appreciative of the effort she devoted to translating parts of the *Etz Chayyim* and the *Temunah* for and with me. Finally, I am indebted to her for the assistance she gave me in understanding certain aspects of Jewish ritual and for the witness she bore to their power.

Of the various other individuals for whose support and aid I am especially grateful, the first I wish to acknowledge is Zalman Schachter-Shalomi, a major figure in the world of Jewish spirituality, whose great heart immediately intuited the nature and importance of my work and gave it his unstinting support. He was also one of two persons to whom I sent portions of the manuscript for review and whose supporting letters have been most helpful. The second person is my physicist colleague at St. John's University, Robert Finkel, to whom I had turned for advice regarding my studies of quantum physics. I discussed with him the ideas that would be developed in chapters 9 and 10, the former a new geometric modeling of all the particles in quantum physics and the latter a new interpretation of quantum cosmology, which in their final form he thought would have an impact on the philosophy of science.

There are a few additional scholars whose personal suggestions or comments to me I have acknowledged in notes, most prominently Stanley Krippner, Martin Samuel Cohen, Robert Zoller, and Santosh Desai. I would also now like to acknowledge the following individuals for their various contributions to this work: Avram Malowicki for his expert aid in Hebrew translation; David Finkelstein, Robert Lawlor, John Anthony

West, Joscelyn Godwin, and Antonio de Nicolás for reading and commenting on individual chapters; and for their most appreciated assistance in helping me to find the right publisher for this unusual work, John Anthony West, Maia Gregory, Richard Falk, William Irwin Thompson, Deborah Foreman, and, most importantly, Gerald Epstein. I also wish to express my gratitude to the editorial staff of Inner Traditions, most notably to Jon Graham, Rowan Jacobsen, and Cannon Labrie for the knowledgeable and sensitive support they have given to my works. I am particularly indebted to Cannon Labrie, for his many helpful suggestions during the final editing of the text.

Finally, I would like to acknowledge my great debt to St. John's University for its generous support of my research, including various research leaves and course reductions as well as help with the final word processing of the manuscript, and to give special thanks for the support given me by the former Vice President Paul T. Medici, the late Dean Fr. Thomas Hoar, C.M., the Associate Provost Willard Gingerich, and my former chairperson, Angela Belli. I would also like to thank the Word Processing Center at St. John's University for the priority that was given to my constantly revised manuscript and to that best of typists, Kathy Leander. Perhaps even more important was the help given me on the computer graphics for this work by the Faculty Support Center, most substantially by its former director, Fr. Frank W. Sacks, C.M. Also of great help to me have been another of its former directors, Robert Lejeune, and its present manager, Louise McKenzie.

There is a final comment I would like to make about the approach of this work since its attempt to validate the substance of the Kabbalah is one that goes counter to the direction of academic scholarship on the Kabbalah, whose primary concern has been with the circumstances of kabbalistic texts and schools in terms largely of cultural history. Though I have both made use of this research and will hopefully contribute something to it at various points in my analysis, my primary concern has rather been to reveal as best I could the vital meaning of this ancient esoteric lore, to show how its main tenets can be substantiated both by an understanding of its original sacred science and by its renewed practice. And I have also tried to show how this ancient science can provide guidelines for modern secular science leading to a truer theoretical formulation of its data, thus providing the needed new paradigm that can synthesize sacred and secular science into a coherent cosmology acceptable to the modern mind.

PART 1

Theoretical
Foundations

1

An Introduction to the Priestly Legacy

A Brief History of the Hebraic Priestly Tradition

Kabbalah is a word meaning "tradition," and it is a major thesis of this work that the tradition this esoteric movement was dedicated to transmit had its origin with the ancient Hebraic priesthood. For the two components of this hidden knowledge, a cosmology linking the processes of cosmic creation to its goal in human transformation and the sacred science that could demonstrate this purpose, can be shown to have either derived from or informed the two major functions of the priesthood: the ritual of animal sacrifice and the consecrating of sacred space. This volume will attempt to recover not only the main features of the priestly lore but its meaningfulness, that which in many guises through the millennia has continued to embody the secret heart of Jewish mysticism and give it vitality. But its explorations of this priestly knowledge and legacy will not stop with the clear textual evidence of this tradition it will trace from the Bible to the Kabbalah; it will also follow new experimental pathways to the sources of this knowledge as well as attempting a synthesis of this sacred scientific tradition with secular science.

The sacred science that engaged the priest-scientists of the Hebrew

Temple, as of so many ancient cultures, was focused on the three areas that could demonstrate the same unification of the finite with the infinite that was the central mystery of their cosmology. These three areas are geometry (both earthly and astronomical), sound (both harmonic and linguistic), and number: geometry involving the realm of the limited, sound of the unlimited, and number of that which can bring these inverse polarities into relationship. It is these same three areas of sacred science that will be shown to underlie the creation account in Genesis 1, the specific details of the numbered days being organized by the esoteric keys of the musical harmonics and the geometric form of the hexagram, the Star of David. The Kabbalah will also be shown to begin with this same conjunction of sound, form, and number in the process of creation, such an assertion appearing in the very first verse of the first extant text of the kabbalistic tradition, the *Sefer Yetzirah*. Thus between the writing or final redaction of the first chapters of Genesis and the *Sefer Yetzirah*, there was a continuity of understanding of the creative relationship of sound, form, and number that points to a traditional body of esoteric teachings and to institutions designed for its conservation.

This first section will attempt to sketch something of the history of Hebraic sacred science from its imputed priestly origins to its partial disclosure in cryptic kabbalistic texts, paying particular attention to the aspect of this sacred science that has had the most continuing importance. This is the geometry that finally surfaces in what would seem to have originally been an initiatic key, that of the kabbalistic Tree of Life Diagram. Introduced at the close of this section will also be the cosmological component of priestly understanding, the secret doctrine at its core. This subject will be explored extensively in chapter 2, which will provide fuller historical justification than what is offered here for a main thesis of this work, the priestly origin of the Jewish esoteric tradition. And following the present, brief survey of this thesis, there will be a further introductory discussion of the surviving elements of such priestly sacred science in the Kabbalah. This will first consider the practice of Gematria and then give more extended treatment to the traditional forms and meanings of the Tree of Life Diagram, both background treatments being essential for the later analyses. Finally, there will be a brief review of the contents and implications of this work.

Beginning this brief history with the point that evidence of a traditional body of esoteric learning implies the existence of institutions designed for its conservation, there seems little doubt that such institutions would have been the priesthood and the Temple, features of Jewish history for over one thousand years that have a natural connection with a geometrically based esoteric science wherever in the world they appear. For it is only the elite group that in any society is entrusted with the study and transmission of ancient geometric knowledge, a knowledge in which science and cosmology are joined, that feels compelled to erect temples, to give architectural form to its understanding of sacred space. Conversely, the erection of such a sacred space requires a knowledge of geometric proportions and the selection of ideal forms—epitomized by the cubic form of the Holy of Holies in the Mosaic Sanctuary—which demands the study of geometry. What is more, since the construction of a temple implies the imaginative grip of geometry upon the minds and hearts of its architects and builders, it follows that both this structure and the order of priests devoted to its service would be dedicated to the continuing study and development of this hidden learning, this in addition to their ritual services for the laity. The fact that entrance into the Hebrew Temple was reserved to the priesthood, and that entrance into the priesthood required an initiatic laying on of hands and other ritualized procedures for the conferral of power, further suggests the characteristics of a secret society devoted to study of the interrelated laws of creation and holy empowerment.

It can be postulated, then, that esoteric study of geometry, though clearly a continuous tradition, was particularly high at the three periods that show an enthusiastic interest in Temple construction: the Mosaically inspired construction of the desert Sanctuary, to whose detailed description so much of Exodus is devoted; the construction of the First Temple by Solomon, a figure noted for his esoteric wisdom and for the related attribution of his use of the hexagram as his seal ring;[1] and the rebuilding of Solomon's Temple after the Babylonian captivity, which had been inspired by the prophecies of Ezekiel during that captivity. The "higher criticism" attributes the first chapter of Genesis to the priests of the Second Temple period, as part of the P document. But a case may perhaps be made either for Solomon, since both this text and sagacious king have special associations with the hexagram, or for Moses. The rabbis tell us that an Oral Torah was given to Moses at Mount Sinai along with the Written Torah. Similarly, it has been said that there was an esoteric wisdom given to Moses, and it can be argued that this wisdom was transmitted privately to the priesthood at the same time as the exoteric writings on history and law were initially promulgated by Moses, becoming and remaining an essential part of priestly training until the final destruction of the Second Temple.

In the last years before the final destruction and exile, the four main groupings within Judaism, as defined by Josephus, showed differing cognitive associations with the various forms of old and new learning. Of lasting importance were the Pharisees, who were to become the rabbinical leaders of diaspora Jewry and who held to the authority of both the Written and Oral Torahs. Of least duration were the Zealots, a patriotic-apocalyptic group thought to have split off from the Pharisees in the last decades of the Temple to revolt against Roman rule. But the most important from our perspective were the remaining two groups, the Sadducees and the Essenes. The Sadducees were associated with the traditional priesthood descended from Zadok, as he ultimately was from Aaron's son Eleazar, who had served as high priests from the time of David until the Hasmonaean (Maccabean) disruption of the Zadokite line. They were noted for their adherence only to the Written Torah and their rejection of a Mosaic origin for the Oral Torah; but I would also suggest that they cultivated the traditional study of a sacred science that may have been passed down directly from Moses and that emphasized a cosmologically encoded geometry. Also significant were the Essenes, who rejected not only the Oral Torah but the Temple sacrifices offered by the politically appointed Hasmonaean high priests and whose communities, as Josephus tells us,[2] were governed by the Pythagorean rule, a rule that would also suggest a dedication to the study of Pythagorean geometry; and with this study of esoteric geometry, the Essenes, like the Zealots, combined a new apocalyptic spiritualism.

Of these four groups, it would seem that both the old priests and the new pietistic Essenes were knowledgeable about the principles of sacred geometry. But the association appears to go deeper, for as Jacob Neusner has shown of the Qumran community, generally identified with the Essenes and believed to be the source of the Dead Sea Scrolls: "The founders of the Qumran Community were Temple priests, who saw themselves as continuators of the true priestly line,"[3] the line of Zadok. Lawrence H. Schiffman supports this view: "when Temple worship was entrusted to a usurper—the Hasmonaean high priest . . .—some pious Sadducees formed a sect and seceded from participation in the ritual of the Jerusalem Temple. . . . the term "Essene" came to designate the originally Sadducean sectarians. . . ."[4] Geza Vermes qualifies this view that the Essenes of Qumran were founded by Zadokite priests, arguing rather that "the 'sons of Zadok, the priests,' members of the 'Zadokite' high-priestly family, took over the leadership of the sect."[5] My discussion of the "Community Rule" scroll in the next chapter should provide further support for the thesis that the Qumran Essenes were led by Zadokite priests, whether or not they had also been founded by such dissident priests, and it will also expand our knowledge of traditional priestly learning.

But whether the Qumran Essenes were founded or taken over by members of the Zadokite priesthood, it may well have been their schooling in Temple geometry that disposed them, either before or after their association with the Essenes, to an embrace of the Pythagorean form of sacred science whose resemblance to their own tradition they could recognize. The Sadducean Essenes may thus be considered to have been knowledgeable about both Hebraic Temple geometry and the Hellenistic form of sacred geometry deriving from Pythagoras, a joint knowledge probably shared by many priests of that epoch. That some such union of Pythagorean-Essenic and priestly geometry was finally effected can be seen in the peculiarly Jewish form of geometric reasoning that, a few hundred years later, comes to light in the *Sefer Yetzirah* and continues to inform all later kabbalistic speculation. But in addition to such disaffected Zadokite priests as may have left the Temple to found the Essenes, most of the traditional Zadokite priesthood continued to serve in the Temple under its politicized high priests until its destruction in 70 C.E.

As the early history of Temple Judaism showed the two faces of an exoteric ritualism of priestly sacrifices, later supplemented by priestly prayer services and instruction of the people in Torah, and an esoteric priestly study of the geometry and associated sacred sciences that could validate their related understanding of the mystical purpose of sacrifice, so the later history of rabbinical Judaism had an exoteric face of talmudic legalism and an esoteric face of kabbalistic geometry and cosmology. But though a talmudic sage like Rabbi Akiba was known for his secret kabbalistic studies, and many Kabbalists were learned Talmudists, there was still this basic difference, that the Kabbalists were somehow able to preserve a link to the ancient priestly lore that was of little interest to the Talmudists. The very fact that the nonpriestly rabbinical tradition shows no interest either in geometry or in temple building (its synagogues evinced no canons of sacred proportions or forms—whether those of the cube, the hexagram, or the Tree of Life Diagram—but were either nondescript or adaptations of the architectural styles of the surrounding non-Judaic cultures) is further evidence that this is a tradition unschooled in the sacred science of geometry. It is unschooled as well in such other priestly practices as meditative chanting, the later analyses of the second line of the Sh'ma,[6] discussed in chapter 5, and of the *Sefer Yetzirah* Sefirot, discussed in chapter 7, showing that there were such meditative practices extending from at least the discovery of Deuteronomy to the codifying and dissemination of this ancient wisdom in the *Sefer Yetzirah*.

Between the Torah, whether ascribed to Mosaic or priestly authorship, and the *Sefer Yetzirah*, there are, then, clear lines of parallel esoteric concerns that argue strongly for a continuous tradition that not only extended through the Temple period but, after the destruction of the Temple and the deprofessionalization of the priesthood, was somehow able to maintain and transmit its learning through forms of loose-knit secret societies. Gershom Scholem has pointed out that "historically speaking, organized closed societies of mystics have been proved to exist only since the end of the Second Temple era,"[7] and it seems obvious that major factors in such a development would have been the survival of some still zealous members of the Essene sect, who had been taught by the Zadokite priests and wished to pass on their secret doctrines, and especially the effects of the deprofessionalizing of the priesthood after the destruction of the Second Temple. Great Temple scholars, who had lost both their income and the institution through which they had expected to hand down their learning, would have been prone for both reasons to become private teachers, and they would also have tried to maintain the hidden nature of their teachings, teachings that had always been the province of a spiritual elite. It is generally agreed that the kabbalistic tradition, especially in its earlier phases, involved the oral transmission of learning from a master to a few disciples, and what I am here suggesting is that it was the esoteric elements of the ancient priestly lore that were so transmitted, surfacing first in the Hekhalot-Merkabah texts and finally in the texts of the Kabbalah.

Though the split between priestly and rabbinical concerns and training was already highly developed during the final centuries of the Temple, we have seen that with the destruction of the Temple the weights between the two traditions shifted dramatically. The rabbis took charge of the Jewish religious communities and set up major schools of learning devoted to the interpretation of Scripture, while, with the loss of the Temple and of the funding of priestly activity, the priestly class virtually disappeared from public view. Its learning, however, would seem to have gone underground, where its esoteric traditions could be secretly maintained among the newer initiates to kabbalistic doctrines, and it sometimes merged in the lives of noted Talmudists, such as Rabbis Akiba and Joseph Karo, the former a major compiler of the Mishnah and the latter the major codifier of talmudic law in his work the *Shulchan Arukh*.

Between the overt and hidden traditions of later rabbinical Judaism there were, then, major differences and also connections, the influence of talmudic modes of thought on kabbalistic thinkers being particularly clear. Indeed, in such a major text of the Kabbalah as the *Zohar*, we may see a synthesis between a geometrically based cosmology and a midrashic mode of interpretation that is perhaps the most characteristic quality of kabbalistic thought. But what distinguishes kabbalistic from talmudic reasoning, despite their similar use of associative interpretation, is that whereas the Talmud takes the biblical text as its model, for the Kabbalah the model is supplied by geometry. In every text of true Kabbalah, the eyes of its authors are ever set upon the diagram called the Tree of Life. Whatever other geometric processes and forms are part of their cosmological thinking and illustrations, it is the Tree of Life Diagram that all texts included within the narrowest definition of the Kabbalah are concerned to explicate.

In such an understanding of the significance of geometric forms, the Kabbalah shares a single ancient wisdom with such other aspects of Western esotericism as Neoplatonism and the hermetic tradition, derived, respectively, from Pythagorean and Egyptian sources importantly devoted to geometry. That both Pythagoras and Moses had associations with Egypt is most suggestive of a common origin of the two geometric traditions that may be said to have resulted from these major founders of Hellenic and Hebraic thought, both cultures as devoted to temple building as the Egyptian, though on a considerably smaller scale. But whether or not there was a common Egyptian source to all of Western sacred geometry, from at least the time of the Essenes and throughout the later history of the Kabbalah there were clear associations between the native esoteric tradition of Judaism and Pythagoreanism that make it difficult to distinguish the elements of geometric knowledge that are native from those that appear to be imported. Both, moreover, develop a geometrically based cosmology emphasizing four worlds or dimensions defined in terms of ten principal constituents, the Pythagorean tradition in terms of the triangular model of ten points called the Tetractys and the Kabbalah of the Tree of Life Diagram. But Pythagorean geometry does not reflect the apparent Hebraic interest in the hexagram, a figure also absent from Egyptian temple decoration but prominently featured in the Indian and Far Eastern symbolism of the geometric diagrams known as *yantras* and *mandalas*. Whatever may be the truth of the cultural contacts between the ancient Hebrews and Indians regarding the dissemination of the hexagram as the paramount symbol of creation, it is one thesis of the present work that, despite the failure of modern scholarship to distinguish a clear symbolic use of the hexagram in early Hebraic sources, a failure that the new evidence offered in chapter 6 should redress, it was the preeminent geometric symbol throughout the long history of the Jewish esoteric tradition, though rarely surfacing, as it is alleged to have done in the case of Solomon's Seal, until, for reasons that have never been adequately explained, it is finally embraced by the whole Jewish people as its symbol. Equally obscure is the origin of the distinctively kabbalistic symbol of the Tree of Life Diagram, though its similarity to the menorah is suggestive of its possible origination with Moses. In any case, it is likely that this whole geometric complex was part of a hidden tradition transmitted by the priesthood, a complex whose constituents will be explored extensively in this work.

Having considered the historical relationship of Hebraic sacred science to analogous Egyptian, Greek, and Indian esoteric traditions, we should close this introductory survey with a similar look at the cosmological principle that all this sacred science was dedicated to demonstrate, the genesis of the divine son. For Hebraic sacred science is centered in that secret doctrine of the son first announced by God when He said: "Israel is my son, even my firstborn" (Exod. 4:22).[8] This also has analogues to similar doctrines in all of the world's great religions, most importantly to the earlier Egyptian figures of the son god Horus and his earthly-divine avatar, the pharaoh, the later figures of the Hindu Krishna and Buddhist Amitabha, and, of course, the conceptualization of Jesus derived directly from this Hebraic tradition. But whether the universal appearance of this same understanding of a conjoined cosmic and human destiny in so many different religious traditions points to a source in a common Neolithic human culture, to more direct influences and cross-fertilizations, or to similar prophetic intuitions, each tradition has developed its own authentic formulation of this salvific belief and its attendant rituals, practices, and proofs. Of all practicing religions, Judaism is the oldest continuous religious tradition embodying this belief, but it has also been the most careful to hide this most enduring element of its mystical understanding and devotions. One reason for this is undoubtedly its feared similarity to the dominant Christianity from which Judaism has ever been vigilant to distinguish itself. But it is also true, and perhaps unfortunate, that in Judaism the doctrine of the son has ever been a jealously guarded secret tradition. Thus this most essential core of the Jewish religion has consistently been both covertly proclaimed for those who could understand it and as openly denied. But from the Bible, through Merkabah mysticism and the Kabbalah, to Hasidism, the central mystery of the son, as of the cosmic process, has ever had but one meaning, *that*

ultimate unification of the human and divine that could effect both the person-
alization of the divine and complementary divinization of perfected humans.

Writing about the time in 1918 when he began his study of the Kabbalah, Gershom Scholem notes how deficient was the scholarly understanding of this subject: "It is true that, judging from the obtuse Enlightenment standard that Jewish scholars have offered on the subject, the
key to their understanding seems to have been lost."[9] But the essential
message just given had never been both as proclaimed and denied as it
then was by the modern Hasidim, the heirs of that most influential reformulation of the Kabbalah effected by Isaac Luria in sixteenth-
century Palestinian Safed. And shortly after the period of Scholem's introduction to the subject, this message would get through to the leading
Jewish religious philosophers of the 1920s: Franz Rosenzweig, Martin
Buber, and Abraham Isaac Kook, the last also the chief rabbi of pre-Israel
Palestine. Rosenzweig expresses this central mystery in terms we will later
come to recognize as deriving from Ezekiel's Throne vision: "In the innermost sanctum of the divine truth, where man might expect all the
world and himself to dwindle into likeness of that which he is to catch
sight of there, he thus catches sight of none other than a countenance
like his own. The Star of Redemption is become countenance which
glances to me and out of which I glance."[10] Buber has a similar understanding of the process and message of revelation, its production of "a
new form of God": "Thus . . . ever new provinces of the world and the
spirit are raised to form, summoned to divine form. Ever new spheres
become regions of a theophany. It is not man's own power that works
here, nor is it God's pure effective passage, but it is a mixture of the divine and the human . . . we shape eternally the form of God."[11] And Rav
Kook, as he was known, relates such individual salvation to the course
and purpose of cosmic evolution:

> However life breaks down into particularization, it continues to draw
> light from the original divine light, and it needs to return to the
> higher realm, together with the essence of our souls. Then we shall
> not ascend devoid of riches. . . . We shall have with us our multicol-
> ored robes we acquired as a result of the proliferation of all life. . . .
> Existence is destined to reach a point when the whole will assimi-
> late the good in all its constituted particulars.[12]

The attempt of all three was to forge a modern Jewish theology from the
esoteric legacy of the Hasidim, itself the final legacy of the ancient Hebraic

priesthood. But as it is now over seventy years since they variously made their contribution to modern Jewish thought, and the message has once more been lost, it may be time to recover the meaning of the "tradition" once more both for Jews and those of cognate traditions who have also lost the esoteric keys to their belief systems and practices. This recovery will do more than such previous attempts, however, in clarifying the meaning of this salvific belief and of the sacred science used to demonstrate its truths. Of the sophisticated sacred science relating geometry, sound, and number that can be attributed to the Hebraic priesthood, little has, however, survived in the Kabbalah. The practices that have survived, use of the interpretaitve techniques of Gematria and of the Tree of The Life Diagram as cosmological model, seem to lack the rigor of a true sacred science. But we should explore these practices nonetheless both to understand the later discussions of kabbalistic concepts and to recover the more complex forms of these practices, in the later parts of this book, for which they hold the key. We will begin with a brief treatment of Gematria that relates directly to the just defined secret doctrine of the Jewish esoteric tradition and then we will proceed to a more extended discussion of the traditional forms and meanings of the Kabbalah's most famous diagram.

Kabbalistic Sacred Science: Gematria and the Tree of Life Diagram

What distinguishes kabbalistic from Pythagorean sacred science is that the three elements of the sacred science they share are understood in the Kabbalah, from at least the time of the *Sefer Yetzirah*, to be contained in the higher dimension of language: in the shape of each letter, in its sound, and in its number. It is the union of the last two of these elements that forms the most enduring branch of Hebraic sacred science, that known as Gematria, though the derivation of this word from the Greek word for geometry implies some original geometric component to the kabbalistic sacred science most concerned with number.

The basis of Gematria is the fact that the Hebrew letters serve not only to form sounded words but also as the numbers used in counting. In this standard Hebrew mode of numbering, the first nine letters signify the units from one to nine, the next nine the tens from ten to ninety, and the last four letters plus five different final forms of previous letters the hundreds from one hundred to nine hundred, one thousand being signified by big Aleph. It is the fact that each word can also be interpreted as a number that forms the basis of the associative technique of Gematria; for two words having the same Gematria number are considered to have a meaningful relationship.

To demonstrate this standard technique, I will use an example of my own.[13] The form of the verb *chayah*, meaning "to be," appearing in the word *vehayah*, normally translated "and it shall come to pass," has the same Gematria number as the Tetragrammaton, the holiest of divine Names, since it simply transposes its letters from YHVH to VHYH, the Gematria value of these letters being 26 (Yod = 10, Hey = 5, Vav = 6, and Hey = 5). But its cognate term *veyehi*, normally translated "and it came to pass," has a Gematria value of 31 (Vav = 6, Yod = 10, Hey = 5, and Yod = 10). What is interesting about this number is that it is the same as the word for God, El (Aleph = 1 and Lamed = 30). The significance that can be drawn from these Gematria equations is that the word referring to a future product of causality is associated with the *personal* name of God, the Tetragrammaton, while that referring to a past causality is associated with the *impersonal* Name, or rather word, for God, El. The associations of the impersonal realm with the past and of the personal realm with the future can be taken to support the main cosmological thrust of the Lurianic Kabbalah, shortly to be rehearsed, that the course of cosmic evolution is toward the development of divine personality, to which we can add such spiritually developed individuals as form the divine son Israel, those whose alignment with the higher will of the personal God can alter the impersonal cause-and-effect mechanism defining past divine causality.

From this example one can see how the standard form of Gematria associations can be used to support Hebraic exegesis. But in the further Gematria relationships of the Tetragrammaton that will be developed in chapter 4, a web of relationships will be developed that will also include the processes of arithmetic, thus suggesting that a more rigorous form of this practice might well have existed. The Tetragrammaton expansions, with their Gematria signifiers, will also be related to the Tree of Life Diagram in chapter 4, and the further association of the Tetragrammaton letters with the Hebrew vowels will lead to a full treatment of the harmonics in chapter 5, again in relation to the Sefirot of the Tree, all of which suggests that there once was a far more sophisticated and complex science of Gematria than that simpler version that has survived in the tradition. This is even truer of the complex of precise geometric diagrams that will be recovered in chapters 6–8 through use of the key of the Tree of Life Diagram in concert with certain geometric clues appearing in kabbalistic texts. It is to this central kabbalistic diagram that we now turn.

The Tree of Life Diagram, that most important model for kabbalistic cosmology, is shown in figure 1.1 in the fully developed form attributed to Isaac Luria that includes his unique assignment of the twenty-two Hebrew letters to the twenty-two paths of this diagram.

The two main elements in the design of the Tree of Life Diagram are the ten Sefirot-named spheres ("sphere" being one etymological derivation of the word *Sefirot*, the plural form of the word *Sefirah*) and the twenty-two paths or channels connecting them, elements that first make their appearance in the *Sefer Yetzirah*. There ten such Sefirot are specified, apparently corresponding to the ten basic numbers, and the twenty-two letters of the Hebrew alphabet are divided into the groups of the three "mother" letters, the seven double letters, and the twelve single letters that complete the formal elements of cosmic creation, this being the book (*sefer*) of the World of Formation (Yetzirah). In his version of the Tree illustrated in figure 1.1, Luria has appropriately correlated its paths with the three categories of letters in the *Sefer Yetzirah*, the three horizontal paths with the three mother letters, the seven vertical paths with the seven double letters, and the twelve diagonal paths with the twelve single letters, thus associating the geometry of the Tree with this seminal text. Although the *Sefer Yetzirah* does not go further to give the Sefirot the familiar names shown in figure 1.1 or to place them clearly in a drawn diagram associated with the Tree of Life, it does define the two essential elements to which the later drawn versions will largely hold, the ten spheres called Sefirot and the twenty-two variously lettered paths connecting them.[14] The recognized names of the Sefirot begin to appear almost one thousand years later, after the *Sefer Yetzirah*, in the *Bahir*, and then in the *Zohar*, but it is not until the work of the sixteenth-century Kabbalists in the Safed community of Palestine that the names and diagrammatic positions of the Sefirot and paths are fully and openly disclosed.

It is in Moses Cordovero's *Pardes Rimmonim* (Garden of Pomegranates), written in 1548 in Safed and first published in 1591 in Cracow, Poland, that the Tree of Life Diagram finally emerges from the obscurity of at least three hundred years of verbal allusion in its generally accepted modern proportions, the previous 1516 publication of the diagram in Paulus Rincius' *Portae Lucis*, a Latin translation of Joseph Gikatilla's *Sha'arei Orah* (Gate of Light), having eccentric proportions. Cordovero's disclosure is most important because it combines a detailed commentary

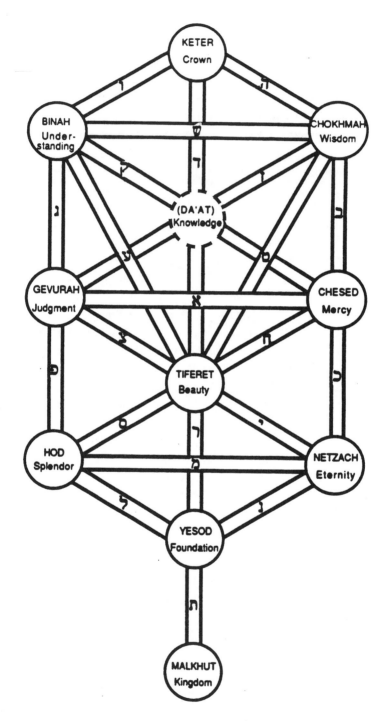

FIGURE 1.1. THE LURIANIC MODEL OF THE TREE OF LIFE DIAGRAM

on the Sefirot and the channels with a drawn diagram depicting them. The discrepancies between this commentary and illustration, shortly to be analyzed, show that together they appear to validate the two major forms of the diagram that have been prominent in the kabbalistic tradition, that which can be associated with Cordovero, since it is consistent with his written commentary, and that which is closer to the illustrated diagram and can be associated with Isaac Luria. It was probably the growing influence of the Lurianic version of the Tree in the period intervening between the writing and publication of the *Pardes* that accounts for the presumed editorial tampering with the original Cordovero diagram to bring it into closer conformity with the different version of the Tree popularized by Luria that had gained in authority during this time.

The distinction between the two recognized forms of the Tree does not only hold between the earlier Zoharic Kabbalah and the later Lurianic Kabbalah but also between the two streams of Kabbalah that begin to diverge from each other during the Renaissance, for the Christian scholars who begin the serious study of the Kabbalah at this time[15] are primarily students of the *Zohar* and the *Sefer Yetzirah*, both of which were published in Latin translations before they appeared in the original. Although the transmission of Lurianic concepts was widespread enough for the able Hebrew scholar John Milton to incorporate Luria's doctrine of the Tzimtzum into *Paradise Lost* within only one century,[16] the major "Lurianic" writings were circulated in manuscript, the most authoritative version of the *Etz Chayyim* (Tree of Life), written by Luria's disciple Chaim Vital, not being published until 1784, and they are still largely unavailable in translation.

It is not only in their primary concepts that the Christian and Jewish Kabbalah begin to diverge at this time but, as just suggested, also in their versions of the Tree of Life Diagram. While the Christian tradition seems to have largely adopted the model as defined in the textual commentary of Cordovero, the Jewish tradition has used the Lurianic version of the Tree almost as exclusively, the version approximated in the drawn diagram of the *Pardes*. Thus both major versions of the diagram may be said to have made their first public appearance in the 1591 publication of the *Pardes*, a fact that authenticates both versions of the diagram as belonging to the genuine Jewish kabbalistic tradition. As the question of geometric proportions and of the disposition of the paths or channels between the ten Sefirot of this diagram is vital to the geometric discussions that make up the central core of this book (part 3), a careful analysis of the Cordovero text will be required.

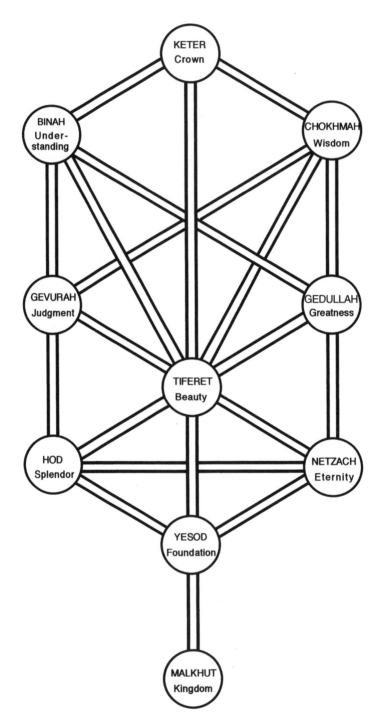

FIGURE 1.2. THE *PARDES RIMMONIM* TREE OF LIFE DIAGRAM

We have seen that it was not until the sixteenth century that the Kabbalists in Palestinian Safed clearly defined all the names and diagrammatic positions of the Sefirot, most importantly in the *Pardes* because of its combination of a written commentary on the Sefirot and their connecting channels with a drawn diagram depicting them. But as we have also seen, this diagram and commentary, rather than resolving all problems, raises the central issue as to the true form of the Tree, for the diagram and commentary do not agree in the placement of all of the channels, and there are differing versions of the text that compound the problem. This can readily be seen if we compare the diagram with the summary commentary that follows it. Figure 1.2 gives the Tree of Life Diagram as it appears in the *Pardes* but with the Sefirotic names in their transliterated Hebrew forms and English translations.

The one obvious error in this version of the Tree is that it only has twenty paths or channels between the Sefirot rather than the twenty-two specified by the text, the missing ones being the horizontal paths between Chokhmah and Binah and between Chesed (given with its alternate name of Gedullah in the *Pardes* diagram) and Gevurah. But the summary commentary reveals that there are other differences and problems, the problems being caused by textual differences between the standard version, which is supported by the longer commentary that follows it, and a different version (referred to in the editorial insertions by the abbreviation "d.v."), which is closer to the drawn version of the diagram than is what seems to be Cordovero's original commentary. In his discussion, Cordovero used the word *tzinnor*, which shall be translated as "channel," although "pipe" would seem to be an even better translation did it not seem inappropriate in this context:

> "*Tzinnor*" is a channel [pipe] in which water travels from place to place and Kabbalists relate this to the influx [Shefa] which runs from Sefirah to Sefirah. . . . The number of channels that flow from Keter are three. One to Chokhmah, one to Binah, and one to Tiferet. Three more (d.v. four) flow from Chokhmah: one to Binah, one to Chesed (d.v. and one to Gevurah), and one to Tiferet. Another two (d.v. three) flow from Binah (one to Chesed), one to Gevurah, and one to Tiferet. Another three flow from Chesed: one to Gevurah, one to Tiferet, and one to Netzach. Two more flow from Gevurah: one to Tiferet and one to Hod. Three more flow from Tiferet: one to Netzach, one to Hod, and one to Yesod. Two more flow from Netzach: one to Hod and one to Yesod and some believe also one to

Malkhut. Another channel flows from Hod to Yesod and some say also to Malkhut. Another one flows from Yesod to Malkhut, making a total of twenty-two.[17]

What is at issue here is the position of two of the channels making the necessary total of twenty-two, the difference in the placement of these two channels defining the two major forms of the Tree of Life Diagram in the kabbalistic tradition.

Without the insertions by the editor Yisrael Yehudah Shapiro, there is simply the issue of the two channels from Netzach and Hod to Malkhut, which Cordovero reports "some believe" to be essential while other Kabbalists must not. On this question, the drawn diagram agrees with those who reject these two channels while the later Cordovero commentary supports those who "believe" these channels to be authentic. The differing version, on the other hand, supplies two additional channels that again conform to the drawn diagram but not to the later commentary, the channels between Chokhmah and Gevurah and between Binah and Chesed. Clearly a choice must be made between these two versions, either of which will supply the necessary twenty-two paths: if the additional crossing channels from Chokhmah and Binah are to be allowed, then those from Netzach and Hod to Malkhut must be rejected, and vice versa. In the later commentary, it is clear that Cordovero chooses the twenty-two channels that include those from Netzach and Hod to Malkhut and makes no mention of possible channels from Chokhmah to Gevurah and from Binah to Chesed:

Another three channels stretch from Chokhmah. One is to Binah. . . . A second channel stretches from Chokhmah to Chesed. . . . The third channel stretches from Chokhmah to Tiferet. . . . The reason may be because Tiferet is the son of Chokhmah and Binah, and there must be something of the influence of the father in the son as well as of the influence of the mother, for a person has three partners [God plus the two parents]. Two more channels stretch from Binah. One is to Gevurah. . . . The second channel is from Binah to Tiferet. This channel is similar to the one explained above, the third channel stretching from Chokhmah to Tiferet. . . . Another three channels go from Chesed, the first to Gevurah. . . . Through this channel Chesed is included in Gevurah and Gevurah in Chesed without including Tiferet, as explained in the Zohar. . . .

> A third channel goes from Netzach to Malkhut. . . . Another two
> channels go from Hod, one to Yesod . . . and a second to Malkhut. [18]

I have presented this evidence at such length because it is crucial in determining the authenticity of both major forms of the Tree of Life Diagram
and because it has not previously been made available in translation.

On the basis of the discrepancies between this extended commentary, for which Cordovero is clearly responsible, and both the drawn diagram and the variant additions to the other version, it seems reasonable
to conclude that the errors in the diagram and variants in the text appeared somewhere in the process of transmission between the manuscript
and printed version and, moreover, were the product of one or more careless editorial attempts to make the Cordovero diagram and commentary
conform to a different version of the Tree of Life Diagram that had gained
in authority during the time between the composition of the *Pardes* and
its publication. The carelessness of these presumed editorial changes is
indicated by the fact that the textual additions lead to a total number of
twenty-four channels, the paths from Netzach and Hod to Malkhut not
having been omitted, while the presumed tampering with the original
Cordovero diagram, which removed the paths from Netzach and Hod to
Malkhut while adding those from Chokhmah to Gevurah and from Binah
to Chesed, also seems to have removed in the process the undisputed
paths from Chokhmah to Binah and from Chesed to Gevurah, with the
result that the diagram is left with only twenty channels. With these last
two paths reinserted, however, the drawn diagram would conform to the
version of the Tree of Life Diagram developed by that most influential of
Kabbalists, Isaac Luria, that in which the three horizontal paths are assigned the three mother letters, the seven vertical paths the seven double
letters, and the twelve diagonal paths the twelve single letters.

As expounded by his disciples, primarily by Chayyim Vital in the *Etz
Chayyim*, there are three main principles of the new Lurianic Kabbalah:
the Tzimtzum,[19] that retraction of the divine substance, following its initial "contraction," which left the primordial circular space in which the
creation could take place; the Shevirah, or "breaking of the vessels" of
the original Sefirot, which were not strong enough to contain the divine
influx; and the Tikkun, the cosmic reconstruction or return by which the
Sefirot are reconstituted as the five divine personalities or Partzufim. Luria
calls the cosmic world of the originally emanated Sefirot the Olam ha-
Tohu, the World of Chaos, because in his system the Sefirot at this stage

existed only as points of light without the connecting paths that could give them structural stability. And when asked to explain the difference between his system and that of Cordovero, he answered that Cordovero's concern was with the Olam ha-Tohu while his was with the Olam ha-Tikkun.[20] Although Cordovero's understanding of the original emanation of the Sefirot is not in accord with that of Luria, the basic distinction made by Luria does hold true. Cordovero, who may be considered the culmination of the earlier Zoharic tradition, is primarily concerned with the cosmic process of emanation, and Luria, who begins the later continuous history of Jewish mystical understanding and practice, is primarily concerned with the cosmic process of return. It is the breach between these two different foci of attention that the Sabbatical cosmic structure to be developed in chapters 6 and 10 hopes to heal by providing the larger cosmic structure that can contain them both. In the later analyses, therefore, both versions of the Tree will be accepted while the difference between them will be maintained, the Cordovero diagram being regarded as the Tree of Emanation and the Luria diagram as the Tree of Return.

Both versions give the same names to the Sefirot: Keter (Crown), Chokhmah (Wisdom), Binah (Understanding), Chesed (Mercy), Gevurah (Judgment), Tiferet (Beauty), Netzach (Eternity), Hod (Splendor), Yesod (Foundation), and Malkhut (Kingdom). But as just shown, they differ in the positions accorded to some of the paths. The Cordovero diagram contains paths from Malkhut to Netzach and Hod that do not appear in the Luria diagram, while the latter has paths from Chokhmah to Gevurah and from Binah to Chesed that do not appear in the former. Both versions, however, feature the three horizontal paths, seven vertical paths, and twelve diagonal paths that may be correlated with the similar divisions of the letters in the *Sefer Yetzirah*, figure 1.1 having shown how the letters are so distributed in the form of the diagram attributed to Luria. Although the writings of Luria's disciples do not contain a drawn version of his diagram, the descriptions of the paths are clear enough, particularly in Luria's commentary on the Talmud and at the end of his edition of the *Sefer Yetzirah*, to enable the construction of such a diagram, and it has appeared without proper identification in more than one modern work on the Kabbalah.[21] Both forms of the Tree are illustrated in figure 1.3.

We have previously been primarily concerned with the disposition of the twenty-two paths of this diagram. But it is the ten Sefirot, no longer signifying just the primary numbers, as they do in the *Sefer Yetzirah*, but in their Sefirot names the divine attributes, with which we will be concerned in the following summary of the main lines of interpretation in

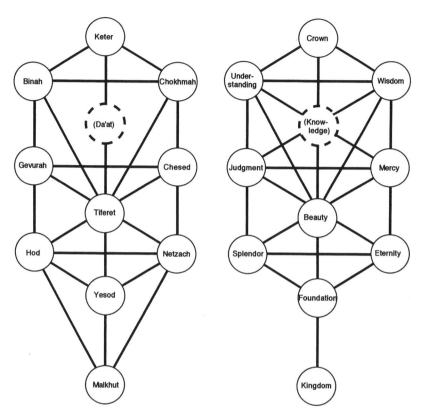

The Cordovero Tree of Emanation   *The Luria Tree of Return*

FIGURE 1.3. THE TREE OF LIFE DIAGRAMS

the kabbalistic tradition, interpretations that will demonstrate the intrinsic relationships of names to forms in the understanding of the Tree and the associative mode of interpretation characteristic of kabbalistic geometry.[22]

We will begin this survey with another version of the Tree, that superimposed on the cosmic figure of the primal man, Adam Kadmon, a version that accords with the formulations of the early Kabbalah. In this form of the diagram, Keter is placed above the crown, Chokhmah to the right of the head, Binah to the left, Chesed on the right arm, Gevurah on the left arm, Tiferet on the heart, Netzach on the right knee, Hod on the left knee, Yesod back up on the genitals (suggesting that an original version understood the cosmic man not to be in the standing position in which he has traditionally been illustrated but in a seated position with the knees raised in the ancient position of prophetic inspiration),[23] and

Malkhut below the feet. The uppermost triad was thus associated with the mind, the middle triad with the emotions, and the lowest triad with the instincts, Malkhut representing the final receptacle of the original divine influx. There is also an eleventh non-Sefirah Da'at (Knowledge) sometimes associated, instead of Keter, with Chokhmah and Binah. But chapters 6 to 8 will show that Da'at is rather the key to a more hidden knowledge of an underlying geometric complex, of which it is the center, with major cosmological implications, particularly regarding the secret doctrine of the Kabbalah. In addition to the division by triads, there was also a tradition that distinguished the upper six Sefirot from the lower four, the upper attributed to the divine and the lower to the human with Tiferet serving to unite the finite with the infinite.

Such identifications have also been variously associated with the three major soul levels in kabbalistic spiritual psychology. In the case of the three triads, the upper mental triad is associated with the Neshamah soul, the middle emotional level with the Ruach soul, and the lower instinctual level with the birthright Nefesh soul. In the second case, all of the upper six divine Sefirot are associated with the Neshamah soul, understood to be the divine higher self, and the lower human four are variously apportioned between the Ruach and Nefesh soul levels. Various attempts have also been made to correlate the four kabbalistic worlds of emanation with the Tree. In the Lurianic Kabbalah, all ten Sefirot are assigned to the first world of Atzilut (Emanation), but in another, more popular version, only the upper triad is so assigned, the middle triad being correlated with the second world of Beriah (Creation), the lower triad with the third world of Yetzirah (Formation), and the final Sefirah with the fourth world of Assiyah (Action or Making).

There is also a slightly different correlation of cosmic worlds to Sefirot based upon a vertical form of the Tetragrammaton arranged to resemble the human body, as seen in figure 1.4. Keter and Chokhmah are here identified with both the head-resembling Yod and Atzilut, Binah with the arms-resembling upper Hey and Beriah, Chesed to Yesod with the torso-resembling Vav and Yetzirah, and Malkhut with the legs-resembling lower Hey and Assiyah.

The purpose of this correlation of Tetragrammaton letters with cosmic worlds would seem to be the establishment of cosmic world parity between the masculine and feminine Sefirot. For in the later Zoharic-Lurianic version, the Sefirot also became identified with the five Partzufim, the divine personalities: Keter with the Partzuf of Arikh Anpin (Long

FIGURE 1.4. THE VERTICAL TETRAGRAMMATON

Face), Chokhmah with Abba (Father), Binah with Imma (Mother), the next six Sefirot from Chesed to Yesod with the single Partzuf of the son, Ze'ir Anpin (Short Face), and the final Sefirah of Malkhut with the Partzuf of the daughter-bride, the Nukvah (Female).

Each Sefirah was also identified with a divine name, the most important being that of the Tetragrammaton (YHVH) with Tiferet and of Adonai (Lord) with Malkhut. In addition, Tiferet was identified with the Holy One, blessed be He, and Malkhut with the Shekhinah, the former the masculine representative of the divine transcendence and the latter the feminine form of the divine immanence. It is also Tiferet that is the defining Sefirah of the six-Sefirot Partzuf of the son, and its position as the bridge between the finite and infinite also defines the cosmic function of this most important divine personality. His six Sefirot may similarly be viewed as uniting his upper divine triad of Chesed-Gevurah-Tiferet with his lower human triad of Netzach-Hod-Yesod. It can thus be seen that as the earlier Kabbalah identified the whole Sefirotic Tree with a single figure representative of the cosmic son, so does the Partzuf of the son emerge as the dominant figure in the Tree of the later Kabbalah, the Tree in both versions having been assimilated within a broader esoteric tradition going back to the ancient priesthood.

With this brief introduction to the traditional forms and meanings of the Tree of Life Diagram, we will be in a better position both to understand the later discussions of the Sefirot in kabbalistic texts and to develop the more logical geometric constructions for whose principles the traditional Tree holds the key. And as this key is used to unlock these underlying diagrams, each new form will prove to be most expressive of cosmological meaning, one whose interpretation will be dependent upon and display the semiotic technique of kabbalistic geometry I have termed "The Science of Expressive Form." With this introduction to the kabbalistic survivals of Hebraic sacred science that will provide the key to recovery of the priestly secret tradition, we can finally turn to a brief survey of the structure and implications of this work.

The Order and Implications of This Study

Each of the following chapters represents an independent scholarly exploration of its subject, but they should all contribute to an enlarged understanding of the priestly legacy that constitutes the Jewish esoteric tradition, and they are divided into four parts that have a logical order. This first part concerns the theoretical foundations of the whole work and, in addition to the present introductory chapter, includes two further chapters. These next two chapters develop the theoretical bases of the twin components of this tradition, its cosmological doctrine of the son and its correlated sacred science. Each of the following three parts takes its point of departure from some aspect of the sacred science defined in chapter 3 and develops this in ways that finally demonstrate some new facet of the mystery that the comprehensive textual study of chapter 2 has defined as the secret doctrine of the son. The second and third parts represent new experimental methods of practicing Hebraic sacred science that not only demonstrate the cogency of its procedures but also discover the roots and meaning of many surviving fragments of the original knowledge. Part 2 (chapters 4 and 5) focuses on kabbalistic linguistics, on the occult correspondences of language, particularly of the Tetragrammaton, the four-letter holiest name of God, while part 3 (chapters 6–8) focuses on kabbalisic geometry, particularly on the various forms and meanings of the Tree of Life Diagram central to kabbalistic cosmology. Where part 3 explores the geometric hints that are to be found in important kabbalistic texts and diagrams, part 2 explores the Hebrew language in ways that have not been so memorialized, including the correlations of the Hebrew vowel letters with the harmonics and the Sefirot. But it begins with that aspect of Hebraic sacred science that has most endured, the practice of Gematria, and it follows most directly from the final analysis of language in chapter 3, a philosophical explanation of the meaning of sacred science whose extended analysis of language and of its natural relationship to objective reality will provide a new understanding of both cosmic structure and human perception. If the foundations of sacred science given in chapter 3 lead in the following five chapters in the direction of a renewed practice of sacred science, in part 4 (chapters 9 and 10) they take another direction. In this part the formulations of sacred science and kabbalistic cosmology are applied to the data of quantum physics and quantum cosmology to produce new syntheses of sacred and secular science. With this map of the work before us, we can now look a bit more closely at some of the discoveries that will emerge from its fresh perspective on the Jewish esoteric tradition.

This book represents a unique approach to study of the Jewish esoteric tradition, one whose respect both for the methodologies employed by this tradition and the conclusions so precisely demonstrated by their use distinguishes it from previous scholarly efforts. Though the research of Gershom Scholem and his students has been invaluable in opening up so much of this tradition's textual history, the exclusive focus of this research on the history of ideas, with little more than an antiquarian interest in its discovered oddities, has left it unable to explain either the persistence of this tradition or its value. For this can only come from scholars of the sacred who are prepared to find a lasting truth in its ritual and literary expressions and to follow all such hints to that central core of knowledge in which rational understanding fuses with mystical experience to illuminate the meaningfulness of our cosmic participation. It is this approach that has here been essayed, and it has led to some remarkable discoveries and conclusions.

Perhaps the most important of these has been the recognition of the secret doctrine of the son as the central salvific belief of the Jewish esoteric tradition from its beginnings and that this origin is to be found in the Temple culture of the ancient Hebraic priesthood. Aspects of this core belief and history have been separately demonstrated by previous scholars, most notably by Scholem in a recent posthumous publication,[24] but nowhere, to my knowledge, have they been put together to provide a coherent understanding of this main tenet of the secret tradition or of its priestly origin, an understanding that not only can give new meaning to study of this historical tradition but also to contemporary spirituality.

Also significant are its contributions to various aspects of biblical studies and their ritual survivals. These range from reinterpretations of the Genesis creation account and the Sh'ma to the form of verbal archeology practiced with regard to the word *ish*. Especially significant is the reinterpretation of the central verse of the Sh'ma in chapter 6, which goes beyond the kabbalistic understanding of it as signifying a unification to the further recognition that it also encodes the priestly doctrine of the son, Israel. All show precise complexes of meaning that reflect a consistent worldview comprehending the interrelated laws of manifestation and human transformation, the understanding of cosmic and spiritual functioning also conveyed through the secret doctrine of the son and the symbol of the hexagram. An important thesis of this work is the intrinsic connection of the geometry of the hexagram with Hebraic sacred science from its priestly origins, constituting perhaps its most hidden aspect but one that can link the biblical creation account to the central geometric model of the Kabbalah, the Tree of Life Diagram. Not only is new light shed on the Bible but also on various other kabbalistic texts, most importantly the *Sefer Yetzirah* and the *Etz Chayyim*, both of which are shown to be centrally concerned with this same doctrine of the son and to reveal their deepest meanings through geometric modeling.

Such analysis would not be possible without the full study here undertaken of the sacred science that the priestly legacy shares with that of Pythagoras, a study that clarifies the core principle of this worldwide ancient science in a way consistent with the first literary product of Pythagorean philosophy, the fragments of Philolaus. But a comparison of this sacred science with the Hebraic secret doctrine of the son can further explain why the relationship of the limited and unlimited pointed to by Philolaus should have been so seriously studied in its objective forms. An understanding of the Pythagorean sacred scientific triad of geometry, harmonics, and number provides, in turn, the esoteric key to the first chapter of Genesis and proof that such esoteric knowledge must have formed an important part of priestly learning.

What distinguishes kabbalistic sacred science from its classical antecedents, however, is its emphasis on language that seems so contrary to scientific reasoning, especially given the current linguistic view of the arbitrary nature of linguistic signification. But the more rigorous use of Gematria practiced here exposes such a web of persuasive associations between words, numbers, and forms as to put in question the standard view and give new support to the Platonic theory of natural language. Beyond this, the various studies of the Tetragrammaton conducted in terms of kabbalistic sacred science have led to ancillary discoveries. The

Gematria equation of the word for son, Ben, with the number 52, has led to a new association of the secret doctrine of the son with the advent of solar reckoning. A Hebrew analogue or source for the Greek earth goddess Gaia was also strongly suggested, providing further evidence of patriarchal suppression of feminine elements in the later Hebraic religion of the Bible. Most importantly, a method was discovered for determining the correct pronunciation of the Tetragrammaton as well as its linguistic meaning that should have widespread importance. The analysis of the number, sounds, and shapes comprehended by the Tetragrammaton should contribute to a new understanding both of the Tetragrammaton and of language in general, an understanding that can only illuminate the greater mystery of their appropriateness. All such discoveries are the result of taking the methodology of the Jewish esoteric tradition seriously and seeing what its rigorous application would prove, an approach that goes far toward validating the deeper interconnections between form, sound, and number posited by sacred science and that can bring us even further, to "a sense sublime of something far more deeply interfused."[25]

In addition to uncovering the correspondences of significant Hebrew words, most importantly the Tetragrammaton, a form of geometric archeology has also been practiced in which textual or diagrammatic hints have been explored to find the underlying geometric logic that can yield their hidden meanings. Even more significant than solution of the geometric enigma of the *Sefer Yetzirah* has been the discovery of the clearest source of the most important cosmological diagram of the Western esoteric tradition, the kabbalistic Tree of Life Diagram. Its demonstrated derivation from a sixfold rotation around its Da'at (Knowledge) point introduces us to a remarkable diagram every line of which contributes to an elegant geometric proof of that geometric problem the Greeks called the "duplication of the cube," and which in Hebrew, as in Greek, geometry seems to have had a primary mythological significance, that of the genesis of the son. In the expanding forms of this "Tree of Knowledge," the cosmic process is graphically portrayed as a movement from divine conception, through interuterine development in the World of Creation, to final delivery of the cosmic son. Analysis of the interrelated geometry of the single, sixfold, and *Sefer Yetzirah* Trees may well be the most important contribution of this work to kabbalistic studies, explaining as never before both the abstract and symbolic meaning of the diagram whose explication has been the primary focus of kabbalistic cosmology.

Not only has the study of Hebraic sacred science revealed much that was previously hidden about the Jewish esoteric tradition, but it also has implications that go beyond historical understanding, implications for the nature of the multidimensional reality it is uniquely fitted to explore. The greatest validation of the ancient sacred science may come, however, from the new illumination it can shed on contemporary physics. In fact, the comprehensive modeling by a kabbalistically derived geometric matrix of all the particles known to quantum physics should make a major contribution to quantum theory by providing new explanations for some previously unvisualizable aspects of this theory, such as the double spin of the quarks and the exclusion principle relative to the nuclear particles. Even more important may be the new perspective on quantum physics resulting from an application of the guidelines of sacred science to its data, enabling us to see in the atom that same numerical balancing of infinite extension and finite localization that sacred science has ever posited as the model for both microcosmic and macrocosmic functioning. So too should the alternative scenario for quantum cosmology, based on its own data, raise some further questions about the adequacy of the received theory and generate new respect for the insights of kabbalistic cosmology. This synthesis of quantum cosmology with the cosmology of Luria projects a course of future cosmic evolution not as dark as that envisioned by quantum cosmologists. Building upon the Sabbatical cosmic model shown in chapter 6 to be archetypally embodied in the Genesis creation account, this final projection is one that sees the cosmos and its son evolving jointly toward that final unification with the infinite in which the finite treasure of particularity is not lost but redeemed.

But if the nine explorations that make up this volume have implications for the secular as well as sacred branches of science and cosmology, it is still of the sacred that they speak most powerfully and with a particular accent. They may provide just the needed support, therefore, for that remythologizing of the Jewish sacred tradition for which Arthur Green, among other Jewish historians, has been calling:

> We have seen the unidimensional flatness and poverty which positivism and historicism have lent to our once sacred existence. The need for demythologizing is past; *a remythologizing of the religious consciousness is what this hour calls upon us to create.* And here it is the Kabbalist, the one who has most successfully accomplished that task in our past, who is to be our historic guide and mentor.[26]

Such a remythologizing of the Kabbalah must understand the Lurianic preoccupation with the Partzufim, particularly with the birthing of the

Partzuf of the son, as pointing a brave new way to human perfectibility: that the divine cosmic child *is* perfected humanity, and that human spiritual growth and transformation into a multiplicity of divine personalities represents the purpose of creation that has ever been the secret doctrine of the Jewish esoteric tradition culminating in the Kabbalah. In revealing its consistent meaningfulness, this work may thus provide contemporary Jewry not only with a past that can deepen its devotions but also with a future.

2

The Hebraic Secret
Doctrine of the Son

Texts of the Biblical Period

At the core of esoteric Judaism lies a complex hidden knowledge that I
have termed the secret doctrine of the son. This chapter will attempt to
reconstruct the historical background for the Hebraic conceptualization
of such a salvific figure, tracing the evidence for this secret doctrine from
its earliest biblical roots through the various later stages of Jewish mysticism. We will begin with the thesis that the Jewish esoteric tradition
culminating in the Kabbalah had its origin in the ancient lore of the
Temple priests, a lore containing the central knowledge transmitted
through the millennia by this tradition and one that the final section of
this chapter will show to have been conveyed as early as the primary
credal affirmation of the Sh'ma.

In the Books of Moses the secret doctrine of the son is most closely
tied to the practice of sacrifice and thus eventually to the holiness of the
priesthood. But it begins in archetypal form with Abraham. The renam-
ing of Abraham, as also of Sarah, can be considered symbolic of the
transformation of personality that signifies such spiritual rebirth as establishes a covenant with the Everlasting. The association of this cov-

enant with sacrifice is variously indicated in the text:

> And when Abram was ninety years old and nine, the Lord appeared
> to Abram and said unto him, I am the Almighty God; walk before
> me, and be thou perfect [*tamim*]. And I will make my covenant
> between me and thee. . . . Neither shall thy name any more be
> called Abram, but thy name shall be Abraham. . . . And ye shall
> circumcise the flesh of your foreskin; and it shall be a token of the
> covenant betwixt me and you. And he that is eight days old shall
> be circumcised; and my covenant shall be in your flesh for an ever-
> lasting covenant. . . . As for Sarai thy wife . . . Sarah shall her name
> be. . . . Sarah thy wife shall bear thee a son. (Gen. 17:1–19)

The covenant requires that Abraham be *tamim,* a whole without flaw or
division, in performing the divine will. Such a sacrifice of that which is
animal in human nature for that which is everlasting is signified by the
rite of circumcision, the token of the covenant, a rite normally to be
performed on that eighth day considered as beyond the seven days of
creation and thus symbolic of eternity. In this case the sacrifice of the
flesh of the foreskin is only symbolic of an inner consecration of the
whole self to divine service, the fruits of sexuality also being devoted to
this higher covenant. But the meaning of animal sacrifice is spelled out
more clearly with respect to the miraculous son who is to be born, against
all the laws of nature, to the divinely renamed Abraham and Sarah.

The meaning of the divinely ordered binding of Isaac is not simply
the final proving of Abraham and through his obedience the transmission of blessing to all humanity: "And in thy seed shall all the nations of
the earth be blessed; because thou hast obeyed my voice" (Gen. 22:18).
It is an instruction as to the use of the substitute sacrifice: "And Abraham
lifted up his eyes, and looked, and behold behind him a ram caught in a
thicket by his horns: and Abraham went and took the ram, and offered
him up for a burnt offering in the stead of his son" (Gen. 22:13). The
individual consecrated to divine service is not to be destroyed but redeemed through the practice of sacrifice, in particular through the practice of the substitute animal sacrifice.

Such a substitution of animal for human sacrifice is not a temporiz-
ing of an originally purer practice that had come to be regarded as too
demanding, but the essence of all religious rites of sacrifice properly
understood. It is rather the use of human sacrifice that represents a
degradation from the true purpose of such rites, the transformation of

the human into the divine through the redemptive sacrifice of that which is animal. But the substitute animal that is sacrificed is not only symbolic of the animal nature of man; it also becomes the vehicle of that sanctification of man by which he becomes holy. This association of the priestly rite of animal sacrifice, the main ritual focus of the books of the Mosaic Law, with the secret doctrine of the son, the soul or souls that have been spiritually reborn in holiness, is further developed in the Book of Exodus.

We begin with God's instruction to Moses as to what he should say to Pharaoh: "thus saith the Lord, Israel is my son, even my firstborn: And I say unto thee, Let my son go, that he may serve me" (Exod. 4:22–23). The religious meaning of the term "son" is first applied to the collective nation of Israel, which through such service will become "a kingdom of priests, and an holy nation" (Exod. 19:6). In the Palestinian Talmud, this special usage of the term "son(s)" is recognized: "At the hour that Israel does the will of the Holy One, blessed be He, they are called sons; and at the hour that they do not do the will of the Holy One, blessed be He, they are not called sons" (Kiddushin 61a). The nation of Israel is not only the divine son but His firstborn, one specially consecrated to the divine service: "Sanctify unto me all the firstborn, whatsoever openeth the womb among the children of Israel, both of man and of beast: it is mine" (Exod. 13:2). But the important distinction between the sancti-fied firstborns of man and of animals is that "All the firstborn of thy sons thou shalt redeem" (Exod. 34:20). The human firstborns are not only to be technically redeemed from death through the substitute of an animal sacrifice, later reduced to a monetary contribution of five shekels to the Temple (Num. 18:15–16), but also through the spiritual efficacy of this practice, that revealed in the instructions for the consecration of those who are to be models for the whole nation, the priests.

The most significant things Moses must do for Aaron and his sons "to hallow them, to minister unto me in the priest's office" (Exod. 29:1) involve the "ram of consecration" (Exod. 29:22). First some of its blood is to be put on the tips of their right earlobes, right thumbs, and right big toes (Exod. 29:20), an act that would appear to symbolize the strengthening of their right, spiritually expansive sides and the integra-tion of the three psychic centers that can be identified with these ex-tremities, the mind with the earlobes, the heart with the thumbs, and the instincts with the toes. Even more significant than their anointing, and that of the sanctuary, with blood and oil is the final use to be made of this ram:

And thou shalt take the ram of consecration, and seethe its flesh in
a holy place. And Aaron and his sons shall eat the flesh of the ram,
and the bread that is in the basket, at the door of the tent of meeting. And they shall eat those things wherewith atonement was made,
to consecrate and to sanctify them; but a stranger shall not eat
thereof, because they are holy. (Exod. 29:31–33)

The sacrificial animal that is offered up to God in a holy place becomes
transformed by the divine holiness of which it partakes; and the eating of
this ritually transformed animal flesh transfers this same holiness to the
participant through ingestion. This is the central mystery of the priestly
practice of animal sacrifice and the essence of the priestly religious understanding.

This understanding is conveyed at the conclusion of the divine instructions for the consecration of the tabernacle and the priesthood:

And I will sanctify the tabernacle of the congregation, and the altar: I will sanctify also both Aaron and his sons, to minister to me
in the priest's office. And I will dwell among the children of Israel,
and will be their God. And they shall know that I am the Lord their
God, that brought them forth out of the land of Egypt, that I may
dwell among them: I am the Lord their God. (Exod. 29:44–46)

Although the key to this priestly understanding is clearly stated in the
Hebrew, the obscuring of its meaning in the translation is a product of
the loss of this understanding that has befallen the Jewish exoteric tradition. For the word twice translated as "among," *betoch,* can be shown in
any Hebrew-English dictionary to have the principal meaning of "within."
What God is here proclaiming is that through the ministrations of the
priest's office, the sacrifice and eating of consecrated animals in a holy
place, God will dwell *within* the children of Israel, such a transfiguration
of man with holiness being the reason that they were delivered from
Egyptian bondage. By partaking of the holy sacrifices during the three
pilgrimage festivals, all of the children of Israel will further be able
to experience the indwelling of the Holy Spirit that is the daily experience of the officiating priests and thus likewise grow in such holiness
as will truly establish Israel as the divine son, as "a kingdom of priests,
and an holy nation" (Exod. 19:6). But it is what must be presumed to
have been the daily experience of the officiating priests, the miraculous
transformation of flesh into spirit through their ritual ministrations and

the communication of its holiness into their own persons, which forms the basis of all the later cosmological developments that can be associated with this priestly knowledge.

We can distinguish two main lines of theoretical development that have their source in the Mosaic Law, those of the prophets and of the priests. The Hebrew prophets have been the more celebrated in Western religious history, but their primary concern was with the ethical behavior of man to man, both individually and collectively, and they showed little sympathy for the Temple sacrifices or understanding of their purpose. The prophets preached an ethical rather than ritual religion, as in these words of Micah: "Wherewith shall I come before the Lord. . . . shall I come before him with burnt offerings, with calves of a year old? . . . He hath shewed thee, O man, what is good; and what doth the Lord require of thee, but to do justly, and to love mercy, and to walk humbly with thy God?" (Mic. 6:6, 8). In contrast to what might be called the "horizontal" concern of the prophets, their antisacerdotal concern with social ethics, those associated with the true priestly lore showed a correspondingly "vertical" concern for individual spiritual transformation. Where the prophets preached the high ideal of a holy society, finally of a Messianic society, the priests were developing their different understanding of human perfectibility, not of humility before God but of salvific unification with the divine. Through ritual purifications and sacrifices, they experienced the God within and must have taught the mysteries of an accompanying spiritual ascent to mystic vision. Evidence of such a developing lore can first be seen through those prophets who can be directly linked with priestly practice, Elijah and Ezekiel.

Of Elijah, who can be dated in the ninth century B.C.E., we have only the historical account appearing in 1 and 2 Kings, written some two centuries later. But that the historians compiling this record were priests would appear from the high valuation they gave to the sacrificial cult and their understanding of its purpose. Thus Elijah's greatest earthly accomplishment involves his drawing down of the divine fire to light his sacrifice and so confound the four hundred and fifty prophets of Baal. His great theophany is of the God who is not in earth-shaking external events but within, in "a still small voice" (1 Kings 19:12). And his end is one of direct translation to heaven in a fiery chariot.

Elijah had told Elisha he would receive the double portion of his spirit that Elisha had requested if he could perceive the way the elder prophet is to pass away: "And it came to pass . . . that, behold, there appeared a chariot of fire, and horses of fire, and parted them both asunder; and Elijah went up by a whirlwind into heaven. And Elisha saw it, and he cried, My father, my father, the chariot of Israel, and the horsemen thereof" (2 Kings 2:11–12). Elijah's translation to heaven is mystically perceived by Elisha, who thus not only becomes Elijah's spiritual son but understands the vehicle of this translation, the chariot, to be the ideal Community of Israel, that which we have seen named by God as His son. As a true saint of the Lord, Elijah becomes one of those who will form the ideal community collectively represented as the divine son, and his passage from life also demonstrates the salvation finally attendant upon a life devoted to the enhancing of spiritual power, the transcendence of mortality. The story of Elijah's life and death is the culminating example of the central truth of the priestly tradition, that there are spiritual practices by which man can become informed with divine power, the power to overcome earthly limitations both in life and beyond it, and that the goal of human existence is the perfecting of such holiness as can achieve eternal endurance.

This central truth of the historical books, which we have just traced from Abraham to Elijah and seen to be derived from the nature of priestly sacrifices, first achieves individual literary expression in the writings of the greatest prophet who was also a Zadokite priest, Ezekiel. It is Ezekiel who clearly brings together the concepts of the son and of the chariot that seemed to be similarly connected by Elisha. As Elisha had a chariot vision that bestowed spiritual power upon him and caused him to recognize his sonship to that formerly human source of power appearing on the chariot, so does Ezekiel, in what would seem to be a literary borrowing. Writing one hundred years after the redaction of 2 Kings, in the sixth century B.C.E., Ezekiel has a chariot vision after which he is addressed by God with the term he made famous, "son of man," and is filled with His spirit: "And he said unto me, Son of man, stand upon thy feet, and I will speak with thee. And the spirit entered into me when he spake unto me, and set me upon my feet" (Ezek. 2:1–2). The phrase "son of man" *(ben adam)*, which is to have a remarkable further history in the later apocalypses, appears eighty-seven times in the Book of Ezekiel in reference to the prophet-priest himself, and it would seem to be directly related to that which he sees on the chariot Throne.

The chariot he sees has four levels—the Wheels, the Living Creatures, the Firmament, and the Throne—"and upon the likeness of the throne was the likeness as the appearance of a man above upon it. . . .

This was the appearance of the likeness of the glory of the Lord" (Ezek. 1:26, 28). The Glory, or Kavod, of God, which he saw seated on the Throne, had "the appearance of a man." The phrase "son of man" used by God of Ezekiel would seem to imply that the prophet is a human son of God, a being derived from man who has achieved the status of divine sonship earlier attributed collectively to Israel. And the essence of this Throne vision, so unlike that of Isaiah—"I saw also the Lord sitting upon a throne" (Isa. 6 : 1)—is not directly of God but of glorified man. It is man in his potentially final state of spiritual transfiguration that would here seem to represent the Glory of God and final purpose of creation, the Glory thus representing the supernal form of the divine son.

The essential meaning of Ezekiel's vision, then, is that the son of man, the human son of God, is he who has achieved the mystical capacity to see the divine nature of his own higher self. This understanding became part of the later kabbalistic tradition that at the highest level of mystical ascent the face one sees on the Throne will be one's own. Thus Abraham Abulafia, the great kabbalistic master of meditation, writes: "When an individual completely enters the mystery of prophecy, he suddenly sees his own image standing before him." And he proceeds to support this claim by quoting from a work of Moshe of Narbonne that refers to this earlier tradition: "When the sages teach that the prophets 'liken a form to its Creator,' they mean that they liken the form which is in the prophet's own soul . . . to its Creator, that is, to God. It is thus written, 'Over the form of the Throne there was a form like an image of a Man' (Ezek. 1:26). These forms and images exist in the soul of the prophet. . . ."[1] This is the essential message of all later forms of Jewish mysticism, for all are derived directly from Ezekiel's vision. The Kabbalists emphasize the four levels of the chariot, which they identify with the four worlds of cosmic emanation, the Merkabah mystics the ascent of the chariot (Merkabah) through the seven heavens to the Throne vision, and the apocalyptic writers the two forms of divine sonship. But all take from Ezekiel his particular revelation of the priestly learning that conveys its most profound meaning.

The mystical tradition in Judaism is, then, the lineal descendent of the learning that we may presume was taught in the Temple as part of the training for the priesthood. In the last chapter, as in the next, I argue that this priestly training also conserved and passed down the ancient heritage of scientific understanding, primarily the laws governing and relating number, form, and harmonic sound but also such astronomy as is necessary for making the religious calendar. Though the later rabbinical tradition derives largely from the prophets, the esoteric-mystical tradition, which has always maintained a hidden but vital existence throughout the subsequent millennia of Jewish religious history, derives just as surely from the priesthood as its tradition was filtered through the main conduit of its great prophet, Ezekiel.

The culminating biblical expression of this tradition, and one deriving most directly from Ezekiel, is that of the Book of Daniel, now thought to have been written in the second century B.C.E. In Daniel's Throne vision, the term "son of man" is directly applied to one of the two supernal beings seen by him:

> The Ancient of days did sit, whose garment was white as snow, and the hair of his head like the pure wool: his throne was like the fiery flame, and his wheels as burning fire. . . . I saw in the night visions, and, behold, one like the Son of man came with the clouds of heaven, and came to the Ancient of days, and they brought him near before him. And there was given him dominion, and glory, and a kingdom, that all people, nations, and languages, should serve him: his dominion is an everlasting dominion, which shall not pass away, and his kingdom that which shall not be destroyed. . . . the saints of the most High shall take the kingdom, and possess the kingdom for ever. (7:9, 13–14, 18)

The two supernal beings are distinguished by age, he who is seated on the chariot Throne being characterized as "Ancient" and having white hair while he who is brought before this enthroned Ancient of Days has the comparative youth associated with the term "son." But this son would seem to be derived from man, if the prior analysis of the term "son of man" in Ezekiel can be applied as well to the Daniel text, and to him is given final dominion and glory in an everlasting kingdom to which "the saints of the most High" are also heir.

Where the association of Ezekiel as "son of man" with the envisioned man on the Throne was only implied, such an implication becomes explicit in the next vision of Daniel: "And it came to pass, when I, even I Daniel, had seen the vision, and sought for the meaning, then, behold, there stood before me as the appearance of a man. . . . he said unto me, Understand, O son of man: for at the time of the end shall be the vision" (8:15,17). The addressing of Daniel, like Ezekiel, as the "son of man" *(ben adam)* makes explicit the identification of seer and seen, since a form of this term had been applied to the supernal being who is to be the final apocalyptic judge and rule the everlasting kingdom.

That such an identification was understood to be the meaning of Ezekiel's vision is made even clearer in a further apocalyptic work, one influenced by Daniel but not included in the biblical canon, that also uses the term "son of man." This is the "Parables" section of the Ethiopic Book of Enoch, now known as 1 Enoch, which postdates the rest of this text by some 100 to 200 years. As R. H. Charles has convincingly deduced: "the date of the Parables could not have been earlier than 94 B.C. or later than 64 B.C. But it is possible to define the date more precisely . . . to the years 94–79."[2] Both Daniel and this second part of 1 Enoch are expressions of a developing priestly cosmology either rooted in interpretation of Ezekiel's vision or given an earlier, more cryptic, expression by Ezekiel himself. As in Daniel, there is the double vision of supernal beings, one older and the other younger:

> And there I saw one who had a head of days, and his head (was) white like wool; and with him (there was) another, whose face had the appearance of a man, and his face (was) full of grace, like one of the holy angels. And I asked one of the holy angels who went with me, and showed me all the secrets, about that Son of Man, who he was, and whence he was, (and) why he went with the Head of Days. And he answered me and said to me: 'This is the Son of Man who has righteousness, and with whom righteousness dwells; he will reveal all the treasures of that which is secret, for the Lord of Spirits has chosen him, and through uprightness his lot has surpassed all before the Lord of Spirits for ever. And this Son of Man . . . will cast down the kings from their throne. (chap. 46)[3]

Of the final Day of Judgment, we were earlier told of this chosen being: "On that day the Chosen One will sit on the throne of glory" (chap. 45). Equally significant is the suggestion of his prior existence: "For from the beginning the Son of Man was hidden, and the Most High kept him in the presence of his power, and revealed him (only) to the chosen; and the community of the holy and the chosen will be sown, and all the chosen will stand before him on that day" (chap. 62). It is not clear whether this supernal "son of man" existed from the beginning or only the plan for his final revelation. But those who, like Enoch, were chosen for final redemption were given a foreknowledge of his role in the last days, as in Enoch's vision: "And he sat on the throne of his glory, and the whole judgement was given to the Son of Man" (chap. 69). Most significant, however, is the clear identification finally made between the human visionary Enoch and this "son of man":

> And it came to pass after this that my spirit was carried off, and it went up into the heavens. . . . And that angel came to me, and greeted me with his voice, and said to me: "You are the Son of Man who was born to righteousness, and righteousness remains over you, and the righteousness of the Head of Days will not leave you." And he said to me: "He proclaims peace to you in the name of the world which is to come, for from there peace has come out from the creation of the world; and so you will have it for ever and for ever and ever. And all . . . will walk according to your way, inasmuch as righteousness will never leave you; with you will be their dwelling, and with you their lot, and they will not be separated from you, for ever. (chap. 71)

The angelic proclamation of Enoch's identification with the "son of man" sitting on the Throne of Glory indicates that the exalted object of his vision is that of his own higher self. This higher self may again have existed from the beginning as his exclusive spiritual guide or as the guide of all the righteous, as their communal soul root, but in any case, it is one that will represent, in its final manifestation, the community of the righteous, the ideal of Israel as the divine son, the consecrated firstborn. The priestly understanding of the laws of purification was always that such observance would endow man with a divine character: "I am the Lord your God; sanctify yourselves therefore, and be ye holy; for I am holy" (Lev. 11:44). And in Enoch's vision, the divinization of man as that son who is to sit on the Throne of Glory is most clearly stated to be the final transfiguration in "the world which is to come" of all the righteous who have followed the path of priestly gnosis.

It is "knowledge" of hidden things, particularly of the process of spiritual transformation by which one can achieve final unification with the divine higher self revealed to one in mystic visions, that is the gnosis transmitted through the generations of priests, probably from the founding of the priesthood. It appears in one quasi-veiled form or another in all the biblical books that they edited, open to "one who is wise, understanding with his own knowledge," the talmudic requirement for mystical studies,[4] and finally begins to emerge in ever less cryptic form in the apocalypses derived from the priestly prophet Ezekiel. In its later Merkabah and kabbalistic forms, it has been viewed by Scholem and others[5] as a product of non-Jewish Gnosticism, but the direction of transmission would appear to have been the reverse.

As we have seen, the Jewish doctrine was complete by the time of 1 Enoch, well before the emergence either of Christianity or of Gnosticism. Jesus, who consistently referred to himself as the "son of man" and rejected the title of Messiah, was clearly influenced by the particular strand of earlier Jewish mysticism we have been tracing. And so was Mani. As Gilles Quispel has shown:

> The Cologne *Mani Codex* seems to be of particular importance in this connection, because it shows how Gnosis evolved out of Judaism, or Jewish Christianity, as a result of a dialectical process.
>
> On the one hand there is no doubt that the Manichaean myth described a Gnostic experience, namely the encounter with the Self. The Codex tells how "the Twin" revealed himself to Mani at the age of 25:
>
>> I recognized him
>> and understood that he was my Self,
>> from whom I had been separated.
>
> On the other hand we now have proof that from the age of four to twenty-five, i.e., before he had this experience, Mani had been—like his father Patek before him—a member of the Jewish Christian Elkesaite sect in Babylonia. . . . We now know that as a child Mani was a Jewish boy, that he was circumcised and celebrated the Sabbath.[6]

The Christianity that Mani accepted was precisely that esoteric form deriving from Ezekiel. As Quispel further shows:

> Mani assumed the name of Apostle because he interpreted his Twin as the Paraclete . . . that Christ would send. . . . He did not indulge in self-deification; not his empirical ego, but his transcendental Self was the Paraclete. . . . The Jewish Christians were entirely convinced that the Holy Spirit was a feminine hypostasis. . . . Mani's religious experience, his encounter with the Self, presupposes and spiritualizes the symbolism of anointment, rebirth and the *mysterium coniunctionis* of Jewish Christian baptism.[7]

Baptism had, of course, a Jewish origin and was a major practice of the Essenes. Scholem reminds us that "we should not dismiss the possibility of a continuous flow of specific ideas from the Qumran sect [thought to be the Essenes] to the Merkabah mystics and rabbinic circles in the case of *Shi'ur Komah* as well as in other fields."[8] Though there may well have been cross-fertilization in the post-Christian era between the esoteric branches of Judaism, Christianity, and Islam, and of all with Gnosticism, it is Judaism that had the temporal priority and a fully developed tradition of esoteric knowledge and practice long before these other offshoots arose, one which it transmitted to them as well as directly to its own continuously developing forms of Jewish mysticism.

Jewish mysticism in the last centuries of the Temple has been generally associated with the Pharisees, the priestly class of Sadducees being thought to have rejected the concept of an afterlife, largely on the testimony of Josephus. But however worldly some of the priests may have become, the evidence that has already been developed would rather argue that the priesthood, at least those priests of the house of Zadok, was the conservator of an age-old mystical tradition and that this tradition became more widely disseminated in this period by some of the more devout of the priests, perhaps just because of the worldliness of the upper hierarchy. That the apocalyptic literature of this period was the product of such anti-Hasmonaean priests is a thesis also advanced by Ithamar Gruenwald:

> For people who considered the temple as being defiled by the hands of an unworthy clan of priests, there was no alternative but to conceive of God as having to withdraw His presence from the earthly temple to the uppermost heaven. . . . Apocalypticism gives, among other things, expression to that criticism of the Jerusalem-priesthood. . . . Moreover, if we take into consideration the fact that Apocalypticism was to a large extent the product of levitic, or priestly, circles then the polemical tones struck therein do not merely have an anti-priestly orientation, but they do in fact echo an inner-priestly struggle for hegemony and authority.[9]

In chapter 1, we saw that Sadducean Zadokite priests were considered by Jacob Neusner and Lawrence H. Schiffman to be the founders of the Qumran community of Essenes, understood to be the source of the Dead Sea Scrolls, and that Geza Vermes, translator of the most authoritative edition of the Dead Sea Scrolls in English, only qualified this view slightly by arguing that Zadokite priests rather took over this community in its formative years, led by one of their number, the Teacher of Righteousness, who defined the teachings of this movement.[10] In "The Community Rule" scroll, formerly known as "The Manual of Discipline," we may not only see such a connection confirmed but learn more about the roles played by the Zadokite priesthood and their secret doctrine:

> The Priests shall enter first, ranked one after another according to the perfection of their spirit; then the Levites; and thirdly, all the people one after another. . . . and (they shall all of them be) sons of the everlasting Company. . . . Whoever approaches the Council of the Community shall enter the Covenant of God. . . . by a binding oath to return with all his heart and soul to every commandment of the Law of Moses in accordance with all that has been revealed of it to the sons of Zadok, the Priests, Keepers of the Covenant and Seekers of His will. . . . concerning His laws that they might know the hidden things. . . . impart[ing] true knowledge and righteous judgement to those who have chosen the Way. . . . the mysteries of marvellous truth.[11]

The "sons of Zadok" not only are accorded respect of place but accepted as interpreters of the Mosaic Torah, of both its ritual specifications and also its "hidden things":

> Then the Priests shall recite the favours of God manifested in His mighty deeds and shall declare all His merciful grace to Israel. . . . The Master shall instruct all the sons of light and shall teach them the nature of all the children of men. . . . the sons of truth in this world. And as for the visitation of all who walk in this spirit, it shall be healing, great peace in a long life, and fruitfulness, together with every everlasting blessing and eternal joy in life without end, a crown of glory and a garment of majesty in unending light.[12]

The most marvelous of the mysteries to be divulged involve the secret doctrine of the son, a word constantly reappearing in the document with such other associations as "light" and "truth" but signifying most importantly the final fruit of "eternal joy." Since this is addressed to a celibate community, the "fruitfulness" referred to cannot be of this world. This meaning is clarified in the translation of the original editor of this scroll, Millar Burrows, who gives the significant reading "sons of man" where Vermes had given "children of men" and who gives the following, more meaningful, translation of the last phrases of the above quote: "and bringing forth seed, with all eternal blessings and everlasting joy in the life of eternity, and a crown of glory with raiment of majesty in everlasting light."[13] Here we have an almost explicit statement of the mystery of the son as the eternal form of the self, a higher self endowed with "a crown of glory" appropriate only to a divine form, though a form whose seed is to be recognized as brought forth or planted in this world. Such redeemed covenanters are collectively called "sons of the everlasting Company," of the selective true supernal Community of Israel understood to be the referent of God's proclamation: "Israel is my son" (Exod. 4:22).

This formerly hidden doctrine is now being revealed to this covenanting community with the hope it will still be kept secret: "the Interpreter shall not conceal from them, out of fear of the spirit of apostasy, any of those things hidden from Israel which have been discovered by him."[14] And the response of the newly enlightened is ecstatic:

> My eyes have gazed
>> on that which is eternal,
> on wisdom concealed from men,
>> on knowledge and wise design.[15]

Though the saving knowledge of the covenanter's final transfiguration may be attributed to personal vision, it is more likely to have been the product of such priestly instruction as we have seen to be prescribed; and this would probably have been supported by the visual evidence of sacred geometry, such a complex of geometric proofs as will be the subject of chapters 6, 7, and 8. The eight copies of the Book of Daniel in the Qumran library attest to the community's interest in the son of man theological concept, though the dualistic notions of predestination found in the sectarian documents also point to a separate development of the separatist priesthood who had left the Temple for the desert. As Schiffman has shown, "Both groups of Sadducees—those who left the Temple to become the sectarians, perhaps included in the term 'Essenes,' and those who remained in Jerusalem—underwent profound changes thereafter."[16]

"The Community Rule" offers us a rare opportunity to see how the Zadokite priesthood functioned in areas of leadership and interpretaion going far beyond their primary cultic rituals of Temple sacrifice, though the concern of the manual with "the sacred food of the masters"[17] shows that the ingestion of food made holy through the ritual of priestly bless-ing—"the Priest shall be the first to stretch out his hand to bless the firstfruits of the bread and new wine"[18]—was still a central feature of the community these priests were governing. Prayer was also important and was viewed by these dissident priests as a proper substitute for the Temple sacrifices: "And Prayer rightly offered shall be as an acceptable fragrance of righteousness, and perfection of way as a delectable free-will offer-ing."[19] Indeed, as Mishnah Tamid 5:1 early recognized, the seminal lit-urgy of the "three-paragraph" Sh'ma and its surrounding blessings was already being offered in a prayer service by priests in the Temple.

At the conclusion of this chapter we shall see how prayer was under-stood in the later kabbalistic and hasidic traditions to accomplish the very transfiguration of the person praying into the divine personality that was the attested goal of the esoteric writings. But it was already under-stood in this way by the priests who developed the liturgy performed in the Temple prayer services. As I have elsewhere shown,[20] this earliest liturgy was centered on the Sh'ma with its commandment to love God, and it already contained the prior benediction "Ahavah Rabbah," con-cerned, as I understand it, with the redemptive character of the divine love ideally experienced in prayer, the love that could transform the pray-ing individual into a member of Klal Yisrael, the divine son of the priestly secret doctrine. Thus theology and practice were developed together as necessary complements by those Temple priests who conserved and de-veloped the hidden spiritual tradition of the priesthood.

Though the priestly governors of the Qumran Essenes developed the secret priestly doctrine of salvation along more dualistic apocalyptic lines, those who remained in the Temple continued their scholarly work of determining, refining, and expounding the biblical canon as well as de-veloping liturgical prayer meetings as an adjunct to the sacrificial offer-ings that offered a new way of effecting the purpose of their inner tradi-tion. For in addition to their exoteric areas of creative religious labor, they also cultivated the esoteric doctrine of individual salvation we have been tracing and the sacred science that could demonstrate its truth, a doctrine first cryptically divulged by their prophet Ezekiel and then more openly in Daniel and 1 Enoch. The differences between these exoteric and esoteric formulations do not signify opposition parties within the priesthood,[21] but rather the distinction any temple culture must make between the doctrines promulgated to the community at large and those reserved for the spiritual elite identified with the institution of the priesthood. Whatever the differences between Daniel and 1 Enoch, the importance of the son of man doctrine to both shows that this was the essential element of priestly theology for at least the five hundred years between Ezekiel and the Parables section of 1 Enoch, and we shall see that it continued to flourish in Merkabah mysticism.

Given the spiritual traditions and training of the priesthood, it is likely that priests not only founded the Essenes but would also have joined the Pharisees and other Jewish sects. Indeed, the Rabbi Ishmael whom we shall shortly see to figure in the *Shi'ur Komah*, as he also does in the *Hekhalot Rabbatai*, was talmudically identified as a high priest.[22] But it is also known that initiatic mystical groups, composed of a teacher and only a few students, also developed in the early tannaic period and that such groups passed the mystic lore down from generation to generation.[23] An important factor in the development of such "cabals" may have been the existence of surviving members of the no longer functioning Essene community who had been trained by the Zadokite priests. But an even greater factor must have been the deprofessionalization of the priesthood after the destruction of the Second Temple, which would have necessitated great Temple scholars becoming private teachers, thereby both preserving their ancient knowledge in its purest form and maintaining its hidden nature.

It is perhaps unfortunate that the Sadducean priests who transmitted the inner tradition of the Temple cult always did so, as with the Essenes, under an oath of secrecy. For had they revealed their secret doctrine to the Jewish populace, it might have changed Jewish destiny in the same way that this doctrine, in a somewhat different form, was taken by Christianity to the world. Or had they made common cause with the Pharisees at the time of national crisis, they might have ensured the popularization of their secret doctrine as the mystical teaching of the future rabbinical tradition. Without such priestly collaboration, however, the talmudic tradition carried over to the people of Israel only the externals of the priestly culture, its code of purity, without its allied secret doctrine of individual salvation, a loss of mystical understanding from which traditional Judaism has suffered to this day. The priestly elite, on the other hand, remained true to its nature and, rather than embracing such populist alternatives, chose to set up the direct, secret chain of transmission—which has always been the source claimed by the Kabbalists—through which an intrinsically Jewish form of gnosis was passed down from the Temple to become the core of that later form of the "tradition" known as the Kabbalah.

The Merkabah Texts

The further development of the secret doctrine of the son in the postbiblical period occurs in such Merkabah (chariot) works as 3 Enoch and the *Shi'ur Komah*, generally dated within the second to fourth centuries C.E., though the origin of this literary tradition is a much contested issue. As Joseph Dan has most recently summarized this controversy, the standard position is that of Gershom Scholem and Saul Lieberman, one that views "Hechalot and *Merkavah* esoteric traditions as a secret stratum of mysticism in the heart of the talmudic-midrashic religious world. . . . as if these ideas . . . were always there, coexisting with the timeless sources of rabbinic literature."[24] Ephrayim E. Urbach is cited as a "lonely voice of dissent from this consensus"[25] before Dan's similar claim that this literature represents a "beginning" that is "unprecedented in its radical nature in rabbinic Judaism" as well as being "a radical departure from anything found in ancient Judaism."[26] We seem to be offered a choice between believing this mystical literature to be an inner talmudic tradition derived only from the traditional sources of rabbinic culture or to have no source.

But Rachel Elior has offered a more suggestive possibility in demonstrating the central importance in these texts of allusions to the Temple priesthood and its practices:

> There is no doubt that Hekhalot literature is replete with direct and indirect allusions to the world of the priests and the Levites in the temple. . . . Thus, though one may dispute the actual relationship between the historical circumstances (the destruction of the temple and abolition of the service) and their indirect literary expression (the tradition of the *Hekhalot* and the *Merkava*), one cannot ignore the focal position of the ritual and liturgical heritage of the temple in Hekhalot literature. . . . and the secrets of its priesthood's ritual heritage.[27]

Elior does not, however, go beyond her significant analysis that the use of Temple imagery, transferred to heavenly worship, was a particular response on the part of later mystics to loss of the earthly Temple. She does not enter into the "dispute" concerning "the actual relationship" between "historical circumstances" and "literary expression" to suggest, as I do, that such priestly "secrets" were actually those disseminated to a mystical elite by members of the post-Temple priesthood and the successive generations of their pupils. For despite the introduction of new elements into the original priestly teachings, as with the Essenes, what is more revealing, I would argue, is the continuity in these works of the priestly secret doctrine of the son.

As we shall now see, the main difference of 3 Enoch and the *Shi'ur Komah* from Daniel and 1 Enoch with respect to this secret doctrine is the substitute name of Metatron given for the figure earlier identified as the son of man. Whether it was the Christian adoption of this latter term that necessitated the need for a new name in Jewish mystical writings, or the need to make the meaning of this figure more explicit as well as more qualified, the new name of Metatron came into general use both in these writings and in the Talmud. The meaning of this name is still unresolved in contemporary scholarship, but the most persuasive argument, to my mind, is that assembled by Hugo Odeberg, the English translator and editor of 3 Enoch who gave this name to the late "Hebrew Book of Enoch."

The derivation finally adopted by Odeberg, that Metatron represents a combination of the two Greek words *meta* and *thronos*, was first advanced by J. H. Maius in 1698 and has since been supported by various authorities. Such a word coined by Greek-speaking Jews would have the meaning of "the Throne after or next to" another primary or higher Throne. For Odeberg, this meaning

> *best accords with the essential character assigned to Metatron in the earliest representations of him, above all in our book.* . . . . on the ground that *the idea of the "throne" plays a central part in the conception of Metatron.*
>
> Hence it may be suggested that the exact interpretation of the word Metatron is:
>
> The celestial being *who occupies the throne next to the Throne of Glory* (the Divine throne), or *the Throne next to the Throne of Glory* (using the early terminology acc. to which "throne" = "occupant of a throne" . . . or lesser Throne (= lesser YHWH; cf. ch. 12).[28]

In 3 Enoch, Metatron explains:

> All these things the Holy One, blessed be He, made for me: He made me a throne, similar to the Throne of Glory. . . . And He placed it at the door to the Seventh Hall and seated me on it. . . . And He called me THE LESSER YHWH in the presence of all His heavenly household; as it is written (Ex. xxiii. 21): "For my name is in him."[29]

If, then, the meaning of the name Metatron indicates the fact that in these later Merkabah works Metatron is not seated directly on the Throne of Glory but, at best, next to it, this would represent an apparent demotion of this figure. In Ezekiel the enthroned man was identified directly with the Glory (Ezek. 1:28, 3:23), and in 1 Enoch it is on the Throne of Glory that the "son of man" sits: "And he sat on the throne of his glory, and the whole judgement was given to the Son of Man" (69:27). But in the *Shi'ur Komah* Metatron's position is "beneath the throne of glory" (J_x 9, 11)[30] while, as just shown, in 3 Enoch Metatron is seated on a throne only "similar to the Throne of Glory" and placed only "at the door to the Seventh Hall." In both works, however, the earlier meaning is suggested by the identification of Metatron with the angel who is to be with the Israelites and lead them to the Promised Land, of whom it is said by God, "my name is in him" (Exod. 23:21). This angel appears to be associated with the later references to the indwelling Presence, the Shekhinah, in Exod. 29:45–46, and to the "Face," generally translated as "presence," in Exod. 33:14–15, which is to lead them.[31] In the *Shi'ur Komah*, reference to this angel comes significantly just before the statement that "the Shekhinah is on the throne of glory in the center" (L 3). But if the angel identified with Metatron is the Shekhinah, then the hidden message is that it really is Metatron who is seated on the Throne of Glory.

The main thrust of the Metatron works is, however, the same as those referring to the son of man, that there are two levels of the divine, the white-haired Ancient and the "son" or "youth," the former understood to be the ineffable Lord and the latter that which can be apprehended, His Glory. In both works Metatron is called "youth," *na'ar*. In 3 Enoch, the answer given by Metatron to the question as to why "they call thee 'Youth' in the high heavens" is: "Because I am Enoch, the son of Jared. For when the generation of the flood sinned. . . . the Holy One, blessed be He, lifted me up. . . . And the Holy One, blessed be He, assigned me for a prince and a ruler among the ministering angels" (4:1–3, 5). Metatron is called "Youth" because he is the transfigured form of the man Enoch, and it is the role of such a transfigured human to serve as a "prince" to the Holy One, blessed be He, who must thus be accounted the "king" of heaven. But since the normal relationship of king to prince is that of father to son, the term "youth" can also be understood to be a euphemism for the concept of the divine son, which its esoteric Jewish author may have felt had been co-opted by Christianity.

In the *Shi'ur Komah*, the term "son" is used not of Metatron but of those, like Rabbis Akiba, Ishmael, and Nathan, who have learned the Measure of the Body. In an earlier, and in this regard preferable, translation of the *Shi'ur Komah*, we are told: "He who knows this measure of our Creator . . . is assured that he is a son of the world to come."[32] Since Metatron is called *na'ar*, the implication is, however, that such a "son of the world to come" will be identified with the son figure of Metatron, also called the "prince of the presence" (J$_x$ 16), though whether this means only that he serves the Shekhinah or is actually to be equated with the enthroned Presence is left ambiguous.

The problem seems to have been that there was originally only one Throne of Glory on which sat the supernal man or two supernal figures, an ancient and a youth. Thus when it was deemed proper to assign the Throne to the ancient figure, now called the Holy One, blessed be He, the youth figure had to be assigned the lesser Throne, which resulted in his needing to be renamed as Metatron. But since the understanding was still that it should be the son or prince figure who represented "the glory of the Lord" (Ezek. 1:28), and thus should be seated on the Throne of Glory, various surreptitious means were employed to equate Metatron with the Shekhinah, a figure more appropriately seated on this Throne and actually occupying this position in the *Shi'ur Komah*.

The problem of the two thrones would seem to have been addressed most directly in the Kedushah, an antiphonal chant deriving from this Merkabah tradition that appears three times in the daily morning service—in the first benediction before the Sh'ma, within the Amidah prayer, and before the final Aleinu prayer—the antiphonal nature of this chant apparently attempting to reconcile the differing Throne visions of Isaiah and Ezekiel. Isaiah sees "the Lord sitting upon a throne" (6:1) and hears "seraphims" (6:2) crying to each other: "Holy, holy, holy is the Lord of hosts: the whole earth is full of his glory" (6:3). Ezekiel sees upon the Throne "the likeness of the appearance of a man. . . . This was the appearance of the likeness of the glory of the Lord" (1:26, 28), and he hears Cherubim saying: "Blessed be the glory of the Lord from his place" (3:12). Isaiah's enthroned being *is* the Lord and is seated above the glory-filled earth; Ezekiel's is this Glory, and its "place," when considered comparatively, would be understood to be beneath that of the Lord. The angelic singers are to be similarly distinguished, the Seraphim being a higher order than the Cherubim, this indicated as well by the number of their wings, the Seraphim having six, a perfect number that may be identified with heaven, and the Cherubim four, the number of the earth. In the Kedushah, both of these angelic orders are portrayed as singing their biblical refrains to each other, the Seraphim praising the divine transcendence and the Cherubim the divine immanence.

It is the singing of the Kedushah that is also the chief activity of the angelic hosts in the Merkabah Throne visions. As Odeberg early pointed out, "the significance of the celestial *Qedussa* is indicated by the stress laid on its performance. . . . It is the symbol of, and, at the same time, the actual realization of the Kingdom of Heaven in the celestial spheres."[33] The most recent editor of the *Shi'ur Komah*, Martin Samuel Cohen, agrees with a similar earlier assessment: "Alexander Altman, in an article on the use of hymns in *hekhalot* literature, has written that 'there can be no vision of the chariot-throne without hymnody.' This assertion is abundantly verified on every page, practically, of early mystic literature. . . ."[34] In the more literal translation of the *Shi'ur Komah* earlier introduced, we are further told: "He who knows this measure of our Creator, and the praise of the Holy One, blessed be He, Who is hidden from the creatures, is assured that he is a son of the world to come."[35] It is not, then, only the "measure of our Creator," the lower figure of Metatron whose size "is the height of the entire universe"(J_x 13–14), but also hymnal praise of the hidden Holy One, blessed be He, which is required to become a "son of the world to come," presumably in the transfigured form of Metatron. But we are then told: "whoever knows this measure of our Creator, and the praise of the Holy One, blessed be He, he will surely be a son of the world to come, provided he learns it regularly every day."[36] The Merkabah texts, with their many incorporated hymns, were meant to be performed orally every day[37] as a means by which the aspirant could experience his unity with the celestial choirs and so achieve, in Odeberg's words, "the actual realization of the Kingdom of Heaven in the celestial spheres."

There seems little doubt that this aspect of the Throne literature was as indebted to the priestly heritage as was its understanding of human transformation. As the latter derived from the practice of sacrifice, so the former derived from the communal prayer services offered by the priests in the Temple. During the heavenly service before the Throne in the *Shi'ur Komah*, reference is made to "the explicit name that the Lad [*na'ar*], whose name is Metatron, utters at that time" (L 162), a clear association of Metatron with the role of the earthly high priest on the Day of Atonement. It is the priests who developed the earliest order of the prayer service, certainly including a section of blessings containing the Sh'ma, as well as various other hymns and musical settings of the psalms, all performed with antiphonal choruses of Levites. And the implication of the *Shi'ur Komah* is that it is through such personal performance of prayer and sacred chanting that the transformation of personality, originally ascribed to the practice of animal sacrifice, is also to be achieved.

This brings us back to our point of origin, the divine renamings of Genesis. For it is not only Abraham and Sarah who are so renamed but also Jacob. And his transformation from Jacob into Israel occurs only after his great moment of prayer. Caught between the animosity of Laban, to whom he cannot by vow return, and Essau coming with troops to meet him, Jacob turns upward for deliverance: "O God of my father Abraham, and God of my father Isaac . . . I am not worthy of the least of all the mercies and of all the truth, which thou has shewed unto thy servant; for with my staff I passed over this Jordan; and I am become two bands. Deliver me, I pray thee, from the hand of my brother" (Gen. 32:9–11). As he wrestles that night with an angel and triumphs over all the liabilities his actions have accumulated during his lifetime, Jacob accomplishes psychologically the same transcendence of his animal nature that is ritually accomplished through animal sacrifice. It is only after this sacrifice of his lower self, that his name is angelically changed: "And he said, Thy name shall be called no more Jacob, but Israel: for as a prince hast thou power with God as with men, and hast prevailed" (Gen. 32:28). Jacob has been transformed into a "prince" (the root meaning of *sar* also incorporated into Sarah's name) of God (El), has been spiritually reborn as a divine son insofar as the relationship of a prince to a king is the same as that of a son to a king, and he has "prevailed," achieved a transcending endurance. This suggestion of a triumph over mortality is further strengthened by Jacob's response to the angel's blessing: "And Jacob called the name of the place Peniel: for I have seen God face to face, and my life is preserved" (Gen. 32:30).

We saw earlier that the "Face of God," the meaning of "Peniel," was one of the biblical expressions that could be identified with Metatron, of whom the God of the *Shi'ur Komah* and 3 Enoch had said, "my name is in him" (Exod. 23:21). The general scholarly understanding is that this represents Metatron's gradual taking over of the role earlier assigned to the angel Yahoel, of which the same statement—"my name is in him"—was made in the Apocalypse of Abraham, chapter 10.[38] But as the names of Abraham and Sarah were changed at their transforming covenantal moment by the assertion of just a Hey into their former names, so a Yod is found in the seven-letter form of Metatron identified with the final transfiguration of Enoch into a divine being. Thus of the three renamed figures of Genesis, Abraham and Sarah have the divine Hey in their names, and Jacob as Israel has the divine name El in him, this last revealing that rebirth as a prince implies the state of being a prince or son of God. But if, as we saw in the Throne visions deriving from Ezekiel, the "Face" one sees on this Throne is one's own, that of one's own higher self in the finally transfigured form later identified with Metatron, then Jacob has been able to survive the usually mortal seeing of God's face because the face he saw was that of his own immortal self, such a vision as was understood in the later Merkabah tradition to give one just this assurance of immortality, of being "a son of the world to come."[39]

The three divine renamings of Genesis imply two things. In the first case of Abraham and Sarah, the implication is that spiritual rebirth is an equal possibility for both men and women, that the collective divine son identified in Exodus with the Community of Israel is androgynous. In the case of the two males so renamed, the implication is of two different methods of achieving such rebirth. For Abraham, this is the method of the substitute animal sacrifice as he came to understand it in his final testing; for Jacob, it is the method of such true prayer as reveals a total abnegation of the lower or animal ego. These are also the two methods of human transformation with which the priesthood was originally identified. For as the priesthood first developed the prayer service as an adjunct to the Temple sacrifices, so did they incorporate in the very words and structure of the prayer service the essence of the priestly gnosis, the esoteric knowledge that the goal of such ritual observances is spiritual rebirth as a divine son. Much of this understanding was passed on to the core of rabbis that continued the development of the prayer services until it quite early achieved the basic form still practiced today. But the full mystical implications of the ritual of prayer were conveyed through that same chain of initiatic mystical groups that also transmitted the priestly cosmology down through the centuries. The subject of mystical prayer is one to which we will return after first tracing the appearance of the priestly model in the successive developments of the Jewish esoteric tradition that together finally become known as the Kabbalah.

Note should first be given to the *Sefer Yetzirah*, a cosmological work arising from the same milieu that produced the Merkabah literature, whose various aspects will be treated throughout this work, most importantly in chapters 3, 7, and 8. Though we cannot here go into a detailed discussion of this seminal work, what these extended analyses should demonstrate is that the secret subject of this work is the generation of the cosmic anthropos, another form of the divine son. Such a generation will be shown to have been integrated with the introduction in this same text of the significant new terminology of the Sefirot that is the defining characteristic of the Kabbalah. This decad was, from the beginning, thus integrally associated with the concept of the cosmic son or divine Glory, Kavod, developed in the prior esoteric tradition, that figure seated on the heavenly Throne who finally came to be called Metatron and with whom the mystic envisioning him could recognize an identity.

But what is obscure in the *Sefer Yetzirah* is openly disclosed in the most important transitional work between the *Sefer Yetzirah* of the third century and the *Bahir* of the twelfth, the *Raza Rabbah*, or "Great Mystery," written between the fifth and eighth centuries and surviving only in quotations from it by the Ashkenazi Hasidim. This work not only combines a table of ten principles with Merkabah entities but in its novel association of Moses with Metatron it does reveal the "great mystery" of the Jewish esoteric tradition. In words attributed to Rabbi Ishmael, this text states: "I saw the faithful envoy and the Prince of the Countenance, and they had the same face, and all of them sanctified and praised the Holy One, may He be praised. . . ."[40] Here again we have a division between a higher and lower supernal figure and an identification between an ascendant spiritual master, Moses, and the lower supernal figure who is strikingly said to have "the same face" as that former human. It is in this identification of the mystic with the supernal object of his vision that the double concept of divine sonship resides, and the text tells us that he who understands this mystery is equally "assured" of being "a son of the world to come," using the same words in the original as appear in the *Shi'ur Komah:*

> Moreover, it is said in the book of the "Great Mystery" that everyone who knows this mystery, which proceeds from the Trishagion [Isa. 6:3] and [the verse Ezekiel 3:12, which follows it in the liturgy of the *qedushah*]: "Blessed is the Presence of the Lord in his place" may be assured of the life of the future world [bliss], and this is the name of the Holy One, blessed be He.[41]

These words appear again in writings of Abraham ben David of Posquieres, known as the Rabad, a founder of Provençal Kabbalism in the twelfth century. As quoted by the Rabad's grandson:

> This refers to the Prince of the [divine] countenance [that is, to Metatron]. . . . And it is He who appeared to Moses and who

appeared to Ezekiel. . . . But the Cause of causes did not appear to any man. . . . And this is the secret, of which it is said in the cosmogony, *ma'aseh bereshith*, "whoever knows the measure of the Creator of the beginning, *yoser bereshith*, can be assured, etc.[42]

Thus we see that there was a tradition apparently going back to the *Shi'ur Komah* that related a particular esoteric knowledge to a linguistic formula assuring one of eternal life with a phrase so familiar it could be recognized simply through allusion, the phrase "son of the world to come," Ben Olam ha-Ba.

But in addition to its appearance in the *Shi'ur Komah*, the *Raza Rabbah*, and the writings of the Rabad, there is another context in which the phrase Ben Olam ha-Ba appears. This is in the *Talmud Megillah* 28b, a passage quoted in the Sabbath Musaf service as follows: "It was taught in the school of Elijah: Whoever studies traditional laws every day is assured of life in the world to come, for it is said: 'His ways are eternal.' Read not here *halikhoth* [ways] but *halakhoth* [traditional laws]."[43] Philip Birnbaum has related the Elijah reference not directly to the prophet but to a later work citing him, the *Seder Eliyyahu*. This work,

> a midrashic collection of mysterious authorship, consists of two parts: *Seder Eliyyahu Rabba* (thirty-one chapters) and *Seder Elliyyahu Zuta* (twenty-five chapters). According to the Talmud (Kethuboth 106a) Elijah frequently visited Rabba Anan (third century) and taught him *Seder Eliyyahu*. This work, which has been named "the jewel of aggadic literature," repeatedly emphasized the importance of diligence in the study of the Torah.[44]

The reference cited in *Megillah* 28b is to chapter 2 in the *Seder Elliyyahu Zuta*,[45] which must therefore be pretalmudic,[46] as the quotation in the Siddur, the prayer book, must be posttalmudic.

The question now arises as to the chronological relationship of the *Shi'ur Komah* linguistic formula related to esoteric knowledge and the talmudic formula related to exoteric knowledge, that of Torah. The *Shi'ur Komah* becomes the source of this whole tradition if we accept the early dating of Gershom Scholem: "The age of this *Shi'ur Qomah* mysticism . . . may now be fixed with certainty. Contrary to the views that once prevailed, it must be dated to the second century, and certainly not later."[47] That the eternal reward for esoteric study should have been transferred by the rabbis to that for study of the Torah seems the more likely direction of transmission, and we can appreciate how the phrase with which we are concerned, Ben Olam ha-Ba, could have been attributed by them to a mystical transmission from the prophet Elijah, whose ascent to Heaven in a fiery chariot would certainly seem to demonstrate the reward "assured" to a "son of the world to come." But the source is reversed if we accept the late dating of the most recent editor of the *Shi'ur Komah*, Martin Samuel Cohen, who posits "an early gaonic date for the composition of the Urtext of the *Shi'ur Qomah*, a date late enough to post-date the redaction of the *Babylonian Talmud*."[48]

Joseph Dan, however, notes that Cohen's late dating is the single exception to the earlier Scholem dating, "now almost universally accepted," and finds his argument "incomplete and unconvincing."[49] But whether the origin of this phrase is the *Shi'ur Komah*, the *Seder Eliyyahu Zuta*, or a source common to both, it was widely disseminated in both the esoteric and exoteric traditions of post-Temple Judaism. And though almost all translators of these texts, because they have lost the key to its esoteric meaning, obscure the reference to "son," *ben*, in their versions, it is the whole phrase that contains the most central meaning of the Hebraic secret doctrine of the son, the assurance that through particular daily mystical practices or study one will inherit eternal life. That this secret doctrine was understood to derive from the Temple priesthood[50] may perhaps be seen in the significant placement of the Siddur passage containing this phrase right after the description of the incense used in the Temple and the listing of the psalms that used to be recited by the Levites in the Temple. The telling use of the word for son in the important phrases Ben Adam and Ben Olam ha-Ba in the pre-Zoharic Jewish mystical tradition would together seem to reveal the essence of the secret priestly doctrine, that the purpose of the son of man is to become a son of the world to come.

The Kabbalistic Texts

In the late twelfth century the esoteric tradition, whose texts and oral interpretations had been transmitted secretly for centuries, emerged almost simultaneously both in circles of the Ashkenazi Hasidism of Germany and the Kabbalists of Provence. Joseph Dan has shown how these twelfth-century esoteric developments relied upon the Merkabah texts we have just studied:

To a large extent, there can be no doubt that the first Jewish mystics in medieval Europe were indeed the followers and revealers of ancient traditions. One of the most meaningful characteristics of Ashkenazi Hasidic mysticism is the rediscovery and revival of ancient Jewish mystical sources, the Hechalot and Merkavah mysticism of the talmudic period. . . . The Ashkenazi Hasidim adapted the myth of the Shiur Komah and made it central to their conception of the divine world; the figure described is a divine one, though not the supreme God. . . . In this case, at least the claim that they follow and reveal ancient traditional secrets seems to be entirely correct. . . . A similar, though not identical, situation can be found in the early kabbalah. The Sefer ha-Bahir and other early kabbalistic works adopted the Shiur Komah anthropomorphism to present the Godhead. . . . combined by the kabbalists with another set of symbols, that of the ten divine emanations (the sefirot) . . . It is certain, however, that the two most important ones [Hechalot texts] for them [the Ashkenazi Hasidim] were the Shiur Komah and Sefer Hechalot (Third Enoch, or the Hebrew Book of Enoch).[51]

Both forms of the Jewish mystical tradition that emerged in the twelfth century were equally derived, then, from the specific Hekhalot-Merkabah texts that we have seen to have been the primary transmitters of the priestly secret doctrine first cryptically divulged in texts of the Second Temple period, those in Ezekiel, Daniel, and 1 Enoch. But as Dan indicates, what distinguishes the major phases of the Kabbalah from the earlier priestly-Merkabah esoteric tradition is the fact that its cosmology is defined in terms of the ten Sefirot on the Tree of Life Diagram. In the following consideration of kabbalistic texts, the earlier discussion with illustrations of this diagram, which appeared in the introductory chapter, should therefore be kept in mind. But first we should look further at the way in which the Sefirot were treated in the earlier history of the Kabbalah.

Scholem has traced a direct line of influence from the transitional Raza Rabbah, through the German Hasidim and the text of the Bahir deriving from them, to the twelfth century Provençal Kabbalists who are responsible for the final redaction of the Bahir and the further elaboration of Kabbalistic concepts, as well as the possibility of reciprocal influence of the Provençal Kabbalists on the German Hasidim.[52] And he shows that in both cases the concept of the ten Sefirot was integrated with the lower of two supernal figures, the major difference being that the Provençal writers continued to apply Merkabah terminology to these figures, primarily that of Metatron to the lower figure, while the Germans employed the terminology of the double Kavod, one invisible and the other visible. Of the hasidic formulations, Scholem says: "In general the sefiroth are located below the divine *kabhod*, but sometimes they are also interwoven with the idea of the *kabhod* itself."[53] Both of the European medieval traditions that emerged in the twelfth century were equally associated with the fragments of the *Bahir* that Scholem argues came first into the possession of the Ashkenazi Hasidim and were transmitted by them to the Kabbalists of Provence. Of this most important source text of the Kabbalah, Scholem says:

> . . . a relation is without doubt established between the old *Shi'ur qomah* speculations and their early kabbalistic reinterpretation in the *Bahir*. . . . All later kabbalists correctly understood the statements of the *Bahir* concerning the sefirot or the forms of God as a mystical interpretation of the old ideas. There, indeed, the limbs of primordial man were described as Ezekiel 1:26 saw him on the throne of the Merkabah.[54]

Thus from its first formulation in the *Sefer Yetzirah* to its Provençal elaboration, the concept of the ten Sefirot was always understood to define the inner workings or potencies of the cosmic anthropos, an understanding that would finally receive graphic representation in the Adam Kadmon version of the Sefirotic Tree. Though the study of the Kabbalah has largely focused on its evolving use of the Tree of Life Diagram, the references earlier given to the *Raza Rabbah*, the *Bahir*, and the Rabad should show that it was rather the continuity of the Merkabah formulations containing the salvific meaning of this esoteric tradition that was finally of more importance.

In the kabbalistic reformulations of the esoteric tradition, what distinguishes the Kabbalah from the older Merkabah formulations are the two factors of the Tree of Sefirot and the still more radical emergence of feminine cosmic principles, both of which first surface in the *Bahir*. But as the Tree was assimilated with the older tradition, so was the sexualizing of the Sefirot also put into the service of that genesis of the son constituting its chief salvific doctrine. This next step appears most clearly in the *Zohar*, the most important kabbalistic work to emerge in medieval Spain and the source of all major further developments in the Kabbalah.

Perhaps the best example of the secret doctrine appears in the sections of the Zohar concerned with the divine "Faces": the *Sifra di-Tseniutha*, or "Book of Concealment"; the *Idra Rabba*, or "Greater Assembly"; *Idra Zutta*, or "Lesser Assembly"; and the *Idra di-be-Mashkana*, or "Assembly on . . . the Tabernacle."[55] The last of the Zoharic sections listed makes the important association between the concept of the Faces and the Tabernacle, and of both with prayer, thereby associating both the concept of the Faces and the related practice of prayer with the priesthood. Alleging to be assemblies in the secret mystical societies of the second-century Rabbi Simeon ben Yohai, these works are centered on detailed descriptions of the two divine Faces, the Long Face ("Arikh Anpin"), otherwise known as the Ancient of Days and the White Head, and the Short Face ("Ze'ir Anpin"). As the former is concealed, so is the latter manifest and in a form that is at once both masculine and androgynous:

> But the conformations of Microprosopus are disposed from the forms of Macroprosopus; and his constituent parts are expanded on this side and on that under a human form, so that there may be manifest in Him the Spirit of the Concealed One in every part. . . . this supernal form . . . is called (*the supernal*) man; the man who comprehendeth Male and Female equally. . . . When the Syntagma of the Supernal Man had been mitigated as to the Holy Body, in Male and Female form, these two were conjoined together. . . . And thenceforth the superior and inferior worlds are bound together under the form of the Holy Body, and the worlds are associated together, and cohere together, and have been made one Body.[56]

The *Idra Rabba*—from which these infelicitously translated quotations are taken—nowhere in all its elaborate descriptions explains the genesis of Ze'ir Anpin and how, through him, "the superior and inferior worlds" of heaven and earth can be "made one Body." But it does faithfully reproduce the main features of the early apocalypses: the existence of two hierarchically arranged divine persons, one an Ancient of Days and the other a son-figure with a humanlike appearance, and the special relationship of this latter to man, particularly the ever more revealed understanding that such a son of man represents the transfigured form of the person who has had a mystic vision of this enthroned being.

It is with such an understanding that the *Idra Rabba* closes: "Who is He, the Holy One of Tetragrammaton? This is Rabbi Schimeon Ben

Yochai, who is called very glorious (*both*) in this world and in (*the world*)
to come."[57] Shortly before this striking statement, the secret revelations
of this assembly have concluded with the enraptured deaths of three of
Rabbi Simeon's companions, whom all see carried by angels through a
heavenly veil and whose voices are heard proclaiming: "'This is the portion of God the most Holy One—may He be blessed!—from the nuptials
of Rabbi Schimeon and his companions.'"[58] Such "nuptials" seem to be
defined as "the just united by the Union of the Diadems,"[59] but no further explanation is here given.

It is in the *Idra Zuta* that an explanation is suggested that goes far
beyond the earlier Merkabah tradition deriving from Ezekiel's Throne
vision, an explanation developing further one aspect of the *Idra Rabba*
text. The *Idra Rabba* is primarily concerned to define an emanationist
cosmology by which the androgynous Short Face is derived from the Long
Face and then its female aspect is separated from its male aspect. But the
purpose of this separation is that they can then come together again, an
association on which the judgments given to both worlds depend: "And
when they are associated together, then are They mutually mitigated in
that day on which all things are mitigated. And therefore are the judgments mitigated mutually and restored into order, both superiors and inferiors."[60] The sexual nature of their association, and that of their newly
defined parents, is spelled out in the last revelations of Rabbi Simeon on
his deathbed, the subject of the *Idra Zuta*. The previously withheld information is now given, that

> When the Most Holy Ancient One, the Concealed with all Con-
> cealments, desired to be formed forth, He conformed all things un-
> der the form of Male and Female. . . . Chokhmah, Wisdom, as the
> Father; Binah, Understanding, as the Mother. . . . *Yod*, I, impregnateth
> the letter *He*, H, and produceth a Son. . . . For in Their conforma-
> tions are They found to be the perfection of all things—Father and
> Mother, Son, and Daughter. . . . the last H, *He*, is called the Bride at
> certain times. . . . For many are the times when the Male is not
> associated with Her. . . . But as to that which pertaineth unto the
> Mother, then the benevolence of Them both is not taken away for
> all eternity. . . . the one is never taken away from the other.[61]

The desire of the original Holiness to achieve particular form is expressed through a distinction and sexualizing of his essence, first into

the parental Partzufim and through them into a son and subsequent daughter, who also then mate. But the distinction between these supernal couplings, a distinction we shall later see to be an important feature of Lurianic cosmology, is that the Father and Mother, traditionally associated with the process of continuous creation, never separate, while those of the Son and his Bride, associated with the processes of Providence, are intermittent.

This last is most important, for not only is the joy of the world dependent upon a supernal joy that can mitigate the otherwise severe Providential judgments, but the joy deriving from the lower coupling is also dependent upon the behavior of earthly man. For when "the Male and Female are united . . . the worlds all and several exist in love and in joy. But whensoever sins are multiplied in the world, and the sanctuary is polluted . . . the Male and Female are separated."[62] The relationship of this cosmology to the priesthood and the proper performance of its duties, whether historically justified or not, is further stressed in the statement that "there is permission granted unto none to enter therein, save unto the High Priest, who entereth from the side of Chesed. . . . And He entereth into the Holy of Holies, and the Bride is mitigated, and that Holy of Holies receiveth blessing. . . ."[63] Through his ministrations, the priest is understood either to couple directly with the Bride, the Shekhinah, or to facilitate her coupling with the Holy One, blessed be He, in either case sharing, as did Rabbi Simeon, in their "nuptials."[64] Her divine mate is identified both with the Sefirah Tiferet and its associated divine name: "then is He called Tiferet. . . . For Tiferet is Tetragrammaton."[65] But it is further said of the priest who properly enters the Holy of Holies: "Thence Chesed entereth into the Holy of Holies; as it is written, Ps. cxxxiii. 3: 'For there Tetragrammaton commanded the blessing, even life for evermore.'"[66] We have seen that Rabbi Simeon was himself identified with the Tetragrammaton and now we can understand the reason for this. As one of those who, like the high priest, has been transfigured through such mystical activities as can facilitate and share in the divine nuptials, he may be said to have been spiritually reborn as a divine son, one whose position on the Tree is that of Tiferet-Tetragrammaton, and thus to have achieved immortality.

The novel element in the Bahiric tradition culminating in the Idrot is the introduction of the feminine into a salvific cosmology hitherto expressed in wholly masculine terms. But this just serves to facilitate the imaginative comprehension of the main element of the priestly teachings with which this apparently new elaboration is so pointedly being associated, the transformation of a righteous man into the divine son. This association is made quite clear in the first description of the generation of the son from Chokhmah and Binah: "And that Son is called the first-born, as it is written, Exod. iv. 22: 'Israel is my first-born son.'"[67] Here, as previously, the lower divine Face or enthroned form is the one associated with human transformation into the divine son, and it is sharply differentiated from an original, and thus older, divine source. But how this supernal man is first generated and how earthly man can achieve unification with it had never before been as clearly specified as the Kabbalah now makes possible with the introduction of the divine feminine elements and of the two levels of supernal couplings.

The various aspects of the Hebraic secret doctrine of the son that we have just seen to inform the Idra sections of the *Zohar* are all brought together in a highly significant passage from the central portion of the *Zohar* in which this doctrine becomes most explicit:

> R. Simeon said: "In the hour when the morning breaks, the Hind (Shekinah) rises and starts from her place in order to enter the two hundred palaces of the King. When a man studies the Torah in solitude at midnight, at the hour when the north wind springs up and the Hind desires to be astir, he is taken with her into supernal realms, to appear before the King. When dawn brightens and he recites his prayers, and unifies the Holy Name in manner due, he is encircled with a thread of grace; he looks into the firmament, and a light of holy knowledge rests upon him. As the man is thus adorned and shrouded with light all things tremble before him, for he is called the son of the Holy One, the son of the King's Palace. . . . Therefore it has been taught that a priest who knows not how to unify thus the Holy Name cannot perform proper service, for on the achievement of that unity hangs both celestial and terrestrial worship. The priest must, therefore, strive to concentrate heart and mind on the attainment of this unification, so that those above and those below may be blessed."[68]

Through such properly concentrated and intentioned prayer as is here attributed to the ancient priesthood, in what is also an early statement of the principle of *kavanah*, mystical intention, man not only can unify the masculine and feminine aspects of the Holy Name, thus blessing "those above," but through this unification can become "the son of the Holy One" and of the Shekhinah, whose desire for unification he has also fulfilled, thus additionally blessing "those below," most specifically by achieving the generation of his own higher self as the divine son.

Another Kabbalist who uses sexual symbolism to explain the mystery of spiritual rebirth as a divine son is Abraham Abulafia, a figure contemporaneous with the appearance of the *Zohar* at the end of the thirteenth century. Moshe Idel's analysis traces Abulafia's erotic imagery from the kiss, through intercourse, the seed, and impregnation, to "The Son and the New Birth," an analysis culminating in the following quotation and commentary: "'the human intellect is the fruit of God, may He be praised, and by way of simile is His seed, and he is in truth His son.' . . . in Abulafia, the appearance of the intellective element is seen as a new birth, which transforms the mystic into a son of the divine."[69] Though Idel stresses the difference between Abulafia's use of this imagery and that of the Zoharic-Lurianic school of Kabbalah, regarding the former as being concerned with the relationship of the human soul to the divine and the latter as concerned only with interrelationships within the godhead, he does show "that the *Zohar* also interprets the appearance of the soul, which is the supernal component within the personality, as a new birth, transforming man into a son of God,"[70] a transformation we have seen to have been depicted at the close of the *Idra Rabba*. And it seems clear that the concept of the son being developed in terms of sexual symbolism in both of the allegedly conflicting "schools" of the Kabbalah[71] had its origin in the priestly-Merkabah tradition.

This new sexualized cosmology both distinguishes kabbalistic speculation from the original priestly knowledge and also connects it with this earlier gnosis. It is usual to identify the Kabbalah as that aspect of the Jewish esoteric tradition that is primarily concerned with the Tree of Sefirot and the four cosmic worlds and so represents a sharp departure from the earlier tradition of apocalyptic or Merkabah mysticism. But when the whole history of the Jewish esoteric tradition is considered, it shows a unity whose emphasis is much older than that of the Tree and the worlds of emanation and that makes these apparently newer concerns seem minor. In fact, quite early and increasingly the diagram of Sefirot was adapted to a modeling of either the cosmic Adam or the Partzufim, the divine personalities, the latter centered on the six-Sefirot personality of the divine son. Where it differed from the earlier Throne vision model was in the aforementioned introduction of feminine and sexual elements, which may either have been there from the beginning but were kept more hidden and were only now being revealed or which represent a truly non-Jewish form of Gnosticism newly imported into the tradition. Whatever the case may be, it is in this latter form that the ancient Jewish mystical tradition is transmitted from the medieval period to the Renaissance, from the Kabbalah of the *Zohar* to that of Luria.

Isaac Luria, the sixteenth-century Kabbalist of Safed, Palestine, known as the Ari, has had the most important influence on the subsequent development of the Jewish esoteric tradition through his reformulation of the Zoharic Kabbalah. Although his treatment of the Partzufim is largely derived from the Zoharic model just described, what he has added to this formulation is a new understanding of the cosmic context of the divine personalities. As expounded by his disciples, primarily by Chayyim Vital in the *Etz Chayyim*, there are three main principles of the new Lurianic Kabbalah: the Tzimtzum, a "contraction" and then retraction of the divine substance that left the primordial circular space in which the creation could take place and into which there then entered a line of the ten Sefirot; the Shevirah, or "breaking of the vessels" of the original Sefirot, which were not strong enough to contain the divine influx; and the Tikkun, the cosmic rectification or return by which the Sefirot are reconstituted as the five Partzufim.[72] In the Lurianic system, the Tree of Life Diagram is reconfigured from the Tree of individual Sefirot, representing the primordial World of Points existing before the Shevirah, into the Tree of the Tikkun, which correlates the Partzufim with the following Sefirot: Arikh Anpin with Keter, Abba with Chokhmah, Imma with Binah, Ze'ir Anptin with the six Sefirot from Chesed to Yesod, and the Nukvah with Malkhut. In this reconfiguration, the Partzuf of the son, Ze'ir Anpin, is clearly dominant. Luria's cosmology will be discussed at length in later chapters, his concept of the Tzimtzum being the focus of chapter 10 and that of the Partzufim a major subject of chapter 7. As this latter will provide numerous quotations from the *Etz Chayyim* detailing the sexual genesis and growth of the Partzuf of the son, this material need not be repeated here, and we can largely rest the treatment of the derivative Lurianic-Hasidic understanding of the secret doctrine of the son on the analysis recently given of its development in the *Zohar*.

But there is one aspect of his teachings that must be considered here. For it is with Luria that the second distinction of the Kabbalah from Merkabah mysticism most fully emerges, a distinction that is to characterize the subsequent development of this esoteric-mystical tradition from the Safed Kabbalists to the eastern European Hasidim. This is the special technology of prayer and its relationship to the concept of the Tikkun, the cosmic rectification, in which it is to play such a central role. Though this greater emphasis on the returning movement of cosmic reconstruction distinguishes the Lurianic Kabbalah even more from that of the *Zohar*, with its emphasis on the outward movement of divine emanation, than from the earlier apocalyptic literature, with its emphasis on eschatology, the Lurianic association of prayer with the mechanics of divine sexuality, already suggested in the Idra sections of the *Zohar*, distinguishes it as sharply from the earlier form of Throne mysticism. This had, indeed, understood prayer to be the mystical practice through which spiritual transformation is to be accomplished, such liturgical praise of the enthroned deity as would lift one to the condition of the angels. But the divine unification this would effect was one of a simple duality, a unification of finite man with his infinite higher self. In the later tradition that derives from the *Idra Zuta*, the divine unification effected by human prayer is threefold.

In Lurianic cosmology the process of the Tikkun proceeds from the bottom up. It is through the prayers of the righteous that the lower male and female Partzufim are aroused to come into union, and this in turn arouses the similar unification of the upper Partzufim that completes the process of cosmic reconstruction. As explained by Chayyim Vital in the *Etz Chayyim:* "This is what remains for us to rectify through prayer. . . . Just as the souls of the righteous raise the female waters for the purpose of uniting the Male and Female, in the same way the Male and Female can raise the female waters for the purpose of uniting Abba and Imma. . . . in the mystery of the unification of 'Hear, O Israel. . . .'"[73] The mystical purpose of prayer is made even clearer in words attributed to the Baal Shem Tov, founder of the later Hasidic movement: "Through his need and his want he knows the want of the Shekina, and he prays that the want of the Shekina will be satisfied and that through him, the praying man, the unification of God with His Shekina will take place."[74] The mystical purpose of prayer, then, is to effect the unification of "God with His Shekina," of the transcendent and immanent aspects of the divine, through the very person of the individual engaged in prayer with such *kavanah*, mystical intention, as will necessarily also include and be expressed through the transfigured personality of the praying individual. As Lewis Jacobs sums up the Hasidic understanding of prayer: "Hasidic prayer is, then, an exercise in assisting the divine unification and participating in it."[75] But as we will see in the final section, this ultimate understanding of the threefold unification to be effected by prayer was already there from the beginning. And what is true of the continuity of such theurgical practice is also true of the history of Jewish esoteric cosmology.

From the earliest to its most recent history, the Jewish esoteric tradition has had but one message, the cosmic birthing of the divine son through the spiritual development of righteous human beings, a generation that fulfills both the divine purpose of the whole creation and the human purpose of spiritual practice, the transcendence of mortality through such human unification with the divine as can endow it with divine personality. But that message has been as overtly obscured as it is everywhere covertly implied. It is rare to see a work like 3 Enoch that openly proclaims the angelic Prince of the Presence, Metatron, to be the transfigured form of a former human, Enoch. But it is just such transfiguration that we have seen to have been implied in every text of Throne mysticism deriving from the vision of Ezekiel, just as it has been in the major kabbalistic texts leading up to and beyond the *Zohar*.

Scholem and the Secret Doctrine

As it is rare to see the secret doctrine of the son overtly expressed in Jewish esoteric texts, so is it rare to see any scholarly recognition of the centrality of this secret doctrine to the whole of the Jewish esoteric tradition. But in the most recent of the posthumous translations of important earlier works by Gershom Scholem, a collection of six essays based on his Eranos lectures from 1952 to 1961 and given the title *On the Mystical Shape of the Godhead: Basic Concepts in the Kabbalah*, Scholem has come closer than ever before or since to recognizing, if not the centrality, then the various facets that together make up what I have designated as the secret doctrine of the son.

In Scholem's essay "Tselem: The Concept of the Astral Body," the essential meaning of the Jewish mystical tradition deriving from Ezekiel's Throne vision is clarified: "R. Moses Isserles of Cracow . . . explicitly cites R. Judah Hayyot (c. 1500), who compares the human shape seen by the prophet in a vision (e.g., as in Ezek. 1:26) to the image which man sees of himself. . . . Even the latest Kabbalists maintain the experience of self-encounter as the ultimate initiation experience into the world of esoteric knowledge."[76] But Scholem shows the self thus encountered, particularly as treated in the *Shushan Sodoth* collection edited by Moses ben Jacob of Kiev, to be a variously interpreted higher self:

> Indeed, there seems good reason to argue that this self is an angelic "I" connected with man's essential nature, a kind of personal angel intrinsically belonging to man, which here becomes visible to him.

. . . The occult experience of the *tselem* as the astral body of the righteous is also mentioned by R. Hayyim Vital, R. Isaac Luria's chief disciple: "The ethereal body of them [the righteous] is [contained] in the secret of the *tselem*, which is perceived by those who have purified vision." . . . the *tselem* of the righteous man is identical with the angel which protects him. This image of the *tselem* does not greatly differ from that of the "perfected nature," with which we became acquainted above.[77]

The upper and lower aspects of this Ezekiel-derived mystical tradition are treated separately, as far as this is possible, in two earlier essays. In the title essay, *"Shi'ur Komah: The Mystical Shape of the Godhead,"* Scholem stresses that "The lower, earthly human being and the upper, mystical human being, in which the Godhead is manifested as shape, belong together and are unthinkable without one another."[78] But his emphasis here is on the upper shape, kabbalistically identified with Ze'ir Anpin and the Tetragrammaton: "the image . . . meticulously described in the *'Idroth* as the shape of the Primal Man, is identical with the name of God. . . . For the *Zohar* . . . Ze'ir 'Anpin is essentially God as He is revealed in the unity of his activity. The true name of God, the Tetragrammaton, befits this level of manifestation and expresses its special structure."[79] What from one perspective is an angelic higher self is from another the active aspect of the divine, the Partzuf of Ze'ir Anpin identified primarily with the Sefirah of Tiferet and the divine Name of the Tetragrammaton associated with this Sefirah.

But it is in the essay devoted to the lower human aspect, that entitled "Tsaddik: The Righteous One," that Scholem comes closest to revealing the hidden gnosis of the Jewish esoteric tradition. This emerges from an understanding of the relationship of the human Tzaddik to his supernal counterpart identified with the ninth Sefirah, especially as defined by the thirteenth-century Spanish Kabbalist Joseph Gikatilla: "As the *Tsaddik* awakens the world to repent or to fix that which is not whole, this attribute is called Peace, mediating for good between *YHVH* and *Adonai*, making peace between them and bringing them near to dwell together without separation or breaking up in the world; and at that hour we find that God is one."[80] Gikatilla understands the human role of the Tzaddik to parallel that of his Sefirotic counterpart. For as the ninth Sefirah of the Tzaddik (Yesod) unifies the male Sefirah of YHVH (Tiferet) just above it with the female Sefirah of Adonai (Malkhut) just below it, so is it the purpose of the human Tzaddik to unify the transcendent and immanent forms of the divine also signified by these Sefirot and further distinguished by gender: "Thus, the sacred marriage of male and female potencies, consummated by means of the *Tsaddik*, the *Sefirah* of *Yesod*, lies at the center of this symbolism."[81] Also significant is the Shefa, or influx, deriving from this Sefirah and requiring a reciprocal receptivity from the human Tzaddik, with important implications: "In this way the lower world can transform the influx from above into a living, active structure, and thereafter to return it as the reflection of its own existence."[82] As a sixteenth-century Kabbalist of Safed, Moses Alshekh, sums up the purpose both of the Tzaddik and of man's creation: "the purpose of man's creation is to make of matter form, and that they be one unity, and not separate things."[83]

These remarkable essays should reveal that the "Basic Concepts in the Kabbalah," in the words of the subtitle of this volume, are all various aspects of the larger, unifying concept that I have termed the Hebraic secret doctrine of the son. But what Scholem has not recognized is the central though ever changing role of the figure of the son as the unifying thread tying all these aspects of the Jewish esoteric tradition together and its origin with the ancient Hebraic priesthood.

In summarizing this tradition, we may say that while the later Kabbalah took over the priestly-Merkabah conception of the two supernal figures and/or Thrones in its own conception of the two divine "Faces," the Long Face (Arikh Anpin) and the Short Face (Ze'ir Anpin), it gave the earlier personifications a greater specificity that could explain their functioning in a way never before possible. The Long Face was understood to be a composite triadic figure and the Short Face a composite dyadic figure. The upper triad was composed of the original unity, Arikh Anpin or the Ancient of Days, and its further sexual distinction into male and female aspects, those of Abba (Father) and Imma (Mother). The subsequent sexual Yichud between them could then explain the generation of the lower Face, something not previously attempted. Although originally androgynous in its conception, this cosmic child was then also further differentiated into male and female personalities, the son figure of Ze'ir Anpin and the daughter-bride figure of the Nukvah. To these latter figures were also attached the principal terms used in the Talmud to express the transcendent and immanent forms of the deity, the Holy One, blessed be He, and the Shekhinah. In much kabbalistic discussion, moreover, the original five Partzufim were simplified into a threefold distinction between Ein Sof (in this formulation identified with the composite figure of Arikh Anpin), the Holy One, blessed be He, and the Shekhinah, these three identified with the major Sefirot of Keter, Tiferet, and Malkhut, respectively. In this formulation, the Shekhinah was identified with the form of divinity that fills the earth, the holy spark immanent in each soul and thing, Ein Sof was regarded as wholly transcendent and inaccessible, and the Holy One, blessed be He, occupied a middle position as the holiness that is apprehensible to mystic vision and with which man can interact, the personal God of Israel.[84]

It is in this latter terminology that the lower male and female Partzufim appear with respect to the remaining aspect of Merkabah mysticism, that of human transformation. As the sexual differentiation of the upper Face could explain the genesis of the lower Face, so can this similar differentiation of the lower Face explain the mystery of human spiritual rebirth. For the mystical purpose of prayer, the form of spiritual practice that has been consistently associated with human transformation in both the Merkabah and kabbalistic texts, is precisely to provide a human vessel for the unification of the divine immanence within the human soul and the divine transcendence beyond it. But since these two forms of the divine are conceived of as sexually differentiated, and since all sexual unions of the masculine and feminine are understood mythologically to be generative, the son being generated by the divine unification taking place within the human soul during prayer would seem to be none other than the higher self of that individual. Furthermore, since this unification is taking place in man, he must also share in its divine nature through the higher self thus generated, the "son of the world to come" and member of Klal Yisrael. How this core of priestly knowledge is conveyed through the oldest of ritual prayers with which the priesthood may be associated, the Sh'ma, we are now to see.

The Esoteric Meaning of the Sh'ma

As the central message of the Jewish esoteric tradition has remained remarkably constant throughout its long history, so has its principle method of spiritual transformation, mystical prayer, an understanding of its hidden purpose having been passed down from teacher to initiated student in concert with the cosmology whose goal it was to effect. The prayer service has different meanings for those schooled only in the exoteric halakhic tradition and those whose esoteric learning allows them to read its hidden message. But such different meanings are particularly true of the original core of the morning and evening prayer services, the credal affirmation of the Sh'ma whose words Israel is commanded to repeat twice daily. We shall see that as the central message of the Jewish esoteric tradition is the ultimate unification of the human with the divine, so is it also the most esoteric meaning of the Sh'ma,[85] that central affirmation of Judaism in which cosmology and spiritual practice are united.

The esoteric meaning of the Sh'ma appearing most prominently in the *Zohar* and consistently repeated throughout the later history of the Kabbalah is that it affirms not a simple divine unity but a divine unification, Yichud, one involving a femininely conceived God who is immanent in multiplicity, YHVH Elohaynu, and a masculinely conceived transcendent God beyond all qualification, YHVH. For Elohaynu, normally translated as the qualified form of "our God," is also a form of the plural divine name Elohim. The *Zohar* expresses this most simply in the statement: "This is the mystery of, 'Hear O Israel, God is our Lord, God is One.' . . . The mystery is that the two are united as one."[86] This meaning is more clearly conveyed through the following translation of the Sh'ma:

Hear, [O] Israel, YHVH Elohaynu [and] YHVH [are] one.

Whether the distinction between the divine immanence and the divine transcendence is understood to be one of generation, as in the earlier model of Throne mysticism, or of gender, as in its later kabbalistic reformulation, the esoteric tradition that had developed such a distinction would have certainly needed to affirm its even stronger belief in the unity underlying these two forms of divinity. So there is no reason not to accept the medieval disclosure of this esoteric meaning as going back to its original formulation in Deuteronomy. But given the analysis earlier offered of Israel's own part in this unification, I would like to suggest an even deeper understanding of these words:

Hear: Israel, YHVH Elohaynu, [and] YHVH [are] one.

Such an interpretation would introduce the central mystery of Israel's cosmic destiny into the primary affirmation of its creed, that it is its divinely appointed role to unify the divine transcendence with its immanence and thus achieve its own deification.

This understanding of the Sh'ma as signifying a threefold unification of the divine transcendence and immanence that both includes and requires the participation of Israel also appears to be suggested in the *Zohar*. This is in that most recondite section on the "Terumah" portion of Exodus that reinforces the association between this esoteric cosmology of divine unification and the center of the priestly vocation, the Sanctuary:

> At the time when Israel is proclaiming the unity—the mystery contained in the Shema—with a perfect intention . . . the Spouse makes ready likewise to enter the Canopy in order to unite Himself with the Matrona. Therefore we proclaim loudly: "Hear, O Israel; prepare thyself, for thy Husband has come to receive thee." And also we say: "The Lord our God, the Lord is one," which signifies that the two are united as one, in a perfect and glorious union, without any flaw of separation to mar it. . . . Blessed is the people which perceives these things, ordering its prayers in accordance with this mystery of Faith! . . . As He united Himself above according to six aspects, so also She united Herself below according to six other aspects, so that the oneness may be completed, both above and below, as it is written: "The Lord will be One, and his Name One" (Zech. XIV, 9): Six words above—*Shema Israel YHVH Elohenn YHVH ehad*, corresponding to the six aspects, and six words below—*baruk shem kabod malkuto le'olam waed* (Blessed be the Name, etc.)—corresponding to the six other aspects. . . . The Holy One, blessed be He, who is One above, does not take His seat upon the Throne of Glory, until She has entered within the mystery of the One in accordance with His very essence of Oneness, to be the One in One.[87]

The *Zohar* here identified Israel with the Shekhinah as the Bride of the Holy One, blessed be He. And it clearly indicates that there are two unifications taking place in the Sh'ma, of Israel with YHVH Elohaynu and of YHVH Elohaynu with YHVH, the former a unification of identities and the latter of dissimilars. The identification of Israel with the Shekhinah is a more general kabbalistic concept, as both are viewed as different aspects of the Sefirah Malkhut, the lowest Sefirah and final receptacle on the Tree of Life Diagram, and this identification is central to the mystical understanding of prayer, Israel's prayers being understood to express the yearning of the Shekhinah for unification with the Holy One, blessed be He.

This Zoharic passage also clarifies other aspects of the divine Yichud. It explicates the famous statement in Zechariah—"The Lord will be One, and his Name One"—making clear that when reference is made to the "Name" of God, it is always esoterically understood to be to the

Shekhinah, and showing how this statement may be viewed as an interpretative key to the Sh'ma. It further shows that the liturgical insertion of the words "Blessed be the Name of the Glory of His Kingdom for ever and ever," following the six words of the Sh'ma in the prayer services, was meant to underscore the esoteric meaning of the Sh'ma as involving a divine unification of the masculine and feminine. For such a reference to the Shekhinah, she who was understood to be the Name, Glory, and Kingdom (Malkhut), would only have been appropriate if the preceding words of the Sh'ma were esoterically understood to imply a Yichud involving the Shekhinah, that the unity proclaimed was a unification.

That such a Yichud was also quite early understood to be threefold may be deduced from the formula introducing the third blessing of the Amidah that follows performance of the Kedushah: "You are holy and Your Name is holy, and holy beings praise you daily, forever." The holy beings who share with God and His Name the divine attribute of holiness may be identified with the angels that the likely priestly authors of the Amidah conceived of as performing the celestial Kedushah, a conception that appears in all the later Throne visions deriving from this priestly tradition. But they may also be identified with the human performers of the Kedushah, the ones actually saying these words during the earthly prayer services, those who by this very practice are becoming Kedushim, the celestial Holy Ones that represent the final form of their transfiguration, as Metatron represents the transfigured form of Enoch. In the very act of performing the earthly Kedushah, then, the celebrant has an experience of unification with the celestial choir in praise of the Holy One, blessed be He, by which he is filled with the same holiness that is his promise of such bliss "forever."

Another indication of the esoteric heart of normative Judaism is given in the prayer with which the devout introduce their various acts of blessing. This, in its most condensed version, may be translated as: "Behold, I am ready and prepared to fulfill the Commandment [Mitzvah] of _____ for the sake of the unification [Yichud] of the Holy One, blessed be He, and His Shekhinah by means of that which is hidden and concealed in the name of all Israel." Here again we may see a threefold unification of the Holy One, blessed be He, the Shekhinah, and the Community of Israel. Indeed, this unification is said to be possible only through something hidden and concealed in the name Israel, understood in its mystical sense as the supernal community of righteous souls. What this something may be would seem to be given in the first definition of the name Israel: "for as a prince hast thou power with God and with men, and hast prevailed" (Gen. 32:28). As earlier shown, the name Israel means a "prince of God," one who can exercise the princely power derived from God and so prevail. The mystical Israel is, then, the community of those souls that have prevailed, overcoming all the impediments to their spiritual evolution while increasing in power until they have arrived at the promised land of salvation, a unification *with* the divine that is also a unification *of* the divine, of the divine masculinity and femininity, its transcendence and immanence, in and through themselves.

In Lurianic cosmology, the whole purpose of creation and definition of the Tikkun is the transformation of the divine ineffable unity into the multiple Partzufim, the divine personalities, a process that requires the spiritual services of man. But a clue to a further human role in this Tikkun can be found in a most telling detail attributed to the *Zohar*,[88] that the most important of these Partzufim, the divine son Ze'ir Anpin, is considered to be twice born. As Chayyim Vital explains the curious three stages of Ze'ir Anpin's maturation in the *Etz Chayyim*, after his first gestation in the womb of Imma and a period of nursing, there is a return to the womb of Imma for a second gestation:

> And now we will explain what the *Zohar* says in Chapter Acharei Mot, p. 65: "After he [Ze'ir Anpin] has finished nursing, he enters a second period of gestation." Ze'ir Anpin returns to the womb of Imma, even though he had already completed for himself a whole Partzuf of six Sefirot in the days of his nursing, to get his brains. And in order not to be astonished over the idea of a second pregnancy [of Imma] after the period of nursing, does it not say: "From my flesh will I see God."[89]

What is most interesting about the "astonishing" circumstance of Imma's second pregnancy with Ze'ir Anpin is that it seems symbolic of the human process of spiritual rebirth and is thus suggestive of some final identification between such spiritually reborn humans and the Partzuf of the twice-born son. As Aryeh Kaplan has recognized, "man is the counterpart of Zer Anpin."[90]

But what Luria and all the Kabbalists and Hasidim deriving from him never say is precisely this implication of the cosmic process, that the multiple Partzufim *are* the personalities given to the divine essence, particularly to the representative figure identified with Tiferet, by those human adepts forming the mystical Community of Israel, Klal Yisrael, those whose fulfillment of the covenant has lifted them to the status of divine sonship. This divine son, who combines in his own nature the transcendent and immanent forms of the divine and endows this synthesis with his own purified personality, may finally be identified with the twice-born form of the supernal divine son, with that increasingly personalized form of divinity whose covenantal interactions with Israel have established it as the God of Israel. But though its ultimate implications are hidden, Lurianic cosmology may be said to complete the long history of this Jewish esoteric doctrine by revealing the larger purpose of creation. For this hidden meaning is not only that the divine son represents a unification of the human with the divine, of purified human personality with the eternally subsisting divine essence, but that it was in order to acquire such multiple divine personalities through the cosmic evolution culminating in spiritually perfected man that the divine spirit first entered into material form, the whole cosmic process having thus been directed to the genesis of this divine cosmic child.

This, then, is the secret gnosis that has informed the Hebrew religion from its foundation, the hidden core of its esoteric tradition through all the ensuing millennia, and the source of the continuing vitality of Judaism. For however hidden it has always been, the texts and the teachers have also always been there, able to satisfy the serious searcher and to infuse communal worship with ever new reformulations of its mystical content. With or without proper *kavanah*, the prayer services and other ritual observances convey a power that touches and can transform the soul, and the biblical and mystical texts whisper meanings that can further instruct the soul thus touched as to the nature and purpose of its experiences, enabling it finally to "hear" the secret message of creation:

Sh'ma: Yisrael, YHVH Elohaynu, YHVH—echod!

Hear: Israel, YHVH Elohaynu, [and] YHVH [are] one!

Sacred Science:
Modes and Meaning

The Pythagorean Mode

In the previous chapter the secret doctrine of the son was traced from its priestly origins though all the later stages of the Jewish esoteric tradition and was shown to inform its central cosmological teachings. But there is another aspect of the priestly legacy that must also be understood if one is to decode the still more esoteric proofs of this central mystery hidden in the texts and diagrams of this tradition. This is the sacred science that the ancient Hebraic priesthood shared with Pythagoras and other ancient cultures, a science focused upon the interrelationship of the three special areas of knowledge that involve the laws of sound (harmonic for the Greeks and also linguistic for the Hebrews), of geometric form (both earthly and celestial), and of number. It is the meaning of this interrelationship that constitutes the central gnosis of sacred science, and its explication will be the main concern of this chapter. In the process this subject will be redefined in a way that will also provide a newly recovered understanding of the structure of reality.

This study of sacred science will begin with the exposition of its Pythagorean formulation, both because of the rigor of the experimental evidence for this science provided by the Pythagorean tradition and because of the clear influence it has been shown to have had on at least the kabbalistic stages of Hebraic sacred science. For the kabbalistic tradition seems to have been as imbued with Pythagoreanism as the gnostic systems that, like it, were fertilized in the rich spiritual soil of the late Hellenistic period. Indeed, the association of the Jewish esoteric tradition with Pythagoreanism goes even further back. Josephus tells us that the Essenes were Pythagorean;[1] Philo Judaeus is known to have employed Pythagorean numerology in his biblical exegesis;[2] and Gershom Scholem considers the first extant work of the Kabbalah, the *Sefer Yetzirah*, to have been "written by a Jewish Neo-Pythagorean."[3] But this text also reveals how the Hebraic practice of sacred science is distinguished from that of the Greeks through its further emphasis on the relationship of sound, shape, and number to the higher dimension of language. And it is language that will prove to be the key to the final explanation of the relationship of these three forms of esoteric knowledge, a key that will give new articulation to the vision of reality that for millennia had provided first the self-evident and then the scientifically demonstrable basis of man's understanding both of his own nature and of the cosmos whose structure is also his own.

This chapter will also provide the basis for most of what follows. The remaining seven chapters have been divided into three parts. Part 2 will continue the final focus of this chapter on the kabbalistic sacred science of language, with emphases on the esoteric correspondences of the Tetragrammaton and on the sacred science of harmonics. Part 3 will return us to the study of geometry, the primary discipline of sacred science, in its distinctively kabbalistic form, beginning with the Genesis creation account, which will be shown to encode the same three areas of esoteric knowledge that inform Pythagorean sacred science—harmonics, geometry, and number. It will continue with explorations of the geometric sources and meaning of the Tree of Life Diagram that will provide perhaps the most important contribution of this work to an understanding of the Kabbalah. Finally, Part 4 will provide syntheses of the sacred science here defined with the secular sciences of quantum physics and quantum cosmology, the former applying the guidelines of sacred science to a new geometric model of all the quanta and the latter finally integrating its scientifically interpreted model of kabbalistic cosmology with the secret doctrine of the son. For it is always this secret doctrine that this book will show to lie at the heart of Hebraic sacred science.

Though it is the Hebraic form of sacred science, with its distinctive manner of relating the interconnections of form, sound, and number to language, that will dominate the remainder of this chapter, we should first examine how this threefold interconnection is apprehended within the Pythagorean tradition and for the reason given earlier, that the conclusions it draws are based upon experimentation and subject to the precise repetition that can still today stand for scientific proof. With Pythagoras, then, the groundwork was laid for the development of the modern science that was to deny the significance of its wisdom.

Yeats reminds us that

> World-famous golden-thighed Pythagoras
> Fingered upon a fiddle-stick or strings
> What a star sang and careless Muses heard.[4]

Whether or not Pythagoras was, as the legend goes, a "golden-thighed" avatar of Apollo, he both worshiped Apollo and played the lyre attributed to Apollo's invention; and on this lyre and the monochord, he developed and/or demonstrated an understanding of numerical ratios that connected the music sacred to the Muses, also associated with Apollo, to the celestial geometry in which the Apollonian sun again figures so prominently, thereby producing a semblance of that which he claimed to be able to hear, the music of the spheres. But this musical or sound equivalent to the measurable distances or lengths of objects in space did not need the evidence of the heavenly spheres to demonstrate its truth; its demonstration was in the musical string itself. For what Pythagoras was able to show is that there is a precise and inverse relationship, expressible in numerical ratios, between the length of the string and the frequency of the tonal pitch it will produce when plucked, that geometrical length is convertible into musical sound through the inversion of fixed numerical ratios.

To give the simplest examples of this, the ratios 2:1, 3:2, and 4:3 define the important consonant intervals of the musical scale: the octave, the fifth, and the fourth, respectively. When these ratios are inverted and expressed as fractions of unity, the corresponding string lengths will produce the tones whose distance from the tonic is represented by their respective inverses. In the first instance, if the string length is halved, it will produce the octave double (2/1) of the tone of its full length. If the string is stopped at the 2/3 point, it will produce the musical fifth (3/2), and at the 3/4 point, the musical fourth (4/3). Another remarkable aspect about the numerical inversion between string length and tonal frequency is that the frequency ratios also express the order of emergence of the harmonics or partials (other terms for overtones, the first overtone being the second harmonic[5]). The second harmonic produced after the fundamental tone is its octave and expresses both the frequency ratio and order of 2:1. The third harmonic is to the second as the interval of the fifth, 3:2. The fourth harmonic is the second octave and is to the third harmonic as the interval of the musical fourth, 4:3. To continue, the fifth harmonic above the fourth, 5:4, is the interval of the major third, and the sixth above that, 6:5, is again the musical fifth, which is a minor third above the previous tone defining the major third.

What is also significant about this ordering is that each new harmonic slices the previous interval in a manner unique to sound, in terms of the non-even proportional division that defines the "harmonic mean." Thus the fifth, in relation to the second octave, divides it into the two uneven divisions of the fifth and the fourth (in the key of C, C to G is a fifth and G to the upper C of the octave is a fourth); the major third divides the fifth into the uneven divisions of the major third and the minor third (C to E is a major third and E to G, the fifth above C, is a minor third); the following "septimal third" divides the interval of the fourth to the third octave into a "septimal third" and a "septimal second," and is a natural or "just" tone a little lower than the B♭ produced through even-temperament tuning (G to such a B♭ being the septimal third and this B♭ to C the septimal second); and so on.

This harmonic mode of producing the mean between two tones is different from the geometric and arithmetic modes of producing means, and it is in these three methods of producing a mediating term that the qualitative differences between geometry, sound, and number can be found. In geometry, as is well known, the geometric mean produced by dividing a square is that of the diagonal, which though irrational with respect to rational sides, produces two equal right triangles, and the geometric progression produced through building squares progressively on the diagonals of preceding squares results in that geometric doubling proportion the Greeks called "analogia," the ratios of 2:4 and of 4:8 in the continuous geometric proportion of 2:4::4:8 being recognized as involving the principle of analogy. In the actual geometric process of producing the diagonal mean, the proportion would be $1:\sqrt{2}::\sqrt{2}:2$; $2:2\sqrt{2}::2\sqrt{2}:4$; and so on. In the geometric proportion, the differences between the extremes and the mean, while truly proportional, are not equal. In the arithmetic progression, however, the differences between the extremes and the mean are equal rather than proportional. The arithmetic mean is, of course, derived by adding the extremes and dividing by two.

These three modes of deriving means can be clarified by the use of algebraic formulae:

Arithmetic mean: $b = \dfrac{a + c}{2}$

Geometric mean: $b^2 = ac$ or $b = \sqrt{ac}$

Harmonic mean: $(a + c)\, b = 2ac$ or $b = \dfrac{2ac}{a + c}$

Let us now apply these formulae[6] to the harmonic tones that can be introjected within the first octave, that is, between the numbers 1 and 2. The arithmetic mean produced by adding these extremes and dividing by 2 is 1.5, or 3/2 ($1 + 2 = 3 \div 2 = 3/2$). The geometric mean produced by multiplying the extremes of 1 and 2 ($= 2$) and taking its square root is $\sqrt{2}$, or 1.414+. . . . Finally, the harmonic mean produced first by multiplying 1 and 2 ($= 2$), then multiplying this product by 2 ($2 \times 2 = 4$), and finally dividing this by the sum of the extremes ($1 + 2 = 3$) is 1.333... , or 4/3. Now from what was earlier established concerning the frequency ratios and corresponding order of the harmonics, we can see that the arithmetic mean between the fundamental tone and its octave is the consonant interval of the perfect fifth, 3:2, while the harmonic mean is the consonant interval of the perfect fourth, 4:3. The geometric mean gives us the inharmonic exact middle of the scale between the fourth (Do-Fa) and the fifth (Do-Sol), the chromatic solfeggio tone of Fi. In figure 3.1 these ratios are expressed in terms of decimals on the number line between 1 and 2 representing the octave.

Various facts can be gleaned from this graph of the three numerical means translated into harmonic intervals. The first is that the harmonic laws of sound, in addition to their own method of establishing harmonic relationships through the harmonic mean, are also able to establish relationships between the laws of sound and those of both geometry and

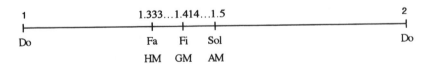

FIGURE 3.1

number. They accomplish this through a tonal structure that can relate these three means to one another. Thus it is not only through number that these three means can be expressed but also through musical sound. But figure 3.1 also shows important differences between these means.

The arithmetic mean that properly comes at the exact center of the number line, as 1.5 is numerically equidistant from 1 and 2, does not represent the exact tonal center of the octave, this being represented by the geometric mean. But where the irrationality of the square root is the characteristic means by which the geometric laws of space define the most pleasing spatial proportions, particularly those proportions involving the √5 that the Pythagoreans called "golden," its musical expression produces an interval dissonant to the ear. The aesthetics of the eye and the ear would seem to work in the same inverse relationship as that numerically given between the length and vibrational frequency of a musical string: what is symmetrically beautiful to the eye being harmonically unpleasant to the ear. And unlike the arithmetic and geometric means, both of which in their different media attempt to make an even division, one of a total number and the other of a total area, the harmonic mean produces tonal beauty by a division in which the differences between *a* and *b* and between *b* and *c* have an equality neither of number, as in the arithmetic progression, nor of proportion, as in the geometric progression.

In the arithmetic progression 2:5::5:8, the mean term 5 between the sum of the extremes, 10, is the same difference of units, 3, above the lower extreme as it is below the upper extreme; in the geometric progression 2:4::4:8, the mean term 4 is the same proportion greater than the lower term, 2 times, as the upper term is greater than it (by formula the mean term 4 is equal to the square root of the product of the extremes, 16). Rather, in the harmonic progression, the extremes and the differences are harmonized so that the number of times that *c* is greater than *a* is also the number of times that the difference between *b* and *c* is greater than that between *a* and *b*. Using the same extremes of 2 and 8, we get the harmonic progression 2:3.2::3.2:8 in which, as 8 is 4 times greater than 2, so the difference between 3.2 and 8, 4.8, is 4 times greater than that between 2 and 3.2, 1.2 (by formula, 32, which is 2x8=16x2=32, divided by 10, the sum of the extremes 2+8, equals 3.2). The ear that discriminates consonance from dissonance has a different aesthetic logic, then, from that of the eye, which appreciates a balancing of the parts, and these qualitative aspects of harmonic and geometric proportions, though distinctively different from each other, are both equally different from the quantitative averaging characteristic of arithmetical mediation.

But it is nonetheless precisely through these mathematical formulae of numbers that the spatial laws of proportion and the temporal laws of harmony can be related and the structure of one be translated into the medium of the other.

Before further developing this understanding of the pivotal role played by numbers, there is a final aspect of the harmonic series that reveals another way in which the laws of sound incorporate the laws of the other two elements of the esoteric triangle, number and geometry. We have already seen the way in which the order of the harmonics reflects the numerical proportions present in the vibrational frequencies of the strings, and we can clarify this relationship further. Thus if the first of two strings tuned to the same fundamental tone is depressed at the halfway point of its octave and the second at the two-thirds point of the fifth above this octave, the first string will have a double frequency of vibration and the second a triple frequency, which will produce the consonant interval of the perfect fifth through the phase coherence of these two frequency cycles of 3:2, as shown in figure 3.2.

But what is even more interesting about this order of harmonic emergence in musical sound is that the reappearance of the same tone at higher octaves always follows the doubling geometric progression of numbers. This is illustrated in table 3.1, which shows the thirty-two harmonics whose emergence through the first five octaves provides the essential tones of the diatonic scale. At the left the sixteen different tones that emerge in the course of these five octaves are listed with ascending chromatic solfeggio whole and composite names, and the corresponding tones in the key of C, the order in which they appear being given in parentheses.

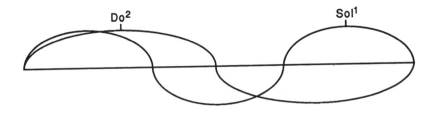

FIGURE 3.2

OCTAVE		I	II	III	IV	V
Do-C	(1)	1	2	4	8	16
Di-C#	(17)					17
Re-D	(9)				9	18
Ri-D#	(19)					19
Mi-E	(5)			5	10	20
Fa-F	(21)					21
Fi-F#	(11)				11	22
Fi/Sol-F#/G	(23)					23
Sol-G	(3)		3	6	12	24
Sol/Si-G/G#	(25)					25
Si-G#	(13)				13	26
La-A	(27)					27
Li-A#	(7)			7	14	28
Li/Ti-A#/B	(29)					29
Ti-B	(15)				15	30
Ti/Do-B/C	(31)					31
Do-C	(2)	2	4	8	16	32

TABLE 3.1. ORDER OF THE HARMONICS

What we see here is a table showing the perfect harmonic fractioning of the octaves and the geometric progression of the tones through successive octaves, but nothing in this table can explain the choice of the seven particular harmonics that make up the diatonic scale.

The diatonic scale does have its own musical logic, one based upon the significance of the major consonant intervals of the octave and the fifth. For the simplest tuning of the eight strings of two tetrachords is first to tune the eighth string one octave above the first and then to tune the fourth and fifth strings by fifths: the fourth string a harmonic fifth below the octave, and the fifth string a harmonic fifth above the fundamental tone of the first string. The question that determines the various musical modes is how the internal strings of the two tetrachords are to be divided, but all are based on some arrangement of the interval that emerges between the fourth and fifth strings, that of the whole tone. The simplest is again that of the diatonic or two-tone arrangement, which divides the intervals in each of the tetrachords into the same two whole tones plus a remainder. This remainder in even-temperament tuning is the semitone and in harmonic tuning is the "leimma," the former having the ratio of 16:15 while the latter has that of 256:243, the slight difference between 1 1/15 and less than 1 1/18. It should be noted that the precise difference of thirteen within the proportion of the leimma has become part of the esoteric lore surrounding the number thirteen. Only two intervals are required, then, to tune the whole of the diatonic scale, the second harmonic of the octave produced by dividing the first string in half and the third harmonic of the fifth produced by dividing or depressing the string at its 2/3 point. The ear can then tune the fourth, fifth, and eighth strings to the harmonics so produced and the remaining strings to the emergent whole tone between the fourth and fifth strings. But why the resulting mode called "Dorian," the counterpart of the modern major scale, should have the cosmic character attributed to it in the Pythagorean-Platonic tradition, that which, according to Macrobius, defines the harmony of the spheres,[7] cannot be explained simply in terms of the acoustic science of harmonics. When Pythagoras "Fingered upon a fiddle-stick or strings/ What a star sang and careless Muses heard," he was engaging, then, in two separable but connected enterprises. On the monochord he was demonstrating the laws of conversion between spatial extension and temporal frequency in terms of inverse numerical proportions, the rational basis of a sacred science relating space and time through number. But on the tetrachords he was playing a celestial music whose origin is unknown and whose persuasive validity rested not on such quantitative relationships but rather on a qualitative appreciation of the beauty of a particular arrangement of those relationships, not on the invariant laws of harmony but on the personal creation of melody, of free variation within the fixed ratios of a scale familiar to the Muses and somehow derived from their sphere.

Like music, number can also be shown to have characteristics that seem more properly to belong to the other domains of this special triad of interchangeable systems. Robert Lawlor has noted one aspect of number which allies it with the vibrational nature of musical sound:

we obtain wholes by linearly adding together discrete units, such as 1 + 1 + 1. In systematizing number in this way we forget that number continuity really only progresses through a wave-like alternation (odd-even), that there are no discontinuous magnitudes nor discrete parts, that a unit can never exist outside of a contiguous form/flow. This is why the Greek word *arithmos* denotes the definite and discrete, but also means rhythm and unbroken interrelatedness. . . . Plato's monadic ontology implies that every number presupposes a definite and discrete unit taken from a limitless, homogeneous field. Contemplation of it thus provides access to the contemplation not only of a limit, but also of the limitless. These extremes are the fundamental tension in Pythagorean thought.[8]

The major distinction of numerical units into the alternating categories of odd and even is taken by Lawlor to convey the rhythmic or vibrational characteristic of number, reflected in the Greek word *arithmos*, through which we may relate number to sound. In the table 3.1 we may see, moreover, a further characteristic of odd and even numbers by which they can be related to the notions of limit and the limitless. It shows that whereas each odd number introduces a new tone, it is the function of the even numbers to resonate this tone in a geometric progression through a potentially infinite number of octaves. Thus the odd numbers are each identified with their own unique tone while the even numbers relate this limited particularity to the limitless through a progression that they neither initiate nor can end. The particularity of the odd and integrative nature of the even is further demonstrated by the fact that odd numbers can only be divided by unity and themselves while even numbers combine larger numbers of factors.

Not only does number reveal a wave-like alternation analogous to sound but also a characteristic that allies it more closely with geometry, though this again will also bring in the third corner of musical harmonics. We still use the category of "square" numbers—those like 4, 9, 16, and 25 formed by multiplying a number by itself, "squaring" it—without normally realizing that they can be represented graphically by the form of a square of units, as in figure 3.3.

But in addition to such square and cube numbers as can be represented by the use of exponents, the Pythagoreans also categorized numbers in terms of other geometric figures, the most important perhaps being that of the triangle and triangular numbers, as in figure 3.4.

4	9	16	25
1 1	1 1 1	1 1 1 1	1 1 1 1 1
1 1	1 1 1	1 1 1 1	1 1 1 1 1
	1 1 1	1 1 1 1	1 1 1 1 1
		1 1 1 1	1 1 1 1 1
			1 1 1 1 1

FIGURE 3.3. SQUARE NUMBERS

Most significant of these triangular numbers is that of the decad known as the Tetractys. This triangular array of ten units became the symbol of Pythagorean thought and its adherents because it most succinctly expressed the unity of number with geometry and music that was the culminating insight of this school. Its relationship to geometry was not simply that of its triangular shape, but the fact that the number of units on each of these lines was taken to represent the progression through the geometrical dimensions. For its ordering of ten "pebble" points in the shape of an equilateral triangle not only provides the numerical ratios of the point, the line, the plane, and the solid, since these four dimensions require, respectively, one, two, three, and four points to define their simplest forms, but also a diagram of the emanation of four successive "worlds." The single pebble on the top signifies the mathematical point that, itself, represents the first world of unity. The two pebble points on the second line signify the mathematical line that can be drawn between them and are representative of the second world of duality, a world of extension into multiplicity. The three pebble points on the third line signify the minimal surface of the triangle, which requires three such points, and are representative of the harmonizing third world. Finally, the four pebble points on the bottom line signify the minimal solid, the four-pointed tetrahedron composed of four triangles, which represents the fourth world of manifest solids. The addition of the pebbles or dots that make up the four "worlds" of the point (1), the line (2), the surface (3), and the solid (4) equals the ten points of the Tetractys. Just as significant was the already suggested harmonic relationship of these four sets of units, which can be seen to express the ratios of the three consonant intervals: the 2:1 relationship of the upper two lines representing the interval of the octave; the 3:2 relationship of the third to the second line that of the fifth; and the 4:3 relationship of the last two lines that of the fourth. As we complete this discussion of the sacred science of Pythagoreanism, we can begin to understand the significance it attributed to the Tetractys.

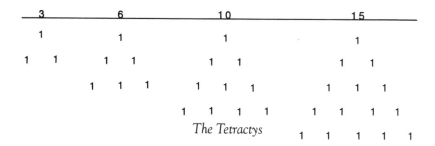

FIGURE 3.4. TRIANGULAR NUMBERS

It is the unique power of geometry, particularly in its Pythagorean form, to provide an archetypal explanation of cosmic functioning that explains the long hold its principles and practice have had in all the Western esoteric traditions; and to the extent that the Western and Eastern traditions can be distinguished, it is largely due to the presence or absence of the Pythagorean leaven. Evidence was earlier noted of the continuous association of the Jewish esoteric tradition with Pythagorean geometry; but before the Renaissance, the geometric content of kabbalistic thought was rendered largely by verbal description or metaphoric allusion. Even the profoundly geometric *Sefer Yetzirah* gives only verbal directions—and these couched in an obscurity probably meant to be penetrated only by the initiate—for what appears to be the construction of a cosmological diagram. The same obscurity marks the geometric aspect of the *Zohar*. It is possible, nonetheless, to recognize the Pythagorean quality of geometric description in these two monuments of kabbalistic thought by the primary geometric concepts they employ, and before turning to the fuller exposition of Hebraic sacred science, we should consider these further Pythagorean aspects of the Kabbalah.

On one level, the *Sefer Yetzirah* provides directions for the mental construction of the cube of infinite space. The full discussion of the *Sefer Yetzirah* Diagram, with a proposed solution of its enigma, will be deferred to chapter 7, it being sufficient at this point simply to observe that the author seems to have derived the structure of his cosmos from contemplation of the mysterious relationship of the diagonal to the side of a cube. This mystery emerges from the fact that when the side of a square is a whole number, such as 1, the diagonal will be an irrational number, in this case $\sqrt{2}$, and it is this irrational element that provides the square with its potential for growth, the new base through which it can multiply its size. It was the incommensurability of the diagonal to the side that was the great secret the Pythagorean initiate was vowed to keep, not as generally taught because this fact destroys the rationality of Pythagorean geometry but precisely because it is a revelation of the vital necessity of the suprarational element in all finite structures, that the square root contains a power whose nature is, in truth, unutterable in terms of finite measure and that points to the deepest of cosmic mysteries.[9] Thus in the relationship of the side to the diagonal of a square we have another measure of that association of the limited and unlimited at the core of Pythagorean thought.

As we have seen, the basic principles of Pythagorean cosmology are contained in Pythagoras' great mystic symbol, the Tetractys, and there would seem to be evidence that the Kabbalists of medieval Provence and Spain were practicing geometers with knowledge of this prime Pythagorean symbol. Gershom Scholem has summarized some of the evidence of geometric concepts employed by the medieval Spanish Kabbalists of Gerona:

> In the Zohar, as well as in the Hebrew writings of Moses de Leon, the transformation of Nothing into Being is frequently explained by the use of one particular symbol, that of the primordial point. Already the Kabbalists of the Geronese school employed the comparison with the mathematical point, whose motion creates the line and the surface, to illustrate the process of emanation from the "hidden cause."[10]

The use by Geronese Kabbalists of the point, line, and surface "to illustrate the process of emanation" would seem to suggest a knowledge of the Tetractys. More significant, however, is the emergence of the related concept of four cosmic worlds in such late thirteenth- and early fourteenth-century Spanish texts as the *Tikkunei Zohar* and the *Massekhet Atzilut*. The connection of this concept with that of the ten Sefirot, in the form first appearing in the twelfth-century Provençal *Sefer ha-Bahir*, is one seen and elaborated upon by almost the whole of the later kabbalistic tradition. The pervasiveness of this union of four worlds with ten constituents in this thirteenth-century kabbalistic tradition indicates something of the importance it must have given to the practice of Pythagorean geometry.

For over one thousand years, then, from the emergence of the *Sefer Yetzirah* as early as the third century to the golden age of Spanish Kabbalism in the thirteenth century, there seems to have been some core of geometric practice and understanding in the kabbalistic tradition that had clear links to the principles of Pythagorean geometry. And in the following discussion, both the links and differences between Pythagorean and Hebraic sacred science will be studied in terms of the seminal work that may be credited with having transmitted the essential lore of the Hebraic priesthood to the later Kabbalah, the *Sefer Yetzirah*.

The Kabbalistic Mode in the *Sefer Yetzirah*

With a greater understanding of Pythagorean science, we can now turn to the Kabbalah and discern in its first extant text, the *Sefer Yetzirah*, a similar intuition into the principal components of creation, an intuition expressed in its very first verse:

> With 32 mystical paths of Wisdom engraved Yah, the Lord of Hosts, the God of Israel, the living God, King of the universe, El Shaddai, Merciful and Gracious, High and Exalted, dwelling in eternity, whose name is Holy—He is lofty and holy—and He created His universe with three books (*Sepharim*), with text (*Sepher*), with number (*Sephar*), and with communication (*Sippur*).[11]

The wisdom with which God, in the ten aspects here named, which may also be associated with the ten Sefirot soon to be defined in this text, created the universe involves three aspects of the Hebrew letter-numbers: their form (*sefer*), their correlated number (*sefar*), and their sound (*sippur*). All three of these Hebrew words, as well as Sefirah, are similar in spelling and sound and are all derived from the same triliteral root of Samekh, Pe, and Resh, the words *sefirah* and *sefer* being distinguishable primarily in terms of gender, the former feminine and the latter masculine.[12] It is, then, through God's ten feminine attributes and three masculine instrumentalities that the universe is here said to have come into being. And as the ten elements of the Tetractys were equally related to number, harmonics, and geometry, so are these ten designations for God related to the same three categories. The relationship with number is directly stated, while "text" can here be taken to refer to form and "communication" to sound. What is most significant, however, is the unique Hebraic awareness that these three aspects of sacred science are all contained in the higher unifying science of language, each of the letters having a numerical correlation, a sound, and a visual form.

Before proceeding further, it may be helpful to explain again the practice of converting words into numbers known as Gematria, a late Hebrew word that also suggests a hidden etymological association with the Greek word for geometry, *geometrein*, and so relates the capacity of words to be interchanged into numbers with a third, geometric, corner. For in Hebrew as in Roman figuring, there are no separate symbols for numbers; rather, the letters of the alphabet also serve as numbers. The first nine Hebrew letters represent the numbers from one to nine; the next nine the tens; and the last four, with the distinctive final forms of an additional five earlier-counted letters, the hundreds; a larger version of the initial letter Aleph being used, finally, to represent one thousand.

It might be pointed out that not only do these twenty-seven or twenty-eight different forms of the letters provide a logical correlation with the decimal numbering system but they also relate to the cycles of the moon, the former number with the mode of "sidereal" computation based upon the fixed stars, and the latter number with the mean between the "sidereal" and the "synodical" method of determining the new moon's position with regard to the also moving sun. The continuing importance of the moon to the Hebraic religious consciousness is shown through the Hebraic use of the moon as the basis of its calendar as well as the monthly religious festival of Rosh Chodesh to welcome the new moon. Given this Hebraic concern with lunar time, and the association of both its numerical cycle with the number of different characters in the Hebrew alphabet and of these letters with a decimal numbering system, it is not too much to suggest that, to the correlation of letters with numbers, there was understood to be an additional correlation to the celestial geometry of astronomy, a correlation that will be considered further in the next chapter and that particularly emphasized the monthly movement of the moon in relation to the position of the sun. In this regard, the moon's steady movement further and further to the left of the sun throughout the month may perhaps explain the Hebrew linguistic practice of writing from right to left.[13]

Thus, despite the fact that Gematria ostensibly involves only the relationship of letters to numbers, there would seem to be a third geometric element necessarily interwoven into this major technique of esoteric explication. But the practice of Gematria goes beyond the simple use of letters for counting, as in the census of Hebrews in the wilderness period. It is based on the further understanding that letters not only signify numbers but that the particular addition of the numerical worth of the letters in any word both defines its character and reveals its subtle connection with any other word or words whose letters add up to the same numerical sum, a connection that can be used to explicate a subtle dimension of the other word and its context not otherwise perceivable.

In addition to their numerical correlation, the *Sefer Yetzirah* also understands the Hebrew letters to have the characteristics of spatial and temporal extension, as shown in the further correlations made for each of the twenty-two letters in their three numerical categories: "Twenty-two foundation letters: three Mothers, seven Doubles, and twelve Elementals."[14] For all of the letters are given correspondences in three further categories related to space, time, and the significant third category of the soul, whose function it would seem to be to mediate between the dimensions of space and time through its own third dimension of spirit. These three categories, or dimensions, of Olam (the universe), Shonah (the year), and Nefesh (the soul) define the essential characteristics that distinguish each of the letters. Thus the spatial dimension of the three mother letters—Aleph, Mem, and Shin—are the elements of fire (Shin), water (Mem), and the air (Aleph) that mediates between the other two, the heavens deriving from fire, the earth from water, and the spirit from air, which maintains its mediating function: "Heaven was created from fire, earth was created from water, and air decides between the fire and the water."[15] On the temporal dimension the three elements result in the three seasonal temperatures of hot, cold, and the temperate balance between them. On the spiritual dimension the element of fire is related to the head area of the mind, that of water to the abdominal area of the senses and instincts, and that of air to the chest area of the mediating heart. The seven double letters are similarly related, the spatial dimension to the seven planets, the temporal to the seven days of the week, and the spiritual to the seven orifices of the head. To complete the list of these correspondences, the twelve single letters are related spatially to the twelve constellations, temporally to the twelve months, and spiritually to twelve bodily members and organs.

Most significant is the final summary of these three dimensions with the new terminology it introduces in proof of the three numerical groupings of letters:

> And the proof of this, true witnesses, are the Universe, the Year, and the Soul. He decreed Twelve, (Ten), Seven and Three, and He appointed them in the Teli, the Cycle, and the Heart. . . . The Teli in the Universe is like a king on his throne, the Cycle in the Year is like a king in the province, the Heart in the soul is like a king in battle.[16]

Though Aryeh Kaplan has translated Galgal as cycle and Lev in its clear meaning of heart, he has left the word Teli untranslated, and this because its meaning is so complex as to require extended commentary. But before we can elucidate its meaning it must first be clarified that the

correspondences of the Teli, Galgal, and Lev are not to the three numerical groups of letters, as might first appear, but to the three dimensions of
Olam, Shonah, and Nefesh, all three categories of letters having these
same dimensions of space, time, and spirit. With this clarification, we
can now proceed to a fuller understanding of these significant new terms.

The Teli—Tuf, Lamed, Yod—literally means "hanging" and is used
in many biblical and kabbalistic contexts with this essential meaning.
But it has a particular referent throughout the history of Hebrew astronomy
to the conjoined astronomical factors of the constellation Draco (the
Dragon) and the path of the ecliptic that circles it, the constellation
Draco circling the northern pole of the ecliptic, the apparent path of the
sun's orbit as seen from the earth's two nodes of the moon. These lunar
nodes are the points at which the plane of the moon's orbit intersects the
plane of the sun's orbit, the ecliptic, to define the northern "Dragon's
Head" and the southern "Dragon's Tail," the names given to these nodes.
The ecliptic pole, therefore, is viewed in kabbalistic thought as defining
the axis of the universe around which the two great circles of the sun and
the moon meet in mystical union. The midrashic tradition of a double
Teli, male and female, refers, in one interpretation, to the masculine Teli
of the constellation Draco around the ecliptic pole as this pole is en-
circled by the feminine ecliptic path. But it can also refer to the nodal
points where the masculine sun meets the feminine moon, and it was the
understanding of both Judah Halevi and Abraham Abulafia that the term
Teli referred to the two nodes of the moon. Abulafia understood the nodes
as the place where the earthly and spiritual achieve a mystical meeting,
and this accords with the modern astronomical understanding of them as
the points where the plane of the moon's orbit around the earth intersects that of the earth's orbit around the sun. The long and consistent
Hebraic use of the term Teli to define the relationship of the constellation Draco to the nodes of the moon is thought, finally, either to be
derived from or reflected in the following biblical verses in which Teli is
translated simply in its literal meaning of "hanging"[17]: "He stretcheth
out the north over the empty place, and hangeth the earth upon nothing. . . . By his spirit he hath garnished the heavens; his hand hath formed
the crooked serpent" (Job 26:7, 13).

If Teli may be said to define space in terms of a universal axis, Galgal,
whose primary meaning relates to the circular, can equally be said to
define time in terms not of linear extension but of rhythmic cycles, the
cycles of the days, months, and seasons. Space is further defined by the
seven doubles and twelve singles in terms of an infinitely expansible cube.

As will be shown in detail in chapter 7, devoted to my solution of the mysterious *Sefer Yetzirah* Diagram, it is through the twelve diagonal edges of the octahedron that the six-sided dualing cube, whose seventh element is "the Holy Palace precisely in the middle,"[18] can be expanded in an infinite series of discrete stages. And it is through the eternal round of similarly discrete periods that time can also be defined. But between this infinity of discrete spatial expansion and eternity of discrete temporal repetition comes the all important mediating faculty of the Lev, the heart.

To return now to the three "books," *sefarim*, with which the *Sefer Yetzirah* begins, it will be remembered that they comprised the triad of "text," or shape, number, and "communication," or sound. Now since the first aspect of the letters implies their spatial dimension of form while the last implies their temporal dimension of sound—and the spatial is associated with the Teli as the temporal is with the Galgal—it follows that the median aspect of number is to be associated with the Lev. This association of number with the heart may well be the most extraordinary concept implied in the whole of the *Sefer Yetzirah* and is perhaps its greatest contribution to the definition of sacred science I am here attempting. For once one contemplates this association of number with the heart, considers the heart as involved in the perception of number, in the process of counting, its justification becomes clear: as the beating organ that establishes the body's rhythm, it provides the norm against which other rhythms can be compared, counted,[19] counting and rhythm again being conjoined, as also in the Greek word for the "art of counting," *arithmetike*. The perceptual system would seem, then, to have a counting faculty, one which the *Sefer Yetzirah* tells us has the power to mediate numerically between the elements of space and time, form and sound, and which is centered in the heart. The Greek word for "arithmetic" implies, however, the "art" of counting, a capacity not only quantitative but, it would seem, also qualitative, one that can distinguish the beautiful from the ugly in spatial and harmonic proportions; and this would also seem to be a special property of the heart, its qualitative ability to discern a personal affinity to some vibrational patterns and aversion to others, and to express these responses to the consciousness in the form of feelings. To seat this quantitative-qualitative faculty of counting in the heart is further consistent with the Hebraic identification of that deeper knowledge known as "understanding" with the heart, as in that *chokham lev* (wise heart) required for the builders of the desert Sanctuary (Exod. 35:10) and for which Solomon prayed (1 Kings 3:9), an understanding more felt than rationally formulated. It is on such a prerational level of consciousness that the human numerical computer must also be lodged, for we are certainly not consciously aware of the complicated numerical computations that are involved not only in the primary perceptions of visual and auditory data but, just as importantly, in the secondary conversions of data from one medium to another. Once the heart has been associated with number, it then becomes possible to understand how the human perceptual system can interconvert the languages of the eye and the ear.

Such understanding is based on an interpretation of the *Sefer Yetzirah* references to the Nefesh as relating to the human soul, an interpretation that is true on a secondary level of analogy. The soul referred to in this text, however, is not primarily human but cosmic; for the three dimensions of Olam, Shonah, and Nefesh define the body and soul of the Yetziric anthropocosmos, that of Adam Kadmon.[20] And all the references to the bodily organs of the Nefesh refer not to its cosmic body of planets and constellations but to its intermediate spiritual or astral body. The cosmos is being defined, then, as extended in space and time and informed by soul. But these two coordinates, between whose numerical proportions the heart of the soul body is the mediator, are not to be understood in modern Cartesian terms.

As Giorgio de Santillana and Hertha von Dechend show in their prodigious work of comparative mythology, in archaic consciousness, and, one might add, also in Einsteinian relativity theory, space and time are not to be separated: "archaic time is the universe, like it circular and definite."[21] And like the cosmic frame implied in the *Sefer Yetzirah*, the basic paradigm they have discovered to inform the mythology of all the preliterate cultures worldwide is that which relates the temporal revolutions of the heavenly bodies to the ecliptic pole and whose mythological image is the "whirlpool":

> The rotation of the polar axis must not be disjointed from the great circles which shift along with it in heaven. . . . The mythical earth *is*, in fact, a plane, but this plane is not *our* "earth" at all, neither our globe, nor a presupposed homocentrical earth. "Earth" is the implied plane through the four points of the year, marked by the equinoxes and solstices, in other words the ecliptic. And this is why this earth is very frequently said to be quadrangular. . . . We think that the whirlpool stands for the "ecliptical world" marked by the whirling planets, embracing everything that circles obliquely with respect to the polar axis and the equator. . . . starting from the idea of the whirlpool as a way to the other world, one must look at the

situation through the eyes of a soul meaning to go there. . . . But in order to leave the ecliptical frame, there must be a station for changing trains at the equator. . . . All "change stations" are found invariably in two regions: one in the South between Scorpios and Sagittarius, the other in the North between Gemini and Taurus; and this is valid through time and space, from Babylon to Nicaragua. Why was it ever done in the first place? Because of the Galaxy, which has its crossroads with the ecliptic between Sagittarius and Scorpios in the South, and between Gemini and Taurus in the North.[22]

The *Sefer Yetzirah* references to the Teli and Galgal are clearly related to this most ancient understanding both of cosmic periodicity and of the means by which it can be transcended, the former defined as the "ecliptical world" and the latter as the nodes where its two great circles meet. And whether the later kabbalistic tradition is correct in its association of the Teli with the lunar nodes, or de Santillana and von Dechend's new analysis is accepted that understands the mythological references to involve the points at which the ecliptic path of the sun intersects the plane not of the moon but of the galaxy, it is through its harmonization of two such great circles of space-time, a balancing performed by its heart, that the world-soul of Adam Kadmon can maintain or regain its connection with the eternal.

The image of the "whirlpool as a way to the other world" can also be associated with the complex of connected concepts and terms in the *Sefer Yetzirah*, most significantly with the triad of elements identified with the three mother letters. These letters were selected for vibrational characteristics (as will be explained in chapter 5), as well as for their sound associations with the Hebrew words for these elements, Shin for Aesch (fire), Mem for Mayim (water), and the silent Aleph for the silent element of air whose Hebrew word is Avir; and their selection had the further effect of reducing the remaining double letters to seven and single letters to twelve, numbers whose astronomical significance cannot be overestimated since they correspond to the seven planets of the older astronomy and the twelve constellations. Now it is my suggestion that the air-balanced elements of fire above and water below, both in the *Sefer Yetzirah* and in the alchemical tradition, were understood to imply the symbol of the hexagram in its elemental form of balanced vortices, the ascending vortex of fire and the descending vortex or whirlpool of water. The resulting hexagram, which chapter 6 will show to have been part of the Jewish esoteric tradition from its earliest origins, would also seem to be implied in the *Sefer Yetzirah*. Once the hexagram can be admitted to the conceptual nexus of the *Sefer Yetzirah*, it can be further associated not only with the northern and southern galactic "change stations" where space and time, Teli and Galgal, are both united and transcended but also with that third heart aspect, the Lev, whose balance can bring the soul to those still points of the changing world. Such an association of the hexagram with the heart also appears in the esoteric Indian system of yoga, which correlates this symbol with the heart Chakra, itself an energy vortex of the astral body with which we are here concerned.

The *Sefer Yetzirah*, then, perpetuates a unified cosmology that goes back to Neolithic times and was spread over the whole globe. And as de Santillana and von Dechend define the essential teaching of this cosmology: "The connections were what counted . . . all things were signs and signatures of each other, inscribed in the hologram, to be divined subtly. And number dominated them all."[23] So also is it Number that defines the "thirty-two mysterious paths of wisdom" through which the *Sefer Yetzirah* explains the creation: the ten ideal numbers of the Sefirot, which constitute the cosmic man, added to the twenty-two letter-numbers used for computation, through which the spatial, temporal, and spiritual dimensions of the anthropocosmos are further distinguished. And it is through the heart that the subtle presence and operations of number can be divined and balanced, this not only for the world soul in the emanation but for such a human soul as Abraham, who can also use numbers creatively and "be successful"[24] in the returning path of the Tikkun.

Meaning and the Complementarity of Shape and Sound

We have seen that the reciprocal relationship of shape and sound as mediated by number was the central focus of both Pythagorean and Hebraic sacred science. But we have yet to consider the more important question of *why* this relationship was so seriously studied. The philosophic implications of ancient sacred science now to be explored through a consideration of the nature and origin of language will not only unlock the deepest mystery of this science but show how it provides an ultimate explanation of the nature of reality.

We can begin with the profound connection that exists between visual imagery and language, a connection with far-reaching implications for sacred science. This is the remarkable fact of their interchangeability, the ability of language to express meanings through the use of imagery and of images to convey linguistic meaning. The former is a recognized property of poetic language and is splendidly illustrated by Archibald MacLeish in "Ars Poetica":

> A poem should be palpable and mute
> As a globed fruit,
>
> . . . .
>
> For all the history of grief
> An empty doorway and a maple leaf.
> For love
> The leaning grasses and two lights above the sea—
> A poem should not mean
> But be.

MacLeish would seem to be arguing here for a definition of lyric poetry that sees it as a paradoxical attempt to use the temporal and auditory medium of language to achieve the atemporal and silent expressiveness of pure form. And with extraordinary success, he gives us two untranslated images whose concrete nature speaks more powerfully to our understanding than would any attempt of verbal paraphrase to explain what they "mean." With just confidence, MacLeish expects us to be able to "read" in the visual facts of an open doorway, empty except for a fallen and uncleared maple leaf, "all the history of grief," and in the pictorial juxtaposition of something as mortal as grasses inclining toward those two lights that have transcended the welter of the sea, we are also expected to recognize the archetypal structure of love. So too would Keats have us believe that a Grecian urn, "the foster-child of silence and slow time," can "express / A flowery tale more sweetly than our rime," more, that we have inner spiritual senses attuned to the perception of such silent meanings:

> Heard melodies are sweet, but those unheard
>   Are sweeter; therefore, ye soft pipes, play on;
> Not to the sensual ear, but, more endeared,
>   Pipe to the spirit ditties of no tone:

It is the high art of lyric poetry that it focuses on the timelessness of a moment rich in implications and holding the promise of such a transcendence of mutability as is given to atemporal form: "Thou, silent form, dost tease us out of thought / As doth eternity."

But if lyric poetry reveals the power of language to translate the expressive potential of images, the opposite is true, as Freud has shown, of dream images, which can translate words and such word plays as puns into concrete images:

> The dream-thoughts and the dream-content are presented to us like two versions of the same subject-matter in two different languages. Or, more properly, the dream-content seems like a transcript of the dream-thoughts into another mode of expression, whose characters and syntactic laws it is our business to discover by comparing the original and the translation. The dream-thoughts are immediately comprehensible, as soon as we have learnt them. The dream-content, on the other hand, is expressed as it were in a pictographic script, the characters of which have to be transposed individually into the language of the dream-thoughts. If we attempted to read these characters according to their pictorial value instead of according to their symbolic relation, we should clearly be led into error. . . . The work of condensation in dreams is seen at its clearest when it handles words and names. It is true in general that words are frequently treated in dreams as though they were things, and for that reason they are apt to be combined in just the same way as are presentations of things. Dreams of this sort offer the most amusing and curious neologisms. . . . for the purpose of representation in dreams, the spelling of words is far less important than their sound. . . . the course of linguistic evolution has made things very easy for dreams. For language has a whole number of words at its command which originally had a pictorial and concrete significance, but are used to-day in a colourless and abstract sense. All that the dream need do is to give these words their former, full meaning or to go back a little way to an earlier phase in their development.[25]

The Freudian method of interpreting dreams first associates a visual form (the dream-content) with a verbal meaning (the dream-thought) and then applies an associative method of interpretation to such a dream "text," a hermeneutic method much like that of kabbalistic geometry, defined later as the Science of Expressive Form. But an additional feature of Freudian theory particularly relevant here is the fact that as the mind seems to have unconscious means of reading the verbal meaningfulness of images, so can the unconscious in its dream-work translate words into a language of symbolic images.

Having recognized the interchangeability of verbal and pictorial meanings, that we are able to render our thoughts and feelings through pictures that are meaningful to another and, as with the English Pre-Raphaelite poet-painters, translatable into poetry, we must now address the more fundamental question of *how* we are able to make such cognitive exchanges between the objects of visual and auditory perception. The first speculative step toward a solution to this problem is suggested by Freud's important insight that "the dream-thoughts and the dream-content are presented to us like two versions of the same subject-matter in two different languages." First there is the simpler recognition of two different languages, the normal language composed of words by which all thought is constituted, waking or underlying dreams, and which thus makes dream-thoughts "immediately comprehensible, as soon as we have learnt them," and the "pictographic script" of symbolic images "whose characters and syntactic laws it is our business to discover," a discovery aided by the translatability of these languages from one into the other. But more important is the recognition that this translatability of one such language into another is most easily explained by assuming a single "subject-matter" or source of meaning. Though Freud does not go so far in positing what might be construed as a unified object of different modes of perception, but first says they are "*like* two versions of the same subject matter" and then, with even more qualification, that "more properly," the dream images are not an original version but a translation of verbal material, it is the least qualified form of this suggestion that constitutes his boldest insight, an insight that we will see to be consistent with the evidence of ancient sacred sciences. Before we can understand the unifying principle within these ancient sacred sciences, however, we should first explore new supporting evidence for this complementarity provided by modern science and technology.

In his comprehensive study of cross-modal sense perception, Lawrence E. Marks has shown one mechanism by which temporal sound waves are translated into spatial form in the process of perception: ". . . sounds of different frequency are represented by different sites of maximal stimulation along the basilar membrane of the inner ear. That is, the sense organ of hearing is extended in space, and sound frequency maps spatially onto it."[26] He also shows the role of number both in the perception of sight and sound and in the transformations of neural to mental processes:

> Denumerability is an attribute of hearing as well as of seeing, but
> primarily through time for the former, through space for the latter.

. . . What does it mean to say that a nonlinear formula translates brain process to sensory experience? Does this very fact not imply that the gap between physiological and mental is bridged through a simple mathematical conversion, a transformation from one scale of numbers to another?[27]

His treatment of the neural bases for cross-modal perception is of particular interest:

> each of the perceived secondary qualities is limited to a single sense, whereas primary qualities may be perceived through several or all, and especially, if we follow Aristotle, through the common sense. . . .The common sense might . . . translate the babel of different senses into a universal language. . . . The unity of the senses creates a network of suprasensory attributes, of dimensions common to all senses, that enter first in the act of perception, then in the act of linguistic representation.[28]

If it is a "common sense" that extracts meaning from all the specific sensory information coming concurrently to it, particularly from the higher senses of hearing and vision, then modern thought has lost the understanding that appeared to be such common sense to the ancients, the understanding of how the evidence of sound and light can be related. But the mechanism of such a relation is the same for the Marks-Aristotle theory of the "common sense" as it is for sacred science, number: "The common sense looks at the frequency of neural impulses, regardless of modality."[29]

Lawlor has made another important association between modern brain research and Greek philosophy:

> Why was the humble activity of counting held to be of such importance by the Greek philosophers? One answer oddly enough comes from modern brain research. All our perceptions begin from an innate capacity in the brain/mind to recognize (count) periodic patterns of energy frequencies which our nervous system has transformed into neural rhythms. . . . The first act of perception is thus a *quantity* recognition of temporal periods which are then transformed, in the case of vision, into spatial fields and qualities set in a spatial context. . . . Intelligence *counts* and then views these tabulations of time as spatial images. If we assume then that qualities are derived from this innate counting, then intelligence can be understood as a

process of transformations back and forth between two inseparable ways of being, quantity and quality. This may be the conceptual intuition which guided the Platonic emphasis on counting, for in Platonic philosophy, as in Hindu philosophy, counting and calculation are proper to man (the Sanskrit word *manas*, man, means "measuring") and relate him to the intelligible world. This in turn must be connected to the Pythagorean influence, where ontology itself was defined as that which is countable.[30]

In Lawlor's analysis, perception begins with the counting of energy frequencies, temporal patterns that it then translates into spatial images in order to "read" their meaning, and number serves as the lingua franca between the languages of soundlike energy frequencies and of form.

It should finally be noted that modern proof of the mediating role of number between the perception of form and sound, as well as their manifestation, is provided not only by brain research and the deductions of cognitive psychologists but more phenomenally by computer technology. For *digital* computers can produce both graphic representations of numerically programmed forms and superb reproductions of numerically recorded music. But though the central mystery of both the Pythagorean and kabbalistic traditions of sacred science can be supported by modern science and technology, it is still to this ancient science that we must turn for final illumination of this mystery.

We have thus far been concerned primarily with the mutual convertibility of forms and verbal sounds, a process we have seen to require the mediation of number. But though thus separable and convertible, the association of form and sound is far more closely connected, and it is, in fact, this intrinsic connection that explains both our need for the dual sense organs through which they are initially apprehended, the eyes and the ears, and for the capacity of mutual translation between the forms of data they provide. In chapter 6 we will see that the opposing orientations of visual and aural perception dominated and defined for Thorlief Boman the contrasting natures of Hebraic and Greek thinking. But in concluding his analysis he also comes to see "the unitary Hebraic manner of thinking and the unitary Greek manner of thinking as two possible and equally necessary reactions to one and the same reality. . . the Greeks describe reality as *being*, the Hebrews as *movement*. Reality is, however, both at the same time; this is logically impossible, and yet it is correct."[31] Thus it may be that the same "object" can appear to our sight as delimited in space while the vibrational pattern of its energy transmits another message to some type of ultrasonic receptor with which we must be equipped and that is probably mediated through the ear, and this message is not one of separate parts but of the whole.

The form of a substance whose nature we can apprehend visually through various light clues would seem at the same time to be announcing its nature through sound clues of a subtlety beyond our normal conscious awareness but that nonetheless are conveying important qualitative information to subliminal levels of perception. This Keats also long ago intuited when he said: "therefore, ye soft pipes, play on; / Not to the sensual ear, but, more endeared, / Pipe to the spirit ditties of no tone." It is to such inner hearing, moreover, that the unlimited aspect of any source of vibrational transmission can be communicated. Thus the subtle clues through which the spirit can apprehend the true nature of that which it senses are as much defined by the nature of the sense that apprehends them, eye or ear and gross or subtle, as by that which transmits these clues, and they present evidence for the complementary nature of such perception. For where the eye picks up evidence for the localization of an object in space, the ear or other receptor of soundlike waves picks up a more subtle message of the extension of such a centering point of energy through all the furthest reaches of space and of its interaction with all other frequency patterns.

Before considering the final implications of the dual messages matter seems to be transmitting through light and sound, we should return to the central focus of Hebraic sacred science, that of language, and the way in which language may be related to such subtle transmissions of sound from material objects. For it is in the nature of language that the final key to the understanding of sacred science will be found and the special emphasis of its Hebrew mode also validated.

Language and the Final Explanation

The modern language theory called semiotics, founded by Ferdinand de Saussure, posits that the linguistic sign is composed of two elements, the signifier and the signified:

> The linguistic sign unites, not a thing and a name, but a concept and a sound-image. . . . The two elements are intimately united, and each recalls the other. . . . I propose to retain the word *sign* [*signe*] to designate the whole and to replace *concept* and *sound-image* respec-

> tively by *signified* [*signifié*] and *signifier* [*signifiant*]. . . . The bond be-
> tween the signifier and the signified is arbitrary. . . . arbitrary in that
> it actually has no natural connection with the signified.[32]

The double nature of the linguistic sign is most important for this investigation, though we shall see reason to dispute Saussure on two essential
points of his linguistic theory, his new equation of the "signified" with
"concept" rather than its older identification with image and his assertion that the relationship of signifier to signified is arbitrary. For the relationship of sound to shape we have been exploring provides a different
key to the understanding of the linguistic sign. If we can identify the
reality to which the sign points with the sense data, primarily visual, by
which the reality of the thing forces itself upon our consciousness, the
signified would then represent both the visual image that largely determines our concept of a thing and the ontological claim that this image
has a necessary connection to its referent. What I, in concert with important linguists, propose to add to the semiotic definition of the sign is a
restoration of the ancient understanding of the visual image as the source
of thought and the origin of verbal meaning, that within the conceptual
aspect of at least those signs that are primary words is a visual image.

But we should first consider the implications of these two aspects
of the sign so defined. If the signifier can be identified with a sound
signal and the signified with a visual image, then we must confront the
fact that words involve the meaningful bonding of the two wholly dis-
similar domains that were also the focus of ancient sacred science, that
at the heart of at least primary words or names is the seeing of similarity
between dissimilars that Aristotle ascribed to metaphor: "a good metaphor implies an intuitive perception of the similarity in dissimilars."[33]
Emile Benveniste, following Saussure in part, holds that "the signifier
is a phonic translation of a concept."[34] How this can be when by concept we understand image is a question we shall leave for later discussion, but that the mind can make such meaningful translations of images into sounds and vice versa is demonstrable in the most elementary
processes of language. And they mark these processes as essentially
metaphorical.

The further development of vocabulary through metaphorical transfers from those more concrete signifiers whose referents are sensible images to those involving abstractions has been pointed out by many, among
them Julian Jaynes:

In early times, language and its referents climbed up from the concrete to the abstract on the steps of metaphors, even, we may say,
created the abstract on the bases of metaphors. . . . Understanding
a thing is to arrive at a metaphor for that thing by substituting something more familiar to us. And the feeling of familiarity is the feeling of understanding. . . . Moreover, things that in the physical-
behavioral world do not have a spatial quality are made to have
such in consciousness. Otherwise we cannot be conscious of them.[35]

All denominations, then, retain some link to the spatial images through
which corresponding sound slices first became capable of generating
meaning. And however dead the metaphoric content of abstract words
may become, their meaningfulness rests on some original metaphorical
connection with a concrete image or process that can often be traced
through their etymologies.

Paul Ricoeur also recognizes that later metaphoric processes may be
the same as those originally responsible for the development of language
when he asks: "could we not imagine that the order itself is born in the
same way that it changes? Is there not, in Gadamer's terms, a 'metaphoric'
at work at the origin of logical thought, at the root of all classification?"[36]
In his main development of a theory of metaphor as the vehicle for "the
creation of meaning in language,"[37] Ricoeur is primarily dependent on
the earlier work of I. A. Richards, Max Black, and Monroe C. Beardsley,
who all tend to view this production of meaning as the result of an interaction between two metaphorically associated ideas. But through the work
of Marcus B. Hester and others, especially Wittgenstein, he later comes
to question this earlier analysis and returns to the central importance of
the image to metaphor as first defined by Aristotle:

the question remains whether one cannot or ought not to attempt
the reverse, and *proclaim the image to be the final moment of a semantic theory* that objected to it as a starting point. . . . What remains to
be explained is the *sensible* moment of metaphor. This moment is
designated in Aristotle by the lively character of metaphor, by its
power to "set before the eyes." . . . The most satisfying explanation
. . . is the one that Hester links to the notion of "seeing as" (which
is Wittgensteinian in origin). . . . Thus, "seeing as" quite precisely
plays the role of the schema that unites. . . the light of sense with
the fullness of the image. In this way, the non-verbal and the verbal
are firmly united at the core of the image-ing function of language.[38]

With this reentry of the image into semantic theory, and the admission that metaphoric processes involving such imagery function at all stages in the development of language, we can return to the earlier definition offered here of the signifier as the sound slice and the signified as the image and understand how together they produce the metaphoric meaning that distinguishes the linguistic sign or word. This suggests, first, that the phenomenal object appearing as image is somehow also responsible for producing its phonic signifier, that it is, indeed, as Benveniste said, its "phonic translation." And it also suggests that the generation of meaning is a direct product of those sounds that are the denotative aspect of words, that as the sound aspect of a word is somehow derivable from the object it signifies, so is it from the recognition of this verbal sound that the mind gains an intuition into the nature of its perception that renders it meaningful.

Before leaving our consideration of the sign, there is one other aspect of the Hebrew tradition that is particularly pertinent and should be considered here, the meaning attached to the Hebrew term for word, *davar*. In his linguistic study of this word, Boman has shown that Hebrew draws no distinction between words and the reality they signify: "*dabhar*—'the word in spoken form,' hence 'efficacious fact,' is for the Semites the great reality of existence."[39] Susan A. Handelman further develops this understanding of *davar*:

> Though *davar* means both *thing* and *word* in Hebrew, it is crucial to point out that *thing* did not have the Greek connotations of *substance*. As I. Rabinowitz puts it, "the word is the reality in its most concentrated, compacted, essential form." . . . Names are not conventional, but intrinsically connected to their referents; the name, indeed, is the real referent of the thing, its essential character—not the reverse, as in Greek thought. One does not pass beyond the names as an arbitrary sign towards a non-verbal vision of the thing, but rather *from the thing to the word*, which creates, characterizes, and sustains it. Hence *davar* is not simply *thing* but also action, efficacious fact, event, matter, process.[40]

When the linguistic sign is interpreted from the perspective of *davar*, it is not simply the relation of signifier to signified that proves necessary but also that from the whole sign to reality. The signified becomes both linguistic and extralinguistic, and the signifier bound by necessity to a dynamic reality made ever more creative through the power of the word.

We saw that Freud suggested some such association of language and images in the subject matter of dreams when he said: "The dream-thoughts and the dream-content are presented to us like two versions of the same subject-matter in two different languages." Also significant was his perception that "for the purpose of representation in dreams, the spelling of words is far less important than their sound." As a material object may be said to be represented in perception through the two different media of image and sound, so too with the dream subject matter, but with this apparent difference, that it is not simply tonal frequencies that are translated by the dream work into images but linguistic sounds. At the risk of being thought to be dreaming, I would suggest that it is not only the images of dreams that may be thought to be speaking but everything that can claim an identity. We come thus to the obscure subject of the origin of language.

If the same object can transmit different messages to the eye and the ear, then certain sound frequencies, though not normally falling within the range of conscious hearing, will have a natural connection to the visual perception of that object as a pattern of light. But to connect such ultrasonic vibrations to linguistic sound, it is necessary to posit some mythical race of more highly attuned sages who could actually "hear" such frequencies, somehow stepped down to the audible range, and that when they were so converted their sound more resembled the unique sounds that compose human speech than those of melodic song—sibilants, fricatives, and the like. It is some such race of original "legislators" that Plato also has need to posit in developing his highly qualified theory of natural language in the *Cratylus*:

> not every man is able to give a name but only a maker of names; and this seems to be the legislator, who of all skilled artisans in the world is the rarest. . . . ought not our legislator also to know how to put the true natural name of each thing into sounds and syllables . . . if he is to be a namer in any true sense? . . . And the legislator, whether he be Hellene or barbarian, is not deemed by you a worse legislator, provided he expresses the form of the name proper to each subject in whatever syllables; this or that country makes no matter.[41]

Once Plato has established such original "legislators" who, in different countries and with different sounds and syllables, could convey "the true natural name of each thing," he then proceeds to analyze the nature of this process:

> Then a name is, it seems, a vocal imitation of any object; and a man
> is said to *name* any object when he imitates it with the voice. . . .
> All objects have sound and figure, and many have colour. . . . But
> the art of naming appears not to be concerned with imitations of
> this kind; the arts which have to do with them are music and draw-
> ing. . . . he has to imitate the essence by syllables and letters. . . .
> That objects should be imitated in letters and syllables and so find
> expression, may appear ridiculous, Hermogenes, but it cannot be
> avoided—there is no better principle to which we can look for the
> truth of first names.[42]

When Plato concludes a name to be "a vocal imitation of any object," he is
implying one of two connected propositions. The first is that the original
"maker of names" could imitate his spatial image of an object in the different medium of vocal sound because, on some level, he knew or could use
the mathematical equivalents between the media of light and sound frequencies as well as the laws permitting the numerical conversions from one
medium to the other, a knowledge that the *Sefer Yetzirah* suggests is lodged
in and mediated by the heart, more properly what can be considered the
"heart" of the astral or subtle body, the Tzelem. Thus he could be said to
have an intuitive apprehension of the right name for any object through
the subtle operations in his spirit of the laws for the numerical conversion of
spatial to temporal measures that, as we have seen, form the central knowledge transmitted through the various traditions of sacred science.

The second meaning of Plato's "vocal imitation," and it would seem
to come closer to the final explanation we have been searching for, would
understand such imitation as involving not the conversion of spatial
images to their sound equivalents but the conversion of the ultrasonic
frequencies coming from the same source as a spatial image to those frequencies within the audible range that can be approximated, imitated,
by the human voice. Perhaps Plato's "maker of names" represented a perceptual capacity even greater, one for whom such sounds were naturally
audible and needed no further subtle processes of conversion. The continuing research into cross-modal perception, or synesthesia, supported
by the latest brain-scanning techniques, has given new support for the
older suggestions that some people can actually hear the sounds of things
and that it is this ability that lies at the root of language.

The work of Dr. Richard E. Cytowic, a research neurologist, takes
us from actual subjects to an important new theoretical framework for
synesthesia:

As one subject explained, "The shapes are not distinct from hearing—they are part of what hearing is." . . .We have known for a long time that the ability to make cross-modal associations is the foundation of language. . . . because of this we can assign names to objects. . . . Cross-modal associations are a normal part of our thinking, although they occur at an unconscious level. In synesthetes . . . it is as if these associations poke through to awareness. . . . *I believe that synesthesia is actually a normal brain function in every one of us, but that its workings reach conscious awareness in only a handful.* . . . synesthesia is localized to the limbic system of the left hemisphere. . . . Synesthesia is a conscious peek at a neural process that happens all the time in everyone. What converges in the limbic system, especially the hippocampus, is the highly processed information from sensory receptors about the world, a *multisensory evaluation of it.* I call synesthetes *cognitive fossils* because they are fortunate to retain some awareness, however slight, of something that is so fundamental to what it means not only to be human, but mammalian! . . . The limbic system gives salience to events. . . . It is also the place where value, purpose, and desire are evaluated. . . .[Synesthesia] is closer to our biological roots than ordinary experience is.[43]

Synesthetes provide actual evidence of a perceptual power that appears to have been general at an earlier stage in brain evolution, a stage at which we may be able to posit the origin of language and recognize it as a natural product of a perceptual mechanism that confers value on sense impressions precisely because of its multisensory character. This modern scientific evidence gives strong support to the ancient intuition that the information conveyed through sight and sound is interconvertible because both forms of information are signals sent by the same source, signals whose passage through different media causes them to be received differently by the senses of sight and hearing designed to pick up such informational transformations.

But if we have developed these dual modes of receiving perceptual information, it must be because there is a complementarity between the messages they are fitted to receive that is necessary for complete comprehension. In the case of a visual object, there is a difference between the conscious awareness we have of its visible form and the subconscious awareness that is here being posited that we have of its vibrational character; and it would seem that it is from the former that we understand the quantitative aspect of a substance and from the latter its qualitative aspect, the former appearing in the form of image and the latter of sound waves that, though normally unheard by the sensual ear, are yet or have been sufficiently apprehended to be capable of vocal imitation. It understands "first names" as having a natural, rather than arbitrary, relationship to the objects so denominated based upon the approximations of their syllabic sounds to those of the energy frequencies emitted by these objects.

But Plato goes beyond this probable association of the sound of the "true natural name of each thing" with its energy frequency, for a linguistic imitation must "imitate the essence by syllables and letters." There must be, on the linguistic end, that same joining of sound and form as is true of the substantial object of such a name. As an object transmits its essence through the dual media of light and sound, so the name through which that object finds "expression" must, for Plato, be able to reproduce both of these aspects through its own appropriate forms and sounds. And the basis on which the form of a letter came to be associated with a particular sound was probably that convertibility of sound into form that is part of the ancient knowledge of sacred science and has been demonstrated more recently in both the study of dream imagery by Freud and the "cymatics" of Hans Jenny. The work of Hans Jenny in the study of wave forms he has called cymatics is particularly important in this regard. For when Jenny subjected certain substances, such as sand, to specific sound frequencies, they assumed special geometric forms that could only be called forth by those frequencies,[44] thus proving the convertibility of sound and form that was the central insight of ancient sacred science.

At the source of language are "roots," having at once a sound, a particular association of letters, and a seminal meaning. Owen Barfield, though he does not consider the relationship of letters to syllables with respect to these roots, does provide an illuminating discussion of the origin of language that is pertinent here:

> We have seen that, in the older doctrine of invented and applied "roots of speech," as pointing to the origin of language, and in the more recent one of "metaphor" as the principal instrument for the growth of meaning, we are saddled with two notions, which are both of them inconsistent with the testimony of language itself. . . . "metaphor" is a misleading concept to apply to any but the later and more sophisticated stages of language. For all the evidence points rather to that sort of "polarization" of an ancient unity into an outer and an inner meaning. . . . it points to the source of language in original participation—and, in doing so, indicates the direction in

which we must look for a true understanding of those mysterious
"roots.". . . Roots are the echo of nature herself sounding in man.
Or rather, they are the echo of what once sounded and fashioned in
both of them at the same time. . . . The Hebrew language . . . is at
the same time, according to some opinions, that one among the
ancient languages in which the roots preserve most clearly (though
still dimly enough) the old unity of sound and meaning. . . . suffice
it to say that the Semitic languages seem to point us back to the old
unity of man and nature, through the shapes of their sounds. We
feel those shapes not only as sounds, but also, in a manner, as *gestures* of the speech-organs.[46]

For Barfield, linguistic roots could only have originated in a state of "original
participation." It is such a state of man in nature that can also be correlated with the myth of a still innocent Adam, that creature capable of
dominating the animal nature through his unique ability to give to each
its true name. For this Adam of Genesis as for the "legislators" of Plato,
the lost power to be a true "maker of names" is thought by Barfield to
reside in an original ability to "hear" the language of nature. As most
beautifully expressed by him: "Roots are the echo of nature herself sounding in man." And Barfield acknowledges that, according to some, it is in
the Hebrew roots that the "old unity of sound and meaning" is most clearly
preserved. But though he also makes a perceptive association between the
sounds of speech and the shape taken by the speech-organs to produce
those sounds, one that will be demonstrated in chapter 5 and that reflects
the same association between the length of a musical string and the tone
it produces made by Pythagoras, it is to the form of the letters that sound
is most closely associated both in Platonic and Hebraic thought. And
what is most distinctive about the Semitic roots is that they are triliteral.

We come here to the most mysterious aspect of the roots, their meaningful association of a sound with exactly three letter-numbers. What are
we to make of these shapes and numbers correlative to the sound that is
here being considered an "echo" of the vibrational definition of an object? Can they be regarded as in some way constituting the measurements
of that object, and, if so, are these the measurements of its three-dimensional localization in space, of the three characteristics of its wave pattern—frequency, amplitude, and phase—or of some form of mediation
between the two? There is no way in which we can any longer decode the
numerical meaning of a linguistic root, the code by which phenomena
become translated into such numbers and the numbers into their charac-

teristic letter shapes. But that there was some original suitability between the sound, shapes, and numbers of the triliteral roots that reflected these same three aspects inherent in the substance being named is the conclusion that seems to follow from all the evidence and analysis recently given in support of the truth of sacred science, that sound, form, and number arise together as separable aspects of the unique signature of any thing and that it is through number that its image can be translated into sound, or vice versa. It is the demonstrable nature of these associations and conversions that can be offered, finally, in support of the ancient Hebraic understanding of the "word," *davar*, as signifying not just a name but its inextricable union with the essence of that which it signifies.

Whether we speak of mythical "legislators," Edenic Adam, or of the now lost condition of "original participation" in which such linguistic creators could divine the nature of first names, those who have affirmed the truth of natural language have understood something of the sacred science whose self-evidence to such originators of language, as of geometry, can alone explain these first achievements of human culture. Edmund Husserl, in his analysis of the origin and subsequent progress of geometry, has shown that "what had given and had to give meaning to all propositions and theories" was "a meaning arising from the primal sources which can be made self-evident again and again."[47] Husserl understands that the tradition inherited by Euclid could never have originated without some primal unity between geometric object and self-evident meaning, that "geometrical idealities arose together with the first 'axiomatic' propositions."[48]

That such understanding is revealed both in Genesis and Platonic philosophy, and continues to inform the traditions of thought deriving from them, has been amply shown, and it underlies the simple assertions of the justice of such Adamic linguistic legislation: "and whatsoever Adam called every living creature, that was the name thereof" (Gen. 2:19). Such assertions imply, then, both a knowledge that all things, and these were all ultimately recognized to be informed with vital energy, have the natural name of this energy pattern and that there were once men who, because they were still totally involved in larger natural and tribal wholes and thus had not yet developed an individualized consciousness, could apprehend that vibrational pattern in its intimate association of sound with numerical periodicity, relate that "heard" information with the form apprehended by the sight, and reproduce the exact nature of this information in a linguistic sign. The knowledge of names and forms would thus seem to have arisen together, each explaining the other with the original self-evidence in which all the later developments of language and geometry are rooted and whose union alone still makes both of these branches of thought fully comprehensible.

If, then, it is sound that contains or imitates the vibratory aspect of the imaged object, that aspect also containing its meaning, it follows that it is the sounded approximation to the unheard auditory vibration that enables the mind to form the concept of the thing producing this vibration. Its spatial image is thus capable of "phonic translation," in Benveniste's words, because both are transcriptions of sense data originating from the same source; and it would also seem that this data can be translated from the language of the eye into that of the ear, as well as the reverse, through the numerical understanding of the heart. Thus it may be said that all forms emit a vibratory signal that is meaningful to the sense of inner hearing and that can be translated into the right words. Conversely, all such words can be translated by the inner sight into symbolic images and narratives of such images. Both form and the sound inherent within it as also sound and the form it can produce are necessary, then, for the production of polysemous meaning: form gives the quantitative measure of an object and sound its qualitative nature, form its outer and sound its inner meaning and value. But this unity of forms with names, from which both geometry and language would seem to have originated and together, and for the reason that form is everywhere in nature co-present with meaningful sound signals, has become obscured in both the Hellenically transmitted study of geometry and the Hebraically transmitted study of linguistic texts.

It was earlier argued that such a symbolic interpretation of geometric forms and laws as would seem to have been taught by Pythagoras, and that continued to inform the Western esoteric tradition deriving from such Greek roots, was also practiced in a distinctively Hebraic form in the long tradition of the Kabbalah, but that apart from these hidden traditions, the study of geometry was completely divorced from all such metaphysical associations. And though the *Sefer Yetzirah* and the *Zohar* show a knowledge and appreciation of general geometric concepts, the later Kabbalah seems not to have retained much general geometric knowledge in its exclusive focus on the geometry of the Tree of Life Diagram.

What it has retained of the ancient sacred science and continues to practice to this day is the study of the equation of letters and numbers known as Gematria. In the words of one of its foremost contemporary practitioners, Carlo Suares: "Instead of consisting of letters having no significance of their own . . . the language of the Qabala fully expresses itself in the whole Autiot [letters], for the Autiot are projections of the vital movement that is both within and without Man."[49] And by the "whole Autiot," Suares means the letters in terms of their numerical "equations."[50] In the next chapter, however, my own extended study of such Gematria relationships will reveal a profound level of association between the letter-numbers and a numerical aspect of geometry, thus returning this surviving kabbalistic practice to what may well be something like its original form as a sacred science incorporating the relationship of the alphabet to both geometry and elementary arithmetic. The more usual form of Gematria is, nonetheless, consistent with the Hebraic emphasis on "hearing" that inner aspect of reality whose structure or "vital movement" is revealed in numerical frequencies. Though I will attempt in this work both to reconstruct the historical evidence for a continuing geometric tradition within the Kabbalah and to engage once more in its serious practice, the greater emphasis more recently paid to the nongeometric study of Gematria and the obscurity into which the geometric tradition has fallen is another reflection of the limited understanding of the Hebraic emphasis of hearing over sight when that emphasis is regarded without the corrective of the inner esoteric teachings.

For the prohibition of graven images and the commandment to "hear" were themselves intended to correct the imbalance that had befallen ordinary human perception after its exile from the Garden of "original participation." In that Garden, man's visual perceptions had been naturally attended by the heartfelt inner hearing that gave him true insight into the nature of all things. In that state of meaningful vision, he could hear each thing speaking its name. But with the growth of individual consciousness, man suffered a loss of sensitivity to this vibratory speech. His perceptual field, which before had hummed a message of interconnected energies, now fell silent, and he recognized himself to be as disconnected as the objects of his sight. So the Prophet came to tell him to stop idolizing only that which he can see and to open his heart to the deeper message attending the state of higher attunement, the message of the all-embracing divine unity.

In associating hearing with unity, the Sh'ma shows recognition of the principal characteristic of sound and all the energetic wave patterns to which it is related and for which it can stand as representative, that such waves are unlimited in extension and mutually interpenetrating, that at the vibratory level all things are infinite and one. This is, indeed, a profound revelation and the most urgent teaching of the Hebrew religion, for it is only by such a redevelopment of vibratory sensitivity that man can redeem the value of his individuality from the meaninglessness to which it now lies forfeit. But this message must not be thought to deny the equal validity of the evidence of sight. If hearing can reveal the underlying unity of all things, sight too has a message, of the unique and irreducible individuality of each part of that larger whole. And as the evidence of sight needs to be attended by the knowledge communicated through such simultaneous hearing, that there is such a whole in which all individuals partake, so that of hearing must admit the truth of its polar opposite, of the meaningful persistence of the particular and limited within the limitless universal. Were this not so, were hearing all that was required for the discernment of the one truth that is both ultimate and here, we would be endowed only with some form of ultrasonic radar and would never have developed eyes. But that eyes have had demonstrable survival value for those species that have developed them is sufficient evidence that they are somehow isomorphic to the reality they are designed to apprehend. If we are equipped with both eyes and ears with which to gain the most significant of sense data, it must be because the reality whose nature determined their structural sensitivity to light and sound patterns is sending dual signals both of which it is necessary that we receive. This is not to say that without one of these senses we would lose all knowledge of the central connection of parts to a whole, for both sight and hearing equally inform us of this connection. Sight informs us that all manifest objects are multifaceted while hearing informs us that each tone is composed of a series of harmonic partials, the overtones. But there is still this all important difference, that the number of faces of a polyhedron will always be finite while the number of a tone's harmonics are potentially infinite. Sight informs us of the limited, then, and hearing of the unlimited.

With this understanding, we can now return to the starting point of this inquiry into sacred science, the science of Pythagoras, better able to appreciate the culminating wisdom with which the earliest of Pythagorean writers, Philolaus, begins his text:

> The world's nature is a harmonious compound of Limited and Unlimited elements; similar is the totality of the world in itself, and of all it contains. . . . All things . . . contain Number. . . . Number instills a certain proportion, and thereby establishes among all things harmonic relations. . . . The composite of these two things, the divine eternally in motion, and of generation ever changing is the World. That is why one is right in saying that the world is the eternal energy of God.[51]

The essential Pythagorean insight is that the cosmos and all entities within it combine three elements, the Limited, the Unlimited, and the Number that can harmonize this opposition, such a composition establishing the divine character of the cosmic order.

The central gnosis of sacred science, then, which is also the most important message transmitted by the dual senses of sight and hearing, is that we, like all things, like the cosmos itself, are at one and the same time, now and forever, both limited and unlimited, like the hexagram having one point on earth and the other in heaven. To regain the capacity to perceive this double truth is to live in the new heaven and new earth of Messianic redemption, not that lost Paradise of undifferentiated wholeness, but the still more blessed state of wholeness recovered without loss of individuality and with that spiritual mastery whose perfection as the divine son is both the subject and goal of the treasured teachings of the Kabbalah. For the ancient truths of sacred science serve precisely to demonstrate the mystery fulfilled by this son, that space and time are interchangeable modes through which the heart can realize its nature as the creative mediator between the power and beauty inherent both in limitation and the limitless.

PART 2

The Kabbalistic Sacred Science of Language

The Tetragrammaton and Hebraic Sacred Science

The Tetragrammaton and the Covenant of Number

MEDIATION AND THE NAME

The previous chapter presented a new thesis concerning the focus and significance of that precise body of ancient knowledge that can be called sacred science. The main focus of such science was shown to be the demonstrable laws of geometry, sound, and number, the first revealing the property of finite localization, the second of infinite extension, and the third of mediation; and its significance was shown to lie in the relationship of these three aspects of ancient concern, that the cosmos and everything within it involves such a balancing of the finite with the infinite as witnesses to its sacred character. It also was shown that from at least the time of the *Sefer Yetzirah* what distinguishes the kabbalistic branch of sacred science from that of the Pythagorean school is its subsuming of the three categories of shape, sound, and number under a more inclusive science of language. The study of the occult correspondences of language has left few signs of the intellectual rigor that must once have informed such effort. Unlike the laws relating musical sound to string length and number that were demonstrated by the Pythagoreans, those relating linguistic sound to form and number can be made demonstrable only by their systematic occurrences. They are, indeed, occult, but they can be caught in the net of circumstance to reveal a level of cosmic functioning beyond our powers of comprehension. It is such a net that the present discussion will throw over the occult correspondences of language, revealing a web of hidden associations so pervasive and precise as to mystify the ordinary intelligence and fulfill the goal of all spiritual practice, the opening of the spirit to a higher dimension of explanation and meaningfulness.

The following analysis is a natural outgrowth of the preceding study of sacred science insofar as it continues its study of the kabbalistic approach to language and relates it precisely to the discoveries of ancient mathematics and astronomy that informed it. The *Sefer Yetzirah* concepts of the Teli, Galgal, and Lev were there shown to relate to the great circles of the sun and moon and to the process of cosmic mediation, but they will here also be related to a Pythagorean concept of mediation, specifically that involving the geometric mean in the geometric doubling proportion, to reveal a new understanding of the Sinai Covenant, one in which the secret doctrine of the son is related to that level of cultural evolution first manifesting the ability to count. The Hebraic tradition will thus be shown to be rooted in a very early stage of human evolution but one in which the essential gnosis of sacred science appears to have already been grasped.

This analysis will also use the special kabbalistic technique of Gematria, an exegetical technique based on the fact that the Hebrew letters also signify numbers. In this system, the first nine letters signify the first nine units, the next nine letters the tens, and the last four letters plus five final forms of previous letters the hundreds, with big Aleph representing one thousand. The technique of Gematria derives from the circumstance that the letters signifying numbers also comprise words, and words sharing the same Gematria number can be interpreted as having special affinities that can be applied to textual exegesis. The present use of this technique will show a new concern with the Gematria number of the word for son, Ben, and for that most important of divine names, YHVH, the Tetragrammaton. But this is not the ordinary technique of Gematria, illustrated with an original example in chapter 1, which involves the association of words carrying the same numerical value of their letters. Rather, this section will expose baffling correspondences of mathematically significant numbers, of numbers in a set multiplication pattern, with the words formed by their letter-numbers, and with astronomical geometry. The chapter as a whole should contribute to a new understanding of the Tetragrammaton, of the secret doctrine of the son, and of language in general, an understanding that can only illuminate the greater mystery of linguistic appropriateness. The importance of the present chapter is that it provides evidence of the validity of Hebraic sacred science, particularly in its linguistic aspect. For it is one thing to show the numerical relationship of string length to harmonic tone, as did Pythagoras, and quite another to show an equally necessary relationship between the sound, form, and number of letters, as asserted in the *Sefer Yetzirah*. Since language does not appear to be subject to the same determinism as has been established for musical harmonics, to prove a real correlation between the processes of at least the Hebrew language and elementary arithmetic must lead to a reexamination of the received assumptions about language and a heightened awareness that there are more things in heaven and earth than are dreamt of in the philosophy of many a Horatio. It is precisely such a hidden web of associations between words, numbers, and forms that this section will demonstrate and, by so doing, validate the inexplicable fact of that conjunction of language and geometry that is not only at the heart of Kabbalistic geometry but of all perception. As the first two sections will be concerned in part with the numerical correspondences of the Tetragrammaton, so will the third and fourth sections throw an equally remarkable light on its sound correspondences, revealing persuasive associations of persons divine and grammatical as well as a new approach to the pronunciation of this most holy Name. But we will allow the later sections to introduce themselves and proceed with this first exploration of the covenant of number.

Pythagoras held that the ultimate reality is number, and it is also through number that what may well be the ultimate gnosis or Da'at of the Hebraic esoteric tradition is uniquely conveyed, a conveyance that incorporates the main features of the ancient sacred science previously traced and that requires a similar knowledge of these features for its perception. In the following discussion, we shall see how all of the preceding material on sacred science is epitomized in a single geometric progression of numbers that can be said to hold the secret key to a deeper understanding of the national mythos of Exodus and of its larger cosmological implications.

It is through associating the Pythagorean emphasis on mathematical mediation with the kabbalistic emphasis on astronomical mediation that we can begin to appreciate the high knowledge contained in a particular geometric progression of three numbers each of which has special esoteric implications within the particular symbolism of the Hebraic tradition. This is the geometric proportion 13:26::26:52. What is immediately most suggestive about this geometric proportion is its mediating term, for

26 is the Gematria of the Tetragrammaton (Yod = 10, Hey = 5, Vav = 6, and Hey = 5). Thus the first implication of this proportion is that the divine power conveyed through this Name can be said to function in a manner somehow analogous to that of the geometric mean, analogy, we remember, being characteristic of the geometric proportion. Kepler said that "God forever geometrizes," and His method of geometrizing would here seem to be that of divine mediation,[1] in particular between whatever it is that the numbers 13 and 52 may be said to represent.

These numbers develop a special set of connotations in the context of the *Sefer Yetzirah*, with its emphasis on the triple factors of the Teli, Galgal, and Lev, those points of space-time where the great circles of the sun and the moon unite with the cosmic heart to mediate the process of spiritual transcendence in a manner consistent with the essence of the worldwide mythology of prehistoric man.[2] Seen in this context, it becomes possible to associate the number 13 with the moon and the number 52 with the sun when the revolutions of these heavenly bodies are seen in conjunction with one another. But these associations, while obvious as soon as noted, are not as simple as might at first appear. Rather, they each convey a whole nexus of cultural-cosmological associations.

The number 13 can be associated with the moon because it is possible to divide the solar year into exactly thirteen months of 28 days each plus an additional day. These 28 days can be understood to represent an approximation of the arithmetical mean between the sidereal lunar cycle of $27^{1}/_{3}$ days and the synodical lunar cycle of $29^{1}/_{2}$ days, the former based upon the interval of the moon's conjunction with a fixed star and the latter upon its conjunction with what, from earth's perspective, appears to be that of the also moving sun. The approximately 28 days of this mean between the two alternate methods of computing the observable revolutions of the moon has another association, however, which may be even more significant in positing any prehistorical use of a thirteen-month yearly calendar, and that is its appearance in the regular menstrual cycle of women. Those anthropologists and mythologists who have followed the lead of Sir James Frazer in positing an earlier, fertility-dominated matriarchal culture preceding the current form of patriarchal society have also suggested its use of such a thirteen-month lunar calendar to stress the identification of the moon with the feminine. Thus the association of the moon with the number 13 also carries with it the derivative associations of the fertility religion of the Great Mother, a religion of resurrection reflected not only in the rebirth of the year in the spring but also of the monthly rebirth of the moon after its three hidden days. Such a rebirth is celebrated in the festival of the New Moon whose observance has been perpetuated in the Hebraic festival of Rosh Chodesh. And in the traditional Hebraic association of 13 with the attributes of divine mercy, can we not also see some recognition of the maternal character of mercy, of mercy as an expression of the feminine aspect of the divine?

Turning now to the number 52, this would appear to be associated with the sun insofar as the solar year can be divided into exactly fifty-two weeks plus the same additional day. Before considering the nature of the week, we should consider the meaning of this number in kabbalistic terms. For the Gematria equivalent of this number is the word *ben* (Bet = 2; Nun = 50), meaning son. We have seen that the first term of this geometric proportion can be taken to symbolize a maternal source and the last term the final product of the son. But the numerical progression with which we began would also seem to suggest some paternal mediation in the derivation of the son from the mother. For if the paternal principle can be associated with the sun and the solar calendar and the maternal principle with the moon and lunar calendar, the final implication of this paternal mediation between mother and son is to permit that independence of the son from the mother signified by the patriarchal transition to the solar calendar. Given these associations, the homonymic identification of "son" and "sun" in English seems no accident but to carry fundamental esoteric meaning. To say that man is a "son of the sun," is to recognize the importance of transcendental mediation in the whole progress of man, from his very inception to his spiritual enlightenment.

Considering the number 26 as the geometric mean between 13 and 52, we should note the further kabbalistic association of the Tetragrammaton, the Gematria equivalent of 26, in terms of the Tree of Life Diagram. Most significant is the assignment of this divine name to the Sefirah Tiferet, the Sefirah also associated with the cosmic heart of Adam Kadmon. Thus the mediating function ascribed to the heart in the *Sefer Yetzirah* is at one with the function of the Gematria number of the Tetragrammaton in the geometric progression from 13 to 52.

Another numerical way of considering the final term of the son is in terms of the equation 13 x 4 = 52. For the Tetragrammaton is not only to be associated with the number 26 but, as indicated by its Greek name, also with the number of its letters, four. Now the generation of a child is also metaphorically related to the arithmetic process of multiplication, and so the symbolic implication of the equation 13 x 4 = 52 would seem to be that the son is a product of the act of multiplication of the heavenly father with the earth mother.

If the number 26 is considered as the central number from which this geometric progression originated, then the whole meaning of the progression becomes one of divine mediation. This can be supported by the mythological research of Giorgio de Santillana and Hertha von Dechend in *Hamlet's Mill*, the major thesis of which is that the essential worldwide myth of earliest man involves the 26,000-year cycle of the precession of the equinoxes: "The time which this prolonged axis needs to circumscribe the elliptical North Pole is roughly 26,000 years."[3] The number 26 appears at a still larger degree of temporal magnification in relation to the recent theory of a "death star," fittingly called Nemesis, proposed by Richard A. Muller with Marc Davis and Piet Hut, whose 26 million year orbit could produce a rain of comets as it thus periodically approached the solar system, which could then account for the mass extinctions of species that the paleontologists J. John Sepkoski and David M. Raup have discovered from the fossil records to occur every 26 million years.[4] The association of the Gematria number of the Tetragrammaton with these vast cycles of cosmic time—26,000 and 26,000,000 years—further reveals the profound appropriateness of this divine name and its number, both to each other and to the precise structure of the cosmos, as well as of the mysterious source of this human knowledge of hidden things.

But there is another way in which this progression can be understood to have originated that can give it a different mythological dimension and explanation. We have thus far seen significant Gematria verbal associations for the numbers 26 and 52 that suggest that, in its imputed original formulation, the first of these three proportional numbers would also have an appropriate Gematria equivalent. For the sake of completeness, we shall accept this premise and follow its suggestive thread where it may lead. If, then, the number 13 is related to its letter equivalents, these would be Gimel (=3) plus Yod (=10). Now these two letters do, in fact, form the Hebrew word meaning "valley," a meaning whose association with the concept of container or vessel and thus with the feminine is borne out by one meaning of the root *well* of the English *valley*: "*wolw-a* in Latin *vulva*, *volva*, covering, womb."[5] Where the letters Gimel-Yod form the Hebrew word *guy* meaning "valley" or "wadi," river basin, the reverse form of Yod-Gimel plus Ayin forms the word *yagaiah* meaning "labor" or "pain." The suggestion is that in its forward form the letters Gimel-Yod can refer to the earth with the female connotation of the womb in its phase of receptivity to the flow of seminal fluid, while in its backward form of Yod-Gimel (the final Ayin in such roots often being dropped) it can refer to the labor pains attendant on the reverse process of childbirth. A similar case of meaningful reverse Gematria is featured in the *Sefer Yetzirah*, 2:4:

> Twenty-Two letters are the foundation: He set them in a wheel, like a kind of wall, with two hundred and thirty-one gates. And the wheel rotates forward and backward. And the sign of the thing is:
> —there is no goodness above pleasure ('NG) and
> —there is no evil below pain (NG').[6]

Dropping the Ayins and focusing on the letter combinations of Nun-Gimel and Gimel-Nun, David R. Blumenthal has solved the puzzle of the "wheel" formation of the 231 gates with computer-generated graphic illustrations of the letters.[7] And as, by this, the *Sefer Yetzirah* is shown to posit cosmic significance to the forward and reverse combinations of letters with their appropriate meanings, so we may see in the same union of opposite processes conveyed through the letters Gimel-Yod and Yod-Gimel' a cycle of fertility linked to the fundamental processes of cosmic creation.

We have seen that the basic Gematria of the number 13, Gimel-Yod, was related through its surviving meaning of "valley" both to a geological feature of the earth and, in virtue of the containment nature of this geological feature, to feminine fertility. This meaning would also seem to be related to a tradition going as far back as Megalithic culture. It has become recognized that some Megalithic mounds, the earliest surviving human constructions, were oriented to receive a beam of sunlight on astronomically significant days, most importantly the winter solstice. Martin Brennan has shown this to be the case with the New Grange mound in Ireland.[8] But what I believe has not been as recognized is the sexual character and function of such a mound, that it represents a vaginal structuring of the earth to facilitate the reception by its feminine divinity of the penetrating light beam from the masculine divinity of the sun. As study of the mystery religions has shown, the purpose of such a *mysterium coniunctionis* was not only the resurrection of the land in the spring but the spiritual rebirth of the initiates who participated in the ritual celebrations of the solstices, and would thereby become reborn as sons of the divinity residing in the earth and sun.

But there is an even more startling cognate to the underlying Hebraic concept of a "Mother Earth" deriving from the Gematria Gimel-Yod of the number 13. This is the Greek mythical figure of Gaia, the earth goddess, a name that seems closely related to the Hebrew Gimel-Yod and may be said to share its Gematria number of 13. Gaia is spelled Gamma-Alpha-Iota-Alpha, that is, Gamma-Iota if we follow the Hebraic practice of eliminating the vowels and regard Iota as a consonant representing the sound Y. That this latter should be permissible is supported by the following etymological information provided in a dictionary listing for Iota: "Greek *iota*, of Semitic origin, akin to Hebrew *yodh*, Yod."[9] Equally pertinent is the fact that although Iota is the ninth letter of the Greek alphabet, the Gematria equivalent given for it in classical Greek lexicons is ten, the same number as Yod, Gamma being the third letter of the Greek alphabet as Gimel is of the Hebrew alphabet. Since Greek Gematria was primarily an early Christian practice, its Hebraic origin seems clear, as is also attested to by the difficulty of assigning the twenty-seven numbers with Hebrew letter-form equivalents to the twenty-four letters of the Greek alphabet, a difficulty that has led to the Greek elimination of the numbers 6, 90, and 900. The foregoing suggests that the Greek goddess Gaia may have derived her name and character from the Hebrew letter-number combination of Gimel-Yod, letters signifying the number 13 associated with feminine fertility through the 13 female menstrual cycles of the solar year. Though these female cycles were previously related to the lunar months, once we move from the abstract number 13 to its Gematria verbal equivalent of the root Gimel-Yod, we encounter the still closer association of female fertility with the planet Earth. But if Gaia can be associated with the Hebrew letters Gimel-Yod, then it may be that the Greek myth of Gaia either preserves a Semitic understanding of the root Gimel-Yod, which explains why it should have the feminine-earth connotation of "valley," or that the Greek letters Gamma-Iota were understood to carry the similar numerical correspondence of 13 associated with the feminine cycle.

In the myth of Gaia, this personification of the earth is the daughter of Chaos and both mother and wife to Uranus, god of the sky, by whom she bears many children, including the Titans and the Furies. The earth as the product of a primeval chaos appears similarly in the creation myth of Genesis; and in the further creation of Adam we may see other features analogous to the Greek myth. For in the Garden story, Adam is shown to be a product of the union of elements from the earth and the air or sky, clay animated by the breath of life. It is interesting that the biblical view that life originated in earthly clay has found scientific support, clay being shown to have the needed ability to trap and intensify energy precisely because it routinely makes mistakes in its crystallization process,[10] the development of life, especially as detailed in the Genesis Garden story, being significantly associated with the capacity for making errors. It is, then, precisely the flaws in this template that permit the previously undifferentiated spirit to form those individual personalities whose preservation, purified of their impurities, is the goal of the cosmic process and the task set for these children of earth and sky, who unite and can bring to their intended perfection the best potentialities of both matter and spirit. Interpreted in this fashion, the Genesis and Gaia myths can provide a new way of understanding the progression 13:26::26:52.

As the firstborn of Chaos, it is from Gaia (Gimel-Yod [Gamma-Iota] = 13) that the chain of creation takes its point of numerically specifiable origin. As the earth, *ge*, is identified with Gaia, so it is appropriate that the numerical progression originating with her numerical equivalent of 13 should be in the form of a geometric proportion, geometry being the study of the earth and a term derived from this Greek word for earth. If, then, the original divine force of creation is to be associated with the earth goddess Gaia, it would begin with her Gematria number 13 and progress through the geometric proportion that defines the logic of terrestrial spatial order. The next number, 26, would then represent as her mate her own offspring, the transcendental sky god Uranus, and the final number of 52 would, as in the Hebrew version (52= Ben or son), represent their child (children). But if Gaia can be accepted as the Greek version of an analogous Hebraic concept of an Earth Mother conveyed through the letters Gimel-Yod, then we are faced with a meaningful progression of Hebraic letter-numbers that is wholly Hebraic in its source: Gimel-Yod (13) is to Yod-Hey-Vuv-Hey (26) as Yod-Hey-Vuv-Hey (26) is to Bet-Nun (52). In this progression not only are all of the numbers arithmetically proper, but all of their Gematria verbal equivalents are both meaningful and appropriate. Gimel-Yod in its meaning of valley, an earth receptacle feminine in nature, represents the earth as contributing parent to the composition of man; the Tetragrammaton is the transcendent divine source that fertilizes the earth as mother with the living soul of man; and Ben is the son of this union of heaven and earth.

If we can accept some historical awareness of the meaningfulness of this numerical progression, the only question would be whether it is 13 or 26 that should be regarded as the originating source of this letter-number progression. Though we have seen vast periods of time associated with the number 26, there is an even greater cosmic number that can now be associated with the number 13. For the latest news from the big bang is that "The universe bursts into existence an estimated 13 billion years ago."[11] Thus we can understand this progression as starting with 13 billion years, the number marking the beginning of the universe, a number that has a feminine connotation and so can be associated with a divine feminine creator or her immanence in the creation. It would then proceed to the progressively smaller periods of 26 million and 26 thousand years associated with the heavenly bodies of a comet and the sun, which can be associated with the divine masculine transcendence, and finally to the mere 52 weeks of the solar year, which we will soon see to define the final product of cosmic evolution, the astronomical counter of this heavenly rotation, the son.

If the matriarchal interpretation of this progression is accepted as original, then the fact that the Hebraic esoteric tradition has retained the clear Gematria associations for the father and son number-words while having lost both the association of the number 13 with the letters Gimel-Yod and of the word they signify with the concept of the earth as mother would seem to imply a patriarchal adoption of the matriarchal myth accompanied by an almost complete erasure of its feminine elements.[12] In the following section, we shall see just such a patriarchal transfer of lunar-feminine elements to the purposes of the solar calendar and consciousness. And the omission of the feminine component is even more marked in the Christian version of this "trinity."

But as there are also cogent reasons for considering the Tetragrammaton number of 26 as the originating number for this geometric proportion, a final argument can be made for the inclusion of both number-concepts in a mathematical-linguistic code. This code can be understood to define the cosmic process as originating with both feminine and masculine elements in a preset ratio and that these then expand to a three-term proportion in whose progression the purpose of cosmic emanation is encoded. The message thus encoded would seem to be that there must be progression from the natural to the supernatural if man is to become, in the words of the *Shi'ur Komah*, a "son of the world to come."[13]

Before proceeding further with this analysis, we should finally consider the peculiar nature of the Gematria equation of the number 52 with the word *ben*. As a later section will show, a traditional part of kabbalistic mysticism involves the four expansions of the Tetragrammaton, that is, the four ways the Tetragrammaton letters can be spelled. Names have been given to these expansions composed of the letters which together add up to the Gematria sums of each of these expansions, these being: Ab (72: Ayin = 70 and Bet = 2); Sag (63: Samach = 60 and Gimel = 3); Mah (45: Mem = 40 and Hey = 5); and Ben (52: Bet = 2 and Nun = 50). As can be seen, *ben* is the only one in which the unit letter-number comes before that for the tens. Since coining the term *neb* would have been more consistent with the terms applied to the upper three Tetragrammaton expansions, the inconsistent choice of the word *ben* for this particular numerical expansion indicates that its meaning as son must have determined its choice. But there is a further problem with applying this meaningful letter combination to the number 52, since the actual word *ben* would require a final Nun whose Gematria number is not 50, as with medial Nun, but 700. Again it is clear that the tradition means to insist upon the equation between the number 52 and the word meaning son despite all the problems of inconsistency introduced with this equation. The best explanation that offers itself for this circumstance is that this equation predated both the practice of Tetragrammaton expansions and also the distinction between medial and final letters, counting not going beyond the number 400 for the last letter Tav. This is not only the most persuasive explanation but it also provides supporting evidence for the existence of this particular progression of numbers, whether implicitly or explicitly, at the inception of that consciousness that may be defined as uniquely Hebraic, a progression that holds a key both to its understanding of the genesis and purpose of human existence and of the particular form of its sacred science, most notably the practice of Gematria.

The chain of evidence that led to the discovery of this progression began with contemplation of what seems to be the most hidden truth of the *Sefer Yetzirah*, the significance of the Teli in its association with the Galgal and the Lev; for what it does is to fix the space-time orbits of the celestial bodies (the Galgal) at precisely those lunar nodes (the Teli) at which the mediating function of the cosmic heart (the Lev) is thought to be present. Contained in this concept, then, is that interrelation of what, from the earth's perspective, appear to be the cycles of the moon and the sun with the mediating power between them; and this could have led to the awareness that the lunar and solar cycles can be associated with numbers that bear a unique mathematical relationship to the Gematria number of the most sacred Hebrew divine name, the Tetragrammaton, that the numbers 13 and 52, which are the half and double of the Tetragrammaton number of 26, can be related to the divisions of the solar year, the former into the lunar months and the latter into the weeks whose derivation we shall shortly be considering but that can finally be considered a product of solar-oriented counting. This geometric progression, however, not only exhibits a Gematria association for its mediating term; its final term also has a Gematria association with the word for son, an association recognized in the later Kabbalah and one that clearly represents another facet of the secret doctrine of the son. But that the first term should, as suspected, also have a significantly appropriate Gematria equivalent is not only uncanny but seems to provide the final proof of the validity of the whole practice of Gematria.

What it seems to show are two things, that numbers and words do have subtle connections and that these connections become significant when they are mediated by the precise laws of geometric manifestation, as here with the law defining the geometric proportion of numbers. In the proportion 13:26::26:52, geometry is a determining factor in the specific relationship of these three numbers in two respects. As just indicated, it relates them in terms of the doubling proportion whose definition is derived from the geometric process of expanding squares through the diagonal, a process of growth that also informs the multiplication of living cells related to the whole question of the genesis of life with which this particular proportion also seems to be concerned. And the relation of the numbers 13 and 52 to the revolutions of the moon with respect to the sun also defines a key phenomenon of celestial geometry, one of particular importance to all the ordering of human affairs on earth that has its origin in the first high human science of astronomical observation. It is, then, in the geometric aspects of these three Gematria terms of letter-numbers that the deepest cosmological truth is revealed, the hermetic principle also central to the Kabbalah that "as above, so below," that the same geometric laws revealed in the relations of the sun and moon also apply to the germination and progress of life, and thus that the movements of the sun and moon can be read as "signs" (Gen. 1:14) to direct the course of human life to the fullest harvest of its potential.

Whether or not the proportion 13:26::26:52 has ever before been so considered, it serves as proof of the truth of sacred science, particularly of that triple association of number, sound, and form with which the *Sefer Yetzirah* begins and that also informs Pythagorean science. And it makes clear that the Hebraic practice of Gematria is, as its name suggests, rooted in some still more subtle form of geometric mediation. Not only does this proportion seem to embody a uniquely Hebraic form of the universal gnosis but its deepest mystery may well concern the number 7, necessarily associated with the number of weeks in the solar year, 52. The significance of this number is at the heart of the Hebrew revelation and one further related to the belief that man can become the spiritual son of the cosmos and the fulfillment of its purpose. In what follows we shall see more clearly how this dual message is contained in the Gematria culmination of this geometric proportion, Ben = 52, a message uniquely Hebraic both in its method of formulation and in its association with the essential ritual observance of the Sinai Covenant.

COUNTING AND COVENANT

We have seen that the numbers of our key geometric proportion all have astronomical correlatives. Thirteen is one way of defining the relationship of the lunar months to the solar year, a way emphasizing the association between the feminine menstrual and lunar cycles; and 26, multiplied by the number of big Aleph (1,000) is equivalent to the twelve "months" of the sun's Great Year through the precession of the equinoxes. But the astronomical significance of the number 52, Hebraically identified with the concept of the son, depends upon the division of the solar year into periods of exactly seven days, and we are here faced with the important question of the origin of this seven-day week, unknown to the Egyptians who, like the Chinese, used ten-day sublunar periods.

The astronomical bases of all the other temporal periods are immediately clear. The day is marked by what appears to be the daily revolution of the sun around the earth, the month by the sidereal or synodical period of the moon, and the year by the circuit of the sun through the constellations. But where are we to find an astronomical definition of the seven-day week? The answer to this would seem to be in the four, approximately seven-day, phases of the moon. If we are to accept this derivation of the temporal period of the week, then the movement from *noting* the phases of the moon, the period between, say, the half and the full moon, to *counting* the weeks of the solar year should probably be regarded as the single most important event in the evolution of human culture. For it marks the process of intellectual abstraction through which man progressed from his fetal-like immersion in natural process to an independence of consciousness that, while exiling him from the prenatal Garden, also carries the promise of true spiritual rebirth in the divine image.

It is of such spiritual rebirth that the whole of the Mosaic and kabbalistic traditions speak, that rebirth of what is always understood to be the androgynous son. As we have seen, the cosmic child known as Ze'ir Anpin was expressly defined in both the Zoharic *Idra Rabba* and Lurianic *Etz Chayyim* as androgynous, his twice-born character in the latter being quaintly explained in terms of his return to the womb of Imma after the nursing phase to receive the upper three Sefirot that constitute his brains or higher consciousness. And in the initial covenant with the ancestors of the Hebrew people, it is not only Abram but also Sarai whose divine change of name signifies that a covenant with God entails precisely such a rebirth in the spirit. If the divine mother Imma may be associated with the divine immanence, and the divine father Abba with the divine transcendence, then the androgynous son Ze'ir Anpin may be associated with the synthesis of this divine polarity, with a transcendence that retains its roots in the immanent, an abstraction without loss of concreteness, as Tiferet may be understood to balance and perfect the existential union of the force of Chokhmah-Abba with the formative power of Binah-Imma. Let us now see how the Sinai Covenant may be viewed as marking an exodus from man's enslavement to nature and an entrance upon his path to spiritual mastery, a transition from a lunar-fertility orientation to one that is solar-social, the "holy nation" being the agent for the emancipation of human consciousness dependent upon its power of abstraction.

This power of abstraction is everywhere associated with solar intelligence, that identified with the left hemisphere of the brain, and marks its difference from such incorporation into unity as distinguishes the lunar intelligence identified with the right hemisphere. The sign of this power of abstraction, as previously indicated, is the ability first to standardize the period of the lunar phases from approximately to exactly seven days and then to divorce it completely from any astronomical observation so that its measure becomes determinable strictly on the basis of human counting.

It is just this capacity for both spatial and temporal measure that is made the prerequisite and test of Israel's readiness for entrance into a divine covenant, and the training of this capacity is presented in terms of a substance with the significant name of *manna*, pronounced "mahn." The Israelites are individually required to gather exactly one omer of manna for five days, two omers on the sixth day in preparation for the Sabbath, and none on the seventh; in God's words, "the people shall go out and gather a certain rate every day, that I may prove them, whether they will walk in my law, or no" (Exod. 16:4). That the ability to measure substance and time, here made a prerequisite for the observance of a freely made covenant, should be defined in terms of the word *manna* suggests some etymological association with the Sanskrit word *manas*, which has, among others, the meanings of "man" and "measuring," rather than the

Egyptian *ma nu*, meaning "what is it?," as previously thought. For as in the Sanskrit *manas*, the Hebrew *man* or manna relates the higher human nature to the capacity for measuring or counting. Moreover, this capacity is immediately related to the discrimination of the Sabbatical week. The sign of the ability to walk in the divine law is the ability to count weeks, with special observance of "the rest of the holy sabbath" (Exod. 16:23), and it is through counting such weeks, that they may rest on the Sabbaths, that the Israelites progress to their great moment of covenant at Mount Sinai. There, in the covenantal Ten Commandments, they are again instructed in the single and most essential of ritual observances, that of the Sabbath, in the Fourth Commandment. Later, Sabbath observance is explicitly made the sign of the covenant: ". . .my sabbaths ye shall keep: for it is a sign between me and you throughout your generations. . . . Wherefore the children of Israel shall keep the sabbath . . . for a perpetual covenant" (Exod. 31:13, 16).

Also significant in this context is the institution of the festival of Shavuot, rabbinically associated with the giving of the Torah at Mount Sinai, which is to be prepared for by such a counting of weeks, specifically seven, as had been originally practiced by the Israelites of the Exodus as they gathered manna at the prescribed rate while en route to the holy mountain: "Seven weeks shalt thou number unto thee. . . . And thou shalt keep the feast of weeks unto the Lord thy God" (Deut. 16:9, 10). Shavuot, meaning "weeks," and the Sabbath both relate the counting and observance of the seventh day to the covenant that is the first fruits of the redemption of Israel from enslavement in Mitzraim, the term for Egypt that also means "narrow." It marks as well that spiritual enlargement consequent upon the shift from lunar to solar attention, from observation of the crescent moon to the wide yearly circuit of the sun.

This, of course, does not mean that the Temple culture of ancient Egypt construed the natural fertility cycles of its rituals as narrowly as was portrayed in the Hebraic myth of Egypt, which saw it as the locus of an enslavement of spirit as much as of body. Indeed, in its concept of the son Horus, it has associated the same faculty of counting as that required by the Mosaic covenant of the Hebrew people chosen to be heir to the Promised Land, that is, to function in the role of son: "Thus saith the Lord, Israel is my son, even my firstborn" (Exod. 4:22). In his quotations from the Pyramid Texts, R. A. Schwaller de Lubicz, though not himself noting the significance of associating Horus with the activity of counting, has given examples of this association in defining the role of Horus with regard to the mythic and ritual renewal of his dismembered father Osiris:

Osiris is also the annual renewal of all vegetation. . . . At the same time, he is the *ka* of Horus, his son:

Horus has come, he has counted [recognized] thee. . . .
Horus has come, he "counts" [recognizes] his father in thee.

   . . . during the rising of Ra, the celebrant—the king—performs the rite of the daily divine cult. . . to recall the *renewal*, the reconstitution of the dismembered body and its resurrection by day. This can occur only by the grace of the mysterious Eye of Horus which is "counted down" (analyzed by the offerings of oil, incense, water, or food). The sacrifice of this Eye of Horus serves as a daily reminder of rebirth.[14]

Where Osiris is tied to the annual round of fertility, extrapolated to the cycle of human reincarnations, Horus is shown to represent the direct path to spiritual liberation,[15] a path that seems to require and reflect the abstracting power of numerical counting, the recognition by the understanding heart of the numerical relationships underlying and ordering all things. This recognition would seem, finally, to be symbolized by the "Eye of Horus," clearly associated with "the rising of Ra," the sun. For Egypt as for Israel, then, the salvific power of spiritual rebirth became related primarily to the capacity for solar reckoning.

   The evidence for such a Hebrew association has thus far been circumstantial, the relationship of the Gematria number 52 of the Hebrew word for "son" with its apparent solar significance, the fifty-two Sabbaths of the solar year whose observance is the sign of the Sinai Covenant. But there is one late Hebrew source that seems to contain some remnant of a tradition going back to the earliest sources of the culture that the Hebrews shared not only with the Egyptians but with all astronomically informed peoples. This is the Book of Enoch in the Ethiopic version also known a 1 Enoch. As discussed in chapter 2, the Enoch legend underwent a major development in this text whereby this figure first has a revelation of a supernatural "son of man" who sits on the Throne and then, after his own death and transfiguration, finally becomes identified with him. But the point I wish to raise here is the additional association of this complex of the transcending man Enoch and of the concept of the son with the importance of correct solar reckoning. A major portion of the Book of Enoch is devoted to an explanation of the wisdom of the solar calendar by Enoch to his son Methuselah, at the close of which Enoch pronounces a blessing that certainly appears to be related to the final salvation of man:

> I have given wisdom to you and to your children. . . . Blessed are all
> the righteous, blessed are all those who walk in the way of righ-
> teousness, and do not sin like the sinners in the numbering of all
> their days in which the sun journeys in heaven. . . . Because of them
> men go wrong, and they do not reckon them . . . exactly. For they
> belong in the reckoning of the *year*. . . . And in those days, says the
> Lord, they shall call and testify to the sons of the earth about the
> wisdom in them. Show (it) to them, for you (are) their leaders, and
> the rewards (which are to come) over all the earth. For I and my
> son will join ourselves with them for ever in the paths of upright-
> ness during their lives, and you will have peace.[16]

Thus it was to solar rather than lunar reckoning that the concept of
spiritual rebirth was primarily related. Though the Torah does accept the
observance of Rosh Chodesh, the New Moon (Num. 10:10; 28:11), it
nowhere specifically institutes it. Rather, the Mosaic Law establishes the
Sabbaths and seasonal festivals, which are both related to the sun. The
fifty-two Sabbaths of the solar year are observed with no reference to
alignment with the lunar phases but rather to the setting of the sun; and
the festivals are related to the spring planting and fall harvesting seasons
also determined by the position of the sun. But all such solar-determined
observances are distinguished from lunar observances by that same abstraction and alteration of the natural as we have seen to characterize the
seven-day week.

The essence of this alteration can be seen in the very word given to
the sun, *shemesh*, Shin-Mem-Shin. The appropriateness of these mother
letters to the Hebrew method of marking the beginning of the day and
the year suggests that their special significance did not begin with the
Sefer Yetzirah but is as old as the language. For if we accept the *Sefer Yetzirah*
identifications of Shin with fire and Mem with water, then incorporated
in the Hebrew word for sun is a circular pattern going from the light of
fire to the darkness of water and back to the light of fire that not only
reflects the peculiar Hebrew method of beginning the day at sundown
but a suggestion of its significance.

The most natural way of marking the beginning of the day is at
sunbreak and of the year is in the spring. That Nissan, the spring month
in which Passover is celebrated, was originally understood to be the first
month is undeniable from the following: "This month shall be unto you

the beginning of months: it shall be the first month of the year to you" (Exod. 12:2). But in the full development of the festival calendar, the beginning of the year, Rosh Hashanah, is deferred to the fall, the year like the day now understood to begin with the dying of the light and continuing on through its later revival. This is as different from the natural method as it is from that which has somehow become the standard for contemporary practice, the day beginning and ending in the darkness of midnight and the year in the coldness of winter. Rather, the Hebrew method of defining the solar day and year is, like the word *shemesh* for the sun, one that goes from the waning of the light, through a period of darkness, to the revival of light, a mental alteration of the natural sequence suggestive of the intervention of symbolic content, of a resurrection motif.

Now such a motif can also be seen with respect to the celebration of Rosh Chodesh, of the return of the crescent moon after its three hidden nights. But what distinguishes Rosh Chodesh from Rosh Hashanah is precisely the naturalism of the lunar symbolism as opposed to the abstracted and manipulated nature of solar symbolism. As with the week, the transfer of the symbolism of rebirth from the moon to the sun reflects a process of abstraction by which the natural is lifted to the level of the supernatural, the eternal round of natural fertility to the level of conscious spiritual rebirth. In manipulating the order of the day and year so that they may symbolize the dying of the old and the revival of the new washed clean of all its impurities, man demonstrates his own ability to transcend the order of nature through the power of reason.

Moving his allegiance from the light that rules the night to that which rules the day, from his old immersion in natural process to his new capacity to abstract his consciousness from its natural origins without loss of the essence of that experience, he becomes the reborn son of the sun, a "Ben Shemesh" who, like that process symbolized in this word for the sun, has gone through the waters of purification to be reborn in the spirit. A similar sequence can be seen in the Egyptian myth of the passage of Ra, the sun god, from day, through a watery *dwat*, back to day.[17] And the son god Horus, whose "eye" we have seen to be ritually associated with Ra, would seem to be a model for such a "Ben Shemesh." The sequence Shin-Mem-Shin through which the sun may be said to pass daily can be understood, on one level, as referring to the waters of the Lower World, also regarded as the feminine waters, through which the sun could have been thought to pass during its night beneath the earth. Passage through such water also appears importantly in two stages of the national epic, in the form of the Red Sea intervening between Mitzraim and Mount Sinai, the mountain of revelation, and in that of the River Jordan between the Moab wilderness and the Promised Land, with its holy mountain of Messianic redemption. The implication is that man can only become a Ben Shemesh by undergoing a process of purification through which the old light of particularizing consciousness is reborn shorn of its alienating egotism and radiating the new light of perfected individuality, of divine personality.

But if the nature of the Sinai Covenant may be said to mark the transition from an immemorial observance of lunar time to a new adherence to solar reckoning, it was a transition that sought to retain the essential values of the old while lifting them to new spiritual heights, as perfume is extracted from the flower and animal sacrifices yield a sweet savor unto the Lord. Indeed, more than any other surviving ancient culture, Judaism has retained an essentially lunar calendar remarkably harmonized with the solar year. It might be pointed out that this harmonization is made in terms of what seems to be a genuine musical consideration. In seven years of a nineteen-year cycle, a thirteenth month is added, these years being in a sequence that appears to reflect the intervals of the diatonic scale: 0, 3, 6, 8, 11, 14, 17, 19. But however this parallel may be explained, the lunar-solar contemporary Jewish calendar shows a mediation between the lunar and solar in which the values of both are recognized and retained.

Another ancient culture that achieved an equally complex though different harmonization of the lunar and solar rounds was the Mayan, and it offers an intriguing analogue to the further association with which this discussion has approached these temporal cycles, that of the Gematria equation Ben (son) = 52. As we have seen, this equation would seem to have originally identified the concept of "son" with that being who can count the approximately fifty-two phases of the moon that make up the solar round and so synthesize the lunar and solar cycles. A similar concept may perhaps be seen in the Mayan calendar, in which the 260-day ritual-lunar cycle (composed of 13 x 20 days) and the 360-day social-solar cycle (composed of 18 x 20 days) complete the "calendar round," marking the reappearance in both cycles of the same day and month names, and this in exactly fifty-two years! Though the concept of the son does not overtly appear in the Mayan calendrical symbolism, it may perhaps be inferred by the unit of 20 used for counting. For this number refers to the Mayan concept of the complete human being: "The Maya counted with the full person, both fingers and toes, and based their system on units of twenty." [18] As with the word *ben* for son and the son god Horus, it was as the counter of heavenly rhythms that the human being was understood by the Mayans to be "full" or, as seems likely, perfected, was on some level understood to combine the polarity he synthesized—that of the feminine moon (13 always representing the feminine-lunar equation) and complementary masculine sun, of the natural and transcendent—and be their product or "son." The number 18 featured in the Mayan solar cycle also has a suggestive Hebrew analogue. It is the Gematria number of the word *chai* (Chet = 8, Yod = 10), meaning life, worn by many as a neck amulet. And perhaps it is some such association of life with the sun, possibly of eternal life, that explains the Mayan choice of 18 as its solar marker. Though these complex sets of associations may have developed independently, they may also point to some worldwide sacred science of the greatest antiquity that associated its advanced science of astronomy with an understanding of the triumphant human role in cosmic history.

To return to our opening geometric proportion, we may now also observe in it such a hidden equivalence as the Hebrew and Mayan calendars are designed to maintain: $13(28) = 52(7)$. In this equation of the extremes, it may even be possible to identify the mediating Tetragrammaton with the symbol of equivalence, if this form of the verb "to be" can be allowed to assume the function of the copula. This final arithmetic arrangement of the numbers 13 and 52 may be further related to the two different forms of number defined in the *Sefer Yetzirah*. It was earlier suggested that the twenty-eight forms of letter-numbers needed for computation could be related to the lunar cycle. Returning to this premise, we may be able to relate the lunar intelligence both with language and with those numbers directly tied to the space-time dimensions of substance. But the Sabbatical number to which solar intelligence would here seem to be allied seems rather to be related to the concept of number conveyed by the term Sefirot Belimah. The word *belimah* appearing after *sefirot* throughout the first chapter of the *Sefer Yetzirah* and seeming to mean "without what" has never been satisfactorily explained. But the present context seems to suggest that it means "without substance" or abstract, that the Sefirot Belimah, the first ten numbers whose letter signifiers cannot be combined to form words, refer quite simply to the fact of abstract numerals. Relating the letter-numbers to lunar intelligence is further consistent with the discussion in chapter 3 of the natural origin of language, of language as the expression of substantial form, words being understood to be the extensions of things, for to hear this speech of living matter is to be still enclosed in the womb of nature. If the number of lunar intelligence (13) can be related through the multiple of its days (28) to the letter-numbers defining both natural language and spatial measurement, then that of solar intelligence (52) can be related through its multiple of days (7) with the abstract numerals that exemplify the intelligible world transcending the natural.

That the number 7 should epitomize the special quality of abstraction characteristic of these numerals was recognized by the Pythagoreans, as the second-century Platonic philosopher Theon of Smyrna has shown: "Another number of the decad, the number seven, is endowed with a remarkable property: it is the only one which does not give birth to any number contained in the decad and which is not born out of any of them, which fact moved the Pythagoreans to give it the name Athena, because this goddess was not born out of a mother and gave birth to none."[19] Athena, the brainchild of Zeus, symbolizes well the abstract conception of pure number in general, but none so well as the number seven, the number Theon shows to be least identifiable with the processes of natural conception and best fitted to symbolize the transcendent state. It was not the Pythagoreans, however, but the Hebrews who saw in the number seven the most essential of cosmic principles.

It was earlier argued that the conception of the Sabbatical week was derived from observation of the phases of the moon, and this also was recognized by Theon and the tradition for which he speaks: "The month is composed of four weeks (*four* times *seven* days); in the first week the moon appears divided in two; in the second it becomes full, in the third it is again divided, and in the fourth, it returns to meet the sun in order to begin a new month and to increase during the following week."[20] But such a derivation could never have assumed the cosmic significance with which the Hebrew tradition has endowed the number 7 if it was not consistent with other sources of knowledge regarding the cosmos. The Genesis account of the fourth-day creation of the sun and moon makes clear that they are to be considered not only as indicators of temporal periods, significantly those determined by the sun, but also as "signs" of something beyond such temporal reckoning: "And God said, Let there be lights in the firmament of the heaven to divide the day from the night; and let them be for signs, and for seasons, and for days, and years" (Gen. 1:14). Similarly the *Sefer Yetzirah* considers the intersecting paths of the sun and moon to be "true witnesses" (6:1) to higher truths of cosmic order and meaningfulness. If the Hebrews, like other ancient peoples, sought to align their personal and communal rhythms with those of the sun and moon, it was not, as with some other peoples, because they worshiped these mythologized astronomical bodies as such but because they could read the revolutions of these bodies as hieroglyphs of a higher order of reality, as a symbolic map that exteriorized the inner structure of that which was its source.

The central fact of this inner structure seems to be its Sabbatical nature. In chapter 6 we shall see that the cosmos whose creation is detailed in Genesis may be understood to have a structure of seven dimensions, the four of space-time produced by the fourth day and the three additional spiritual dimensions established through the remaining "days," a structuring of cosmic dimensions further developed in chapter 10. Such a projection of additional imperceptible dimensions, amounting to ten, is now being hailed as the ultimate solution looked for in the unification theories of quantum physics known as "superstrings." As Murray Gell-Mann has explained such superstring dimensions:

> Superstrings reduce to four dimensions, if one supposes that the ten dimensions spontaneously collapse into four, with the other six rolled up into a little ball at every point in space-time. In superstring theories or super-gravity, we have generalizations of Einstein's theory of gravitation that give possible ways of unifying everything with a single superfield that contains examples of all the kinds of particles that we need. . . . Superstring theory seems to require nine spatial dimensions instead of three (plus the dimension of time). The extra dimensions would not then be perceived as such but would affect the spectrum of the elementary particles and the character of the cosmology of the very early universe.[21]

No less arcane than kabbalistic cosmology, the latest efforts of modern physics support the model of a multidimensional universe we will see to be encoded in the sacred science of the Genesis creation myth. And it may even be that the conflict of numbers between these two projections can be resolved. For on the kabbalistic Tree, there are three Sefirot above those lower seven definitive of the seven days of the cosmic world, which might be viewed as constituting transcendent dimensions above the cosmic seven and would thus raise the total number to that of the ten Sefirot.

In our study of sacred science, we have seen that matter sends a double message of its both limited and limitless nature, the message transmitted both through light and ultrasonic vibrations, for which we need our dual senses of sight and hearing. And we have also seen that the message of localization given by form and that of universal extension given by sound was mediated by a numerical counting processed by the beating and emotionally responsive heart, a counting at once quantitative and qualitative. So far, we have been primarily concerned with a particular expression of this numerical mediation that seems to show such mediation to be a function of the divine, the geometrical proportion 13:26::26:52. If this progression may be said to contain the fundamental Da'at (Knowledge) at the heart of the Hebraic esoteric tradition, then this tradition may also be said to emphasize the sacred nature of this science, seeing its ordering and interrelating of the separate logics of form, sound, and number as everywhere revelatory not only of cosmic precision but also of divine mystery, and it is less concerned with further developing the subtleties of this science than it is with the development of the sacred scientist. For the "son of the world to come," who may be said to represent the product of the above divine proportion, is none other than just such a sacred scientist, a scientist of the sacred cosmic order and also himself sacred. It is the achievement of such divine personality that may well be said to have been the guiding spirit behind the Sinai Covenant, that divine covenant whose first requirement of man was that he learn to count weeks[22] and observe the holiness of their Sabbaths, learning a mode of numerical abstraction that retains the qualitative within the quantitative and that integrates the knowledge of the head with that of the heart.

If the proportion 13:26::26:52 may be said to define the cosmic extremes of concreteness and abstraction, then the mean that mediates between them may truly be said to have the characteristics of geometry, for geometry has both the concreteness of particular form as well as its abstraction from material manifestation. And the sacred scientists—they who represent the culminating purpose of this divinely mediated progression from concreteness to abstraction, who can so abstract and liberate the particular from its imprisonment in the concrete that its universal character stands revealed—are they who can receive this truth precisely because they have achieved the saving knowledge of their own limitless particularity. Thus the extremes of concreteness and abstraction that geometry can divinely mediate represent both an equation and a progression. Coded in terms of the months and weeks of the solar year (13 x 28 and 52 x 7), they can be recognized in their equality, but coded in terms of their mythological associations with the Earth Mother (13) and the cosmic son (52), they represent a progression mediated by heavenly grace. It is the mystery of this progression from concreteness to universality without loss of the equality between these extremes that is the final knowledge transmitted by the geometric proportion whose mean is the number of the Tetragrammaton, this proportion testifying to a mystery beyond its power to explain and one that can finally only fill the sacred scientists capable of comprehending such messages with awe at the cosmos that has given its enlightened sons and daughters the privilege of somehow contributing through this achieved knowledge to its mysterious purposes.

The Tetragrammaton Expansions

In the course of our investigations, we have seen a curious numerical relationship between the Tetragrammaton and the word for son, *ben*, that their Gematria numbers of 26 and 52, respectively, are in the doubling geometric proportion, with significant theoretical implications. But there is another area of the Kabbalah in which they are also importantly related, that of the Tetragrammaton expansions, the four ways in which it has traditionally been thought that the letters composing the Tetragrammaton can be individually spelled. For as we have seen, the Gematria equation of Ben = 52 appears as one of the Tetragrammaton expansions.

To summarize this important cosmological concept and practice, there are four such expansions of the Name whose different numerical counts are referred to by the sounds these letter-numbers form: Ab = 72 (Ayin = 70 and Bet = 2); Sag = 63 (Samakh = 60 and Gimel = 3); Mah = 45 (Mem = 40 and Hey = 5); and Ben = 52 (Bet = 2 and Nun = 50). Now there are two things that should be apparent from the above listing. The first, as earlier noted, is that the fourth expansion, Ben = 52, does not conform to the upper three expansions in the order of its letter-numbers, being the reverse of ordinary counting with the units here preceding the tens. The second, which also relates to Ben, is that its number has no relationship to the upper three numbers, not only being out of proper sequence with them but also not displaying the one factor that relates the other three. This is that they are all multiples of nine: $72 = 9 \times 8$; $63 = 9 \times 7$; and $45 = 9 \times 5$. A clue to what this may signify can perhaps be found in the following discussion of the Tetragrammaton expansions by Chayyim Vital. In this summary of an aspect of Lurianic spiritual practice, the definition of Ab is especially noteworthy:

> The Tetragrammaton expanded with Yod's, adding up to 72 (Ab), motivates the union of Chokhmah-Wisdom (Father) and Binah-Understanding (Mother), through the Neshamah of the Neshamah of the saint. It is associated with Chokhmah-Wisdom.
>
> The Tetragrammaton adding up to 63 (Sag) then elevates the Feminine Waters through the Neshamah of the saint. This is associated with Binah-Understanding.

The Tetragrammaton adding up to 45 (Mah) then motivates the union between Tiferet-Beauty (Male) and Malkhut-Kingship (Female) through the Ruach of the saint. [It is associated with Tiferet-Beauty (*Zer Anpin*)].

The Tetragrammaton adding up to 52 (Ben) then elevates the Feminine Waters through the Nefesh of the saint. This is associated with Malkhut-Kingship (the Female Partzuf).[23]

What is especially significant about the Lurianic explanation of the Tetragrammaton expansions is its association of Ab with the union of Chokhmah and Binah, an association that has just been shown to have a numerical basis, namely that 8 x 9 (the numbers of Binah and Chokhmah when counted in ascending order) = 72.[24] There may also have been some surviving association of Mah with Tiferet, the fifth Sefirah in ascending order (5 x 9 = 45—Mah). But the numerical explanation of these associations has clearly been lost. Working with these two remnants of an original explanation that would seem to have become obscured through the very secretive and cryptic methods by which some elements of an original mystical doctrine were passed down, Luria or Vital appears to have regularized these two expansions with each other and then fitted in the remaining two in accordance with older traditions regarding the four Tetragrammaton letters. Thus Mah is said to feature a lower sexual union to parallel the upper such union of Ab, and Ab is said to be associated only with Chokhmah as Mah is with Tiferet. Once these two expansions have been thus regularized, Sag and Ben can be easily identified with the female Partzufim involved in these unifications. But what this does is simply equate the four expansions of the Tetragrammaton with the prior identifications of its four letters without adding any special intelligence from the Gematria numbers of these expansions or their names.

It needed not such numerical complication to tell us that Chokhmah is to be identified with Yod, Binah with Hey, Tiferet (and the other five Sefirot of Ze'ir Anpin) with Vav, and Malkhut with the lower Hey, and it leads to the incongruity of identifying the expansion of the son, Ben, with the Sefirah of the daughter, Malkhut. What we have seen, however, is that a remarkable web of correspondences arises as soon as one assumes that the numbers associated with esoteric doctrines and practices always have a sound arithmetic or geometric basis, and one begins to explore this hidden mathematics. It can only be deplored that the traces of sacred science found throughout the authentic elements of the Jewish esoteric tradition ceased to be passed down as a pedagogical discipline by the conservators and innovators of the later Kabbalah, and so its true mysteries became misunderstood or lost. Even the element that it did retain, Gematria, was devoted largely to its linguistic aspect, the association of words on the basis of their numerical equivalence, without any real appreciation or study of the significance of such an equation of letters and numbers. The significance of the numbers and names attached to the Tetragrammaton expansions is passed over in silence while other explanations are sought to fill this gap in understanding.

Now if the earlier deduction was correct that the numbers 9 and 8, whose product equals the number 72 of the Tetragrammaton expansion named Ab, are to be identified with the Sefirot so numbered when counted up from Malkhut, then this same principle should also apply to the expansions named Sag and Mah. As Ab can thus be identified with the multiplication or unification of Chokhmah (9) and Binah (8), so can Sag be identified with the unification of Chokhmah (9) and Chesed (7), and Mah with that of Chokhmah (9) and Tiferet (5). These three expansions would seem to signify, then, at the very least, three levels of Wisdom, Chokhmah, a subject to which we shall shortly return. Furthermore, since the development of wisdom is a mental process, and it is the mind that is involved in meditation, these three levels of wisdom, whose number signifiers would seem to correspond to the upward count of Sefirot, can be understood to define three ascending levels of spiritual development that are to be reached through appropriate forms of meditation.

What, then, of the expansion called Ben, whose letter-numbers do not contain a multiplication of nine, the number of Chokhmah-Wisdom, and are given in reverse order? If the Sefirot identifications of the upper three expansions imply an ascending order, and this ascent is associated with the normal order of the letter-numbers, may it be that the reverse order of the letter-numbers in Ben is meant to equate this name with the very process of reversal, that Ben signifies that "son of the world to come" who is to reverse the process of spiritual descent into the process of return or Tikkun by engaging in the upward spiritual path signified by the other three expansions? If this can be accepted, then Ben is set apart from the other expansions in both form and significance, both of which would seem to have been established long before the four Tetragrammaton expansions had developed their final shape.

For the equation of the name Ben with the number 52 would seem to have been quite ancient. As recently suggested, the secret doctrine of the son was probably originally associated with the Gematria equation

Ben (son) = 52 in relationship to this number of Sabbaticals (weeks) in the solar year, the "son" with whom God entered into a covenant at Sinai being he who could count weeks and so be made holy through ritual observance of the sign of this covenant, the Sabbath. The son, Ben, divinely adopted in the Exodus from Egypt that he might participate in this covenant—"Thus saith the Lord, Israel is my son, even my first born" (Exod. 4:22)—can, therefore, be considered to represent that potential for covenantal relationship that marks the beginning of the spiritual growth of Israel.

We have now to consider how Av or Ab, signifying 72, could have become associated with the name Ben, and it would seem that it is the linguistic significance of these names that first provided justification for such a linkage. For as Ben means son, so does Ab or Abba mean father. Though this involves a Hebrew pun between the similarly sounding Ayin-Bet (signifying 72 and the word for cloud) and Aleph-Bet (meaning father), insofar as the number 72 identified with Ayin-Bet can be associated with the Sefirah Chokhmah, as previously shown, it can also be associated with the Partzuf identified with this Sefirah, Abba. What is more, since this number can be viewed as the product of 9 x 8, it can also be understood to signify the Yichud of Abba (Chokhmah) and Imma (Binah). And it is this union whose fruit can finally be identified with the son, Ben. The names of Ab and Ben can thus be naturally associated with the supreme cosmic mystery, the generation of the cosmic child by the sexualized forms of the supernal godhead, Abba and Imma.

These names are not, however, found independently associated but only in the context of the four Tetragrammaton expansions. But when these expansions are examined closely, only one has a natural validity, Sag. For when Yod, Hey, Vav, and Hey are spelled out, it is only the combination of Yods and Aleph inserted as vowel-letters, which adds up to 63 or Sag, that provides a true pronunciation of each of the Tetragrammaton letters. Since the other three ways of spelling out these four letters are artificial and seem to be motivated only by the Gematria numbers thus produced, it would seem that the name Sag provided the nucleus around which the complex of four Tetragrammaton expansions developed in accordance with other considerations. Once it was noticed that the natural expansion of the Tetragrammaton, Sag, and the expansion adding up to 72, Ab, both involved multiplications of the number 9 that could be related to the upward count of Sefirot, it was seen that a Tetragrammaton expansion using only Yods could be fashioned that would produce the number 72. So also, one using only Alephs could produce the number 45, which would relate the true Sefirah of the son, Tiferet, to that of the father, Chokhmah. Finally the reversed-order name Ben was produced using only inserted Heys. Although production of the name Mah (= 45) rendered that of Ben superfluous as a signifier of the son, its probable earlier association with the name of Ab, as previously suggested, would seem to have carried the name of Ben over to the Tetragrammaton expansions. But because of the marked distinction between Ben and the upper three expansions, in both numerical terms and the reversed order of its letter-numbers, this name could only be taken to signify something different from the rest, most easily the human son who has to reverse directions and engage in the meditative practices that can lift him to the three levels of the divine represented by the upper three expansions.

Considering the process first as a progression through various levels of wisdom, we are first struck by the aptness of the names of the Sefirot that couple with Chokhmah in the middle two expansions, Tiferet or Beauty for Mah and Chesed or Mercy for Sag. These seem to take us through that same progression from the aesthetic to the ethical that the Danish religious philosopher Søren Kierkegaard was to write of with such penetration in his work *Either/Or*. And with the final ascent to Ab, we arrive at that union of Abba and Imma that may be said to define the mystical level of wisdom. But if Mah, Sag, and Ab can be thus said to define the aesthetic, ethical, and mystical levels of wisdom, then they do so not only in their numerical associations with particular Sefirot but also in the linguistic meanings conveyed through these letter-numbers. And it is here that the earlier historical analysis begins to fall apart, only to reveal a deeper level of mystery. For not only may these numbers be correlated with the geometry of the Tree of Life Diagram but their signifying letters also form meaningful words consistent with the prior Sefirot identifications, that same triple association of number, form, and sound that we saw to be the central teaching of sacred science and the measure of its wisdom.

The name for the number 45, Mah, is a common Hebrew word with a most pertinent meaning, "what." The question posed by the word Mah—"What is the meaning of this?"—has a clear relation to the aesthetic level of wisdom defined by the multiplication of Tiferet-Beauty (5) with Chokhmah-Wisdom (9) since it is just such an expression of uncomprehending awe that marks the aesthetic response at its highest, the response to the sublime, a response that the Greek philosopher of the sublime, Longinus, found in the Hebrew psalms. And it is the psychic elevation arising from this perception of a sublime beauty and order to nature that may well be considered the root from which the more defined forms of religious experience can blossom.

The next stage of such religious development will be that in which the initial question is met with a satisfying answer, and this answer would seem to be contained in the name for the number 63, Sag. This again can be correlated with a word composed of only the consonants Samakh and Gimel, with the vowel-letters being permitted to go uncounted. In this case the Hebrew word composed of these consonants that seems most appropriate to the level of wisdom being associated with the number 63 is the word *sagi* (Samakh-Gimel-Yod), a word one of whose meanings is "great" and that signifies a general concept of abundance and expansiveness. Now what is most remarkable about this meaning is that another word for greatness, Gedullah, which is probably derived from the same root as *sagi*, is an alternate and older name for the Sefirah more usually called Chesed, that whose seventh ascending position, when multiplied by the ninth position of Chokhmah, yields the number 63, whose name Sag can be related to the word for great, *sagi*. The answer given by this higher level of wisdom to the question "What?" would thus seem to be that the cause of something so wondrous can only be something still *greater*. Translated into spatial size, it is such Gedullah that informs the Merkabah concept of the "Shi'ur Komah," that vast divine body whose measurement is the achievement marking a "son of the world to come." As Ben rises in wisdom from an initial questioning of the cause of the cosmos, Mah, to an apprehension of the greatness of its source, Sag, he becomes the "son of the world to come" who can pierce the cloud, Av or Ab, to gain the mystic vision of that unification of Abba and Imma through which he has been spiritually reborn.

What is also most significant about the selection of Sefirot in the three upper expansions that involve the multiplication of the number 9 is that this process of Tikkun pointedly excludes the missing number 54, that entailing the Sefirah of Gevurah or Din, which is sixth in the order of ascent. But as the discussion of the Tzimtzum in chapter 10 will show, it is precisely the elimination of the quality of Din, or Severity from the divine nature that Luria understood to be the purpose of the Tzimtzum.[25] Thus the ascent from Tiferet to Binah and Chokhmah by way of Chesed would seem to accomplish that purpose of eliminating Gevurah, which can also be taken to define the proper course of the Tikkun. The skipping of 54 in the passage from 45 to 63 can be seen, therefore, to prescribe a returning path by way of the right side of the Tree, of Chesed rather than Gevurah. And it might also be pointed out that the expansiveness of

Gedullah at the divine heart level would lead precisely to the quality of Chesed by which this heart Sefirah is primarily known, the quality that can finally give an ethical dimension to the answer provided by Sag, that the source of creation is both great and good.

Of the complex web of associations that has just been developed by focusing on both the numerical and linguistic implications of the letter-numbers for the four Tetragrammaton expansions, little has, however, come down through the explicit texts of the kabbalistic tradition. But what the explorations undertaken in this chapter have demonstrated is a consistently meaningful correspondence between symbolically significant numbers and the linguistic roots associated with the letter-numbers by which they are expressed. Thus in the first investigation devoted to the geometric progression 13:26::26:52, there were the clear Gematria associations of 26 with the Tetragrammaton, of 52 with the word for son, Ben, and of 13 with the Hebrew word *guy* meaning "valley," an analogue to the Greek name Gaia signifying the earth goddess. Whether this last association is the product of cultural influence, an earlier source to both, or separate emergences, it is certainly suggestive. And more recently we have seen significant meanings emerging from the letter-numbers for 63, not to speak of such more obvious words as Mah and Ben. What is even more startling are the geometric correspondences to these equations of numbers and words, in the case of the above mentioned geometric progression to the celestial geometry involving the great circles of the sun and moon and in that of the Tetragrammaton expansions to the geometry of the Tree of Life Diagram. Science may not have addressed such occult correspondences but neither can it explain them. Faced with such a network of meaningful correspondences, we can do no more than ask and answer the question they raise on the model provided by the Tetragrammaton expansions that just again revealed this mystery. To the question "Mah?" ("What is the explanation?"), the only answer is "Sagi," a logic of such great complexity and power as cannot be comprehended on this side of the cloud of unknowing.

To transcend that cloud to a mystic apprehension of the ultimate unity in which each participates is the goal of all spiritual practices, and this too is the highest goal of the Kabbalah. As Abulafia has shown:

> The Kabbalah . . . is generally divided into two parts. One part deals with knowing God through the method of the ten *sefirot*. . . .
> The other part involves knowing God through the method of the

twenty-two letters of the alphabet. . . . Undoubtedly, the first category of kabbalistic study must precede the second, but the second is of greater importance than the first. The latter was the goal in the creation of the human species, and the one who attains it is the only one whose mental faculties have reached complete self-realization. It is to him that the Lord of all existence has revealed Himself and disclosed His secret. . . . Thus the mastery of the knowledge of the ten *sefirot* precedes the additional knowledge of the names of God, and not vice-versa.[26]

In his discussion of spiritual practices, Abulafia has indicated just such an association of divine names with Sefirot as I have shown could best explain the spiritual significance of the Tetragrammaton expansions. But as Abulafia has further made clear, effective use of these practices can only be made by one whose knowledge of kabbalistic theory has informed him of their true purpose. For the cosmology contained in the model of the Sefirotic Tree defines just such a unification of the divine that it is the purpose of man to facilitate and share through his spiritual practice. As Abulafia stresses, "it is the *sefirot* that manifest the secret of divine unity,"[27] and it is this "secret" that will be disclosed to those through whose spiritual devotions the "goal in the creation" has been achieved. This is the secret of the unification of the transcendent and immanent forms of the divine in the persons of those self-realized humans who are assured of being "sons of the world to come."

What this chapter has thus far shown is that the Tetragrammaton is composed of letter-numbers that so focus strands of cosmologically significant numbers, sounds, and forms as to provide a unique key to the unraveling of cosmic mysteries, particularly the mystery of just such occult correspondences as are demonstrated by its own letters. Using this key, two different doors have been unlocked that have offered different entrances to a hidden dimension, one at which the different logics of sound (particularly in its linguistic form), shape, and number all are integrated by a metalogic beyond our power to explain but whose existence can be demonstrated by the correspondences that can be uncovered among these three factors permitting perception. It is this capacity for demonstration that entitles the study of such correspondences to be considered a science. Since these correspondences are truly occult, however, leading not to a rationally constructed theory of explanation but rather to mystery, it must also be considered a science of the sacred, of that realm defined by the Tetragrammaton itself.

Our investigation of the mysterious meaningfulness and power of the Tetragrammaton is now to take a completely different direction, revealing ever new facets of this holiest Name of the divine and taking us even further back than that early stage of man's cultural evolution in which he developed the ability to count. It will take us to that earliest stage in which his power of vocal communication consisted entirely of vowels, and it will lead to a new understanding both of the meaning of the Tetragrammaton and its pronunciation, an understanding of this holiest Name resulting from the investigation of its sound correspondences. These further explorations will also lay the foundation for the treatment in the next chapter of the vowels in relationship to spiritual practice. Thus our exploration of the mysteries of the Tetragrammaton is only beginning.

The Tetragrammaton and the Vowel-Letters

CONSONANTS AND VOWELS

The Hebraic definition of the son as one worthy of entering into a divine covenant was shown to be related to the capacity to count the 52 Sabbaticals of the solar year. But this equation of a number with the word formed by its signifying letters, Ben = 52, indicates a further association between the nature of the counting numbers and letters, particularly the consonantal letters of the Hebrew alphabet. For numerical discrimination involves the same level of mental and social development as that articulation of thought in speech made possible by the consonants. Words and numbers equally reflect the same power of mental discrimination, of particularization, that marks the advent of a true human culture, and they seem to have emerged both together and interconnected. Number was divided by the very nature of this system into two classes, the abstract numbers, like the "Sefirot Belimah" of the *Sefer Yetzirah* and perhaps the Sefirot of the Tree, which could be signified by the first ten single letters and so could not be translated into words, and most subsequent numbers, which required that combination of letters to be signified as numbers that could also be read as words. The first ten numbers would thus have acquired a mystical character as being beyond the descriptive power of language; and as evidenced by their appearance in the Pythagorean Tetractys and kabbalistic Tree of Life Diagram, they were held to be unique conveyers of cosmic structure and meaning. But the very ability of most subsequent numbers to be translated into appropriate words was held to be just as revealing of mystery within that realm of particularity that could be specified by number and name. Thus the union of number with the consonantal letters could be taken to demonstrate both the divine transcendence and immanence, and these two forms of number became the focus of the main forms of kabbalistic contemplation, those involving study of the Tree and of such letter manipulations as Gematria.

But there is another aspect of language that takes us still further back in human development, to that precultural stage of inarticulate sounds in which man is still animal and an indivisible part of nature. It is in such sounds that the human heart first conveyed its own understanding, and such meaningful sounds still form what has been called the soul of language, its vowels. Language combines the fixed articulation of the consonants and the inarticulate continuity of the vowels, the first conveying the understanding of the mind as the second conveys that of the heart. The following discussion will be devoted to these vowel sounds and their significant relationship to the Tetragrammaton, a relationship that will prove the foundation for the varied further explorations of the Hebrew vowels in chapter 5. But the final section of this chapter should prove even more revelatory, being no less than a new attempt to uncover the original pronunciation of the Tetragrammaton, the holiest divine Name that we soon will see to have an essential relationship to the very vowel sounds through which its own pronunciation can be definitively determined and a new interpretation of its meaning suggested.

In this study we shall be going back, then, to the origin of human experience and understanding and shall discover it to have been already fully informed of the nature and purpose of existence, a knowledge that the esoteric tradition has been at pains to conserve and transmit. Such transmission may be seen in the form of linguistic expression that most preserves the primitive significance of the vowels, prayer. Some features of the prayer service[28] will provide our point of entry into the significance of the vowels.

THE VOWEL-LETTERS AND PERSONS GRAMMATICAL AND DIVINE

The prayer service may be divided into three stages, an introductory ascending stage, the central plateau comprised primarily of the Sh'ma and the Amidah, and a closing descending stage. And each of these stages is characterized by one of what we shall shortly see to be the three primitive vowels, the sounds of *ee*, *ah*, and *oo*. These sounds predominate in the ordered stages of the service because they appear at the close of the personal pronouns with which these stages can be associated, *ee* with the first person singular, *ani*, *ah* with the second person singular masculine, *atah*, and *oo* with the first person plural, *anachnu*. We bring our egos into the introductory stage of prayer (marked by such passages as "Ma Tova," "Adon Alam," and "Ashray," which feature the first person *ee* sound), rise to the plateau of Devekut, communion, in which God addresses us as "you" in the Sh'ma and we address Him similarly in the Amidah (thereby featuring the *ah* sound of the second person masculine), and then descend to a New Earth transfigured by our achieved sense of holy community, the *anachnu* of the first person plural ending in the *oo* sound (as conveyed through such passages as "Avenu Malkanu," "Ain Kaylohaynu," and "Alaynu"). The first clue as to the larger meaning of the primary vowels is, then, their association with what we would now call the concept of grammatical person. The expressive sounds of the primary vowels would seem to have arisen from that stage of emotional development in which the self was first differentiated from the other but also recognized as being able to achieve new forms of both individual and group relationship. They express the self in its need to communicate with the other and so create a society.

Not only may the three primary vowels be related to the concept of grammatical number but also to geometry, as we would expect from our study of sacred science. A statement by Owen Barfield quoted earlier is again pertinent here: ". . . the Semitic languages seem to point us back to the old unity of man and nature, through the shapes of their sounds. We feel those shapes not only as sounds, but also, in a manner, as *gestures* of the speech-organs. . . ."[29] These "gestures" may be related to the essential geometric distinction in Lurianic cosmology between the creative activity of the circle and the line, particularly in the Tzimtzum, the divine contraction at the start of the creative process to be treated in chapter 10. For the *ee* sound is produced by the narrowest opening of the lips and teeth in the form of a line while the *oo* sound involves the most complete rounded contraction of the lips. Between these two extremes of linear and circular lip openings, and mediating the transition from one to the other, is the most relaxed *ah* sound, produced by a full opening of the mouth. William Chomsky has represented the Hebraic vowel system graphically by means of the following triangle, to which he has added a most instructive comment:

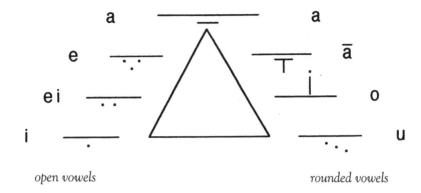

open vowels   rounded vowels

> This vocalic triangle is based on a well-established principle in pho-
> netics, according to which all "culture languages," without excep-
> tion, must have the three vowels on the apices of the triangle,
> namely, *a, u, i*. These are the original or primitive vowels. The vow-
> els on the sides of the triangle are secondary and may be lacking in
> one or another language. In Hebrew the four secondary vowels on
> the sides evolved out of the three primitive vowels . . . and repre-
> sent mere shadings or modifications of them.[30]

The vowel sounds associated with the letters *i, a,* and *u* are, indeed, primitive, expressing the most primitive of emotions. The *ee* sound related to
the first is expressive of fear, a product of a mental self-consciousness seen
to be under threat, and is well defined by an English word in which it
appears, "shriek." The middle *ah* sound is expressive of deep satisfaction.
And the final *oo* sound can itself be considered a low moan of pain.[31] We
shall later see that the beginning consonants of the English words *shriek*
and *moan* have a special connection with the *ee* and *oo* sounds they both
characterize in these words and complete in terms of mouth movement.
One can also see how these sounds of extreme feeling could have become
the signifiers of grammatical person, fear being a product of the sense of
self, satisfaction the product of a loving involvement with the other, and
pain an experience leading at its highest to a sense of compassion, the "I,"
"you," and "we" previously distinguished in the prayer service.

Chomsky has discussed these vowel sounds in terms of the Masoretic
system of dots and lines that developed in the seventh century C.E. as a
means of specifying the vowel sounds of a language whose alphabet consists wholly of consonants. But an even more fascinating view of these
vowels is presented when one turns to the intermediate category of the
vowel-letters. As explained in one of the finest of Hebrew grammar books:

long before the introduction of the vowel-signs it was felt that the main vowel-sounds should be indicated in writing, and so the three letters ו, ה, י were used to represent the long vowels, thus:

> ה represents a, so that מה reads ma.
> י represents i and e, so that מי reads mi or me.
> ו represents u and o, so that מו reads mu or mo.

Because these three letters—ו, ה, י—represent both vowels and letters they are known as VOWEL-LETTERS.[32]

It is surprising that no grammarian who has discussed the vowel-letters has noted the signal fact, which should be apparent to any intelligent five year old (especially if he has already begun to study Hebrew), that the vowel-letters are the very letters of the Tetragrammaton! And though the vowels have long been felt to provide the soul or spiritual dimension of the language, this has never been related to any connection of the main vowels to the Tetragrammaton. But what is most surprising about this correlation is that both these vowel sounds and the Tetragrammaton letters used to express them can be related to the concept of persons, grammatical in the first case and divine in the second.

Before considering what correlation may be made between these two sets of persons, a short review of these vowel sounds is in order. Of the seven sounds represented in the triangular model, all except the short e (eh) and the short a (awe) were originally indicated by the vowel-letters. Of the five remaining long vowels, the Yod represented the primary i sound, as in the English me, and the secondary diphthong e, as in the English may; the Hey represented the single long a sound, as in the English diminutive for mother, ma; and the Vuv again represented both a primary sound and a secondary diphthong, the primary u, as in the English sound imitative of the lowing of a cow, moo, and the diphthong o, as in the English nickname "Moe."

Interestingly, these numbers may also be related to the Partzufim identifications of these Tetragrammaton letters: the Yod identified with both Arikh Anpin and Abba, that is, with Keter and Chokhmah; the intermediate Hey only with Imma or Binah; and the Vav always with Ze'ir Anpin and, in much Lurianic discussion of the first birth of Ze'ir Anpin, also with the Nukvah, the constituents of this originally androgynous Ze'ir Anpin being the lower seven Sefirot. As there are five long vowels represented by the Tetragrammaton letters, so do these letters represent an equal number of Partzufim. It would simplify our preliminary discussion, however, to concentrate upon the three primary sounds and the Partzufim normally associated with these three Tetragrammaton letters, the divine father Abba and what we will now be calling the *i* sound with the Yod, the divine mother Imma and the *a* sound with the Hey, and the divine androgynous child Ze'ir Anpin and the *u* sound with the Vav.

As we have already seen, the *i* sound indicates the first person singular in both its pronoun and various inflections, the *a* sound indicates the second person masculine singular, and the *u* sound indicates the first person plural. But the present context reminds us that the *u* sound is also the indicator of the third person masculine singular, its pronoun being *hu*. On this basis, it seems clear that there is some implicit identification of the Yod as Abba with the first person, the Hey as Imma with the second person, and the Vav as the androgynous Ze'ir Anpin with the third person. This is the ordering of these Partzufim-identified letters in the Tetragrammaton and also of the grammatical persons identified with the vowel sounds they signify.

We are thus led into a grammatical analysis of the divine personalities in which Abba, as the first person, defines himself by speaking the word "I," Imma, as the second person, defines herself by addressing the word "you" to Abba, and Ze'ir Anpin as the third person, defines himself by speaking the word "he" that reveals his distance from the object of his thought, presumably also Abba. But our understanding of these divine personalities will be enhanced by looking, in this context, at the extraordinary shapes of these three letters, the Yod, the Hey, and the Vav, reading them from right to left:

Looking at the shapes and ordering of these letters, it is clear that if Imma is to give her reply of direct address to Abba's declaration of selfhood, she must turn around to face him. Such a need has been the subject of much Lurianic mythologizing. As will be developed at length in chapter 7, Imma was conceived with her back turned to Abba, and the whole process of the Tikkun or cosmic rectification is understood to involve such an arousing of her female waters by the prayers of the righteous as will cause her to face Abba so as to engage properly in the act of Yichud. It now seems obvious that this aspect of Luria's cosmology derives from a meditation on the shapes of these letters, which we will see does not begin with him. For still concentrating on these shapes, we can see that when she so turns around, there is a space between the Dalet portion of her Hey and its unattached line of a size and position just suitable for the Yod of Abba to enter. Such a recognition also appears in an important Zoharic passage relating the concept of Yichud to the Sh'ma:

> This is the mystery of Unification (Yichud). The individual who is worthy of the World to Come must unify the name of the Blessed Holy One. . . . This is the mystery of "Hear O Israel, God is our Lord, God is One," . . . Yod is the mystery of the Holy Covenant. Heh is the chamber, the place in which the Holy Covenant, which is the Yod, is concealed. And even though we have stated [elsewhere] that this is the Vav (ו) [in the Tetragrammaton, YHVH (יהוה)] here it is a Yod. The mystery is that the two are united as one.[33]

The identification of the Yod with the "Holy Covenant" is an apparent allusion to circumcision and the revealed glans, that which can be "concealed" in the Heh when it is turned face-to-face with the Yod, the position signifying the Tikkun in the later Lurianic Kabbalah. Thus from at least the time of the Zohar, the Yichud of the upper Partzufim was understood to be graphically depicted in the Tetragrammaton letters identified with them. Not only this, if we now imagine the Yod so placed on the unattached vertical line of the Hey, we can see that it forms the very shape of the Vav. As Abba and Imma become unified in the first person plural, the "we" of anachnu, so do they produce the third person, the "he" of hu, this u sound completing the descent of the sound from the high i of ani ("I") through the intermediary a of atah ("you," masc. sing.).

But there is more to the shape and vowel sounds of the Vav in relationship to the grammatical and divine persons that can be associated with this vowel-letter. For the pronoun of the still internal Nukvah, the divine daughter, is also significant in terms of sound. This is the Hebrew word he meaning "she," a word having the same vowel sound as that of the first person, the Yod of Abba. And if we look closely again at the Vav, we can see that its "head" is just such a Yod. An aspect of Lurianic sexual cosmology is the identification of the Yesod of Ze'ir Anpin with just the shaft of the penis and of Malkhut-Nukvah with its head.[34] The Lurianic description of the Yesod of each has a more striking resemblance, however, to these two parts of the Vav than to human physiology, particularly in the case of the female, as can be seen in the following quotation

from a Lurianic work of the eighteenth century, the *Sha'arei Gan Eden* of
Jacob Koppel: "The Yesod of Atik . . . is combined of male and female in
a wonderful unity. . . . And it happens that the Yesod of the Female is
short and wide and the Yesod of the Male is lean and long."[35] This "wonderful unity" of shapes would seem to describe the Vav and to have arisen
from Luria's contemplation of the Vav, the letter identified with Ze'ir
Anpin and indicating its androgynous nature.

Returning now to the current usage of the Vav as a vowel-letter, the *u*
sound of the Vav is indicated by a dot at the left midpoint of its shaft and
its *o* sound by a dot just above its head. There seem, therefore, to be grounds
for associating the *u* sound of the Vav with the divine son and its *o* sound
with the divine daughter, the son deriving his initial form from the mother
as the daughter derives her initial form from the father. But in this crossing of gender types from one generation to the next, a crossing also to be
revealed in the geometric modeling of these Partzufim undertaken in chapter 7 in terms of the *Sefer Yetzirah* Diagram, there is a subtle modulation of
these parental influences. The *i* sound of the father and daughter pronouns, earlier associated with fear, has in the female part of the Vav been
transmuted into the *o* sound indicative of awe, "oh," the more sublime
reverential emotion that is, however, suggestive of safe distance from what
might otherwise inspire a starker fear. As the sound of the daughter's pronoun is the same as the final vowel of the first person singular, so that of
the son's is identical with the final vowel of the first person plural. This
again represents a modulation of the quality characterizing the mother.
Where her *atah* ("you") involved a complete negation of her selfhood, the
making of herself wholly into a vessel to contain the other, the association of the *u* sound of the son's pronoun with that of the first person plural
shows an identification with the collective in which the personal is not
lost, the "I" being contained within the "we." In the androgynous child
there is, then, a polarity between the personal definition of the feminine
aspect and the collective definition of the masculine aspect, both aspects
of which are not only necessary attributes of all aspects of creation but
would seem to represent the purpose of creation, the purpose of that Yichud
of the more partial Abba and Imma that produced this cosmic child.

There is yet another way of looking at the distinction between the
primary *u* sound and secondary *o* sound of the Vav; for these are also the
sounds that distinguish between the third person masculine singular pronouns signifying the subject (Hebrew *hu* and English *he*) and the object
(Hebrew *oto* and English *him*). Since the Hey is also the sign of the old
accusative case ending once signifying the object and now signifying

motion toward something (as in the turning of this letter to face the Yod), it can be argued that there is an association between the object and the feminine, particularly in the sense of sexual object. In the internal dialogue between the masculine and feminine aspects of the Vav, then, it could be said that the *u* sound signifies the subjective and the *o* sound the objective and objectifying aspects of the personality, Binah being traditionally associated with the concretization of the original creative energy into form. The association of the feminine Hey with the sound of the object is strengthened by the fact that, of the subject pronouns, it is only that of the second person, here associated with this Tetragrammaton letter, that begins with the same two letters beginning all of the object pronouns, Aleph and Tav, the first and last letters of the Hebrew alphabet that together form the word for "letter" or "sign." Thus it is through language that the mind can objectify its experience, transforming its initial fear into the awe that can compose psalms of praise.

Whether we distinguish the sexuality of the shaft or head of the Vav in terms of its form or pronominally associated sound, there is good reason, then, to identify the *u* sound of the shaft with the masculine and the *o* sound of the head with the feminine. The difference between these two approaches is that in the former case, that of form, there was a crossing of gender characteristics between the generations and in the latter case of sound a direct transmission of gender distinctions. Combining these two approaches provides a more complex view of both the masculine and feminine sides of the androgynous child while still maintaining the essential polarity between a personal center and the capacity to relate to that which is beyond it, a capacity that marks all aspects of creation and, on the conscious level, its purpose.

Though the associations between the Hebrew long vowels, pronominal sounds, and the Tetragrammaton vowel-letters may be surprising, it seems hard to dismiss their uncanny appropriateness as mere coincidence. Rather, there seems to have been an original appropriateness of both the geometry (forms) and sounds of language not only to the particular significances of individual words but to the whole order of creation. For now we can further see that the very structure of language—with its union of sound, form, and grammar—contains the key to the divine nature of the reality that the Hebraic tradition maintains was produced through language. In particular, we have just seen that the very letters of the Tetragrammaton contain the seed of the whole of kabbalistic cosmology, and that Luria, as the last of a long line of speculative Kabbalists, did not invent such cosmological relationships but discovered those that were implicitly there.

These considerations have relevance to the subject of the prayer service with which we began. For if the descent of the creative energy into material form may be said to have been mediated through some form of "language" whose sound frequencies (numbers) contained the potential of form inherent within them, then the ascent of this formed energy to more immaterial being must also be mediated by language, the language of prayer. In the previous discussion of the order of the service, the main concern was with the three primitive vowel sounds, *i*, *a*, and *u*. But between the *i* sound of the introductory phase, accomplishing the purification of the ego, and the *a* sound of the Sh'ma and the Amidah, of the state of Devekut, comes the *o* sound of the Kedushah (Isa. 6:13), the greatest expression of human awe at the glory of God and that primarily responsible in the service for arousing the fear of God, a fear that must be retained even during the height of Devekut. Since such awe can only result from the strong sense of self with which the service begins, we may say that during the ascending phase we go up with the daughter to the height of the Kedushah, which is her highest expression. For the ascent can only be made by the element of creation that, having developed a personal center, now wishes for that highest expansion of the self resulting from such a reconnection with its source as involves both fear and love of God, personal survival within this larger unification. And in such Devekut with its source, it also achieves a communion between the two halves of itself, the need for both individuation and connection having been met. From such an achieved sense of wholeness that also partakes of the holy, the divine Presence unifying all, a descent can now be made by that element of the self identified with the son, his sense of collective identity being carried down from the divine to the human realm with the imbued sense of community resounding through the *u* sound of the concluding communal prayers.

As we come to the close of this investigation into the use of the Tetragrammaton letters to indicate the long vowels, there is a final subject that demands our attention, one which I approach more hesitantly than any other in this study because it involves a practice long forbidden to Jews. This is the question of the proper pronunciation of the Tetragrammaton. My excuse for reopening what has long been an essentially closed subject is that the special focus of this investigation has provided new clues for solving a major mystery of Western religion that can further illuminate the nature of the deity so named. It is, then, with the end of understanding rather than of practice that we now enter the sacred precincts of the Name.

Pronunciation of the Tetragrammaton

Although pronunciation of the Tetragrammaton has been prohibited since at least the third century B.C.E. for all except the high priest on Yom Kippur and after his experience in the Temple's Holy of Holies, a final exception that itself ended with the destruction of the Temple, there are now two well-recognized pronunciations of the Tetragrammaton, one promulgated by modern biblical scholarship and the other rejected by it. The pronunciation now universally accepted by biblical scholars is *Yahweh* and that equally discredited by them is *Jehovah,* and both the advancement of the one and discrediting of the other seem to have begun with Jean Astruc, physician to Louis XV, who may be said to have originated the "higher criticism" in 1753 by distinguishing two strands in Genesis marked by the use of Elohim or "Yahweh," the latter advanced in place of what he regarded as the incorrect form of the popular Jehovah. It is now standard dogma, repeated uncritically in all books of respectable biblical scholarship by Jews and Gentiles alike, that the Jehovah pronunciation is a product of the ignorance of Gentile Hebraists regarding a Jewish scribal practice, that of indicating the substitute term of Adonai by the vowel points of this name placed beneath the letters of the Tetragrammaton. And it is equally proof of their own enlightenment, again by all such Jews and Gentiles, to proudly make use of the "correct" form, Yahweh.

How our study of the vowel-letters can help to resolve this standoff between the popular and scholarly Christian traditions of pronunciation, the Jewish tradition being silent on this matter, was suggested to me by a remark coming from a completely different quarter, from Rudolf Steiner:

> If one ascends to the spiritual world . . . one can say that it consists entirely of vowels. Lacking the bodily instrument, one enters a tonal world colored in a variety of ways with vowels. . . . This is why you will find in languages that were closer to the primeval languages that the words for things of the supersensible world were actually vowel-like. The Hebrew word *"Jahve"* for example, did not have the J and the V; it actually consisted only of vowels and was rhythmically half-sung.[36]

Steiner shows his modernity by using the accepted pronunciation Yahweh, though with Germanic consonantal forms. But his belief that the divine Name "consisted only of vowels" opens up a new possibility of pronunciation. Though his spiritual pronouncements may be unverifiable, that regarding the vowel-like nature of words in the earliest languages, particularly of the supersensible, has a ring of truth. When man was still more mammalian than human, the emotional-limbic system then in predominance would have produced a more lyrical language of vowels. And though consonants later developed to represent the greater precision of cortical cognition, the most sacred of words could have been expected to maintain their most traditional forms, those consisting largely of vowels.

Once the Tetragrammaton is accepted as consisting only of vowels, its pronunciation becomes obvious. For we know what vowels are conveyed through its letters. Since the Yod represents the long *ee* sound, the Hey the long *ah* sound, and the Vav the long *oo* sound, the pronunciation of the four letters that can initially be essayed is *Ee-ah-oo-ah*. But it is a fact that the *ee* and *oo* sounds do have consonantal endings, the former a Y, *eeyuh*, and the latter a W, *oowuh*. Thus a more descriptive transliteration of the Name would be *Ee-yah-oo-wah*. But if the Yod and Vav can now be understood to begin with a vowel and end with a consonant, it would seem that the same should be true for the Hey. And, indeed, if one lets out a long sigh, it can immediately be recognized that it begins with the voiced vowel sound and ends with the aspirated consonant, as still represented in the word for a sigh, *ah*. If the consonantal ending of H is now included and joined with the next vowel, the final, fully expressed form for the Name would be *Ee-yah-hu-wah*.

It is Eyahuwah, with the accents placed rhythmically on the two *ah* syllables of this four-syllable word, that may lay claim to be that most ancient pronunciation of the Name that was ritually preserved by the priesthood for delivery on Yom Kippur, a recital indeed associated with deliverance as part of the atonement service. The tradition recounted during the Avodah service of the more modern Yom Kippur liturgy describes each of the high priest's recitations of the Name as so prolonged that the community had time to respond with a long phrase during its delivery, an indication that it was musically intoned.

But during the millennium or more that general pronunciation of the Name was allowed, it is likely that its four fully expressed vowels were variously truncated to permit a quicker or easier rendition. The simplest such shortening, produced by sliding or slurring over the initial portion of the Yod and Vav vowels, would result in one of the following forms: 'Yah'wah or 'Yahuwah. Each has a striking resemblance to one of the two forms of modern pronunciation, but also a significant difference. It is clear that 'Yah'wah, which must finally have been reduced simply to Yahwah, is close to the modern version, Yahweh, but the difference would seem to favor Yahwah since there is no discernible reason why the two Heys should be differently pronounced. Similarly, 'Yahuwah, which might have been further simplified to Yahowah since the *oh* sound is easier to produce than the more contracted *oo* sound, is close to the supposedly inaccurate Jehovah, with the preference again being in favor of Yahowah and for the same reason that the two Heys should have identical pronunciations. Since the Jews were separated in various locales, the two kingdoms as well as Babylon, it seems likely that various local traditions of pronunciation would have developed. That the Name was in general use is indicated by the Third Commandment against its vain use, in curses and ill-considered oaths. But its use in sacred oaths, blessings, and prayers would have been common and continuous enough to have permitted the various forces of linguistic change to operate upon it in the two main ways already traced.

Now the first thing that would seem to be proved by the ability to derive something like Yahweh and Jehovah from an understanding of the Tetragrammaton as composed solely of vowel-letters is that this must have been the original signification of these letters. That *Y, H,* and *W,* which are the consonants identified with these letters, should also be the concluding sounds of the vowels later thought to be signified by these same letters seems too coincidental to be simply accepted as a late product of linguistic convenience. And it seems clear that they were always vowel-letters, that is, forms which, because they originally conveyed a vowel-consonant combination, could be used either in their original vowel forms or to express the truncated sound of only their final consonants.

Thus it would appear that the Hebrew language, like the Greek and the English, was originally composed of letters signifying both vowels and consonants. In addition to the three Tetragrammaton letters, which still appear in many Hebrew words as signifiers of the three main long vowels, there are also the two now-silent letters of Aleph and Ayin, which also are often signifiers of vowels in Hebrew words, the former as in Adonai and the latter as in Sh'ma. As English has five vowels out of twenty-six letters, so would it seem that Hebrew had five vowels out of twenty-two letters. But the fact that most of the vowels were not linguistically expressed led to the development of the Masoretic vowel points, which rendered the vowel-letters superfluous. The continuing appearance of these vowel signifiers in words, however, led, in turn, to the dubious theory of later grammarians that the vowel-letters were an intermediate step before the development of the Masoretic points, a late product of literary convenience involving the choice of handy weakened consonants to supply a need for vowel signifiers. But rather than representing weakened consonants, their consonantal use appears to have been the result of a weakening and final dropping of their initial vowel sounds, exactly such a result as can be seen in the popular pronunciations of the Tetragrammaton that appear to have so developed.

The second thing that such derivation seems to prove is that Jehovah is no less valid a product of normal linguistic change in popular usage than is Yahweh, and, conversely, that Yahweh cannot be claimed to be either the correct abbreviation or the original pronunciation of the Tetragrammaton. Jehovah is, of course, the correct pronunciation of the Name indicated by the Masoretic pointing of the Tetragrammaton letters in the Bible, once allowance is made for the Anglicizing of the Hebrew Y to the English J and the conversion of the Vav into a primary consonantal signifier of the V. What appears is a *sheva* under the Yod, indicating the dropping of the vowel or its reduction to *uh* with the consequence that the accent is thrown to the next syllable, and a double pointing of the Vav, the *cholam* dot above it indicating the *oh* sound with respect to the Hey before it and the *kamatz* below it indicating that the long *ah* sound follows the consonantal Vav: הֹ וֹ הֹ יְ . Reading the letters strictly as consonants, the Yod with a *sheva* would yield *yuh*, the Hey with the *cholam* an accented *ho*, and the Vav with the *kamatz* a *vah*, the whole word reading *Yehovah* or the Anglicized *Jehovah*.

But if we assume for the moment that the Masoretic scribes were not only trying to indicate the traditional pronunciation of the Tetragrammaton that had come down to them but also that they were aware of the vowel character of its letters, then the indicated pronunciation would be somewhat different. The *sheva* below the Yod could now be taken to indicate a dropping of the initial *ee* vowel and its reduction to just the consonantal form of the Y, a reduction that would throw the accent to the next vowel-letter and join it as *yah*. The second syllable would be the same *ho* but the third would begin with the consonantal ending of the previous *oh* sound, the W rather than the V, and be pronounced *wah*. The whole could thus be rendered as 'Yahowah, differing from the deduced original pronunciation only by the eliding of the first vowel and the lifting of the vowel sound signified by the Vav from the primary *oo* to the secondary *oh* sound. This form would probably still be accented on the first and third syllables since the shift of accent to the second syllable in Jehovah is the result of reading the Yod not as a vowel-letter but as a consonant, a reading that also changes the first vowel from *ah* to *eh*. Taking the radical position that the scribes were trying to indicate what they considered to be the proper pronunciation of the Tetragrammaton, one that had already suffered some change from the then forgotten priestly rendering, we have arrived at a close enough approximation of the original to suggest that this was, indeed, their intention.

But let us now consider the standard view that the Masoretic points are meant to indicate the vowels of Adonai. The word *adonai* is pointed as follows: אֲ דֹ נָ י . The *patach* under the initial Aleph indicates a short *a*, one still further shortened by the *sheva* before it that throws the accent to the second syllable. The *cholam* dot above the following Dalet indicates the *oh* sound, as previously. But the *kamatz* below the Nun does not indicate the long *ah* sound since it is followed by the Yod that converts it to a diphthong, *ah-ee*, becoming the sound of the letter *I*. Though it could be argued that the omissions of the *patach* under the Tetragrammaton Yod and of any indicator of a conversion of the *kamatz* under the Vuv to the diphthong *I* do not pose serious problems in regarding the Tetragrammaton pointing as signifying the vowels of Adonai, it is still obvious that the fit is not exact. For it would result in the pronunciation: *Uhdonah*. Not only would Adonai have to be understood as the substitute but also that the Sheva be understood to be followed by a missing *patach* and the *kamatz* to be followed by a missing Yod. Quite a lot of understanding in the absence of any real evidence of Masoretic intention! Though there is no way of resolving the question, it may be that the Jewish contention of Gentile ignorance in understanding the substitute pointing, a contention accepted by Gentile biblical scholars, was really an attempt to prevent the Christian disclosure and use of a pronunciation of the Tetragrammaton they recognized to be traditional. And it may have worked, since the substitute pronunciation of Yahweh which then developed is probably not as close as Yahowah or the Christianized Jehovah to the original form. Both involve a change of vowel sounds, but that from *oo* to *oh* in Jehovah is within the range of the letter Vuv and a move to easier articulation while that from *ah* to *eh* in Yahweh cannot be compassed by the same letter Hey and results in a harder articulation. If there is any superiority in Yahweh, it is in the vowel of its first syllable and in restoring the double accent to what probably was originally a four-syllable Name. What it is hoped the preceding discussion has shown is that both Yahweh and Jehovah, despite some inaccuracies, can be derived from the original fully expressed vowel pronunciation of the Tetragrammaton through various normal processes of linguistic change, but that neither is this original form. What we have now to see is what this original pronunciation can tell us about the nature of the deity.

Beginning from the premise that the Tetragrammaton letters were not converted to vowel signifiers but were always signifiers of the three long vowels, the original full pronunciation can be unequivocally given as EYAHUWAH. What this first indicates is an association of the deity it signifies with the heart language of the vowels, the musical source of language that Genesis tells us was there from the beginning of creation. It is through such understanding of the heart that prophetic messages may also be transmitted. But beyond such general identification with the source of language and its power both to create and to communicate, the associations of the individual vowels of the Name are also most telling.

In the next chapter, the vowels will first be identified with the Sefirot and then with the harmonics, and these correlations will indicate where the vowel sounds should be placed in both macrocosmic and microcosmic man. On this later to be established basis, we can now assert that in both the cosmic and the human man, the *ee* sound is to be placed in the head, the *ah* sound in the heart, and the *oo* sound in the abdomen and below. Thus the first three Tetragrammaton letters can be read as synthesizing or harmonizing the upper and the lower powers or expressions of the divine, what might be considered its transcendent and immanent forms, through the mediation of the middle, the divine heart. It is not surprising, therefore, that the position of the Tetragrammaton on the Tree of Life Diagram should be in the Sefirah of Tiferet, the predominant Sefirah of the divine heart. But if this were the final meaning of the Tetragrammaton, it would not require four letters.

Once the four letters are considered, the iambic accenting previously given suggests that the Name be broken up into two metrical units, *ee-ah* and *oo-ah*. In the kabbalistic cosmology of the Partzufim, these units can be related to two levels of divine coupling, that signified by the Yod and upper Hey to the Yichud of Abba and Imma and that by the Vav and lower Hey to the Yichud of Ze'ir Anpin and the Nukvah. But though the symbolism is sexual, the association of both the upper and lower couplings with the heart sound of *ah* further suggests that these are unifications of and through the heart. One can go still further and see the upper union as that of the upper mental faculties with the heart and the lower union as that of the lower instinctual faculties with the heart. Finally, we can see both dyads as defining forms of the heart, the *ee* and *oo* sounds seeming to qualify that defined by the *ah*, as adjectives do a noun. Seen in this manner, *ee-ah* could be interpreted as the upper heart and *oo-ah* as the lower heart. A concept of the "double heart" exists in the Jewish tradition with reference to the two "inclinations" to which the heart is thought to be subject, the good inclination (*yetzer ha-tov*) and the bad (*yetzer ha-ra*). But both here and in the next chapter, a different understanding of the "double heart" will be developed that rather comprehends two different levels of the heart. The full name, *ee-ah-oo-ah* or Eyahuwah, can be understood, then, as that which unifies the double heart or in which they are unified. The latter would define the nature of God as that in which the transcendent and the immanent are united in a love that permeates both, and the former would define His salvific nature in terms of the grace that can unite the double heart in man.

How such a unification of the double heart can accomplish the salvation of man can be better understood in terms of the major concept of rebirth. As previously shown, the Partzuf identified with the Sefirah Tiferet of the Tetragrammaton, Ze'ir Anpin, is understood by Luria to be twice-born, and one can say that the unification of the double heart, particularly as achieved through prayer, also accomplishes a spiritual rebirth for man, further, that neither is possible without the other, that the human and the divine are working out a joint salvation by which both will be blessed, one through which the transcendent and the immanent forms of God will be forever united by and with man in harmonious love. As seen through the vowel-letters that make up the Tetragrammaton, this personal Name of the God of Israel conveys the precise nature of the salvific power of divine love that has ever been attributed to the personal God throughout the Jewish esoteric tradition.

It should also be clear that the various correspondences that have been pointed out in this chapter between these vowel-letters and the Tetragrammaton reveal a web of associations far too complex to be the product of accident or simple convenience. These letters may be said to be signifiers of an existence understood to be both vital and divine just because they focus such a profound web of connections, one that can only fill us with awe at this hidden dimension of correspondences whose explanation is beyond the capacity of the human mind to fathom but through whose evidences we can begin to develop, in the words of Wordsworth, "a sense sublime of something far more deeply interfused."[37]

5

The Sacred Science
of Sound and
Spiritual Practice

The Vowel Sounds and the Body

This chapter derives directly from the final concern of the previous chapter with the Hebrew vowel-letters in their significant relationship to the Tetragrammaton. As we have seen, the individual Tetragrammaton letters also serve to signify the vowels in Hebrew writing, the Yod signifying the *i* (ee) sound, the Hey the *a* (ah) sound, and the Vav the *u* (oo) sound. In applying these sounds to the question of the pronunciation of the Tetragrammaton, an important implication was the suggestion that this divine Name signifies the concept of a higher "double heart," a concept thought to be reflected in the spelling of the word for heart, Lev, with two Vets in many significant biblical contexts, as in those concerning the circumcision of the heart in Deuteronomy. In this chapter we will be further exploring this concept, not in its usual understanding of the human heart as involving the good and evil inclinations, the *yetzer ha-tov* and the *yetzer ha-ra*, but rather as unifying the upper and lower hearts of the more spiritual dimensions.

The identification of the Tetragrammaton with the heart is also significant with respect to the Tree of Sefirot, since this divine Name is assigned to the Sefirah of Tiferet, and in the Adam Kadmon version of the Tree superimposed on an anthropomorphic body, Tiferet is identified with the heart. The heart is also associated with a sound in the *Sefer Yetzirah*, with the *a* sound of the mother letter Aleph. For in addition to the three different Tetragrammaton letters, there is also a fourth generally recognized vowel-letter, the Aleph: א. This letter has been associated with divinity in view of its position at the beginning of the alphabet and the fact that it can be broken up into three parts that can be equated with other letters. The diagonal line is correlated with the Vav and the two short branches emanating from it with Yods, the Gematria sum of these two Yods (10 x 2 = 20) and the Vav (6) equaling the 26 of the Tetragrammaton. In view of the threefold shape of this letter, a shape, moreover, in which a median part serves to connect and balance an associated polarity, this letter can and has been taken to characterize the threefold nature of the One, that also indicated by the three different letters of the Tetragrammaton. In fact, the Aleph can be viewed as the unified form of the divine, in contrast to the divided form suggested by the Tetragrammaton, and it has been kabbalistically identified with Ein Sof, the ultimate source, in further contrast to the Partzufim identifications of the Tetragrammaton.

Now what is even more interesting about this fourth vowel-letter is that it normally signifies the same *a* sound as the Hey, though in a different position. Where the Yod and the Vav signify two vowel sounds apiece, the *a* sound would seem to require two different vowel-letters. For unlike the Yod and the Vav, which signify their two vowel sounds in both the medial and final positions in words, the Hey is normally used to designate a final *a* and the Aleph, a medial *a*. Though the Aleph is also more identified with the short form of the *a*, the primary distinction is one of placement within a word, and we are faced with the fact that the sound associated with the upper torso location of the heart in the *Sefer Yetzirah* is identified with two separate vowel-letters, a further support for the concept of such a higher double heart in the Jewish esoteric tradition as I have here been developing.

In the *Sefer Yetzirah* the three mother letters are associated with areas of the body: the Shin with the head, the Aleph with the upper torso, and the Mem with the lower torso. Now if we can identify the Hey sound with the heart area on the basis of its sound equivalence to the bodily defined position of the Aleph, it seems reasonable to identify the remaining Tetragrammaton letters with the body positions of the other mother letters that can be associated with them, the Yod with the head position of the Shin and the Vav with the abdominal position of the Mem. In relating these remaining mother letters and Tetragrammaton vowel-letters, the linguistic indications further support and refine the associations just made, indicating that the Shin and the Mem should be placed at the extremes of the *i* and *u* vowel sounds. For when this is done, it becomes apparent that they do, in fact, complete the progression of mouth movements through the vowels. As the linear narrowing of the mouth for the *ee* sound is completed by the closing of the teeth for the *sh* sound, so the rounding of the mouth for the *oo* sound is completed by the closing of the pursed lips for the *mm* sound.

On the basis of their correlations with the body-related mother letters, the Yod can be identified with the head, the Hey with the heart, and the Vav with the abdomen, identifications consistent with those first made of their associated vowel sounds with the three most basic of primitive emotions. As seen in chapter 4, the *ee* sound of the Yod is expressive of the emotion of fear and so implies the sense of a threatened self that can be associated with mental awareness. The most relaxed *ah* sound is similarly expressive of satisfaction and so can be associated with the fulfilled heart. Finally, the *oo* sound is expressive of pain and seems localized in a contraction of the gut, an experience that can lead to the empathy conveyed through the biblical references to the "bowels of compassion."

The Hebraically derived associations of vowel sounds with bodily locations will provide the basis of the further analyses relating these sounds first to the Sefirot and then to the harmonics, correlations leading to the development of a spiritual practice involving the intoning of such vowel sounds based upon the understanding of the effectiveness of this practice in most spiritual traditions. In the previous chapter we also saw that the Hebrew prayer service emphasizes specific vowel sounds in its various parts that knowingly convey the tenor of the emotional progression through the service. But an older example of such knowing construction of the words of prayer to facilitate the purpose of which they speak can be found in the oldest of Hebrew ritual prayers, the core element of the prayer service that developed around it, the essential Sh'ma itself, and it suggests a knowledge on the part of the Hebraic priesthood of the effect of certain vowel sounds upon specific physiological areas of the body. It is the recently completed correlation of the *ah* vowel sound with the organ of the heart that can now illuminate the second verse of the Sh'ma (Deut. 6:5) specifically concerned with the very opening of the heart that the intoning of this sound is thought in many spiritual traditions to effect. And the following treatment of this verse would suggest that such understanding was also part of the knowledge of the Hebrew priesthood.

It has become traditional to give special importance to the saying of the first verse of the Sh'ma (Deut. 6:4), which begins with the word Sh'ma, and its words are often lengthened in delivery, whether said or sung to a traditional melody. But it has not been recognized that the words of verse 5 have a special formulaic quality in Hebrew, forming five rhyming lines. Verse 5 can be broken down into the following five rhyming phrases:

Ve-ah-hav-ta	And you shall love
Et A-do-nai E-lo-he-kha	The Lord your God
Be khol le-va-ve-kha	With all your heart
Uh ve-khol naf-she-kha	And with all your soul
Uh ve-khol me-o-de-kha	And with all your might

What is most interesting about these five phrases concerned with the loving of God is that they each end with the sound of *ah*, a sound that can be associated with the opening of the heart. It would thus seem that this second verse of the Sh'ma contains a power to open the heart to the divine when properly delivered and that it was for this reason its twice-daily performance was commanded. If, then, the opening of the heart to God can be aided by production of the *ah* sound in the twice-daily repetition of the second verse of the Sh'ma, then it would seem to have been knowingly constructed in this fashion for precisely this purpose. It would thus also seem best to perform this verse skillfully by resonating the "ah" frequency through the body so that it can have this desired effect on the heart, to which it is in special attunement.[1] Before turning to the fuller practice of vowel intoning to which the following analyses will lead, we should first continue the association of the vowel sounds with the Tree of Sefirot as understood to model the body.

We have seen that the three major vowel sounds appear in a significant sequence through the three major sections of the prayer service.[2] But though the vowel sounds, especially when melodically chanted, resound through the air, what is more important are their internal resonances. And here we come to an important aspect of these intoned vowels in relation to spiritual practice. For it is clear that the composers of the earliest elements of the service were knowledgeable about the whole range of spiritual science, not simply about the esoteric correspondences between form, sound, and number but also about how these can be used for spiritual development. To aid in the recovery of one such practice, we shall have to investigate the bodily associations of the Sefirot more closely.

Such a placement of Sefirot depends upon use of the anthropomorphic body traditionally ascribed to the Adam Kadmon form of the Tree of Life Diagram. In this version, the Sefirotic Tree is superimposed on the crowned body of Adam Kadmon, the original cosmic man, in such a way that Keter covers the crown, Chokhmah is placed on the right side of the head or brain, Binah on the left side of the head or brain, Chesed on the right arm, Gevurah on the left arm, Tiferet on the heart, Netzach on the right knee, Hod on the left knee, Yesod back up on the genitals, and Malkhut below the feet. In this system, the upper triad is associated with mental, the middle triad with emotional, and the lower triad with instinctual functioning, the last Sefirah generally being treated as the final receptacle of the above.

Knowledge of the correlation of certain spiritual energy centers with specific areas of the human body is not unique to the Hebraic tradition and informs all authentic forms of spiritual practice. A particularly close analogue can be found in the Chakra system of the Indian tradition of yoga. This Hindu tradition may well have had some ancient ties to the early Hebraic spiritual culture, so close are their understanding of the relationships of form to language in defining the human and cosmic body, but it has developed and practiced this science far more intensively in the intervening years and so can deepen our understanding of the spiritual physiology of the Sefirotic system.

The Chakras are understood to be the spiritual energy centers of the subtle body aligned along the line of the physical spine and acting upon the major glands of the physical body, and a clear correlation can be made between the Chakras and the Sefirot concerning their placement in the human body. Such a consideration has independent value in showing a parallel between the great Hebrew and Hindu spiritual traditions, one that will prove to be just the first of other such parallels that will emerge in this chapter, most notably the comparative study of the homonyms pronounced *ish* in both the Bible and Sanskrit texts. The correspondences between the Sefirot and Chakras we are now to consider will also lead to a new and fuller understanding of the concept of the "double heart."

The Sefirot, the Chakras, and the Double Heart

Any comparison of the Sefirot and Chakras must begin by noting the most important difference between the two systems, that of number, the Chakras usually numbering seven and the Sefirot ten. But despite this difference, the similarities between the psychological aspects of these two systems are striking and should prove mutually illuminating. The parallel between the three lowest and three highest Sefirot and Chakras is particularly strong and clear. Because that between the fourth or heart Chakra and the fourth through seventh Sefirot is more problematical, it will be reserved for a later point in this comparative study. It should also be pointed out that the numbering of the two systems is the reverse of each other, the Chakra numbers going from bottom to top and the Sefirot numbers from top to bottom.

Beginning, then, with the first Chakra, Muladhara, and the tenth Sefirah, Malkhut, we can see an identification of both with the earth and the organs associated with it, for the former the anal region and for the latter the feet. Both are also associated with the feminine, the first Chakra through its yonic symbol of an inverted triangle and the last Sefirah through the feminine associations of Malkhut as the Partzuf of the daughter-bride. Though the first Chakra is primarily concerned with issues of survival and security, it is also at this root Chakra, located at the base of the spine, that the Kundalini energy lies coiled. Symbolized in the form of snake, it is this Kundalini energy that is understood to be the source and vehicle of all spiritual evolution. As Malkhut is kabbalistically understood to be the source of the returning path of Tikkun through the Tree, we can see a further correlation between this lowest Sefirah and the first Chakra. Turning now to the second Chakra, Svadhisthana, and the ninth Sefirah, Yesod, both are associated with the genitals, particularly of the male, and may be identified with qualities of personal identity and of free choice, in that choice of sexual partners based upon subtle principles of attraction that are rooted in the individual personality and constitute its preferences. Together the two lowest Sefirot-Chakras are most representative of the Nefesh soul in its primary definition as the instinctual-intuitive body.

The third, or Manipura, Chakra is centered in the solar plexus and seems to be clearly related to the ego power-drives and quick mentality generally associated with the Sefirah Hod. But though a popular approach has been to associate the second Chakra with Freudian psychology and the third Chakra with Adlerian psychology, both, like the first Chakra, are more properly defined in terms of their higher spiritual aspects, in this case as the storehouse of higher spiritual power. A problem of comparison for the third and also fourth lowest Sefirot concerns their traditional bodily identification with the legs, particularly the knees, whereas the third Chakra is identified with the solar plexus. A possible solution is that, although the Adam Kadmon diagram shows the body in a standing position, the placement of the knee Sefirot above the genital Sefirah on the Tree rather suggests that the original model of the human Tree was based either on the prophetic position of the head between the bended knees[3] or on the lotus posture associated with Eastern meditation, in either of which position the solar plexus would be located between the knees. We will later see how the Sefirah Netzach can also be associated with this solar plexus area while distinguished from the third Chakra, but first we should continue with the easier associations of the upper three Chakras and Sefirot.

The association of the Sefirah Binah with the fifth, or Visuddha Chakra, located in the throat, of Chokhmah with the sixth, or Ajna Chakra, located at the point between the eyebrows commonly depicted as the "third eye," and of Keter with the seventh, or Sahasrara Chakra, located at the crown of the head, is remarkably close when the characteristics of these Sefirot and Chakras are compared. This is particularly true in a circumstance noted by Gershom Scholem: "Sometimes the three Sefirot, Keter, Hochmah, and Binah, are not depicted in a triangle, but in a straight line, one below the other."[4] But the comparisons hold however the Sefirot are portrayed. The fifth Chakra is the source of creative intelligence and, like the Understanding of Binah, combines the faculties of mind and heart. The sixth Chakra, like Chokhmah, is the source of mystical insight and prophetic utterance. It is completed in the transcendence experienced with the opening of the seventh or crown Chakra, the crown also being the meaning of the highest Sefirah, Keter. The higher mental-mystical Sefirot of Binah, Chokhmah, and Keter, so clearly correlated with the higher three Chakras, are commonly associated with the Neshamah soul body.

We come now to the difficult problem involving the fourth, or Anahata, Chakra, a problem arising from the difference between the number of Chakras (7) and Sefirot (10). The two possible solutions are to correlate the fourth Chakra with only one Sefirah or with all four of the remaining Sefirot. If the first alternative is chosen, the most obvious correlation would be with Tiferet, identified with the heart on the Adam Kadmon version of the Tree. But the fourth Chakra can also be correlated with Netzach. In the latter case, the four lower Chakras could be equated with the four lowest Sefirot as could the three highest Chakras with the three highest Sefirot. The three Sefirot left out of this account could then be assigned another function also related to the heart Chakra, that of mediation. And since Tiferet is also associated with the Partzuf of Ze'ir Anpin, the omitted Sefirot may well signify the influx of divine grace needed to turn the consciousness from a worldly to a heavenly orientation.

In this last we may see the way to a second and more satisfying solution to the problem of correlating Sefirot with the heart Chakra. For it is the Sefirot of Chesed, Gevurah, and Tiferet that can be identified with both the divine heart and the heart of the Neshamah soul. The sacred science of harmonics will later be found to provide a firmer basis for the correlations of soul levels to Sefirot here being developed; and on this basis Netzach can now be identified with the Ruach heart as the three remaining Sefirot can be identified with the Neshamah heart. Thus these two different soul levels of the heart, representing the levels of the perfected human personality and its higher divine personality, can be related to the Hebraic concept of the double heart. Though normally understood to refer to the two "inclinations" of the heart, the *yetzir ha-ra* and the *yetzir ha-tov*, believed to incline the heart to evil or to good, an esoteric understanding of the correlation of soul levels with Sefirot would rather suggest that on the higher spiritual planes the double heart refers to the unification of the Ruach and Neshamah hearts, both of which are good, though oriented in different directions. Such an interpretation of the double heart is in keeping with the similar analysis of the two levels of the divine heart developed in discussing the pronunciation of the Tetragrammaton at the conclusion of the last chapter, and the emergence of this same concept in such different contexts gives further support to its validity.

In the yogic tradition the fourth or heart Chakra is identified with the hexagram, the geometric figure known in the West as Solomon's Seal or the Star of David, which will be a major focus of the next chapter. And this identification also seems to support the understanding of the spiritual heart center as composed of such integrated upper and lower halves as is symbolized by the two interfacing triangles of the hexagram, upper and lower halves that can then serve the further mediating function of integrating the upper and lower three Sefirot-Chakras. Indeed, such mediation would seem to be impossible without the prior integration of the Ruach heart with its Neshamah twin whose primary definition is in terms of such harmonization of opposites, Tiferet mediating between Chesed-Mercy and Gevurah-Justice. Though these latter Sefirot are associated with the arms, as Netzach and Hod are with the legs, it is a common understanding of esoteric physiology that the arms are an outward expression of the heart, whether in Chesed love or Gevurah anger, as the legs are the primary expression of the increased mobility of the animal over that of the plant. The Taoist medical system, whose meridians for the heart are in the arms and for the solar plexus organs in the legs, is closer in these respects to the system of the Sefirotic Tree. By combining the three elements of the Neshamah heart with that of the Ruach heart, we would thus seem to arrive at the most satisfactory correlation of Sefirot to Chakras.

The concept of the double heart can also be related to the two physiological areas in which emotional experience is most localized. In addition to the heart itself, the Bible associates the bowels with compassion. This can be correlated with the Oriental understanding of this visceral area, called the *hara* by the Japanese and the lower *tan t'ien* by the Taoists, as the source of spiritual energy and also of the quality of empathy. This same solar plexus region is identified with the yogic third Chakra, and we saw that the comparable Sefirah of Hod could be associated with this area insofar as the left knee with which it was identified could, in a crossed leg or bent head position, be related to it. Now since the Sefirah of Netzach is identified with the right knee in the Adam Kadmon Tree, its locus could similarly be ascribed to the solar plexus. Identification of the leg Sefirot with the solar plexus can be further correlated with traditional Chinese physiology since its two organ pairs for this area, liver–gallbladder and spleen-stomach are associated with emotions that parallel these Sefirot, the former with such anger as can be related to the ego and the power-oriented Hod, the latter with the sympathy that can be said to characterize Netzach. This area may be recognized to have a double character, therefore, both the "guts" involved in such individual assertion as may be associated with the liver, the third Chakra, and the Sefirah Hod, and the "gut" reaction of empathic pain that may be associated with the spleen and the Sefirah Netzach. Thus both the mind and the heart of the Ruach soul, identifiable with Hod and Netzach on the Tree, can be localized in this same physiological area and be understood to reflect its double nature.

As the gut area has a double character, so the spiritual heart can be ascribed a double location, each serving a different function. Its lower visceral half serves as a receptive center and its upper heart-located half as the center of its outgoing emotions, both movements being necessary and complementary. In contrast to such visceral relating of the Ruach heart, the localization of emotion in the physiological heart is always indicative of some participation by the higher Neshamah soul. When the heart is filled with the recognizable emotion of love, it is because one's own Neshamah has, however fleetingly, perceived and responded to the Neshamah of another and desires only to unite its fullness with that of the other in a true soul mating. But whether demanding or responsive, the lower "heart" has the receptive nature of the viscera while the upper "heart" has that quality of outgoing flow that is characteristic of the activity of the physiological heart, circulation. Further support for this use of the concept of the double heart in the correlation of Sefirot with Chakras can be found in another aspect of the vowel letters, which brings us back to our initial point of departure, the question of spiritual practice.

There is a final locus in which we may be able to find further support for this new interpretation of the double heart as signifying the union of the Ruach and Neshamah hearts and this is in a kabbalistic interpretation that may be given to the Name of forty-two letters. It is generally agreed that the Name of forty-two letters is either derived from or exemplified in the ancient prayer Ana Bekhoach, ascribed to the second-century figure Nechunya ben ha-Kana and composed of seven lines containing six words apiece, each word of which begins with an initial of this divine Name. The structure of this prayer indicates that the number 42 is to be understood as the product of multiplying 6 by 7, numbers that can be most immediately correlated with the six workday and Sabbath divisions of the creation week and whose multiplication can thus be understood to signify the generative unification of the immanent and transcendent forms of the divine. But another way of understanding these numbers, suggested by the previous analysis, is in terms of their Sefirot correspondences, Tiferet, which is the defining Sefirah of the Neshamah heart, being the sixth Sefirah, and Netzach, the Sefirah that can be identified with the Ruach heart, the seventh. The structure of Ana Bekhoach, whether so initially intended or not, can be taken, then, to symbolize just such a unification of the divine and human levels of the heart as we have understood to be signified by the concept of the double heart.

Ana Bekhoach is a particularly significant prayer since it appears in the prayer book right after a description of the priestly practice of sacrifice and so can be understood to represent prayer as a substitute form of divine service. But if Ana Bekhoach can thus be considered the very archetype of prayer, and its multiplication of 6 by 7 can be taken to signify the unification of the double heart, then prayer can be understood as the process by which the upper and lower hearts come into the multiplicative or generative relationship whose product is a new integrated heart. This number of letters also appears in other important sections of the liturgy, as in the first blessing of the Amidah, and would seem to distill the understood purpose of prayer, the unification of the finite and transcendent forms of the divine identified with the numbers 6 and 7, a unification symbolized by the fruitful union or multiplication of these significant numbers. Thus it would seem that the purpose of prayer, whose word number is ideally 42, is precisely to unify the sixth and seventh Sefirot that represent the essential elements of what is here being identified with the double heart. But if the purpose of prayer is to unite the double heart, it is because such a unification can also effect the Yichud of the immanent and transcendent aspects of the divine that may be identified with these two hearts, prayer thus effecting a divine unification of and through the heart.[5]

The introductory discussion attempted to recover what may well have been a Hebraic priestly practice of vowel intoning, one involving the *ah* sound that is significantly repeated five times in the second verse of the Sh'ma concerned with the very opening of the heart this sound is thought to effect. But there is a fuller practice of intoning all the vowels that can also be developed, and to this we now turn.

Introduction to the Practice of Vowel Intoning

Once one identifies both the Hey and the Aleph with the *a* sound and the heart Sefirot, it becomes clear that the heart center can be understood as the mediator not only between high and low but between two different divisions of the upper and lower centers. For as the Hey is the intermediary between the Yod and the Vav of the Tetragrammaton, so is the Aleph the intermediary between the Shin and the Mem that, together with the Aleph, form the three mother letters of the *Sefer Yetzirah*. A similar association of letters may perhaps be seen in the important Hindu spiritual word *soham*, containing the whole of this esoteric tradition in its meaning, "you are that." This noted mantra also begins with S, concludes with M, and has an H in the middle, and there is reason to suspect that the final identifications of vowel sounds, tones, and Sefirot I will soon be outlining may have been part of an original tradition of spiritual practice common to both Hebrews and Hindus.

As earlier indicated, in relating the remaining mother letters to their Tetragrammaton counterparts, the Shin and the Mem should be placed at the extremes of the *i* and *u* vowel sounds, in this way completing the linear narrowing of the mouth for the *ee* sound by the closing of the teeth for the *sh* sound and the mouth rounding of the *oo* sound by the closing of the pursed lips for the *mm* sound. But there is the important difference that the Shin still permits the passage of breath through the teeth whereas the Mem does not, and, conversely, that a tone can still be sounded with the Mem but no longer with the Shin. The first difference seems most significant with regard to a descent through the sound frequencies and the second to an ascent through this sequence.

The passage of breath from the *sh* through the *ah* to the *mm* sounds of the three mother letters seems to recapitulate the traditional analogy to the process of glassblowing used to explain the three major soul levels. In this analogy, God is the glassblower, His breath the Neshamah soul, the glassblowing tube through which the breath passes the Ruach soul, and the final glass vessel the Nefesh soul. So, too, the *sh* sound is a pure indicator of breath, and its lack of specific tonality is suggestive of divine transcendence, whereas the closed *mm* sound gives physical form to the symbol of the vessel as the final product of the descent of the breath. Viewing this descent as not only passing through the psychic centers related to the three soul levels but also as a reenactment of the process of creation, there are important further associations with both the Hindu and Hebraic esoteric traditions. The final portion of the descent, whether taken from the median *ah* or from the lower diphthong *oh*, also signified by the Vav, and continuing through the *oo*, the primary signification of the Vav, to the *mm*, gives us the most significant sound Aum or Om, considered in the Hindu tradition to have been the original sound of creation. The analogue in the Hebraic tradition is the word *omayn* (Amen), now understood to be simply a concluding expression of pious assent. The beginning portion of the descent is also significant. The English word *she* initially formed is not far from the mark. For if the Shin is connected not with the primary signification of the Yod vowel-letter, the *ee* sound, but with the intermediate diphthong it also signifies, the *ay* sound, and completed with the final Mem, we get the Hebrew word for the Name, *shaym*, which we have seen has the esoteric significance of the feminine Shekhinah, understood to be the actual agent of the creation.

It might be further pointed out that not only is the Shekhinah primarily identified with the Sefirah Malkhut but also the divine name Adonai, interesting in the present context because Adonai has been traditionally substituted for the Tetragrammaton in biblical reading. Though the principle reason given for such corrected reading, *qere*, of the text as written, *kethibh*, is reverence, it may be that here, as elsewhere, such as the various inserted liturgical reminders of the "Glory of the Name of His

Kingdom," *Shaym Kavod Malkhuto*, the true subtext involves an esoteric substitution of feminine for masculine divine references. The explanation for this may be that the Tetragrammaton was regarded as unutterable because of its very association with the divine transcendence while the divine names connoting the feminine were regarded as utterable precisely because of their association with the divine immanence, with the descent of spirit into discrete form. Thus whether the esoteric explanation of the substitution of the pronounced Adonai for the written Tetragrammaton can be assigned to the originators of this practice or to such a later kabbalistic interpretation as may be considered responsible for the kabbalistic assignment of Adonai to the Sefirah Malkhut, such an implication is clearly present in the esoteric tradition. The significance of this association of the descent with the feminine will become clearer after consideration of the ascent through the vowels.

The ascent through these sounds is equally significant in terms of cognitive associations, particularly in its final phases. If it be taken from the *ay* sound through the *sh* in one syllable, we get the word *aysh*, meaning "fire," which is the element assigned to the Shin in the *Sefer Yetzirah*. This is significant in terms of the mental center defined by both the Shin and the upper Sefirot correlated with the vowel sounds of the Yod. For it can be taken to signify the electrical activity of the brain, and it can also be related to the spiritual light from which all was created and to which the enlightened man aspires to return. But even more significant is the word formed by combining the primary sound of the Yod vowel-letter, the *ee*, with the final *sh*, the word *ish* meaning "man." The full ascent can thus be viewed as a progression from the lowing of a cow, *moo*, to the final affirmation of fully realized humanity.

In the next chapter, a model of the Hexagram of Creation will be developed in which the point of the descending triangle is defined as the Mem and that of the ascending triangle as the Shin, the water triangle of the Mem being associated with the descent of spirit, and being a clear yonic symbol of the feminine, and the fire triangle of the Shin being associated with the ascent of man, and in its upright form also serving as a phallic symbol. In the descent of the sounds to the circular and ascent to the linear, we may now see the same distinction between the feminine and the masculine that these forms suggest.

As the descent ends with the sound of creation, *om*, so the ascent ends with the sound of that which fulfills the purpose of creation, *ish*, man. If the former can be associated with the divine mother, so can the latter be associated with the Hebraic secret doctrine of the son. For side-by-side with this developing concept, the Kabbalah also developed the concept of the divine creative mother, Imma. As with the development of Christian Mariology, the esoteric tradition within Judaism sought to develop a radical theology involving the relations of mother and son, seeing the mother as the agency of the creation and the son as the agent through which that world of nature is to be perfected, that same round of descent and ascent through the letter sounds by which the soul can become alternately immersed in the mystery of creation and of its purpose.

The six Hebrew letters that form these vocalic progressions combine the three letters of the Tetragrammaton with the three mother letters in a way that seems to be suggested by the *Sefer Yetzirah*. At the conclusion of its first chapter, in the description or instruction for the sealing of the six directions of the cosmic cube, we are told in most editions that three simple letters are to be variously placed in the three letters of the Tetragrammaton, a condition made more precise in the edition attributed to Luria by the specifying of these three simple letters as the mother letters.[6] In the *Sefer Yetzirah*, the six directions of this cube, sealed with various unifications of the mother letters with those of the Tetragrammaton, again suggestive of the union of feminine and masculine, represent the body of the cosmic man, and the creation of such a spiritual body can also be said to be the purpose of such spiritual practices as can utilize these sounds to open and energize the various psychic centers in resonance with them, practices that could have been shared by the Hebraic and Hindu traditions, as the emergence of both Hebrew and Hindu words from the progressions of vowel sounds would seem to suggest. The simplest of such practices would involve the intoning or chanting of the sound series going from *mu* to *ah* to *ish* and the reverse descent to *aum* or *om*. Such a circular pattern would emphasize the essential double cosmic motion culminating alternately in the *om* of the materialization of spirit and the *ish* through which the respiritualization of matter can accomplish the purpose of this cosmic process, the development of such purified individuality as can transmute the initial shriek of fear-tormented primitive man into the "eureka" of mentally discovered connections. This practice of descent and ascent through the vowel series has two further ramifications that should be explored in view of their extraordinary richness of implication, the first extending the vowel-Sefirot identifications to include the harmonics and the second exploring the culminating sound of the ascending series, Ish, in both the Hebrew and Hindu traditions.

Vowel Intoning, the Harmonics, and the Sefirot

Though the practice of vowel intoning may be simple to initiate, it is more difficult to perfect, and the present section will develop a still higher form of this practice with important theoretical implications. The possibility of a more skillful performance of this practice arises from a fact that will prove to be of enormous significance, the fact that when the vowel series is continuously intoned, the effect of the mouth positions that form the vowel sounds is to distinguish sequentially the various partials or harmonics that are part of the fundamental tone. It would thus seem to be one of the functions of the vowel sounds to form the geometric angles that can separate out the harmonic tone with which it is in resonance from the tones of music or speech. One can go further and say that the vowels are the expression of the pure harmonics whose precise sequence provides one of the most basic of cosmic laws. And it is through the vowels that we are now able to correlate these harmonics with the human bodily centers we previously saw to be in resonance with these vowels. More properly, it is the harmonics produced by the vowel sounds that provide the resonances able to affect these various centers. In what follows, I will attempt a correlation of vowels with the harmonic series that we will see to have great significance with respect to the Sefirot. The final theoretical implication of this correlation of Sefirot to harmonics depends, however, on the experiential evidence arising from the ability to produce harmonics by the human voice, an ability that has long been demonstrated by the devotees of various spiritual traditions.

It may have been Huston Smith who made the first recording of such harmonic chanting by Tibetan monks, among others, and thus introduced this practice to the Western world; but it is David Hykes who has perfected and extended the vocal production of harmonics into a new form of Western spiritual music. As the composer of the Harmonic Choir, which he founded and with which he performs, and as a teacher of harmonic singing to many, including myself, he has done more than anyone else to make this vocal possibility known and available for more general use in spiritual practice.

The basic technique is simply to go through the vowel sequence on a continuous fundamental tone and listen for any harmonics that may be produced. It is that attentive hearing called for in the Sh'ma that then becomes one's personal teacher for the harder work of perfecting this practice, instructing one as to the mouth positions through which one has produced a particular harmonic so that it can then be reproduced more skillfully, by this means turning the human vocal apparatus into a kind of flute. As the harmonics are produced with slight differences by different practitioners and at different pitches, I will now be speaking primarily of my own experience in the following correlation of harmonics with the vowels.

Beginning, then, with a fundamental tone at midrange and intoned to the sound of *mm*, one can produce the first overtone or second harmonic with the smallest opening of the lips for the *oo* sound, this harmonic, however, being the hardest to produce or distinguish from the fundamental tone one octave below it. Easier to produce is the third harmonic of the fifth above the octave, Sol_1, produced either with a more open *oo* or one moving toward the shortest *oh*. The fourth harmonic, or Do_3, can be produced with the still more open lips resulting in the short *a*, of *awe*, that which when followed by *u* yields the true diphthong *oh*. The fifth harmonic, Mi_1, is produced by a yet wider form of the short *a* moving toward the long *a*, of *ah*. But it is the sixth harmonic, Sol_2, which is most closely identified with the full *ah* sound. With the seventh harmonic, $Tay-_1$, the minus sign signifying that this harmonic is slightly flatter than its even-tempered counterpart, the movement from the most constricted to the most open circular mouth positions begins to change into the complementary movement toward increasing linearity, this harmonic being most easily produced by the short *e* sound of *eh*. From this point on, one has simply to form the *i* sound that will also produce the intermediate diphthong of *ay* in the process. If one can separate out the components of this diphthong, it might be possible to associate the eighth harmonic, Do_4, with the *ay*, the ninth harmonic, Re_1, with the purest *ee*, and the tenth harmonic, Mi_2, with the *yuh* that concludes the full *ee* sound, but it is really difficult to distinguish them and it seems best to associate the eighth through tenth harmonics simply with the long *i* that follows the short *e* by which I, at least, have been best able to produce the seventh harmonic.

Now what is most startling about the process of producing harmonics is that an almost impenetrable wall seems to appear after the tenth harmonic. Whereas the third through the tenth harmonics are fairly easy to produce once one has learned the basic technique, any further harmonics are produced only with the greatest difficulty or training. A novice like myself can get to the twelfth harmonic, Sol_3, though with great strain and poor sound quality, and an adept like Hykes to around the twentieth harmonic, Mi_3, all such higher harmonics being produced by the same *ee* sound with ever more intensity of breath. But the fact remains that normal human production of the harmonic series by the voice extends only through the tenth harmonic.

Given the prior associations of the vowel sounds with the Sefirot, there now seems to be a basis for the further association of the harmonic series with the Sefirot. Though the Sefirot were earlier correlated with the Chakras, the experience of producing the harmonics suggests that there is a more precise correlation between the harmonic series and the Sefirot than with the Chakras, except as these latter can be correlated with the Sefirot, this in view of the same number ten for both the primary harmonics and the Sefirot. But a stronger reason for restricting the following correlations of the harmonics just to the Sefirot is the fact that the Chakras are traditionally associated with different sounds. Listing them from the first to the seventh Chakras, these seed syllables, known as *bija*, are as follows: *lung, vang, ram, ung, hung, om, ah*. As can be seen, these sounds do not correspond to the acoustic science of harmonics as do the vowels, earlier correlated to the Sefirot on various bases drawn from Hebraic sacred science. So we will proceed with this discussion of the harmonics only in relation to the Sefirot.

The correlation of harmonics to Sefirot not only provides a spiritual practice by which to resonate the Sefirot coordinates within one's own psychic body of that cosmic structure with which they are in tune, it also provides a key to what may well be the deepest signification of the Sefirotic Tree. As we explore the theoretical ramifications of this new dimension of the Tree of Life Diagram, it would help to review both the form of the Tree, as given in figure 1.1, and table 5.1 which shows the various relationships already developed in this analysis of the harmonics first to the vowel sounds and letters, and then to the Sefirot.

The first level of signification with which we should be concerned is the correlation between the harmonic Sefirot and the bodily centers, and it is best to examine this in terms of the division of the octaves. Such a division will also be seen to provide both a needed sacred scientific basis for the correlation of soul levels to Sefirot earlier developed and a further illumination of the distinctive natures of these soul levels.[7] As can be seen in table 5.1, the first octave, from Do_1 to Do_2, corresponds to the Sefirot of Malkhut and Yesod. Now if there is any validity in identifying soul levels with the harmonic octaves, then the lowest octave would determine the constituents and nature of the lowest Nefesh level of the soul. These constituents would be the same Malkhut and Yesod identified with the Nefesh soul in earlier analyses but now assigned on a firmer basis, and its nature would be that of the simple and undivided unison represented by this first octave, one which suggests that this primitive animal soul is meant to function in unison with the collective whole of Nature. The difficulty in distinguishing the second harmonic may, in fact, signify the essentially autonomous nature of this sensual soul, even the sexual function most characteristic of its associated Sefirah Yesod being largely beyond the control of the will.

HARMONIC	VOWEL	SEFIRAH
1—Do_1	(mm)	Malkhut
2—Do_2	oo (Vuv)	Yesod
3—Sol_1	oo-o (Vuv)	Hod
4—Do_3	awe (Hey)	Netzach
5—Mi_1	awe-ah (Hey-Aleph)	Tiferet
6—Sol_2	ah (Aleph)	Gevurah
7—$Tay-_1$	ah-eh (Aleph)	Chesed
8—Do_4	ay-ee (Yod)	Binah
9—Re_1	ee (Yod)	Chokhmah
10—Mi_2	ee-yuh (Yod)	Keter
10+	(sh)	

TABLE 5.1. HARMONIC CORRESPONDENCES

As the first octave may be identified with the Nefesh soul, so may the second octave be identified with the Ruach soul. What distinguishes the second harmonic octave is its division by the fifth, the third and fourth harmonics no longer producing a unison but with the difference that the fourth is still in unison with the harmonics of the first octave whereas the third, Sol_1, represents a radical departure from it. This is consistent with prior analysis of the Sefirot of Hod and Netzach corresponding to this second octave and so the proper constituents of the Ruach soul on this analytic basis, Hod having been identified with the Ruach mind and its individual will whereas Netzach is identified with the selfless Ruach heart. But though the second octave is divided, it is by a tone that produces what are called "perfect" intervals, that from the second to the third harmonic defining the "perfect fifth" and that from the third to the fourth harmonic the "perfect fourth." They are called "perfect" because these intervals do not have the emotional distinction of major and minor, producing rather an open quality, and such a quality would seem appropriate in characterizing the Ruach soul, with its openness to the "wind" of "spirit," the two meanings of the word *ruach.*

Because the harmonics of the octave resonances of the fundamental tone have dual natures, completing one octave and beginning another, the Sefirot with which they are identified should also be able to demonstrate this capacity. In the case of the second harmonic, Do_2, whose Sefirah is Yesod, this would seem to be true since Yesod is often kabbalistically linked with Hod and Netzach in defining the three centers of the human as opposed to the divine soul, its instinctual, mental, and emotional centers, the upper six Sefirot being identified in such a modeling with the divine. But it is even more true of the Sefirah Netzach identified with the fourth harmonic, Do_3, which, though it may like Hod be located in the abdomen, also forms a part of what we have here been designating as the double heart, that emotional center defining the third octave for which its harmonic is the foundation.

As with the previous two octaves, entrance to the third octave again marks the beginning of a new soul level, that of the Neshamah soul. But here the correlation of harmonic octaves with soul levels begins to break down, for the beginning of the fourth octave will not mark the start of a new soul level but rather of a higher level of this same Neshamah soul. Yet it is still remarkable that the differences we are now to observe between the third and fourth harmonic octaves should so precisely discriminate between those Sefirot identified with the heart and those identified with the mind of Adam Kadmon, these six Sefirot also generally identified with the divine Neshamah soul.

But to return to the transitional role of Do_3 identified with the Sefirah Netzach, and its relationship to the Sefirot of the third octave, what is most significant about the four harmonics identified with the double heart is that they do, in fact, harmonize, forming the notes of the harmonic minor seventh chord: Do, Mi, Sol, Tay–. That it is the nature of the heart to harmonize, particularly in its perfected double form, seems almost too obvious, but it is surely remarkable that this characteristic of the heart center should be so borne out by its associated harmonics. It is the fifth harmonic, Mi_1, that makes this harmony possible, transforming the perfect fifth interval between the fourth and sixth harmonics, Do_3 and Sol_2, into the major chord. And this is also extremely fitting for its associated Sefirah of Tiferet, whose primary characteristic is that of harmonizing, most particularly the polarity of Chesed and Gevurah but also that of the upper and lower Sefirot. It may well be considered the harmonic center of the Tree.

The seventh harmonic, that slightly flatter tone than the even-tempered minor seventh, also plays a transitional role and one perhaps even greater than that of the octaves. Its first effect is to convert the broken major chord of Do-Mi-Sol into the minor seventh chord, an important qualitative change from major into minor. But this minor seventh chord has a further transitional function, its suspended quality demanding resolution through a modulation into a new key, the key of the subdominant. The minor seventh is a modulating tone, and what it is here modulating is the transition from the harmonically associated Sefirot of the heart to those of the mind. As it completes the harmonic chord so does it initiate the quality that characterizes the fourth octave, the linear progression of tones to form scales that can make possible the production of melody. And despite the fact that the harmonics from the eighth to the sixteenth make a somewhat more recognizable scale, though one of nine rather than eight tones, the scale formed from the seventh to the fourteenth harmonics, though somewhat stranger, is lovely and has exactly eight tones.[8] The four tones of this scale appearing on the Tree take us from the augmented or septimal second between Tay_{-1} and Do_4, to the major second between Do_4 and Re_1, and finally to the minor second between Re_1 and Mi_2.

The lyric progression of tones in the fourth octave is most appropriate to the Sefirot of the higher mind. For unlike the harmonizing Sefirot of the double heart, those of the Neshamah mind can play their own melody. Where the harmonics of the Ruach and Neshamah hearts define a chord in which the whole may be said to take precedence over the parts, those of the Neshamah mind define a linear progression that must be kept separate from each other to avoid dissonance. This distinction between the harmonics of the third and fourth octaves again seems remarkable when applied to their associated Sefirot, for it precisely defines the difference between the functioning of the heart and mind that these Sefirot also signify.

If correlating Sefirot and harmonics has proved illuminating with regard to the soul levels with which they can be identified, it is even more so with respect to their Partzufim identifications. Beginning with the fundamental tone, and observing the Sefirot positions of the four Dos on the Tree, it is apparent that both the source tone and its three higher octaves have a primary correspondence with the divine feminine. Do_1 and Do_4, the first and eighth harmonics, are identified with the two feminine Sefirot on the Tree, Malkhut and Binah, respectively. And even Do_2 and Do_3 can be related to the feminine, at least in the sexual stereotypes that inform all mythology. Do_3, Netzach, represents the selfless Ruach heart, a quality of the heart that is generally considered feminine, and though Do_2, Yesod, would seem to be particularly associated with the masculine, signifying as it does primarily the male sex organ, the nature of sexual responsiveness involves a sensitivity that may also be considered a feminine characteristic, and it is certainly directed toward the female. The association of the feminine Sefirot, Malkhut and Binah, with precisely the harmonics of Do seems hardly to have been an accident and again suggests that Kabbalists were familiar with the law of harmonics and understood the divine feminine to be the agent and source of creation. Similarly precise are the placement of the principal male Partzufim on the Tree with respect to the order of the harmonics, for the Sefirot representing the two such principal Partzufim, Ze'ir Anpin and Arikh Anpin, are also both represented by the same tone, Tiferet by Mi_1 and Keter by Mi_2. The highest position on the Tree given to the Mi tone also suggests an association of the divine masculine with transcendence, as the lowest position of the Do is suggestive of the divine feminine as immanent in the creation. These correspondences were enough to support the contention that the Sefirot, in general, and their Partzufim identifications, in particular, were knowingly arranged in accordance with the harmonic series.

But there is another tone whose positioning on the Tree also appears to be significant, that of Sol. It seems appropriate to identify this with man, that Ish whose further identification with the secret doctrine of the son we shall see to emerge naturally from the very progression of harmonics with which we are here concerned. This identification of man with the Sol tone also follows from the correlation of this tone with man in the harmonic analysis of the Genesis creation account appearing in the next chapter. Thus there is a curious association that can be made between the Sol tone and man that seems expressive of the same tension between man and creation as appears musically between the tonic and dominant tones of the scale, a tension that can be attributed to the very free will of man that has been taken to demonstrate his creation in the divine image. Furthermore, if Do can be identified with the divine mother, then that which first emerges from the creative matrix as something other than it, Sol, can be called the son. But what comes between Do and Sol in musical terms is Mi, the tone of the transcendent father.

Now what is most startling about this musical logic is that it is totally consistent with the implications of the numerical logic studied in the previous chapter. There the geometric progression of 13:26::26:52 was shown to have significant Gematria implications. Thirteen was shown to have a Gematria meaning whose cognate is the Greek earth goddess Gaia; 26 is, of course, the numerical equivalent of the Tetragrammaton; and the Gematria of 52 is Ben, meaning son. So this numerical proportion could be said to define a progression from mother earth to realized man, the "son of the world to come," mediated by the transcendent father, the number of the Tetragrammaton being the geometric mean between these two extremes. It is most remarkable that the masculine symbols of the divine, the Tetragrammaton and the Partzufim of Ze'ir Anpin and Arikh Anpin, should emerge in the same mediating role from the evidence of both number and sound, the Gematria of the Tetragrammaton, 26, being the geometric mean between the extremes of divine mother, 13, and human son, 52, and the tone of the main male Partzufim, Mi, being the harmonizing intermediary between the tones of this same mother, Do, and son, Sol.

In terms of this mediating function, it matters little whether or not the feminine connotation of the originating term in both cases implies that the transcendent father is also a product of this cosmic womb and develops through interaction with the son, or even that this is just a map of the Tikkun defining how the development of divine personality requires an interaction between earthly man and a transcendent spirit. For the indication from both the laws of number and of sound, as these interact both with each other and with geometry—a geometric proportion deriving from the process of expanding squares, in the first case, and the Tree of Sefirot, in the second—is that it is the function of the transcendent form of the divine to mediate the passage of man from his immersion in nature, in the divine immanence, to his final supernatural state. In terms of harmonics, this final state may well be identified with Sol_3, the twelfth harmonic to which the moderately trained human voice can with great difficulty break through and which stands above even the Mi_2 of Keter. But through a second harmonic "wall" arises after the twelfth harmonic that may lead the novice to believe that the "son of the world to come" represents the pinnacle of cosmic achievement, the adept shows that it is possible to progress still further, to the twentieth harmonic, Mi_3, which discloses the still overriding presence of the divine transcendence.

What these laws also show is that the divine transcendence is disclosed to man at a particular point in his own evolution. If man's cosmic position on the Tree is with the Sefirot identified with the tone of Sol, then the harmonic series can tell us much about his spiritual condition. Carrying this identification of the Sol tone with man into the harmonically redefined Tree, we see that its associated Sefirot are Hod and Gevurah, those corresponding to the third harmonic, Sol_1, and the sixth, Sol_2. Again it seems appropriate to identify the emergence of true man with Hod, since this is the first Sefirah above those of the Nefesh animal soul and represents that which most distinguishes man from the animals, his mind, this being the Sefirah of the Ruach mind, the level at which it would appear that man was intended to function. But the identification of the more developed form of Neshamah man with Gevurah is surprising, especially since it is its sixth harmonic that is most clearly associated with the most relaxed of vowel positions, that of *ah*.

If this identification can be accepted, it gives support to the kabbalistic tradition deriving from the *Temunah* that the *shemitah*, or era, of our universe is that of Gevurah, this fact perhaps explaining why man should feel most relaxed in this most constricted of Sefirot. If, then, both undeveloped and developed man can be placed on the left, constricted side of this cosmic map, and his most relaxed breathing takes place in Gevurah, this would explain why it is so difficult for man to expand his consciousness, to leave the psychic enclosure in which he feels safe for the transforming power of Chesed. But the harmonic series also provides the clue to his liberation. At his first appearance, Sol_1-Hod, he is totally enclosed in the natural, able to apprehend the divinity within it only at second hand. Surrounded by Do_2-Yesod and Do_3-Netzach, he is equally removed from the lower divine feminine at Do_1-Malkhut and its higher manifestation at Do_4-Binah. But he can encounter the divine immanence in a veiled form through the sexual ecstasy afforded by Yesod and the experience of human community afforded by Netzach. His primary Hod energies, however, are expended in mastering nature through mental understanding of its laws. For true spiritual growth to occur, the transcendent must intervene between man and his absorption with nature, between Do_3 and Sol_2, between Netzach and Gevurah.

The availability of grace at precisely the point at which it first becomes operative is most significant. For Mi_1-Tiferet, the harmonizing harmonic and Sefirah appearing at the heart center, is, indeed, the Sefirah that most characterizes the heart. What this tells us is that the mediating role of transcendental grace occurs at the heart level, that the heart is where we first encounter the transcendent when it has been opened to such an experience by the intervention of divine grace. But the form of the divine transcendence that the heart encounters is also significant. Since Tiferet is identified with the lower Face of God, Ze'ir Anpin, and this has been further identified with the God of Israel, the suggestion is that what the heart experiences is the personal God, the God of Abraham, the God of Isaac, and the God of Jacob, identified with the Sefirot of Chesed, Gevurah, and Tiferet, respectively. This seems right, that the only God the heart can know and love, its natural response, must be personal. So, also, the form of transcendence manifested by the upper Face, Arikh Anpin, the Partzuf of Mi_2-Keter, would appropriately be that which the head can apprehend, this being the position of the harmonics and Sefirot identified with the brain, the abstract God of philosophy who is beyond all personal attributes.

In concluding this discussion of the harmonics, it is well to consider what they can teach us about the opening of these higher centers. If it is true that the psychic centers resonate to the frequencies of specific harmonics and that production of such harmonics can serve to activate and purify these centers, making them into more crystalline-like receivers of subtle vibrations, then that which enables us to produce such spiritually enhancing harmonics, the vowels, is of central importance. And vowel production is a result of the use of language. In its most normal form, then, it is the use of language, that which most characterizes human society, that begins the development of the higher centers of the heart and mind. It is surely significant that the harmonics easiest to produce, those from four through ten, should be the ones specifically related to those higher centers needing such development. While it is obvious that the social activity of speech would cause a necessary development of feeling and thought, what is not obvious but surprising is that the form of speech that human beings have evolved is one that can also have a more subtle effect on the physical organs productive of such emotion and cognition, sensitizing them to more refined responses through harmonic resonance.

But the vowels produced through ordinary speech, even when separated from the consonants and held, do not have the same resonating power as when sung to a musical tone. Whatever harmonics may be produced through speech, and they certainly are so produced and do have some effect upon the body, are slight and, for the most part, inaudible compared to the intoning of vowels. It is for this reason that all religious traditions have taught the practice of chanting, the melodic performance of a liturgy. For meaningful words charge melodic sound with greater power of penetration, and melodic sound provides the vehicle by which the harmonics shaped by the linguistic vowels can be distinguished and have their most powerful effect in enhancing spiritual development. Still more potent is that form of chanting in which full breaths are used and the tones carrying the vowels are held for longer durations. We have already seen how the second verse of the Sh'ma can be so performed, and I will suggest some further meditative use of what can be considered kabbalistic mantras in chapter 7, but at this point I will just make some final comments on the practice of producing the harmonic series in ascending and descending order from a single fundamental tone.

In the earlier discussion we saw that the vowel series, when begun and ended with those mother letters Mem and Shin that do complete the mouth positions from the circular to the linear, forms sounds that have been accepted as spiritually significant words in both the Hindu and Hebrew traditions. And it is well in producing the harmonic series to emphasize the significance of these verbal sounds. Even if one cannot produce the actual harmonics from a fundamental tone, a practice of singing the tones of at least the fourth through tenth harmonics, though at a convenient pitch, would still establish an attunement to the resonant frequencies of the higher heart and mind centers. These tones— Do, Mi, Sol, Tay, Do, Re, Mi—are well within the normal vocal range and could also be sung with the appropriate vowels that, when bounded by *mm* or *sh*, can produce significant words. If one prefers to remain exclusively within Hebraic verbal connotations, and this whether the harmonic pitches are produced from a single fundamental tone or sung, the ascending series would conclude with Ish, Man, and the descending series with Shaym, the Name. Having correlated harmonics with Sefirot, we can now better appreciate how such a correlation can support the traditional identification of the Name with the divine feminine, for it is the word *shaym*, also often pronounced "shem," which is precisely spelled out by the harmonics of the feminine Sefirot. Beginning with that Shin that is beyond all sexual differentiation, this word can be spelled out by emphasizing the harmonic-producing vowels of just the eighth and first Sefirot in descending order, the *ay* which can be associated with Imma-Binah and the *mm* of the Shekhinah-Malkhut.

If done as a stretching exercise, a practice that can effect an immediate energizing of the nervous system, it would be symbolically appropriate to conclude the ascent on tiptoes and with spread out fingers and concealed thumbs, a hand position that would symbolize the form of the spiritual four-branched Shin (such as appears on the box of the phylactery meant to be placed on the forehead directly above the "third eye"), the tiptoe and outstretched hand position further suggesting a reaching out for connection with the divine transcendence, the divine father. The descending bend or bow could also conclude by touching not the toes but the ground before them, thus symbolically reestablishing one's connection with the divine mother immanent in the earth. Practiced as a circular pattern, one would thus rise with man, Ish, to the unutterable transcendence signified by Mi_2-Keter, the rest being the tonal silence of the Shin, and descend either in the presence of the Name that can be uttered, Shaym, or to a reabsorption in the original sound of creation, Om, this new linguistic power enabling one to reencounter the source of one's being with growing understanding.

With this final return to the practice with which the past two sections have been concerned, the intoning of the descending and ascending vowel sequences whose primary verbal extremes are the Sanskrit *om*, its Hebrew cognate being *omayn*, and the Hebrew *ish*, we are finally in a position to address the question of whether *ish* also has a Sanskrit cognate. A positive answer would allow this practice to be integrated into either Jewish or yogic spiritual disciplines and would suggest a deeper historical association between the Hebraic and Hindu spiritual traditions. In the concluding section this question will be answered through a comparative study of biblical and Sanskrit texts that will provide new insight into the meaning and promise of man in both spiritual traditions.

Ish in Hebrew and Sanskrit

Once the question is raised as to whether the Hebrew word *ish*, normally translated as "man," has a Sanskrit cognate, a possibility that arises only because of its exact verbal opposition to the sound which Sanskrit recognizes as that of creation, Om, answers emerge that are illuminating for both the Hebrew and Hindu traditions. Not only does Sanskrit prove to have a word of identical pronunciation, one normally transliterated as *īśa* (the accented *s* being pronounced *sh* and the final *a* being silent) but it is a word of great theological significance. Generally translated as Lord, the meaning also of the divine name Adonai substituted in reading for the Tetragrammaton, its major signification is that of the divine with qualities, the divine person or personal god, as opposed to the qualityless Brahman.

The word first appears or surfaces in the Upanishads, particularly in the Īśa Upanishad dated as early as the eighth century B.C.E:

1. By the Lord (Īśa) enveloped must this all be—
Whatever moving thing there is in the moving world.
5. . . . It is within all this,
And it is outside of all this.
16. . . . What is thy fairest form—that of thee I see.
He who is yonder, yonder Person—I myself am he![9]

In the Sanskrit word *īśa* there can be seen to be a triple identification of the divine as transcendent, immanent, and also as that divine Person in whom the mystic can recognize his higher and truest self.

It is *ish* or *ishvara* that is the term for the divine predominating in the later devotional cults dedicated to Shiva and Vishnu. It appears importantly in the Bhagavad-Gita, probably written in the third century B.C.E., as the term for both the transcendent Vishnu and his human avatar Krishna. Vishnu represents the cosmic form of Krishna that he reveals to his devotee Arjuna in the central eleventh chapter:

7. Behold today the entire world of the moving and unmoving,
Standing in unity here in my body . . .
24. Having seen you touching the sky . . .
I find no firmness or peace, O Viṣṇu.
37. Boundless Lord of Gods, Abode of the World,
You are the imperishable which is beyond existence and non-existence
And that which is beyond both.
38. You are the first of gods, primal *puruṣa;*
You are the supreme treasure-house of all this.
You are the knower and what is to be known,
And the supreme goal, O Infinite Form!
44. Therefore having made obeisance before you and prostrated my body,
I seek your grace, O Lord;
Please bear with me, as father with son, friend with friend, lover with beloved.
45. I am delighted, having seen what was not previously seen,
But my mind trembles with fear.
Show me that other (human) form of yours, O Lord;
Be gracious, Refuge of the World.
50. The great one, having become again the gracious form,
Comforted him in his fear.

The Blessed One said:
54. . . . by single-minded devotion *(bhaktya)*, O Arjuna, I can, in
that form, be known and be seen in essence, And be entered into,
O Foe-Destroyer.[10]

The Lord of love and grace, who appears in both incarnate and cosmic
form, is also that which the devotee can become. From the Upanishads
through the Gita to the present day, the great Hindu devotional cults
have addressed their deity as Īśa,[11] pronounced "ish."

But though most Hindus are less aware of it, the Sanskrit Īśa can be
applied not only to the divine but also to humans, and not just those
humans who have recognized their union with the divine. A Sanskrit
dictionary gives the following six definitions of *īśa*:

1) Owning, possessing, sharing, master or lord of;
2) One who is completely master of anything;
3) Capable of (genitive);
4) Powerful, supreme;
5) A husband;
6) A title of Viṣṇu and Śiva.[12]

Whether human or divine, *īśa* refers to the male in his role as lord or
master, even of a wife, in human terms to man at a higher level of power.
Even less well known is the feminine form of this word, pronounced
"ishah" as in Hebrew, which has the following two major categories of
meaning:

1) Supremacy, greatness;
2) Name of the Goddess Durga, a woman having
   supremacy, a rich lady.[13]

But though the word *īśa* and its feminine form *īśah* have both human and divine referents, the Hindu tradition has emphasized the divine
meanings.

The opposite seems to have been the case with the Hebrew word *ish*,
which is universally translated simply as "man" though it can be seen to
have a wider cluster of meanings with significant similarities to those of
its Sanskrit cognate. Like the latter, the Hebrew word *ish* has traditionally been recognized to refer to man in his higher development, his lower
form being signified by the word Adam when the two terms appear in the
same context, as in the much commented upon reference in Psalm 49:3
to *"gan benai Adam gan benai ish,"* translated in the King James Version

simply as "both low and high." Since the complex meanings of Ish have not previously been studied and together provide a unique access to the heart of biblical religious understanding, it would be useful to attempt such a study here. The method will involve a tabulation of the categories of meaning that emerge from consideration of all the uses of Ish in one book of the Bible, Genesis, to which some other major usages will be added.[14] From this analysis, four major meanings of Ish will emerge.

In its first biblical uses, Ish defines man in his relationship to woman. The formerly androgynous Adam redefines himself in terms of the now feminine side of himself that had been separated out from his former wholeness, when he says: "she shall be called Woman [ishah] because she was taken out of Man [ish]" (Gen. 2:23). As Ish is spelled Aleph-Yod-Shin and Ishah is Aleph-Shin-Hey, and the Aleph and Shin in both words form the word for fire, Aesh, while the remaining letters together spell the divine name Yah, the famous midrashic interpretation of the relations of the sexes is that the divine should be part of the sexual act and that when it is removed only fire remains. This interpretation is supported by the next verse: "Therefore shall a man [ish] leave his father and his mother, and shall cleave [davak] unto his wife [ishtoe]: and they shall be one flesh" (Gen. 2:24). The purpose of the distinction of the sexes is that they should be able to achieve a higher reunification than that which was lost, one which by also including the divine Yichud of the masculine Yod (later associated with the Partzuf of Abba) with the feminine Hey (associated as well with the Partzuf of Imma) can lift the union of man and woman to the state of Devekut, communion with the divine. Such sexual union partakes of the divine in yet another sense, that it is generative, as can be seen in a later use of Ish: "And Adam knew Eve his wife [ishtoe]; and she conceived, and bare Cain, and said, I have gotten a man [ish] from the Lord [et-YHVH]" (Gen. 4:1).

J. H. Hertz notes that there are two conflicting interpretations of Eve's words: "The traditional interpretation makes 'a man' refer to Cain; and the words an expression of thanksgiving for her child. Others refer 'man' to husband (cf. XXIX, 32)."[15] In the first interpretation, Adam and Eve could be related to their divine counterparts, Abba and Imma, and the *ish et-YHVH* would refer to the generation of that which, like the label here affixed to it, represents the higher development of man, the divine son. That it can be looked upon as a label is suggested by the hyphen between the form word Aleph-Tav, the first and last letters of the Hebrew alphabet that are sometimes taken to symbolize the beginning and end or all-inclusiveness of something, as well as the

Tetragrammaton. It appears in this untranslatable form in the first sentence of Genesis before the word for heaven and that for earth. So understood, Eve's words can be taken to mean: "I have gotten or begotten a human form of the all-inclusive divinity." However meaningful Eve's words may be when applied to her son, they seem even more apt when applied to her mate. As the title Ish was only applied to Adam in the context of their projected sexual union, it would seem most fitting that it be used to celebrate Adam's new stature upon its generative consummation. Translated into the vernacular, Eve could be saying that she has made a man of him. But "man" here should be understood to represent the human form of the divine insofar as the human power of generation reenacts and extends the divine power of creation.

In his sexual relationship with woman, then, man is first lifted above his earthly origin to partake with her in a higher unity. As in the Sanskrit, the word is also taken to mean husband, and is so translated in Gen. 3:6, 16; 16:3; 20:7; 29:32, 34; 30:15, 20. It is also used in that derived sense preserved in the English translation of Ish as "husbandman" in Gen. 9:20. But unlike the power implications of this meaning in the Sanskrit, in the Hebrew the use of Ish and Ishah to signify husband and wife does not imply a hierarchical power relationship but rather one informed by sexual mating. Indeed, the terms Ish and Ishah are even applied to mated animals in Gen. 7:2. And it is man as actual or potential sexual mate that is signified by Ish in these further passages: Gen. 19:8, 31; 24:16; 26:10; 29:19; 34:14; 38:25.

The second major meaning of Ish can be viewed as an extension of the first, not man in relationship with woman but in relationship with one or more others. It appears often in the phrase translated in Gen. 11:3 as "one to another" and is otherwise exemplified in Gen. 11:7; 13:11; 26:31; 31:49; 37:19; 42:28. It is also used to signify one of a group or the simple plural "men" in the following: Gen. 32:7; 33:1; 34:20, 25; 39:11, 14; 40:5; 41:44; 42:25, 35; 44:11, 13; 45:1, 22; 47:20; 49:6, 28. It is even applied to a thing in relationship to others in Gen. 15:10. All such references seem to derive from the first such usage in Gen. 9:5, which refers to "every man's brother" and seems to imply a concept of the brotherhood of man. In this second meaning, then, Ish refers to that higher development of man reflected in his capacity to form larger social bonds.

In the first two meanings of Ish, man is lifted above his birthright condition by the simple process of forming larger sexual or social bonds, of coming by these means into a higher unity that seems to partake of the divine. We have already seen how the sexual union of Adam and Eve could be interpreted in this light, and such an understanding of society will appear in the concept of Israel as a holy nation. But with the third meaning of Ish, we come at last to the higher development of individual men. Though this can be understood in the power sense that pervades its Sanskrit counterpart—particularly in Gen. 23:6; 26:13; 30:43; 39:2, which refer to the prosperous man or the ruler—this is not its primary meaning. At its lowest level, it refers to anyone who has distinguished himself sufficiently for us to take notice of him, as in "a certain Adullamite," Canaanite, or Egyptian (Gen. 38:1, 2; 39:14). At the next higher level are the individuals called Ish without additional qualifying adjectives. The first is Lot in his role as protector of the angels (Gen. 19:9). Next is the reference to Isaac in Gen. 24:65, though this seems to be identified with his position of "master" in the same verse. Essau, in contrast to Jacob, is also called Ish without further specification of its meaning in Gen. 25:27.We come next to the unnamed man who helped Joseph in Gen. 37:15, 17, apparently a sufficient reason to lift him to the status of Ish, as is the simple fact of brotherhood to Joseph in Gen. 44:17 or stewardship to him in Gen. 43:17, 19, the latter also an example of power status.

The next higher level may perhaps be first associated with those who have the capacity for language (Gen. 10:5) and for counting (Gen. 13:16). But it is best represented by those of higher moral quality, specifically Noah and Jacob. Noah is called "a just man and perfect" (Gen. 6:9), *ish tzaddik tamim*. So too is Jacob called an *ish tam* (Gen. 25:27). Most important in determining the significance of this higher level of Ish is the meaning of *tam* or *tamim*, translated in the case of Noah as "perfect" but "perfect" understood in the sense of wholeness. This meaning is also suggested in Gen. 42:11, 13, where Jacob is called an Ish-echod, which seems to represent him as some form of unified man. If, then, an *ish tam* can be interpreted as a whole man, then it would seem to harken back to that first definition of an Ish as someone whose feminine side had been taken out of him and who needed to recover his original wholeness through becoming one flesh with his now separated Ishah. Where the simple Ish can only recover his sense of original wholeness through his participation in larger collective wholes of a sexual or social nature, the *ish tam* would seem to be one who has reintegrated the feminine, more intuitive side of his nature into a psyche of new wholeness. Indeed, Hertz translates *tamim* in Gen. 6:9 as "whole-hearted."[16] He has recovered wholeness through his higher spiritual development; and with this new wholeness of being, he can now enter into the still higher unity of his relationship with God: "and Noah walked with God" (Gen. 6:9).

One should probably not go higher than this example of perfected individuality and can assume that the highest level now to be considered is contained implicitly within it. But there are two characters to whom the term Ish is applied an extraordinary number of times, and they do seem to represent a level of spiritual mastery beyond the communion experience of Noah, that which can direct the highest of spiritual energies in accordance with its will. The first of these is Eliezer, so referred to in Gen. 24:21, 22, 24, 26, 29, 30, 32, 58, and 61. Sent by his master Abraham to find a suitable wife for his son Isaac, Eliezer prays for success in carrying out his mission and then sets up a scenario through which God can give him a sign as to the right choice, one that is enacted exactly as previously scripted and that is taken as a proof of divine cooperation and support. It also seems to justify Abraham's earlier assurance to Eliezer, which he repeats to Laban: "The Lord, before whom I walk, will send his angel with thee, and prosper thy way" (Gen. 24:40).

But it is Joseph who, in Genesis, represents the highest definition of an Ish, the term being applied to him a record thirteen times: Gen. 41:2, 33, 38; 42:30, 33; 43:3, 5, 6, 7, 11, 13; 44:15, 26. Representing by the end the height of both social and spiritual power, he is one whose mastery of prophetic dream interpretation leads to his identification as "a man in whom the Spirit of God is" (Gen. 41:38). His spiritual mastery is further revealed when he states as obvious that "such a man as I can certainly divine" (Gen. 44:15). Joseph, like Eliezer, is one who knows how to use spiritual energies to good effect, but his exemplification of the highest human level of Ish goes beyond such use to reveal the presence of the divine spirit within. In this culminating form of the third level of meaning of the word Ish, man is conceived of as not only walking with God but containing Him.

Though Laban appears to distinguish between the categories of Ish and God when, in making his covenant with Jacob, he says: "no man is with us; see, God is witness betwixt me and thee" (Gen. 31:50), this distinction is blurred not only in the case of Joseph but most radically in the use of the term Ish to define angels. This can be seen when Jacob wrestles with the angel: "And Jacob was left alone; and there wrestled a man [ish] with him until the breaking of the day" (Gen. 32:24). Jacob recognizes the divine nature of this Ish when he says: "I have seen God face to face, and my life is preserved" (Gen. 32:30). So also are the three angels who appear to Abraham called by the plural of ish, anashim: "And the Lord appeared unto him in the plains of Mamre . . . And he lifted up his eyes and looked, and, lo, three men stood by him" (18:1-2). Of later references to angels as Ish, only one need be noted here, that in Judges 13:6 in which the angel who announces the coming birth of Samson is called an Ish Elohim. As with its Sanskrit cognate, then, Ish is a term that can be applied to the divine, most significantly to a similar definition of the deity in terms of its manifestation not simply in terms of form but most specifically of the human form. When God interacts with man in the human forms of the angels, He is called Ish, the human form of the divine being perfectly expressed in the term Ish Elohim.

Having considered every reference to Ish in Genesis, it seems clear that this word comprehends a complex understanding of that level of consciousness in which the human and divine can meet. As man rises through levels of sexual, social, and psychological wholeness to the point where he can first commune with God and finally internalize the divine spirit, so does God descend in the angelic human form to interact with man at that highest level of his development in which he truly becomes the image of God. Though spelled out more clearly in the Īśa Upanishad and the Bhagavad-Gita than in Genesis, the remarkable similarities that have been demonstrated by this verbal exploration would seem to argue for some very early cross-cultural interaction between the Hebrews and Hindus, possibly between the Abrahamic core of the Hebrew tradition and the Aryan invaders as they passed through Babylonia on their way to India. But whether or not this was so, the root meaning of Ish followed different courses of development in these two traditions. As the Hindus emphasized the divine side of the human-divine nexus comprehended by this term, so did the Hebrews emphasize the human side, and as the Hindus emphasized its lordly, power aspect, so did the Hebrews emphasize its association with wholeness. Despite these differences, however, both language traditions employed the verbal sound of highest frequency, *ish,* to convey that reciprocal and interactive personalization of the divine and divinization of the human whose ultimate point of unification would seem to represent the purpose of creation. It is this same understanding of human potential that also informs the Hebraic secret doctrine of the son, and it is fittingly represented by the word *ish* that culminates the ascending vowel series. With this return to the suggested spiritual practice of intoning the vowel series, it should now be more fully apparent how the complex meanings of Ish are related to its high frequency sound and how the production of this sound can serve as both tenor and vehicle for the spiritual perfecting of man.

In closing this discussion of the vowel-letters, it is clear that it has opened up a trail of occult correspondences that has led us far from our point of departure, the correlation between the vowel-letters and the Tetragrammaton, taking us to such further subjects as the correspondence of harmonics to Sefirot, which has added a new dimension to our understanding of the Tree. But our exploration of the Tree of Life Diagram is just beginning. The next part forms the vital center of this work, and it will show the geometric model of the Kabbalah to be the surviving product of a Hebraic sacred science whose sophistication was the rival of any in Egypt and Greece, a geometric complex variously related to the Tree of Life Diagram and enshrining the core meaning of the Hebraic priestly legacy, the secret doctrine of the son.

PART 3

The Kabbalistic Sacred Science of Geometry

6

Kabbalistic Geometry and the Cosmic Genesis

In this part we shall be exploring the unique qualities of the kabbalistic geometry encoded in the major texts of the Jewish esoteric tradition going back to the Bible. Only one major form of this geometry has thus far emerged in this tradition, that of the Tree of Life Diagram, the most famous cosmological diagram in the Western esoteric tradition, but in these chapters a larger geometric complex will be recovered and one that can be further related to the hexagram, the Star of David, thus revealing this "Jewish star" to have been an intrinsic element of Hebraic sacred science from its biblical origins.

This chapter will show how the Genesis creation account can be linked to the Tree of Life Diagram through the hexagram form, the form whose initial construction and further expansion into a succession of enlarging hexagrams will be seen to model the processes of cosmic creation as these processes have been detailed in the major cosmological texts of this tradition. As this analysis develops, we will find the biblical creation account to encode the three essential aspects of Pythagorean sacred science—geometry, harmonics, and number—thus completing the proof, begun in the earlier consideration of sacred science, of the parallel and ancient nature of its Hebraic mode. But as there indicated, the geometry it encodes differs from the Pythagorean in its direct cosmological context and its hexagram form, the latter of which should help to establish the early association of this form with Hebraic sacred science.

The diagram of expanding hexagrams, whose development will follow the esoteric exploration of the Genesis creation acount, will not only provide a model for the emanation of the four cosmic worlds of the Kabbalah but also serve as a powerful analytic tool for determining the cosmic world correlations of the further diagrams to be developed in this part. And in decoding the geometric secrets embedded in the major cosmological texts of the Hebraic tradition, Genesis, the *Sefer Yetzirah*, the *Bahir*, the *Zohar*, and the *Etz Chayyim*, the interpretative strategy of this part will involve the same linking of form to text that is the hallmark of kabbalistic geometry, the form providing a model for the text and the text reciprocally serving to name and explicate its various geometric features.

The solution proposed in the next chapter for the geometric enigma of the *Sefer Yetzirah* will result in a diagram that can model the genesis of the cosmic son as that genesis was later conceptualized in Lurianic cosmology. Even more significant will be the diagram produced in the concluding chapter of this part through the simple sixfold rotation of the Tree of Life Diagram around its Da'at (Knowledge) point. In this diagram, each of its lines will be seen to be necessary for the Hebraic solution of a problem that stumped the Greek geometers, one called the "duplication of the cube," and it will show such duplication to encode the central gnosis of Hebraic sacred science also encoded in the *Sefer Yetzirah* Diagram, the genesis of the son. The connections that will be established between the *Sefer Yetzirah* Diagram and the other diagrams derived from that of the Tree of Life suggest that all of these diagrams were once part of a single body of geometric knowledge probably dating back to the Hebraic priesthood. In this part, then, we will be tracing the whole course of cosmic evolution from its origin to its goal through geometric models the clues for which have lain embedded for millennia in the texts and major disclosed diagram of the Kabbalah, that of the Tree of Life, the source of all the diagrams developed in this part. And it will show how geometry was used in this tradition to demonstrate the cosmological principles of the Hebraic priesthood, demonstrations that will take us from the beginning of the cosmos to its goal in the generation of the son. Perhaps the most remarkable feature of the geometric complex to be here derived from the key of the Tree of Life Diagram is the fact that its precise geometric forms and processes are everywhere expressive of cosmological meaning. This phenomenon requires some theoretical explanation if such interpretations of formal properties are to be allowed, and so this exploration of kabbalistic geometry should begin with an attempt to validate both its significance and its methodology.

The Science of Expressive Form

That geometry is particularly expressive of cosmological meaning was understood by the Greeks as well as the Hebrews. Plato developed his cosmology in the *Timaeus* on the basis of the earlier geometric insights of Pythagoras, and such a core of geometrically encoded knowledge is to be found in the whole of the Western esoteric tradition, including the Kabbalah. For it is geometry that can provide the meaningful structure to cosmological and related areas of speculation that seems to partake of absolute truth, the truth inherent in the processes and forms of geometric construction. If geometry holds a central position in Western esoteric thought, it is because of its unique ability to supply an explanation, a blueprint, of those laws of existence that seem to apply equally to the processes of immaterial thought and to the material objects of such thought, an explanation of how consciousness and the world of material solids can be but different aspects of a coherent cosmos ordered by intelligible functions. It is through geometry that the mind can embrace with rational precision and clarity those universal principles that otherwise appear so paradoxical to reason, such mystical paradoxes as that expressed in the hermetic formula, "as above, so below," the laws of universal correspondence in an all-embracing and unified cosmos that is the secret gnosis of esoteric spirituality.

The average liberally educated persons of today have so lost touch with the discipline of geometry, however, that even if interested in the Jewish branch of esoteric mysticism, they will not normally be attracted to its geometric aspect and, if they are, will feel themselves ill prepared to engage in its study. To overcome such hesitancy, there can be no more inspiring introduction to the spiritual importance of geometric constructs than the lines of the Romantic poet William Wordsworth as he meditates on the special attraction that geometry has ever held for him:

Yet may we not entirely overlook
The pleasure gathered from the rudiments

Of geometric science. Though advanced
In these enquiries, with regret I speak,
No farther than the threshold, there I found
Both elevation and composed delight:
With Indian awe and wonder, ignorance pleased
With its own struggles, did I meditate
On the relation those abstractions bear
To Nature's laws, and by what process led,
Those immaterial agents bowed their heads
Duly to serve the mind of earth-born man;
. . . there, recognized
A type, for finite natures, of the one
Supreme Existence, the surpassing life,
Which . . . is,
And hath the name of, God. Transcendent peace
And silence did await upon these thoughts. . . .
And specially delightful unto me
Was that clear synthesis built up aloft. . . .
In verity, an independent world,
Created out of pure intelligence.

(The Prelude, 6. 115–67)

Though not even a rudimentary knowledge of classical geometry will be necessary to follow the discussions of geometric form and meaning that constitute the core of this book, the reader should come to share something of Wordsworth's awe at the power of geometry to convey ultimate truths.

If all esoteric traditions have held geometry to be sacred, it is because their adepts understood it to encode the basic principles on which the cosmos is founded, and their geometric practice with the compass and ruler instructed them in its meaning. This dual practice of construction and interpretation provides a technique for the discovery of cosmic principles that it seems fitting to name the Science of Expressive Form. It can be considered a science because its basis is not arbitrary but determined by the discoverable geometric laws involved in geometric construction. But the forms produced by such construction are also expressive of meanings that go beyond their purely mathematical properties and whose interpretation can be considered an art. The Science of Expressive Form, of sacred geometry, has always required, then, a synthesis of analytic and intuitive capacities. John Michell, who has himself contributed importantly to recent efforts at recovering the ancient esoteric tradition, has spoken similarly of both its ancient and modern practitioners: "Its masters are both mystics and logicians, insisting that nothing be accepted as true that cannot be proven so in two ways: by reason and poetic intuition." And he further asserts that "there are no esoteric schemes of geometry, no secret laws of mathematics, lost chords or musical harmonies which may not be discovered by searching."[1]

That the Jewish esoteric tradition was schooled from its biblical origins in the same sacred sciences that informed the Pythagorean tradition will be demonstrated in the new reading of the first chapter of Genesis appearing later in this chapter. But in addition to such use of precise geometric processes to model creation as this chapter will show can be found in Genesis and the *Zohar*, the Kabbalah developed its distinctive approach to geometry in which form could not be separated from cosmological interpretation. The Tree of Life Diagram is not simply an arrangement of various circles and the lines connecting them; its parts are named and their spatial relationships are given an associative mythological interpretation. Thus kabbalistic geometry, though having certain historical links with Pythagorean geometry, can also be distinguished from it in its quasi-talmudic approach to geometric form as something very much like a literary "text," one whose meanings must be grasped not through logical demonstration but through mythological association. In relating its major speculations to a specific visual model, the Kabbalah has shown unusual sensitivity to the correlation between form and meaning and to the possibility of conveying this meaning through language. The question of the methodology of kabbalistic geometry is closely related, then, to the explanation earlier offered of sacred science as focused on sound and form mediated by number, and we shall shortly see how that explanation can go far toward validating a linguistic method of geometric interpretation by suggesting how it is possible to "read" a geometric form as a sign, to construe its meaning and translate its absolute truth into the secondary order of mythological explanation that permits it to be verbalized.

We can begin our attempt to validate this methodology by considering the distinction between Hebrew and Greek modes of thought developed more fully by Thorlief Boman in his definitive study *Hebrew Thought Compared with Greek*, a study that expands upon the thesis of E. von Dobschutz on the contrast between the spatial quality of thought for the Greeks and the temporal quality of Hebrew thought:

It is astounding how far clear thinking depended for the Greeks upon the visual faculty. As evidence we may cite not only Euclid's Geometry, Aristotle's Logic, and Plato's Doctrine of Ideas, but we should also recall the quite metaphysical significance that Plato accords to the study of geometry—through geometry the highest earthly being is perceived, and true being, i.e. divine being, is betokened. . . . Quite as decided in the Old Testament is the emphasis upon the significance of hearing and of the *word in its being spoken*. . . . For the Greeks truth, negatively expressed, is that which is unveiled . . . that which is seen clearly. . . . The corresponding Hebrew concept of truth is expressed by means of derivates of the verb *aman*—"to be steady, faithful." . . . the Hebrews really do not ask what is true in the objective sense but what is subjectively certain, what is faithful in the existential sense. . . . Greek thinking is clear logical knowing; Israelite thinking is deep psychological understanding.[2]

It is in kabbalistic geometry, however, that the best of the Hebraic and Hellenic traditions are uniquely synthesized to provide what may well be our surest guide to cosmic understanding. For to the spatial logic discernible by the eye that defines the primary mental orientation of the Greeks, the Kabbalah brings the special interpretative sensitivity of that linguistic logic tied to the laws of hearing that, for Boman, is the characteristic mark of the Hebrew genius. But this union of precise geometric construction with a linguistic explication of its felt meaningfulness would also seem to have been true of the Pythagorean mode of philosophical geometry, Pythagoras having been the first to call himself a philosopher as well as being the first independent thinker to ground philosophy on geometric principles. And these principles also inform the linguistic dialectics of Plato. The Pythagorean-Platonic tradition of geometrically based cosmology is as opposed to the empty deductions of Euclidian geometry as is the tradition of the Kabbalah.

But if on both sides of the Hebrew-Greek divide there were schools of esoteric knowledge that exemplified a synthesis between the orientations of the ear and the eye, in its later tradition of kabbalistic geometry the Hebraic approach can be distinguished from the Greek in two important respects. The first is the unique contribution of the Kabbalah to the whole corpus of Western esotericism, the Tree of Life Diagram. But it is not alone in its exclusive focus on the geometry of the Tree that the Kabbalah can be distinguished from its sister form of sacred geometry practiced by the heirs of Pythagoras. It is also in its peculiarly Jewish mode of interpreting this diagram, a mode that can only be called talmudic. With eyes ever fixed upon a geometric model so well known to its students that they never needed actually to draw it in their manuscripts, the Kabbalists applied a form of associative reasoning markedly similar to the modes of talmudic interpretation in which they were doubtlessly as well studied.

In her analysis of the relationship of language to hermeneutics, particularly with respect to rabbinical interpretation, Susan A. Handelman has placed this connection within the context of contemporary literary theory:

> What such thinkers as Derrida, Freud, Ricoeur, Gadamer, and Levi-Strauss are seeking is to recover the innate logic of language itself. . . . Perhaps this is why a consideration of Rabbinic thought is so appropriate, for Rabbinic thought always gave primacy to the text, the word, and Greek thought to the mathematical figure. How does one discover, however, the inner living life of language without superimposing the conceptual framework which one seeks to penetrate? Ricoeur and Gadamer have looked to metaphor precisely for the reason that it represents the ordering act of language prior to the classifications of scientific logic, the seeing of resemblances where science had decreed separations.[3]

The methods used in the Talmud to interpret the meaning of biblical law and proof texts are shown by Handelman to differ from the deductive modes of Greek logic precisely in that they follow a logic of their own that seems to parallel the associative processes of metaphorical thought intrinsic to language. For it would seem that the same metaphoric processes involved in the creation of linguistic meaning are also responsible for our ability to interpret a text, to grasp and order its meanings, a process we shall see to be comparable to the kabbalistic practice of geometric interpretation.

Not only can the methodology of kabbalistic geometry be related to rabbinical hermeneutics but to all forms of literary interpretation. How the practice of interpreting geometric constructs may be related to that of literary texts is further suggested by the analysis of E. D. Hirsch, Jr., in his attempt to distinguish validation from interpretation:

> the complex process of construing a text always involves interpretative guesses as well as the testing of those guesses against the text.

... There can be no canons of *construction*, but only canons which help us to choose between alternative meanings that have already been construed from the text. . . . What Schleiermacher calls the "divinatory function" is the productive guess or hypothesis for which no rules can be formulated but without which the process of inter-pretation cannot even begin.[4]

The modern study of hermeneutics founded by Schleiermacher, though devoted to the divining of sacred texts, has also become a basis of con-temporary literary theory, and both may be related to the interpretative processes of kabbalistic geometry. But what is more surprising is the fur-ther similarity between the kabbalistic approach to geometric form and the scientific use of models.

Max Black has shown that the pervasive use of models in scientific theorizing reveals the root of such reasoning to be the same as that in-volving all symbolic or linguistic thought: "To speak of 'models' in con-nection with a scientific theory already smacks of the metaphorical. . . . Use of theoretical models resembles the use of metaphors in requiring analogical transfer of a vocabulary. Metaphor and model-making reveal new relationships. . . ."[5] Scientific reasoning begins, then, as a herme-neutic discipline; it must interpret its disordered data through divining their structural similarity to another, more familiar, domain, and this struc-tural similarity can best be apprehended through the cognitive medium of an image, a visual model. Most useful for this purpose is the constructed analogue model:

An analogue model is some material object, system, or process de-signed to reproduce as faithfully as possible in some new medium the *structure* or web of relationships in an original. . . . [It is] a sym-bolic representation of some real or imaginary original, subject to rules of interpretation for making accurate inferences from the rel-evant features of the model. . . . The inventor of a theoretical model is undistracted by accidental and irrelevant properties of the model object . . . but he is deprived of the controls enforced by the attempt at actual construction.[6]

It is precisely the controls involved in the actual construction of geomet-ric models that give to such models a truth value lacking in an arbitrarily "invented" theoretical model. And it is also through the attention paid to the "accidental" properties of the model that new insights can be generated regarding the structure of the domain intuitively recognized to be isomorphic to the model: "A promising model is one with implications rich enough to suggest novel hypotheses and speculations in the primary field of investigation—in short, to *see new connections*.[7] Black's analysis of the scientific use of models, like Hirsch's analysis of the interpretative process, is shown to begin with "interpretative guesses" and then to move to the canons of validation by which they can be tested: "We can determine the validity of a given model by checking the extent of its isomorphism with its intended application."[8] In its use of models, then, scientific theorizing approximates the interpretative methods used in the construing of a literary text, not the processes of logical syllogism but the more intuitive processes of associative reasoning, a metaphorical apprehension of similarity between apparent dissimilars.

It is such a union of the techniques of literary interpretation with those of geometric construction that may be said to define traditional kabbalistic geometry, and this is also true of my own methodology in this work. The geometry practiced here may justly claim a place in the long tradition of kabbalistic geometry for the two reasons that it uses the same methodology and that its own geometric constructions are most specifically derived from the kabbalistic diagram of the Tree of Life. Here, as in earlier kabbalistic works, the main effort has been spent on the association of a particular geometry with biblical and kabbalistic texts, the geometry serving to order and validate concepts of the specifically earlier Jewish tradition, and these concepts provide a reciprocal enlargement of each diagram's power of signification by demonstrating its power to model them.

But between the pure geometry of these diagrams and their use to model a linguistically expressed domain that had an original coherence apart from any such geometric modeling, there is the all-important step unique to kabbalistic geometry, the nongeometric naming of geometric elements. The very definitional impossibility of separating the geometric elements from their names is consistent with Edmund Husserl's general hypothesis for all geometric genesis—that "geometrical idealities arose together with the first 'axiomatic' propositions,"[9] forms together with their signifying meanings—and it certainly would seem to provide evidence for this hypothesis. Not only this, as the diagrams with which we will be concerned are configurations expressive of linguistically conceptual meanings, the explication of their significance is as intrinsic to their definition as is the naming of their parts. And since this significance is not limited to the internal laws and rules of their geometric construction

but also extends to the cosmological correspondences of these constructions expressible in language, the explication of such geometric constructions cannot be one of logical proof but must be that interpretative method
appropriate to linguistic formulations that is based upon association.

The methodology of kabbalistic geometry can be considered to be
essentially talmudic not only in its associative approach but also in its
conception of the relationship of "text," geometric in this case, to interpretation. Handelman has further shown that in talmudic practice "interpretation is not essentially separate from the text itself—an external
act intruded upon it—but rather the *extension* of the text, the uncovering
of the connective network of relations, a part of the continuous revelation of the text itself: at bottom, another aspect of the text."[10] And as
interpretation and text form one unity in talmudic understanding, so
also is it impossible to separate the geometry of a kabbalistic diagram
from the full explication of its meaning, the interpretation being understood, rather, to be an "*extension* of the text," the expression of its geometrically formulated significance.

We have so far seen that interpretation of the expressive forms of
kabbalistic diagrams involves the same associative process of grasping
meaning as makes possible such diverse modes of cognition as the construing of literary texts and the modeling of scientific theories. Thus it
would seem that the same validity should be granted to the methodology
of kabbalistic geometry as is normally accorded to these other disciplines.
But we should now take up the final issue of the ontological relationship
of geometry to the generation of mythological interpretation and what it
is that gives such mythology its truth value. Granted that geometry provides less arbitrary constructions than language, the fact that persuasive
correlations can be made between them would seem to argue that, to
paraphrase a famous law of genetics, *mythology recapitulates geometry*. This
is not to deny the truth of such mythology but to recognize it as a second
order of truth, one based upon the absolute truths of its geometric models, models subject to a variety of such mythological interpretation and
giving to each systematic interpretation the quality of secondary or symbolic truth. Nonetheless, the ability to give such mythological "readings"
of geometric form shows geometry to be a type of language that expresses
ideas the deep structures of the mind can recognize intuitively and for
the reason that this deepest level of mental perception seems to be encoded in such geometric archetypes. The persuasiveness with which geometric forms can be associated with mythological symbols further suggests that the mythological and geometric levels of the mind lie close

together and that it is in terms of such mythology that the mind first translates its geometric understanding into linguistic symbols. Whether or not the revelation of such meaning first arises in the mind at the primary geometric level or at the secondary level at which geometric forms have already become translated into mythological symbols and narratives, the coherence between such narratives and geometric construction shows that such a geometric base is implicit in these narratives, a fact that serves to validate their mythology as symbolic expressions of absolute truths. One geometric symbol that has long been felt to express cosmological meaning is the hexagram. But before developing its significance for Hebraic Sacred Science we must first consider the problematic relationship of the hexagram to the early history of the Jewish esoteric tradition.

The Hexagram and Hebraic Sacred Science

Variously called the Shield of David (Magen David), the Star of David, and Solomon's Seal, the hexagram has come to be the symbol most identified with the Jewish people. Composed of two oppositely pointed equilateral triangles whose apexes are defined by the radial arc points of a circle, this six-pointed star is an important esoteric symbol, associated with the heart Chakra in tantric yoga and discovered in the ground plan of Stonehenge.[11] It has long been thought that it was Arabic alchemy that in the West most popularized this symbol of equilibrium between the opposed spiritual forces of fire (the expansive force represented by the upward-pointing triangle) and water (the contractive force represented by the downward-pointing triangle). Since it was only in the early Middle Ages that the hexagram began to be featured prominently in Jewish magical texts and amulets, most modern historians have concluded that it was probably through this Arabic source that the hexagram was most directly transmitted to the medieval Spanish Kabbalists. But since in the Arabic literature employing this symbol the hexagram is normally given a Hebrew derivation through the terms "Solomon's Seal" or "Shield of David" by which it is called,[12] another possibility is that there was a continuous association of the Jewish esoteric tradition with this esoteric symbol of David and Solomon that preceded Islam. The talmudic reference to the hexagram engraved on the seal ring of Solomon[13] supports this possibility of an early association of the hexagram with Jewish esoteric understanding and practice reaching as far back as the biblical period, and this chapter will provide further grounds for such an association.

Gershom Scholem supports the contrary view that "the hexagram is not a Jewish symbol." He does admit that this figure and its names, "Seal of Solomon and Shield of David . . . go back to pre-Islamic Jewish magic," but considers that the hexagram "had one and only one purpose in its career as magic: to serve as protection against demons." More allegorical treatment of the hexagram by the few later Jewish authors he cites is set down by him to the "use of alchemistic symbolism,"[14] apparently of Arabic origin. But Raphael Patai, in his important recent work *The Jewish Alchemists*, has traced a very different history for the alchemical tradition that must cause a major revision of the received opinion concerning the relationship of Jews to alchemy and its hexagram symbol. As he reveals: "The first nonfictitious alchemists of the western world lived, as far as can be ascertained, in Hellenistic Egypt. And the earliest among them was Maria Hebraea, Maria the Hebrew, or Maria the Jewess, for whom our chief source is Zosimus the Panopolitan. Zosimus is the first Greek alchemical author whose actual writings have survived. He lived in Hellenistic Egypt, about 300 C.E. . . . We can thus tentatively assign her to the early third century C.E. at the latest.[15]

In quotations from Maria's teachings by Zosimus and others, we will recognize cosmological principles that appeared to emerge only later in the kabbalistic revisions of the priestly secret doctrine:

> "One becomes two, two becomes three, and by means of the third and fourth achieves unity; thus two are but one. . . . Join the male and the female, and you will find what is sought. . . . If you do not render the corporeal substances incorporeal, and the incorporeal substances corporeal, and if you do not make the two bodies one, nothing of the expected will be produced." . . . She [Maria] said: "The philosopher (Pseudo-) Democritus said . . . 'Transform nature, and make the spirit which is hidden inside this body come out.' . . . "Destroy the body, and make it become water, and extract that which is in it. . . . The 'water' which I have mentioned is an angel, and descends from the sky, and the earth accepts it on account of its [the earth's] moistness. The water of the sky is held by the water of the earth." . . . And as for her statement "[The water] descends from the sky," she meant by this the child which they say will be born for them in the air, while conception had taken place in the lower [region]; this being [through] the higher celestial strength which the water has gained by its absorption of the air.[16]

Maria Hebraea reveals alchemy to be a sacred science much like the more theoretical sacred sciences of geometry, harmonics, and number, the precise procedures of metallurgy, the first human technology, being studied and valued not only for their mundane usefulness but for what they can reveal of the principles governing both natural law and cosmic possibility. Her first quoted rule, which we are told "the Hebrew prophetess shrieked,"[17] seems to foreshadow the kabbalistic doctrine of the Partzufim: "One [Arikh Anpin] become two [Abba and Imma], two [Abba and Imma] becomes three [Ze'ir Anpin], and by means of the third [Ze'ir Anpin] and fourth [the Nukvah] achieves unity [a metaphorically sexual unification]; thus two are but one" [the Yichud of the transcendent or "incorporeal" with the immanent or "corporeal"]. It is this "sexual" union that generates the air-born "child" that the tenth-century Arabian alchemist Ibn Umail understood Maria to mean by the descending water or angel through which nature can be transformed to realize the spirit within it. In chapter 2 we saw a similar reference in the Essene "Manual of Discipline" scroll to "bringing forth seed, with all eternal blessings and everlasting joy in the life of eternity." The earthly conception of such an eternal seed is, then, a spiritual goal that goes back to the tradition of the Zadokite priestly founders of the Essenes. But it was not yet formulated in terms of the sexual model contained in Maria Hebraea's teachings. This sexual model, imputed not only to humans but to metals, is important because it sees the object of the Great Work of alchemy as such a unification of the opposing metallurgic procedures for dissolving the fixed and coagulating the volatile as can generate a more precious new being, one whose perfection consists precisely in the conjunction of both of these purified qualities—truly a new definition of the Hebraic secret doctrine of the son.

Maria Hebraea's alchemy also seems already to suggest use of the hexagram model, the descending "water of the sky" not only denoting the descending triangle of the hexagram but also the concept of the upper and lower waters in the Genesis creation account, which we will later see can also be modeled by the hexagram and in a way whose clarification of otherwise inexplicable features of the biblical account reinforces the early association of the hexagram with the sacred science of the Hebraic priesthood. The alchemical revelations of Maria Hebraea would seem, then, to be a direct outgrowth of an earlier and continuing Hebraic sacred science and to provide a link to the later theoretical elaborations of this tradition in the more sexually generative form of kabbalistic myth.

Patai provides much evidence to show "that Jewish alchemists were the teachers of both Muslim and Christian alchemists in the Middle Ages, just as they had been of Hellenistic alchemists in antiquity."[18] One Arab work, falsely attributed to Khalid Ibn Yazad, is particularly indebted to Maria Hebraea, as can be seen in the following quotation:

> But this dissolution and congelation, which I mentioned, is the dissolution of the body and the congelation of the spirit, and they are two but have one single operation, because the spirit cannot be congealed except with the dissolution of the body, and similarly the body cannot be dissolved except with the congelation of the spirit. And the body and the soul, when they are joined at the same time, each acts on its partner, making it similar to itself. . . . For the composition in this artifice or magisterium is the conjunction or matrimony of the congealed spirit with the dissolved body.[19]

Again this essential alchemical marriage of opposites seems suggestive of the hexagram model, the "dissolved body," signified by its ascending triangle, "joined at the same time" to the "congealed spirit," signified by its descending triangle, a conjunction that represents the culmination of the Great Work of alchemy, the production of the "philosophers' stone." As Patai indicates, in considering the alchemical legends surrounding Solomon:

> The close association between Solomon and the philosophers' stone is shown by the fact that the materia prima of the stone was sometimes represented as the two interlaced triangles of "Solomon's seal." . . . the sign of the "fiery water," since it consists of a combination of two symbols: that of fire, which rises upward and hence is symbolized by the upward pointing triangle, and that of water, which descends from the sky and is represented by the downward pointing triangle. The old midrashic interpretation of the Hebrew word for heaven, *shamayim*, namely that it is a combination of the words *esh*, fire, and *mayim*, water, was known and restated by the alchemists.[20]

Recognition of the coherence between the doctrines of alchemy and the Kabbalah appears in a Jewish sixteenth-century treatise entitled *Esh M'Saref* (The Refiner's Fire):

But know that the mysteries of this wisdom [i.e., alchemy] do not differ from the supernal mysteries of the Kabbalah. For just as there is a reflection of predicaments in sanctity, so there is also in impurity. And the sefirot which are in Asilut. . .are also in 'Asiya. . ., yea, even in that kingdom which is commonly called Minerals, although on the supernal plane their excellence is always greater. . . . Gehazi, the servant of Elisha, is of the type of the vulgar students of nature who set about contemplating the valleys and profundities of nature, but do not descend into its secrets, wherefore they labor in vain and remain servants forever. They give counsel about procuring the son of the wise, whose generation is impossible for nature, 2 Kings 4:14. But they can contribute nothing to this generation.[21]

The great secret shared by both the Kabbalah and alchemy is that which I have termed the secret doctrine of the son, that "son of the wise, whose generation is impossible for nature," and who unites the essential qualities of the higher and lower planes, of the infinite and the finite. And they would seem to share this secret doctrine because both are similarly derived from an earlier Hebraic priestly culture.

In arguing that in the Western esoteric tradition the hexagram had a Hebrew origin as well as a Hebrew name, I have shown that the imputed alchemical source for its spiritual symbolism not only does not preclude a Jewish source earlier than that of Arabic alchemy but demands it. In the Maria Hebraea of second or third century C.E. Alexandria, we may see a union of Hebraic priestly teachings with some seed elements of an Egyptian Hermetic practice of metallurgy that bore the new ideological fruit of alchemical formulation. But at the same time in Palestine there was a parallel theoretical development that showed a similar concern with the opposing qualities of fire and water and so with the possible employment of the hexagram to symbolize their union. This is in the most important text of Hebraic sacred science, the *Sefer Yetzirah*.

As we have seen in chapters 3 and 5, the third and fourth Sefirot of this text's first chapter derive water from air and fire from water; and in its third chapter, fire is further correlated with the mother letter Shin and the head, water with the mother letter Mem and the abdomen, and the air, which mediates between these opposed elements and their upper and lower locations, is correlated with the mother letter Aleph and the chest. As in alchemy, though differently, the ten Sefirot and the twenty-two letters of this text define the process of generating the cosmic man.

Given that in the later alchemical tradition, the circumstances of upper fire and lower water betoken the model of the hexagram, it does not seem too much to find a similar hidden reference to the hexagram in the *Sefer Yetzirah*, concerned as they both are with the same sacred scientific quest to study those features of theoretical or technological science whose precise processes appear to reveal the structure and purpose of existence. One difference between these teachings, however, is that Maria Hebraea synthesizes Hebraic sacred science with some earlier development of metallurgy in Egypt while in the *Sefer Yetzirah* Hebraic sacred science is synthesized with the Pythagorean sacred science of Greece.

Following in the tradition of Heinrich Graetz, Abraham Epstein, and Louis Ginzberg, Scholem concludes that "the main part of *Sefer Yezirah*, though it contains post-talmudic additions, was written between the third and sixth centuries, apparently in Palestine by a devout Jew with leanings toward mysticism."[22] But Aryeh Kaplan has argued that, since many authorities consider the *Sefer Yetzirah* to be referred to under the term *Ma'aseh Bereshit* in the Mishnah, redacted in 204 C.E., its written form must precede this date, and he sketches an earlier oral history going back to Rabbi Akiba, the Essenes, and still earlier figures.[23] The most important point to be made is that sometime during the second and third centuries C.E., there was a separate flowering of Hebraic sacred science both in post-Temple Palestine and diaspora Alexandria whose similarities would seem to imply the same source. As earlier argued in the introductory chapter, this source is most likely to have been the members of the priesthood deprofessionalized after the destruction of the Temple, who would have become private teachers of what must have been a long tradition of Temple sacred science. And one feature of this ancient science that appears to have surfaced alike in the teachings of Maria Hebraea and the *Sefer Yetzirah* is a peculiar joint definition of a fire above and water below, which in the later alchemical tradition was identified with the figure of the hexagram and given a Hebrew origin in the names by which it was known, Solomon's Seal and the Shield of David. As with the discovery of Troy just where Homer had claimed it to be, so it seems reasonable to conclude from the long association of the hexagram with the Hebrew kings that this symbol was, indeed, a particular aspect of the Jewish esoteric tradition going back at least to the Temple priesthood. The remainder of this part will not only assume this to be true but add important new evidence to support this thesis.

Hexagram Construction and the Zoharic Account of Creation

As the geometric construction of the hexagram involves basic geometric processes that must be understood to comprehend some of the later discussions in this chapter, and as it will explain both the importance of actual geometric practice to the adepts of Western esoteric mysticism and its association with their understanding of the primary processes of creation, it is appropriate to introduce the form of the hexagram at this point and review the method by which it is geometrically constructed. It shall be seen to be a method that recreates the primal acts of creation as they are defined from these very geometric processes in the texts of Hebraic sacred science extending from the Bible to the *Zohar*.

We begin with that marvelous instrument, the compass, whose features the poet John Donne thought a fitting symbol for the mysteries of spiritual love[24] and which the poet John Milton employed in his depiction of the creation:

> One foot he centred, and the other turn'd
> Round through the vast profundity obscure,
> And said, Thus far extend, thus far thy bounds,
> This be thy just Circumference, O World.
> Thus God the Heav'n created, thus the Earth,
> Matter unform'd and void.
>
> (*Paradise Lost*, 7:228–33)

Observing with Milton the creative workings of the compass, we may say that the compass is an instrument that unites in a larger functional whole a fixed foot and a moving foot, the fixed foot pointing always to the unmanifest center of unity represented by the mathematical point and the moving foot creating the mathematical line that measures the shortest distance it has traversed in its movement away from the center. The compass, which can be taken as a symbol of the One from whom all creation emanates, has a threefold nature that may be defined as: (1) the point or unitary center established by the fixed foot; (2) the line or extension into duality, difference, and multiplicity, produced by the movement of the movable foot; and (3) the circular plane, a third, larger whole that contains and harmonizes the polarity of point and line into the complementarity of circular line, and which is produced by rotating the line about the point to form a circumference.

Having produced a bound expanse, the first primordial space, through its three successive manifestations as contracted point, expansive line, and harmonizing circle, for its second action, the One may be said to multiply itself as point through the interaction of its other two aspects as (2) line or radius and (3) circumference, which is why the creative process would seem to require these other two aspects of unity. The interaction of the second and third aspects or steps, in other words, the measuring of radial arcs on the circumference by moving the fixed foot to the circumference, results in the production of six and only six points, the multiplication of 3 x 2 equaling 6. It is precisely because the compass, without changing the established distance of the radius between its two hinged feet, will mark off exactly six equidistant points on the circumference of a circle that the number six is accorded such a high place in numerology. Not only is it a "perfect" number, as the sum of its factors, but it can also be considered the number of creation, an association reflected in the biblical six days of creation, because it is from these six points that the first manifest lines of the hexagram model of creation can be drawn.

The work of the compass has been to establish the basis for manifestation but all its actions may be associated with the premanifest level of such creation as can be modeled by this mode of diagram construction. For once these six points have been determined, the circle needed for their establishment can be erased. At this point the work of creation can be handed over from the compass to the straightedge, which will be used for drawing straight lines between the already established points and adding extensions of these lines to newly established vertices. The switch from the geometry of the circle to that of straightedged surfaces, from what might be considered the unmanifest to the manifest aspects of creation, is required for precision because the circle and any curved line is, in every sense of the word, immeasurable. The world of the determinate is the world of straight lines, and such straight lines can be found within the general curvature of nature, as in the crystalline form of all chemical substances and in the lines that can be drawn between the centers of circular cells in organic matter to reveal its determining geometric structure.

From the six points that have been established through the use of the compass, our divine geometer or human counterpart will now most logically draw the hexagram, for it is the figure that most perfectly represents the six-pointed product of 3 x 2, the unmanifest operations of unity just detailed. As the union of two triangles, the hexagram represents both twoness and threeness around a center, the inner hexagon. It further represents two essential principles of the cosmos, the threefold manifestation of unity in the form of the triangle—which incorporates the contraction of the point, the expansion of the line, and the harmonizing surface that contains them—and the principle of the inverse. The ascending triangle can also be taken to represent heaven, the descending triangle, the earth, and the hexagram the symbol of their interconnection. From the preceding discussion, it should now be clear how the process of constructing the hexagram could become symbolic of the primordial acts of creation to a practicing geometer, and the hexagram itself the paramount symbol of the creation.

With this understanding of the basic geometric processes involved in the construction of the circle and the hexagram, we should be better able to appreciate the geometric descriptions of creation in the *Zohar*. At the start of the section called "Bereshit," the basic geometric progression from point, through line, to circle, and then to the marking of radial arc points is described in relation to the first processes of creation: "The Most Mysterious struck its void, and caused this point to shine. This 'beginning' then extended, and made for itself a palace for its honour and glory. . . . From this point onwards *bara shith*, 'he created six.'"[25] The interpretation of the first word of the Torah, "Bereshit," as signifying "he created six," has a long tradition prior to the *Zohar*, going back at least to the Baraita de Ma'aseh Bereshit (c. eighth century): "In the beginning God created the heaven and the earth; you shouldn't read BERESIT as *in the beginning* but BERA SIT, *He created six*. And in effect you will find that it is written *He created six*.[26] Early in the *Zohar* there is a geometric elaboration of this interpretation:

> What is the meaning of *Bereshith*? It means "with Wisdom", the Wisdom on which the world is based, and through this it introduces us to deep and recondite mysteries. In it, too, is the inscription of six chief supernal directions, out of which there issues the totality of existence. From the same there go forth six sources of rivers which flow into the Great Sea. This is implied in the word *BeReSHITH*, which can be analyzed into *BaRa-SHiTH* (He created six). And who created them? The Mysterious Unknown.[27]

In this reference, the meaning "He created six" ascribed to Bereshit is directly identified with the "six chief supernal directions, out of which there issues the totality of existence." It has, then, a geometric meaning and derivation.

As we have seen, the work of the compass can be distinguished from that of the straightedge, the former being the instrument of immeasurable unity and the latter the instrument of precise measure through which the second linear world can be constructed. The two quotations from the *Zohar* depict the creative work of the compass by the "Mysterious Unknown," leading through the successive stages of point, line, and circle to the final work of premanifest, primordial creation, the fixing or creation of the six radial arc points on the circle.

But the creation of the first hexagram requires a dualistic instrumentality, that which is or uses the straightedge. This creative instrument is, in the *Zohar* as in Genesis, given the plural divine name Elohim. Continuing an earlier quotation that detailed the progression from supernal point through its extension into a palace (geometrically the circle), we can see the identification of Elohim with this third manifestation of the "Most Mysterious" as circle: "This palace is called *Elohim*, and this doctrine is contained in the words, 'By means of a beginning (it) created Elohim.'"[28] The interpretation just given of the first three words of Genesis, "*Bereshit bara Elohim*" presents the startling but by no means unusual esoteric conception that the creator God of the heavens and the earth is not the ultimate source of all being, here the mysterious Ein Sof, but a derived aspect of its plurality harmonized with its unity (the symbolic meaning of the circle), here called Elohim.

But if "Bereshit," normally translated "In the beginning," is understood in its other kabbalistic interpretation as "He created six," then a preliminary reading of the first seven words of Genesis could be: "The Mysterious Unknown created six; Elohim created the heavens and the earth." Now if these six are given the simple geometrical significance of the six points made by the compass on the circumference of the circle, then the form of the heavens and the earth created by the straightedge would most logically be the hexagram joining these six points in the interconnected ascending triangle, signifying the heavens or the spiritual fire that is their source, and the descending triangle, signifying the earth or its source in the spiritual waters. The hexagram is, then, a fitting supernal symbol of the process of creation defined in the first sentence of Genesis: "*Bereshit bara* [created] *Elohim et ha-shammaim* [the heavens] *ve-et ha-aretz* [and the earth]." And from the foregoing analysis, it becomes possible to give the following completely geometric reading to the first seven words defining creation: "By means of the six [points] He [the "Mysterious Unknown" (?)] had created, Elohim created the heavens [signified by the ascending triangle of the hexagram] and the earth [signified by the descending triangle of the hexagram]."

This analysis should be sufficient to show that the Zoharic treatment of the first seven words of Genesis relates them to the basic geometric processes thought to have been involved in the process of cosmic creation. It should also show how the hexagram can provide the geometric model of the creation as developed in the Genesis account. Further, as the first verse of Genesis provides a summary of the creation that may be modeled by the hexagram, so may the remainder of the first chapter be understood as a progressive revelation of this hexagram form. The esoteric nature of the creation account can be demonstrated by its apparent employment of two organizing keys drawn from what we have seen to be the most essential of esoteric sciences, geometry and music. We shall begin this exploration with the latter and then conclude by analyzing the geometry of the full creation account.

The Hexagram of Creation:
Recovering the Esoteric Keys to Genesis

The key to the peculiar chronological order of creation is so remarkably simple that it is a wonder it has never before been recognized. It is none other than the harmonic series of overtones or partials. In the earlier treatments of the harmonic series, most recently in chapter 5, we saw that when a tone is sounded (1), its first overtone or second harmonic will be the octave (2), followed by the fifth (3), the next octave (4), the third (5), the next fifth (6), and the minor seventh (7). This can be represented by the following solfeggio names and tones: (1) Do-C, (2) Do-C_2, (3) Sol-G, (4) Do-C_3, (5) Mi-E, (6) Sol-G_2, (7) Tay-Bb. Now what is astonishing about this series in conjunction with the creation account is that the first, second, and fourth positions in which the Do tone is sounded are the same chronological positions in which reference is made to heavenly creation; the third and sixth positions in which the Sol tone is sounded are the same in which reference is made to earthly creation; and the remaining tones of the fifth and seventh positions relate to neither of these creation categories. Let us follow the account chronologically through the days of creation.

The first day can be associated with heaven (Do_1) insofar as it involves the creation of the supernal light. In the second day, the firmament then created is specifically called "Heaven" (Do_2). The third day gives us the creation of the dry land called "earth" (Sol_1). The fourth day returns us to the creation of the "lights in the firmament of the heaven" (Do_3). The fifth day takes us to the creation of the creatures inhabiting the flowing elements of water and air (Mi). The sixth day returns us to the earth (Sol_2) with the creation of the animals and man. And the seventh day brings us to the Sabbath sanctification that may well be associated with the modulating interval of the minor seventh, what in harmonic theory is more precisely defined as that flatter interval of the septimal seventh. Thus the peculiar reversal of the third and fourth days, in terms of which the logical progression of heavenly creation is interrupted by that of earthly vegetation, can be explained and would seem to have been motivated by the overriding consideration of the parallel to the harmonic series. The importance of such a parallel would further suggest that Hebrew cosmology is like the Hindu in tracing the creation back to an original sound. For Hindu cosmology it is the sound Om or Aum; in the biblical account it is the sound produced by the voice of God, an original vibration resulting in a form of supernal energy that can be associated with light. If all of the creation is implicit in the creative activity of the first day, as the opening seven words would suggest, then this original sound, which may be what Israel is twice daily called upon to "Hear" (*sh'ma*), would implicitly contain the harmonic series that is to be progressively expressed through the remaining days of creation and provide its order of manifestation.

The immediate translation of sound waves into a patterning of light, ascribed to the first day of creation, reveals an esoteric understanding of the relationship of musical harmonics to geometric form that is being increasingly substantiated by modern experimentation. The work of Hans Jenny in what he has called "cymatics" is most important here. For what Jenny has demonstrated is that when sound is applied to certain substances, they assume special geometric forms that only such sound frequencies can call forth. As Jenny explains:

> we see in front of us the result of complex periodic vibration, a musical tone becoming a "visible" figure in which one or more intervals are featured. One must always bear in mind that these phenomena are generated by sound. If the sound is removed the whole picture along with its dynamics will disappear and return again immediately when the sound is restored. These phenomena are subject to definite laws and are repeatable at any time. . . . The resultants of harmonic vibrations are at all times so strictly law-ordered

that it is possible to draw up a systematology of morphogenesis. What one must bear in mind is that under this or that quite specific set of conditions Nature produces this form only and no other. Nothing here is diffuse and indeterminate; everything presents itself in a precisely defined form. The more one studies these things, the more one realizes that sound is the creative principle. It must be regarded as primordial.[29]

Among the beautiful photographs taken of such symmetrical patterning there are some that reveal clear hexagram forms, as in the extraordinary photograph by Jenny reproduced in figure 6.1.

One explanation of this association of harmonics with geometric form is derived by Robert Lawlor from the work of Hermann Helmholtz:

> In order to hear a particular partial which is normally blended into the whole or "fundamental" tone, Hermann Helmholtz designed small cup-like resonators. These, when held to the ear, at somewhere between a forty and a forty-five degree angle to the eardrum, allow one to hear separately—to "phenomenalize"—these partial tones, the particular partial heard depending upon the shape and size of the little cup. . . . It follows from this, not only that every whole tone is a simultaneous combination of all its partials, such that the shift in the angulation of the resonator allows one to hear the different partials contained in it, but also that there is a relationship between the structure of audible sound and geometry, in which the geometric angles act as a controlling device to release certain potential qualities locked within a holistic sound pattern.[30]

If Lawlor is correct in his conclusions, then the process of creation can be explained by the conjunction of a fundamental tone and the reciprocal effect upon it of the geometric angulation produced by the feedback of its derivative form. The ability of the hexagram form to provide such a secondary key to the Genesis account further suggests that it was precisely the sound that could cymatically produce the hexagram that was understood to have been emitted by the divine voice "in the beginning."

Now if the creation of the heaven and the earth referred to in the first verse can be understood to denote the resonating of the fundamental tone of creation, then this tone would not only have implicit within it the whole series of overtones related to its frequency but also a precise geometrical form. If we can further postulate that this implicit or virtual

FIGURE 6.1. A CYMATIC HEXAGRAM FORM. From Hans Jenny, *Cymatics*, 2 vols. (Basel: Basilius Press, 1974), 2,106.

form is that of the hexagram, then we should be able to observe its progressive spatial unfolding through the days of creation in the same way that these days revealed the chronological phenomenalization of the harmonic series. The earlier analysis of the first seven words of Genesis showed that they could be read as defining the six radial arc points on the circumference of a circle and their interconnection in the hexagram form. If these are now understood to refer to a premanifest circle and a virtual hexagram, then we can begin the progressive manifestation of the hexagram whose form is already virtually present. Figure 6.2 shows the finished model of creation whose stages it is better first to define.

We begin, then, with a circle that represents "the face of the deep" and that is filled with "waters" that are "without form and void" (Gen. 1:2). Into this circle, a cone of light may be thought to emerge from the

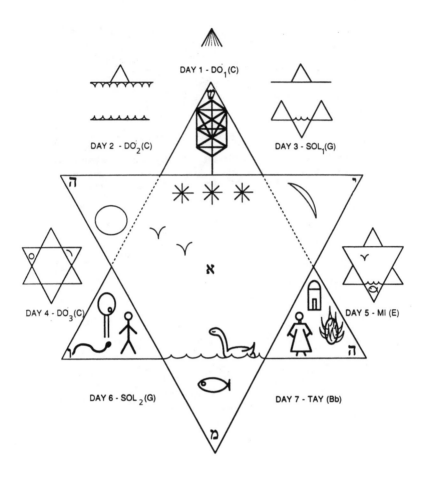

FIGURE 6.2. THE HEXAGRAM OF CREATION

uppermost radial arc point to fill and manifest the upper sub-triangle of the hexagram and to complete the creative process of the first day. On the second day, the firmament that divides the upper from the lower waters can be said to manifest the upper and lower bars of the hexagram and to fill the space between them. It is the special circumstances of the third day that spatially as well as temporally argue strongly for the esoteric keys being here provided: "And God said, Let the waters under the heaven be gathered together unto one place, and let the dry land appear" (Gen. 1:9). In terms of the hexagram model, the place of the lower waters would be beneath the lower bar of the hexagram, which is the base of its full ascending triangle, and the "one place" where they can be gathered would be in the hexagram's lowest sub-triangle, the point of its full descending triangle. The lower two sub-triangles of the full ascending triangle would then provide the twin mountain forms in which the "dry land" could appear. Continuing with the account, the fourth day would now complete the manifestation of the hexagram form, the remaining two upper sub-triangles of the full descending triangle providing the spaces within the firmament in which the sun and moon can be set. The circumstances of the fifth day can be better understood if the descending triangle is thought to overlay the ascending triangle in a single unbroken form, for the fish and fowl created on this day can then be placed within the water of its lower sub-triangle and the air that can be understood to fill the adjoining inner hexagon. With the sixth day, the separated earthly mountains, which had earlier been covered with vegetation, can now be given their animal and human inhabitants that complete the work of creation. Though the Sabbath adds no new elements, its holiness is suggested in the final design of the Hexagram of Creation by the way the fourth-day elements are illustrated. The simultaneous appearance of the setting sun and three stars is meant to suggest that most holy twenty-fifth hour of the Sabbath occupying the period from just before sunset, when the Sabbath began on the previous evening, to the time at which the first three stars can be seen on the following evening, which officially closes the Sabbath.

The Hexagram of Creation does more than reveal the geometric structure of the Genesis account. It also provides a key to understanding much of biblical imagery as well as major aspects of the Jewish and other esoteric traditions. The first is particularly true of the scheme it provides for the elements of the third day. Its graphic representation of two mountains separated by water is echoed by the position accorded these elements in biblical narrative, law, and prophecy. For Jewish history can be viewed as progressing from one mountain to another, from Mount Sinai where the Law was given to the Holy Mountain of Messianic Jerusalem where it is to be fulfilled. To move from the first to the second mountain, however, requires a spiritual purification both symbolized and accomplished through the ritual bath of the *mikvah*.

The manner in which the hexagram can arrange the elements of the whole creation account also suggests a parallel between this account and the cosmology that has been ascribed to the more universal shamanic tradition, a parallel that only this Hexagram of Creation can enable us to perceive. For its descending triangle, associated as it is with the flowing elements of water and air, can be related to the shamanic Lower World, and its ascending triangle, associated with the elements of mountains and fire, can be related to the shamanic Upper World.[31] The descending triangle can be further associated with the consciousness of such a shamanic "Lower World" and the ascending triangle with that of such a shamanic "Upper World." The consciousness of such a "Lower World" may also be associated with the Way of God, the *derekh ha-shem*, and that of the "Upper World" with what is above and directs its flow, such "Lower World" consciousness with submergence in this flow and "Upper World" consciousness identifiable with spiritual dominion.[32] The forms of these two major triangles can also deepen the usual interpretation of them by which the descending triangle is identified with divine descent and the ascending triangle with human ascent, showing the unity of the divine flowing force and the segmented nature of human ascent, its movement from the mountain of imperfect man through the waters of purification to the mountain of perfected man and finally to the transcendent mountain of divine light. The association of the uppermost sub-triangle, and so the entire ascending triangle, with light or fire, and of the lowest sub-triangle, with the entire descending triangle of which it is a part, with water shows further coherence between the hexagram model of creation and its later use in alchemy. This again suggests that it was not from Arabic alchemy that medieval Kabbalists were introduced to the hexagram and that the alchemical tradition was correct in attributing an earlier Hebrew origin both to this form, and, as we earlier saw, to its metallurgical principles.

In the artistic design of the illustrated Hexagram of Creation, the uppermost sub-triangle of fire is designated by the Hebrew letter Shin, the lowermost sub-triangle of water by the letter Mem, and the central point of air by the letter Aleph, these three letters having been given these connotations in the *Sefer Yetzirah*, which classifies them as the three "mother letters." To complete the design, the remaining four sub-triangles have each been correlated with one of the letters of the Tetragrammaton. Trees also figure in each of the ascending sub-triangles, the Tree of Knowledge on the left mountain of post-Edenic man, the burning bush on the right mountain of perfected man, and the Tree of Life Diagram on the central mountain of transcendent light, the diagram that will provide the further key by which the Hexagram of Creation can generate a yet more complex and precise cosmological model.

We come finally to what may be the most significant fact about the hexagram modeling of the creation account, the fact that the full manifestation of the hexagram is completed by the fourth day of a seven-day process. This permits us to integrate the four-stage process of kabbalistic cosmology within the larger Sabbatical structure that Genesis projects for the cosmos and that would seem to be the more authentic cosmological model of the Jewish esoteric tradition. But associating the four days of creation needed to manifest the hexagram form with the four cosmic worlds of the Kabbalah leading to the manifestation of the physical world will call for a radical reinterpretation of the biblical account. These four worlds are defined as Atzilut (Emanation), Beriah (Creation), Yetzirah (Formation), and Assiyah (Making). Associating the first world of Atzilut with the first day offers no problem since both may be said to represent a divine emanation not really separable from its divine source. It is with the second world of Beriah that creation may be properly said to begin from the kabbalistic perspective, and the separation of creation from Creator would also seem to be the function of the firmament created in the second day. The identification of the garden world of the third day with Yetzirah can also be supported since this world is kabbalistically associated with the Garden of Eden and the Adamic transgression leading to the materialization of the fourth world. The major problem that arises is with the fourth day, the day identified with the creation of the sun, the moon, and the stars. But an observation made by the *Zohar* on this text can help to resolve this problem: "Observe that stars and planets exist through a covenant that is the firmament of the heaven, in which they are inscribed and engraved."[33] If the major lights, the sun and the moon, can be related to the "stars and planets," which is what they are, indeed, then the fourth day can be understood astronomically to represent all the physical components of the cosmos, that with which the fourth kabbalistic world can be precisely correlated. This leaves the last three days of creation to define the more subtle dimensions of consciousness that can be associated with the concept of the Tikkun, the cosmic process of rectification developed by the sixteenth century Kabbalist Isaac Luria. On this model, the first and last three days would define supernal creations with only the fourth day representing the physical dimension of creation.

The first three days may further be viewed from a Pythagorean perspective, for the progressive unfolding of hexagram elements also reveals a numerological progression through geometrically defined worlds. The first day may be said to disclose a point of light radiating a certain distance into the medium of chaotic waters. The second day not only brings us to the second world of the line but of the number two, for it manifests the two linear bars of the hexagram. Since these bars are meant to clear the area between them of "waters," they may be further thought of as providing some mode of magnetic attractor that might cause the intervening medium to collect about them. In the process, the upper bar would close off the portion of the upper "waters" that may be thought to have transformed the fundamental tone of creation into a conical pattern of light. Finally, with the third day we arrive at both the third world of the triangular plane and the triple number of such triangles, the arrangement of which also suggests the quality of balance associated with the triadic. It is only the unfolding of these three supernal worlds—defining the archetypal elements of unity, duality, and the balance between them that is also generative—that can allow the fourth world of material solids, informed by these functions, to be manifested.

Beyond this, the creation account may be understood to project the virtual fields of higher consciousness. The Kabbalah understands the soul to be composed of three basic levels, those of the Nefesh, the Ruach, and the Neshamah soul levels, and these may be related to the fourth, fifth, and sixth cosmic worlds or "days" of a Sabbatical cosmic structure. If the fourth day is now to be identified with the fourth of the kabbalistic cosmic worlds, then it would not only represent the mineral elements of creation but all the constituents living in the physical world in accordance with their natural endowments. For man, this natural spiritual endowment is the Nefesh or vital animal soul. In the biblical account, the fourth day contributes a level of creation under "rule," one which may be supposed to exhibit matter under the control of natural law and spirit largely under the control of the instinctual appetites. This latter may be said to define the Nefesh level of the soul. The fifth and sixth days bring us to two higher soul levels, both of which are termed "blessed" in the Genesis account. The fifth day and world would now be correlated with the Ruach soul dimension and define it as that which enters into the divine flow. The sixth day and world would then be correlated with the Neshamah soul and define it as that in which man has moved from a condition of being controlled, through one of participating in such control, to a final state of spiritual "dominion." In such a state, man can enter into the Sabbatical day and world to experience the fullness of that holiness with which he has been briefly visited each earthly Sabbath.

We have seen that the first chapter of Genesis is informed by esoteric keys of musical harmonics and geometric form that reveal a deeper logic underlying and ordering the progression of its elements. The harmonic series can explain why the evolution of heavenly creation was interrupted on the third day for the creation of earthly life, and the hexagram elements that can model the biblical specifications regarding the relative positions of the sea and land can reveal the symbolic character of this creation. It shows how the descending sub-triangle, whose form has always been symbolic of the spiral vortex of water, can explain the unnatural condition that the waters are to be gathered into one place, the place that its position in the hexagram would seem archetypally to provide. And the two ascending triangles at its sides not only can be associated with the dry land but give to this association the added visual impression of mountains. Since this triple geometric formation can be taken as signifying two mountains separated by water, and since the structure of Jewish history and the purification process necessary for its proper evolution can be interpreted in terms of this symbolism, knowledge of the geometric code can illuminate the symbolic nature of the biblical text, showing how the account of the third day provides a supernal or archetypal model of the plan that the whole of earthly history is to follow. In the same way, the whole seven days can be understood to develop the plan of cosmic history, to program the perimeters within which the creation can achieve actualization. That this program not only can be modeled but decoded by the hexagram form would seem further to demonstrate that the association of the Jewish esoteric tradition with the hexagram goes back to its earliest biblical origins.

The foregoing analysis is not the first attempt to derive a Sabbatical cosmic structure from the creation account in Genesis. Such a structure also appears in the Merkabah tradition of the seven heavens, in the *Temunah*, an influential kabbalistic text from the fourteenth century developing the concept of the *shemitot* (Sabbaticals) as world-eras, and most importantly in the Talmud, which understands the seven days of the Genesis account to involve a spiritual creation preceding physical manifestation and providing its plan of development.[34] What this analysis further attempts is to integrate such a Sabbatical cosmic structure with both the classical kabbalistic concept of the four worlds of emanation and the concept of future worlds projected by the earlier normative tradition and the later kabbalistic tradition deriving from the cosmology of Isaac Luria. The normative tradition deriving from the prophets and Talmud projects two future eras or states, that of the Messianic Age and of the World to Come, while the Lurianic tradition combines such future states into an all-embracing future world of the Tikkun. Thus the geometric analysis of the creation account provides a means of integrating the kabbalistic four worlds into a larger Sabbatical cosmic structure. But the Jewish esoteric tradition can only be so integrated with the creation account because of the discovery of the esoteric keys that both inform it and connect it with the later strands of esotericism that have maintained

some understanding of their meaning. As the function of the Jewish esoteric tradition is the preservation of this knowledge, it should not be
surprising that the best means of decoding it would be through the very
geometry on which this knowledge is based.

The previous discussion of the Hexagram of Creation has shown the
hexagram to be the basis of a Sabbatical cosmic structure whose progression is outlined in the first chapter of Genesis, a Sabbatical structure that
can accommodate all aspects of the Jewish esoteric tradition and show it
to be a cohesive whole informed throughout by a basic hexadic geometry. In the geometric analyses to follow, all that will be required is the
ability to distinguish between two geometric terms and figures, the
hexagram and the hexagon, shown in figure 6.3, and to have that confidence in one's ability to follow a discussion of such simple geometric
figures as will keep the mind from wandering and focus it on the diagram
under consideration. If God is a geometer, as Kepler asserted, the principles of His operations can be taught to an intelligent kindergarten class,
as indeed Rudolph Steiner has shown in the practice of the Waldorf schools
he founded. And as in such a kindergarten the students will be expected
to make their own geometric drawings, so it is hoped that the readers for
whom these diagrams and the given explanations have meaning will not
be content simply to appreciate the illustrations provided but will get
themselves the tools of a geometer, a compass and straightedge, and make
their own diagrams, with all the individual illumination the process can
afford. For these diagrams, however beautiful their form, constitute a form
of geometric meditation that reveals its cosmic secrets only to the person
who engages in such construction. It is precisely for this reason that esoteric geometry in its most vital form—and in this form it is a great power
capable of inspiring a culture to the construction of pyramids and cathe-
drals—has always been a practice, a form of spiritual discipline. But the
geometric forms that have been most enlarging to the consciousness have
been the circular, symmetrical mandalas and yantras whose cosmological
records the mind can remember when lifted by such geometric medita-
tions to its higher powers. The hexagram, honored by so many sacred
traditions, is a mandala that the Jewish people have made their own.

Derivation of the Tree of Life Diagram

It is from the simple geometric process of constructing larger hexagrams
from the point-hexagon of a smaller hexagram—a process derived from
the very nature of the hexagram, whose two equilateral triangles overlap

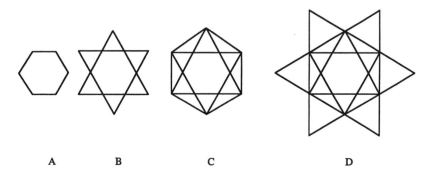

A   B   C   D

FIGURE 6.3.
(A) The hexagon; (B) the hexagram; (C) a hexagram within a hexagon; (D) a second hexagram built on the point-hexagon
of a smaller hexagram.

in such a way as to form an inner hexagon—that a key to the geometric derivation of the Tree of Life Diagram can be found. If, as earlier argued, the initial geometric processes associated with creation involve the drawing of a hexagram from the six radial arc points of an original, premanifest circle, then the further acts of creation might reasonably be expected to involve the building of ever more complex patterns of hexagrams upon this primordial base. But when a third hexagram is constructed by this process, the extension of the lines of the point-hexagon of what is now the second hexagram so that these lines meet to form a six-pointed star, a remarkable inner pattern is revealed, as illustrated in figure 6.4.

When three hexagrams are constructed one upon the point-hexagon of the other, the simplest way of building an enlarging structure of hexagrams, the remarkable inner pattern they may be shown to form is none other than the Tree of Life Diagram in almost all the details of that form of the diagram identified in chapter 1 as the Tree of Emanation. There we saw that there were two major forms of the Tree in the kabbalistic tradition, one identified with Cordovero as the Tree of Emanation and another identified with Luria as the Tree of Return. The emerging form of the Tree in figure 6.4 is clearly that of the Tree of Emanation, but as the fuller form of this hexagram model develops, we will see that it can accommodate the Tree of Return as well. The following construction and analysis of the hexagram diagram underlying the traditional Tree will be facilitated by illustrating the Tree again in its two traditionally recognized forms, as given in figure 6.5.

FIGURE 6.4. THE EMERGING TREE OF LIFE DIAGRAM

The two main constituents of both forms of the Tree are its ten Sefirot-named spheres and the twenty-two paths connecting them. Both versions give the same names and positions of the Sefirot. From top to bottom these are: (1) Keter-Crown, (2) Chokhmah-Wisdom, (3) Binah-Understanding, (4) Chesed-Mercy, (5) Gevurah-Judgment, (6) Tiferet-Beauty, (7) Netzach-Eternity, (8) Hod-Splendor, (9) Yesod-Foundation, and (10) Malkhut-Kingdom. What distinguishes the two versions is that the Tree of Emanation has paths between Netzach and Malkhut and between Hod and Malkhut but no paths between Chockmah and Gevurah and between Binah and Chesed, whereas the opposite is true of the Tree of Return. A non-Sefirah named Da'at (Knowledge) is

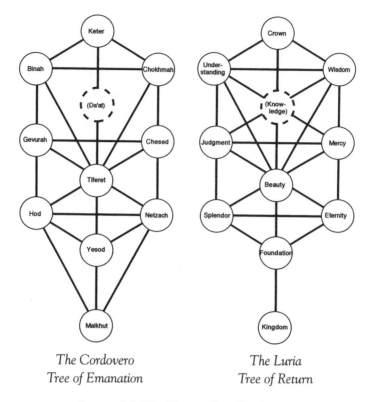

The Cordovero
Tree of Emanation

The Luria
Tree of Return

FIGURE 6.5. THE TREE OF LIFE DIAGRAMS

also featured on both versions of the Tree. With this brief review of the dual forms of the Tree of Life Diagram (presented with much more historical detail and interpretive commentary in chapter 1), we can continue with the construction of the hexagram diagram for whose principles the traditional Tree holds the key. We will thus see that the hexagram, which has been the most universally accepted contribution of the Kabbalah to Jewish life, has an intrinsic connection to the Tree of Life Diagram, which has come more and more to symbolize the secret wisdom of the Kabbalah as a stream separate from the main flow of Jewish communal history. Because this underlying diagram will, in turn, explain features of the Tree that appear to be arbitrary, it would almost seem as if the Tree, though itself long hidden from public view, was meant to serve as an exoteric key to a yet more esoteric complex of cosmological diagrams, of which the one now to be developed is the most fundamental, and which only the initiate would be able to unlock.

Whatever the case may be, the developing hexagram diagram can already unlock one major puzzle of the Tree, the relationship to the ten Sefirot of the eleventh non-Sefirah called Da'at, which is traditionally placed at the otherwise conspicuously empty spot at the center of the upper kite shape. For Da'at, which is translated as "Knowledge," and which signifies for the Kabbalist the knowledge of ultimate reality that lies outside of manifest creation, is located at the exact center of the larger diagram from which the Tree would seem to have been derived. Although the particular association of Da'at with Chokhmah and Binah goes back at least as far as the *Idra Rabba* section of the *Zohar*[35] and informs the "Chabad" tradition founded by the original Lubavitcher Rabbi, all those who attempt to make a triad of Chokhmah and Binah with Da'at (the three words composing the name Chabad) rather than with Keter are normally careful not to claim it as a Sefirah. The placement of the non-Sefirah Da'at at this precise spot has never been satisfactorily explained, nor the reason why it cannot be treated simply as another Sefirah, but it should now be clear that the source of its special treatment lies in its position at the true center of an underlying diagram and that, though this knowledge has now been largely lost, there must have been some who once could claim it.

If we look again at the Tree of Life Diagram that emerges from this construction of three hexagrams, it can be seen that it lacks only the Sefirah Yesod, with the two paths connecting it to Netzach and Hod, and the three paths of the central line between Keter and Malkhut, sometimes called the pillar of equilibrium. Now if the working hypothesis is accepted that the Tree of Life Diagram is, indeed, derived from a more basic geometric construction composed of hexagrams, then it would follow that these missing elements of the Tree diagram should also be somehow produced by hexagrams, though this cannot be accomplished through the simple addition of the fourth hexagram in the previously established mode of progression. But if one allows that the complete diagram underlying that of the Tree is composed entirely of hexagrams, that every line in it must be a line of a hexagram, one can then proceed to construct the necessary additional hexagrams using the Tree of Life Diagram as a key to such further construction.

To do this, one should begin by drawing lines along those established between Netzach and Hod with Yesod, lines that cross the site of Yesod and extend until they meet lines joining them from the other five directions of the diagram (for this diagram produces not one but six radiating Trees from the same central point of Da'at, a subject that is the focus of chapter 8). The hexagram thus formed can be seen in figure 6.6.

FIGURE 6.6. THE YESOD CROSSING

As figure 6.6 shows, the hexagram whose construction manifests the previously missing Yesod with its two paths to Netzach and Hod discloses another principle of hexagram construction than that by which the first three hexagrams had been formed. These could be built in an inward or outward direction by the same simple procedure of either inscribing a smaller hexagram within the inner hexagon formed by an originating hexagram, as in figure 6.3C, or by extending the sides of its outer hexagon until they form a new enlarged hexagram, as in figure 6.3D. We may call this most natural way of building infinitely larger or smaller hexagrams the whole-step progression, and it involves an alternation of orientation at each whole step. This change of orientation is determined by the very structure of the hexagram, whose inner hexagon defines a different orientation from that of its points. Since the outer hexagon formed from aligning two of the hexagram points becomes the inner hexagon of the next larger enclosing hexagram, we are really talking only

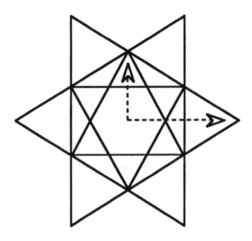

FIGURE 6.7

about the dual-oriented nature of the hexagram, which rotates 90° at each whole-step progression of hexagram construction, as illustrated in figure 6.7.

The Yesod hexagram, however, involves a second important way of constructing hexagrams that can be called the half-step progression inasmuch as it has produced a hexagram that, though larger than the previously constructed third hexagram, is not as large as the hexagram that can be formed from the point-hexagon of this third hexagram in the regular whole-step progression. Rather than a product of the third hexagram, it seems to be, like the third hexagram itself, built upon the base of the second hexagram, but with a different manner of construction. Although discovered through plotting the Yesod crossing, the hexagram thus formed would seem to be most easily constructed directly from the single points of the second hexagram.

There are, then, two ways of constructing larger hexagrams that are both first demonstrated in relationship to the second hexagram of this developing diagram. From this second hexagram, two larger hexagrams can be formed, as shown in figure 6.8. The smaller of these two hexagrams is formed by the lines connecting two of the points of the second hexagram in the whole-step progression, as in figure 6.8A. The larger of these hexagrams is formed by drawing a line through a single point of the second hexagram parallel to the lines of this second hexagram in the half-step progression that maintains the same orientation of the second hexagram, as in figure 6.8B.

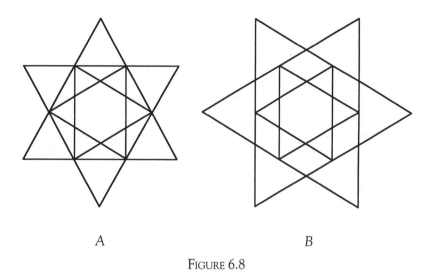

A   B

FIGURE 6.8

The whole-step progression (based upon an alignment through two points) extends the orientation of the inner hexagon, while the half-step progression (based upon an alignment through a single point) extends the orientation of the points. But since the half step is measured as a half step past the previous whole step, it is really one and one-half steps beyond the hexagram from whose single points it is constructed. What is most significant about this difference in construction, however, is that the whole-step progression produces a more stable hexagram than the half-step progression since the direction of a line connecting two separated points is clearly defined while that based on a single point is uncertain, and in terms of construction, harder to draw with accuracy. This distinction can more easily be appreciated if we move from a two-dimensional line to a three-dimensional board, such a board being obviously more precariously balanced on one pivot than on two. In terms of visual appearance as well, these lines convey different aesthetic qualities to the symbolic understanding of the mind, the dual-supported line conveying an impression of stable balance and the singly supported line an impression of precarious tension. There is no doubt that something novel is being introduced to the diagram by this fourth hexagram, and its expressive form can help to reveal both its encoded meaning and, through this, the first principle of interpreting this diagram of hexagram expansion.

We have seen that the half-step hexagram following the third hexagram gives an impression of instability, and further, that it is connected by the key of the Tree of Life Diagram with the Sefirah Yesod.

Now this is the Sefirah that the kabbalistic tradition associates with sex, for in the version of the Tree placed upon the cosmic body of Adam Kadmon, primordial man, it defines the site of the sexual organs. The association of sex with instability would seem to take us to the myth of Adamic transgression. In the earlier discussion of the creation account, we saw that the garden world was a product of the third day and that this could be associated with the third world of Yetzirah, which is, indeed, where a kabbalistic tradition places the Garden of Eden and the transgression of Adam to which the materialization of this fourth world is attributed. I have hitherto avoided the standard Western terminology for this cosmic catastrophe, that of the Fall, but as we enter the subject of kabbalistic cosmology, this terminology, taken simply as a symbolic name without its further association with Original Sin, becomes the handiest signifier for interpreting the Edenic myth because of its larger cosmic consequences,[36] and I will use it from this point on to convey the cosmic catastrophe leading to the present condition of man.

Continuing with the analysis of figure 6.6, the association of instability with the fourth hexagram would suggest an association of the kabbalistic cosmic worlds not only with the days of creation but also with the progression of whole step hexagrams developed from the key of the Tree of Life Diagram. Now if this whole-step progression of hexagrams can be thus associated with the cosmic worlds, then the geometric descriptions of these hexagrams can also serve as archetypal definitions of the first three of these worlds. Thus the world of Atzilut (Emanation) can be seen to define the basic cosmic functions associated with the hexagram, those of expansion, contraction, and balance; the world of Beriah (Creation) to define a basic shift of orientation to a creative dualism, creative of the two differently oriented hexagrams that it spawns and that express and synthesize the basic differences of orientation between the first and second hexagram worlds; and the world of Yetzirah (Formation) to be made up of its two resulting parts, one stable and one unstable. On this basis, the third hexagram, constructed through the more stable dual supports of the whole-step progression, would seem to be identifiable with the unfallen state of Yetzirah, while the fourth hexagram, constructed through the more precarious single support of the half-step progression, seems to signify a predisposition to the Fall and to be identifiable with a protolapsarian stage still contained within the third world but transitional to the fourth world and leading to its further fracturing of unity into multiplicity.

The peculiar characteristics of the fourth hexagram not only suggest an analogy between the developing diagram and the worlds of the Kabbalah but also one to music. For the movement of one whole step from a starting point, followed by another whole step and then a half step, has an obvious musical analogue in the tonal intervals of the rising diatonic scale, which begins with the similar progression of two whole tones followed by a half or semitone that is easily recognizable through their familiar solfeggio names: Do, Re, Mi, and Fa. But if we can so associate this first tetrachord of the diatonic scale with the hexagrams earlier associated with the first three kabbalistic worlds, this would seem to mean that the diatonic scale contains a second key for further construction of the hexagram diagram, one that reinforces the earlier implications of the geometric-musical keys to the creation account. Where the creation account would appear to associate the hexagram form with a Sabbatical cosmic structure, the analogue of the diatonic scale seems to suggest an octave structure that would bring the hexagram diagram to the same seventh world of the Sabbath. If each of the future worlds are to be as tonally complete as the third world, having what can be considered two semitone hexagrams in accordance with this model, this would bring the extrapolated form of the complete fourth world to the correlated Sol tone and place the octave within the first half of the seventh such world, giving to this seventh world a special character as that which both consummates and transcends the cosmic octave. In any case, it suggests that the developing diagram could be extended beyond the four worlds of the classical Kabbalah in accordance with the two modes of harmonic progression that seem to be part of the esoteric cosmology here being decoded, a cosmology based on a triple association of harmonics, geometry, and number and on the mythological interpretation of the laws they reveal. In the creation account, a seven-day pattern is inextricably tied to both the harmonic series and the hexagram form; and the further expansion of the single hexagram diagram into one of multiple hexagrams would seem to relate the progression of hexagrams to the structure of tones appearing in the major diatonic scale, a structure that has long been held to contain a cosmic code.

In this scale the various tones that emerge in the harmonic series are organized into a particular succession of intervals introjected between the fundamental tone and its first octave overtone. Unlike the discoverable laws of the harmonic series or of "gnomonic" hexagram construction, that in which a geometric expansion results in a form similar to the original, the diatonic scale is like the Tree of Life Diagram in having an apparently arbitrary arrangement of its parts. And yet it is the two apparently arbitrary structures of the Tree of Life Diagram and the diatonic

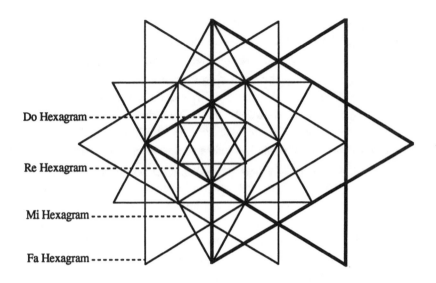

Do Hexagram

Re Hexagram

Mi Hexagram

Fa Hexagram

FIGURE 6.9. THE MIDDLE PILLAR AS A HEXAGRAM CONSTITUENT

scale that prove to be the twin keys capable of unlocking the construction principles for what would seem to be the ultimate cosmological diagram. Because the diatonic scale appears to be so closely correlated with the hexagram progression of this diagram, and this despite the numerical incongruence of harmonic and root 3 geometric proportions, the solfeggio names of its tones will henceforth be adopted to define their hexagram counterparts, a procedure that will not only simplify the identification of hexagrams but also reveal their analogous harmonic relationships. This is particularly useful in the case of the fourth or Fa hexagram at which these twin keys meet.

In the developing hexagram diagram derived directly from that of the Tree of Life, the unique geometric process needed to define the fourth hexagram is one that goes counter to the rules of the whole-step progression otherwise everywhere in force. For it is not on its basis that we are brought to the fourth world of Assiyah by the key of the Tree of Life Diagram. And the way this key will bring us to a fourth world hexagram form exactly a whole step beyond the third or Mi hexagram will further reinforce the suggestions of a contrary quality to the Fa hexagram arising from this key. But this is jumping ahead, for we have yet to derive the Tree of Life Diagram from the underlying construction composed wholly of hexagrams. There remains the decisive middle pillar or line between Keter and Malkhut.

To derive the missing line between Keter and Malkhut, we should, as earlier, simply proceed to draw it, extending the line beyond Keter, situated at the tip of the Do hexagram, as far upward from the central Da'at point as it goes down from it to Malkhut, at the lower tip of the Mi hexagram, for symmetry is one of the guiding principles of this diagram. This line should extend from point to point of the third hexagram. But since the first rule of this diagram is that all its lines must be parts of a hexagram, we must now construct an equilateral triangle using this line as its base and then cross it with its inverse triangle. This can be easily done by aligning the other two lines of this triangle with two points of the third hexagram and its inverse triangle with the angle formed by a point of the second hexagram, as shown in figure 6.9.

This completes the Tree of Life Diagram with lines formed only from hexagrams but it clearly unbalances the diagram. The procedure has obviously to be repeated on the other side of the vertical line forming the middle pillar and then on the other two axes of symmetry passing through the points of the first and third hexagrams, which follow the same orientation, a procedure that will lead to the drawing of six hexagrams. But the drawing of these six hexagrams produces a veritable explosion of hexagrams. It looks as though a "big bang" has suddenly taken place in the diagram. And then the wonder of the diagram manifests itself. A seventh star can be seen to form itself without geometric work from the six drawn hexagrams, larger than all of them and located exactly a whole step beyond the third hexagram, the whole step that brings us finally to the kabbalistic fourth world. It seems fitting to name it the Sabbath Star and the diagram after it. It also seems clear that the six worked hexagrams and the seventh embracing star of consummation, which together form the constellation of hexagrams named the Sabbath Star, are symbolic of the creation of the material world as it has been numerologically projected in the first chapter of Genesis. Because of the importance of the Sabbath Star construct, it will be presented first by itself in figure 6.10, a version that will make it easier to distinguish its parts, each of its six component hexagrams being marked by a different form of dashed or dashed-and-dotted lines within the unbroken form of the seventh embracing star.

Though such a construction is not featured in any text of practical or spiritual geometry of which I am aware, it is a potential construction inherent in the recognized geometric progression of one to six to seven: six derived from unity will magically produce or contain a seventh. We have already seen how six is the first geometric expression of the unity of the

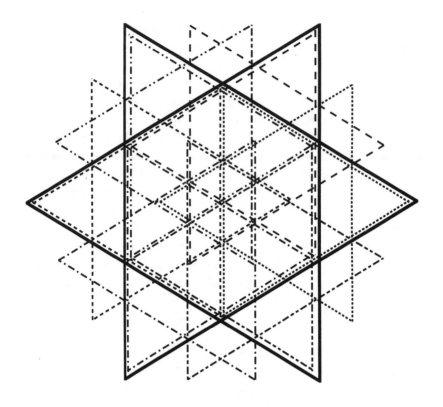

FIGURE 6.10. THE SABBATH STAR

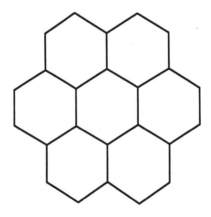

FIGURE 6.11

circle. Now if we join the six points that the radius defines on the circumference of a circle not in a hexagram, as previously, but in a hexagon, and build other hexagons of the same size on each of its sides, we will find that these six close-packed hexagons define the outline of the central hexagon: in a two-dimensional drawing, the six outer hexagons can be thought of as producing the inner seventh, as shown in figure 6.11.

Six circles will equally enclose a seventh. And this is a geometric property only of sixness. It does not apply to five, seven, or any other number of hexagons or circles. But the magical power of six derived from unity to manifest a seventh is perhaps nowhere so dramatically expressed as in the Sabbath Star we have just seen produced from six symmetrically arranged hexagrams whose bases diametrically connect the six radial arc points of a circle. If Pythagoras was right in asserting that the ultimate nature of reality lies in numbers, by which he meant in part the various functions and qualities associated with unity, duality, triadicy, and so forth, then the manifestation of the One into multiplicity would follow the laws of geometry and in some sense the universe would have been produced through the workings of six—six acts that together formed the completeness, the harmony, the peace, the sacredness of seven.

Having studied the Sabbath Star separately, we can now place it in the completed Sabbath Star Diagram, the diagram composed of the minimum number of hexagrams, consistent with symmetry, needed to manifest the Tree of Life Diagram with all its paths and Sefirot. And this also proves to be the number necessary for the Sabbath Star Diagram to define the four kabbalistic worlds culminating in the material world of Assiyah. If we now translate the whole-step progression magically produced by the Sabbath Star construction into the musical terminology of solfeggio, the tone signified by its larger seventh hexagram would be that termed Fi, corresponding to F# in the key of C, and we can speak of the whole construction as the Fi Sabbath Star. Since this Sabbath Star is necessary to complete the derivation of the Tree of Life Diagram from the underlying Sabbath Star Diagram, it may also be possible to associate it not only with the big bang of material creation but more specifically with the evolution of embodied life in the cosmos, that life for which the tree has ever been symbolic.

In figure 6.12, the completed Sabbath Star Diagram is illustrated with the superimposed Tree of Emanation, the form of the Tree associated in chapter 1 with Cordovero, but without the further discrimination of its parts that might mar the visual impression of the whole. It

FIGURE 6.12. THE SABBATH STAR DIAGRAM WITH
THE TREE OF EMANATION

should also be noticed that the Fi Sabbath Star overlays the second or Re hexagram signifying Beriah, the world of Creation, and might thus be said to incorporate in manifest form the Berian archetypes from which the creation was generated. But though the Sabbath Star of the fourth world completes the Tree of Emanation, it also contributes those lines crisscrossing the central Da'at point that, with the central column, suddenly manifests the complete Lurianic Tree of Return as well.

The Sabbath Star Diagram, then, provides a geometric derivation for both major forms of the Tree of Life Diagram that have been present in the kabbalistic tradition since at least sixteenth-century Safed. But in addition it shows that the Tree of Emanation is particularly relevant to the process of emanation up to and including the fourth world of manifest solids and may have its greatest significance with regard to the third world, whose mythologically represented Garden of Eden was the specified place of the Tree of Life. And it further shows that the Tree of Re-

FIGURE 6.13. THE SABBATH STAR DIAGRAM WITH
THE TREE OF RETURN

turn has its origin at that very central seventh tone of the spiral octave of creation, after which all is Tikkun. This can be easily seen in the twelve tone progression of the ascending chromatic solfeggio scale: Do, Di/ Re, Ri/ Mi, Fa/ **Fi**, Sol/ Si, La/ Li, Ti, /Do. It would thus seem that both versions of the Tree are relevant to discussions of the fourth world, but that the Tree of Emanation has more relevance to an understanding of the earlier cosmic worlds, which are the focus of the Zoharic Kabbalah, while the Tree of Return has more relevance to the Olam ha-Tikkun, the future process of return that is the focus of the Lurianic Kabbalah. This latter Tree is represented in figure 6.13.

Although it was earlier suggested that both versions of the Tree are equally validated by the final form of the Sabbath Star Diagram, it can be equally argued that the fourth-world Sabbath Star effects a change in the Tree diagram, eliminating Malkhut's former paths to Netzach and Hod and adding the paths crisscrossing Da'at that are to serve a specifically

FIGURE 6.14. THE MENORAH WITHIN THE SABBATH STAR DIAGRAM

fourth-world function. Further discussion of this point will be part of the larger reinterpretation of the Tree of Life Diagram in chapter 8.

Before concluding this discussion of the Sabbath Star Diagram, there is an additional feature that needs to be observed, and it is one that takes us back to the very first geometric form to be incorporated into the ritual of Jewish observance, the form from which the Tree of Life Diagram has itself been thought to have been derived, that of the menorah. Figure 6.14 shows us how the form of the menorah exactly fits into the lines of the Sabbath Star Diagram.

The seven-branched candelabrum can be seen to fit exactly onto the vertical lines that meet at the upper bar of the Mi hexagram. The connection between this earliest external emblem of the Jewish people and the later emblem of its esoteric spirituality can be seen most immediately by comparing the three essential aspects of both. In both we can find right and left sides and a central shaft that joins and may be said to harmonize them. Moreover, in the description of the menorah given in Exodus 25:31–40, there are further numerical correspondences to be observed. In addition to the shaft and three pairs of branches, there are also ten knobs or spheres and twenty-two bowls. Although there is scholarly dispute about the exact arrangement contemplated by the text, and whether the menorah depicted on the Arch of Titus conforms to it, what can be determined from the text is that each branch contains one sphere with flowers and three bowls while the central shaft contains four spheres with flowers and four bowls. Not only do the branches and flowers suggest a tree, then, but the ten spheres suggest the ten Sefirot and the twenty-two bowls the twenty-two paths of the Tree of Life Diagram, which, like the menorah, is divided into central, right, and left parts. Moses was shown the menorah in a vision on Mount Sinai and told that it should be constructed on this visionary pattern: "And look that thou make them [the ark, table, and menorah] after their pattern, which was shewed thee in the mount" (Exod. 25:40). Moses was further instructed to have the menorah made of a single piece of beaten gold by Bezaleel, "in whose heart the Lord had put wisdom" (Exod. 36:2). The menorah, then, was conveyed to Israel through two levels of prophetic vision, first that shown to Moses on the mountain and then that directly communicated to the heart of the inspired craftsman Bezaleel. We can never know the exact nature of the vision on the mount, but it seems not beyond possibility that the "pattern" of the menorah shown to Moses included the underlying Sabbath Star Diagram and revealed the relationship between the menorah and the Tree as both were seen to be contained within it.

In the *Zohar* allusion is made at the very beginning to a diagram underlying all of creation, a diagram whose existence in the supernal thought is said to have been first disclosed through the direct revelation of Elijah:

> This mystery remained sealed until one day, whilst I was on the seashore, Elijah came and said to me . . . "When the most mysterious wished to reveal Himself, He first produced a single point which was transmuted into a thought, and in this He . . . graved within the sacred and mystic lamp a mystic and most holy design, which was a wondrous edifice issuing from the midst of thought. This . . . was the beginning of the edifice, existent and non-existent, deep-buried, unknowable by name. . . . And upon this secret the world is built."[37]

The fact that the name of this "most holy design" is said to be "un-knowable" suggests that it is not the famous Tree of Life Diagram, whose name would already have been known by the author or final redactor of the *Zohar* in thirteenth-century Spain. It seems not impossible that it might be taken as an allusion to the Sabbath Star Diagram, since another passage from the *Zohar* seems further to describe the basic pro-gression and structure of this diagram:

> R. Simeon proceeded: "See now, it was by means of the Torah that the Holy One created the world. . . . He looked at the Torah once, twice, thrice, and a fourth time. . . . indicated by the verse, 'Then did he see, and declare it; he established it, yea, and searched it out.' (Job. XXVIII, 27). Seeing, declaring, establishing and search-ing out correspond to these four operations which the Holy One, blessed be He, went through before entering on the work of cre-ation. Hence the account of the creation commences with the four words *Bereshith Bara Aelohim Aith* ('In-the-beginning created God the'), before mentioning 'the heavens," thus signifying the four times which the Holy One, blessed be He, looked into the Torah before he performed His work."[38]

In the Sabbath Star Diagram there are also "four operations" to be done "before entering on the work of creation," the drawing of the four hexagrams that precede the explosion of six hexagrams in the Sabbath Star signifying "the work of creation," all drawn in accordance with the hidden laws (Torah) of this diagram: that all its lines be formed from hexagrams; that the progression be from the first to the second to the third hexagram by whole step or whole tone; that the progression to the fourth hexagram be by the half step or semitone; and that this be fol-lowed by the remarkable configuration and transmutation of six hexagrams into seven of the Sabbath Star.

If we can accept Zoharic discussion of Sefirot in connection with "paths" and "columns" as denoting a specific diagram because a model of just such a diagram surfaced three hundred years later called the Tree of Life, might we not also find in the Zoharic quotations just referred to allusions that would equally seem to point to the existence and knowl-edge of the Sabbath Star Diagram had such a diagram ever surfaced in the tradition? But whether or not these quotations suggest a knowledge of the Sabbath Star Diagram by the author of the *Zohar* and others before him, they should show that there was some geometric model that the Kabbalist associated with the processes of creation, that this "mystic and most holy design" existing in the supernal mind not only contained the processes of emanation and material creation but also their meaning, and that this divine geometry could be discovered on all levels of the cosmos and reveal its mystic secrets to the knowing. Whatever its origin, the Sabbath Star Diagram seems deeply connected with a basic hexadic geometry at the very heart of the kabbalistic tradition, one that expressed itself most overtly in the two geometric symbols popularized by the Kabbalah since the seventeenth century, the hexagram, or Star of David, and the Tree of Life Diagram. It may perhaps explain the secret of their connection.

7

Kabbalistic Geometry and the Genesis of the Son

Decoding the *Sefer Yetzirah* Diagram: The Sefirot and Meditation

In chapter 6 a geometric derivation of the Tree of Life Diagram, named the Sabbath Star Diagram, was proposed that employed an expanding grid of hexagrams and that proved to have suggestive correspondences with the kabbalistic cosmology of four worlds. In the next two chapters we will study two further diagrams and these analyses will profit from use of the key provided by the Sabbath Star Diagram for determining the cosmic world correlations of their geometric parts. As we proceed with these analyses, we will see that the various associations of these three underlying diagrams both with one another and with the finally disclosed Tree of Knowledge Diagram argue strongly for their all being part of one system of Hebraic sacred science probably going back to the Temple priesthood.

This chapter will offer a solution to the geometric enigma of the *Sefer Yetzirah*. For this first extant work of the Kabbalah has long been held to allude to a diagram or construction of a cube, one that it has thus far proved impossible to explain in satisfactory geometric terms. But before decoding the implicit geometry of the *Sefer Yetzirah*, its equally encoded instructions for meditative practice will first be recovered. In addition, this chapter will study the major text of the Lurianic Kabbalah, the *Etz Chayyim* of Chayyim Vital, making much of this text available in English for the first time. And we will see that the complete *Sefer Yetzirah* Diagram, one expanded to contain that of the Tree of Life in accordance with such a reference a millennium later in the *Sefer ha-Bahir*, will prove to be a precise model for Lurianic cosmology, particularly regarding the generation of the Partzufim, the divine personalities. Furthermore, Luria's concept of the twice-born Partzuf of Ze'ir Anpin, as modeled by this diagram, will have significant ramifications with respect to the Hebraic secret doctrine of the son.

It is the modeling of the Partzufim and their various relationships by the full *Sefer Yetzirah* Diagram that will be the main focus of this chapter, and this will necessarily involve a close study of their sexual relations, A. E. Waite having rightly concluded in his monumental study of the Kabbalah that "the Supreme Wisdom is a Mystery of Sex."[1] Our understanding of Lurianic cosmology will depend, then, on our mastering the intricacies of Luria's sexual mythology. But it is the final interpretation of the fully expanded *Sefer Yetzirah* Diagram as a model depicting the generation of the cosmic son that will prove especially enlightening, not only regarding the geometric-cosmological implications of the *Sefer Yetzirah* Diagram but also of the Tree of Life Diagram, particularly in its sixfold rotated form, the final subject of this part. In the process, we should also gain greater appreciation of the *Sefer Yetzirah* as both the culmination of the earlier Jewish esoteric tradition and fount of the later Kabbalah. But it is now time to turn to its encoded wisdom, beginning with its encoded meditative technique.

In its first chapter, the *Sefer Yetzirah* identifies the first four Sefirot "Belimah" (an untranslatable term that has been taken to mean everything from the infinite to nothingness but probably signifies the abstract nature of the numerals) with the Holy Breath and the elements of air, water, and fire, elements associated in chapter 2 of the *Sefer Yetzirah* with the three mother letters: Aleph, Mem, and Shin. The following are these definitions of the first four Sefirot:

> 1:9. Ten Sefirot of Nothingness: One is the Breath of the Living God [*Ruach Elohim Chayyim*], blessed and benedicted be the Name of the Life of worlds. Voice, Breath and Speech. This is the Holy Breath (*Ruach HaKodesh*).

1:10. Two: Breath from Breath [*ruach me-ruach*]. With it engrave and carve twenty-two foundation letters—three Mothers, seven Doubles, and twelve Elementals—and one Breath is from them.

1:11. Three: Water from Breath [*mayyim me-ruach*]. With it engrave and carve chaos and void [*tohu and bohu*], mire and clay. Engrave them like a garden plot, carve them like a wall, cover them like a ceiling.

1:12. Four: Fire from Water [*aesch me-mayyim*]. With it engrave and carve the Throne of Glory, Seraphim, Ophanim, holy Chayot, and Ministering angels.[2] (My brackets)

The normal translation of the *Sefer Yetzirah* is a third person account of God's creation of the supernal worlds through the third world of Yetzirah. But Aryeh Kaplan, taking advantage of an ambiguity in the verb forms has, in his appendix, translated the "short form" of this text completely in the imperative mode, thus making the reader a potential cosmic creator and the whole a manual for spiritual development through meditation, a possibility strengthened by the verse just preceding those quoted, in 1:8: "Ten Sefirot of Nothingness: Bridle your mouth from speaking and your heart from thinking. And if your heart runs, return to the place."[3] Thus from the third person perspective we are told that the creation proceeded from the Ruach ha-Kodesh, from which the twenty-two letters were formed, that with these foundation letters the three dimensions were engraved and carved out of *tohu* and *bohu*, and that from these three dimensions the Throne of Glory and all the heavenly hosts were formed. In the next verse the six directions of three-dimensional space are "sealed" through various unifications of the three mother letters—Aleph, Mem, and Shin—and the three different letters of the Tetragrammaton—Yod, Hey, and Vav. But with the alternate perspective made possible through the imperative translation, it becomes possible to read these verses as providing instructions on meditation, and I would like to suggest that they contain instructions on a particular technique combining what, from the yogic tradition, might be called *pranayama* and mantra, special breathing with silent repetition of a name of God or formula containing such a divine name. In what follows, this decoded technique will be presented as a lesson for the modern meditator, and it can be used in conjunction with the harmonic stretching practice given in chapter 5.

In chapter 3 of the *Sefer Yetzirah*, it is shown that breath is associated with the mother letter Aleph and with the chest in man, that water is associated with the mother letter Mem and the lower torso, and fire with the mother letter Shin and the head. Our meditator begins, then, inspired, in all senses of the word, by the Holy Breath and repeating the name of the first Sefirah: *Ruach Elohim Chayyim*. He then begins a slow chest exhalation, silently repeating *ruach me-ruach*, which is completed with an abdominal contraction that expels the last of the breath to the words *mayyim me-ruach*. A new breath is now inhaled to the head, the words *aesch me-mayyim* accompanying this expanded state, and then the breath is held for the divine influx through the crown that reinspires the consciousness with the Holy Breath as the mantralike phrase containing the divine name, *Ruach Elohim Chayyim*, is again repeated. As this pattern of breathing becomes a continuous flow, the mantralike names of the first four Sefirot form a rhythmic and rhyming pattern:

Ruach me-ruach
Mayyim me-ruach
Aesch me-mayyim
Ruach Elohim Chayyim

With such a meditative technique, which I believe to be the hidden instruction in these verses, the meditator who thus bridles his mouth from speaking and heart from thinking of anything but these special words is using breath and language to order the chaotic consciousness so that it can ascend to the Throne of Glory and be one with the heavenly hosts. Through such practices the higher Ruach level of the soul can be perfected and, with it, its spiritual body, that supernal cube in which Yetziric Adam is to be completed:

1:13. Five: With three of the simple letters seal "above." Choose three [the Lurianic edition here adds "in the mystery of the three Mothers Aleph Mem Shin"] and place them in His great Name: YHV. With them seal the six extremities. Face upward and seal it with YHV.
Six: Seal "below." Face downward and seal it with YVH.
Seven: Seal "east." Face straight ahead and seal it with HYV.
Eight: Seal "west." Face backward and seal it with HVY.
Nine: Seal "south." Face to the right and seal it with VYH.

Ten: Seal "north." Face to the left and seal it with VHY.[4] (My
brackets)

If the first four Sefirot may be said to inspirit Adamic man, filling his
chest, lower trunk, and head with the divine breath, with the last six he
becomes fully animate, moving upward and downward with his head,
forward and backward with his legs, and out to the right and left with his
arms. We can thus see how these verses have been taken to refer to the
mental creation of an artificial man or robot, the Golem of legend. But as
with the mundane misinterpretation of alchemy, so here it would seem
that what is being created or transmuted is nothing of earthly use, but
rather is of the spirit.

Whether the *Sefer Yetzirah* is understood to define the process by
which the supernal Adam was divinely created or that by which the
spiritual adept can recreate himself in the image of this cosmic man, it
shows a continuity of emphasis with the earlier form of Jewish
esotericism known as the Merkabah tradition, that deriving from the
Throne vision of Ezekiel in which the mystic envisioned the cosmic
Glory not only as the supernal man but, as Abraham Abulafia is later
to reveal, as one exhibiting his own face. As I have argued, from Ezekiel,
through the *Shi'ur Komah* and *Sefer Yetzirah*, to the Kabbalah of the
Bahir, Abulafia, and beyond, the Jewish esoteric tradition has maintained a continuous understanding of the cosmic man as the center of
both its gnosis and practice. Suffice it to say here that whether envisioned as enthroned or with a body composed of the Sefirot, the contemplative "measurement" of such a cosmic body was the very means
by which the mystic attempted to recreate himself in this divine image.
The concept of the Golem as an externally created magical being was,
then, a vulgarization of what the true adept always knew to be the hidden meaning of the source texts of this legend, the understanding that
the entity to be mystically created was the mystic's own higher self. But
let us now return to and conclude this treatment of the *Sefer Yetzirah* as
a meditative text. Progressing, then, from the first four to the last six
Sefirot, the soul of the meditator, recreated in the divine image through
the Ruach ha-Kodesh, can now enclose itself in its resonant crystalline
body through a contemplative facing of each of its six directions and,
seated within the sacred space of this imaginatively constructed cube,
can experience the infinite expansion made possible through the mystery of its twelve diagonals.[5]

Solution to the Mystery of the
Sefer Yetzirah Diagram

The *Sefer Yetzirah* has been understood to allude to a cubic diagram because its first chapter closes with a definition of the six directions of space. It has hitherto proved impossible to explain its construction, however, because the definitions it provides for the twelve diagonals of this cube seem rather to define its twelve edges:

> Twelve Elementals: HV ZCh TY LN SO TzQ. . . . Their measure is the twelve diagonal boundaries: the north-east boundary, the south-east boundary, the upper-east boundary, the lower-east boundary, the upper-north boundary, the lower-north boundary, the south-west boundary, the north-west boundary, the upper-west boundary, the lower-west boundary, the upper-south boundary, the lower-south boundary. They continually spread for ever and ever. They are the Arms of the Universe.[6]

That the solution to this enigma was known and, further, that there existed a tradition of interpreting the esoteric *Sefer Yetzirah* cube as containing the Tree of Life Diagram is suggested by a historically significant reference to the above passage in the next important work of the Kabbalah, the *Bahir*:

> The Blessed Holy One has a single Tree, and it has twelve diagonal boundaries:
>
> > The northeast boundary, the southeast boundary;
> > The upper east boundary, the lower east boundary;
> >
> > The southwest boundary, the northwest boundary;
> > The upper west boundary, the lower west boundary;
> >
> > The upper south boundary, the lower south boundary;
> > The upper north boundary, the lower north boundary;
> >
> > They continually spread forever and ever;
> > They are the "arms of the world"
>
> On the inside of them is the Tree.[7]

Though the identification of all twelve diagonals with the twelve edges of the cube is the way the *Sefer Yetzirah* cubic diagram is most often dismissed,[8] I am going to propose a radically different approach to the *Sefer Yetzirah* diagonals that assumes its compilers used the geometric term for diagonal, *alakhson*, because they were practicing geometers who understood the spiritual difference between the diagonal and the edge and intended to differentiate the irrational measures from the rational.

Although our concern is primarily with the infinite diagonals of chapter 5 of the *Sefer Yetzirah*, whose description was just given, the earlier discussion of its equally encoded meditative technique has been necessary to indicate the significance of the cube that is being imaginatively constructed in the course of this *sefer*, or book, for this cube is the subtle container of the higher cosmic worlds and defines both the process of divine emanation and of spiritual return. But since this is the Book of Yetzirah, the third kabbalistic world associated geometrically with the second dimension, the cube to be thus constructed would not be an actual solid, rather a two-dimensional representation of such a cube. This distinction seems to be implied in a Zoharic passage quoted earlier that should be repeated here:

> What is the meaning of *Bereshith*? It means "with Wisdom," the Wisdom on which the world is based, and through this it introduces us to deep and recondite mysteries. In it, too, is the inscription of six chief supernal directions, out of which there issues the totality of existence. From the same there go forth six sources of rivers which flow into the Great Sea. This is implied in the word *BeReSHiTH*, which can be analyzed into BaRa-SHiTH (He created six). And who created them? The Mysterious Unknown.[9]

In this reference, the meaning "He created six" ascribed to "Bereshit" is directly identified with the "six chief supernal directions, out of which there issues the totality of existence." But since these "supernal directions" precede existence, they cannot be identified with the world of created solids, with the six directions that define the sides of a cube. Rather, the "six chief supernal directions" would have to be those defined by the six points inscribed on the circumference of the primal circle in the regular geometric progression of hexagram growth detailed in chapter 6, and the "cube" that which joins them in an orthogonal projection. It is, I believe, such a diagram that forms the basis of all kabbalistic references to the six supernal directions, and it is central to the construction

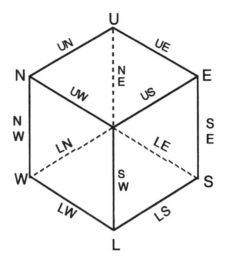

FIGURE 7.1. THE TWELVE EDGES OF THE *SEFER YETZIRAH* CUBE

of the *Sefer Yetzirah* Diagram. In figure 7.1, the six sides of the cube "sealed" in chapter 1 are illustrated in this "supernal" form, the visible faces represented by complete lines and the invisible faces by broken lines.

At the six radial arc points of the enclosing premanifest circle the six directional letters can be found that indicate upper, east, south, lower, west, and north. If any one of these directions is chosen, it can be seen that there is a corresponding plane in which its letter figures in all four of its edges. Thus the visible southern plane, bounded by the four points *E*, *S*, *L*, and that which can be placed at the center, has four edges marked *SE*, *LS*, *SW*, and *US*. Once this diagram has been understood, we can proceed to the next, which adds the diagonals in their normally recognized form, a subject requiring some explanation.

Since each side of a solid cube is a square, if this square were to be given an edge size of 1, its two diagonals would have the length of √2. In addition to the twelve √2 diagonals for the six sides, there are also four √3 diagonals in a cube, as in that from the upper northeast corner to the lower southwest corner. In this diagram the fourth √3 diagonal cannot be seen as it goes through the two corners located in this orthogonal projection directly at the center, the upper southwest and lower northeast corners. But it is with the twelve √2 diagonals that we must be concerned since this is the number of the diagonals specified in the *Sefer Yetzirah*. Now if we attempt to insert these twelve diagonals into the orthogonal

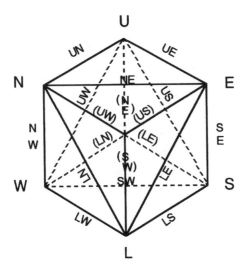

FIGURE 7.2. The Twelve "Diagonals" of the *Sefer Yetzirah* Cube

projection of a cube that it was determined was the form of the cube implied in this text, we will find that half of them are already there, for the three visible faces of figure 7.1 these are the dashed lines, their solid extensions providing similar diagonals for the three invisible faces. But when we then insert the remaining six diagonals, what becomes manifest is the significant form of the hexagram. Thus in the encoded geometry of the *Sefer Yetzirah* there is the same hexagram form we also saw in the last chapter to be encoded in the Genesis creation account. If the first stage in solving the enigma of the *Sefer Yetzirah* cube was the recognition that it must be a two-dimensional projection, the second stage is accomplished simply by adding the twelve diagonals of the six sides of such an orthogonal cube. We shall soon see that this can only solve half of the problem once the *Sefer Yetzirah* directions are applied to these diagonals, but it is the logical way to start, and it will finally lead to the correct solution.

In figure 7.2 these twelve diagonals have been given the letter names for the directional points that they join. Thus the diagonal crossing the southern plane, which joins the E and L points, is now called the *LE* or lower east infinite diagonal. Now the interesting thing about this and all the other hexagram diagonals is that they bisect an edge with precisely the same directional name, the *LE* diagonal bisecting the invisible *LE* edge of the lower plane. In figure 7.2, the identifications of the bisected edges are given in parentheses while those for the diagonals are not in parentheses.

This last diagram has defined six of the infinite diagonals: *LE, LN, NE, US, SW,* and *UW.* This leaves us with the need to establish the other six diagonals: *UE, SE, LS, LW, NW,* and *UN.* If we look at figure 7.2, it can be seen that these correspond to the six sides of the outer hexagon that, in figure 7.1, defined six edges of the cube, edges that cannot also function as the diagonals of the same cube. On the other hand, the six edges that cross the earlier established diagonals and give the visual appearance of diagonals already have the directional identifications corresponding to the previously established diagonals. Now if the diagram is intended to have twelve diagonals distinguished from the twelve edges of the cube, then another solution must be found than has yet been offered in the commentaries on the *Sefer Yetzirah* for the six missing diagonals.

The solution I would offer does not differ in form from the single successful attempt, of which I am aware, that has previously been made to construct the *Sefer Yetzirah* Diagram. This is the diagram that appears without commentary in the translation of the *Sefer Yetzirah* made in a publication by the "Work of the Chariot"[10] that is reproduced in figure 7.3.

In this diagram, the six lines of the hexagram and the six lines of the enclosing hexagon are given the letter identifications corresponding to the twelve single letters associated with the twelve infinite diagonals, but the seven double letters have been identified only with the center and the six directions of space radiating from it rather than with the six planes that form a cube, an omission that renders meaningless the very concept of diagonals. To restore the cube of which the other twelve lettered lines are presumably the diagonals, it would be necessary to divide the six double letters that are here restricted to the directional lines so that one form of the letter remains with the six lines radiating from the center, the center that rightly contains the seventh double letter, and the other form of these first six double letters is assigned to the six sides of the outer hexagon. But this brings us back to the problem with which we began and that obviously stumped the Kabbalists who call themselves the Work of the Chariot—the necessity of distinguishing between the edges and diagonals of a cube. For if the first six double letters were thus divided to form the twelve edges of the cube, six of the cube's edges would also have to function as its diagonals. This apparent absurdity can be resolved, however, if the two sets of letters are understood to belong to different and

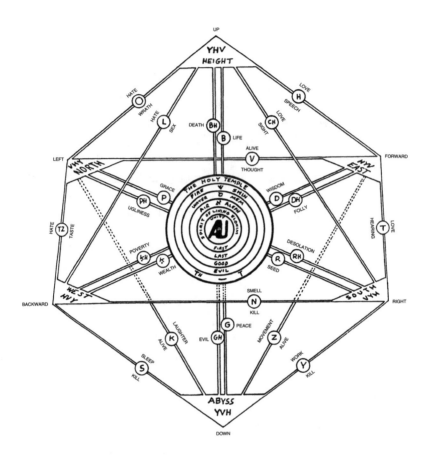

FIGURE 7.3. THE WORK OF THE CHARIOT VERSION OF THE *SEFER YETZIRAH*
DIAGRAM. From *Book of Formation (Sefer Yetzirah):*
The Letters of Our Father Abraham (Hollywood, Calif.:
Work of the Chariot, 1971), chap. 5, fig. 5.

interpenetrating geometric forms, one of which could contain the enlarging diagonals of the other.

It is this possibility that I offer as the solution to the twelve diagonals
whose names, at the beginning of the fifth chapter in the *Sefer Yetzirah*,
seem rather to correspond to the edges than to the diagonals of a three-
dimensional cube: NE, SE, UE, LE, UN, LN, SW, NW, UW, LW, US,
and LS. For though a diagonal might be construed as going from the NE
corner to the SW corner, it could not, except in an orthogonal projection, be conceived of as going from north to east or as in any way joining

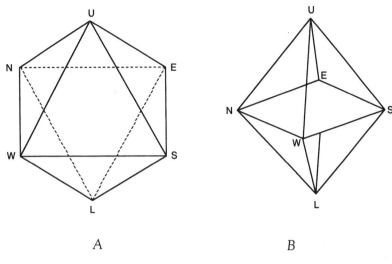

A   B

FIGURE 7.4

these two directions in the manner of the cubic edge. But even the orthogonal projection can only account for the hexagram diagonals, which
comprise only half the required number. If the hexagram and its enclosing hexagon are considered separately, however, they can be taken to
represent an entirely different solid, that of the octahedron, shown in
figure 7.4A. For our present purposes, however, it is important to view
the octahedron also in its on-point or dual pyramid position, as shown in
figure 7.4B.

As can be seen in figure 7.4B, the octahedron has an upper point, a
lower point, and four additional points at the four corners of an intermediate square that can be identified with the four compass points of north,
east, south, and west. The six vertices of the octahedron correspond to
the six sides of the cube, just as the eight vertices of the cube correspond
to the eight triangular sides of the octahedron. The two solids can thus
dual each other in the sense that each can exactly contain the other:
when the octahedron is within the cube its vertices touch the center of
the cube's sides, and when the cube is within the octahedron its vertices
touch the center of the octahedron's sides. Both solids, however, have
twelve edges that can be defined by the same twelve letter names given
for the twelve diagonals in the *Sefer Yetzirah*. If these be rearranged to
correspond to the illustration of the on-point octahedron, we can then
identify the four edges going from the upper point to the intermediate

square as UE, US, UW, and UN, the four edges going from the lower point to the intermediate square as LE, LS, LW, and LN, and the four edges of the square as NE, SE, SW, and NW. What is most significant, however, is that, unlike the right-angled edges of the cube, the edges of the octahedron are all diagonals. They are all also the sides of equilateral triangles, the other sides of which they meet individually at oblique or diagonal angles of 60°. Thus even the edges of the intermediate square, which divides the octahedron into two facing pyramids, are also diagonal sides of triangles and reveal their diagonal nature as soon as the octahedron is turned on another of its points. With this in mind, we should now return to the phrasing of the *Sefer Yetzirah* regarding the twelve single letters: "Their measure is the twelve diagonal boundaries: the north-east boundary, the south-east boundary," and so on. The reference here seems clearly to point to the diagonal edges or boundaries of the octahedron. And it suggests that its author was well aware of an octahedron method of enlarging the cube.

The enlarging of the sides of a cube is not a problem since this can be done practically through measurement and geometrically through the diagonal method of square expansion, one of the most basic procedures of plane geometry: a square with a side of 1 is enlarged to a square with a side of 2 through an intervening square whose side is the same as the diagonal of the first square, $\sqrt{2}$, and whose own diagonal will provide the length of the side on the surrounding square, 2. If these three squares are nested one within the other and the middle square is drawn diagonally to the other two, it can be seen how the diagonal of the smaller square is equal to the side of the one enclosing it, as in figure 7.5.

But though a cube can thus be expanded through expansion of its square sides, this is still a method of plane geometry applied to solid geometry; and if appropriately sized cubes are placed one within the other, they will not be distributed proportionally through the space but all sit on the bottom of the largest cube. The more elegant solution is to use the dualing octahedron, which *can* hold the smaller cube centered within it even as it is centered within the larger cube, and which can also provide the needed diagonal measurement. For as we have just seen, the octahedron is composed of four upper and four lower triangles meeting at a square, the diagonal of which is equal to the side of a surrounding cube. This can also be illustrated by figure 7.5 if the three squares are revisualized so that the inner square with a side of 1 is taken to represent the upper and lower sides of an inner cube, the outer square with a side of 2 the same sides of an outer cube, and the middle square with a side of √2 the square in the intervening octahedron.

Not only is use of the dualing octahedron in the expansion of the cube a method more appropriate to the geometry of solids; it also indicates a far more sophisticated knowledge of geometry, in particular the geometry of the regular Platonic solids, which have various dualing and other relationships with each other and from the beginnings of Greek geometry have been held to have implications with regards to cosmic genesis and the basic elements of material manifestation, the cube being correlated with earth and the octahedron with air. If we look again at figure 7.4A, we can see how the octahedron could be considered the three-dimensionalization of the two-dimensional hexagram, an important fact in associating the hexagram and the cube.

We have explored the cosmological significance of the hexagram in the Genesis creation account, and the cube is the form understood to be designated in Exodus for the Holy of Holies in the Sanctuary and future Temple, this being the site of the yearly atonement of man with God that may be said to fulfill the purpose of creation. If these first two books of the Torah may be said to reflect the priestly tradition of Hebraic sacred science, then this esoteric tradition would seem to have accorded major cosmological significance to the hexagram and the cube, understanding them to define not only the origin and turning point of the cosmic process but also the distinction between the two-dimensional world of Yetzirah and the three-dimensional world of Assiyah. It follows that the form of the octahedron, which is magically manifested by the simple interfacing of an orthogonal cube and a hexagram, and which can both mediate between these two and three dimensions and serve in the expansion of the cube, would also have assumed geometric importance. Thus if the *Sefer Yetzirah* is defining both the genesis of the cube of earth and the complementary process by which it is to be infinitely expanded with the increasing spiritualization of man, we can understand the insistence of this text on this expansion being mediated by the aerial form of the octahedron. But whether the geometry of the *Sefer Yetzirah* was derived from the ancient Hebraic tradition of sacred science, from the Platonic tradition, or from their interaction, and this at any time from the fifth century B.C.E. to the third century C.E., it seems evident that it was the cosmological implications of the regular solids, most explicitly the dualing relationship of the cube and octahedron, that accounts for its hidden instructions stipulating the use of the dualing octahedron to expand the cube, a

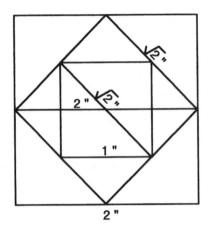

FIGURE 7.5. EXPANDING SQUARES

stipulation that demonstrates an advanced knowledge of geometry. With this further understanding, we can conclude this initial presentation by turning again to figure 7.5, now understood as a diagram of these dualing solids.

Figure 7.5 can be understood to provide a two-dimensional cross section of three-dimensional solids that, though they may enclose and be enclosed in other three-dimensional shapes, cannot occupy the same space. But if I am correct about the *Sefer Yetzirah* Diagram, then its orthogonal projections of a cube and octahedron *are* interpenetrating and do occupy the same space. Since this diagram is a product of the two-dimensional world of Yetzirah, it may be viewed as operating in a dimension above that of our normal space-time frame of reference, a dimension in which the paradox of both/and can be seen to be graphically validated. On this basis we can now proceed with the proposed solution of the *Sefer Yetzirah* Tree.

To satisfy the requirements of the *Bahir*, the minimal *Sefer Yetzirah* Diagram established in figure 7.2 must be further expanded in accordance with rules of self-generation that can be derived from it, the only apparent solution being to have interpenetrating cubes and octahedra at each phase of cosmic growth, as in the original model. This means that with each enlargement of the octahedron, the cube will be automatically enlarged. The two-dimensional enlargement of the octahedron offers no difficulty since it is actually composed of a hexagram surrounded by its point-hexagon, that on which the next hexagram in the whole step or double-point method of progression can be built, itself to be surrounded by its point-hexagon to produce a two-dimensional version of the octahedron. All that is now required to convert this into an interpenetrating octahedron and cube is to add the center-radiated lines that define the orthogonal cube. Such an enlargement of the diagram to Beriah and then Yetzirah by what we can still call the whole-step progression produces all of the Tree of Life Diagram with the exception of the pattern breaking Yesod with its two paths. So if we are to accept the *Bahir*'s word that the Tree is "inside" the diagonals, it would appear that its tradition of constructing the *Sefer Yetzirah* Tree understood the principle of the half-step progression through which it must be formed, that in which a hexagram is built on the single points of a preceding hexagram with its bars parallel to those of the smaller hexagram. But though the whole- and half-step progressions still build their enlarged hexagrams on the double or single points, respectively, of smaller hexagrams, as in the Sabbath Star Diagram, the difference in constructing the *Sefer Yetzirah* Diagram, as already indicated, is that in addition to the enlarged hexagram, the outer hexagon that transforms the hexagram into a two-dimensional representation of an octahedron must be added as well as the six lines radiating from the center to the points of the new enlarged hexagram that provide its dualing cube.

With this understanding of the simplest method of producing the version of the *Sefer Yetzirah* Tree of Life Diagram being here proposed, we can now turn to the finished product as reproduced in figure 7.6. This gives us the Tree completely enclosed within a cube that contains all twelve of the curiously designated diagonals in the *Sefer Yetzirah* tradition, and it includes all the possible whole and half steps through the cube of the Fa-point hexagon that fully manifests the cosmic world of Yetzirah, as these worlds were defined in the last chapter by the expanding hexagrams of the Sabbath Star Diagram. The most important difference between the cubic and Sabbath Star method of deriving the Tree of Life is that the cubic method produces the central column within Yetzirah, with no need of a fourth world of material creation to complete the cosmic process. This sense of producing the "unfallen" world of Yetzirah— using the terminology of the Fall from this point on in the purely metaphorical sense earlier introduced in the analysis of the unstable Fa hexagram of the third world depicted in figure 6.7—is everywhere present in the creation manual that is the *Sefer Yetzirah*, whose mother letters represent only the higher three elements with no mention of the fourth element of earth. And meditation on its mandala is the way it would seem to prescribe for a spiritual return to this higher cosmic world, where the Tree of Life may still be seen to flourish.

The analysis thus far has attempted to solve the geometric riddles of two early but most significant kabbalistic texts. Its solution of the suggested *Sefer Yetzirah* Diagram was through the orthogonal projection of a cube and interpenetrating octahedron. The further riddle suggested by the *Bahir*, that the Tree of Life Diagram is contained within the diagonals of the *Sefer Yetzirah* Diagram, was then solved by enlarging the minimal diagram in figure 7.2 through the methods of hexagram enlargement earlier employed in constructing the Sabbath Star Diagram but adapted to include the additional lines necessary for the two-dimensional projections of the interpenetrating octahedra and cubes, the final enlargement that could contain all the required lines of the Tree being given in figure 7.6.

This may be as far as one should go both in terms of the explicit suggestions within these two kabbalistic texts and the normal processes of geometric construction. But another mode of interpreting these geometric forms and processes suggests itself from our point of origin, the octahedron method of cubic expansion. We have seen that awareness of the dualing relationship of the cube and the octahedron indicates a sophisticated understanding of solid geometry that would logically include a similar knowledge of the remaining three regular solids—the tetrahedron, icosahedron, and dodecahedron.

To understand why these five solids should have developed such profound cosmological significance it might help to review their construction. The minimal solid that can be constructed is the tetrahedron, which has three triangular faces meeting at a vertex. The octahedron has four such faces at each of its vertices and the icosahedron five such faces. It is impossible to construct a solid with six triangular faces meeting at a vertex because it would become flat. As the tetrahedron has three triangles meeting at its vertices, so the cube has three such squares and the dodecahedron three such pentagons. A figure with three hexagons at a vertex would again be flat. Thus there can be no more than five regular polyhedra. This exposition may also help to explain why there are exactly five Partzufim, no more, no less.

The association between the five regular solids and the five Partzufim is reinforced by another similarity between them, one arising particularly from the fact that in the minimal *Sefer Yetzirah* Diagram the cube and octahedron are not only dualing but interpenetrating, a circumstance

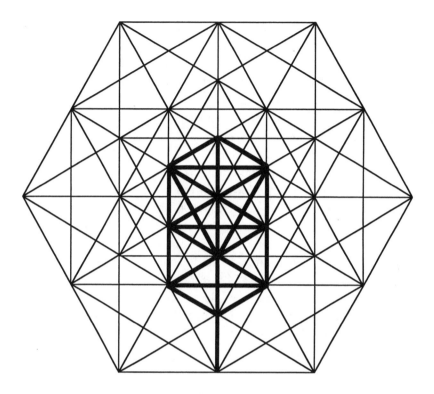

FIGURE 7.6. THE *SEFER YETZIRAH* TREE OF LIFE DIAGRAM

suggestive of the principal activity of the Lurianic Partzufim, that of sexual unification or Yichud. Of the five Partzufim, we will see that the forms produced through the whole-step progression of cube-octahedra can be correlated with the differentiated aspects of Arikh Anpin, Abba, and Imma: Abba with the cube, Imma with the octahedron, and Arikh Anpin with the star tetrahedron, also emerging in this diagram, in which they are unified. The dualing relationship of the icosahedron and dodecahedron will also be seen to be one that can be correlated with the lower Partzufim couple of Ze'ir Anpin and the Nukvah, these forms similarly proving to emerge in the *Sefer Yetzirah* Diagram, this time through the half-step progression needed to manifest the sexual Sefirah Yesod.

While there is no clear evidence that the author or authors of the *Sefer Yetzirah* were aware of concepts that surfaced later in the kabbalistic tradition, such as the Tree of Life Diagram and the Partzufim, this does not mean that later Kabbalists did not use the *Sefer Yetzirah* cubic diagram in their own cosmological contemplations and that their interpretive extensions of the diagram did not contribute to the mythological details of their later concepts. Evidence of just such a use would seem to be present in the Bahiric statement that "The Blessed Holy One has a single Tree, and it has twelve diagonal boundaries. . . . on the inside of them is the Tree." For whether or not such an extension of the diagram had been contemplated by the author(s) of the *Sefer Yetzirah*, the diagram certainly had been so extended by the time of the *Bahir*. Similarly, it may well be that Zoharic and Lurianic concepts of the Partzufim were developed in part through contemplation of the fully expanded *Sefer Yetzirah* Diagram, in which such concepts appear to be geometrically grounded. For we will see that the Lurianic definitions of the Partzufim can be laid out on the *Sefer Yetzirah* Tree in terms of these five regular solids and their geometric interactions. It would, indeed, seem that many curious aspects of the nature and history of the Partzufim that the *Etz Chayyim* details can only have had their source in study of this diagram. Such a possibility will be assumed in the following step-by-step mythologized interpretation of the *Sefer Yetzirah* Diagram as containing an interpenetrating cube and octahedron.

The *Sefer Yetzirah* Diagram and the Lurianic Partzufim

THE UPPER THREE PARTZUFIM

We will begin the mythologized interpretation of the *Sefer Yetzirah* Diagram in the manner just suggested by associating the cube and octahedron in their distinguished forms with the sexually distinguished aspects of Arikh Anpin, the cube with Abba and the octahedron with Imma, assignments whose rationale will shortly be apparent. If we can view the outer hexagon that they share as representing their predistinguished unity within Arikh Anpin, then the geometric features that appear to give them sexual differentiation would be the six center-radiated lines of Abba and the six hexagram lines of Imma, the outward thrust of the center-radiated lines complementing the circular origin and nature of the hexagram, as the Yesods of these male and female Partzufim may be said to complement each other. Once we make this step and identify these distinguishing features with the Yesods of Abba and Imma, then their Yichud or coupling would take the form of interpenetrating or star tetra-

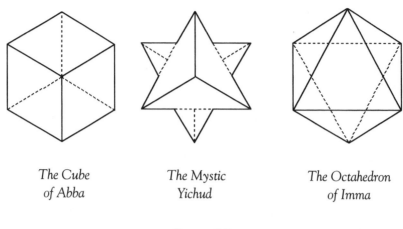

| The Cube | The Mystic | The Octahedron |
| of Abba | Yichud | of Imma |

FIGURE 7.7

hedra, the third of the five Platonic solids thus far manifested by the *Sefer Yetzirah* Diagram in its reformulation as a diagram of creation through the agency of the supernal Partzufim. In figure 7.7 these three solids are distinguished, the cube of Abba, the octahedron of Imma, and the interpenetrating tetrahedra in which they are mystically reunited in the heart of Arikh Anpin.

The three illustrated solids are all simultaneously present in the minimal *Sefer Yetzirah* Diagram of figure 7.2, which, in the theoretical chronology of the Sabbath Star Diagram on which such assignments are being based, can be associated with the first cosmic world of Atzilut. In their first Atzilutic manifestation, therefore, the Partzufim of Abba and Imma may already be seen to be engaged in the eternal act of coupling thought to create and sustain the cosmos. Nonetheless, one can distinguish different stages of this simultaneous process by selecting different features for display. As earlier suggested, the full eighteen-line figure of the minimal *Sefer Yetzirah* Diagram can be taken to represent the cubic body of Arikh Anpin with the infinite diagonals by which it can be expanded. At this stage the secondary Partzufim of Abba and Imma may be considered only potentially present within the higher unity of Arikh Anpin. At a second logical rather than chronological stage, the differentiated cube of Abba and octahedron of Imma may be considered to separate out of the primal unity that had previously contained them and to have assumed an orientation that, by focusing upon their individual distinctiveness, had placed them in an ungenerative back-to-back position.

Finally, and this may be considered a definition of the Lurianic Tikkun, Abba and Imma may be conceived to have turned into the face-to-face position that can permit a coupling in which they find a higher unity both with each other and with their source without the loss of their personalities.

In Lurianic cosmology, the Abba and Imma of the second stage, though often called by these Partzufim names, are to be understood as the originally emanated Sefirot of Chokhmah and Binah in the world of points. Although these Sefirot were not broken with the influx of the light, we are told that Binah was only able to receive the light by turning her back to it and thus also to Chokhmah, who had received it face-to-face from Keter. Thus they must also be included in the Rectification that, for them, involves the turning of Binah into a face-to-face position with Chokhmah and their reconstitution as Partzufim. Quoting from the very beginning of the *Etz Chayyim*:

> When it arose in His will, blessed be His name, to create the world in order to be good to those He created, and that they should be able to recognize His greatness and merit, being a chariot of the supernal, to be attached to Him, the Blessed One, He emanated one point, which included ten, and they are the ten Sefirot of the points that were in one vessel, and they were invisible. . . . And know that when the ten dots mentioned above spread out, Keter was able to absorb this light but Abba and Imma were not equal because Abba received the light face-to-face from Keter and he had within him the ability to absorb the light but Binah only received the light from Chokhmah back-to-back because she could not absorb it. . . . Chokhmah and Binah also needed rectification because is it not so that Binah initially was receiving the light back-to-back because she was not able to tolerate [the light] face-to-face.[11]

Rectification for the breaking of the vessels is accomplished by "spreading the light":

> And, therefore, from the point that was Keter, there was a spreading out to become a single, complete Partzuf composed of the ten Sefirot that were included in it from the beginning. . . [the Partzuf] called Arikh Anpin. Similarly, from the point of Chokhmah, one complete Partzuf was made from ten Sefirot, and then it was called Abba. Similarly, from Binah, one complete Partzuf from ten Sefirot

was made, and it was called Imma. . . . And after the complete Partzuf of Arikh Anpin was made, [the] two Partzufim of Abba and Imma were made. And this is the meaning of the *Idra Zutra:* "As one they came out and as one they exist and they are never separate." And the meaning is that Chokhmah and Binah were not emanated like the Male [Ze'ir Anpin] and Female [the Nukvah] inasmuch as the Female came out from behind the chest, between the arms, but Abba and Imma [came out] as one. At the time of their birth the two of them came out together and one did not precede the other. And they live together as one because [unlike] the Male and Female [who, when they first] came out [were] back-to-back, Abba and Imma live as one, face-to-face.[12]

In these lengthy quotations, extended because this material is not available elsewhere in translation, we see that Chokhmah and Binah are recreated by the Tikkun in such a manner that there is no longer that difference between them that, as Sefirot, caused Binah to turn her back to Chokhmah; rather, they now come out together, face-to-face, neither preceding the other, and, reconstituted as Partzufim, "as one they exist and they are never separate." But in the advanced cosmic sexology of Luria, their procreative coupling is dependent on a second factor in addition to their face-to-face position: "this is the mystery of the female waters," *mayyim nukvah*, that arousing of Imma through the elevation of the sparks that produces her "female waters [thus enabling her] to unite with Abba."[13] The ongoing creative process of the cosmos is made dependent, then, on an equality between the supernal male and female divine personalities that results in the female's new receptivity toward the male. Commenting parenthetically on this cosmological circumstance, I would add that if the back-to-back position of Binah toward Chokhmah, consequent upon that hierarchical disparity between their original positions that rendered her inadequate to receive his light, is the kabbalistic symbol of the fragmented nature of this world, and Imma's face-to-face receptivity to Abba, consequent upon their recreation as equal Partzufim, is the kabbalistic symbol of the Tikkun in the Messianic Age, then as the pious are wont to say of any such Messianic tidings, "May it come speedily to pass and in our time"!

In discussing the creative sexuality of the parental Partzufim in geometric terms, we must first distinguish between its two forms, the whole-step progression that builds its hexagon base upon the double points of a preceding hexagram and produces clonic but ever enlarging replications of the originating forms, and the half-step progression that builds its hexagon base upon the single points of a preceding hexagram and produces distinctively new geometric entities. It seems appropriate to identify the first form, as in the Sabbath Star Diagram, with the generation of new cosmic worlds. We shall later see that the second form can be precisely identified with the children Partzufim, Ze'ir Anpin and the Nukvah, but it seems better to discuss these two different forms of generation separately, beginning with the sexual process that takes us from the ideal Atzilutic consummation to the creation of the new world of Beriah.

Figure 7.8A begins with the *Sefer Yetzirah* Diagram of creation, the orthogonal projection of an interpenetrating cube and octahedron that may be said to represent the Yichud of Abba and Imma, a coupling further understood to forever combine the excitement of arousal with the ecstasy of consummation. The former is represented by the interpenetrating tetrahedra in which their Yesods are united and the latter by the surrounding hexagon that completes and returns them to their individual bodies. We have thus far been considering Abba and Imma in the inseparable Atzilutic union of their first creation as Partzufim. But for the further creation of the lower cosmic worlds with that Tree of Life that is to join the supernal Father and Mother with their children, Ze'ir Anpin and the Nukvah, Abba and Imma must grow sexually through two discrete acts of coupling. Thus the first Atzilutic Yichud must also be considered generative of the second world of Beriah as the second Berian Yichud is generative of the third world of Yetzirah.

In figure 7.8B we may read a symbolic representation of the necessary first step in this process, the arousing of the female waters, a mode of arousal that actually only becomes necessary with the second Berian Yichud. As we will see in the later analyses of the Lurianic text in relation to the generation of the children Partzufim, there is a first purely mental conception and a second conception requiring the female waters. But since the first purely mental arousal *is* generative, we may consider figure 7.8 to be an ideal representation of a sexually expressed process defined first at a more subtle level and secondly at one less subtle. The discrete stages by which the Do cube-octahedron of Atzilut may be enlarged to the size of the Re cube-octahedron of Beriah can be interpreted in terms of sexual mythology if we apply the equations earlier made of the center-radiated lines with the Yesod of Abba and of the circular derivation of the hexagram with the Yesod of Imma. What figure 7.8B shows us is that the hexagram, as sexual vessel, can be geometrically unfolded from the cube of Abba if this latter is reconceptualized as a plane figure of

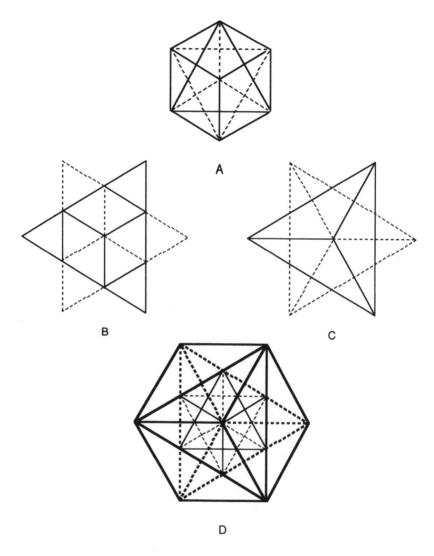

FIGURE 7.8. THE GENERATION OF BERIAH

six equilateral triangles within a hexagon. If Abba and Imma may be thought to return to the second dimension after the projected third dimension of their Atzilutic union, then the process of unfolding the hexagram form from the six enfolded triangles of its inner hexagon may be mythologized to suggest just such a response of Imma's mind to Abba. The significance of identifying the enfolded form with the supernal masculine and the unfolded form with the supernal feminine will be

considered more theoretically below; but first we must continue this sexualized reading of the method chosen to expand the cube-octahedron construction from Do to Re size, a method that can provide a geometric
model of this aspect of Lurianic cosmology.

Returning, then, to the allegorical reading of figure 7.8B, it may further be said to convey the consciousness of Imma in two successive phases.
In the first phase, the attention would be exclusively on the bodily form
of Abba, composed in this instance of six equilateral triangles. From such
contemplation, her desire to be his symmetrical opposite may be thought
to unfold, opening her to an enlarged receptivity to his renewing force,
an ideal representation of what at a lower level can be considered the
arousal of her female waters. In figure 7.8C we may see that Imma's prepared vessel has rearoused Abba to new depths of penetration, her expanded receptivity leading to his reciprocal expansion of power in the
heightened passion of their renewed Yichud. Finally, the magical child of
this passion, that third entity formed by their Yesods and figured here in
the interpenetrating tetrahedra, results in the new conception accompanying consummation and represented by the surrounding hexagon that,
in figure 7.8D, completes the generation of Beriah.

If we look at our second generation diagram in figure 7.8D, there are
a few points to be observed. The first is the shifted axis of the Berian
octahedron-cube. It is the capacity for such double-axis activity that can
be mythologically interpreted as giving our supernal Father and Mother
such a constantly renewed sexual appetite, for while one axis may be said
to be discharging its energy, the other axis may be considered to be re-
charging. Thus the completion of the procreative process in figure 7.8D,
with the newly created world of Beriah, just sets the stage for what can be
considered the true arousal of Imma's female waters upon her contemplation of the new splendor of Abba's enlarged body. Once again the six
triangles of his two-dimensional body, which the surrounding hexagon
completes, can be viewed as unfolded by her aroused desire into the enlarged capacity of her ever expanding receptacle, the symmetrical triangles
that form her hexagram Yesod. And this enlarged and prepared receptacle may finally be viewed as stimulating the small Yesod of Abba's original axis to a growth complementing the size of Imma's new vessel so that
by their renewed coupling they may conceive the third world of Yetzirah.

The *Sefer Yetzirah* Tree is formed, then, from a series of expanding
double-axis cubes, whose principle of infinite expansion is contained in
the interaction between these cubes and their diagonal counterparts, the
octahedra, an interaction that depends on the "masculinity" of the former's

center-radiated lines and the "femininity" of the latter's circularly derived hexagrams. This protosexual distinction between linearity and circularity may also be seen in the primary acts of Lurianic cosmology, the first acts of creation in the Tzimtzum involving a circular retraction of the Limitless Light and then the emanation of a linear ray of light directly from the Ein Sof into the circular space thus vacated. If Lurianic cosmology places the dualism of circle and line at the very beginning of the creative process, the *Sefer Yetzirah* Diagram would seem to show a later evolution of this geometric distinction in its two-dimensional projection of the complex structure of supernal space.

A most interesting point about this structure is that it takes us just to the point at which the second and third dimensions meet. As we have already seen in discussing figure 7.8B, the inner hexagon with the six lines within it can be described as either an orthogonal projection of a three-dimensional cube or as a two-dimensional plane figure of six equilateral triangles within a hexagon. Now if we look at this same inner hexagon as it appears in figure 7.8D, we will find that the shifted axis of the enlarged cube has added six lines to the original cubic diagram of figure 7.8A, which converts it into a matrix of equilateral triangles with their three lines of symmetry expressed, a matrix whose significance in the present context will be developed at the end of this chapter and whose larger geometric significance for quantum physics will be explored in chapter 9.

The Lower Two Partzufim

Figure 7.8 has shown us how the *Sefer Yetzirah* Diagram of an interpenetrating cube and octahedron can be expanded from one cosmic world to the next by a variant on the whole-step progression. But the Tree that can be manifested by this progression will still lack the two paths leading to the vertex of Yesod, a deficiency that must seem ironic after the highly sexualized nature of the preceding analysis. In the earlier discussion of the *Sefer Yetzirah* Tree, the inclusion of the Ri and Fa half-step progressions was alluded to without further comment. In this more detailed analysis, it will be necessary to construct the first half-step progression of Ri on the basis of the minimal *Sefer Yetzirah* Diagram as given in figure 7.8A. In figure 7.9, we shall discover an important new facet of the *Sefer Yetzirah* Tree as a diagram of the Partzufim.

When the octahedron-cube of Ri is added to that of Do by the half step or single-point progression, the startling figure that emerges in figure 7.9D is the fourth of the Platonic solids, the icosahedron. This regular polyhedron is composed of twenty faces of equilateral triangles so arranged that any five triangles meeting at a vertex can be bound by a pentagon. In figure 7.9D, the ten visible faces of the icosahedron have been emphasized by darkened continuous lines and the ten hidden faces with darkened broken lines, the darkened lines selecting those elements of the Do and Ri octahedron-cubes that together form the faces of the icosahedron. What is significantly omitted from the lines necessary for the icosahedron is the cube of Do. But if the cube's six center-radiated lines are connected with the single-point Di hexagon, as shown in figure 7.9B, what emerges is a rudimentary form of the dodecahedron, the fifth Platonic solid that is the dual of the icosahedron. The dodecahedron is a regular solid composed of twelve pentagonal faces with twenty vertices, and it duals the icosahedron since each of its twenty vertices touches the midpoint of one of the twenty triangular faces of the icosahedron, while each of the icosahedron's twelve vertices touches the midpoint of one of the dodecahedron's twelve pentagonal faces. The reason that figure 7.9B can be considered only a rudimentary form of the dodecahedron is that it provides an orthogonal projection of only three visible and three hidden pentagonal faces, the remaining six faces, which can be identified with the Di hexagonal sides, appearing only in cross section. This undeveloped dodecahedron may be thought of, however, as contained within and still a part of the Ri icosahedron. But the Ri icosahedron does not complete the *Sefer Yetzirah* Tree of Life Diagram, though it does provide the Sefirah Yesod in a disconnected form. To provide the two paths that connect Yesod to Netzach and Hod, another figure correlating to the Fa hexagram of the Sabbath Star Diagram is required. And here we meet an unexpected problem.

We have seen that the whole-step or double-point progression can result in an enlarged alternate axis replication of the original figure, in this case of interpenetrating octahedra and cubes. The single-point progression that fills in the half step or semitone accidentals has a different character, however, in this case resulting in the creation of the new form of the icosahedron from the materials of which it is composed, the originating octahedra and cubes. If we now wish to maintain the association of the single-point progression with the icosahedron as this form is enlarged to the Fa-sized figure, we find that this cannot be accomplished by the simple whole step progression from Ri to Fa, since this will only produce the alternate axis replication of the original octahedron-cube. To provide a Fa-sized icosahedron, we must rather return to the Re octahedron-cube and construct it by the single-point progression from this base.

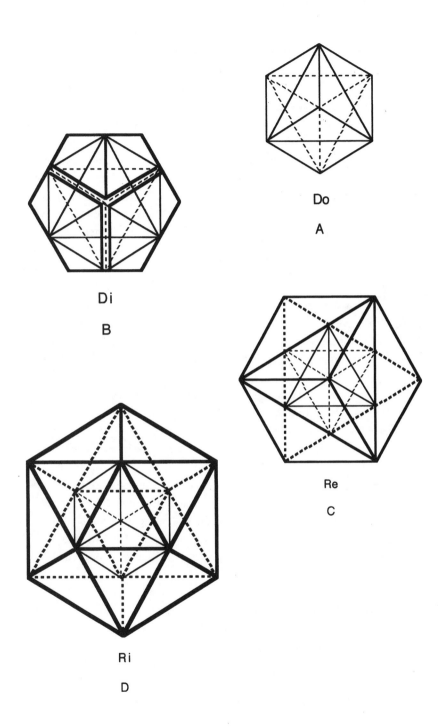

Do

A

Di

B

Re

C

Ri

D

FIGURE 7.9. THE FIRST GENERATION OF ZE'IR ANPIN

Thus from the Do octahedron-cube is constructed both the Re octahedron-cube and the Ri icosahedron, containing a primitive Di dodecahedron, and from the Re octahedron-cube there likewise is constructed both the Mi octahedron-cube and the Fa icosahedron, the latter resulting as well in an enlarged but still incomplete dodecahedron, deriving from the Re cube.

When we return to our mythologized interpretation of these Platonic solids as the geometric archetypes of the Partzufim, we are led to the earlier suggested irresistible conclusion that, as the cube represents Abba and the octahedron Imma, so the icosahedron must represent Ze'ir Anpin and the dodecahedron the Nukvah. Once these identifications are made, some startling correlations can be seen between the stages of construction of these figures and the Lurianic discussion of the maturation processes undergone by Ze'ir Anpin and the Nukvah. Beginning with the growth of Ze'ir Anpin, we discover that Lurianic cosmology assigns three very curious stages to this process. There is a first gestation in the womb of Imma, a period after birth of nursing, and then a return of the womb of Imma for a second gestation, as explained in the *Etz Chayyim*:

> And now we will explain what the *Zohar* says in Chapter Acharei Mot, p. 65: "After he [Ze'ir Anpin] has finished nursing, he enters a second period of gestation." Ze'ir Anpin returns to the womb of Imma, even though he had already completed for himself a whole Partzuf of six Sefirot in the days of his nursing, to get his brains. And in order not to be astonished over the idea of a second pregnancy [of Imma] after the period of nursing, does it not say: "From my flesh will I see God." . . . So is it with the supernal Imma, who becomes pregnant a second time with the souls of the Male and Female, who are renewed in the mystery of the new brains which were given to them.[14]

The concept of a second pregnancy for Imma with Ze'ir Anpin, so astonishing that even Chayyim Vital feels called upon to express our presumed amazement, seems explainable by the geometric processes required for the icosahedron to grow from Ri to Fa size in the *Sefer Yetzirah* Tree.

In our earlier discussion of the whole-step progression as a sexual process by which successive cosmic worlds are created, the Do and Re octahedron-cubes were seen as representations of the eternal and generative couplings of Abba and Imma. In figure 7.8, however, these same Do and Re constructions should be viewed as representing the womb of

Imma. Indeed, just as the chapters of the *Etz Chayyim* concerned with the maturation of Ze'ir Anpin omit almost all discussion of Abba in their exclusive focus on the relationship of the supernal Mother to her child, so the icosahedron representative of Ze'ir Anpin omits from its construction only the lines representative of Abba, the Do cube, while requiring the lines of the Do hexagram that give Imma her maternal capabilities. Viewed from the perspective of the child, therefore, the mother functions not as the sexual partner of the father but as the womb from which he emerged and to which, in this mystery of divine revelation, he is permitted to return, a perspective to be more fully developed in the conclusion. From this perspective, then, figure 7.9A would represent the first phase of Ze'ir Anpin's maturation, his first gestation in the womb of Imma; figure 7.9D the second phase of his maturation, the nursing phase; and figure 7.9C the third phase of his maturation, his second gestation in the womb of Imma from which the fully mature Ze'ir Anpin of the Fa icosahedron will finally emerge in figure 7.11. Because the icosahedron in this diagram cannot replicate itself through the whole-step progression but must always be based on a figure one and one-half steps or a tritone smaller, it can only be enlarged by returning to a prior stage of cosmic development. Thus if Ze'ir Anpin is to be identified with this diagrammatic icosahedron, then his maturation will have to follow the peculiar geometric processes by which the precarious icosahedron can be permitted to grow in this diagram, processes that demand that every such enlargement be a rebirth consequent upon return to a maternal womb.

In discussing the two births of what is still the androgynous Ze'ir Anpin, we should look at how the *Etz Chayyim* has defined these two conceptions. As earlier suggested, the original relationship of Abba and Imma is not only ideal because the pair is engaged in constant coupling but because the nature of this coupling is truly "ideal," that is, its essence is mental even in those aspects that seem most analogous to human sexuality. Indeed, the first conception of Ze'ir Anpin and the Nukvah, we are specifically told in the *Etz Chayyim*, was based on the purely mental arousal of Abba and Imma:

> the Yesod of Arikh Anpin, after it was incorporated into the [upper] half of Tiferet, behold, it there gave out a vapor in the midst of Tiferet. And that very vapor divided into two parts. The one on the right side became the brain of Abba and the one on the left side became the brain of Imma. And due to the fact that they have brains, a desire for union develops in Abba and Imma. And this union is

without the female waters; it is only a [product of the] operation [Torah] of kindness [Chesed], as it says: "I have said the world is built on Chesed."

And thus, when the Male and Female go up into the womb of Imma, they then make there female waters for Binah [to be able] to have union with Abba. By means of this union, the brains for the Male and Female are given birth to and brought down.[15]

Just as the brains of Abba and Imma derive from the Yesod of Arikh Anpin, so the differentiating brains of the lower Partzufim, referred to simply as the Male and Female, appear to have their source in the sexual differentiation that on all levels of cosmic refinement seems to be an essential part of the cosmic process.

The second, sexual conception of Ze'ir Anpin and the Nukvah has two results; it results in the sexual maturity of the parents at the same time that it produces children that develop differently from the mental preconception earlier had of them. In the first, mental conception, the complete Partzuf of the son was endowed with six Sefirot while that of the daughter was endowed with only one Sefirah. In this second, sexual conception, however, these Partzufim both develop their full complement of ten Sefirot each, which for Ze'ir Anpin significantly adds the higher mental Sefirot, though the Nukvah's ten Sefirot will still be contained in her one original Sefirah, Malkhut, until her final emergence from Ze'ir Anpin.

The text first tells us of "the ten Sefirot [of Ze'ir Anpin]"[16] that grow during Imma's second pregnancy and then later tells us of the Nukvah's similar development of ten Sefirot during this second pregnancy: "Afterward [after the nursing phase], with the growth of the brains, she also grew and became a complete Partzuf."[17] Finally, we have the double birth that distinguishes the later relationship of Ze'ir Anpin and the Nukvah from that of Abba and Imma; the androgynous Ze'ir Anpin comes out of the womb of Imma and then the Nukvah comes out of the back of his chest and for a period remains connected back-to-back with him: "the Male and Female are connected together with one wall."[18] The passage defining the different forms of birth for the two couples was quoted in part before but bears repeating:

And this is the meaning of the *Idra Zuta*: "As one they came out and as one they exist and they are never separate." And the meaning is that Chokhmah and Binah were not emanated like the Male and Female inasmuch as the Female came out from behind the chest, between the arms, but Abba and Imma [came out] together and one did not precede the other. And they live together as one because [unlike] the Male and Female [who, when they first] came out [were] back-to-back, Abba and Imma live as one, face-to-face. And that which is said [about Abba and Imma], that they are never separate, [distinguishes them from their children] because the union of Ze'ir Anpin and Malkhut is not constant, as it says in the *Zohar*, Chapter Vayikrah.[19]

These two different modes of Partzufim generation are certainly related to the two different versions of the creation of man in Genesis. The first, equal generation of male and female in the divine image—"So God created man in his own image, in the image of God created he him; male and female created he them" (Gen. 1:37)—can be correlated with the generation of Abba and Imma, just as the unequal generation of Adam and Eve—"And the rib, which the Lord God had taken from man, made he a woman" (Gen. 2:22)—can be correlated with the unequal generation of Ze'ir Anpin and the Nukvah. It is to these two different modes of Partzufim generation that the *Etz Chayyim* clearly attributes the difference between the sexuality of the older and the younger couples, the equal generation of Abba and Imma resulting in their continual sexual relations and the originally unequal generation of Ze'ir Anpin and the Nukvah causing their sexual relations to be only intermittent.

In summary, the Yichud of Atzilutic Abba and Imma (the Do octahedron-cube) leads to Imma's pregnancy with Ze'ir Anpin and the generation of the cosmic world of Beriah in which their natures are replicated, the reproduction of a cosmic world being viewed in this context as the world in which either the gestation or postnatal growth of the child is taking place. Imma's first pregnancy is followed by the birth and nursing of Ze'ir Anpin (the Ri icosahedron). There now occurs a second Berian Yichud which reimpregnates Imma with Ze'ir Anpin even as the personal growth of the parents is reflected in the enlarged estate of Yetzirah (the Mi octahedron-cube). Again the single-point progression precedes that of the double-point progression in constructing from this base the two aspects of the mature world of Ze'ir Anpin. The mature Ze'ir Anpin is reborn as the Fa icosahedron and is provided with the world of Yetzirah (the Mi octahedron-cube) that will be his final inheritance. From the foregoing analysis, construction of the complete *Sefer Yetzirah* Tree becomes a process detailing the maturation of Ze'ir Anpin from first conception to final rebirth, thus providing a graphic depiction and contemplative model of perfected man, reborn through his "new brains" into a state of higher consciousness.

Since Ze'ir Anpin is generally associated with the cosmic world of Yetzirah and the Nukvah with the cosmic world of Assiyah, it is not surprising that the Sefer Yetzirah Tree, concluding as it does with the world of Yetzirah, should not provide a model of the mature and differentiated Nukvah. But this again is consistent with the Lurianic discussion of the early growth of the Nukvah in the Etz Chayyim: "Malkhut is included with the Vav [the Tetragrammaton letter signifying Ze'ir Anpin] during the nursing phase as well."[20] This can be seen to parallel what has already been shown regarding the relationship of the female dodecahedron to the male icosahedron, that the former is only in a rudimentary stage and should be thought of as contained within the latter, figure 7.9B (the Di dodecahedron) within figure 7.9D (the Ri icosahedron). These two solids, which correspond to the inner and outer hexagons of the Ri hexagram, are both based upon the Do Yichud of Abba and Imma, the Nukvah drawing her essence from the Yesod of Abba (the center-radiated lines) as Ze'ir Anpin draws his essence from the Yesod of Imma (the hexagram). This cross-sexual relationship of children to parents, which was well known to both Sophocles and Freud and would seem to be validated by the geometry of this diagram,[21] is specifically noted in the Lurianic text. We are told that "the middle line of Ze'ir Anpin is made from Imma's Yesod"[22] and that the entire Partzuf of the Nukvah derives from Abba: "Malkhut of Ze'ir Anpin derives from the speech of Abba."[23] The one part of the Do cube with its octahedron diagonals, the minimal Sefer Yetzirah Diagram, that Ze'ir Anpin and the Nukvah do not incorporate into their bodies from their parental sources is the outer Do hexagon, earlier identified in its interpenetrating form as completing the body of Arikh Anpin and in its differentiated forms as completing the cubic body of Abba and the octahedron body of Imma. This again conforms to the process of earthly procreation, for a child derives its body's distinctive nature from the union of its parents' Yesods and not from the remainder of its parents' bodies, just as its fetal nourishment in no way impairs the functioning of its mother's body.

Although we are told of the Nukvah's final and curious emergence from the body of Ze'ir Anpin—"Her head comes out from his back and not from a facing position"[24]—the Sefer Yetzirah Tree is completed before this emergence and seems to depict the rebirth of Ze'ir Anpin as a spiritually perfected but still androgynous being, supernal Adam in the unfallen state of Yetzirah where grows the still accessible Tree of Life. Indeed, the association of this stage of Ze'ir Anpin and supernal Adam is insisted upon in the *Idra Rabba* section of the *Zohar*, where we are told that "this supernal form which is called (*the supernal*) man . . . comprehendeth Male and Female equally."[25] With the final Yetziric rebirth of androgynous Ze'ir Anpin, the Partzuf of this divine child becomes clearly identified with the supernal androgynous Adam before Eve is similarly removed from his chest area, the kabbalistic discussions of the final emergence of the Nukvah being closely related to the biblical account of Eve's later separation from Adam in the Garden of Eden. In the Kabbalah, the Garden of Eden story is usually situated in the third world of Yetzirah, which thus makes it primarily a study of supernal Adam as Ze'ir Anpin. The problem that arises in this context is that whereas Eve must somehow be introduced into Yetziric Eden, the Nukvah cannot properly emerge from the androgynous Ze'ir Anpin until the fourth, material world of Assiyah that she informs. Thus the *Sefer Yetzirah* Tree must conclude with the final, androgynous Ze'ir Anpin-Adam of unfallen Yetzirah.

One final word about the Nukvah's identification with our terrestrial fourth world is that it is only in this three-dimensional world that the dodecahedron and icosahedron can come into a true dualing relationship with each other. In the two-dimensional world of Yetzirah, which is the cosmic source of all the diagrams in this part, a grid based on enlarging hexagrams can be accommodated to accurate orthogonal projections of the tetrahedron, octahedron, cube, and icosahedron, but it cannot accommodate an accurate orthogonal projection of the dodecahedron without altering some of the lines of the hexagram grid. Thus if the hexagram grid is to be taken as a model of the creation, as the analysis of Genesis 1 in chapter 6 attempted to show, then its exclusion of a true orthogonal projection of the dodecahedron seems to argue that this form cannot be perfected in the two-dimensional supernal model but, for its true expression, must await and contain the three-dimensional cosmos and, in particular, this earth.

The association of the dodecahedron with the subtle structure of the earth has been a commonplace of spiritual philosophy going back to Plato, but recent students of the subject, while continuing this identification, have also provided evidence that the earth's subtle structure is more complex:

In 1973, three Russians—historian Nikolai Goncharov, construction engineer Vyacheslav Morozov, and electronics specialist Valery

Makarov—announced in the science journal of the Soviet Academy of Sciences, *Khimiya i Zhinzn* (Chemistry and Life), their discovery of a geometric "grid" pattern which spans the globe. The lines of this "grid" pattern, they revealed further, are the lattice edges of a great crystal—a crystal that is nothing less than the Earth itself. The structure of the planetary crystal is in dual form: an *icosahedron*, made up of 20 equilateral triangles, interconnected with a *dodecahedron*, composed of 12 pentagons—or an "icosa-dodeca' for short. . . . When Goncharov, Morozov, and Makarov placed the icosa-dodeca lattice grid over the surface of the modern globe, they were startled to find that the points coincided with locations of natural planetary phenomena . . . the twenty nodes of the dodeca lattice pinpoint centers of high and low barometric pressure areas in the Earth's atmosphere, where storms, hurricanes, and typhoons originate, and move along the crystal edges. Prevailing winds and oceanic current patterns also "flow" with the grid pattern. . . . Concerning the solid Earth itself, the icosa-dodeca crystal grid also delineates patterns of a definite geologic nature—namely the major fracture zones of the Earth's crust. . . . Without a doubt the most convincing testimony to the Ancients' awareness to [*sic*] the world crystal web is the fact that, located along the web lines and centers we find *the major monuments built by man.*[26]

If we can accept this evidence, then the dodecahedron becomes more than just a geometric symbol of Mother Earth; it conveys the true essence of this planet and, it would also seem, of the divine personality immanent within it. Moreover, it is only in terms of this world that the earthly Nukvah can mate with her more transcendent partner—more transcendent because the icosahedral form of Ze'ir Anpin can adapt to the two-dimensional hexagram model as well as to an actual three-dimensional construction, whereas the dodecahedral form of the Nukvah cannot achieve perfect expression in terms of the hexagram model of creation and is thus earthbound. But if the final dodecahedral form of the fully emergent Nukvah cannot be expressed within the grid lines of the *Sefer Yetzirah* Tree, it can be so drawn as to contain it. In figure 7.10 we can see the only true orthogonal projection of the dodecahedron that can be geometrically allowed in relation to the *Sefer Yetzirah* Tree since it is beyond this diagram and contains it, and we may contemplate as well its final dualing with the Fa icosahedron of Ze'ir Anpin (shown separately in figure 7.11), which can represent both the Yichud

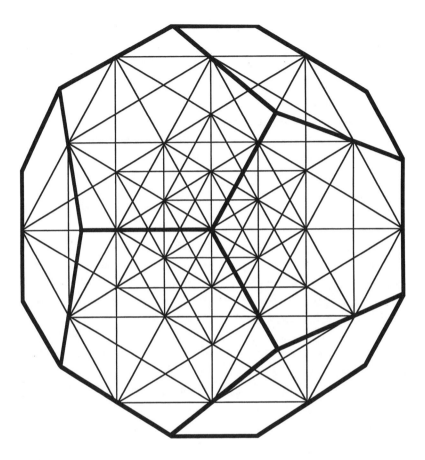

FIGURE 7.10. THE DODECAHEDRON ENCLOSING THE *SEFER YETZIRAH* TREE
OF LIFE DIAGRAM: A MANDALA OF PERFECTED EARTH

of these Male and Female Partzufim and also the icosa-dodeca crystalline pattern of this earth.

In figure 7.10, showing the *Sefer Yetzirah* Tree enclosed within an
orthogonally projected dodecahedron, we may read the consummation
of the cosmic mating of Ze'ir Anpin and the Nukvah toward which the
entire process has, in Lurianic cosmology, been progressing. In this cosmology, such a Yichud is dependent upon the commencement of the
Tikkun, and this is also borne out by the geometry of the interconnected
Sefer Yetzirah Tree and Sabbath Star Diagram. For if this final dodecahedron is to be given a tonal name, it can be seen to be contained within
the inner hexagon of the Fi Sabbath Star, that feature of the Sabbath
Star Diagram that marks what can be considered the turning point of the

cosmic octave between Tzimtzum and Tikkun. Figure 7.10 may thus be considered a mandala of the earth as it is being perfected by the Tikkun. Before proceeding further a comment must finally be made about the anthropomorphic representation of Partzufim sexuality in the Kabbalah and the resulting explicitness of this analysis.

The analyses of this chapter have followed the *Etz Chayyim* in its primary cosmological focus on the sexuality of the Partzufim. But even as we make such connections, we must realize that the Partzufim were conceptualized in this manner to explain specific cosmic processes. For it is through such an interface of the sustained threefold Yichud of Abba and Imma in the heart of Arikh Anpin and the intermittent twofold coupling of Ze'ir Anpin and the Nukvah that the functioning of the cosmos can be explained, specifically how the universal laws can be fine-tuned to the new circumstances constantly arising from the exercise of freedom. The anthropomorphic details relating to these Partzufim and the similar mode by which they have been interpreted thus provide us with an understandable mythology through which we may begin to comprehend the awesome mysteries of the cosmos.

But the *Sefer Yetzirah* Tree is not intended to model the more earthly, intermittent relations of Ze'ir Anpin and the Nukvah. Its more ideal culmination is with the Fa icosahedron of androgynous Ze'ir Anpin. In the remainder of this chapter, we will further develop the implications of this simpler identification of the Fa icosahedron, and so of the *Sefer Yetzirah* Tree that it completes, with the perfected form of the twice-born cosmic child, the ultimate goal of the cosmic process that is the focus alike of the *Sefer Yetzirah* text and of the diagram to which it alludes.

Final Implications of the *Sefer Yetzirah* Tree

If the twice-born Ze'ir Anpin of the completed *Sefer Yetzirah* Tree can be said to represent the final perfected stage of cosmic manifestation, we can conclude this analysis by returning to this diagram as completed by the Fa icosahedron and without the addition of the enclosing, fully projected dodecahedron. For the *Sefer Yetzirah* Tree of the five regular solids and their Partzufim analogues can take us only as far as the rebirth of androgynous Ze'ir Anpin into higher consciousness. But the preceding analysis may help us to appreciate why such a being should be manifested geometrically as the Fa icosahedron.

Some review will, however, be required concerning the meaning of the Fa hexagram, as developed in the earlier discussion of the Sabbath

Star Diagram, and its possible association with Ze'ir Anpin. As shown in the last chapter, the Fa hexagram can be identified with a cosmic Fall that first becomes manifest in the third world of Yetzirah and the person of supernal Adam. Now what distinguishes Ze'ir Anpin, earlier identified with this supernal Adam, and the Nukvah from Arikh Anpin and his sexually differentiated aspects, Abba and Imma, is that the Sefirot from which this latter triad were reconstituted as Partzufim did not suffer a Shevirah or Breakage while the next six, from which Ze'ir Anpin was reconstituted, were completely broken, the final Sefirah reconstituted as the Nukvah being only partially fractured. It is, in fact, because Malkhut does not completely break that it, like the highest triad, can be reconstituted as a complete Partzuf: "And it does not entirely [break] like the previous [Sefirot] but it becomes a single Partzuf after the Rectification (she was worthy of becoming a complete Partzuf in spite of being only one point, which the six Sefirot [of Ze'ir Anpin] did not merit to become)."[27] Thus of the ten original Sefirot, it is only the six associated with the future Ze'ir Anpin that are completely shattered and that represent the Lurianic version of the cosmic Fall known as the Shevirah.

It is, then, from the broken or fallen supernal Adam of the Fa hexagram that Ze'ir Anpin may be considered to be reconstituted as the Fa icosahedron, and this may be the reason for its off-balanced appearance. From this we may draw the next inference, that the Sabbath Star Diagram of hexagrams, at least in the elementary version of it developed in chapter 6, is to be associated with the original process of emanation through the four worlds and the *Sefer Yetzirah* Tree of the regular solids with the subsequent reconstitution of the higher three worlds consequent upon the final manifestation of the material world. If we look at the Sabbath Star Diagram, given in figure 6.12, it can, indeed, be seen that the Fi Sabbath Star of the fourth world transforms the original Do hexagram of Atzilut into the interpenetrating octahedron-cube that defines the minimal *Sefer Yetzirah* Diagram and that forms the basis of the *Sefer Yetzirah* Tree apparently known to the later kabbalistic tradition.

In the preceding analysis, we have seen that the Fa hexagram should be associated with the Fall of supernal man and the Fa icosahedron with his recreation as a perfected being. But in both the hexagram and Platonic solids diagrams, the construction that has been identified with the Fa tone is required for the Sefirah Yesod of the Tree of Life Diagram, the diagram whose derivation both of the aforementioned diagrams seek to explain. Moreover, both the Fa hexagram and Fa icosahedron define this Sefirah as dualistic insofar as their contributions to the Tree are the two paths that manifest the dualism of Yesod. This dualism does not only refer to the sexual differentiation of male and female, however, but also to the two aspects of its position on the cosmic cycle of the Tree. As the sexual nature of Yesod can pull us downward toward the physical fourth world, so can it become the Foundation (the literal meaning of Yesod) for the spiritual rebirth of the Righteous One, the Tzaddik Joseph (also kabbalistically identified with Yesod), the foundation for the harmonizing or conversion of sexual energy to divine purposes. And the mandala of perfected supernal man presented in figure 7.11 can be a contemplative aid to such a return.

As we contemplate this mandala of Yetziric Ze'ir Anpin containing Atzilutic Arikh Anpin, as it further contains the central point to which all that derived from it shall return, we can retrace our steps from the dualism of this world, which the androgynous dyad of Ze'ir Anpin may be said to represent, through that higher consciousness in which all polarities are seen as complementary aspects of a larger mediating whole, which the androgynous triad of Arikh Anpin may be similarly seen to represent, to that highest consciousness in which all distinctions are resolved in unification. This cosmic movement back and forth from unity to duality mediated through triplicity and mythologically associated with the generation of the cosmic man Ze'ir Anpin may also be demonstrated in the form of the human body, for which Ze'ir Anpin is one archetype. If we imagine a beam of light passing through the human body, as in the original emanation it passed through the vessels of the Sefirot said to constitute the body of the yet higher anthropocosmos Adam Kadmon, the beam would pass in unity through the head and throat, then divide into the three parts of the trunk and the two arms, and the portion in the trunk would then again divide to pass into the remaining two parts of the legs. In the *Sefer Yetzirah* Tree we may see his supernal model spanning the upper three cosmic worlds and teaching us the way to our own perfection.

In contemplating this mandala of Yetziric Ze'ir Anpin and Atzilutic Arikh Anpin, we should also observe the function of the intervening Berian world; for as figure 9.1 will show, it is in the two triangles of the Fa icosahedron that together form the Re hexagram that there can be found a most significant matrix of equilateral triangles with their three lines of symmetry expressed, twelve such triangles in all. One meaning of *matrix* is "womb," and this matrix would seem to have a special association with creation since this diagram restricts it to the second, Berian world of Creation (the meaning of Beriah). With this understanding of the matrix, we can now simplify the more precise earlier analysis into the three

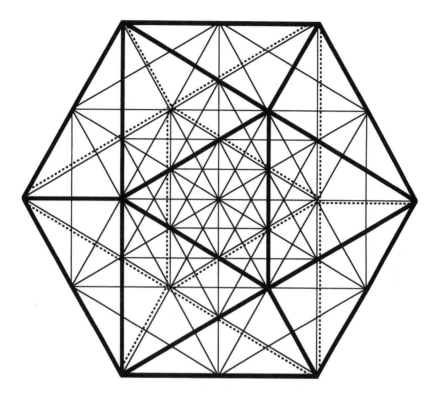

FIGURE 7.11. THE FA ICOSAHEDRON OF THE *SEFER YETZIRAH* TREE OF LIFE
DIAGRAM: A MANDALA OF PERFECTED SUPERNAL MAN

essential stages of the generation and growth of supernal man. We may
thus say that the Yichud of Abba and Imma in the Atzilutic world of
Emanation fertilizes and enlarges the Berian womb of Creation until it
delivers into the Yetziric world of Formation the still larger, fully formed
and perfected cosmic child; the *Sefer Yetzirah* Tree of Life Diagram thus
depicts the conception, the median growth in the cosmic womb of creation, and the final deliverance of Ze'ir Anpin, as of us all.

The matrix emerging in the *Sefer Yetzirah* Tree will be featured in
figure 9.1, and chapter 9 will develop its further significance as a model
for all the particles and their associated forces defined by quantum physics. At the moment, however, an understanding of the position of the
matrix in the *Sefer Yetzirah* Tree can also give support to the traditional
Tetragrammaton pattern of Partzufim distribution, illustrated in figure
1.4, that which identifies Arikh Anpin and Abba with the Yod representative of Atzilut, Binah with the Berian upper Hey, Ze'ir Anpin with the

Yetziric Vav, and the Nukvah with the Assiyic lower Hey. If, as just suggested, the *Sefer Yetzirah* Tree is finally to be simplified into the three stages of the insemination, interuterine enlargement, and final delivery of Ze'ir Anpin, then the first stage can be seen to be a function of the father as the second is of the mother, insemination being dependent on the potency of the father as interuterine growth is on the adequacy of the maternal womb to carry the fetus to term. From this perspective, the higher masculine Partzufim, Arikh Anpin and Abba (for Arikh Anpin, though understood to be androgynous, is always referred to as male), may both be identified with the enfolded paternal seed, Arikh Anpin with its ultimate source at the diagrammatic central point and Abba with the Atzilutic cube. Imma would not now be viewed as Abba's Atzilutic partner but in her Berian maternal role, as the womb in which the seed develops, unfolds. We can then conclude, as does figure 7.11, with the birth of the androgynous Ze'ir Anpin in Yetzirah or continue onward, as in figure 7.10, to the fourth world of Assiyah in which the Nukvah, who may be considered to inform the physical earth, separates herself from her male consort, permeating the heavens. But the *Sefer Yetzirah* Tree extends only to the Fa icosahedron of the androgynous Ze'ir Anpin, the cosmic man who is the archetype of cosmic manifestation and who carries in his nature the defining parental principles of dynamic enfoldment and unfolding, of contraction and expansion held in the divine balance, the principle of his central Sefirah of Tiferet, that permits existence.

With this last point before us, we can see a final geometric explanation and validation of the Tetragrammaton arrangement of the parental Partzufim that places them in different worlds. For it is not only the diagrammatic center that can be associated with the enfolded state of the seed; the cube of Atzilutic Abba may also be viewed as an enfolded form. If we look again at figure 7.8B and its accompanying commentary, we can see a symbolic representation of what the British physicist David Bohm has called the "enfolding-unfolding universe."[28] It will be remembered that the discussion of the female waters focused upon the unfolding of the hexagram of Berian Imma from the six equilateral triangles that comprise the cube of Atzilutic Abba when this projected cube is viewed simply as a plane figure. Viewed in this way, the six triangles within the Atzilutic border hexagon may be taken to represent the enfolded state of the cosmos and the six triangles of the Berian hexagram its unfolded state, the former identified with the masculine form of the divine as the latter is with its feminine form. The view of Abba and Imma as respectively representing the enfolded and unfolded states of the cosmos can be further strengthened by renewed contemplation of figure 7.11. For to the simple diagram of six enfolded triangles and six unfolded triangles joined by a median hexagon, given in figure 7.8B, this final illustration adds the new feature of the Berian matrix that transforms the hexagram of Beriah into the womb of creation and specifically associates it with the maternal aspect of the feminine divine. It is, then, with such a cosmic endowment of power and particularity that Ze'ir Anpin, the cosmic child, will finally be delivered in Yetzirah.

In figure 7.11 we can see that the matrix of Beriah does become the true womb of the glory of Yetzirah, the perfected supernal man that the *Sefer Yetzirah* teaches us God in the beginning created and we in the present can become. With this point we come to the final surprising congruence in this study of surprising correlations, that the diagram suggested by the *Sefer Yetzirah* and this "Book" of Yetzirah should have the same focus. For the point to which both arrive is the spiritual creation of perfected man in the world of Yetzirah. This remarkable agreement between diagram and text suggests that it is the diagram, whose geometry does not have the arbitrary character of words, that inspired the text of the *Sefer Yetzirah* and is the source of its wisdom, as it may also be of the *Bahir* and the *Etz Chayyim*.

It is hoped that this analysis of the *Sefer Yetzirah* Tree has not only served to unlock the secret kabbalistic diagram long thought to be alluded to in this first extant kabbalistic work but also to suggest connections between this diagram and later periods of kabbalistic history from the *Bahir* to the *Etz Chayyim*, thus providing added force to the thesis that there was an ongoing geometric tradition, extending for well over one thousand years, between the *Sefer Yetzirah* and the Safed Kabbalists. That this ongoing geometric tradition had important links to Pythagorean thought is attested to by the central importance it appears to have given to the five regular solids for which both Plato and the later Kabbalists were at least partially indebted to Pythagoras. From the foregoing analysis it seems clear that the complete *Sefer Yetzirah* Diagram was meant to show both the nature and interrelationships of the five Platonic solids and how these five solids could model the basic principles of kabbalistic cosmology, particularly with regard to the cosmic restitution from the effects of the Shevirah symbolized by the Partzufim.

In this regard we might take a final glance back at the *Sefer Yetzirah* Tree that figure 7.11 represents as culminating in the Fa icosahedron of Ze'ir Anpin. For if Ze'ir Anpin is to be associated with the principle of divine balance represented by his central Sefirah of Tiferet, his appearance lacks the erect posture of his Atzilutic father, whose cube is balanced on a point. His stability, rather, seems to have been achieved at the price of a fall, just such a Fall or Shevirah as the Lurianic tradition has largely identified with the six original Sefirot of Ze'ir Anpin. This cosmic son, fallen and yet reborn, is the mythological paradigm of the cosmic process in which we are all engaged. And in tracing its evolution through forms of geometric modeling derived from the clues within authentic kabbalistic sources, we may have understood more fully why the Fall into material manifestation was necessary for that ultimate reconstitution of the conscious source into the divine personalities that fulfill the purpose of creation.

Kabbalistic Geometry and the Tree of Knowledge

The Sixfold Tree of Knowledge

We come now to the culminating study of kabbalistic geometry that will connect all the previous strands of investigation to its central Tree of Life Diagram. We have seen how the Tree of Life Diagram can function as a key to unlock the secret existence of what would seem to be a still more fundamental diagram of cosmic emanation, as well as how this Sabbath Star Diagram provides a further key to the diagram depicting the genesis of the son encoded in the *Sefer Yetzirah*. In this chapter we shall continue the geometric exploration of this central principle of the Hebraic esoteric tradition.

We begin this last geometric exploration with the most startling and significant of the diagrams derived directly from the evidence of the Sabbath Star Diagram. As was demonstrated in chapter 6, the center of this underlying hexagram diagram is the point of the Tree of Life Diagram marking the position of the non-Sefirah Da'at (Knowledge). Taking this as a key to the ultimate gnosis of the Tree, that this is the center of the sixfold rotated form of this diagram that conveys its ultimate meaning, a cubic diagram will emerge with profound cosmological implications for that central tenet of the priestly tradition, the genesis of the son. The full explication of the meaning of this Sixfold Tree is dependent, however, upon our understanding of the second of these diagrams, that derived from hints in the *Sefer Yetzirah*, as developed in chapter 7.

For the final analysis of the Sixfold Tree will prove it to be a simplified version of the *Sefer Yetzirah* Tree, which is why it has had to be deferred until after that diagram had been fully developed and interpreted. Both diagrams have close associations with Greek geometry whether through influence or as analogues, the *Sefer Yetzirah* Tree developing its genesis of the son through a geometric generation of the five Platonic solids and the Sixfold Tree through a geometric solution of what Greek geometers called the "duplication problem." The Sixfold Tree can fittingly be called the Tree of Knowledge since it involves a sixfold rotation of the Tree of Life Diagram around its Da'at (Knowledge) point, and its "knowledge" will prove to be none other than the central gnosis of Hebraic sacred science, the geometric means of demonstrating the secret doctrine of the son.

The geometric connections between the Sixfold and *Sefer Yetzirah* Trees further serve to link the Tree of Life Diagram to the *Sefer Yetzirah*, and we shall later consider the whole question of the relationship of the single as well as sixfold forms of the Tree to both the *Sefer Yetzirah* text and the diagram previously shown to be encoded in it. Since this earliest extant work of the Kabbalah seems to condense the cosmology of a whole prior tradition, which it claims to have originated with Father Abraham, an analysis that could correlate its hidden diagram with that of the Tree of Life, which surfaced only in the sixteenth century, would support the claim that there was a continuous geometric tradition at the heart of the Kabbalah whose model inspired the great moments of kabbalistic history, the periods of the *Sefer Yetzirah*, of the *Zohar*, and of the Safed school resulting in the work of Isaac Luria.

The Sixfold Tree, shown in figure 8.1, is formed by a simple rotation of the Tree of Life Diagram around its Da'at point without the addition of any other lines. The form of the Tree to be so rotated is that attributed to Luria, which was illustrated in figure 1.1. And the reason this must be the form used for the Sixfold Tree is that the rotated central column produces the paths from Chokhmah to Gevurah and from Binah to Chesed. Since it was demonstrated in chapter 1 that these paths cannot coexist with those from Malkhut to Netzach and Hod, which appear in the alternate form of the diagram, as shown in figures 1.3 and 6.5, this not only

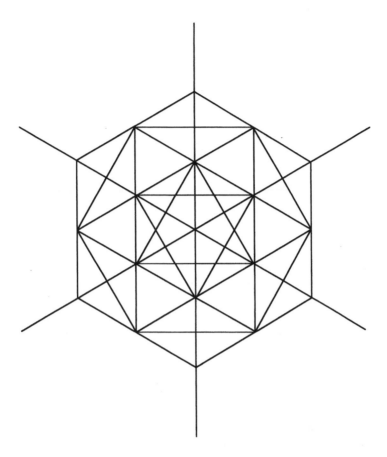

FIGURE 8.1. THE TREE OF KNOWLEDGE DIAGRAM

shows that it is the Lurianic form of the Tree that must be used for this rotation but gives further support to the greater validity of this form.

The stunning form of the Tree of Knowledge Diagram, with the startling emergence of a cube with extended root 3 diagonals, should indicate that this is, indeed, a significant esoteric diagram with special relevance to the kabbalistic tradition. As we have seen, the primary source for the importance of the cube to the whole Hebraic tradition is to be found in Exodus where directions are given for the construction of the Holy of the Holies in which to house the Ark of the Covenant, this central component of the future Temple, as recognized in *Bareitha* 4, to be in the form of a perfect cube. And we also saw that the primary geometric focus of the *Sefer Yetzirah* is a hidden instruction for the construction and infinite expansion of the cube. Thus the first text and the central diagram of the

Kabbalah would both seem to be encoding the same mystery of the cube as the archetype of creation. But though the final analysis of the Sixfold Tree will profit enormously from the analysis of its *Sefer Yetzirah* counterpart, it is best to begin its analysis more innocently. Thus we will first take up those elements that can be understood without reference to the *Sefer Yetzirah* Diagram, and then move on to a more detailed analysis of the Sixfold Tree. But let us now turn to the preliminary analysis of the cubic formations in the Sixfold Tree.

The cube is the solid that signifies the element of earth in the esoteric geometric tradition; and since it is the three lines crossing at the center that transform the diagram of a hexagram within its single-point hexagon into a cube, these lines could be taken to represent the three dimensions of the solid world. This association is reinforced by their correlation to what we know to be elements of the Fi Sabbath Star, identified with the fourth world of material manifestation in the Sabbath Star Diagram. But the large cube of the Sixfold Tree does not represent this fourth world, rather the effect of the fourth world upon the third, the sides of this cube being a product of the form that can be correlated with the inner hexagon of the third-world Fa hexagram. It represents part of that reconstitution of the supernal worlds through the agency of the fourth world known in Lurianic cosmology as the Tikkun. For in addition to the large cube of the reconstituted third world, the lines defining the three dimensions of Assiyah also transform the Atzilutic hexagram into a hidden cube one-eighth the size of the larger cube containing it. Moreover, the Atzilutic cube is a perfect version of the cube, the combination of the Atzilutic hexagram within the Berian inner hexagon plus the three lines of Assiyah producing an orthogonal cube with all twelve of its $\sqrt{2}$ diagonals and all four of its $\sqrt{3}$ diagonals, three explicit and one implicit. Figure 8.2 shows the same Atzilutic cube, now of the sixfold Tree, that we have met before in figure 7.2, where it proved to be the starting point of the solution there offered to the geometric enigma of the *Sefer Yetzirah*.

Each side of a cube has two $\sqrt{2}$ diagonals, and in such an orthogonal projection one of these diagonals is represented by a hexagram side, as in that from east to lower, while the other half is represented by what can here be called a half "Assiyah" line, as in that from the center to south. The full "Assiyah" lines form the $\sqrt{3}$ diagonals, as in that from the upper northeast corner to the lower southwest corner, the fourth $\sqrt{3}$ diagonal not being seen as it links the two corners located in this orthogonal projection directly at the center. In comparison to the perfect cube of Atzilut, the double cube of Yetzirah is imperfect, lacking the six $\sqrt{2}$ diagonals of

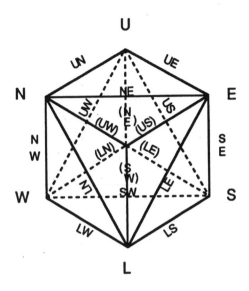

FIGURE 8.2. THE ATZILUTIC CUBE OF THE SIXFOLD TREE

the missing hexagram from what would be a second unmanifest stage of Beriah. This contrast between the perfect inner or concealed cube and the imperfect outer or disclosed cube is surely significant of both the connection between the hidden and disclosed worlds and also the difference between them.

The significance of these two cubes, one hidden and one disclosed, one perfect and one imperfect, can be better appreciated by the treatment of the cube in the *Zohar*:

> From this point onwards *bara shith*, "he created six," from the end of heaven to the end, thereof, six sides which extend from the supernal mystic essence, through the expansion of creative force from a primal point. . . .

> . . . when God came to create man. . . . the source of all lights shone forth and opened the gate of the East, for thence light issues. The South displayed in full power the light which it had inherited from the commencement, and joined hands with the East. The East took hold of the North, and the North awoke and spread forth and called aloud to the West to come and join him. Then the West went up into the North and united with it, and afterwards the South

took hold of the West, and the South and the North, which are the fences of the Garden, surrounded it. Then the East approached the West, and the West was rejoiced and said to the others, "Let us make man in our image, after our likeness," embracing like us the four quarters and the higher and the lower. Then the East united with the West and produced him. Hence our Sages have said that man emerged from the site of the Temple. . . .

Let us make man in our image, after our likeness, i.e. partaking of six directions, compounded of all, after the supernal pattern, with limbs arranged so as to suggest the esoteric Wisdom, altogether an exceptional creature. "Let us make man": the word *adam* (man) implies male and female, created wholly through the supernal and holy Wisdom. "In our image, after our likeness": the two being combined, so that man should be unique in the world and rule over all.[1]

In the first passage quoted, the whole of creation is figured as an infinitely expanding cube proceeding from a primal point. In the second passage "man" is conceived of as created in the form of a cube, which is also the cube of the Holy of Holies in the Temple. The third passage makes it clear that this Adam is not a human being but a supernal androgynous Adam, and that this higher Adam, formed in the likeness of a cube, is itself a reflection of a still higher supernal pattern that, correspondingly, must also be represented by a cube. Having made this association between the cubic formations in the Sixfold Tree and the Zoharic identification of the cube with the divine form and its supernal image, it now seems possible to go one step further and associate these higher and lower cubes with the hidden and disclosed divine personalities or Partzufim that, in the later section of the *Zohar* known as the *Idra Rabba*, are given the names of Arikh Anpin and Ze'ir Anpin. Although in the full elaboration of this concept within the kabbalistic tradition the Partzufim number five, it is this first distinction between the original Arikh Anpin and the derived Ze'ir Anpin that is most essential and may be said to contain the others, Arikh Anpin containing Abba and Imma (Father and Mother) as Ze'ir Anpin contains the Nukvah (Female of Ze'ir Anpin).

In the Lurianic tradition, the transformation of Sefirot into Partzufim is both the product and definition of the Tikkun, the reconstitution of the divine perfection that requires the spiritual efforts of earthly man. The Kabbalistic teaching that the material world can have effects upon the higher worlds seems to receive graphic demonstration from the implied evolution of the Sixfold Tree through the four worlds, the manifestation of the fourth world of solids being necessary to complete the perfection of the first world. The transformation of the Atzilutic hexagram into a cube through the action upon it of the three lines of Assiyic dimensions may be said, then, to encode the reconstitution of the originally emanated Sefirot into the first and all-containing Partzuf of Arikh Anpin. In the *Etz Chayyim*, the major work of Lurianic cosmology written by Chayyim Vital, a similar identification of Arikh Anpin with Atzilut is made: "Arikh Anpin is the soul of all of Atzilut and spreads out and is clothed in all of it."[2]

What is most interesting in the present context about the Lurianic identification of reconstituted Atzilut with the Partzuf of Arikh Anpin is that it leads to a revised numeration of the Sefirot of Atzilut matching that in the geometric analysis being presented here. How the Lurianic analysis converts the ten Sefirot that originally constitute Arikh Anpin, as they finally do all the Partzufim, into the six Sefirot corresponding to those on the Atzilutic hexagram of the interfaced Sabbath Star and Sixfold Tree diagrams will require some discussion.

As explained in the *Etz Chayyim*, the three highest Sefirot in this Partzuf, distinguished by the name Atik (the Ancient One), constitute the soul essence of Arikh Anpin, and the seven lower Sefirot, distinguished by the name Atik Yomin, his soul body. It is from the upper trunk of Arikh Anpin that the soul essences of Abba and Imma are constituted, Abba from the right arm (Chesed) and right half of the chest (a portion of the upper half of Tiferet) and Imma from the left arm (Gevurah) and left half of the chest (another portion of the upper half of Tiferet); and they are considered to cover and thus clothe the upper trunk of Arikh Anpin. This leads to the problem of the uncovered lower trunk of Arikh Anpin:

> And, behold, there remains the lower half of the Tiferet of Arikh Anpin and its Netzach, Hod, [and] Yesod [that] are exposed without having clothing. . . . And to rectify this, the Emanator had to arrange it so that the legs of Arikh Anpin would be included in its arms. Its Netzach, Hod, [and] Yesod are within its Chesed, Gevurah, [and] Tiferet, three within three, and also the lower, exposed half of Tiferet [the trunk] is included in the upper half of Tiferet; and Netzach is included in Chesed, and Hod in Gevurah; and Yesod, and the lower half of Tiferet, are in the upper half of Tiferet. . . .
>
> Malkhut was also included in each of the three upper [Sefirot]—Chesed, Gevurah, and Tiferet.[3]

After one has worked through the anthropomorphic convolutions of the inadequately clothed Arikh Anpin, it becomes clear that Luria's concern is to establish that the final form of this highest Partzuf and soul of Atzilut manifests just the six upper Sefirot, exactly the number that my geometric derivation of the Tree of Life Diagram can also be considered to have disclosed regarding the Sefirot of Atzilut, those that can be located on the six points of the Do hexagram in the Sabbath Star Diagram identified with Atzilut.

But Luria is also concerned to distinguish between the supernal triad identified with Atik and the lower triad of Chesed, Gevurah, and Tiferet, which itself contains the still lower tetrad of Sefirot, this lower triad identified with Atik Yomin, the soul body of Arikh Anpin from which the Partzufim of Abba and Imma are formed. In this context it should also be pointed out that it is not the Atzilutic or Do hexagram alone that the three lines of Assiyic dimensions transform into a cube; for such a cube to be orthogonally projected, it is also necessary to incorporate the inner hexagon of the Berian Re hexagram. For the Sefirot can all be associated with two cosmic worlds, the world of the hexagram on whose points they are first manifested and the world of the next whole-step hexagram whose inner hexagon they touch and that may be said to be their containing vessel or body.

The correlation of Sefirot to cosmic worlds is a much disputed subject in the Kabbalah, and it is well to consider at this point what intelligence the Sabbath Star Diagram can contribute to this issue, a correlation that would be helped by consulting figure 8.3 of the Sabbath Star Diagram containing the Lurianic Tree, with all its Sefirot and hexagrams marked.

In correlating Sefirot to hexagrams, we can see that Netzach and Hod, which appear on two points of the Berian Re hexagram, are first manifested in the second world and touch the third; that though Yesod should properly appear on the points of a Ri hexagram of the second world, since this is unmanifest in both the Sabbath Star Diagram and the Sixfold Tree, it only appears with its two paths on the inner hexagon of the Fa hexagram of the third world and so should be considered a Yetziric Sefirah; and, finally, that though Malkhut appears on the tips of the Yetziric Mi hexagram in the alternate form of the Tree of Emanation featured in figure 6.5, in the Lurianic form here being used, it appears rather to be manifested by the central columns of the Assiyic Fi Sabbath Star and so should be considered a fourth world Sefirah, as, indeed, it has been traditionally considered.

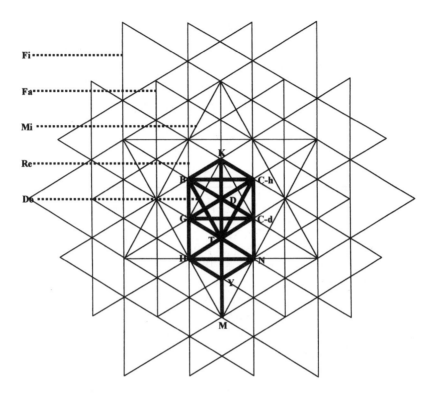

FIGURE 8.3. THE WORLDS OF THE SABBATH STAR DIAGRAM INTERFACED
WITH THE SEFIROT OF THE LURIANIC TREE

Returning from this fuller correlation of Sefirot with cosmic worlds
to the question of Arikh Anpin, it may be possible to associate the supernal triad, as the soul of Arikh Anpin, with the first world of Atzilut, and
the lower triad, as the body of Arikh Anpin and soul of Abba and Imma,
with the second world of Beriah. Nor is the distinction between the upper and lower triads of Arikh Anpin purely mythological; it can also be
grounded in the geometry of the Sixfold Tree. If Da'at is recognized, as it
must, to be the originating point of the Sixfold Tree, it will be seen that,
as in the Sabbath Star Diagram, the three supernals of formal thought
are projected above Da'at and the first three inferiors of qualitative measure below it, as are the remaining four inferiors of materialization. The
Chesed-Gevurah-Tiferet triad can be figured, then, both with the three
supernals with which it forms the Atzilutic hexagram and with the four
further inferiors that, whether or not they are considered to be contained
in the lower Atzilutic triad, as in the above Lurianic interpretation, can
be represented as appearing, like them, below the Da'at point.

If the Sixfold Tree can be looked upon as a diagram of the reconstituted Partzufim, as well as of the originally emanated Sefirot, it can then be argued that Arikh Anpin is to be primarily associated with the Atzilutic Star and Abba and Imma with the containing garment of the Berian inner hexagon, though not with its full hexagram, both configurations being transformed into the hidden cube of Atzilut representative of the three higher Partzufim by the influence of the fourth material world. Similarly, it can be argued that Ze'ir Anpin, which it was earlier suggested could be represented by the disclosed double cube, is to be associated primarily with the third world of Yetzirah, since it is the action of the three Assiyic lines upon the Yesod hexagon that transforms this Yetziric structure into the double cube. But the transformation of the Yesod hexagon into the cubic body of Ze'ir Anpin leaves the Nukvah (Malkhut) exiled from the body of her Lord[4] at the very tip of the lines defining the three dimensions of Assiyic space, which may also be said to constitute that furthest extension of emanation at which the third and fourth worlds meet. In the geometry of the Sixfold Tree, then, we seem to be able to decode both the functioning of the Sefirot in the originally emanated cosmic worlds and their reconstruction as Partzufim after the turning point of fourth-world materialization. And the method of geometric analysis adopted in this work also provides a new approach to perhaps the most unsettled subject in the Kabbalah, the correlation of the Sefirot with the concept of the four worlds. This is as far as we can go in the analysis of the Sixfold Tree without the further intelligence provided by the diagram suggested in the *Sefer Yetzirah*, and to this we now turn.

Relationship of the Sixfold and
Sefer Yetzirah Trees

The new understanding of kabbalistic geometry gained from study of the *Sefer Yetzirah* and *Etz Chayyim* texts in chapter 7 is not only relevant to the structure of the *Sefer Yetzirah* Tree, permitting the five regular solids that can be distinguished in this diagram to be interpreted in terms of the five Partzufim and of their interrelationship from the conception to the final delivery of Ze'ir Anpin, the cosmic son; it can also provide further insight into the geometric-cosmological implications of the sixfold rotated form of the Tree that can well be called the Tree of Knowledge, and it will prove to be true to its word by bringing us to our deepest understanding of kabbalistic cosmology. Let us, then, retrace our steps and see what further understanding of the Sixfold Tree can be gained from the previous analysis of the minimal *Sefer Yetzirah* Diagram shown in figure 7.2, whose twelve marked diagonals were later identified with the edges of an interpenetrating octahedron.

If we reexamine the more recent illustration of this diagram in figure 8.2, the Atzilutic cube can now also be understood to contain such an interpenetrating cube and octahedron as was earlier posited for the minimal *Sefer Yetzirah* Diagram. And from this generative source, the Yetziric cube of the complete Sixfold Tree would seem to have been enlarged through the same method of the intervening octahedron employed in the *Sefer Yetzirah* Tree except that it is given in discrete stages. The Re hexagram with its surrounding inner Mi hexagon can now be viewed as a two-dimensional representation of an octahedron, but this Berian octahedron lacks those center-radiated lines that could produce an interpentrating cube, just as the Yetziric cube lacks the hexagram lines, from the missing Ri hexagram, that could produce an interpenetrating octahedron. The Berian octahedron can be discerned more clearly in figure 8.4, which should be studied together with figure 8.2 of the interpenetrating cube and octahedron of Atzilut and figure 8.7 of the double cube of Yetzirah.

It is, then, from the interpenetrating cube and octahedron of Atzilut that the generation of the Sixfold Tree can now be extrapolated in the discrete stages of the Berian octahedron and the Yetziric double cube. The final feature of the Sixfold Tree is also significant in the present context. This is the extension of those lines beyond the Yetziric cube that were previously viewed as comprising its diagonals, their full lengths within the inner Fa hexagon defining its $\sqrt{3}$ diagonals and their half-lengths six of its twelve $\sqrt{2}$ diagonals. For their extension beyond the enlarged Yetziric cube is suggestive of such infinite diagonals as are described in the *Sefer Yetzirah:* "They continually spread for ever and ever."[5]

What we have thus achieved by rotating the Tree of Life Diagram around its Da'at point to produce the Sixfold Tree can now be seen to be a diagram of cubic enlargement through the method of the intervening octahedron with the suggestion of its capacity for infinite growth. And what is particularly remarkable about the Sixfold Tree is that it would seem to contain the same geometric focus as can be imputed to the encoded *Sefer Yetzirah* Diagram, the significance of the dualing relationship of the octahedron to the cube. Without the textual clue offered

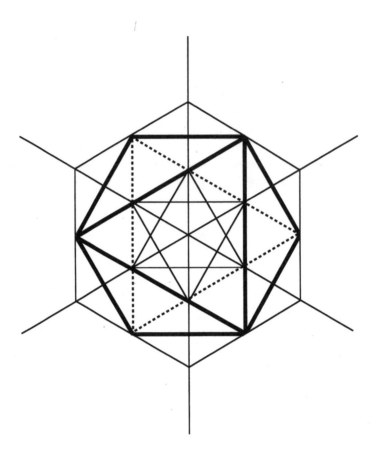

FIGURE 8.4. THE BERIAN OCTAHEDRON

by the *Sefer Yetzirah*, however, there would have been no way of recogniz-ing the appearance here of the octahedron. For it is only the curious definition of the cubic diagonals in this text that made it possible to recognize the hexagram lines as signifying not the normal √2 diagonals of a cubic square side but the dualing solid of the octahedron.

Given the emergence of this advanced geometric concept in both the major disclosed and hidden diagrams of the Kabbalah, the disclosed Tree of Life Diagram, now understood to be a key not only to the Sab-bath Star Diagram but also to its own sixfold rotated form, and the more hidden *Sefer Yetzirah* Diagram, the geometry of the cube would appear to have been an essential aspect of the sacred science informing the Jewish esoteric tradition from its beginnings. The reason for this is not far to seek. Since the cube is the ideal solid that has always been identified with the material world, the secret of its expansion would have been understood to convey the still greater mystery of cosmic genesis and its infinite expansion. From the first geometric definition of the Holy of Holies in Exodus to that of the supernal man in the *Zohar*, the cube has been a central geometric concept used both to represent and to explain the process of divine creation in the Jewish esoteric tradition that, with the *Sefer Yetzirah* and the Tree of Life Diagram, finally comes to be called the Kabbalah. And as we have just seen, both seem to contain the same hidden knowledge of an octahedron method of enlarging the cube.

The question now arises as to why the Sixfold Tree should not be considered, in and of itself, to be the very diagram suggested in the text of the *Sefer Yetzirah*, a question to be raised again in the concluding section. In terms of the present analysis, the reason that it cannot be considered to be more than an analogue to the diagram of the Tree stipulated by the *Bahir* is twofold. As can be seen, the Tree of Life Diagram extends beyond the cubic formation of its sixfold form, rather than being "inside" of the twelve cubic diagonals. Nor does the Sixfold Tree provide any principles by which its cubic form can be further expanded to contain the single Tree.

What is more, though the Sixfold Tree reveals the same geometric method of expanding the cube as does the *Sefer Yetzirah* Tree, that involving use of the intervening octahedron, it cannot take us further to the generation of the remaining two regular solids. It provides a simpler geometric model, then, for kabbalistic cosmology, one that takes us from the Atzilutic coupling of Abba and Imma, represented by the interpenetrating forms of their Do cube and Do octahedron counterparts, through the Berian womb, its octahedron representative being composed of the Re hexagram surrounded by the Mi inner hexagon, to the final Yetziric delivery of Ze'ir Anpin, as represented by the double cube manifested through the Fa inner hexagon, the Nukvah remaining outside of this cubic formation on the tips of the $\sqrt{3}$ diagonals of the fourth world, which may be considered to extend to infinity in accordance with the *Sefer Yetzirah* dictum: "They continually spread for ever and ever." Though the form of the cosmic man in the *Sefer Yetzirah* Tree is the Fa-point icosahedron rather than the simpler inner Fa double cube of the Sixfold Tree, the simplified interpretation of its cosmology to which we arrived at the conclusion of the previous chapter is exactly comparable to that which can be derived from the expanding cubic diagram of the Sixfold Tree once its additional octahedral forms have, through the hindsight of the *Sefer Yetzirah* Tree analysis, been recognized. The Sixfold Tree, unlike its

Sefer Yetzirah counterpart, is not a self-generating geometric construct, but its elements would seem to have been selected from such a more rational construction and with an exquisite precision, a precision having not only cosmological but also geometric significance. Since it is only by understanding its geometric message that we can properly gauge the true importance of this diagram to the Jewish esoteric tradition, it will be necessary to give a somewhat more detailed analysis of its features than was previously offered as well as of the comparable features of the *Sefer Yetzirah* Tree.

It was earlier said that both forms of the Tree display the same geometric method of expanding the cube, but this is not quite accurate. For the double-point progression by which the cube-octahedra were enlarged in the *Sefer Yetzirah* Tree resulted in a tripling of the cubic edge lengths[6] while the process employed in the Sixfold Tree leads to a true doubling of these edges. Though we have seen that the mode of interpretation adopted for the *Sefer Yetzirah* Diagram was most illuminating in defining the development of the five Partzufim in terms of their correlation with the five regular solids, it cannot in these terms also demonstrate the precise doubling of the cube. But it is precisely this that the Sixfold Tree does demonstrate, its single cube having an edge length of 1 and its double cube an edge length of 2. Before analyzing the details of this cubic doubling in the Sixfold Tree, it would be helpful to understand the significance of this process in the geometric thought of both the ancient Hebrews and Greeks.

Greek geometry had three classical problems insoluble by its tools of compass and straightedge: the squaring of the circle, the trisection of the angle, and the duplication of the cube. Of the last there are two legends. The earlier involves the mythical King Minos, whom an obscure Greek poet represented as ordering that the cubic tomb of his son Glaucus be doubled in size, a task the poet felt to be accomplished by a simple doubling of each dimension of the tomb but with which geometers of the time were dissatisfied. The later story involves the cubic altar of Apollo and the instruction by the oracle to the Delians that they must double the size of this altar to rid themselves of a plague, a task they did not accomplish to the satisfaction of the oracle because the workmen again simply doubled the length of the edges. The Delians were reputed to have then taken the problem to Plato, in whose Academy it was to remain a standard problem. Clearly the simple solution of doubling the edge lengths of a cube was beneath the consideration of the Greek geometers and what interested them was the more sophisticated problem of determining the edge length if the *volume* were doubled, the modern solution for such a cubic edge with a volume of 2 being the cube root of 2, or slightly more than 1.2599. It may be, however, that Greek geometers mistook the nature of the "duplication" problem; Theon of Smyrna quotes the geometer Eratosthenes to the effect that Plato understood Apollo not to be interested in the actual doubling of the size of his altar but rather in increasing the respect of the Greeks for geometry.[7]

That the duplication problem had a symbolic rather than practical or even mathematical significance is suggested by the parallel concern that Hebrew geometers would seem to have had with the same problem. And if Greek secular geometers might have laughed as much at their Hebrew counterparts as they did at the workmen for being content simply to double the edge lengths, the Hebrew sacred geometers would have been equally bemused at the vain efforts of their Greek counterparts, who had forgotten the sacred meaning of the cube and the symbolic significance of its earthly duplication. The difference in their understanding and solutions of this problem does, indeed, mark the difference between the growing desanctification of Greek geometry, especially in its Euclidean form, and the preserved symbolic character of both ancient and kabbalistic Hebrew geometry, the recognition, which one would think the Apollo of the legend shared, that geometry was worthy of study precisely because it does convey cosmological meaning. How, then, can we compare the cubes of Greek legend, the tomb of the son and altar of the god, with the major cube of the Hebraic tradition?

As was shown when first discussing the cubic formations of the Sixfold Tree, the Holy of Holies in the Sanctuary and future Temple is to be constructed in the form of a cube.[8] This cubic housing of the Ark of the Covenant is also an oracle, for here, as God says to Moses: "I will meet with thee, and I will commune with thee" (Exod. 25:22). It is here also that the high priest is to enter only on the Day of Atonement to meet with the Holy Presence and to draw from thence atonement for Israel. The Holy of Holies cube is thus both the embodiment of the Holy Presence and the means by which man can be elevated to the atoning communion with the divine through which he can express, even as he pronounces, the Holy Name. This central salvific message seems to be suggested as well, though in more fragmented form, by the two Greek legends of the cube, that of the young oracular sun god and son of Zeus, Apollo, signifying a descent of the divine into communication with man, and that of the human son Glaucus a complementary ascent, a resurrection motif. It is significant that what is demanded is not a simple doubling but a "duplication," a copying of a model. Considering the Delian case first, if the model is that of a divine altar and the plague that of the natural condition of mortality, then the way the Delians can rid themselves of this plague is by an *imitatio dei*, by sacrificing the animal in their nature to embody the divine form, a duplication of the cube. Such a duplication, implying a transcendence of death, appears to have been accomplished in the case of the son Glaucus. It was the double cube that seems to have been the original symbol for that elevation to divine sonship—"Israel is my son, even my first born" (Exod. 4:22)—achieved through the imitation of God: "ye shall therefore be holy, for I am holy" (Lev. 11:45). But though Greek geometers trivialized, even as they complicated, the duplication problem because they had lost the key to its mythic meaning, this key was preserved in the heart of Hebrew sacred geometry, in the Sixfold Tree. Having established the symbolic importance of the doubling of the cube in its simplest geometric terms, it remains only to show that the guiding principle in the design of the Sixfold Tree was this geometric problem, for the Hebrew geometers the problem of how this precise doubling could be demonstrated in a two-dimensional projection based on an expanding hexagram grid.

We have noted that the precise doubling of the cube cannot be accomplished in terms of the whole-step progression of hexagrams that marks the expansion of the cubes in the *Sefer Yetzirah* Tree, but this is only true if it is built through the double-point progression. If we look at the Sixfold Tree in figure 8.8 with all its measurements inserted, the Fa inner hexagon that defines the sides of the double cube can rather be seen to be built on the single points of the Re hexagram. In the *Sefer Yetzirah* Tree, it was such single-point construction that led to the different solid of the icosahedron identified with the Partzuf of the son, an identification that corroborates the earlier identification of the double cube of the Sixfold Tree with this same Partzuf. What distinguishes this double cube from the former icosahedron, however, is that it lacks the Ri hexagram necessary to transform the cube into such an icosahedron, its definition solely through the Fa inner hexagon establishing it as a Yetziric form. But whether as the double cube or first icosahedron, such single-point construction seems to signify the generation of the divine son. Once this identification can be accepted, then the reverse implication also becomes true, that it is only the generation of the form of the child that can allow for the doubling (copying) of the cube. The geometric process of doubling the cube becomes important, then, just because it signifies the generation of the son. Figure 8.5 will help to explain the precise process of this generation in the Sixfold Tree.

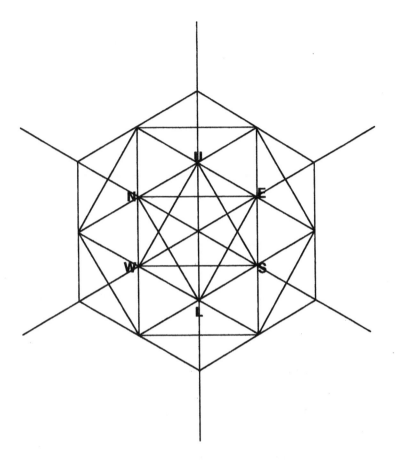

FIGURE 8.5. THE DUALING RELATIONSHIP OF OCTAHEDRON AND
CUBE IN THE SIXFOLD TREE

If the octahedron interpenetrating the single cube is viewed within the double cube, it can be seen that each of its vertices touches the point corresponding to the exact center of one of the sides of the double cube in the proper dualing relationship of these solids, the upper point touching the center of the upper side, the east point the center of the hidden right rear eastern side, the south point the center of the visible right front southern side, and so on. What is more, if we continue to observe this octahedron in its on-point position, the "square" formed by its two meeting pyramids would be that $\sqrt{3}$ rectangle between the hexagram points earlier identified with east, south, west, and north, whose actual drawn sides are 1 and $\sqrt{3}$ rather than the $\sqrt{2}$ that the sides of such a three-dimensional dualing octahedron would have. This median "square" can

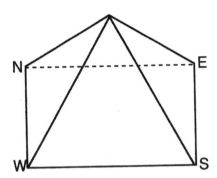

FIGURE 8.6. THE MEDIAN "SQUARE" OF THE OCTAHEDRON

be more easily visualized if the upper pyramid is viewed as composed of the ascending triangle of the Do hexagram plus the two obtuse triangles formed by the two converging lines of this same ascending triangle with the lines of its point hexagon, the fourth triangle not being visible, as in figure 8.6.

It has been necessary to define this median "square" so carefully because the wonder of the present construction is that the diagonals of this rectangle, those going from east to west and north to south, nonetheless have the length of 2 that the diagonals of the intermediate square of a √2 octahedron would have, such an octahedron as would enclose a cube of length-1 sides and be enclosed by one whose sides measure 2 in the proper dualing relationship. And the magic does not end here, since the cube of side 1, which, if properly dualing the intermediate √2 octahedron (given with two sides of √3 in this figure) would be drawn one and one-half steps smaller than the Do octahedron, at the previous La stage, is here presented as interpenetrating this Do octahedron. Yet when we examine it in relationship to the double cube, as in figure 8.7, we see that it occupies exactly the correct one-eighth of the volume of this double cube, corresponding to the progression of 1^3 to 2^3.

So both the Do cube and the Do octahedron are in exactly the right relationship to the inner Fa double cube despite the fact that they interpenetrate rather than dual each other. It can already be seen that the magical method adopted for the doubling of the cube was probably designed to produce just this sense of wonder at the divine mystery it was conveying. But the demonstration, with all its cosmological suggestiveness, is not yet complete.

Though the correct length of the double cube has been provided by the true diagonal of length 2 that can be derived from the Do octahe-

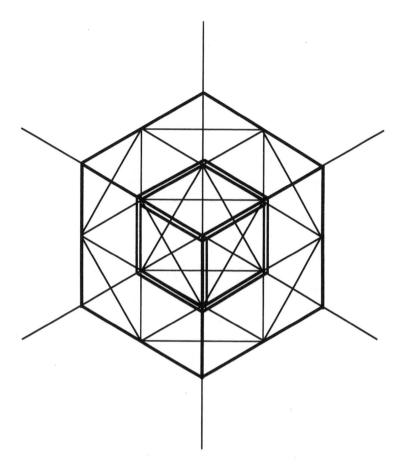

FIGURE 8.7. THE YETZIRIC CUBE OF THE SIXFOLD TREE

dron, there is still no way that the double cube can be constructed from the single cube. Its proper position can only be determined by the single points of the intermediate Re octahedron. This octahedron, however, contains none of the numbers that can be correlated with the double cube. As we shall soon see, its outer hexagon, like the lines of the Do hexagram, measure √3 while its own Re hexagram lines measure 3, the measure as well of the unconstructed Mi point/Fi inner hexagon. And while it may thus be said to carry the "genetic code" of the triple inner Fi cube, it does not do so for the double inner Fa cube, whose genetic code is provided by the Do octahedron interpenetrated by the Do single cube. These geometric facts seem most expressive of the interpretation earlier given these features as signifying the sexual generation, interuterine development, and final delivery of the cosmic child. The conception of this

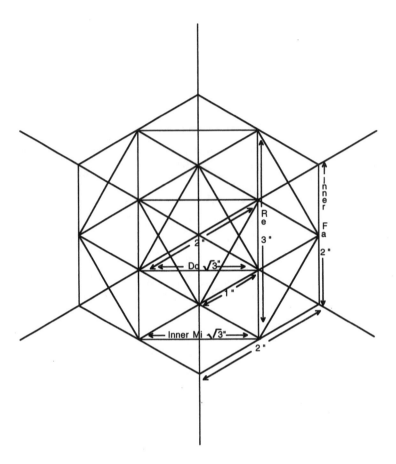

FIGURE 8.8. THE MEASURED SIXFOLD TREE

child, which gives it its genetic code, can be understood to be a product
of the interpenetrating Do cube and Do octahedron of Atzilut, the cube
signifying the father as the octahedron does the mother; and the Berian
Re octahedron, which enlarges the size of the fetus without contributing
any genetic information to it, seems clearly comparable to the womb,
from which the final delivery of the son will be accomplished with the
double cube of Yetzirah. This remarkable diagram is again illustrated, with
all its recently discussed measurements included, in figure 8.8.

A further feature of the Sixfold Tree that figure 8.8 should help to
illustrate is the fact that its two hexagrams would seem to designate two
different contributions of the female to the birth of the child. When it is
interpenetrated by a cube, as with the Do octahedron, it signifies the
female as sexual partner and genetic contributor, but when it is not so

interpenetrated, as with the Re octahedron, it signifies the feminine womb, a form here given in an appropriately enlarged size. Finally, the lack of the Ri hexagram within the point hexagon of the double cube suggests the childlike nature of this final product, its lack of sexual maturity or definition.

Reading this analysis back into that of the *Sefer Yetzirah* Tree, it would now appear that the succession of the interpenetrating Do, Re, and Mi cube-octahedra should be taken to represent overlapping generative actions and that the earlier finished Re octahedron should first be understood to represent the womb carrying the product of the Do generation before the completed Re cube of Abba is considered to reimpregnate Imma with a second conception. In both diagrams, however, the child is figured by a form built through the single-point method of construction.

In concluding this fuller study of the Sixfold Tree, we can see that this diagram does a few remarkable things. It gives us a simplified form of the cosmology developed with much greater detail in the *Sefer Yetzirah* Tree, being like it in also combining the two major geometric forms of Hebrew sacred geometry, the hexagram and the cube. Since its construction is based upon use of the two-dimensional hexagram expanded through both the double- and single-point methods of hexagram expansion, and is a product of the sixfold rotation of the traditional Tree, it clearly establishes as well a central concern of the Jewish esoteric tradition with the geometry of the hexagram. Finally, it provides what the *Sefer Yetzirah* Tree cannot, an elegant demonstration of the doubling of the cube, a problem similar to that of Greek geometry, and perhaps historically associated with it, but likely to have native roots going back as far as the priests of the Hebrew Temple, whose most holy construction was in the form of a cube.

This connection is important, for if the cube of the Holy of Holies was designed to play such a transformative role in the cosmic process as was earlier outlined, the very fact of its human construction would imply the necessity of a supernal model whose duplication could ensure its potency. And if the power of the Sanctuary cube was dependent upon its duplication of a supernal cube, then an essential element of priestly sacred science would have to have been the geometric process for the duplication of the cube. Thus long before Apollo commanded the Delians to double the size of his cubic altar, as the story goes, and set the geometers of Greece to work on what appears to have been a wrong construction of the problem, however fruitful their attempts proved to be in ancillary discoveries, the priests of the Hebrew Temple would seem to have also been at work on this problem. And it also seems likely that their wonderful solution was contained in the Sixfold Tree, all of whose lines are necessary for the minimal demonstration of this cubic doubling as well as the suggestion of its infinite expansion.

We come now to the most important conclusion that can be drawn from the geometric analysis of the Sixfold Tree and the reason for its detailed examination, the relationship of its design to that of the Tree of Life Diagram. Simply stated, the very fact that all of the lines of the Sixfold Tree have geometric justification while the design of the Tree of Life Diagram appears arbitrary seems to prove that this latter diagram was simply carved out of the Sixfold Tree and used as an initiatic symbol, the initiates understanding that it was to be rotated around its Da'at point, probably the only point initially named, to reveal the true mystery of creation, while the noninitiate would have no such "knowledge" of the more rational geometric explanation of its form. Between the traditional form of the Tree and that which can thus be carved out of the Sixfold Tree, there is only one difference, that the two paths from Chesed and Gevurah to Keter have been eliminated in the traditional Tree, lines that the sixfold rotation of the Tree restores. In the disclosed symbol, then, the possibility of such a final ascent to the Crown of godhead has been suppressed.[9] But it is just this possibility that is the revelation the initiate would receive when the key of the Tree of Life Diagram was knowingly placed within the source diagram of its sixfold rotated form.

An important further effect of this suppression of the ascending triangle of this Do hexagram is the emphasis it gives, in the later Sefirot definitions of the Tree, to the relationship of the three Sefirot associated with the remaining descending triagle of this initiating hexagram: Chokhmah, Binah, and Tiferet. This triangle may cause some perplexity because these three Sefirot are not normally considered together, all the more surprising since they do form one of the two dominating triangles in the Cordovero model of the Tree of Life Diagram and the only large triangle of the Luria model. Rather, Chokhmah and Binah are normally considered to be parts of a supernal triangle with either Keter or the quasi-Sefirah of Da'at, both such triangles variously signifying the divine mind. Similarly, Tiferet is normally considered in its triangular relationship with Chesed and Gevurah, a relationship signifying the divine heart. But a quotation given earlier from Cordovero's *Pardes Rimmonim* casts a different light on this triangular relationship:

> The third channel stretches from Chokhmah to Tiferet. . . . The reason may be because Tiferet is the son of Chokhmah and Binah

and there must be something of the influence of the father in the son as well as of the influence of the mother for a person has three partners [God plus the two parents]. . . . . Another three channels go from Chesed, the first to Gevurah. . . . Through this channel Chesed is included in Gevurah and Gevurah in Chesed without including Tiferet, as explained in the *Zohar*.[10]

Cordovero makes a point of treating Chesed-Gevurah as a dyad formed by the line connecting them and does associate Tiferet with Chokhmah and Binah as their son. Thus it is the large equilateral triangle emphasized by the present method of geometric analysis that would seem to encode the most profound of cosmic meanings. For as understood by Cordovero, the three Sefirot in question are each related to one of the Partzufim, Chokhmah to Abba (Father), Binah to Imma (Mother), and Tiferet to their originally androgynous child Ze'ir Anpin, Tiferet being the central and defining Sefirah of this six-Sefirot Partzuf. The triangle of the Tree of Atzilut would seem to hold the key, then, to the essential mystery of the Kabbalah encoded in its Tree of Life Diagram, the genesis of the cosmic son.[11] How this mystery is still further encoded in the Tree of Life Diagram we will see in the following discussion.

Relationship of the Tree of Life Diagram to the *Sefer Yetzirah*

Though the Tree of Life Diagram can now be understood to be a key provided initiates to unlock the more comprehensive geometry of creation, even for such initiates the simpler sign of the mystery of their esoteric science would have needed to undergo its own interpretative development to enable it to convey the essential meaning of its source diagram, that related to the generation of the cube as the signifier of the dual-aspected cosmic son, he in whom the divine descent and human ascent are unified. If we are to seek evidence for such a cubic reconceptualization of the simple or single Tree of Life Diagram, the first place to look would be in the very place where the concept most associated with the linear diagram of the Tree, that of the Sefirot, first surfaces, the *Sefer Yetzirah*. Now this is also the text with cryptic directions for the construction of a cube expanded through the diagonals of its dualing octahedron, a cube whose minimal form also appears at the center of the Sixfold Tree from which it was just deduced the Tree of Life Diagram is most immediately derived. So the question that naturally arises is the relationship of both the single and sixfold forms of the Tree to the *Sefer Yetzirah* and whether the Sixfold Tree is not, in fact, the primary diagram implied in this text. Though all conclusions concerning the prehistory of the Tree of Life Diagram and its relationship to both the cubic Sixfold Tree and the *Sefer Yetzirah* must remain purely speculative, if suggestions regarding both of these forms of the Tree could be found in this earliest extant text of the Kabbalah, this would go far to supporting the probability of such a prehistory.

Given the fact that the Sixfold Tree contains the same interpenetrating cube and octahedron design that was earlier advanced as the minimal *Sefer Yetzirah* Diagram, while its extended √3 diagonals give graphic illustration of the words "they continually spread for ever and ever," the simple answer would seem to be that there is good reason to accept the whole of the Sixfold Tree as the diagram indicated in the later chapters of the *Sefer Yetzirah*. The only argument against this derives not from this text but from the *Bahir*, a work of almost a millennium later that tells us the Tree is contained "inside" of the diagonals, a containment that must be based on its own rules of self-generation since the Sixfold Tree can provide no rules for its further expansion. We shall return later to consideration of what now might better be called the Bahiric Tree; but whether or not this Bahiric Tree was the most complicated diagram implied by the *Sefer Yetzirah*, with the Sixfold Tree now being considered a simplified version of it, the remaining question involves the most simplified product of this geometry, the traditional form of the Tree of Life Diagram, and whether it too can be linked to the *Sefer Yetzirah*. If it were possible to show that the form of the traditional Tree is consistent with the definitions of the Sefirot in this text, this would argue strongly for the case that the esoteric tradition condensed in this brief epitome not only had knowledge of both the Sixfold Tree and its single counterpart but understood their necessary relationship.

The presence of what seem to be directions for two different forms of diagrams in this text supports the thesis being advanced here of an inextricable connection between the Tree and its sixfold rotation such that an encoded reference to the latter would presume an allusion to the former. On the one hand, there are the directions in the *Sefer Yetzirah* for construction of an expansible cube whose six sides are associated with the seven double letters defined in its fourth chapter (the seventh identified with the center), whose diagonals are associated with the twelve single letters defined in its fifth chapter, and whose key of the octahedron method of expansion may be inferred from the definitions of the three mother letters defined in its third chapter in terms of the elements of fire and water associated with the hexagram in alchemy. On the other hand, there are the definitions of the ten Sefirot in chapter 1 of the *Sefer Yetzirah* and the further association that may be made of the three mother letters with the horizontal paths of the Tree, of the seven double letters with its vertical paths, and of its twelve single letters with its diagonal paths, Luria having given just such a distribution of letters to paths in the form of the diagram attributed to him and illustrated in figure 1.1.

That these two diagrams are distinct follows from the nature of the ten Sefirot, which have no logical correlation with the geometry of such a cube as is manifested by the minimal *Sefer Yetzirah* diagram or either of its expanded models but which do have a historical relationship to the form of the Tree of Life Diagram that emerged later in the kabbalistic tradition. The names are clearly different, but the final question is whether the specifications of the ten Sefirot in the *Sefer Yetzirah* are coherent with the form of the Tree finally disclosed in the sixteenth century, more specifically, whether these names and their different numerations can be made consistent with the Lurianic version of the Tree. Not only do I believe that this can be done, a possibility that would show still greater historical continuity between the cosmology of the *Sefer Yetzirah* and the *Etz Chayyim* as well as suggesting a predating of the form of the Tree of Life Diagram to this earliest of kabbalistic texts, if not before it, but this final version of the Tree will prove to be even more illuminating of the ultimate cosmological message of the Kabbalah.

As we saw at the beginning of this chapter, Lurianic cosmology ascribes six Sefirot to Ze'ir Anpin, those from Chesed to Yesod, an association probably mediated by the identification of this Partzuf with the third letter of the Tetragrammaton, the Gematria number of this letter Vav being six. In the *Bahir*, this crucial significance of the letter Vav is further associated with the cube of the cosmic Adam being constructed in the first chapter of the *Sefer Yetzirah*:

> 30. They said to him: But what is *Vav*?
> He said: The world was sealed with six directions.
> They said: Is not *Vav* a single letter?
> He replied: It is written (Psalm 104:2),
> "He wraps Himself in light as a garment."[12]

That the Sefirot normally associated with Ze'ir Anpin were already understood in the *Bahir* to define a cosmic man can be seen by the clear further identifications of Chesed and Gevurah with his right and left hands and of Yesod with his sexual organ.[13] As historically mediated by the *Bahir*, though with some rearrangement of their numerical order and the substitution of different names, the six Sefirot identified with the lowest male Partzuf and the Vav were, then, associated as well with the cube of the *Sefer Yetzirah*. Though the numerical order of the Sefirot defining the six directions of this cube in the *Sefer Yetzirah* is that going from the fifth to the tenth, let us see what form of the Tree will emerge if we rather adopt the numerical ordering of the later Kabbalah, which uniformly identifies Ze'ir Anpin with the six Sefirot numbered four to nine, but picture their arrangement as defining the cube also associated throughout this tradition with Ze'ir Anpin.

Ze'ir Anpin can be recognized in his cubic form if we identify his Sefirot with the six directions of space in the following manner: Tiferet-upper, Yesod-lower, Chesed-east, Hod-west, Netzach-south, and Gevurah-north. These so-defined Sefirot can produce an orthogonal version of the cube if the lines of the Lurianic Tree meeting at Da'at, which is not one of Ze'ir Anpin's Sefirot and so cannot be identified with one of these cubic directions, are included (see figure 8.9). Although the lines between these directionally identified Sefirot will not yield all of the correct cubic edges—as they can if the upper direction is placed at the upper point of the hexagon, in this case at the Da'at position—and certainly none of the diagonals, they do give us a graphic representation of a cube, and that perhaps is sufficient.

Once we have assigned the six Sefirot of direction to the fourth through ninth places normally assigned to Ze'ir Anpin, this leaves only the first three and final spheres on the Tree for the four *Sefer Yetzirah* Sefirot named *Ruach Elohim Chayyim, Ruach me-Ruach, Mayyim me-Ruach,* and *Aesch me-Mayyim,* these being the positions normally assigned to the remaining four Partzufim. Let us begin, however, by considering them primarily in their own terms and see whether these place assignments of the first four *Sefer Yetzirah* Sefirot make any sense on the traditional form of the Tree. We can start to see the rationale for this if the last terms of these phrase names are identified with the essence of these Sefirot and the first terms with what they are to give the Sefirot to follow.

Thus the essence of Keter would be identified not with the whole of the first name, Ruach Elohim Chayyim (Breath of the Living God), but only with the essential divine name Elohim Chayyim, while the *ruach* part of this name would be understood to be that which it transmits to the Sefirah in the Chokhmah position. Similarly, for the second name,

Ruach me-Ruach (Breath from Breath), the essence of Chokhmah would be identified only with the final *ruach* derived directly from the Elohim Chayyim, while the *ruach* deriving from Chokhmah, perhaps better taken in its alternate meaning of wind and thus of air, would be understood to be its transmission to the third placed Sefirah of Binah. Again in the case of the third name, Mayyim me-Ruach (Water from Wind), the essence of Binah would be identified with the lower *ruach* of wind or the element of air, and the water derived from this would be what it transmitted to the fourth of these Sefirot, now placed in the lowest position of Malkhut. Finally it is this water that would be identified with the essence of Malkhut in the last of these names, Aesch me-Mayyim (Fire from Water), and the fire deriving from it would be transmitted upward to the originating point of Keter. This is certainly a most suggestive arrangement in several regards.

First it is appropriate that the three supernal Sefirot of the upper triad should all be identified with the various degrees of *ruach*, or air, since it reinforces their association with the sky, heavens, and transcendence. Secondly, it is surely significant that the two Sefirot identified with water should be those also associated with the two female Partzufim, Binah-Imma and Malkhut-Nukvah, the concept of the "female waters," *mayyim nukvah*, being central to the understanding of their functioning. And thirdly, the identification of Aesch me-Mayyim with Malkhut underscores the traditional understanding of Malkhut as the cosmic turning point between Emanation and Return. For as water follows a descending motion, so does fire define an upward vortex, this double motion being symbolized by the hexagram itself. If Binah and Malkhut can now be identified with the upper and lower waters of the Genesis creation account, then Malkhut can, as traditionally, be identified with the earth and thus with the immanent aspect of the divine. But the fact that fire is here being shown to derive from this lowest Sefirah, and that this by definition signifies an ascent, is a most telling detail. What it tells us first of all is that the emanation process is not an end in itself but the basis on which a higher purpose is to be achieved, that the materialization of spirit, of *ruach*, is to be followed by the ascending fire of spirit as it has been cosmically developed.

If we follow the *Sefer Yetzirah* order in which the ten Sefirot are unfolded, then its first four Sefirot may be considered to occupy the first three and the tenth positions on the traditional Tree before its last six Sefirot occupy the fourth through ninth positions, thus reconciling the difference in numeration. As we explore the iconographic image in the following figure 8.9, it should be remembered from the previous chapter that these first four Sefirot also encode a meditative technique that can bring one into the state of altered consciousness whose mandalic representation, the intermediate cube of cosmic man, may be further considered to be the very image of the meditatively constructed mental cube signifying one's higher spiritual body.

If the first four Sefirot may be said to define the cosmic process quite literally in its most elemental terms, then this process would follow a transformative downward path from air to water and a transformative upward path from water to fire. In figure 8.9, however, these elemental transformations not only result in a returning product different from that of its origin, the original air having been transformed by the cosmic process into fire, but this cosmic gain is shown to be mediated in both phases by the cube of cosmic man. Thus in its downward or emanation phase, the unlimited form of divine consciousness must first be given a personalized form before and through which the material creation can take place, the form more generally of the all-inclusive primordial man, Adam Kadmon, and most specifically of the Partzuf of the son, Ze'ir Anpin. But the returning path, which fulfills the purpose of creation in the ultimate transformation of cosmic consciousness, must also be by way of a cosmic man, not that original contraction into divine personality but the new Adam arising from the spiritual expansion of man, that Community of Israel, the supernal collectivity of all the righteous, embraced by God as His son. In the single cubic form, then, is figured the two phases of the divine son as this personality has been variously understood and denominated in the Jewish esoteric tradition. And their joint appearance within this one form also suggests something of the nature of their cosmic commingling, that the perfected human personalities who rise into communion with the preexisting field of the divine Presence give as well as receive, giving to this intelligence a further personalizing and focus even as their own personalities become ever more perfected embodiments of the divine holiness with which they have been touched. In the crucible of transformation figured by this cube, there is signified, then, that joint sanctification of man and personalizing of the divine that the Jewish esoteric tradition has ever understood to fulfill the purpose of creation.

This exploration of kabbalistic geometry is ending as it began, with the key of the Tree of Life Diagram. And the remarkable meaningfulness of the diagram formed by placing the *Sefer Yetzirah* Sefirot names on the form of the Tree as it later emerged in the kabbalistic tradition, particularly in the Lurianic form that also understood it to represent the five

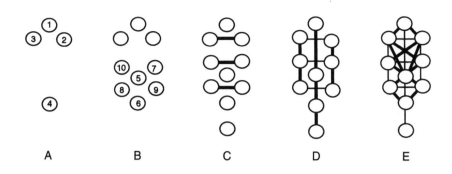

A   B   C   D   E

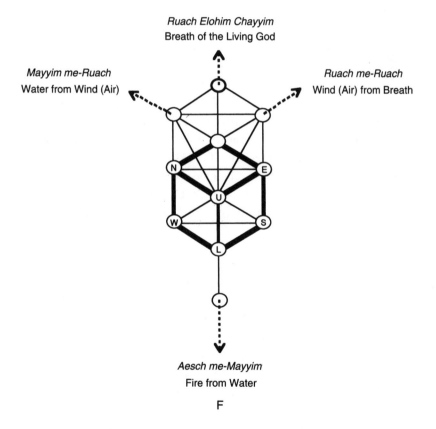

FIGURE 8.9. THE TREE WITH THE SEFER YETZIRAH SEFIROT
(A) The first four Sefirot; (B) the last six Sefirot; (C) the three mother
letters; (D) the seven doubles; (E) the twelve singles;
(F) the Tree with Sefer Yetzirah Sefirot.

Partzufim, suggests that the form of the Tree of Life Diagram was already known to the tradition culminating in the *Sefer Yetzirah*. It thus seems reasonable to claim: (1) that the Tree of Life Diagram was originally an initiatic key to the geometrically more rational diagram of its own sixfold rotated form; (2) that it was later interpreted to reflect the cosmological meaning of the duplication of the cube generated in its sixfold form; and (3) that both the single and sixfold forms of the Tree, as well as their relationship, were part of the initiatic knowledge transmitted in the *Sefer Yetzirah*, their two forms being separately implied by the various geometric details of the text.

Some knowledge of the cubic counterpart of the single Tree diagram, that here named the Sixfold Tree, and its necessary association with the single Tree seems to have been retained almost a millennium later in the *Bahir*, the transitional work in which the newer names of the Sefirot were beginning to become fixed. But thereafter the cubic form of this diagram seems to have been largely lost to this tradition, though the Zoharic references to the duplicate cube of Adam indicate some such knowledge. If the *Bahir* can be trusted, however, in its imputation that the diagram of the Tree within the diagonals of a cube was actually a part of the body of geometric practice reflected in the *Sefer Yetzirah*, then it would appear that the tradition of sacred geometry that devised the original diagram of the duplication of the cube, the Sixfold Tree, not only developed an initiatic key to this geometric demonstration, the Tree of Life Diagram defined at least by its paths, but also a self-generating form of this two-dimensional cubic geometry.

It is impossible to determine absolutely whether a self-generating diagram such as the *Sefer Yetzirah* Tree was a source diagram for the Sixfold Tree or one that derived from it. But it seems more logical that the incomplete form of the Sixfold Tree would have represented a selection from the complete self-generating diagram of the regular solids, a selection made to tell the cosmologically expressive story understood to be conveyed through the geometric duplication of the cube. From the historically disclosed key of the Tree of Life Diagram, it is possible, then, to reconstruct two prior stages of geometric derivation, that of its own sixfold rotation around its Da'at point, which adds no new lines, and then the self-generating source diagram that further satisfies the Baharic stipulation of the Tree within the diagonals of a cube.

As it is thus possible to derive the Tree of Life Diagram from the *Sefer Yetzirah* Tree, for whose existence there is a kabbalistic tradition extending from the *Bahir*, it finally seems necessary to address the nature of its relationship to the Sabbath Star Diagram, the geometric construction first advanced as the source of the Tree of Life Diagram. Since it is possible to derive the Tree of Life Diagram from both constructions, and the *Sefer Yetzirah* Tree has the added advantages of defining the geometry of the Partzufim and being definitely alluded to in the kabbalistic tradition, an argument could be made for dispensing with the Sabbath Star Diagram altogether rather than maintaining that it represents the ultimate kabbalistic diagram from which all the others are derived—the *Sefer Yetzirah* Tree, the Sixfold Tree, and the finally disclosed Tree of Life Diagram—the four successive diagrams forming what was probably one body of initiatic knowledge.

The main basis for the claimed superiority of the Sabbath Star Diagram as the ultimate source of kabbalistic geometry is that the "diagonals" by which the cubic *Sefer Yetzirah* Tree can be infinitely expanded are actually the hexagram components of this diagram and that such expansion is thus based upon the principles of hexagram expansion. In fact, the "passenger" cube forms a rather clumsy addition to the simple elegance of this hexagram expansion, an addition necessitated not by the requirements of such geometric expansion but only by extraneous considerations, primarily the desire to give two-dimensional representation to the generation of the regular solids, rather than, as with the Sabbath Star Diagram, exploring the complexity native to the second dimension. In addition, the double-point expansion of hexagrams in the Sabbath Star Diagram provides a clearer definition of the kabbalistic cosmic worlds than do the point hexagons of the *Sefer Yetzirah* Tree and the still more incomplete hexagons of the Sixfold Tree. The reason for this is that we have no way of knowing, apart from their interfacing with the Sabbath Star Diagram, whether the hexagons defining the shapes of the cubes in these latter two diagrams should be identified with the world of the hexagrams they enclose or of that of the larger hexagrams whose inner hexagons they constitute, a circumstance also true of the Sefirot. It is for this reason that the hexagrams of the Sabbath Star Diagram have formed the basis of all analyses of geometrically defined worlds in this and the previous two chapters. If we can posit, then, that a diagram of hexagram expansion must have provided the geometric method for developing the more unwieldy orthogonal diagram in the Bahiric tradition, one which at each stage of hexagram expansion requires the addition of both the six center-radiated lines and a point hexagon, then an argument can be made for the existence of both diagrams from the early beginnings of the Jewish esoteric tradition.

As previously shown, the hexagram and the cube were the two most important geometric symbols of this tradition, the hexagram symbolizing creation and the cube redemption. It is thus reasonable that Hebrew sacred geometers would have wanted to explore the generative properties of both forms, of the hexagram informing the Genesis creation account and of the cube of atonement whose physical construction is commanded in Exodus, the former the work of God and the latter of man. This difference may also account for the wider dissemination of the cubic form, whose significance is implied by its disclosure in Exodus, the *Sefer Yetzirah*, the *Bahir*, and the *Zohar*. In contrast, direct reference to the hexagram is almost nonexistent in this tradition, figuring most importantly in the Talmudic reference to this form on Solomon's seal ring and in later magical amulets. But its presence can be detected in two significant texts, in the first chapter of Genesis, as demonstrated in chapter 6, and it would seem in the third chapter of the *Sefer Yetzirah*, in the definitions it gives to the three mother letters, the Shin being associated with both fire and heaven, the Mem with both water and the earth, and the Aleph with the balance between them, these also being the correspondences that later surface in the alchemical tradition to define the hexagram it calls "Solomon's Seal," a tradition that was shown in chapter 6 to go back to Jewish sources, most importantly the Maria Hebraea contemporary with the *Sefer Yetzirah*. The fact that the hexagram can be detected in the *Sefer Yetzirah* as well as diagrams of an expansible cube and of ten Sefirot shows them all to be elements of a single body of geometric knowledge, one whose long continued hidden existence is implied by both the complexity and cryptic nature of its geometric references and whose most hidden element was the hexagram. That it was kept so carefully hidden was probably due to its identification with "the secret things [that] belong unto the Lord our God" (Deut. 29:28). But if the prior derivations of the disclosed Tree of Life Diagram, first from the Sixfold Tree and then from the self-generating diagram here called the *Sefer Yetzirah* Tree, are accepted, then the hexagram method by which that latter diagram can alone be expanded implies the prior development of the Sabbath Star Diagram, a diagram that might have originally represented the highest and most secret level of a four-stage process of Temple initiation.

We have seen that the Sixfold Tree conveys the central knowledge of the generation of the son, which this work has argued was the secret doctrine of the Hebraic priesthood. But the final importance of the Sixfold Tree is the proof it offers concerning the significance of Da'at, the center from which the six Tree of Life Diagrams have been shown to rotate in this model. On the basis of this evidence, the Tree of Life Diagram should now be recognized as emanating from the central point of Da'at, the non-Sefirah, and not from Keter, the first emanated Sefirah. The most important implication of recognizing that the Tree of Life Diagram emanates from Da'at emerges, however, from reflection upon the meaning of Da'at—Knowledge. For what the Sixfold Tree centering on Da'at accomplishes is precisely the transformation of the Tree of Life into the Tree of Knowledge. In a kabbalistic tradition recorded by Eleazar of Worms in the *Sefer ha-Shem*,[14] the Tree of Knowledge was held to be not intrinsically evil. Rather, the error of Adam and Eve consisted in eating of its fruit prematurely, on the sixth day instead of the seventh. Had they waited and eaten of the fruit with Sabbath consciousness, it would have been a Tree of Life for them; the central Sabbath column would then have harmonized the duality of good and evil that the right and left columns of the Tree of Life can represent and without which it becomes a destructive Tree of Knowledge.

As it was through a dualistic pursuit of knowledge that Adam and Eve may be said to have lost Paradise, so it is through the proper understanding of Knowledge, Da'at, that the descendants of Adam and Eve were shown the way out of the bondage of this destructive dualism. In the great Exodus saga, God delivers to Moses the following message for the people He would make His own: "I will rid you out of their bondage, and I will redeem you with a stretched out arm, and with great judgments: And I will take you to me for a people, and I will be to you a God: and ye shall *know* that I am the Lord your God, which bringeth you out from under the burdens of the Egyptians"(Exod. 6:6-7; my italics). Redemptive knowledge is that understanding by which one can "know" (a form of the word Da'at) God and the Way of His "great judgments," that the way of redemption from the lower bondage of dualistic knowledge is that service to the highest source of being in which all dualities achieve unification. Where such service is redemptive, resistance to the "great judgments" leads to destruction. God tells Pharaoh to "Let my people go, that they may serve me" (Exod. 9:1), while recognizing that "the Egyptians shall *know* that I am the Lord, when I stretch forth mine hand upon Egypt and bring out the children of Israel from among them" (Exod. 7:5; my italics). But in its deepest sense, Da'at involves more than such rational understanding. It may be said to signify such knowledge of God as not only recognizes that to follow the Way of God is self-fulfilling and to resist it self-defeating but is so exalting that it makes such service to the divine will the only desire and converts the Tree of Knowledge into its intended Sabbatical consummation as the true Tree of Life. What this part has hopefully accomplished is just this union of the Tree of Life to the Tree of Knowledge through the Sabbath Star Diagram that disclosed the Knowledge, the Da'at center, through which the single Tree of Life could be transformed into the Sixfold Tree of Sanctified Knowledge with its revelation of the redemptive generation of the divine personality of the son.

PART 4

Syntheses of
Sacred and
Secular Science

9

A Synthesis of Sacred Science and Quantum Physics

The Matrix Model

We have thus far considered Hebraic sacred science from both theoretical and practical perspectives, exploring those of its aspects that distinguish it from its Greek counterpart, particularly its interest in the occult correspondences of language and in the cosmological interpretation of geometric form. We are now to embark on a new direction, the attempt to synthesize such sacred science with its modern secular heirs, quantum physics in this chapter and quantum cosmology in the next. This first attempt will draw upon both the theoretical framework of sacred science and one product of the experimental kabbalistic geometry practiced in part 3, the matrix that emerged in the diagram of the *Sefer Yetzirah* Tree as decoded from the cryptic references in early kabbalistic texts. As the theoretical framework will provide guidelines leading to a reinterpretation of the data of quantum physics, so will the Kabbalistic matrix provide a modeling of all the particles of the quantum realm, one that will give new graphic form, with great explanatory power, to aspects of quantum theory which have thus far proved impossible to visualize and so to become acceptable to the intuitive imagination.

This synthesis of sacred science and quantum physics will begin with the central concept of reality advanced by sacred science, the balancing of the two opposed conditions of finite localization and infinite extension. For every system that can claim individuality is understood to be compounded of both such finite localization as can be identified with a particle nature and such infinite extension as exhibits the nature of a wave. Once this distinction is put in these terms, it is clear that the new quantum description of matter should be susceptible to a similar interpretation.

Having the dual nature of a particle and wave is something that quantum physics attributes most readily to the electron and its associated electromagnetic force, theory and experiment agreeing in the complementary manifestation of both the electron and light as both wave and particle. Thus the material electron can be analyzed both as a quantum particle and a wave packet and the electromagnetic force as both an energy wave and a compound of quantum particles known as photons. But the problem of applying the mathematical tools of both quantum mechanics and wave mechanics to both matter and energy is that it destroys the distinction between the localization of matter and infinite extension of energy that nature seems determined to demonstrate. This problem is further compounded by the attempt to apply the approach of quantum electrodynamics to the other major form of matter, the nuclear particles and forces, primarily the protons and neutrons and the strong force that confines the yet more elementary quarks within them, an attempt that goes by the name of quantum chromodynamics.

The primary motivation behind this theoretical attempt to combine leptons, such as the electron, and hadrons, such as the nuclear particles, as well as their associated forces, into one formula of quantum interactions would seem to be a philosophical positivism that views all physical forces with suspicion—the suspicion that a spiritual character attaches to force that must be disallowed by a thoroughgoing materialism. But the picture with which quantum physicists are left is one that, however descriptively adequate, can explain nothing. If a proton is pictured as throwing a colored gluon back and forth with a neutron and a photon back and forth with an electron, this does not explain how the force particles that are now absorbed by one or another hadron or lepton can bind that particle to the one from which it was just emitted. Calling it a "gluon" cannot explain the glue that forms a continuous connection between atomic particles, binding the hadrons together to form the atomic nucleus and the leptons to them to form the atom.

But the discussion of sacred science should have shown two things most relevant to the impasse to which quantum physics would seem to have brought the human imagination. The first is that there is nothing about physical force that makes it more spiritual than matter, that both can be assimilated to either a spiritual or materialist interpretation of phenomena. And the second is that, regardless of the philosophical orientation adopted, both matter and forces are necessary for an adequate description of reality. What is needed, then, is a model that can contain all the particulars defined by modern physics while retaining the capacity to distinguish both between matter and force and between the forms of these associated with hadrons (the nucleons) and leptons (the electrons). Such a model can be found in the matrix that emerged in the *Sefer Yetzirah* Tree, one called the "matrix of creation" because it was contained in the stage of this diagram identified with the second kabbalistic world of Beriah (Creation). It should also be noted that the central point of this matrix in the *Sefer Yetzirah* Tree, a cosmological diagram incorporating the traditional kabbalistic diagram of the Tree of Life, is precisely the point defining the position of Da'at (Knowledge) on the superimposed traditional Tree. In this matrix, then, an association is being made between the womb of creation—the word *matrix* meaning "womb"—and the ultimate knowledge it might be thought to carry, the essential knowledge of the sacred science that can provide the guidelines for a new understanding of secular science and in view of which this chapter, with a nod to Fritjof Capra's *The Tao of Physics*, might well be called "The Da'at of Physics"! Though this matrix can be defined independently of this construction, we will begin by considering it in the context of this kabbalistic diagram, with its suggestive associations. In figure 9.1 twelve large triangles and an inner hexagon are highlighted to facilitate the later discussion of this matrix.

If we begin by examining what appears to be the elementary particles of the matrix, the twelve highlighted triangles, we will see that they are by no means the simple structures we might have assumed. Rather, they make manifest the two aspects of any equilateral triangle, its defining outline and its implied lines of symmetry. Without the actual drawing of the triangle, it would not have formal existence. But its three lines of symmetry have an implicit existence whether or not they are drawn; they are the lines along which the triangle may be folded to produce two symmetrical halves, lines perpendicular to a base that can be dropped from any one of its apices. Because such lines describe the path along

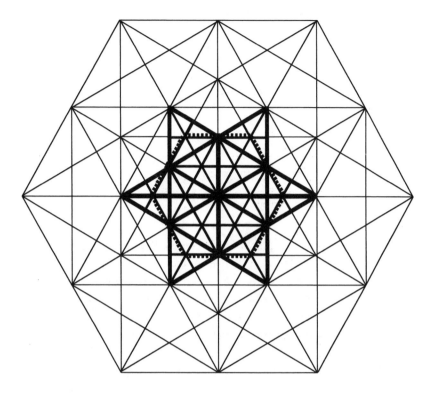

FIGURE 9.1. THE MATRIX OF CREATION IN THE *SEFER YETZIRAH* TREE

which force can travel with the least resistance, they can be considered to represent the triangle's lines of force. In contrast, the triangle's outline can be considered to represent its lines of form.

This subtle inner structure of the triangle can be demonstrated if we move from two to three dimensions. When a tetrahedron constructed out of copper wire is immersed in a soapy solution and then withdrawn from it, the inner planes formed around the four invisible lines leading from the vertices to the center will all magically manifest out of the soapy film. In figure 9.2, depicting one such tetrahedron side, these inner planes can be suggested if the central point is visualized as extending backward in depth to the center of the tetrahedron.

In a pyramid, similarly, it is these same force lines of its triangular sides that give to this structure its famous "pyramid power." Thus the lines of symmetry of the equilateral triangle may truly be said to convey force. The matrix triangles we have been considering represent, then,

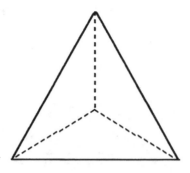

FIGURE 9.2

the most perfect minimal plane figure, the equilateral triangle, with its two aspects of form and force fully manifested. It is the perfect symbol of the necessary coexistence of force and form in any conceivable entity.

In the analysis of these matrix triangles, the distinction between form and force seemed clear and immutable. But if we look more closely at the portion of the matrix pattern within the dashed inner hexagon high-lighted in figure 9.1, we will see that this discussion involved only its macrostructure and that there is an entirely different microstructure to the matrix that interfaces with the macrostructure in such a way as to invert the significance attached to the latter's lines of form and force. This microstructure is formed of small equilateral triangles, one-third the size of those in the macrostructure and with the all-important difference that these microtriangles exhibit only one of their lines of symmetry. Though an equilateral triangle intrinsically has three lines of symme-try—that is, it can be folded into symmetrical halves using any one of its sides as a base—what is distinctive about the particular interfacing of these triangles in the pattern of the matrix is that it explicitly defines all three of the lines of symmetry in its macrotriangles but only one of them in its microtriangles. The microstructure can be discerned by focusing on the central hexagram produced by the force lines in the macrostructure, that whose inner hexagon contains six microtriangles and provides the bases of six more microtriangles while its point-hexagon contains six macrotriangles and provides the bases of six more macrotriangles. As the inner hexagon of a hexagram has a different orientation from the outer hexagon that connects its points, the grid of the microstructure will nec-essarily be differently oriented from that of the macrostructure, the mi-crostructure here following a vertical orientation as the orientation of the macrostructure is horizontal.

Once we distinguish the distinctive appearance of the microtriangles, what is immediately apparent is that the outline of a microtriangle is formed from the force lines of the macrotriangles, its perpendicular lines of symmetry, while its single power line is derived from a macrotriangle's formal outline. In the microtriangle, then, the significance of the form and force lines of the macrotriangle would seem to be inverted. But if we retain the perspective of the macrostructure, it would then appear that in the matrix system the outlines of the macrotriangles provide both the form that defines these larger entities and the force lines that run through the microtriangles and may be thought to bind them into the larger macrotriangular wholes. The outlines or form lines of the microtriangles could also be viewed as defining the mass that fills the larger forms of the macrotriangles. This definition of the matrix will be most useful in developing the matrix model of the hadrons. It is not necessary to make such an identification of the microtriangles with mass, however, since the matrix can be defined in terms of true reciprocity between its two levels, that which provides the defining form of one level also contributing a force to the other level. But once it is realized that the matrix will function equally well whether the planes of the microtriangles are filled in or left blank, it will then be seen that the filling in of the microtriangles opens up an important new possibility. What it does is enable the reconstruction or reconceptualization of this two-dimensional matrix in the three dimensions of space.

In such a construction, the difference between inherent and expressed lines of symmetry becomes crucial. For while the macrotriangle's three lines of symmetry would hold it rigidly in place, the microtriangle would be free to spin about its single axis. The nature of such a three-dimensional reconstruction, then, would be one in which the macrotriangles would provide an immovable grid of tubing around which each distinct and solid microtriangle would be free to spin. Once their differing capacity for movement is recognized, it is not necessary to continue working with a three-dimensional model. It is enough to realize that the single axis of the microtriangle creates the potential for free spin in such a three-dimensional model while the triple axes of the macrotriangle create its stabilizing rigidity. The matrix provides a model, then, of a system that confers freedom to the members of the lower level microstructure, the freedom to spin, within the constraints of that larger whole defined by the higher level macrostructure. For whatever area is being considered and whatever its hierarchical level, the microstructure may be said to represent the level of particular individuality and the macrostructure the level of the collective whole. Both may be said to conform to different laws, the microstructure to the law of freedom and the macrostructure to the law of determinism. This is the most important single point that can be made about the matrix. For this very union of individual freedom within a larger deterministic structure has significant theoretical implications.

It may first be said to define the rule of probability whose operations can be everywhere observed, a subject whose larger philosophical implications will be treated in the epilogue to this chapter. And it can also model the primary tenet of general systems theory, that there is a cosmic hierarchy of dual-leveled systems, the lower level of which demonstrates the freedom characteristic of the individual members of a larger whole and the higher level the constraint that the power of its higher organization imposes on such individuals; these systems thus demonstrate the Aristotelian principle that the whole is more than the sum of its (lower-level) parts. Given its modern redefinition by Ludwig von Bertalanffy,[1] general systems theory has not enjoyed the vogue in recent years it earlier had, due in large part to its inability to generate the new investigations on which the physical and social sciences thrive. The leading edge of systems thinking has moved instead to the study of such dynamic systems as feature a growth in chaos or complexity and which use the computer as the tool of a new experimental mathematics. But as we shall see, it is not the newer systems theorizing—which emphasizes conditions of turbulence, catastrophe, and self-organization, horizontal and unstable rather than hierarchical and stable structuring—that holds the key to a proper understanding of fundamental physics but the by-passed theory of general systems. For the simple triangular matrix just defined is capable of modeling all of the particles and forces known to quantum physics in a form that demonstrates the cogency of general systems theory and in a way that will shed new light on some of the most opaque aspects of this field, opaque because they have not previously been subject to a geometric modeling through which they can be grasped by the imagination.

In addition, the very constraints of such geometric modeling will provide a new way of understanding the quanta. They will reveal the essentially inverse relationship of the hadrons (such as protons) and the leptons (such as electrons) and why the hadrons are better modeled as quanta and the leptons as waves. The advantage of this model is that it provides a geometry whose own structure can explain the inherent relationships among the two types of particles and their related forces, something that the purely descriptive Feynman diagrams of particle interactions cannot accomplish. And it can do this by restoring to physics the main distinction between the localization of particles and extension of waves that, through the related categories of shape and sound, also defines the central insight and contribution of sacred science. This new geometric description can both distinguish and explain all these various elements while at the same time providing a visual model that can once more bring theory and the intuitive imagination back together. Because of the potential importance of this model for particle physics, the matrix modeling of atomic particles will be developed at some length, separate models being provided first for the hadrons, then for the leptons, and finally for their atomic interrelationship.

The Hadron Model

It is the particular way in which the microstructure of this matrix system is related to its macrostructure that makes it most immediately applicable to quantum physics as a model of hadron structure, for this interfacing can be understood to model the relationship of parts to a whole that defines the hadrons, no longer considered to be elementary particles but to be themselves composed of the theoretically more elementary particles known as quarks. At the atomic level, quarks come in three different "colors," called red, blue, and green, this quality representing their susceptibility to the strong nuclear force, and two different electrical forms, the "up" quarks that carry a charge of +2/3 and the "down" quarks whose charge is −1/3. Hadrons also come in two different varieties, the baryons, to which the class of protons and neutrons belong, and the mesons, at this nuclear level only the pions, or pi-mesons, and these are distinguished by the type and number of quarks by which they can be mathematically defined. The baryons are composed of three differently colored quarks, their red, blue, and green "colors" canceling out to a colorless white, while the mesons are composed of a quark and antiquark of a color and its same anticolor, such as blue and antiblue, this combination also being understood to form a colorless combination. With respect to electrical charge, the proton is composed of one down quark and two up quarks (the addition of one −1/3 and two +2/3 charges equaling the +1 charge of the proton) while the neutron is composed of two down quarks and one up quark (the two −1/3 charges being canceled by the one +2/3 charge to equal the zero charge of the neutron). The pions come in three electrical forms: the positive pion whose +1 charge is produced by the combination of an up quark (+2/3) and an antidown quark (+1/3); the negative pion whose -1 charge is produced by combining a down quark (−1/3) with an antiup quark (−2/3); and the more numerous neutral pions produced by combining either a down quark (−1/3) with an antidown quark (+1/3) or an up quark (+2/3) with an antiup quark (−2/3). We shall begin with a simple modeling of the quark-baryon interface and then extend this to include the mesons in diagrams of increasing complexity, which may be regarded as modeling the "fields" of individual protons and neutrons.

Fritjof Capra has pointed out the following essential problem in developing a quark model:

> If quarks are held together by strong interaction forces, these must involve other particles and the quarks must consequently show some kind of "structure," just like all the other strongly interacting particles. For the quark model, however, it is essential to have pointlike, structureless quarks. Because of this fundamental difficulty, it has so far not been possible to formulate the quark model in a consistent dynamic way which accounts for the symmetries and for the binding forces.[2]

Since quarks have not only never been observed experimentally but, making a virtue of necessity, are now considered to be so trapped by the strong force within the structure of the hadrons as to be theoretically unobservable, it may be that the only way out of the difficulty already encountered in formulating an appropriate quark model would be to accept the theoretical implication that quarks do have "some kind of 'structure.'" But since baryons are thought to be bound together within the nucleus by mesons, and mesons are composed of a quark and an antiquark, this means that antimatter must be present within the nucleus and in such a form that it is prevented from annihilating the matter to which it is so closely bound. Our quark model must be capable, therefore, of containing both matter and antimatter within its newly ascribed structure. Once these two conditions are accepted, it becomes possible to model the quark-baryon interface in terms of the geometric symmetries of the matrix.

In its simplest terms, this interface can be modeled by a single macrotriangle within a hexagon of microtriangles, the macrotriangle representing the baryon, in the first case a proton, and the microtriangular parts within it the sum of three differently colored quarks. The modeling solution here posed is that the count of the three unobserved quarks is to be construed as actually composed of two symmetrically opposed half quarks in each of the three required colors. Such a solution is possible in terms of the matrix because each of the microtriangles is bisected by the form of the macrotriangular outline passing through it. Since the quarks are only to be formed of the two similarly colored half microtriangles within the macrotriangular outline signifying a baryon, and since the model must also provide for antiquarks, the full solution of quark-antiquark modeling is to consider each microtriangle as composed of a material half, that lying within the macrotriangular outline of the baryon, and an antimaterial half, that lying beyond this macrotriangular outline and completing the form of the microhexagon. If the third defining characteristic of quarks in addition to their electric and "color" charges is to be considered, that of spin, we can further design our model so that the material half of the side of the microtriangle facing us is understood to be backed by antimatter on the opposite side of the microtriangle facing away from us, with the reverse circumstance holding true for the antimatter half of the microtriangular front face. Given such a construction, we may say that as a symmetrically opposed pair of microtriangles spins on its axes, only the material halves of each will be within the confines of the macrotriangle at any one time, these two halves comprising the count of one whole quark. As we shall later see, the remaining antimaterial halves of these same two similarly colored and electrically defined microtriangles also combine to form the antiquark half of a virtual pion, part of the cloud of virtual pions thought to surround baryons and bind them together within the atomic nucleus. In the following three hadron figures, the up and down quarks are signified by the letters U or D and their antiquark counterparts by these letters with a bar over them. Colors are indicated by the words red, green, or blue or their letters, R, G, or B, not as attractive an expedient as the illustration of these actual colors would be but one that perhaps may be excused by the fact that they are supposed to cancel out to a colorless white. The simplest modeling of this interface appears in figure 9.3.

As can be seen, the macrotriangle representing the proton is in a reciprocal relationship with the six halves, lying within its borders, of the six microtriangles with which it is interfaced, those three pairs of complementary halves from which the count of one down and two up quarks of three different colors can be assembled. In this relationship it is the quarks so defined by the matrix that contribute to the proton both its mass and electrical charge, but what makes a proton whole out of these three quark parts is just the form it imposes upon these parts. Since in

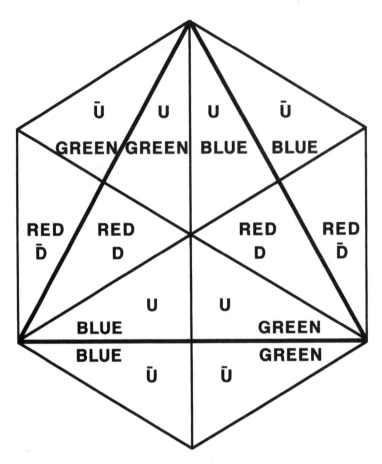

Figure 9.3. The Quark-Baryon Interface Model

quantum theory it is the strong force that is thought to bind quarks into baryons, we may now equate the macrotriangular boundary that defines this baryon with the strong force. As the macrotriangular outline may be equated with the strong force, so may the microtriangular outline be equated with one of the fractional electric charges carried by the quarks. To complete this definition of matrix parts, it is the colored interior planes of the microtriangles that may be equated with the mass of the quarks. If we can imagine the microtriangles as solid chips spinning on the tubular outline of the macrotriangle by which they are bisected, and of the strong force as flowing through this tubing, then we have a model in which such a baryon as the proton here pictured can be recognized to be a composite of matter and force.

In this model the mass can be seen to be entirely contributed by its quark members while the form defining the proton whole and binding these parts into its higher level unity is that contributed by the strong force. The geometry of this relationship would further suggest that *when force meets mass it becomes transmuted into form*, its power to mold and delimit mass being exercised through the geometry it imposes on such previously unconstrained mass as may be postulated but never observed. As the macrotriangular form may be considered both to define the proton whole and to carry the strong force with respect to its interaction with the microtriangles it symmetrically bisects, so may the microtriangular form be considered both to define the quark entities and to carry the electric charge they jointly contribute to the baryons. Since it is only in terms of the baryons that the fractional quark charges achieve the full integer values that nature alone demonstrates, there would seem to be some support for the geometrical distinction being suggested here between the dual nature of triangular outlines as defining both the form of one level of triangle and the force it communicates to the level with which it is interfaced. Thus it may be further argued that it is only within such a larger hadron form as can give integer values to electric charges that the quark form can serve to conduct the electric charge potential in its mass.

But the matrix also indicates that the electric charge contributed to the baryons by the quarks is not on the same hierarchical level as the strong force contributed by the baryons to the quarks, that *charge* represents a lower dimension than *force*. Electric charge may be considered to be of a lower dimension than the strong force insofar as its form aspect serves to define the lower-level quarks, whereas the form aspect of the strong force defines the higher level of the baryons. Since electric charge relates a particle to the electromagnetic force, this would further suggest that the electromagnetic force represents a lower dimensional force than does the strong force, a subject to be more fully developed later in this chapter and in chapter 10. In the matrix modeling of the leptons, we shall also see reason to identify the electromagnetic force with the third dimension, and we can postulate that all of the physical forces may best be understood as the product that the geometry of a higher dimension imposes upon the material constituents of a lower dimension. The lepton matrix model will also show that the electric charge of the electrons is subject to the higher controlling power of the electromagnetic force with which it is associated, that for the leptons as for the hadrons, charge is subject to, and distinguishable from, force. It can be further postulated that as long as the electric charge is contained within the nuclear particles, it does not have the scope necessary to develop the third dimension in its complementary electromagnetic force and that this force appears in such particles only in what the physicist David Bohm has called an implicate or enfolded form.[3] It can only so develop this third dimension when it either is in a position surrounding the nucleus or in the nonatomic free form it can also assume. In the former atomically bound case, the electromagnetic force may further be said to supply the atom with the three-dimensional form that then allows the more weighty mass of the nucleus to add the fourth dimension that relativity theory tells us can curve space-time. Thus we may read this two-dimensional model of the nuclear particles as representing the enfolded forms of the higher dimensions of those forces with which both the electric and color charges of the quarks can couple in a complete atomic model. By themselves, the nuclear particles may be considered to be as truly two-dimensional as in their matrix representation but to be so related that they demonstrate the hierarchical relationship of the enfolded dimensions associated with the quark parts and their baryon whole.

In this model we have seen how the geometry of the matrix can explain the relationship of matter to force within a baryon without recourse to the added category of bosons into which quantum theory understands the various forces to be "quantized." Since it is a characteristic of such force quanta, however, to be massed together in the same space so as to form a continuous wave, the distinction between the old wave concept of force and the new quantum concept seems to come down to little more than a question of semantics, of preferring to view the forces as composed of continuously massed quanta rather than of waves. If such a view is preferred, then the matrix model can, of course, be interpreted entirely in quantum chromodynamic terms with the macrotriangular outlines now being identified with colored gluons and their planes with the quark-composed baryons. But such an understanding of these outlines as representing the hypothesized "messenger" particles called bosons, none of which have been observed within the limits of the nucleus, destroys the distinction between matter and force that the matrix can so graphically illustrate and that is more coherent with our intuitive understanding.

We have seen that it is the strong force, thought to bind quarks into baryons, that can be identified with the macrotriangular outline without recourse to the superfluous category of the bosons, a matrix modeling that preserves the distinction between matter and force that is analogous to the central truth of sacred science. But there is another aspect of this modeling that we must now consider. For quantum theory tells us that the strong force is also neutral between matter and antimatter, being that which not only binds quarks into protons and neutrons but also antiquarks into antiprotons and antineutrons. And since we have seen that the hadron model includes antimatter, the antimatter in the mesons we will be studying in the next section, we may go further and say that when matter and antimatter are placed in contiguity within the geometry of the atomic nucleus, the strong force to which they are both attached will also serve to neutralize the opposition between them so that they do not annihilate each other.

Perhaps the most spectacular product of this attempt to design a model of the quark-hadron relationship that includes mesons as well as baryons is the emergence of antimatter particles, not just of mesons but of antibaryons. In fact, what the expanded hadron field model of figure 9.4 immediately reveals is that material baryons are surrounded on all sides and points by antibaryons, a situation exactly reversed for the antibaryons, and that in a large enough field, as in figure 9.5, there is an exact numerical parity between baryons and antibaryons. Before examining the complexity of these field models, we should review the subject of antimatter.

It was Paul Dirac who first posited the existence of antiparticles, specifically the antielectron or positron. And as Heinz R. Pagels has shown, "Soon it was realized by physicists that the Dirac equation, in implying the existence of the antielectron, was offering but one specific example of the general consequence of combining quantum theory with the principle of relativity—namely the existence of antimatter. . . . For every particle that can exist, the laws of physics imply that an antiparticle can also exist."[4] What is most interesting about antimatter is that its existence emerges as the theoretical "consequence of combining quantum theory with the principle of relativity," of combining particles with the geometrical definition of force, particularly of gravity, that is the central achievement of relativity theory. Dirac's work, be it noted, was not based on the quantum but on the wave properties of the electron and it implied the existence of a substratum that exerts some controlling force over quantum freedom, of the coexistence of deterministic force with the individual freedom of quanta. In summarizing the implications of Dirac's quantum mechanics, Sir James Jeans concludes "that the fundamental laws of nature do not control the phenomena directly. We must picture them as operating in a substratum of which we can form no mental picture."[5] Again the matrix model may accomplish what previous models have failed to do by providing a mental picture of the relationship of free particles to constraining forces that would also seem to combine quantum with relativity theory. But it does this not by positing an unimaginable substratum to phenomena, rather by relating the observable phenomena of quantum theory to the superstratum of force identified with a higher geometric dimension, this relationship achieving graphic form through the interface of the two dimensions represented by the microstructure and macrostructure of the matrix. For as just seen in the matrix modeling of the hadrons, the macrostructure is identified with the strong force and further understood to represent the enfolded form of the fourth dimension posited by relativity theory. *Where there is mass, there is, then, the relativistic geometry of force with its consequence of antimatter.*

Not only does the matrix model show baryons to be surrounded at all their points of contact by antimatter and in a manner that prevents their mutual annihilation (the neutralizing effect of the strong force when it appears in such a regular geometric configuration as that of the matrix), but it would also appear to explain the "exclusion principle" first enunciated by Wolfgang Pauli and now extended to all fermions. As summarized by Paul Davies:

> All quarks and leptons are fermions, each having spin of one-half a unit. It is the fermion's spin which so taxes the imagination with its double-rotation property. . . . The fermions . . . are possessed of a sort of xenophobia and do not permit their siblings to come too close. . . . In contrast to the isolationist behavior of fermions, bosons positively love to get together. . . . No exclusion principle operates here, and so the behavior of massed bosons is completely different from their fermion cousins. . . . This means that bosons tend to be associated with *force*, whereas fermions are associated with *matter*.[6]

What the matrix suggests is that the reason that baryons, and also leptons, as we shall later see are prevented from coming too close together is that the "space" immediately surrounding each such particle is completely occupied by antimatter, this antimatter forming a sort of moat around each material particle whose "space" might be thought to have the power to annihilate (in geometric terms, to redefine) any particle of matter that intrudes upon it.

A final power of the matrix model to give imaginable shape to theoretical properties that have hitherto taxed the imagination may be seen in the way it can explain the half-integer spin of the quarks, the fact that they must rotate twice to come back to the same spot. Since in this model the quark is understood to be composed of two halves, each of which rotates on its own axis, the addition of the single rotations of each may be considered to result in the double rotation of the whole composite quark. Thus the matrix model can explain the fermion attributes of exclusion and double spin in the case of hadrons by distributing them between the baryon wholes (exclusion) and their quark parts (double spin). Having already considered the easily observed modeling of the baryon-antibaryon relationship soon to be featured in figure 9.4, we can now explore the way in which this relationship allows for the representation of those virtual pions by which the nuclear baryons come into relationship with each other. I should, however, also warn nonscientific readers at this point of the increasing complexity of the following analysis of pion modeling and suggest that they might want to move directly to the lepton model.

The Hadron-Field Model

There is one type of force-related quanta postulated by quantum theory that must be capable of discrete modeling by the matrix if the matrix is to be offered as an adequate model for the interrelationship of the nuclear particles. This is the category of pi-mesons known as pions, the other category of nuclear hadrons beside the baryons, which are considered to be composed of quarks and their antiparticles. To understand the relationship of pions to baryons in matrix terms, we shall need an enlarged model minimally composed of a complex of thirteen macrotriangles. In this model the matrix solution being offered to the pion modeling is in terms of a new assemblage of microtriangular halves, those outlined with a variety of dots and dashes in figure 9.4.

As both theory and modeling show, the nuclear pions must be considered virtual rather than real. Although mesons have been experimentally produced outside of the nucleus, within the nucleus they are accorded only a virtual status, the theoretical product of an energy loan financed by the Heisenberg "uncertainty principle." Only the huge energies available in particle accelerators can give real existence to such virtual particles. As in the theory, so in the model those microtriangular halves that can be assembled to represent the varieties of virtual pions may already claim a prior existence as constituents of the previously assembled baryons and antibaryons. Their virtual existence is a product, then, only of a geometric pattern that can be superimposed on another more basic pattern whose parts it rearranges into a new configuration.

And yet this superimposed configuration, though having only virtual parts of its own, has a real function in determining the disposition of the baryons and antibaryons defined by the model.

Such a model of a central neutron and its associated field of virtual baryons and pions is shown in figure 9.4. In this and in figure 9.5, the baryon type—proton, neutron, antiproton, or antineutron—will be indicated by the letters P or N, with or without the upper bar that conventionally indicates an antiparticle, these letters appearing within a *circle* placed at the meeting point of the three lines of symmetry in the macrotriangle indicating a baryon. The colors of the quarks or antiquarks—red, green, or blue—will be indicated by the letters R, G, or B within a *square* placed on the line of symmetry within the microtriangle of such a color, the two halves of such a microtriangle constituting a half quark and half antiquark of the same color. Finally, the type of quark— up, down, antiup, and antidown—will be indicated by the letter U or D, with or without the upper bar indicative of an antiparticle.

We can begin to understand the way in which the matrix model defines the pions by comparing it with the earlier quark-baryon modeling of figure 9.3. In that modeling, two microtriangles meeting point-to-point within the limits of a macrotriangle were accorded the same color and charge, and so their complementary halves within these limits were considered to form one quark. As the parts of these two microtriangles within the macrotriangular boundary were understood to form a quark, so their remaining two halves may now be understood to form an antiquark. The object then is to find another similarly colored pair of microtriangles with whose two quark halves these two antiquark halves may join to form a pion.

The most satisfactory candidate for this corresponding pair of microtriangles will be the one where the two antiquark halves may meet two quark halves at a shared point, for then each of the separated quark-antiquark halves of the pion can form a joined configuration, one in the shape of a forward or reversed closed figure K, while these two pion halves may also be considered to be joined in view of the connection between the antiquark halves and their microtriangular mates within the macrotriangular boundaries. In the matrix, a pion may therefore be identified with all such closed-K and reversed closed-K facing configurations.

Whether we are speaking about neutrons or protons, the assembly of the three pions here being associated with each baryon will follow certain rules. The odd quark of the baryon (up for the neutron and down for the proton) will always have its antiquark other halves connect with an op-

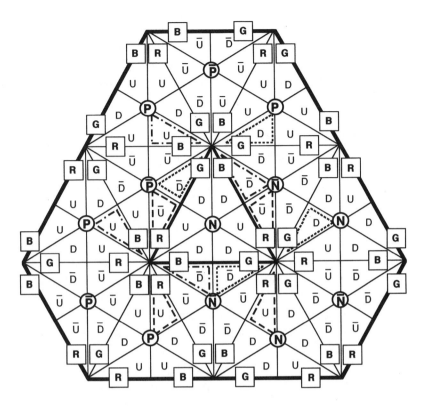

FIGURE 9.4. THE BARYON-PION INTERFACE MODEL

positely charged quark to produce a neutral pion. Of the two even quarks, the antiquark other halves of one will also connect with an oppositely charged quark to produce another neutral pion (antiup with up or antidown with down). But it is the third quark, which cross-connects to produce either a positive or negative pion (for the neutron an antidown with an up making a positive pion and for the proton an antiup with a down making a negative pion), that has the crucial role, in effect establishing the whole geometry of what can be considered the virtual particle field.

It should be pointed out that this is the only arrangement of pions permitted by the matrix modeling of the hadrons. The cross-connection of the associated odd antiquark is impossible because, in a field of thirteen macrotriangles, one of these macrotriangles would always contain a nonparticle arrangement of either three ups or three downs or their antiparticle complements. Less serious but still forbidden is the cross-connection of both of the associated even antiquarks because this would have the effect of unbalancing the parity in the field between matter and

antimatter, this over and above the present unbalancing that is due simply to the odd number of macrotriangles in a field of thirteen. But the
correct way of establishing the hadron field demonstrates something even
more significant, an essential lack of determinism with respect to which
of the two even antiquarks will "choose" the more dynamic path of cross-
connection. As with photon polarization, to which we will return in the
conclusion, the initial determination as to which of the even antiquarks
will cross-connect to form a nonneutral pion is essentially stochastic.
But once this initially free determination is made, the organization of
the rest of the field will follow a determined path, establishing ever larger
symmetries.

In figure 9.4 we may see the form of the three pions resulting from
the procedure prescribed above. The two antiup red halves of the odd
antiquark combine with the two similarly colored up halves directly below them to form one neutral pion. The two antidown green halves combine with two similarly colored down halves facing to their right to form
the second neutral pion. Finally, the two antidown blue halves cross-
connect with two up halves facing to their left to form a positive pion.
As we shall see in figure 9.5, this is the preferred direction, not for an
antiquark but for a draftsperson who wishes to make a symmetrical arrangement in the smallest compass permitting such symmetry, a predrawn
hexagon containing twenty-four macrotriangles. Such a hexagon will
establish itself whichever direction is chosen, but it will then have to be
built up in the process, not predrawn. A comparison between figures 9.4
and 9.5 will show that the thirteen macrotriangle complex of figure 9.4
does not have the numerical parity between matter and antimatter that
could render it such a complete model as that given in figure 9.5. It is
composed of three neutrons, three antineutrons, three antiprotons, and
four protons. But as figure 9.5 shows with respect to an initiating proton,
the full design is not that in which the initiating baryon is centered but
in which the hexagon formed of three such baryons and their antiparticles is centered within a larger hexagon that surrounds the smaller hexagon with a ring of eighteen macrotriangles signifying the other variety of
baryon. Thus in figure 9.5, the hexagon containing six macrotriangles of
protons and antiprotons is surrounded by a ring of eighteen neutrons and
antineutrons, each ring showing exact parity between matter and antimatter. What we see in figure 9.4, then, must be understood to be part of
a larger design, its seven protons and antiprotons, which there half-circle
the hexagon of neutrons and antineutrons in the lower right of the diagram, representing but a portion of the ring of evenly matched protons

and antiprotons that in a more complete diagram would fully surround the hexagon of the initiating baryon.

But figure 9.4 is still an important model because it represents the way in which one nucleon may be supposed to situate itself with respect to other nucleons within an actual atomic nucleus. These models do not represent any possible nuclear arrangement but the virtual fields of individual baryons that may be understood in one of two ways. First, they may be understood as mathematical models that explain the various characteristics and interrelationships ascribed to the hadrons by quantum theory in terms of the way they can be arranged in a purely geometric space. But it would also seem that the geometric program that can be so unfolded from each individual baryon would have an actual effect were that baryon to be placed alone in a vacuum, arranging its space and potential contents so as to give them the virtual form being here designated. But whether in the nucleus or a vacuum, what we are concerned with is a single real baryon in a virtual field.

This formulation has some similarity to the quantum field theory developed by Werner Heisenberg and Wolfgang Pauli, as explained by Steven Weinberg:

> They showed that material particles could be understood as the quanta of various fields. . . . There was supposed to be one field for each type of elementary particle. Thus, the inhabitants of the universe were conceived to be a set of fields—an electron field, a proton field, an electromagnetic field—and particles were reduced to mere epiphenomena. In its essentials, this point of view has survived to the present day.[7]

Whether particles are understood to be the mere epiphenomena of quantum fields or the fields to be a real or virtual emanation from the particles, we may postulate that every "particle" that experiment and theory tell us is to be found in a particular atom may be understood to be accompanied by its own at least *geometric* field, an implicit arrangement that defines the ways in which it can relate to other particles within the atom. And since each such particle has its own similarly associated field, the situation of particles with respect to one another will depend on their finding mutually appropriate places in each other's overlapping fields, the whole forming one lattice of intersecting fields with such a final mutual accommodation as forms a pattern contained in no one particle field but defining the pattern of the larger nuclear and atomic wholes. What the virtual pions in each field are doing, then, is neither holding the various baryons together nor being tossed back and forth between them but rather designating the appropriate place for each in the others' fields that can give stability to the whole.

If we look more closely at figure 9.4, we can see that it reflects the essential counterpart of three against two that is central to the quark analysis of the hadrons.[8] For the two categories of hadrons, as we have seen, have just this distinction, the baryons being composed of three quarks (the antibaryons of three antiquarks) and the mesons of two parts, a quark and an antiquark. In the matrix, this distinction is revealed not only in the composition of the configurations identified with the baryons and the mesons but also in the colors of overlapping hexagons. Each microhexagon that contains a macrotriangle representative of a baryon or antibaryon is composed of the three colors identified with its three quarks or antiquarks. But each of the microtriangles contributing to the formation of the initiating baryon also forms a part of a larger microhexagram configuration; and within each of these microhexagrams is an inner microhexagon not housing a macrotriangle but instead six microtriangles of only two colors, the two other than the color of the surrounding microhexagram. These three microhexagrams also set the pattern for the ever enlarging model whose structure will become clearer upon examination of figure 9.5.

But the final counterpart of two against three is most important for the arrangement of nucleons being proposed here. This involves the inner arrangement of quarks within the baryons. There are three ways in which these quarks may be arranged, with the odd quark appearing (1) in the horizontal position, (2) in that going from right to left, or (3) that going from left to right. Now it can be seen that all of these ways are represented among the neutrons in the neutron-antineutron hexagon of figure 9.4, but that only two of these ways are represented among the four protons there shown, the horizontal position and that going from right to left. What this signifies is that the neutron-proton linkage is more restricted than the neutron-neutron linkage, that only two-thirds of the protons and neutrons in a nucleus can be placed in adjacent positions in terms of each other's fields but that any neutron can be placed next to a neutron or proton next to a proton. As figure 9.5 will show, the same arrangement holds for a proton center of the comparable thirteen macrotriangle portion of the larger model, but it is only this smaller model that can define the immediate relations between nucleons. For the three pions that a baryon may be said to generate from the surrounding field define the only six places to situate other baryons with which it can form a direct bond. It is the function of mesons in quantum theory to mediate the strong force not within a baryon but between them. This the matrix mesons may be said to do. Their antiquark portions are strung on the outer sides of a baryon border carrying the strong force, while their quark portions are situated along the inner sides of such borders of neighboring baryons; and at the vertex points of these baryons, where the quark and antiquark portions of these mesons meet, this strong force may be thought both to neutralize their opposition and to enfuse them with its power. Thus the microtriangular halves that have been designated as comprising the virtual pions may be said to bond baryons together through the strong force insofar as they can be considered its carriers. But what the model also shows us is that the strong force *is* a geometric power. It is the form of the macrotriangle defining the larger entity of the baryon that so strongly confines the microtriangle portions within its boundaries and so defines them as its three quarks. So also is it the geometric rearrangement of microtriangular halves whose definition of the virtual pions permits them to accomplish their task of integrating the baryons into a larger whole. To complete the analysis of the matrix modeling of the hadrons, we should now turn to the more precise examination of the enlarged symmetrical model given in figure 9.5.

If we first observe the inner macrohexagon, we can see that its form is defined not by the initiating baryon of this twenty-four macrotriangle model, the highlighted proton to the upper left of the inner macrohexagon, but by its cross-connecting blue antiquark complement with an up charge. This establishes the blue micro*hexagram* of up-antiup charges that is to center all further enlargement of this proton field. Returning to our initiating proton, its red antidown complement couples with the red down-quark halves below it, while its green antiup complement couples with the green up-quark halves to its right to form the two neutral pions. From this point on the colors of these quark and antiquark parts will never vary as to their charge; red will always signify the down-antidown charge and green the up-antiup charge, and they will form microhexagrams of these colors and charges throughout the infinitely expansible field of this proton. In figure 9.5 the red microtriangles form two down microhexagrams on the left side of the diagram and one such microhexagram at the mid-portion on the right, while the green microtriangles form two similar up microhexagrams on the right side of the diagram and one at the mid-portion on the left. But the original two blue antiup-antiquark halves, which cross-connected with the two blue down-quark halves to their left to form the negative pion, define the

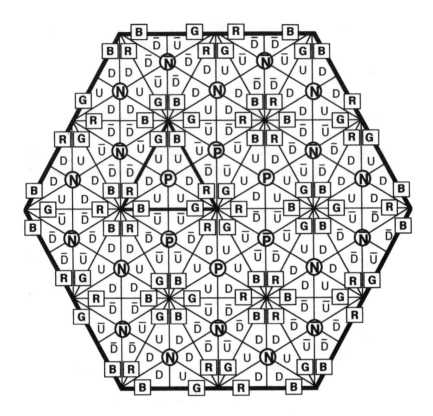

Figure 9.5. The Hexagonal Model of the Baryon Virtual Field

double charge characteristic of the blue color that will continue to be attached to this color and, through this attachment, give this baryon field its final form. If the central blue microhexagram is observed, it will be seen that each of its antiup points meets two other blue microtriangular halves with their cross charge of down. It is in the two-color microhexagons—such as that directly at the center with alternating green and red microtriangles—that the points of the colored microtriangles meet, three points of one color always alternating with three points of another, with a red down microtriangle always meeting two other red down microtriangles and a green up microtriangle two other green up microtriangles. But the situation differs for a blue up microtriangle— such as that alternating with green in the microhexagon directly to the right of the previously designated central microhexagon—that will always meet two other blue down microtriangles, which will in turn form new blue down microhexagrams.

As the model is further expanded in accordance with these rules, what emerges is a pattern of space-filling six-macrotriangular macrohexagons each of which contains only one form of baryon and its antiparticle. Moving now from counting macrotriangles to counting macrohexagons, what emerges is a ring pattern of such space-filling macrohexagons of the following alternating character. In the case of an originating proton, the central proton macrohexagon is circled by a ring of neutron macrohexagons, which in turn is circled by a ring of alternating proton and neutron macrohexagons, followed by a ring of just neutron macrohexagons once more. Thus rings composed just of neutrons alternate with those showing combinations of neutrons and protons, the reverse pattern developing in the case of an initiating neutron. Within an actual atomic nucleus these differences would balance out, since for every proton field from the helium atom on up there would be a complementary neutron field.[9]

This discussion of hadron modeling has centered on the nuclear hadrons because of my belief that the structural principles informing material reality are not to be found on the quantum level but only on the level of the atom. Thus my primary concern is with those particles that form the stable structures of our manifest four-dimensional world. But before leaving the hadron model, it should be pointed out that this model will work as well for all the strange- and charm-filled baryons and mesons whose microsecond existence has been actualized in the particle accelerators. If we return to figure 9.4, it can be seen that the model can easily be adapted to these more exotic particles simply by substituting a "strange" or "charm" quark for a down or up quark of its same color, and this in any of the proportions defining these new baryons.

Thus, if we wish, for instance, to turn the neutron there featured into a neutral sigma particle (composed of up, down, and strange quarks), we have only to change one of the down quarks to a strange quark. If the cross-connecting blue quark is chosen, the unification of its strange antiquark complement with the same up-quark halves that had formerly formed a positive pion will now form a positive kaon, one of the family of "strange" mesons. Such a substitution of any or all of the three baryon quarks by strange quarks or even by a combination of strange quarks (with $-1/3$ charge) with charm quarks (with $+2/3$ charge) will give us the initiating baryon from which its whole field can be built up in the manner indicated for the neutron and proton fields. But as long as these artificially produced higher resonant hadrons are still operating on the lower resonant fourth dimension of the strong force, they will be too unstable to form atomic nuclei. In the next chapter we shall consider the possibility of such higher dimensional forces, but now we must conclude this discussion of hadron modeling.

The modeling being presented in this chapter gives us a new view of the quantum level of matter when taken out of its natural systemic connections to the macroscopic layers of distinguishable objects. Though it cannot explain the higher organizational principles that define each higher level of the systems hierarchy, since this is precisely what is lacking at the quantum level, as a model for quantum theory, it may be conceded that the matrix succeeds where other models have failed in providing a geometric picture of hadron-particle interactions that have previously defied the visual imagination and that imparts to such interactions as have been formulated in quantum theory the support and illumination of its own geometric logic. It would be enough just to have shown how the matrix can model the quark constituents of the hadrons and the further interactions of the baryons and mesons with the antiparticles that they constitute. But as we shall now see, it provides just as remarkable a model for the lepton branch of matter and one whose comparison with the previously offered hadron model may illuminate as never before the inverse character of these two necessarily different categories of matter.

The Lepton Model

The difference between hadrons and leptons is that the hadrons are most adequately explained in terms of quantum mechanics whereas the leptons are subject to two different interpretations, those of quantum mechanics and of wave mechanics. That is, both the electron and the electromagnetic force to which it couples can be interpreted in terms of both forms of mechanics, the electron being associated with a definite wavelength and the electromagnetic force being quantized into photons. Because the wave picture provides a more accurate picture of our knowledge of the particles and forces associated with the lepton category of matter, it has itself been subject to dual interpretations, either as the correct theory replacing that of quantum mechanics or as the pictorial representation of the quantum mechanical understanding with which its mathematical formulation is in agreement. In this last view, which synthesizes quantum and wave mechanics, the particles rather than the waves are granted reality and the waves are interpreted to represent probability rather than matter, the probability of finding an electron or a photon at any particular point in its associated wave pattern, a probability, it might be pointed out, that once again shows geometry to be exercising a controlling force over the free movement of particles. As Jeans has shown with regard to the electron waves of Louis de Broglie and Erwin Schrödinger:

> These waves form the subject-matter of the wave mechanics, and at the same time, as we have seen, provide a pictorial representation of Heisenberg's quantum mechanics. The fact that the mathematical wave-lengths (although never physical waves) show their presence experimentally provides confirmation both of the truth of the quantum mechanics and of the validity of the wave mechanics as a pictorial representation of it.[10]

There are, then, two different interpretations of wave mechanics, the original Schrödinger interpretation that it represents the true picture of the wave nature of matter and the probabilistic interpretation of these waves offered by Max Born. Pagels makes clear this theoretical conflict:

> Schrödinger himself offered one of the first interpretations: The electron is not a particle, he argued, it is a matter wave as an ocean wave is a water wave. According to this interpretation the particle idea is wrong or only approximate. . . . Born interpreted the de Broglie-Schrödinger wave function as specifying the probability of finding an electron at some point in space. . . . The electron is always a true particle and its Schrödinger wave function only specifies the probability for finding it at some point in space. Born realized the waves are not *material*, as Schrödinger wrongly supposed; they are waves of *probability*.[11]

But whether the Schrödinger or Born interpretation of wave mechanics is accepted, and I would prefer to accept Schrödinger's view as the correct one, it is clear that the leptons are best represented pictorially in terms of wave mechanics. Thus the lepton wave model will have to differ significantly from the hadron particle model, this difference reflecting the irreducible distinction between hadrons and leptons.

But there is another difficulty that would seem to attend the present attempt to provide such a wave model of the leptons in terms of the same matrix previously used to model the hadrons, the fact that the mathematical descriptions of both the undulatory theory of light and of the electron wave-packet have implications regarding the geometric dimensions that would lift their representation beyond the two dimensions of the matrix model. In the explanation offered by Jeans,

> The waves of the undulatory theory need a space of only three dimensions for their representation, so that we may conveniently and legitimately represent them in ordinary physical space. The waves of a single electron can also be represented in a space of three dimensions, but the waves of two electrons need a space of six dimensions, three for each electron, while the waves of a million electrons need a space of three million dimensions. Thus the wave-picture of even the simplest group of electrons, or of other particles, cannot be drawn in ordinary space.[12]

To picture a group of electrons either within an electric current or within a complex atom we would have to have a model that could accord each electron its own three dimensions of space.

There is still another difficulty with the representation of this space, for the field surrounding the electron is that of the electromagnetic force and its energy is calculated to be infinite. As Davies explains,

> The observed mass of a real electron will be composed of two pieces: its bare mass plus the mass of the electric energy generated by the field. The embarrassment is that the electric energy part is calculated to be infinite. . . . In practice the theorist simply adjusts, or "renormalizes," the zero-point on the scale used for measuring mass by an infinite amount. . . . By this mathematical sleight-of-hand the description of the electron can be rid of the infinite terms that at first threatened to reduce the theory to absurdity. . . . The problem now centers on the nature of virtual photons. . . . In the quantum description of an electron . . . the electromagnetic field which clothes the particle must be viewed as a retinue of virtual photons fussing around the electron, clinging to it, and forming a tenacious shroud of energy. The photons come and go very rapidly. Those that remain close to the electron, near the centre of the shroud, carry considerable energy; in fact, when the total energy of the photon shroud is computed, it again turns out to be infinite. . . . When this horrendous sequence of infinite terms is packaged up the right way (mathematically speaking) it so happens that the whole lot

can be disposed of in one go. . . . Without it the theory would crumble into meaningless nonsense.[13]

Though quantum physicists view infinities with the same horror they display toward forces, the "mathematical sleight-of-hand" of "renormalization," which is heralded as the great triumph of quantum electrodynamics, may rather be viewed as masking another significant distinction between the leptons and the hadrons that an adequate model should be able to contain. Not only should leptons be characterized as waves and hadrons as particles, but the particle description of the hadrons should define their nature as finite while the wave description of the leptons should define their complementary nature in its true infinity.

Translating Davies' quantum description back into the wave mechanics that can serve as its pictorial representation, we may say that the electron wave-packet is surrounded by the waves of the electromagnetic force, the former of which can be understood to contain a single electron of unspecified position, while the latter can be similarly understood to be crowded with the photon class of bosons, and that both the inner and surrounding waves have an infinite character. But since one set of infinities is surrounding another, this already reveals that the infinities involved must admit of degrees, must be that intermediate form of infinity between the absolutely infinite and finite that Georg Cantor has redefined by the term *transfinite*:

> The actual infinite arises in three contexts: *first* when it is realized in the most complete form, in a fully independent other-worldly being, *in Deo*, where I call it the Absolute Infinite or simply Absolute; *second* when it occurs in the contingent, created world; *third* when the mind grasps it *in abstracto* as a mathematical magnitude, number, or order type. I wish to make a sharp contrast between the Absolute and what I call the Transfinite, that is, the actual infinities of the last two sorts, which are clearly limited, subject to further increase, and thus related to the finite.[14]

If we can understand the renormalization process not as a means of doing away with infinities regarded as leading to "meaningless nonsense," but rather as the means of revealing their Cantorian transfinite nature, then we can accept both the infinite character of the electron and its force as well as the degrees of such mathematically calculated infinities as can permit the different quantum states or orbits of the atomically bound electrons.

We have seen that three characteristics are required for an adequate lepton model: that it portrays both the electron and its surrounding electromagnetic force field as waves; that each such lepton particle field be accorded its own three dimensions of space, and that this force-filled space be recognized to have a transfinite quality. This set of requirements would seem to ensure that such a lepton model, in the words of Jeans, "cannot be drawn in ordinary space." And yet it is precisely this peculiar set of characteristics that provides the clue as to how the matrix can be reconceptualized into a lepton model that preserves these distinguishing qualities. The secret is to view the microhexagon not as a two-dimensional composite of six microtriangles but rather as a two-dimensional projection of the three-dimensional cube, the twelve lines that had hitherto defined the microtriangles now being understood to define the twelve edges of this cube. It is within this private force-field of three-dimensional space that the electron wave-packet is to be pictured, and this may be as easily identified with the macrotriangle contained within this microhexagon as the microtriangles can be identified with the three-dimensional shape of a cube. Thus we can see how the same matrix can be used to define the three-in-one nature of the hadrons (three quarks in one baryon) and the one-in-three nature of the leptons (one electron in its own three dimensions of space). This reconceptualization of the matrix as a lepton model takes the minimal form seen in figure 9.6.

In this model the plane of the macrotriangle may be identified with the mass of the electron, its outline with the electric charge it gives to its surrounding force-field, and the outlines of the microtriangles with the electromagnetic force defining this surrounding cube of space. Using the same matrix to model both the hadron and lepton fields enables us to see as perhaps never before the inverse symmetries belonging to these two contrasting categories of matter. Most significant is the different relationship of mass to force demonstrated in these two models. In the case of the hadrons the force is contained within the nucleons while in the case of the leptons the force surrounds the electrons. In both cases force may be said to surround charged mass. But since the nucleons can themselves be understood to represent the force-fields of the quarks, the distinction between the hadron and lepton models with respect to the relationship of mass to force still holds as these two aspects are differently defined in the two models. Whereas in the hadron model force is identified with the macrotriangle and charged mass with the microtriangles, in

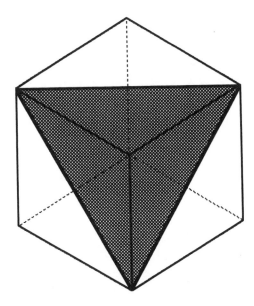

FIGURE 9.6. THE LEPTON-WAVE MODEL

the lepton model it is charged mass that is identified with the macro-triangle and force with the microtriangles.

There is a further symmetry between these models with respect to the implied presence in both of antimatter. We have seen that the had-ron model required the presence of antimatter to account for the anti-quarks necessary for the composition of the mesons. So too the lepton model must be able to accommodate the positrons that also couple to the electromagnetic force. How it can do this we can see in the multiple lepton model shown in figure 9.7.

In modeling the hadrons and leptons, opposite macrotriangles have been chosen to represent the hadrons and leptons depending on the domi-nant charge of their atomic nonneutral material particles. Thus the posi-tive charge of the protons led to the choice of the ascending macrotriangles to signify the baryons and of the descending macrotriangles to signify the antibaryons. For the leptons, the descending macrotriangles were chosen to signify the negative charge of the material electrons and the ascending macrotriangles to signify the antimatter positron's positive charge. Thus these dual models can distinguish between the nuclear and nonnuclear atomic constituents in yet a third way. In addition to their particle-wave discrimination, the particles containing force and the waves being con-tained by it, and their situation in two- or three-dimensional space, they

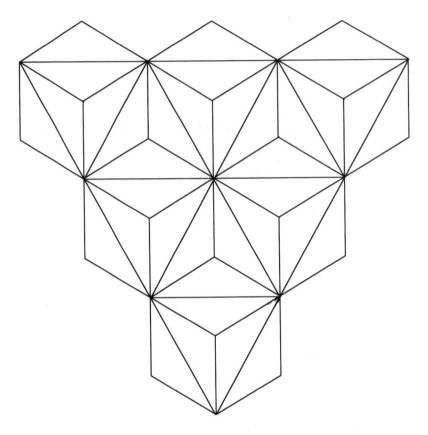

FIGURE 9.7. THE LEPTON-WAVE FIELD MODEL

can also distinguish between the positive charge of the nucleus and the negative charge of the surrounding atomic space.

But there would seem to be a problem in considering the lepton model to contain positrons as well as electrons. For where the matrix of the hadron model provided room and substance for each of its baryons and antibaryons (the room of the macrotriangles and the substance from the sum of the three differently colored quarks or antiquarks that the microtriangular halves contained within these macrotriangles could be said to constitute), all of the matrix lines in the lepton model would seem to be used up to designate the electrons in their separate spaces, and there is no portion of the matrix left to define or house the positrons. This is true—but only as long as the matrix is still taken to represent two-dimensional space. If the honeycomb of cubes in figure 9.7 is observed more carefully, it can be seen that its projected third dimension does leave room on all six implied directions of each cube for the insertion of another such cube already housing its own fully defined positron. Each such imagined additional cube can be seen to contain the outlines of an independent positron within its own distinguishable space. Though the edges of this positron are technically joined to those of the surrounding three electrons, if we can view the electromagnetic walls housing the electrons as also providing the walls of the positron cubes adjacent to them, then the optical illusion created by the projected third dimension insists that we consider the inhabitants of distinguishable spaces also to be distinguishable.

The final model, then, is one in which transparent, three-dimensional cubes of electromagnetic force are arranged in a honeycomb pattern alternately containing electrons and positrons, the appearance of antimatter wave-packets on all sides of the matter wave-packets again explaining the exclusion principle that fermions—electrons as well as protons and neutrons—everywhere demonstrate. The ability of such matter and antimatter to exist together without annihilating each other can again be explained by the same principle in both the hadron and lepton models, that what binds the matter and antimatter geometrically together in these models is also that which is neutral between them and can be considered to neutralize their opposition. For the hadrons this is the strong force carried by the macrotriangular outlines and for the leptons the electromagnetic force carried by the microtriangular outlines. And as the strong force that defines the baryons and antibaryons was also understood to neutralize the opposition between them, so the electromagnetic force defining the separate spaces housing the electrons and positrons can similarly be understood to permit their neutralized cohabitation in those circumstances in which the geometric structure of their natural cohabitation has not been wrenched apart by the violence of subatomic experimentation.

If we can accept the fact that electrons are best represented by a wave model, whether it be understood to be a physical or probability wave, as hadrons are by a particle model, then the matrix would seem to provide the best visual model yet offered to explain the complementary natures of these atomic constituents. Further, its very power so to define, distinguish, and correlate them would suggest that these major types of matter take the forms they do precisely because of the workings of such an underlying geometry.

But as with the hadron model, such a lepton model would have no place for the bosons. The simplest solution would be just to reject these bosons as a redundant theoretical complication disallowed by the matrix model and to permit the forces, into which they had been thus unnecessarily quantized, to do their own designated work once more, a possibility to be considered more theoretically in chapter 10. Or the colored gluons for the strong force, the photons for the electromagnetic force, and the weak gluons for the weak force could be understood to be massed unseen within the matrix lines defining these forces. But as with the electron in the probabilistic interpretation of the lepton-wave model, such a lack of graphic representation would raise the same question as to their true existence.

We come to the final possibility, which is to design a separate matrix model showing the internal interrelationship of these forces to their associated bosons. But such a model would have to show a complementary exclusion of their associated fermions, whether hadron or lepton. In this case as with the hadron model, the macrotriangle would represent the force field and the microtriangles would now represent the bosons. There is no problem in the further modeling of the bosons for the strong and electromagnetic forces. Since they do not have antiparticles, each could be identified with a single microtriangle and thus be accorded the single spin attributed to the bosons in quantum theory. The case of the weak bosons is more complicated since there are three such bosons, the negative particle W^-, the positive antiparticle W^+, and the neutral particle Z°. The solution here, as in gauge-field theory, is to assign a separate field for each of these weak bosons, one with the same geometric structure as in the more inclusive force-boson model.

This force-boson model is as successful as the hadron model and for the same reason that it defines the relationship of parts to a whole, the bosons being understood to constitute the forces as the quarks are understood to constitute the hadrons. But the problem with such a quantum model of the forces is that it cannot explain just that for which it was designed, the action of forces upon particles. It was already suggested that the picture provided by quantum physics of fermion particles throwing boson particles back and forth between them could not explain the nature of their interaction. And this failure of the theory is illustrated by the problem encountered in the matrix modeling of the fermions and bosons, the necessary complementarity between modeling the relationship of the forces to their fermions and to their bosons. We can see the way force constrains fermions or the way in which force is constituted by quanta, but we cannot see the way in which the force quanta influence fermion behavior. Thus the Feynman diagrams of electrons exchanging a photon satisfy neither our intuitive understanding of electric repulsion nor the constraints imposed on the modeling of these particles by the geometry of the matrix. And it would seem that the matrix geometry provides a better model.

We have, then, two different quantum models, the first representing the relationship of the quarks either to the baryons or to the strong force, which in this case are identical, and the second of the bosons to their forces. These models are similar, however, in depicting the same relationship of freedom to determinism through their attribution of the characteristics of free spin to the microtriangles and of rigidity to the macrotriangles. But this relationship is of two different kinds. There is, first, the relationship of free parts acting within the constraints of a controlling whole, as in the relationship of the quarks to the baryons and of the bosons to the forces. And second, there is the relationship of free fundamental particles acting within the constraints of controlling forces, a circumstance that gives to this relationship a systemic quality similar to that of parts to a whole. In either case, it is the matrix quantum model, rather than its wave model, that can truly be said to model the relationship of freedom to determinism whose product is the probability thought to be characteristic of the quantum realm. This is not the complementarity of Niels Bohr, which explains the appearances of electrons as either waves or particles depending on whether their momentum or position is being measured, that is, as the effect of the limitations inherent in the measuring devices, but never doubts that an electron particle is somewhere to be found and that the wave measurements signify only probabilities. Rather, it displaces the workings of probability from the leptons to the hadrons and forces, to those elements of the quantum realm that feature a systemic relationship of parts to a whole. But we have so far examined the hadron and lepton models in isolation from each other and have yet to see if they can be brought together to provide a new model of the higher systems level of the atom.

The Atomic Model

The major problem that an atomic matrix model would seem to face is the fact that the macrotriangle of the lepton model is supposed to represent the entire wave pattern associated with a particular electron quantum state or orbit, and that this is understood to circle the atomic nucleus. But since its projected three dimensions of space are limited in the matrix to a single microhexagon, there seems to be no way in which it can contain even a single proton, much less a whole nucleus of multiple protons and neutrons, each such nucleon being equal to it in matrix size. The way out of this dilemma is to reverse the solution upon which quantum electrodynamics is based, the "miracle" of renormalization. But this new form of renormalization would not transform infinities into finities; rather it would understand its finite modeling to represent relative infinities. Returning to figure 9.7, we can now understand each three-dimensional cube of space as a minimum finite representation of the infinite extension of its force wave in all six of its directions. Thus we can imagine it as expanding sufficiently to contain a comparatively minuscule nucleus at its center. But its infinite expansion must be recognized to be relative insofar as it must also be contained within the larger infinity of the electron wave occupying the next higher quantum state. That this difference does not inhere in the wave but in its state is shown by its demonstrated ability to leap to higher states when excited. Thus the lepton pattern given in figure 9.7 can be viewed as also defining the geometric spaces available to any real electron wave in such a virtual field, each level representing a quantum state and only those on the next higher or lower levels contiguous to it and containing descending macrotriangles being able to offer it accommodation. Again each real electron wave may be understood to be accompanied by its own virtual field and to associate with those in higher or lower quantum states in terms of the mutual accommodation they afford each other in their respective fields. As seen in figure 9.8, this can be diagrammatically represented as a curving string or staircase of such stacked lepton-wave patterns, each one of which is to be understood to contain the nucleus and the lower electron waves centered within it.

The boron atom was chosen for modeling because its atomic number of 5 allows for the most symmetrical pattern of protons, neutrons, and electrons. The nuclear constituents are not as fully drawn as previously, but their pattern reflects the rules earlier established for proton-neutron joinings, that only two-thirds will be accommodated by each other's fields with the remainder attaching to their own kind. Thus only seven out of ten are touching in this matrix model of the boron atom. But though this model can be interpreted in terms of the old solar-system model, the picture that actually emerges from applying all of the constraints arising from theoretical physics as well as the prior matrix modeling offers a far different image, not of a solar system but of a bunch of grapes hung from a twisted stem. Which is the truer picture of how the atom achieves its three-dimensional form from its electromagnetic field is hard to say, since

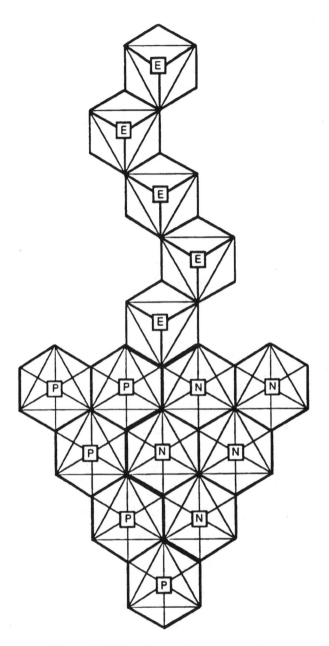

FIGURE 9.8. THE ATOMIC MODEL: BORON

any macroscopic portion of any element would contain so many atoms that its three-dimensionality could be supplied only by the outermost electron cube where it attaches to that of the adjacent atom. Thus we can still keep the model proposed in figure 9.8, but should recognize it as involving a pattern not from above to below but from without to within, from the outermost point of the highest electron cube to the innermost point of the lowest proton. It is only this outermost electron cube that may be supposed to become attached to the outermost electron cube of another atom either of its own element or of another element, thereby forming molecules of simple or compound chemicals. It is the electromagnetic force binding all these electrons together that also supplies the three-dimensionality of the molecular level of matter. But how the outermost layer of these electrons is related to the inner layers of electrons and to the nucleus there is no way of knowing—perhaps as in a solar system, perhaps as in a bunch of grapes. Perhaps all of nature is engaged in one festive Bacchanalia with the "winos" of supersymmetry leading the celebration!

We have seen that the lepton model could only be fitted into the structure of the atom by accepting the infinite nature attributed and then denied to its waves by modern physics, that is, by accepting the full implications of the wave model of the electron. Now if the matrix modeling of the hadrons, leptons, and atom can be accepted as given, then we should be ready to accept the intelligence of its structure, that the geometric possibilities and constraints it provides have a logical validity that should be heeded. And the message that this matrix modeling of the atom seems to be delivering is that *the atom, like the cosmos it epitomizes, unites in electrical balance two radically different forms of matter, the particle nature of the hadrons and the wave nature of the leptons.* The success of the wave model in terms of both theoretical physics and the matrix raises the question as to whether one really needs two different descriptions of the leptons, and it would seem to argue strongly against the validity of any quantum description of either electricity or light, to argue, rather, that the original Schrödinger interpretation of his wave function should be preferred to that of Born.

In discussing "the initial mistake of depicting radiation as identifiable photons," Jeans has argued that

> What is true of radiation is true also of electricity. We know that electricity is always transferred from place to place by complete electron-units, but this does not justify us in replacing a current of electricity by a shower of identifiable particles. . . . the atomicity does not reside in these ingredients but in the events which affect them. To return to our former analogy, all payments into and out of a bank

account are by complete mathematical pence, but they do not consist of bronze pennies flying hither and thither.[15]

Since evidence for individual electrons and photons outside of the atom occur only at the points where electricity or radiation meet a material surface,[16] their apparently discrete nature need not be attributed to the structure of such a current or beam but either to the material surface by which they are absorbed and emitted or to the mechanical device used to measure these effects. In the former case, it is the macroscopic objects that may be considered to be equipped to absorb or emit energy from a continuous stream only in discrete units, this being the form of the receptors or dischargers designed by nature to facilitate the cosmic bookkeeping required to maintain the conservation of energy. In the latter case, it may be the very measuring devices used by human investigators that serve to quantize a physical wave into those units they are alone equipped to read. And since the wave picture is more successful than the particle picture for the "electrons" within the atom,[17] the principle of Occam's razor would seem to require that we finally dispense with the attempt to apply to the lepton branch of matter the quantum description applicable only to the hadrons, a misapplication leading to all those paradoxes that have so perversely delighted quantum physicists. If we can accept the evidence provided by theory, experiment, and the matrix that, at least when in the atom or when travelling through empty space, the lepton branch of matter and force must be regarded as constituting physical waves, then we need not accept the probabilistic interpretation of these waves as housing real particles, and we can return to the simple single description given by both the mathematical and matrix models. But if genuine complementarity is to be sought in this realm, it is to be found in the relationship of leptons to hadrons, the natural condition of an electron being that of a wave as that of a nucleon is to be a particle. *In the atomic numerical balancing of the infinite waves of the electrons and the finite particularization of the nucleons, we may see, then, an extension of the same complementary joining of the finite with the infinite that sacred science has recognized for millennia to define both the nature of physical reality and its goal.*

Concluding Comments

Before considering some final philosophical questions that emerge from the theories of quantum physics, there are some further points that should be noted. There is, first, the significant associations of the primary wave model of the electron with the major kabbalistic text of Hebraic sacred science, the *Sefer Yetzirah*. Though it may not be surprising that a matrix derived from the diagram encoded in the *Sefer Yetzirah* can be associated with this text, the correspondences between the use of this matrix to model the electron and its original formulation are, nonetheless, astonishing. For the minimal cosmic diagram that chapter 7 demonstrated to be encoded in the *Sefer Yetzirah* has proven to be none other than the precise matrix wave model now developed for the electron. Such a correspondence is itself remarkable since the considerations leading to its development in such alien contexts as a third-century kabbalistic text and twentieth-century quantum physics are so completely different. But the further correspondences between the attributes given this same model by contexts so different are such that they can only be called uncanny. For the cube indicated in that classic text, whose mysterious diagonals prove to be the edges of its dualing octahedron when the two are joined together in the same space of such a two-dimensional orthogonal projection, has the identical property of infinite expansion that characterizes the electron cube. Of its twelve diagonals, it is said: "They continually spread for ever and ever. They are the Arms of the Universe."[18] In addition, the association between the *Sefer Yetzirah* and the electron cubes has further implications in terms of the scientific cosmology that will be traced in chapter 10 and related in another manner to kabbalistic cosmology. As will be shown there, before the universe had cooled to the 3,000° Kelvin point, it was dominated by radiation, that same combination of electron waves and electromagnetic force that are figured in this design. Now if the matter-dominated universe that follows this 3,000° Kelvin point can be identified with the fourth cosmic world of the Kabbalah, and the radiation-dominated universe with the third kabbalistic world of Yetzirah, then we find that the esoteric diagram so mysteriously and yet precisely alluded to in this text is an exact geometric model of the physical constituents of the world of Yetzirah that is its subject. Such correlations demonstrate that the observations of the ancient sacred science and its modern secular counterpart are equally precise and that both reveal the same underlying geometry.

In the matrix modeling of all the particles known to quantum physics, a solution emerged to a problematic area of quantum theory that also deserves some concluding comment. This involved a symmetrical modeling of antimatter and matter with widespread theoretical implications. We have seen that the postulation by quantum theory of mesons to bind the nuclear baryons together implies the existence of antimatter within all nuclei, since the pi-mesons of the atomic nucleus are composed of a quark and antiquark combination. To account for this, the hadrons were so modeled by the matrix that the final picture was one containing equal proportions of matter and antimatter in a symmetrical arrangement that could then account for such previously unexplained features of fermion behavior as double spin and exclusion. And since such a matter-antimatter pairing is as true of leptons as of hadrons, this feature of the hadron model was carried over to the lepton model as well. To then account for the stability of the atom, it was further argued that the atom must have some such geometric structure as that of the matrix, a structure that could permit the cohabitation of matter and antimatter without that mutual annihilation to which they are subject when produced in the laboratory without such atomic containment. This is perhaps the most radical implication of this matrix modeling of subatomic particles, challenging some settled convictions of quantum physicists.

The discovery of antimatter with its apparent power to annihilate any matter with which it comes into contact has had two major theoretical implications. It has led to the projection of a mirror universe of antimatter with perhaps also some clumps of antimatter in unknown portions of the material universe. And it has led to various theoretical attempts to explain the asymmetry of matter to antimatter, that minute surplus of matter over antimatter proposed to account for the very existence of our universe of matter. The theoretical model being here advanced, on the other hand, rejects the idea of two mirror universes, rather seeing all the "material" objects of the one universe as composed of equal proportions of matter and antimatter arranged in such atomic and molecular geometric structures as can prevent their mutual annihilation by permitting the discrete and inviolate space of each material fermion. Though such subatomic antimatter can no more be detected in the unexploded atom than can quarks in a proton, it can explain and refine certain features of the quark model, perhaps most importantly the origin of the antiquarks within the nuclear mesons, and give us a view of the universe exemplifying the symmetry of matter to antimatter found by experiment to be true of quantum interactions as well as in the mathematical symmetries of the Dirac equation.

Such a view of subatomic structure within the atom is coherent with recent large-scale attempts to model the universe, quantum physics and cosmology having long found points of theoretical intersection that distinguish them from the "middle range" for which Newton's formulations still seem to work. The first such attempt is the "sponge" model of cosmology put forth by some astrophysicists:

> This new conception holds that a surprisingly complex arrangement of clustered galaxies stretches in connected tubes and filaments from one end of the universe to the other and that galaxy-free voids form an equally complex, equally well connected structure. . . . Further, many astrophysicists believe that the new picture, sponge-like topology, will help connect present-day structure, on scales of millions and billions of light years, to submicroscopic events in the theoretical Big Bang. . . . To some theorists, the symmetry between clumps and voids is what gives sponge-like topology its appeal.[19]

The picture that has emerged is of a honeycombed universe whose structures are not as easily explained by big bang cosmology:

> Astronomers have discovered more than a dozen evenly distributed clumps of galaxies stretching across vast expanses of the heavens, suggesting a structure of the universe so regular and immense that it defies current theories of cosmic creation and evolution. . . . A honeycombed universe is the picture that some astronomers draw from these observations. Each dense clump of galaxies is about the same distance from the next, and in between is a region of equally uniform size that has only a sparse population of galaxies.[20]

Whether or not these new models of the universe are compatible with the early particle interactions projected by quantum cosmologists, a subject to be further considered in the next chapter, such symmetry between galactic clumps and voids can find a parallel in the connecting structure of matter and antimatter that is here being proposed for the little universe of the atom. Though the middle range of macroscopic objects formed of such atoms appear to us as wholly material and not as confined to a larger symmetrical structure, at the two ends of the spectrum—the interior of the unviolated atom and the overall intergalactic structure of the universe—a symmetry emerges between clumps and voids that on the subatomic level, and perhaps equally on the level of cosmic geography, can be identified with the positions of matter and antimatter, but which, in any case, reveals a similar geometric ordering between the constituents of the atom and the universe. It should also be noted that the honeycomb model of the universe is the same suggested in figure 9.7 for the lepton-wave field model, a most significant correlation since it is such lepton fields that would seem to give matter its three-dimensional appearance.

The parallel made between the atom and the universe again reveals the importance of making atomic structure, rather than the unhoused behavior of violated quanta, the model of cosmic functioning. For in addition to its cosmic mirroring of symmetrically arranged clumps and voids, it is this atomic structure that can also be said to exemplify the cosmic truth taught by sacred science, the numerical balancing of infinite extension with finite localization that not only applies to the relationship of leptons to hadrons but also of force to form. Indeed, just as the matrix can assign atomic positions to both matter and antimatter, so does this dual-leveled matrix provide a rational model for the relationship of quanta to force that should take the spookiness out of the concept of material forces and permit their theoretical return to the quantum realm, it being their exile that rather accounts for the true spookiness of this realm.

In the preceding discussion of theoretical physics, we have seen that a more coherent picture of its experimental results can be achieved if the guidelines of sacred science are appreciated and observed. For the philosophic failure of quantum physics to define a cosmos that makes sense to our ordinary experience can be seen to result from a mistaken attempt to achieve unity through homogeneity rather than through the balancing of an irreducible polarity. As long as we are observing a reality that, however explained, exhibits the multiplicity and hierarchical levels that form part of the physical description of nature, our attempts to achieve a simplified description of such phenomena cannot be reduced to unity but only to that triadic balance most perfectly modeled by the triangle, the same form that has been the basis of the matrix modeling here attempted.

But reality, as in all things, gets the last laugh, and the attempt of theorists to exclude all forces and waves from their explanation of physical objects and processes has not rid matter of those aspects thought to signify a superstitious spiritualism. Its effect has rather been to fill matter with new and more impish ghosts. One response has been the development in theoretical physics known as quantum logic. In a demonstration drawing upon the earlier work of John von Neumann and Garrett Birkoff,

David Finkelstein shows how the law of distributivity is violated by photon polarization and a new quantum logic manifested:

> The situation is bizarre enough to merit demonstration. The classic one is photon polarization. Here are two polarizers A and B. . . . A and B are identical but turned 90° relative to each other about the direction of the light. Then all the light from A is stopped by B, practically. . . . The paradox is that if a filter passes light from A and light from B it will also pass light from C, a third polarizer at an angle of 45° . . . when C is between A and B. . . . These effects, the Heisenberg uncertainty relation, and Bohr's principle of complementarity are all manifestations of the breakdown of one logical principle, distribution.[21]

The "bizarre" behavior attributed here to photons depends, of course, on our conceding that the observable effects are due to the quantum nature of light rather than the quantizing effect of the experimental apparatus, the polarizing lenses. But accepting this hypothesis for the purposes of this demonstration, let us review the facts in this strange case of apparent quantum illogic, paying particular attention to its geometric details.

Finkelstein begins with two polarizers, one held before the light vertically so that all vertically aligned photons can pass through it and the other held horizontally so that all horizontally aligned photons can similarly pass through. He then proceeds to show that while the effect of placing the horizontal polarizer in front of the vertical polarizer, that is, at right angles to it, is to stop most of the light, if a third polarizer is placed *diagonally* between these two polarizers, some of the formerly blocked light is thereby enabled to pass through all three polarizers, thus providing a classic example of the strange laws of quantum logic. This involves a violation of the law of distribution since the either/or of light passing though vertical and horizontal polarizers is transmuted into a both/ and equation by the addition of the median placement of the diagonal polarizer. In accordance with Bohr's principle of complementarity, which, in this instance, demonstrates that the diagonal polarizer is complementary to both the vertical and horizontal polarizers, we may say that the former polarization of vertical and horizontal has been brought into complementarity by means of the diagonal.

While all of this may shock the proponents of Aristotelian logic, it is hardly surprising to the student of Pythagorean geometry and numerology. What it shows is that the extreme polarization characteristic of duality can be harmonized through a triplicity that contains the mean between these dualistic extremes, a mean, such as the diagonal of a square, that introduces a suprarational element capable of harmonizing such discord. The quantum concept of coherent superposition, which in Finkelstein's formulation states that "any 'set' that contains the two 'points' A and B contains a third point C as well distinct from A and B,"[22] might be considered, then, a modern, scientific reformulation of the ancient rules by which the various means—arithmetic, harmonic, and geometric—are derived, rules by which extremes are shown to be mediated. The paradox of photon polarization can be resolved only by understanding the unutterable truth contained in the incommensurability of the diagonal to the sides of a square, the truth of the irrational or "suprarational" element within all finite structures,[23] a truth of which it would seem to be a classic example. For what the vertical, diagonal, and horizontal polarizers are demonstrating by this placement is none other than a translation into quantum mechanical action of the geometric laws governing the generative power contained in the diagonal of the square.

A few books have recently been written drawing the parallels between the new quantum physics and such Eastern forms of mystical knowledge as Taoism, but a still closer association can be drawn to the sacred geometry of Pythagoras and the Western esoteric tradition analogous or largely derived from it. Such particles as mesons and baryons have been shown to be ordered in neat hexagons (called "octets" because of the two particles assigned to the center of the hexagons) and the baryon decuplet is even arranged in the form of the Pythagorean Tetractys. Not only does the ordering of such particles reveal a higher level of geometric logic, but the "bizarre" behavior of photons in negotiating a series of polarizers can also be seen to follow a logic based on the laws of geometric functioning, laws involving the relationship of the diagonal to the sides of a square.

The standard historical view of Pythagoreanism is that it kept the fact of irrational numbers a secret because this "unutterable" truth destroyed the rational foundation of a philosophy based on whole integer numbers. Whether or not this is the true explanation of this practice among the Pythagorean brotherhood, it is our modern scientific brethren who can be said to display just such an ostrichlike attitude toward the equally unutterable truth both of the reality of physical forces and waves and of their infinite character. But however "renormalized" or "quantized" they may be, the irrational behavior of the substituted quanta reveals the very truth they were designed to conceal, the existence of real forces demonstrating the logic of the infinite. Nor is there any escape from this dilemma. For the alternative to believing in the reality of physical forces and waves is a belief in the physical power of purely geometric forces. In ridding themselves of the demon of electron waves, quantum physicists have only let in the demon of probability waves that exert a real influence on the free movement of particles.

It is in this very quantum doctrine of probability that the antispiritualism of quantum physics receives its final comeuppance. This is not a problem to be avoided simply by rejecting the Born interpretation of the Schrödinger electron waves. For the quantum models provided by the matrix for both the hadrons and the bosons graphically portray the interrelationship of free particles to the deterministic wholes or forces constraining this freedom whose outcome is the probabilistic order characterizing every level in the cosmic hierarchy of systems. Jeans has earlier addressed the philosophic implications of the quantum doctrine of probability, showing how it both resolves the classical problem of freedom versus determinism while adding the mental dimension of the observer to that of the matter under observation.[24] But he has not addressed the further philosophic problem raised by the very fact of such a probabilistic order functioning in a material cosmos. So I may be excused for addressing this same issue in the following epilogue, one that will relate the matrix model of probability to the human as well as quantum realm and so again reveal the coherence of all aspects of the cosmos.

Epilogue on Probability

To the perennial philosophic question as to the universality of freedom or determinism, the matrix answers that both are real and together produce the universal law of probability. For the law of probability, recognized equally by the physical and social sciences, implies two necessary factors, the uncertainty of individual action and some force that influences the great majority to act in ways consistent with the contours of the bell-shaped curve of statistical probability. The force that can so influence individual response that it freely conforms to the statistical limits of probability is a mystery to the sciences that place such ready faith on the reliability of statistics, but it should fill them with awe. For despite the free choice of direction quantum theory attributes to its photons, exactly half will choose to be left polarized and the other half to be right polarized, just as the freedom individual voters feel in their choice of a candidate does not prevent a CBS computer from telling us who will be president when only 1 percent of the vote has been counted. The Heisenberg uncertainty principle does not imply that the position of a subatomic particle will be random but rather in accordance with a probability pattern. And history follows laws of compensation as exact as those attributed to matter by quantum theory. While not necessarily compensating individuals in strict accordance with their merits, and while being notoriously sloppy at the edges, the "judgment of history" follows laws of probability with regard to the disposition of large numbers as it works mysteriously to maintain a dynamic equilibrium. Moreover, the movements of history seem to reflect a Zeitgeist, or spirit of the age, that shapes trends and cultural patterns in accordance with the bell-shaped curve, one composed, like a moving inch worm, of an avant-garde, a majority that later adopts its new forms, and the stragglers who cling to these forms after the creative energy has been passed to yet newer forms.

There would seem, then, to be a shaping force of determinism that so influences individual freedom that it universally conforms to the laws of probability. No other explanation of probability is possible. For without such a force, individual freedom would result in the randomness of true chaos rather than a probabilistic order. That we live in such a probabilistic cosmos is attested to by the nature of the human mind, whose most elementary functioning is geared to the construction of order out of the fragmentary clues of perception. Perception involves a process of fitting new particulars to previously constructed generalities in such a way as to produce meaning, whether according to old or revised models. Our innate tendency to expect such meaning often catches us up, as in the writer's bogy, proofreading. In proofreading, no matter what absurdity the typographical error might produce, the mind will tend to perceive a meaningful word. Proofreading is wearying because it causes the mind to work against its grain, to look for absurdity rather than for meaning. The mind perceives an ideal order behind the particularities of nature that has both meaning and beauty. Any planned or accidental changes in the order of nature only produce the grotesque, not simply because of our habituation to cultural norms of beauty but because of the mind's innate preference for harmonic proportions. Isolate a mind from all clues in an environment specially constructed to simulate randomness and it will become filled with anxiety-produced mental and physical disease.

The anxiety of modern culture is a product of the false conclusions it has drawn from the curve of probability, conclusions based upon a myopic focusing on possibilities reflective only of its extremes. Applying the probability curve to this very question of cosmic meaning, a question that we have seen must arise to explain the universal phenomenon of probability, we might say that the curve allows for the possibility of random meaninglessness along its edges but that its central thrust favors the probability of meaning. Thus there is a possibility, allowed for by the probability curve, that the scientific reduction of reality to those aspects its instruments can measure, quantitative measurements that cannot reveal qualitative values or meaningfulness, is correct, and the world an accidental product of random forces, though these forces somehow do not act according to pure randomness even in the experiments upon which the conclusion of cosmic meaninglessness is based. But such a possibility, if correct, induces in the mind that embraces it an unhealthy angst, unhealthy because the stress of such distressing news produces the symptoms of disease. The natural condition of the human mind would thus seem to be the serenity founded on the good news of the probability of meaning. Such a belief is not only conducive to good mental and physical health, with greater satisfaction for the self and generosity to others, but these effects provide further evidence of the suitability of this orientation to the structure of reality, further evidence that the foundation for such a belief is probably true.

In the gospel according to probability, the cosmos is founded on the two real principles of freedom and determinism, neither of which can be discounted as illusion in favor of the exclusive dominion of the other. Given the real existence of freedom, not all events can be explained deterministically. If a person is good and also careful, he will probably be able to cross the street safely. But there is a possibility that he will be killed by a car that comes careening around the corner. In such an event, there will be no good purpose that need be deduced from this death. Some form of gross justice will probably be meted out to the drunken driver that will in no way compensate the victim. But if the subtle influence of determinism on freedom leads, on the gross level, to probabilities that allow for disastrous possibilities, on the subtle level, which is its proper domain, its workings are exact and just. Thus the effect of the driver's imputed brutality is to brutalize him and the effect of the pedestrian's imputed fineness is to refine him. There is, as the *Sefer Yetzirah* suggests, a moral fifth dimension,[25] working as surely to define the structure of events as space and time, and this fifth dimension ensures that on the spiritual level we reap what we sow. Though the refined person has no more guarantee than the brute against the gross injustices resulting from freedom, the superior quality of such a life will be its own reward here—and probably hereafter.

The influence of a higher deterministic structure upon the world of gross matter and multiplicity, which might be viewed as the influence of the macrocosm on the microcosm, can only be shown within the law of large numbers on which statistics is based. But within the large numbers and time frames of historical process, a force very much like that which has traditionally been termed Providence can be seen ever working mysteriously to restore a dynamic equilibrium through the polarity of action and reaction that leads to constantly renewed forms of creative vitality. The process is one that, from the longer perspective of eternity, is unforgiving in its judgments upon societies that have grown morally corrupt. But the probabilities are that in such judgments, as in such societies, there will be many innocent victims, that the price of freedom is not only vigilance but also local injustice. Nonetheless, it is not the deterministic structure alone but the freedom whose existence it makes possible that gives meaning to the cosmos and purpose to its evolutionary processes. The attempts of many spiritual thinkers to reduce all reality to a deterministic unity, consigning individuality and freedom to the realm of illusion, is as simplistic an understanding as the secular view, whose contrary illusion is that only matter exists in a world ruled by chance. From both reductions of the greater complexity of reality, the matrix may provide a conceptual way out. In its interface of freely spinning microtriangles within the sacred space of stably fixed macrotriangles, we may see a higher dimension of determinism working within the realm of individual freedom to maintain equilibrium, the balance that is both just and beautiful, and to achieve its perfection.

10

A Synthesis of Kabbalistic
and Quantum Cosmology

Tzimtzum vs. the Big Bang

In the last chapter we saw that the data developed by theoretical and experimental physics could be given a more satisfactory modeling and explanation by applying to its constructs both the geometry and guidelines that can be derived from the Western tradition of sacred science. The geometry, which provided a coherent model for all the particles postulated by quantum physics, was that of the matrix produced through construction of the *Sefer Yetzirah* Tree, itself derived from the kabbalistic Tree of Life Diagram. The guidelines of sacred science caused us to look not to a simple unity for a fundamental explanation of material reality but rather to a complex unity that balances the polarities of infinite extension and finite localization. The model of such unity was seen to be the atom, and the numerical balance it achieves to be that between the infinite extension characteristic of the wave model of the leptons, the electrons, and the finite localization characteristic of the quantum model of the hadrons, the protons and neutrons. In this chapter we shall see that the cosmos can also be best understood, both in its nature and history, by recognizing that it forms just such an atomic system, one that unites the finitude of the hadrons and infinity of the leptons without destroying their necessary and irreducible differentiation.

In terms of cosmology we shall again find the model that can make the best sense of the scientific evidence not to be that developed in science but in the esoteric tradition. The scientific model will be defined primarily by Heinz R. Pagels and by Steven Weinberg, both of whom may be said to represent the voice of orthodox science. The esoteric model will be that of Isaac Luria, the sixteenth-century speculative Kabbalist who has had the most profound influence on the more modern development of the Kabbalah. The synthesis of the Lurianic model with the scientific evidence put forward by modern cosmologists will finally lead to a further synthesis of quantum physics with a conceptualization of the higher dimensions that can be integrated with kabbalistic concepts of the cosmic future. But we should begin by defining the principles of scientific and Lurianic cosmology and seeing which can provide a more adequate explanation of the scientific data.

The major theory of modern scientific cosmology is that of the big bang, which Pagels shows to rest on two forms of experimental evidence:

> The first is the discovery of the expansion of the universe by Edwin Hubble in 1929–31. . . . The second major experimental finding is the microwave background radiation discovered by Arno A. Penzias and Robert W. Wilson in 1964. These researchers at Bell Laboratories found that the black empty space of the universe was not absolutely cold; it has a slight temperature of three degrees Kelvin above absolute zero. This temperature is due to a radiation bath of photons that permeates all of space. . . . The interpretation of this radiation bath is that it is heat left over from the big bang.[1]

The two major facts seem to be of a universe whose matter is expanding and whose space is a special form of vacuum permeated with "a radiation bath of photons." The discovery of the microwave background radiation within what was formerly thought to be "black empty space" can, however, be given another interpretation than that "it is heat left over from the big bang." Rather, it can be explained as preceding the big bang on the basis of Lurianic cosmology. Furthermore, it is only some such concept that can explain the vacuum in which Pagels would like to find the origin of the cosmos:

How did this big bang happen? What was the origin of the primordial soup of quarks, leptons, and gluons? Where did *that* come from? Certainly this is not a question physicists can confidently answer on the basis of experiment and theory. However, we can speculate. There is an answer which I am attracted to based on the rules of physics as we now know them. The answer to the question "Where did the universe come from?" is that it came out of the vacuum. . . . Until recently, an obstacle to the idea that the universe was created out of a vacuum was explaining where the protons in the universe came from.[2]

Pagels bases the deduction that the universe originated from a vacuum on the new theoretical understanding that has developed regarding the nature of the vacuum:

physicists came to a new concept of the vacuum—it is not empty; it is a plenum. The vacuum, empty space, actually consists of particles and antiparticles being spontaneously created and annihilated. . . . physicists could now confidently calculate the interactions of virtual photons with electrons and compare the results with experiments. The agreement was remarkable. . . . Of all the modern quantum field theories, quantum electrodynamics is the exemplar of success.[3]

The only unqualified success among modern quantum field theories is that of quantum electrodynamics, which concerns itself only with the leptons and their electromagnetic force. The hadrons are missing from this experimentally successful model of the new physics of the vacuum, a reason why it has been difficult to explain the origin of the universe from a vacuum.

But what is true of the only vacuum that can be studied experimentally, the kind of vacuum produced in the laboratory, is that it has boundaries from within which all matter has been exhausted. Thus if such a vacuum is to be proposed as a model for the original state of the universe, then it should conform to these same conditions, a bound space from which matter, largely in its hadronic form, has been withdrawn, leaving only the virtual quanta that, with the addition of a new source of energy, could be actualized as an electromagnetic field. How these conditions are fulfilled in the model proposed by Isaac Luria we shall now see.

The fundamental concept of Lurianic cosmology is that of the Tzimtzum, or divine contraction. In Gershom Scholem's review of this concept, the authentic Lurianic doctrine of the Tzimtzum is shown to involve a divine contraction not only "*in* a place, but its withdrawal *from* a place. The place from which He retreats is merely 'a point.' . . . This place is primordial space, and it is called *tehiru*."[4] The primordial space within which creation is to occur, and from which the light of Ein Sof (the Limitless One who figures as the transcendent godhead of the Kabbalah) is to retract, will not, however, be wholly devoid of the divine light. A residue of this light will remain to fill all of the primordial space and to mingle with the roots of Din, or Gevurah, the aspect of the divine consciousness that had become concentrated in that portion of the infinite divine space from which the subsequent divine retraction is to take place and that represents the principle of constriction. Thus "the power of *Din* that was left in primordial space . . . intermingled in a confused fashion with the remnants of the light of *Ein-Sof* that had remained behind even after *zimzum*, like the drops of oil that remain in a vessel after it has been emptied. This residue was called *reshimu*."[5] The establishment of the initial point represents the first stage of creation and the retraction from it the second, these prior stages setting the stage for the third act of creation: "Into this inchoate mixture, which is the hylic aspect of the future universe, there descends from the primordial, space-encompassing *Ein-Sof* a *Yod*, the first letter of the Tetragrammaton, which contains . . . the power of formation and organization."[6] As Scholem summarizes this doctrine:

> Creation, therefore, is conceived of as a double activity of the emanating *Ein-Sof* following on *zimzum*: the Emanator acts both as a receptive substratum through the light of the *reshimu*, and as a form-giving force which descends from the essence of *Ein-Sof* to bring order and structure to the original confusion. Thus both the subject and the object of the process of creation have their origin in God but were differentiated from each other in the *zimzum*.[7]

We shall begin this discussion of Lurianic cosmology by showing how its doctrine of the Tzimtzum can better explain than the scientific theory the specific characteristics that can be legitimately attributed to the vacuum if it is to serve as at least the most immediate source of the universe. For in the Tzimtzum, the withdrawal of an infinitely extended substance called divine from a finitely enclosed space left not a complete vacuum but one filled with residual light. Greater consideration will soon be given to the first two steps of the Tzimtzum, but we shall now more briefly consider its salient feature. This is that the exhausting force effecting the retraction of the infinite substance left within the finite primordial space only an electromagnetic field primarily in the form of light radiation—not the virtual electrons and photons of the electrodynamic model but actual free electrons and electromagnetic force. It is this more modern reformulation of the Lurianic Reshimu that may be considered to leave the microwave background radiation filling this space after the disappearance of the free electrons, shortly to be explained.

How, then, could the protons enter this electromagnetic field to begin the formation of atomic matter? The most satisfying answer would seem to be that suggested by Luria, that they reentered the primordial space in some ball of hadronic matter—why not call it a Yod?—condensed only to the point that would still permit the mutual repulsion of these proto-hadrons, a ball subsequently to be precipitated out from the surrounding infinite light. The cause of such a discharge can be set down to the destabilizing effect of the imbalance between quarks and leptons in the post-Tzimtzum surrounding infinite light due to the remainder of some leptons within the Tehiru, the primordial space. It is this surplus of quarks in what had previously been a balanced whole that must now be discharged from the infinite light if it is to regain its equilibrium. And in a single discharge of this unbalancing energy through the membranelike boundary of space, the ball of condensed hadronic matter, containing all the quarks with their higher resonances that are henceforth to combine with the already present leptons to form the matter of the universe, may be imagined as streaking through space in a radiant line until it reaches the gravitational center of this space, one whose development will later be traced. It may further be imagined as streaking through this space with a force of such strong power that it both prevented all interactions with the surrounding field of leptons and accomplished the binding of the elementary quarks previously inhabiting the infinite light into the composite particles of protons and neutrons, all this during its passage to the gravitational center of the universe. Only then would its positive energy have attracted an equal quantity of negative electron energy from the surrounding cosmic field, their union causing an immediate expansion of the condensed hadron ball, the sound of which could be heard throughout the universe not as a big bang but more of a whimper.

The reason for this sound differential is that this moment comes much later in the chronology of modern cosmology than that usually assigned to the cosmic beginning, not at that above $100^{32°}$ Kelvin but at a temperature of a mere 3,000° Kelvin, the point that marks the transition from a radiation-dominated universe to one dominated by matter. As Steven Weinberg has noted: "It is striking that the transition from a radiation to a matter-dominated universe occurred at just about the same time that the contents of the universe were becoming transparent to radiation, at about 3,000°K. No one really knows why this should be so. . . ."[8] It is particularly difficult to explain this sudden transition if it has been felt theoretically necessary to assume "a small contamination of matter" in a universe "composed chiefly of radiation,"[9] difficult because there is no scientific basis for assuming that hadronic matter can be derived from the electromagnetic field that can be more justly extrapolated from the present microwave background radiation to the cosmic period preceding 3,000°K.

But, in fact, all projections beyond that 3,000°K threshold are subject to another difficulty. Weinberg explains that with the formation of atoms at this temperature, the thermal equilibrium that had been projected onto the previous eras was broken: "The sudden disappearance of free electrons broke the thermal contact between radiation and matter, and the radiation continued thereafter to expand freely."[10] The laws of thermodynamics, on the basis of which all previous eras of cosmic history have been explained by big bang cosmology, can only be proved to apply, however, at the macroscopic level at which true heat can be assigned. As Weinberg is forced to concede: "the first three minutes are so remote from us in time, the conditions of temperature and density are so unfamiliar, that we feel uncomfortable in applying our ordinary theories of statistical mechanics and nuclear physics."[11] But though Weinberg also admits that "the universe has never been in perfect thermal equilibrium, because after all it *is* expanding" and that "it is crucial to the argument of this book that the universe has once passed through a state of thermal equilibrium,"[12] he, nonetheless, proceeds onward undaunted by the fact that all the theoretical bases for this argument are flawed.

Thus scientific cosmology cannot take us further back than the two eras surrounding the 3,000°K transition point that may be correlated with the two phases of Lurianic cosmology earlier defined; and it would seem that the latter can more satisfactorily explain the origin and chronology both of the radiant field of leptons and of the later manifestation of the hadrons, the explanation of "why this should be so." For as we have seen, in this quantum-modified Lurianic model the main purpose of the cosmic genesis involving the Tzimtzum, the creation of a light-filled primordial space, is precisely to differentiate the leptons from the hadrons. Pagels says: "Physicists have no idea why the quarks and leptons exist."[13] But as we have seen in the previous chapter, it is exactly the wave nature of the electrons and particularity of the nucleons that together permit the stable structures they can form to contain such a unity of the infinite with the finite as would seem to be the purpose of the whole process of cosmic evolution. Before proceeding to chart this further cosmic process, however, we should examine the first two steps of the Lurianic Tzimtzum.

The definition of a circle requires two geometric steps prior to its manifestation, the establishment of a central point and then its radial extension as line to the point marking the circumference. And so is it also with the Tzimtzum. If we now begin the cosmic process with these two prior steps, we will arrive at a cosmological explanation both coherent with the proven facts of modern science and more satisfying in its definition of initial conditions. It is more satisfying because, unlike both the new scientific cosmology and the older kabbalistic cosmology of the *Zohar*, Luria saw that a definition of the cosmic process that began with a point of substance emerging out of nothing did not provide an ultimate explanation of origin. Rather he postulated the eternal existence of an infinite light and tried to define a finite cosmos consistent with such an infinite origin:

> Know that before the emanated things were emanated and the created things were created, the pure, divine light filled all existence. . . . Then *Eyn Sof* contracted Himself into a central point with His light in the middle. He contracted this light and then removed Himself to the sides encircling the point at the center. . . . This contraction, equidistant all around the point at the center, formed a void in such a way that the vacuum was spherical on all sides in equal measure. . . . Then, one straight line descended from the light of *Eyn Sof*.[14]

This exposition of Chayyim Vital in the *Etz Chayyim* makes clear the main stages of the Tzimtzum: the initial establishment of a centering point to the limitless light, the equidistant retraction away from it to form a bounded sphere, and the entrance back into it of a different form of the surrounding infinite light following a linear trajectory. Let us now translate this sequence into quantum mechanical terms.

We begin with an infinite light the substance of which can be defined much as quantum cosmologists have postulated, as an undifferentiated soup of all particles and forces in a state of dynamic equilibrium, with the major exception that instead of it being infinitely condensed, it is infinitely expanded. But a beginning is finally made with the fixing of a central point. If the infinite can be identified—as, of course, it is in all religious traditions—with infinite consciousness, then the establishment of such a point could also be understood to reflect the will of such a consciousness to achieve a personal center. But it is also possible to explain the abrupt definition of an orientation point as a result of a random fluctuation, if chance is preferred to purpose, just as Pagels would like to explain the possibility of the big bang emerging spontaneously from the vacuum on the basis of pure statistics: "Since no one is waiting for the event to happen, even if it has an infinitesimal but finite probability, it is certain to happen sometime."[15]

Now since this point is not established in nothingness but in infinite substance or being, it will connect with whatever power is present at that point, and this power will begin to act differently than it could have before the establishment of this point, as a force of gravity. This would seem to follow from certain conclusions of Isaac Newton, as explained by Weinberg: "Newton admitted that if the matter of the universe were evenly distributed in a *finite* region, then it would all tend to fall toward the center, 'and there compose one great spherical mass.' On the other hand, if matter were evenly dispersed through an infinite space, there would be no center to which it could fall."[16] For Newton, a gravitational center implies "a *finite* region" while "infinite space" implies the impossibility of such a center, these implications following from his premise of a static universe. But once one begins "dealing with the dynamics of an infinite medium,"[17] there would seem to be other implications that can be drawn from Newton's distinction. If we can postulate such a spontaneous definition of a center to infinite space as is asserted in Lurianic cosmology, then the Newtonian implications of such a center can be applied to the "region" that can be shown to fall under its influence. For the mere definition of such a centering point to the infinite radiant space would have the effect of "finitizing" its surrounding region by producing a gravitational force capable of controlling what can be called, by analogy to animal behavior, its "territory."

This is not, however, such a point as that postulated by scientific cosmology, which would have all the subsequent matter of the universe condensed within it in a manner far outstripping the medieval attempt to force myriad angels together on the head of a pin. It would not contain anything but its own unprecedented self-definition within the infinite medium, this indeed the only content that can be assigned to a truly infinitesimal, and thus geometric, point. As we shall later see in the further ramifications of this principle, it would seem to be precisely such self-definition that gives to this centering point its attractive force. In Lurianic cosmology, this central point will, in the subsequent emanation of the Yod-ball, be identified as the Sefirah Malkhut, further identified with the feminine Shekhinah. It is with the fourth kabbalistic world of physical reality, Assiyah or Action, that we can identify the Lurianic emanation of that ball here being defined as filled with condensed hadronic matter, as will later become clear. But we are now in the first kabbalistic world of Atzilut, Emanation, a world not yet separated from the infinite light of Ein Sof but that would now seem to define the first, singular step of creation, the self-definition of the feminine Shekhinah within the otherwise undifferentiated substance of Ein Sof in the form of a point, a point whose very quality of definition would have the effect of giving to the infinite force at which it is located a finite limit.

It is the radiation out from this center of the force of its gravitational attraction that may now be said to define the second cosmic world of the Kabbalah, that of Beriah, Creation. Significantly, it is this kabbalistic world, whose inhabitants are considered to be the Kochot, the Forces, that can be correlated with the linear dimension and so give a dynamic description to the force of gravity. It is the force of gravity traveling in the direction of such lines whose final attenuation marks the circumference that will become the circle of the Tzimtzum in the next stage. On the basis of later cosmological developments, we can say that this circle will be marked at precisely that point of radial extension at which two circumstances of this later development will combine to make possible a certain result. The first of these is that the amount of matter remaining in the residual light after the Tzimtzum and matched by the subsequently emanated ball of quarks will be below the critical point at which it could define a universe whose boundary closed it to further expansion and required it to rebound to the center. The second is that the ball of synthesized hadrons that combines with the free electrons to produce the small bang of cosmic expansion should be expanding with a velocity sufficient to escape the force of gravity. It is interesting that in his description of the Alexandre Friedmann modification of Einstein's general theory of relativity, one that transformed Einstein's static model to the current dynamic model of big bang cosmology, Weinberg speaks of this as "the velocity which a galaxy at the surface would have to have to be able just barely to escape to infinity."[18] The problem posed by this cosmology of what infinity it would be escaping to, of what is outside the expanding universe as well as before it, would seem not only to imply such a surrounding infinity as that proposed by the Lurianic model of the Tzimtzum but to require it. It is, then, at the point that will later prove to be consistent with the relationship of cosmic density to the velocity required to permit the "escape to infinity" that the gravitational force of the cosmic center may be said to reach the precise limit that can define a circular boundary within an infinite space still undifferentiated except for the definition of a centering point and the attractive force it radiates. This boundary that may also be said to establish the third kabbalistic world of Yetzirah, Formation, that of the plane. With the definition of this boundary, we return to the third stage of Lurianic cosmology with which we began and can now examine it more closely.

It is the very establishment of such a boundary that produces the dynamics of the next stage, for it establishes a power differential between two neighboring regions that will cause a flow of matter from the lesser to the greater source of power. Before this boundary was established, the power was everywhere equally infinite so that equilibrium was maintained between the energy and particles that had been forever transmuting themselves from one form to the other. But once a boundary differentiated a finite region within infinite space, the power on the surrounding infinite side of this boundary would clearly be far greater than that enclosed within its finite limits. Thus would be generated an infinite force stronger than the finitely limited force of gravity that would have immediately exhausted all matter from that enclosed space except for some remnants of light, Lurianically described as being "like the drops of oil that remain in a vessel after it has been emptied." These lepton droplets may be considered to be those for whom the attraction of a center would still be powerful enough to hold them fast within its gravitational field. But the residual light now permeating all of the primordial space within the finite limits of the Tzimtzum would find itself in a new condition. No longer sharing infinite space with infinite numbers of both its own and other species of particles in a form of equilibrium that permitted no differentiation, it could now define its own characteristics as a field of electromagnetic-weak force, whether or not it is thought to be composed of massless photons, and the slightly massive form of electron-positron wave-packet pairs.

It is when the heat of this sparsely spread electromagnetic field has dropped to approximately 3,000°K that the ball of hadronic matter may be said to suddenly perforate the finite cosmic boundary and streak to the center in the form of already synthesized nucleons to initiate the fourth world in which we are physically situated. Arriving at the cosmic center, each of these nuclear particles would then become informed with that which defines this center, previously identified with the Shekhinah, the indwelling spirit of God, and signifying the property of self-definition. With the fourth kabbalistic world of Assiyah, that of the solid, the demonstrable history of the cosmos would thus begin some few seconds, at the most, after the first spontaneous emergence of a centering point in the infinite medium, for each of the intervening stages would have to have been virtually immediate. And the force its three spatial dimensions may be said to define is the strong force that can hold such individual nucleons together. The positive charge of such newly synthesized protons would now become as attractive to the negatively charged electrons as the cosmic center had been in whose gravitational field they had become enmeshed. And they would rush to embrace these nucleons with the bonds of their own electromagnetic force, each atom so produced revealing what may well be described as the archetypal unification of the Holy One, blessed be He, with His Shekhinah, that unification of "male" lepton with "female" hadron providing the model for all further potential developments at still higher dimensions. It is this unification of all previously free electrons with the nuclear particles thus precipitated into their midst in a highly condensed ball that may now be considered to begin the expansion of the universe at the atomic level at which it had persisted until the advent of nuclear physicists, an expansion whose subsequent evolution can also be shown to be coherent with the explanations of the various branches of modern science.

Before we can proceed to chart such a further evolution, however, a theoretical foundation will first have to be laid that will build upon this theoretical model of quantum-synthesized Lurianic cosmology, a model that has included the traditional identification between the four cosmic worlds and the progression through the dimensions. We will first consider how our understanding of these dimensions can be enlarged to define the expanded model of a seven-dimensional cosmos, a model with deep roots in the Jewish esoteric tradition.

Dimensions of the Sabbatical Cosmos

To speak of the cosmic future in terms of specifically defined worlds is not without precedent. Isaac Luria's term "Olam ha-Tikkun," the World of Rectification, refers primarily to the Messianic Age, while the generally used term "Olam ha-Ba," the World to Come, normally refers to the completely spiritual world that is to follow the destruction of the purified though still physical world of the Messianic millennium. Both concepts have long histories going back to apocalyptic and talmudic literature, as these were themselves inspired by the Hebrew priests and prophets; and they have continued to exert considerable force in kabbalistic thought whether in traditional terms or as related to the doctrine of the *shemitot*. This doctrine, fully developed in the anonymous kabbalistic work the *Sefer ha-Temunah*, The Book of the Image, which was written sometimes after 1300 C.E.,[19] represents the latest elaboration of a Sabbatical cosmology whose ultimate derivation must be the creation account in Genesis. An early such elaboration was the Merkabah concept of the seven halls or heavens through which the soul must journey to achieve the height of mystical experience, the Throne vision.

There were, then, two different concepts of cosmic time that developed within the Jewish esoteric tradition. The biblical conception of seven "days" of creation exerted a strong influence on cosmological time sequences as developed from the Talmud through the *Temunah* to the Sabbationists in terms of the theory of the *shemitot*. But this older view of cosmic time was gradually supplanted in kabbalistic thought by the newer doctrine of the four cosmic worlds of emanation. Suggested in the *Tikkunei Zohar* and fully developed in the fourteenth-century *Massekhet Atzilut*, it became the accepted doctrine of sixteenth-century Safed Kabbalism, both Cordovero and Luria rejecting the alternate theory of the *shemitot* and making that of the four worlds standard for later Kabbalists. The problem with the four-worlds doctrine, however, is that it makes no allowance for that Olam ha-Tikkun so central to the Lurianic Kabbalah. The future orientation of Luria's thought requires a larger cosmic structure to accommodate its vision.

Such a structure, I would suggest, can be found within the broad outlines of the Sabbatical cosmology that maintained its hold on the Jewish esoteric tradition from its enunciation at the beginning of the Hebrew scriptures until at least the seventeenth century. For despite the rejection of the Safed Kabbalists, the understanding of cosmic history based upon the *shemitot* concept continued to exert an influence in periods of Messianic tension, such as that which produced the powerful movement centered around Sabbatai Tz'vi, and it continues today in the expectation of many that the Messiah will appear within 250 years, in the year 6000 of the Jewish calendar. Though the concept of future worlds does, then, have precedents, what is without precedent is the attempt being made, both here and elsewhere in my works, to connect the two main concepts of cosmic time that developed separately in the Kabbalah, those of the four cosmic worlds of emanation, an apparent product of Pythagorean influence, and of the seven cosmic worlds, or their multiples, which form the concept of the *shemitot*.[20] As elaborated in the *Temunah*, each cosmic world or cycle endures for a *shemitah* of 7000 years dominated by a particular Sefirah and the reading of the Torah appropriate to it, our *shemitah* being under the dominance of the Sefirah of Gevurah or Din, the Sefirah signifying rigorous judgment. This basic Sabbatical concept of cosmic time, of six world-cycles followed by a seventh period of consummation, is one that can be assimilated, with some qualification, to the more standard kabbalistic concept of the four cosmic worlds.

Such an assimilation is aided by the fact that the Messianic future was treated, for all intents and purposes, as a separate *shemitah*, a cosmic world with its own Torah, as was the Edenic past.[21] It is this theoretical elaboration that can permit us to identify the *shemitah* of the present with the cosmic world similarly identified with the present, the fourth, and so to establish a coherence between these two competing kabbalistic concepts of cosmic time. But this can only be done by separating the Sabbatical cosmology of the *shemitot* from that of the Sefirot, not as radical a proposition as it might seem, since the incorporation of the Sefirot in the *shemitot* doctrine appears to have been primarily serving a hidden Messianic agenda, the emergence of a more lenient reading of the Torah, rather than aiding cosmological understanding. Such a separation of *shemitot* from Sefirot is necessary for our synthesis since the *shemitot* are generally understood to proceed through just the seven Sefirot from Chesed to Malkhut, and this would place us in the *second shemitah* of Gevurah in a seven-week cosmic Jubilee cycle, a position inconsistent with our placement in the *fourth* world of the four-worlds doctrine. Accepting this separation, however, we can simply equate the concept of cosmic worlds with the Sabbatical number of the *shemitot* deriving from the Bible and so extend this concept to include future worlds. Identifying the present with the fourth cosmic world of Assiyah and placing this within a larger cosmic structure of seven worlds would thus allow us to extend the concept of cosmic worlds to include just the additional three such worlds that can complete the Sabbatical cosmic model originally defined in Genesis and shown in chapter 6 to define a spiritual archetype of the whole cosmic process and model of its subtle infrastructure, an understanding also shown to be coherent with Talmudic interpretations of the "days" of creation. Thus it is the biblical core of the later talmudic-kabbalistic concept of the *shemitot*, rather than its details, that can provide the model for a more comprehensive Kabbalist cosmology consisting of seven cosmic worlds.

But if the establishment of coherence between the four cosmic worlds of emanation and the Sabbatical concept of the *shemitot* provides for a limited extension of the former, such an extension must also take into consideration the implicit definition of the four cosmic worlds of the Kabbalah as a series of expanding dimensions. Though nowhere insisted upon, the Greek geometric source or analogue to this kabbalistic concept led to an understanding of these worlds as proceeding through the dimensions of the point, the line, the plane, and the solid, and it seems probable that it was the conceptual difficulty in expanding the dimensions beyond the spatial three of our solid world that prevented previous attempts to reconcile the two outstanding theories of cosmic history in the Kabbalah.

The key for such an expansion of the dimensions already existed, however, at the start of the whole kabbalistic tradition, in the *Sefer Yetzirah*. In the fifth verse of chapter 1, we are told: "Ten Sefirot of Nothingness: Their measure is ten which have no end. A depth of beginning, a depth of end; a depth of good, a depth of evil; a depth above, a depth below; a depth east, a depth west; a depth north, a depth south. The singular Master, God faithful King, dominates them all from His Holy dwelling until eternity of eternities."[22] In this remarkable passage, we are taken from the three dimensions of space to the fourth dimension of time and from there still further to a fifth dimension, a moral dimension woven into the fabric of existence that ensures that as we sow so shall we reap, a dimension of purposive causality that can be called Providential. But the passage does not stop there; it gives us yet another dimension, the knowledge that the justice working itself out within the frame of space-time cannot be reduced simply to a mechanism, however marvelous, but is itself controlled by a higher power, a dimension that invests the cosmic mechanism with meaningfulness. And beyond this sixth dimension, itself one of eternity, is the final dimension of Sabbatical rest, the "eternity of eternities" that sums up and contains the endless measurements of what can aptly be called "the lower depths."

If the *Sefer Yetzirah* key to the higher dimensions can be accepted, and we can identify the fifth dimension ("a depth of good, a depth of evil") with the fifth cosmic world, then we are led to a curious coherence between the number of dimensions and the number of the world they define that must cause us to examine the question of dimensions still further. The legacy of Einstein has been to teach us that we are inhabiting a four-dimensional world at present, that space-bending time is as real a dimension as those of height, width, and depth. But if the fourth cosmic world of the Kabbalah is now to be defined by four dimensions, then we should consider whether the three prior worlds could also be defined by dimensions corresponding to their number, a redefinition that would increase the number of dimensions in each of these worlds by one. We are left with the question as to what this new dimension might be that could lift the nondimensional point to one dimension, the one-dimensional line to two dimensions, and the two-dimensional plane to three.

The answer to this question would seem to lie in the Einsteinian insight into the status of time as a dimension. But just as this insight had already been formulated in the *Sefer Yetzirah* ("a depth of beginning, a depth of end"), so it may be that time does not first appear in the fourth world but was there from the beginning. Furthermore, it may be that what "Bereshit" really signifies is that "In the beginning" there was only the beginning, time, and that it was out of this beginning point of time that all the other dimensions of being were spawned, seven in number. If we now look at the other dimensions as actually defining dimensions of time, we will arrive at a far more complex notion of time than is ordinarily granted to this dimension and yet one that will seem familiar. Thus the first dimension of time can be considered that of the nondimensional point, the instant in which alone we exist but that is itself beyond or outside of time, the timelessness of the infinitesimal moment. If the first world can now be defined by this first dimension of instantaneous time, so the second world can be characterized by the second, temporal dimension, that of linear time, vectors moving directly out from the instantaneous source. Similarly, the third world would provide a container for this linear force, curving it into the third dimension of circular time. With the addition of the third spatial dimension of the fourth world, time would also add a dimension that would lift the circular into the spiral, the form of time with which we are most familiar but which actually contains each of the more ideal dimensions preceding it. Composed of instants, it traces a circular path through the seasons while nonetheless moving onward in chronological sequence; though recurrence may facilitate a timeless insight into pattern, with each birthday we are a year older.

But if each cosmic world is to be defined as a dimension of time, then this will also have to prove true of the three additional worlds we wish to add. We have seen that the *Sefer Yetzirah* identified the fifth dimension with such operations of cosmic morality as can also be associated with

Providence; and such a Providential order of causality might be further understood to express itself through the synchonicity of events that may be said to define the fifth dimension of time. If, then, the fifth dimension of time may be considered to be that which reveals mysterious patterns shaping the direction of discrete lines of causality so that they will meet in surprising conjunctions, the phenomenon that has been termed synchronicity,[23] so may the sixth dimension of time be understood to reveal the totality of the future pattern being woven today. The fifth temporal dimension would thus extend our four-dimensional perception of causality to include the subtle factors that influence interpersonal connections, but as these still are observed from the perspective of past causality. The sixth temporal dimension, however, would contain the eternal possibility of the completed pattern and make this future completion prophetically present. Seeing the larger pattern, perception would also be illuminated as to the meaning and ultimate purpose of any smaller piece of the pattern that, until such vision, must seem more of a puzzle. But however ultimate the knowledge contained in the sixth dimension may seem, it is still only a knowledge of cosmic functioning, and its timelessness may well be related to Georg Cantor's mathematical concept of the "transfinite." The seventh dimension of time can place even this within a larger context, that of the infinite. It may be said to be that highest dimension in which all opposites are brought into a generative unification, one generative most particularly of the highest level of the soul, the ultimate divine son and goal of creation who can achieve in his own nature that unification of the finite with the infinite in which the holiness of this seventh dimension is defined.

We have seen how the four cosmic worlds of the major kabbalistic tradition can be expanded to include the additional number contained in the alternative kabbalistic concept of the *shemitot*. And as each of these seven cosmic worlds are further shown to define a different dimension of time, which can also be considered a dimension of consciousness, so can they finally be seen to represent seven dimensions of available experience: the four dimensions of space-time that inform Nefesh consciousness; the fifth dimension of Providential causation, whose workings the Ruach consciousness can comprehend and master; the still higher level of Neshamah consciousness that, comprehending the purpose of creation, invests all experience in which it participates with the sixth dimension of meaningfulness; and the final levels of Chayah and Yechidah consciousness, in whose unifications of opposites, ultimately of the finite with the infinite, the seventh dimension of holiness is generated.

GUT Cosmology and the
Four Cosmic Worlds

Having defined the structure of a seven-dimensional cosmos, we can now consider the further equation of these dimensions with the concept of the forces and see how this can be related to the latest understanding of quantum physics. A similar identification of the binding forces with the dimensions of space was developed in the 1920s by Theodor Kaluza and Oscar Klein, and it has recently been utilized in the new multidimensional extension of gauge-field theory known as supersymmetry. As explained by Paul Davies in relation to Grand Unification Theory (GUT),

> In GUTs, the theorists' ability to subsume three very different sorts of forces under a single conceptual umbrella hinged . . . on the discovery that all three forces involved can be described in terms of gauge fields. The central property of these gauge fields is the presence of certain abstract symmetries, which is how they attain their power and elegance. The presence of symmetries in the force fields already hints strongly at some sort of hidden geometry at work. In the revitalized Kaluza-Klein theory the gauge field symmetries become concrete; they are the geometrical symmetries associated with the extra space dimensions. . . . Einstein's dream of a unified field theory built out of geometry has come very close indeed to realization. In the modern Kaluza-Klein theory all the forces of nature, not merely gravity, are treated as manifestations of spacetime structure. What we normally call gravity is a warp in the four spacetime dimensions of our perceptions, while the other forces are reduced to higher-dimensional spacewarps. All the forces of nature are revealed as nothing more than hidden geometry at work. . . . The mathematical "miracle" that the same laws which govern the forces can be expressed in terms of some previously obscure geometrical properties of a multidimensional space must be considered amazing. The order that is being revealed here has not been imposed, but has emerged from lengthy mathematical analysis.[24]

The theory being proposed in the present analysis is similar to that of the reformulated Kaluza-Klein theory in treating "the forces of nature . . . as nothing more than hidden geometry at work."

But the point made in Davies' summary of a complete identification of the forces with the geometrical dimensions has not been understood in its full implications by most quantum theorists, who would still hold on to the now more than ever unnecessary category of the gluons. Thus Pagels' summary of the same gauge-field symmetries would still keep this category whose redundancy was demonstrated in chapter 9:

> As physicists came to understand the mathematical symmetries of field theory they discovered that these symmetries actually required the very interactions they had observed among the fields and their associated quanta. The remarkable insight that symmetry itself implies the existence of gluons that mediate the interactions among quarks and leptons is . . . an example of how the simple and beautiful ideas of symmetry lie at the very foundation of the complex quantum interactions.[25]

Symmetry only "implies the existence of gluons," however, if one is unable to make the theoretical leap epitomized in the statement of John A. Wheeler, "*Physics is geometry.*"[26] If we can make this leap, then we can understand "complex quantum interactions" wholly in terms of the geometrical conditions of their dimension. This does not mean that physicists cannot continue to use the mathematical fiction of gluons to express what are understood to be the functionings of geometric conditions. But they should not be postulated as actual particles of matter.

Even such a use to define geometric symmetries, reversing Pagels' formulation of the relationship of the gluons to geometry, leads, however, to theoretical difficulties. The first is philosophic. For it negates the main Aristotelian principle of general systems theory, that the whole is greater than the sum of its parts, by making possible a model of particle interaction located exclusively on the quantum level, rather than one including the higher systems level of the atomic whole, this indeed seeming to be its primary purpose. The second is the violation of the intuitive imagination it effects by asking us to imagine the binding forces as various gluon balls with which the particles play tennis. Even greater is the violation posed by the masses of the X-particle gluons of supersymmetry. As Davies notes: "The mass of the X comes out at about 10^{14} proton masses, a colossal value."[27] A final objection to the X-particle is its claimed ability to change quarks into leptons, something our study of sacred and secular science has shown should particularly be avoided by a true fundamental theory, and it is upon this proposed X-particle that Grand Unification Theory is built.

But if Grand Unification Theory can only be constructed in such a manner that it violates every principle by which matter can be seen to operate and the mind to understand such operations, then this must surely prove such a theory to be false. Though GUT is mathematically possible, it is a possibility forbidden by the nature of material manifestation, a nature that can be validly modeled not by the freer language of algebra but only by the actual constructions of pure geometry. It is from such geometric study that the formulations of sacred science were derived that can now be called upon to falsify the claims of GUT—and indeed of quantum theory in general—to provide a complete explanation of material reality. Weinberg has said that *"the essential reality is a set of fields* subject to the rules of special relativity and quantum mechanics; all else is derived as a consequence of the quantum dynamics of these fields."[28] It is impossible, however, that "all else" can be so derived since, as Pagels has rightly indicated: "there is a qualitative difference between the microworld and macroworld—the macroworld can store information while the microworld cannot."[29]

But even with all the objections that have just been raised to the formulations and implications both of quantum theory and its GUT development, the further extension of GUT into cosmology is an area that should be explored because of its interesting correspondences with kabbalistic cosmology. This further exploration of the cosmology developed by secular science will, however, again follow the guidelines derived from sacred science, guidelines through which alone it is possible to understand the relationship of microworld to macroworld. For as the earlier examination of sacred science showed number to be the mediating power between the infinitely extended and finitely localized, so is it also through number that the dual levels of material systems are defined. In a manner not explained by quantum theory, a numerical code determines how many hadrons and leptons must be bound together to form the atom of a particular element and how many of which atoms must be so bound to form a particular molecule.

In such a systems understanding of matter, the hadrons and leptons are the only quanta that need be recognized, and even the latter are rightly understood to be wave-packets. That which binds them together to form the numerically coded higher atomic and molecular systems is the macro systems level of the whole, at which a dimension higher than the micro level of the quanta, and exerting a control over the freedom of these system parts, may be said to operate—the level at which geometry and force, as shown in the hadron matrix model of the last chapter, become identified. It is such an identification of gluons with geometry that Pagels seems finally to imply when he says that "one of those gluons, the photon—light itself—is also a consequence of symmetry. If we could go back to the beginning of time, to the primordial fireball of quarks, leptons, and gluons, when the gauge symmetries were as yet unbroken, instead of Fiat Lux—'Let there be light'—we might have heard 'Let there be symmetry.'"[30] Let us, then, return to that beginning and see how the cosmology developed from the geometrically informed gauge-field theory can be correlated with the dimensions of a Sabbatical cosmos as previously defined.

GUT cosmology begins from the premise that the four forces or interactions—the gravitational, weak, electromagnetic, and strong—were once unified and that through a process of successively broken symmetries (echoes of the Lurianic Shevirah?) one after another of these forces, in the reverse of the order listed above, separated out from the previously more collective whole. The concept of a spontaneously broken symmetry was developed separately by Steven Weinberg and Abdus Salam in 1967 as the basis of their gauge-field unification of the electromagnetic and weak forces. This model was followed in 1977 with the theoretical unification proposed by Howard Georgi and Sheldon Glashow of the strong nuclear force with the previously unified electroweak force. But such a unification is based on the questionable postulation of the superheavy X-gluons previously considered; and these are "superheavy gluons that will never be detected"![31] Though the gravitational force has yet to be given even such a questionable unification, it is assumed that it must be theoretically possible and that all four forces must once have been one grand force. In what follows I will not assume that the four forces have been reduced to less than three, or that they emerged successively from a collective whole, but I will accept the premise that they should appear in the order given and see what will emerge if we add to the temporal definition of the dimensions earlier advanced a further identification with one of the forces. Of course, as soon as we enter the atomic and molecular levels of matter, the laws of subatomic quantum behavior lose their definitive explanatory power, for these larger and larger wholes have organizational properties not reducible to the sum of their quantum interactions. Nevertheless, there are some features of development at the fourth and higher dimensions that seem to retain characteristics manifested at lower dimensions, particularly as these were defined in the quantum-synthesized Lurianic model presented earlier.

The simple assignments of the gravitational force to the second world, the electroweak force to the third world, and the strong force to the fourth world, which thus identified these forces with the dimensions associated with these worlds, were earlier made without further elaboration. But a curious support can be found in the geometry of the Sabbath Star Diagram developed in chapter 6 and there shown to be deeply related to the cosmological geometry of the Kabbalah. This is the model that the third world of the Sabbath Star Diagram can provide for the original and only unification of forces that has thus far unquestionably been made. For the theory that Weinberg and later Salam gave for the unification of the weak and electromagnetic forces may be said to work precisely because it is occurring on the same dimension.

The Sabbath Star Diagram was developed to provide the most rational geometric source for the kabbalistic Tree of Life Diagram, and it proved to be a model as well for the emanation of the four cosmic worlds of the Kabbalah. In this model, composed entirely of hexagrams, a double-point hexagram expansion was equated with a cosmic world and considered a whole-step progression while a hexagram expansion based on the single points of a prior hexagram was considered a half-step progression because it could not define the full progression to a further cosmic world. In the Sabbath Star Diagram the progression of the first four hexagrams was from an initial hexagram, through two whole-step progressions, to a half-step progression, and was seen to be analogous to the first four tones of the diatonic scale, those given the solfeggio names of Do, Re, Mi, and Fa, names subsequently transferred to these four hexagrams to better define their spatial relationships. In this model, the Do hexagram was considered to give a functional definition to the original world of Atzilut through its own characteristic harmonization of its dual opposing forms: the ascending triangle that has traditionally symbolized such archetypes as the heavens, fire, and expansion as the descending triangle has symbolized the earth, water, and contraction. What the Re hexagram of the second world of Beriah next defines is primarily a change of orientation, one that can also be said to signify the change from the centeredness of point to the expansiveness of line and that the earlier analysis in the present chapter further identified with the force of gravity. Continuing this further synthesis of the Sabbath Star Diagram with the previously quantum-synthesized Lurianic model, it is with the third world of this diagram, that of Yetzirah, that we arrive at the first forms of lepton particles through a progression of hexagram expansions that may be said to display the broken symmetry that Weinberg himself first proposed to explain the relationship of the weak and electromagnetic forces and to argue for their original unification. For it is in the third world of this diagram that the whole-step progression of hexagram-worlds is first "broken" by the introduction of the half-step progression, this world being defined by the two Mi and Fa hexagrams, the latter of which also seems suggestive of that cosmic catastrophe that many Kabbalists have ascribed to this third world of Yetzirah. Now since construction of the third world is a two-stage process, we may say that in the first stage of the Mi hexagram the weak and electromagnetic forces were unified and that it is only with the manifestation of the second-stage Fa hexagram that this unity was broken, the Mi hexagram subsequently identified with the weak force and the neutrino particles that feel its force while the Fa hexagram becomes identified with the electromagnetic force and the first lepton particle with significant mass, the electron, to which it couples. It is with the electromagnetic force that matter, in the sense of mass, first makes its cosmic appearance, a factor that may be equated with something like the metaphor of the "Fall" also identified with this stage. If this model holds, therefore, we may expect that there will be no equally successful unification of either the gravitational or strong forces with those of the third world already unified.

Before leaving the model of the Sabbath Star Diagram, there are two additional points that should be made about what it can tell us of the further worlds of its own potentially expanded form. The derivation of the Tree of Life Diagram from an underlying diagram composed wholly of hexagrams took us just to that Sabbath Star form whose enlarged and undrawn seventh hexagram was exactly a whole-step progression beyond the Mi hexagram and so brought us to the fourth world with a burst of hexagrams that is most suggestive of the big bang of scientific cosmology. But the model of the third world further suggests that the fourth should also have a stage built on the Fa hexagram, one that would bring it from the stage of the Fi Sabbath Star to that of Sol. And if all such self-generated further worlds are to have two similar major stages, this would have particular significance for the seventh such world in terms of the analogue of the diatonic scale; for the upper Do hexagram, which could be said to conclude the cosmic octave and around which the circle of the Tzimtzum could appropriately be drawn, would come at the midpoint of the seventh world, thus defining the seventh world as that in which the finite and the infinite are unified, a definition already suggested and one that will shortly be further developed. But to return to the fourth world, whose concluding stage was just identified with the Sol Sabbath Star, this would also seem to have further intermediate stages in a fully self-generated form, given the ever greater sizes of each expansion. In fact, such a fully generated fourth-world diagram world can be shown to have exactly four such stages. But if the model of the third world is accepted and the stages of such a world may be said to define separate forces that can be unified, then the same principle should hold for the fourth world as for the third.

Whether or not we continue to use the Sabbath Star Diagram model,[32] we can accept the usual understanding of the four-dimensional earthly realm as composed of the four levels of the minerals, plants, animals, and man. The first stage of the fourth world would, then, be that which can be identified with all the levels of inorganic matter, and the new force demonstrated by this stage can be identified as the strong force. Each of the subsequent stages of the fourth world, however, also contains a new type of force that cannot be simply identified with the strong force unless the strong force is understood to contain them potentially. These are: for the plant level, the life force; for the animal level, the force of the will, willpower; and for the human level, the mental power of consciousness. Each of these forces are evolutionary powers capable of overriding the physical laws specifying the increase of entropy-producing thermal equilibrium through their own capacity to produce ever more highly organized structures.[33] But they can also be understood as further elaborations of the essential power of the strong force to bind together the composite structures of quarks defining the hadrons. With this final definition of the strong force as implicitly containing all the powers of the life force, we will be in a position to proceed to a consideration of the higher dimensions of a Sabbatical cosmos.

We have thus far taken the cosmic process to that fourth dimension of space-time in which atomic fusion can be accomplished and seen that this dimension can be defined by the expanded understanding of the strong force that emerges at this level, one that can be appropriately termed the "strong-life force." If this model is now further applied to the more subtle dimensions that both the earlier given interpretation of the Genesis creation account and superstring theory ascribe to the cosmos, we will then be able to see what further syntheses of quantum theory with the higher dimensional worlds of a Sabbatical cosmos can be made to define a more comprehensive cosmology consistent both with secular and sacred science. For as we move beyond the fourth world of consensus reality, we will not so much be leaving the physical definition of reality behind as moving to the dimensions of its successively higher resonances.

And in defining these, we can again call upon the experimental results of quantum physics. In fact, as we enter the fifth and higher dimensions, we will seem to be entering more and more deeply into the weird circumstances discovered to be operative in the quantum realm.

Quantum Cosmology and the Future Worlds

It is the higher resonances of the elementary particles, which have been successively discovered through the use of ever more powerful accelerators, that can best explain the material constituents of the higher worlds in a manner that can support the premise of a coherent multidimensional cosmos. If we look at such charts of hadrons and leptons as those provided by Pagels,[34] we can see suggestive matches between their higher resonances. Turning first to the elementary hadron quanta, the quarks, it is essential to begin by distinguishing their varieties or "flavors." At the level that can be identified with the fourth world of stable and relatively stable hadrons, the protons and neutrons, respectively, they consist of up quarks, with electron mass of 2 and electric charge of +2/3, and down quarks, with electron mass of 6 and electric charge of −1/3. The characteristic that led to their names is clearly that of electric charge, positive charge being equated with the "up" direction above a neutral line and negative charge with the "down" direction below it. These were the first quarks postulated in the original theory of Murray Gell-Mann, but discovery of new particles required the postulation of quarks with higher masses to account for them in terms of this theory. In the previous chapter the primary focus was on the up and down quarks of the nuclear hadrons and what were called the higher resonant quarks were but briefly glanced at, though it was shown that they could be accommodated by the same quantum matrix model used for the nuclear hadrons. But the argument now to be developed would be aided by a fuller definition of all the higher resonant particles.

The third postulated quark, called "strange," has been ascribed an electron mass of 200 and a charge of −1/3, and in various combinations with the previously defined quarks can explain the properties of the various new hadrons that, together with the proton and neutron, can be given the symmetrical arrangement called the baryon octet. A fourth quark was suggested for theoretical reasons by Sheldon Glashow and named the "charm" quark. With an electron mass of 3,000 and a charge of +2/3, it later seemed to explain the characteristic of a newly discovered meson. Still later, in 1978, the discovery of the more massive meson named "upsilon" required the postulation of a fifth quark, called "bottom" or "beauty" but, in any case, symbolized by a *b,* and having an electron mass of 9,000 and charge of −1/3. Meanwhile, on the other side, new leptons had also been discovered with the same −1 electric charge as the electron but proportionately larger masses, the "muon" with an electron mass of 207 and the "tauon" with an electron mass of 3,491. As suggested, there seems to be some correlation between these new hadrons and leptons, the correlation of strange hadrons with muons and of charmed hadrons with tauons. But the problem is that they are so unstable they decay into more elementary particles before they have a chance to unite in a new form of strange or charmed atomic structure, a decay attributed to the weak force. What is needed, then, is a new force capable of overcoming the weak force, a new force not likely to be found in the laboratories of quantum physicists. What can this be?

Pagels comes close to suggesting such a force when he says:

> Physicists do not yet know if there really exist ultimate laws that express the final conditions of all existence. Perhaps there is no absolute law which governs the universe and life in that universe. . . . Conceivably, life might be able to change those laws of physics that today seem to imply its extinction along with that of the universe. If that is so, then might not life have a more important role in cosmology than is currently envisioned? That is a problem worth thinking about.
>
> In fact, it may be the only problem worth thinking about.[35]

In discussing the fourth world, we saw that its defining strong force had to be understood to contain, at least potentially, the combined forces of a living, conscious will.[36] But at the level of Nefesh consciousness, the animal soul of man defining the psychological dimension identified with the kabbalistic fourth world, such a will is directed toward the manipulation of the familiar and uncharming particles of the material world for the better satisfaction of its primarily physical needs. It is only as we move to the higher levels of the soul distinguished in kabbalistic soul psychology, the Ruach soul level that can be identified with the fifth dimension and the Neshamah soul level identifiable with the sixth dimension, that we can project a life force at levels of power sufficient to unify the massive hadron and lepton higher resonant particles into relatively stable super-atoms.

To use terms that have already cropped up in this discussion, it seems appropriate to name the force that can be associated with the fifth dimension as the "strange-life force" and that for the sixth dimension as the "charmed-life force," the former connecting strange hadrons with muons and the latter charm hadrons with tauons. The possibility of such atomic fusion through the power of various levels of consciousness would go far to explain the formation of the increasingly more subtle soul bodies believed to accompany spiritual development in many religious traditions including the Kabbalah, in which it is referred to as the Tzelem. Indeed, such spiritual interpretations of the most subtle psychological states, particularly in their more usual mythological form, may be viewed as but a more fanciful way of explaining higher dimensional processes that can also be phrased using scientific terminology. In what follows, I will be projecting such a possible explanation of the functioning of the higher dimensions in terms of this union of successively higher levels of consciousness and of material particles, projecting it without excuse as a possibility for contemplation that would effect the final synthesis of sacred and secular science with which this and the previous chapter have been primarily concerned.

Since we will be talking about more subtle states of matter and spirit than are experienced by normal consciousness, even the language of quantum mechanics is bound to sound somewhat alchemical, given the names of the quarks. But there is a difference between the use of such language with reference to the higher dimensions and its conventional use in terms of quantum interactions; for at the quantum level the particles do not form into stable atoms—indeed, this level is only revealed through the smashing of the atom and its nucleus—while the higher dimensions can only be thought to "materialize" to the extent that the massive particles emerging at these levels of power can be held together by the still more powerful forces of higher consciousness. It is spiritual bodies and environments that these higher powers of heart and mind may be thought to be bringing into more subtle forms of existence through their imputed ability to synthesize the higher resonant forms of hadrons and leptons into stable structures not simply atomic or molecular but organic, structures in which higher modes of conscious life can be centered. Thus it is unavoidable that the attempt to explore and describe these higher dimensions will have to employ a terminology increasingly associated with spiritual traditions; but this terminology need not be any less precise or logical for this reason than that of contemporary science and has clear parallels to it.

To return to the more orderly investigation of the higher dimensions, we shall have to consider more closely the nature of both the time and force that can be identified with the fifth dimension of Ruach consciousness. As has been suggested, the fifth dimension of time can be associated with the phenomenon of synchronicity, a phenomenon involving such an interaction of separate lines of causality as is normally ascribed simply to coincidence but that seems to be more Providential. It is the workings of such Providence that may be said to characterize and reveal the influence of the fifth dimension upon the lower four. To one operating on the fifth dimension, there seems to be a constant meeting of exactly what is needed. The normal inconveniences of space and time disappear just as in a dream, just as in what Australian Aborigines call "dream-time." Now what is interesting in this regard is that the telepathic quality of such states of altered consciousness as are referred to by the term "dream-time" is similar to one aspect of quantum reality, its theoretical violation of local causality as formulated in a thought experiment by Einstein, Podolsky, and Rosen and later verified by Bell's experiment. Einstein thought he was disproving the very foundations of quantum theory by the flawless logic of his presentation, as his comment on this thought experiment revealed: "It seems hard to look in God's cards. But I cannot for a moment believe that he plays dice and makes use of 'telepathic' means (as the current quantum theory alleges He does)."[37] But all arguments that have been offered to undermine the conclusions of Einstein, Podolsky, and Rosen, and those of Bell, seem less cogent then their arguments in favor of instantaneous action at a distance, of synchronicity. It is at the fifth dimension, however, that this feature of quantum behavior can come under conscious control. Such paranormal powers as telepathy may, in fact, be partly explained by the imputed ability of Ruach consciousness to use the higher resonances of the quanta at this level, most probably the muons, since the experiments just referred to were based on electrons and photons, and infuse their power with its will. But such Ruach use would represent a lower form of fifth-dimensional power since it does not effect a synthesis of its hadrons and leptons but employs them only in their quantum state.

It is what I have called the strange-life force that can represent the true, synthetic form of fifth-dimensional power, and its prime quality can be considered to be its power to negate the weak force that had destabilized the strange hadrons and muons at the fourth dimension. In addition, it is the power that can be thought to unite such hadrons and leptons into stable atoms of strange elements. But to understand the kind of life it can confer on the bodies thus formed, it is necessary to understand its difference from the charmed-life force that may be identified with the sixth dimension.

Like the fifth dimension, the sixth can also be identified both with a form of time and of force. Neshamah consciousness can be understood to define and exist in a transformative moment, a present in which past and future become transparent to reveal that ideal form of the self for which its past patterning can be sacrificed in a continuous alchemical-like sublimation of the soul. As the Ruach soul lives in a temporal flow of marvelous synchronicity, the Neshamah soul lives in the fullness of a continuous here and now. And it may be thought to do so in a body of charmed life. Like the strange-life force, the charmed-life force can be considered to be able to counteract the effects of the weak force to produce stable bodies compounded of charmed hadrons and tauons. But in addition, it can be conceived of as also able to overcome the further effects of gravity, and it is in this that the major distinction may be made between such strange-life and charmed-life states.

Strange-life bodies may be thought to be still tied to the earth whereas charmed-life bodies are not. However high a strange-life body might be able to soar, it would always fall back to earth; a charmed-life body would not need to. This distinction would also seem to apply to various other areas. While such bodies are operating within the physical bodies of the fourth world, this distinction can be seen in such matters as religious and psychic experiences. In the former case, a Ruach soul would primarily follow the rhythm of the week, soaring with the holiness of the Sabbath and falling back to earthly pressures during the intervening six days of work; but a Neshamah soul would be permanently established in the divine love that its daily prayers are continuously sustaining. In terms of psychic experiences, a Ruach soul would be able to engage in various forms of telepathic communications with other souls on earth while a Neshamah soul would be able to leave the earth in out-of-body experiences.

But the most important difference involves the question of an afterlife. If the human body, composed of normal hadrons and leptons, is as mortal as the Nefesh soul that inhabits it is thought to be, it would seem fair to attribute some form of immortality to the souls that have developed strange-life or charmed-life subtle bodies, this then constituting their principal strangeness or charm. But if strange-life bodies can be considered both immortal and tied to gravity, then they would seem to have a form of immortality that must periodically return to earth, as with their soaring. The conception that comes closest to these circumstances is that of reincarnation, a concept accepted by the Kabbalah and called Gilgul. And it is because it is still so tied to the earth that the very possibility of such life beyond the physical body must seem strange. Charmed-life bodies, however, may be granted that true immortality in which the personality can hold itself together permanently beyond the decay of the physical body. It is charmed, indeed, beyond the power of all earthly forces to disturb its peace. And the possibility of such out-of-body existence does not seem strange to the Neshamah soul both because it has had such charming experiences while in life and because its world is closer to the infinity of the seventh world than to the finitude of the fourth.

We come finally to the seventh dimension, a dimension that can be ascribed the unique power connecting the finite to the infinite. If we are to continue to use quark language to define this force, we will have to choose between bottom and beauty. The latter has definite possibilities since the Hebrew word for beauty is Tiferet, the Sefirah on the Tree of Life Diagram that has been variously identified with the Tetragrammaton, the Holy One, blessed be He, and Ze'ir Anpin, the Partzuf of the divine son. It is the combination of the substance of the Holy One, blessed be He, and the Shekhinah—the former of which can also be understood as the *Reshimu* or residual background radiation and the latter as the holy sparks immanent in all creation, which, in turn, can be understood to be the highest resonant leptons and hadrons[38]—that defines the beautiful life of the seventh dimension and the still higher soul levels comprising it. These are the Chayah and the Yechidah soul levels, the former linguistically associated with life as the latter is with unification, the former further associated in this model with the finite aspects of this dimension as the latter is with its infinite aspects. The holiness that cannot be separated from the seventh dimension may be said to consist precisely in the unifying life force expressed in the divine name Elohim Chayyim, the Living God, a power that can accomplish the very unification of the finite and the infinite that would seem to fulfill the ultimate aim of that first self-definition of a point in the infinite substance here proposed as the origin of the cosmos—the goal of generating the androgynous cosmic son.

This original distinction between centering point and expanse has persisted in the successive stages of the cosmos in which these complementary opposites have achieved some form of union. In this model of cosmology, it next occurs in the fourth world, that which can provide the first dimension of time capable, like that of infinity, of eternal extension. For the three stages following the establishment of a centering point—the radial extension of gravitational force from this central point, the fixing of the circle of the Tzimtzum that effected the exhaustion of all matter from the space it enclosed with the exception of the residual light, and the discharge back into that now finite space of a ball of hadronic matter capable of just balancing the number of free electrons in that space—would have each been effected with virtually instantaneous speed. It is, then, in our four-dimensional world of macroscopic reality that the free energy of the electron and the centered mass of the proton can first join to form the hydrogen atom and all the atoms of the more numerically complex molecules out of which still more numerically complex molecules will be formed, these atoms preserving the primary distinction between the central stability of the proton and the infinite extension of the electron, the distinction as well between the electromagnetic force of third world radiant energy and the strong force of fourth-world material solidity.

It is not, then, to the quantum level or the unbroken symmetries imputed to the first one-hundredth second of the universe that we should look to find the simplest law underlying creation but to the organization of matter as we find it in the real world, in the atom. For all the higher dimensions can be viewed as only more powerful expressions of the threefold law of nature expressed archetypally in the hexagram and physically in the atom, the necessity for a harmonious union of infinite with finite power, of the infinite range of the electromagnetic force with the exceedingly limited range of the strong force. Equally eternal products of the original infinite medium, the electrons and protons express the irreducible polarity of expansiveness and contraction within this medium that alone could give rise to that first definition of a point at which a cosmic beginning can be grasped by thought. In the beginning, the polarity of infinite expanse and contracted point gave rise to a cosmic dialectic that at every stage was to provide new syntheses of this complementary opposition, syntheses that could only be accomplished through the numerical-geometrical power of the fourth and higher dimensions. All that distinguishes the atoms of the four-dimensional world from those theoretically projected for the higher dimensions is the mass of their constituents and the power needed to bring the opposed natures of these constituents into a harmonious and stable union. And it seems hard to avoid seeing in the exponential growth in the masses of the higher resonant leptons and hadrons a further connection with the expanding size of the universe, these greater domains seeming to require proportionately larger bodies to navigate successfully through their ever vaster expanses and to contain their ever increasing power.

But if the only power capable of synthesizing material atoms out of these massive particles is that of consciousness, then from the fifth dimension on we may see a new form of creator emerge on the cosmic stage, the highly developed soul, which is capable of synthesizing the atomic constituents of the living bodies of its higher modes of consciousness out of material particles, just as in the biblical account of the creation of the living soul body of Adam from the dust of the earth. Though secular science may have difficulty in fitting these higher dimensional worlds into its paradigm, this analysis has shown how they may be conceived as having a material aspect that is just what one would expect from the recent discoveries of high-energy physics and that is coherent with the scientific model. More than this, we can see that the model of secular science is incomplete without such an understanding, both of this world and its higher dimensions, as can only be provided by the long tradition of sacred science. For what our study of sacred science has revealed is precisely the same interrelationship of the infinite and the finite mediated by number as can be seen to inform all the levels of structured matter.

In the kabbalistic *Sefer Yetzirah*, number is not only shown, as in Pythagorean science, to mediate between the infinity of sound and the finity of form but to correspond to the heart in its mediating role between the circle (Galgal) and the line (Teli), a distinction that gains new meaning in the context of the Lurianic cosmology developed more than a millennium later. In mediating between the infinite-finite polarity of circle and line, the heart not only provides the numerical counter of its rhythmic beating but a capacity for feeling that is the most important gateway to the highest levels of consciousness. On a symbolic level it might be argued that the real "gluon" connecting the infinite and finite in all material bodies from the most gross to the most subtle, is that of love, and that love itself is but a name for the ultimate force of connection at all levels of the cosmos. Though Stanley Kubrick has forever prevented the possibility of the fifth-dimensional force being called "strange-love," at the level of the seventh dimension this force might well be called the "love-of-beauty." For the Sefirah whose name means "beauty," Tiferet, is also identified with the heart of that reconstituted anthropocosmos, whose Sefirot were emanated from the Limitless Light in the line of light that first perforated the circular boundary of the Tzimtzum, a line also pictured kabbalistically as a series of ten or forty widening rings containing the Sefirot of the Trees of one or four cosmic worlds, Sefirot that can be equated with the infinite body of the Yechidah soul, the true and final form of the androgynous cosmic son. It can further be suggested that the holy love of such a Yechidah soul is particularly aroused by contemplation of the beauty of the total cosmic design that is only fully revealed at this seventh dimension. Cosmologists are increasingly resting their theoretical claims on the grounds of aesthetics, the beauty of the underlying order revealed by their mathematical formulations. But our cosmological model has a final lesson to teach us, the way in which the higher heart of the seventh dimension can achieve the ultimate purpose of the cosmic process initiated by that first point.

We have seen that no synthesis of matter can take place without the leptons and their electromagnetic force that provide a foundation for all later developments derived from the "broken symmetry" of the third world, but that the proposed effect of all higher dimensional super-atomic synthesis is to overcome successively the earlier manifested forces, the weak force and, finally, the force of gravity. If this pattern is to hold at the seventh dimension, then its force must be one capable of overcoming what had been present at the first, when the original point appeared in the infinite medium. In the earlier discussion of the nature of the original infinity, I accepted the analysis of the new cosmology that it was an undifferentiated soup of the various quantum particles prevented from achieving a stable atomic synthesis because any such atom that might have formed would have been blown apart by the infinite heat. Now if the full implications of the original point are to achieve realization at the seventh dimension of its geometric unfolding, then the power of this seventh dimension must be one capable of overcoming the continual operation of atomic and hadronic fission. It must be a power of consciousness capable not only of preserving itself from incineration but also of synthesizing beautiful quarks into hadrons and these with complementary leptons yet undiscovered to produce the body of that true cosmic son who can unite a finitely conceived personality with infinite power.

Once the power of the humanly developed mind enters the picture of cosmic development, its last frame need not be either an incinerating return to its original source or an infinite expansion into a frozen and annihilating darkness. If this analysis has any cogency, then we need not conclude as Weinberg does, in his deep reflection on these alternative endings of scientific cosmology: "The effort to understand the universe is one of the very few things that lifts human life a little above the level of farce, and gives it some of the grace of tragedy."[39] Rather, we can understand cosmic history as an epic process in which we have a heroic part to play, that which can redeem the infinite potential for achieving divine personality. Whether the original self-determining point was a product of infinite will or infinite possibility, it is the point at which our limited reasoning about the cosmos must begin. And as we have followed the speculative unfolding of its exponential powers, it is impossible not to share something of Einstein's sense of religious awe: "My religious feeling is a humble amazement at the order revealed in the small patch of reality to which our feeble intelligence is equal."[40] Again, if we can accept the reality of the higher dimensions of consciousness that have originated on this beautiful earth in this awesome material universe, it is unimportant whether or not they are thought to represent a phenomenon permeating all of infinity or only a local region of growing order, for it *is* growing and has given a purpose and direction to further cosmic development that seems irresistible. The personalizing of the infinite into a conscious unity composed of multiple, still particularized, centers seems destined to continue its organic development through ever greater expansion of its power of organization, an expansion through which an undifferentiated infinite power will be transformed into the ever higher powers of divine personality whose dimensions are truly infinite and whose ways we may be jointly privileged to discover.

Notes

Chapter 1

1. See Gershom Scholem, *Kabbalah* (New York: New American Library, 1978), pp. 362–68.
2. Josephus, *Jewish Antiquities*, trans. Ralph Marcus, 9 vols., Loeb Classical Library (Cambridge: Harvard University Press, 1963), vol. 8, p. 179.
3. Jacob Neusner, "Varieties of Judaism in the Formative Age," *Jewish Spirituality: From the Bible through the Middle Ages*, ed. Arthur Green (New York: Crossroad, 1988), p. 186.
4. Lawrence H. Schiffman, *Reclaiming the Dead Sea Scrolls* (Philadelphia: Jewish Publication Society, 1994), pp. 88, 89. Schiffman provides definitive proof of the Sadducean origins of the Qumran community (see pp. 83–95) while distinguishing the later apocalyptic dualism of this community from the original form of Zadokite priestly beliefs (see p. 157).
5. Geza Vermes, ed. and trans., introduction to *The Complete Dead Sea Scrolls in English* (New York: Penguin Putnam, 1997), p. 28.
6. *Sh'ma* is the first word of the credal affirmation of the divine unity contained most essentially in Deut. 6:4. The next verse, Deut. 6:5, contains the commandment to love God. Here, and throughout this study, I have chosen to use initial capitals rather than italics to distinguish such Hebrew words as Sh'ma used more than a few times from English words as being less visually obtrusive.
7. Scholem, *Kabbalah*, p. 10.

413

8. Here and throughout, unless otherwise noted, I have used the King James Version for biblical translations because of its greater literalness.

9. Gershom Scholem, "A Candid Letter About My True Intentions in Studying Kabbalah" (1937), in his *On the Possibility of Jewish Mysticism in Our Time & Other Essays*, ed. with intro. by Avraham Shapira, trans. Jonathan Chipman (Philadelphia: Jewish Publication Society, 1997), p. 4.

10. Franz Rosenzweig, *The Star of Redemption*, trans. William W. Hallo (Boston: Beacon Press, 1971), p. 423.

11. Martin Buber, *I and Thou*, trans. Ronald Gregor Smith (New York: Charles Scribner's Sons, 1953), pp. 111, 117, 118.

12. Abraham Isaac Kook, *The Lights of Penitence*, trans. and intro. Ben Zion Bokser (New York: Paulist Press, 1978), pp. 87, 221.

13. See the concluding comments to the appendix on *vehayah* as a biblical power word, which compare *vehayah* and *veyehi* though not with the following Gematria associations, in my book *Renewing the Covenant: A Kabbalistic Guide to Jewish Spirituality* (Rochester, Vt.: Inner Traditions, 1999), pp. 243, 257.

14. The *Sefer Yetzirah* will play an important role in chapters 3 and 8, and will be the subject of chapter 7.

15. See Joseph Leon Blau, *The Christian Interpretation of the Cabala in the Renaissance* (Port Washington, N.Y.: Kennikat Press, 1965; orig. pub. 1944 by Columbia University Press); Frances A. Yates, *The Occult Philosophy in the Elizabethan Age* (London: Routledge & Kegan Paul, 1979); and Gersham Scholem, *Kabbalah*, pp. 196–201.

16. Milton's lines are as follows: "Boundless the Deep, because I am who fill/ Infinitude, nor vacuous the space,/ Though I uncircumscrib'd myself retire,/ And put not forth my goodness . . ." (7. 168–71).

17. Moses Cordovero, *Pardes Rimmonim*, ed. Yisrael Yehudah Shapiro (Jerusalem: Rabbi Atiah, 1969), 7:32a, p. 316. My translation.

18. Ibid., 7:32a–b, p. 316.

19. The Tzimtzum will be discussed further in chapter 10; see also chapter 4 of *Renewing the Covenant*.

20. See Scholem, *Kabbalah*, pp. 420–28.

21. See, for instance, Aryeh Kaplan's translation of *The Bahir* (New York: Samuel Weiser, 1979), p. 155; and his *Sefer Yetzirah*, p. 29.

22. For a full analysis of kabbalistic geometry that attempts to validate this associative mode of interpretation, see the first section of chapter 6.

23. See Aryeh Kaplan, *Meditation and the Bible* (New York: Samuel Weiser, 1978), pp. 70–74.

24. See Gershom Scholem, *On the Mystical Shape of the Godhead: Basic Concepts in the Kabbalah*, trans. Joachim Neugroschel, ed. and rev. Jonathan Chipman, foreword by Joseph Dan (New York: Schocken Books, 1991), and the extended discussion of it in the fourth section of chapter 2.

25. William Wordsworth, "Tintern Abbey," ll. 95–96.

26. Arthur E. Green, "The Role of Jewish Mysticism in a Contemporary Theology of Judaism," *Shefa Quarterly: A Journal of Jewish Thought and Study* 1 (Sept.,

1978): 40. Green has reiterated this hope in a more recent review in the *New York Times Book Review*, 30 October 1988, sec. 7, pp. 32–33. See also Yosef Hayim Yerushalmi, *Zakhor: Jewish History and Jewish Memory* (Seattle: Washington University Press, 1982), pp. 98, 99, 103.

Chapter 2

1. Abraham Abulafia, *The Rose of Mysteries [Shoshan Sodoth]*, trans. Aryeh Kaplan, in *Meditation and Kabbalah* (York Beach, Maine: Samuel Weiser, 1982); pp. 109–10. See also note 21 below.
2. R. H. Charles, ed. and trans., *The Book of Enoch or 1 Enoch* (Oxford: Clarendon Press, 1912), p. 67.
3. *The Ethiopic Book of Enoch*, ed. and trans. Michael A. Knibb (Oxford: Clarendon Press, 1978), vol. 2. All further references in the text are to this new edition.
4. In *Chagigah* 14b; see discussion in Kaplan, *Meditation and Kabbalah*, p. 19.
5. See Gershom Scholem, *Major Trends in Jewish Mysticism* (New York: Schocken Books, 1961), pp. 49, 65, 74–75; for a less extreme position, see his later *Kabbalah*, pp. 8–13, 21–22; see also Joseph Dan, ed. *The Early Kabbalah* (New York: Paulist Press, 1986), pp. 5–7.
6. Gilles Quispel, "The Birth of the Child: Some Gnostic and Jewish Aspects," *Eranos Lectures 3: Jewish and Gnostic Man* (Dallas, Texas: Spring Pub., 1973), pp. 5–6, 15. See also Ithamar Gruenwald, *From Apocalypticism to Gnosticism* (Frankfurt am Main: Peter Lang, 1988), who likewise recognizes "the role Mani's heavenly twin-brother plays in these revelations and the fact that Mani's revelations are viewed in the framework of the Jewish (and partly Christian) apocalyptic tradition" (p. 255).
7. Ibid., pp. 12, 23, 26.
8. Scholem, *Kabbalah*, p. 16.
9. Gruenwald, *Apocalypticism*, pp. 130, 138–39.
10. See Vermes, *Complete Dead Sea Scrolls*, pp. 18, 28, 63n.
11. "The Community Rule," trans. Vermes, ibid., pp. 100, 104, 111.
12. Ibid., pp. 99, 101, 102.
13. "The Manual of Discipline," trans. Millar Burrows, in his *The Dead Sea Scrolls* (New York: Viking Press, 1956), pp. 374, 375.
14. "The Community Rule," *Complete Dead Sea Scrolls*, p. 109.
15. Ibid., p. 115.
16. Schiffman, *Reclaiming the Dead Sea Scrolls*, p. 157.
17. "The Manual of Discipline," *Dead Sea Scrolls*, p. 379.
18. "The Community Rule," *Dead Sea Scrolls*, p. 105.
19. Ibid., p. 110.
20. See my discussion of this Temple service in chapter 4 of *Renewing the Covenant*, pp.177–79.
21. Gabriele Boccaccini, following Ben Zion Wacholder, has argued in his book *Beyond the Essene Hypothesis: The Parting of the Ways between Qumran and Enochic Judaism* (Grand Rapids, Mich.: Wm. B. Eerdmans, 1998) that "At the roots of

the Qumran community, therefore, is an ancient schism within the Jewish priest-hood between Enochians and Zadokites. . . . The Enochians were an opposition party within the temple elite" (p. 78). But his argument that the Qumran Essenes were anti-Zadokite Enochians (p. 77) seems most questionable in view of the position given to "the sons of Zadok" in "The Community Rule," and the fact that the post-Qumran "Enochians" who wrote the parables section of 1 Enoch (missing from the Qumran library because of its late date of composition) were in accord with the Zadokite model of Daniel. I would rather argue that the priests who wrote 1 Enoch were developing the core secret doctrine of the Zadokite priesthood.

22. In *Major Trends*, Scholem shows, however, that it was actually his father Elisha who was the high priest and that Ishmael was only a boy when the Temple was destroyed, p. 356, note 3.

23. See Scholem, *Kabbalah*, p. 10, and the discussion of this subject in the previous chapter.

24. Joseph Dan, *Jewish Mysticism*, vol. 1, *Late Antiquity* (Northvale, N.J., and Jerusalem: Jason Aronson, 1998), pp. 75, 84.

25. Ibid., p. 83.

26. Ibid., pp. xviii, xxi, 103.

27. Rachel Elior, "From Earthly Temple to Heavenly Shrines: Prayer and Sacred Liturgy in the *Hekhalot* Literature and its Relation to Temple Traditions," *Tarbiz* 64 (April–June 1995), p. vi.

28. *3 Enoch or The Hebrew Book of Enoch*, ed. and trans. by Hugo Odeberg (1928; reprint, New York: Ktav Publications, 1973), pp. 137, 138.

29. Ibid., 10:1, p. 27; 10:2, p. 28; 12:5; p. 33.

30. *The Shi'ur Qomah: Liturgy and Theurgy in Pre-Kabbalistic Jewish Mysticism*, ed. and trans. by Martin Samuel Cohen. All further references within the text are to this edition and preserve Cohen's subscript references.

31. In Exod. 29:45–46, the root of the word translated and meaning "dwell" is the same as that for the Shekhinah, whereas in Exod. 33:14–15 the word translated as "presence," *panai*, clearly means "My Face." Though Onkelos' rendering of it as the Shekhinah seems to have been adopted by the King James translators, this involves an interpretation of its implications. Such an interpretation can be supported contextually, as I have suggested, but the use of the term for "face" is also significant. This is especially true since it is most immediately surrounded by direct references to the Face of God (Exod. 33:11, 20), which can or cannot be seen in mystic vision by Moses. As we have seen, the beholding of a face on the Throne is a central aspect of the Merkabah tradition and the concept of upper and lower "faces" will be met again in the *Zohar* and the Lurianic tradition deriving from it.

32. This quotation is taken from the version of the *Shi'ur Komah* translated by The Work of The Chariot and appearing in *The Secret Garden: An Anthology in the Kabbalah*, ed. David Meltzer (New York: Seabury Press, 1976), and is superior to the more recent scholarly edition of Martin Samuel Cohen, from which most of the other quotations have been taken, insofar as it retains the literal mean-

ing here of the Hebrew word *ben*, meaning "son." Cohen did confirm in private correspondence to me that "the Hebrew word *ben* in the expression *ben ha'olam haba'* . . . does appear in virtually all of the manuscripts of the Shiur Komah known to me." All references to this expression will, therefore, use the literal translation, "a son of the world to come," appearing in *The Secret Garden*, p. 32.

33. Odeberg, *3 Enoch*, p. 186.
34. Cohen, *Shi'ur Qomah*, p. 88.
35. From the translation by Work of the Chariot, *The Secret Garden*, p. 32.
36. Ibid., p. 32.
37. See Cohen, *Shi'ur Qomah*, pp. 175–76.
38. See Scholem, *Major Trends*, p. 68.
39. An important form of this secret doctrine, which envisions the image of Jacob engraved on the Throne, derives from the Talmud, from Targum Yerushalmi on Genesis 28:12 and Targum Pseudo-Jonathan on the same verse. Elliot R. Wolfson, in his important monograph "The Image of Jacob Engraved upon the Throne: Further Reflection on the Esoteric Doctrine of the German Pietists," appearing in his book *Along the Path: Studies in Kabbalistic Myth, Symbolism, and Hermeneutics* (Albany: State University of New York, 1995) has traced the remarkable history of this motif in the later tradition of the medieval German Hasidim, primarily Eleazar of Worms, and of such Spanish Kabbalists whom they influenced as Jacob ha-Kohan, demonstrating that in their writings "the aggadic image of Jacob engraved upon the throne replaces the biblical image of the human form seated upon the throne" (p. 8) and is variously further identified with Metatron (pp. 16–25), the Presence (p. 27), the Glory (pp. 29–62), and the Sefirah "called *Tif'eret Yisra'el*" (p. 24). This last is especially interesting. In the fuller words of the Spanish Kabbalist Jacob ha-Kohen: "Know, my son, that the upper glory . . . is that which is called *Tif'eret Yisra'el*, and the image of Jacob engraved in the holy creatures is the glory that is below the upper glory, and it is likewise called *Tif'eret Yisra'el*" (pp. 24–25). The standard kabbalistic identification of the Sefirah Tiferet as Jacob, the defining Sefirah of the six-Sefirot Partzuf of the son, Ze'ir Anpin, is given a most compelling pre-history by Wolfson that can relate it to the essential Throne mysticism of the priestly doctrine of the son. For on the basis of my previous analysis, it should be clear that the reason underlying and prompting the use of Jacob to replace such previous occupants of the Throne as the son of man and Metatron must have been the precise double identification of Jacob's transformed self as the divine son Israel, the identification we have just seen to be implied in the meaning of the name Israel as prince or son of God (Gen. 32:28) and that also appears in Israel's denomination by God as His son (Ex. 4:22). The man Jacob, like Daniel and Enoch, is considered in this aggadic tradition to see his own image on the Throne (p. 18), the glorious apparition of his transfigured self as the divine son Israel that provides the perfect model for the priestly secret doctrine that had earlier unified the seer and the seen under the term "son of man." Eleazar of Worms gives just such a definition of this most important term: "Therefore Ezekiel and Daniel were called the 'son of man' *(ben 'adam)*, i.e., one who knows that you have seen the image of a

human (*demut 'adam*)" (p. 10). The "son of man" is thus one who has gained the mystical knowledge of his own ideal transfiguration into the divine son. In the texts of Eleazar we also find "that Jacob's image bears the title 'God of Israel,' for the name Israel designates the lower power in the divine realm"(p. 35) and that "the cherub, also called 'the image of Jacob,' is the divine power revealed to prophets, and it is the glory that sits upon the throne" (p. 61). Wolfson further shows that "in the writings of Eleazar it is clear that the motif of the image of Jacob is covered and cloaked in utter secrecy" (p. 2 et passim). But where Wolfson later attributes this secrecy to Eleazar's suggestions of the androgynous nature of Jacob's enthroned image (see p. 51), a nature we will see to have also been attributed to the kabbalistic Ze'ir Anpin, the Partzuf of the son, in the Zoharic Idrot and the Lurianic *Etz Chayyim*, I would attribute it to the very identification of Jacob with the esoteric Hebraic doctrine of the divine son that was probably felt to have been coopted by exoteric Christianity and so had particularly to be wrapped in secrecy.

40. As quoted in Gershom Scholem, *Origins of the Kabbalah*, trans. Allan Arkush, ed. R. J. Zwi Werblowsky (Princeton: Jewish Publication Society and Princeton University Press, 1987; orig. German publ., 1962), p. 120. Scholem comments on this quotation: "That Moses, the 'faithful envoy,' has the same face as the angel Metatron, the 'Prince of the Countenance,' and together with him conducts the celestial liturgy is an idea that is not found in the Merkabah texts known to date" (p. 120).

41. Ibid., p. 110. Scholem states of this quote: "the formulation: every man who knows this mystery can be assured of bliss, is exactly the same as that given in the beginning of our fragment of the *Shi'ur Qomah*" (p. 110).

42. Ibid., p. 212.

43. Philip Birnbaum, trans. and ed., *Prayer Book for Sabbaths and Festivals* (New York: Hebrew Publishing Company, 1978), p. 228.

44. Ibid., pp. 227–28n.

45. Nissen Mangel, trans. and ed., *Siddur Tilillat Hashem* (Brooklyn: Merkos L'Inyonei Chinoch, 1982), p. 83n. This Lubavitcher Siddur includes the quotation from *Megillah* 28b in the daily morning service as well as the Sabbath Musaf Service, although the Artscroll Siddur includes it only in the Sabbath Musaf Service.

46. But see *The Encyclopedia of the Jewish Religion*, ed. R. J. Zwi Werblowsky and Geoffrey Wigoder (New York: Holt, Rinehart and Winston, 1965), p. 346, which says this work was "probably written in the 10th cent. although it has been assigned to the Talmudic period."

47. Scholem, *Origins of the Kabbalah*, p. 20.

48. Cohen, *Shi'ur Qomah*, p. 65. Though he gives as one reason for his dating "the fact that the *Shi'ur Qomah* seems to echo some passages in the *Babylonian Talmud*" (p. 66), and cites some similar passages noted by previous scholars, both he and they have failed to note the passage in *Megillah* 28b and the Siddur that parallels much of the *Shi'ur Komah* linguistic formula on the eternal reward for daily study of a particular subject of knowledge.

49. Dan, *Jewish Mysticism*, vol. 1, p. 82, 82n.

50. Though Scholem does not suggest such a priestly source, he has supported the view, in his recently translated important work, *Origins of the Kabbalah*, that there were ancient Jewish sources of medieval esoteric doctrines: "The language and concepts are the same, and we look in vain for an answer to the question how this terminology could have originated or been re-created anew in the twelfth century, unless there was some filiation to hidden sources that were some-how related to the old gnostic tradition" (p. 69). Though it is lamentable that Scholem should take such pains to attribute central kabbalistic concepts either to classical and Christian Neoplatonism or non-Jewish Gnosticism, he does of-ten consider the possibility of hidden Jewish sources, going so far as to suggest that "perhaps, there once existed entire systems of a Jewish character parallel to the classic systems of Gnosticism" (pp. 90–91). In this work I have suggested that the origin of the entire Jewish esoteric tradition, as of non-Jewish Gnosti-cism, is in the inner tradition of the Temple priesthood; and it seems strange that apart from the growing scholarly consensus for such an origin of the Essene cult, the existence of a large body of deprofessionalized priests in Jerusalem after the destruction of the Second Temple should be generally ignored by contem-porary scholars in their search for the origins of Jewish esoteric doctrines, doc-trines we have seen to go back to the historical legend of Elijah and the Throne vision of the prophet-priest Ezekiel and that also inform the priestly liturgy for the prayer services held in the Temple, as attested to in Mishnah Tamid 5:1. For my fuller treatment of the esoteric meaning of the core of the liturgy and its priestly origins, see chapter 4 of *Renewing the Covenant*.

51. Joseph Dan, *Jewish Mysticism*, vol. 2, *The Middle Ages* (Jason Aronson: Northvale, N.J., and Jerusalem, 1998), pp. 31, 33–34, 36, my brackets. In this discussion, Dan has seemed to support the probability of the secret transmission of esoteric traditions, particularly with respect to the Kalonymus family, whose claim to have transported an ancient Eastern esoteric tradition from Italy to Germany in the ninth century has been generally accepted by scholars; and he discusses a ceremony used for such transmission: "This ceremony undoubtedly reflects an old tradition of transmitting secrets from generation to generation, probably practiced by the Kalonymous family" (pp. 27–28). But Dan has also disputed the line of direct continuity Scholem has drawn between Merkabah mysticism and medieval mysticism, indeed, even as in the first volume of this work on late antiquity, seeming to deny as well the significance of the biblical and Enochian sources of the Merkabah texts of talmudic times: "The Jewish European mystics of the High Middle Ages relied on the extant texts of the ancient Jewish mys-tics of Late Antiquity, who flourished in the talmudic period. . . . Yet the mys-tics and esoterics of the High Middle Ages cannot be regarded as a continua-tion of the ancient schools of Jewish mystics. They represent a new beginning, and a void of several centuries, in which mysticism was almost completely ab-sent from Jewish culture, separate them. Jewish mysticism, one may say, has been invented twice—once in Late Antiquity and once in the High Middle Ages" (pp. x–xi). But "inventions" that rely on ancient mystical texts imply some necessary form of textual transmission in ages before there were printed

books and esoteric libraries. These texts had to have been copied and reverently passed down from teacher to disciples through the centuries for them to have survived. We have seen that one source of such transmission, generally accepted by modern scholars, was that of the Kalonymus family. And in the twelfth century, the most prominent writer of this family, Rabbi Eleazar of Worms, in the introduction to his first esoteric work, the *Sefer ha-Chokhmah*, feels it necessary to offer "an apology for the writing of esoteric teachings" (p. 138). Thus their previous oral transmission, in part as interpretations of ancient texts like the *Sefer Yetzirah* that would have been secretly passed down with such oral teachings, is the only reasonable explanation for the reliance of these teachings on ancient texts. But Dan refuses to accept this logic without the historical proof of texts that the esoteric tradition denies were previously written down and that he has admitted may have perished for this reason: "There can be no doubt that many secrets that were regarded as such did not reach us because they were never written down" (p. 28). He is often, therefore, left in a quandary. One example is the appearance of "the term *havayot* . . . in a central place in the works of two esoteric writers in the beginning of the thirteenth century who knew nothing about each other—Rabbi Eleazar of Worms and Rabbi Isaac ben Abraham, 'the Blind,' of Provence. Both of them use it in the context of commentaries on the *Sefer Yezira*. . . . It should be explained by the existence of a common source, but this source . . . cannot be identified" (pp. 142–43). Dan's inability to explain his own evidence in terms of his strict historical methodology should indicate the inadequacy of this construction of historical methodology to explain the often hidden history of Jewish mysticism.

52. Scholem, *Origins*, pp. 97–98.
53. Ibid., p. 213.
54. Ibid., p. 139.
55. See Scholem, *Major Trends*, p. 160.
56. *The Kabbalah Unveiled*, trans. S. L. MacGregor Mathers (London: Kegan Paul, Trench, Trubner, 1926), pp. 173, 227, 246. I would have preferred another translation to this, but since this is the only one available of these most important texts, I thought it better to use it rather than to make a direct translation since it would be more accessible for checking by non-Hebrew scholars. This is the reason I have used published translations throughout where available.
57. Ibid., p. 257.
58. Ibid., p. 256.
59. Ibid., p. 257.
60. Ibid., p. 240.
61. Ibid., pp. 281, 282, 286, 287.
62. Ibid., p. 295.
63. Ibid., p. 338.
64. For a further historical discussion of this understanding of the Holy of Holies, see Raphael Patai, *Man and Temple in Ancient Jewish Myth and Ritual*, 2nd ed. (New York: Ktav, 1967), p. 89.

65. *The Kabbalah Unveiled*, pp. 336, 337.

66. Ibid., p. 339.

67. Ibid., p. 289.

68. *The Zohar*, trans. Harry Sperling, Maurice Simon, & Dr. Paul P. Levertoff, 5 vols. (London, Soncino Press, 1978), vol. 3, pp. 175–76 (2. 56b–57a). Here and throughout, the volume and page references to the Mantua edition appear in parentheses following those to the Soncino edition.

69. Moshe Idel, *The Mystical Experience in Abraham Abulafia*, trans. Jonathan Chipman (Albany, N.Y.: SUNY Press, 1988), pp. 195, 197.

70. Ibid., p. 201.

71. Idel's distinction between what he regards as two conflicting schools of Kabbalah has been more fully developed in his *Kabbalah: New Perspectives* (New Haven: Yale University Press, 1988).

72. For further background information on Luria, see Scholem, *Kabbalah*, pp. 420–28.

73. Chayyim Vital, *Etz Chayyim*. (Tel Aviv: Kitve Rabbeinu ha-Ari, 1959), chap. 1, vol. 1, pp. 2–3. My translation.

74. As quoted in Martin Buber, *The Legend of the Bael-Shem*, trans. Maurice Friedman (New York: Schocken Books, 1969), p. 27.

75. Lewis Jacobs, *Hasidic Prayer* (New York: Schocken Books, 1978), p. 76.

76. Scholem, *Mystical Shape of the Godhead*, pp. 258, 272.

77. Ibid., pp. 254, 266, 269.

78. Ibid., p. 45.

79. Ibid., pp. 48, 51.

80. Ibid., p. 104.

81. Ibid., p. 108.

82. Ibid., pp. 110–11.

83. Ibid., p. 132.

84. For this understanding of the personal God of Israel, see Gershom Scholem, *Sabbatai S'evi: The Mystical Messiah*, trans. R. J. Zwi Werblowsky, Bollingen Series 93 (Princeton: Princeton Univ. Press, 1973), pp. 119–20.

85. The esoteric meaning of the Sh'ma I am about to uncover was rehearsed in an abbreviated form in the section on the prayer service in chapter 4 of *Renewing the Covenant*, pp. 175–81, an earlier discussion that complements the present one by placing the Sh'ma within the larger context of the priestly liturgy, as defined in Mishnah Tamid 5:1, of the full mandated section including the Amidah, and of the complete prayer service, contexts which reinforce the priestly origins of the esoteric implications of this service and the mystical purpose of prayer. See also chapter 2 of *Renewing the Covenant* for further treatment of the Sh'ma, including my musical setting of its first two verses, pp. 62–74.

86. *The Zohar*, 2:216a, as quoted in Kaplan, *Meditation and Kabbalah*, pp. 33–34.

87. *The Zohar*, 3:380–82 (2:133b–134a); 3:385–86 (135a–135b).

88. The attribution of this concept to the *Zohar* certainly involves an interpretative leap on the part of Luria or Vital. There are two references on this Zoharic page that, singly or together, might have provided the seed of this idea. The

first refers to the period between midnight and dawn and to the angelic choir presiding at that time: "Then that 'lad' who sucks from his mother's breasts rises to purify them and enters to minister. That is a time of favour when the Matrona converses with the King, and the King stretches forth [65a] a thread of blessing and winds it round the Matrona and all who are joined with her. These are they that study Torah at night time after midnight" (V, 55). The "lad" here mentioned can refer to Ze'ir Anpin as well as to its clear verbal association with Metatron, and the sequence from the nursing of this "lad" by Imma-Matrona to her sexually understood "conversation" with Abba-King could be taken to refer to a new or second conception of that same "lad," though such a connection is far from being explicitly suggested. Shortly thereafter, cosmic conception is related to three or four stages: "R. Eleazar then asked his father to explain to him the name EHYEH ASHER EHYEH (I am that I am). He said 'This name is all comprehensive.[65b]. . . First came Ehyeh (I shall be), the dark womb of all. Then Asher Ehyeh (That I Am), indicating the readiness of the Mother to beget all. Then, after the creation had commenced, came the name Ehyeh alone (ibid.), as much as to say: Now it will bring forth and prepare all. Finally, when all has been created and fixed in its place the name Ehyeh is abandoned and we have YHVH (Ibid. 15), an individual name signifying confirmation" (V, 56-57). The use of the two different Names to signify Creation, Ehyeh and YHVH, again suggests a sequence of two different orders of that which is created. That signified by YHVH clearly suggests the Partzuf of Ze'ir Anpin associated on the Tree with this "individual" or personal divine Name. And this culminating product of Creation is preceded by the less individualized, preparatory product, signified by Ehyeh, itself dependent on the "readiness of the Mother to beget all." This striking statement of the feminine nature of divine Creation could refer to Lurianic concepts later to be encountered in chapter 7, either the "feminine waters," *mayyim nukvah*, which must be aroused for Yichud to take place, or Imma's first, purely mental, conception of the androgynous Ze'ir Anpin. But it is hard to find in this passage a reference to an intermediate period of nursing between two period of gestation for Ze'ir Anpin in Imma's womb. So this radical concept would seem to have originated with Luria, however willing he was to attribute its source to the *Zohar* or actually felt it to have been inspired by one or both of these passages.

89. Vital, *Etz Chayyim*, chap. 4; vol. 1, p. 8.
90. Kaplan, *The Bahir*, p. 132.

Chapter 3

1. Josephus, *Jewish Antiquities*, 8. 179.
2. See S. K. Heninger, Jr., *Touches of Sweet Harmony: Pythagorean Cosmology and Renaissance Poetics* (San Marino, Calif.: Huntington Library, 1974), pp. 243–44.
3. Gershom Scholem, *On the Kabbalah and Its Symbolism*, trans. Ralph Manheim (New York: Schocken Books, 1969), p. 167. Scholem here dates the *Sefer Yetzirah* as written "some time between the third and sixth century." See also his *Kabbalah*, p. 25.

4. William Butler Yeats, "Among School Children," ll. 45–47.

5. There are three competing systems of nomenclature currently being used to refer to what I am calling the "harmonic series." These are the terms "overtone," "partial," and "harmonic." Overtone is the popular term but, as it clearly cannot be considered to include the fundamental tone, being "over" it, it is no longer used in scholarly discourse on the subject. This is desirable since the numbers that we will see to emerge in the harmonic series, numbers which depend on the fundamental tone being considered as the first in this series, cannot be correlated with the series of overtones. Most scholarly discourse—as in the writings of W. A. Mathieu, Robert Lawlor, Joscelyn Godwin, and Andre VandenBroeck—has adopted the term "partial." But this term is subject to the same objection as pertains to the term "overtone," that the fundamental or whole tone *cannot* be a partial form of this tone. The kind of confusion that can arise in use of the term "partial" can be seen in the following treatment by VandenBroeck, from his book *Philosophical Geometry* (Rochester, Vt.: Inner Traditions, 1987), p. 52: "It is evident that by halving again the string length 1/2 which produces C_2, a tone will be found [C_3] standing in relation to C_2 as C_2 stood to C_1, namely as a second partial if C_2 is considered as fundamental or first partial. . . . C_3 also constitutes the 4th partial of C_1," (my brackets). C_3 can certainly be considered as a "second partial if C_2 is considered as fundamental or first partial," but C_2 cannot be considered the fundamental tone; and so VandenBroeck shortly ends up calling C_3 the "4th partial," which would make the fundamental tone the first partial rather than whole tone. It is for this reason that I have chosen to go against the style of contemporary harmonic theorizing by using the more appropriate term of "harmonic" that *can* denote the first, whole, or fundamental tone of the harmonic series. This was the way I was taught harmonic theory by David Hykes, the foremost practitioner and composer of harmonic music in our time, and to my mind it is the most precise. That I am not alone in using this terminology can be seen in Dane Rudhyar's *The Magic of Tone and the Art of Music* (Boulder, Colo.: Shambhala, 1982), whose table of "harmonics" gives C_1 as the first harmonic (p. 71).

6. For further treatment of these means, see Robert Lawlor, *Sacred Geometry* (New York: Crossroad, 1982), pp. 80–83.

7. Theon of Smyrna, *Mathematics Useful for Understanding Plato*, trans. from the Greek/French ed. of J. Dupuis by Robert and Deborah Lawlor, ed. Christos Toulis, (San Diego: Wizards Bookshelf, 1979), p. 37, n. 7.

8. Robert Lawlor, "Pythagorean Number as Form, Color and Light," *Lindisfarne Letter: 14; Homage to Pythagoras* (West Stockbridge, Mass.: Lindisfarne Press, 1982), pp. 32, 34, 35, 36-37. This whole volume of the *Lindisfarne Letter* is recommended reading for students of Pythagorean thought and can be ordered from the Lindisfarne Press, R. D. 2, West Stockbridge, Mass., 01266.

9. See Simone Weil, "The Pythagorean Doctrine," in *Intimations of Christianity*, trans. Elisabeth Chase Geissbuhler (London: Routledge and Kegan Paul, 1957), p. 162.

10. Scholem, *Major Trends in Jewish Mysticism*, p. 218.

11. *Sefer Yetzirah*, p. 5 (1:1). I have here rendered Kaplan's unpunctuated verse translation in prose form, adding the punctuation that appears on p. 261 in his prose translation of the short form of this text, modifying the capitals to fit this prose form, and adding the bracketed extra word that appears in that latter version.

12. See Kaplan's excellent notes on these Hebrew words, ibid.,pp. 19–21.

13. For the relationship of the Hebrew alphabet to the Moon, and for the later discussion of the Hebrew triliteral roots, I am indebted to a private communication from Robert Zoller, astrologer and author of *Lost Keys to Prediction* (New York: Inner Traditions, 1980).

14. *Sefer Yetzirah*, p. 262, (2:1).

15. Ibid., p. 263 (3:3).

16. Ibid., pp. 266–67 (6:1–2).

17. See Kaplan's full scholarly discussion of the Teli, in *Sefer Yetzirah*, pp. 231–39.

18. Ibid., p. 264 (4:3).

19. The Egyptian language suggests a similar association insofar as the word for counting, *ip*, is similar to the word for the heart, *ib*, and R. A. Schwaller de Lubicz, in *The Temple of Man*, trans. Deborah Lawlor and Robert Lawlor (Rochester, Vt.: Inner Traditions, 1998), 1.403–4, shows that they are connected in "The Edwin Smith Surgical Papyrus." There the doctor, who is a priest of Sekhmet, is instructed in what clearly seems to be the diagnostic technique of taking the pulse. Schwaller explains the reference "'if you examine a man,' this is counting [*ip*] someone." As he shows, "The word *ip* is used in mathematics in the sense of enumerating. . . . The insistence on the word 'counting' leaves no doubt that the doctor must count the pulsations of the injured person to deduce the state of his heart. . . . The heart itself is called *ib*, a synonym of 'dancer,' an image expressing very well the rhythmic movements of this organ." But the activity of counting is attributed here only to the doctor, not to the heart itself. Thus though the Egyptian language may seem to suggest such an association as I am making of number with the heart as the organ of numerical perception, this is not an association that Schwaller has made.

20. The term *anthropocosmos* is fundamental to the Egyptian sacred science that R. A. Schwaller de Lubicz has uncovered and presented with such comprehensiveness in *The Temple of Man*, especially 1.61-71. But such a concept is as central to the Jewish esoteric tradition as to other such ancient traditions, and it can be seen most explicitly in the Merkabah work *Shi'ur Komah*, where "measurement" of this cosmic man is the means prescribed for becoming, in its words, "a son of the world to come."

21. Giorgio de Santillana and Hertha von Dechend, *Hamlet's Mill: An Essay on Myth and the Frame of Time* (Boston: Gambit, 1969), p. 340.

22. Ibid., pp. 231, 233, 235, 239, 240, 241.

23. Ibid., p. 9.

24. *Sefer Yetzirah*, p. 267 (6:4).

25. Sigmund Freud, *The Interpretation of Dreams*, trans. James Strachey (New York: Basic Books, n. d.), pp. 277, 295–96, 4–6, 407.

26. Lawrence E. Marks, *The Unity of the Senses: Interrelations Among the Modalities* (New York: Academic Press, 1978), p. 122.

27. Ibid., pp. 36, 179.

28. Ibid., pp. 13, 175, 255.

29. Ibid., p. 175.

30. Lawlor, p. 32.

31. Boman, *Hebrew Thought*, pp. 207–208.

32. Ferdinand de Saussure, *Course in General Linguistics*, trans. Wade Baskin (New York: Philosophical Library, 1959), pp. 66, 67, 69.

33. Aristotle, "Poetics," *The Basic Works of Aristotle*, ed. Richard McKeon (New York: Random House, 1941), p. 1479 (1459a).

34. Emile Benveniste, "The Nature of the Linguistic Sign," *Problems in General Linguistics*, trans. Mary Elizabeth Meek (Coral Gables, Fla.: University of Miami Press, 1971), p. 45.

35. Julian Jaynes, *The Origin of Consciousness in the Breakdown of the Bicameral Mind* (Boston: Houghton Mifflin, 1976), pp. 49, 51, 52, 60.

36. Paul Ricoeur, *The Rule of Metaphor: Multi-Disciplinary Studies of the Creation of Meaning in Language*, trans. Robert Czerny (Toronto: University of Toronto Press, 1977), p. 22.

37. See the subtitle of Paul Ricoeur's *The Rule of Metaphor*, given above in note 36.

38. Ricoeur, *The Rule of Metaphor*, pp. 207, 209, 211, 212, 213. My brackets.

39. Boman, *Hebrew Thought*, p. 184.

40. Handelman, *Slayers of Moses*, p. 32.

41. Plato, *Cratylus*, in *The Dialogues of Plato*, trans. B. Jowett (Oxford: Clarendon Press, 1953), 3.47, 48.

42. Plato, 3.86, 87, 89.

43. Richard E. Cytowic, *The Man Who Tasted Shapes: A Bizarre Medical Mystery Offers Revolutionary Insights into Emotions, Reasoning, and Consciousness* (New York: Putnam, 1993), pp.76–77, 96, 163, 166, 167, 168, 175. See also the more recent review of the subject of synesthesia and of Dr. Cytowic's theoretical contribution to this field by Erica Goode, in "When People See a Sound and Hear a Color," *New York Times*, 23 February 1999, p. F3.

44. See Hans Jenny, *Cymatics*, 2 vols. (Basil: Basilius Presse, 1974). For further information on Jenny's work, see my discussion of figure 6.1 in chapter 6.

45. Owen Barfield, *Saving the Appearances* (New York: Harcourt Brace Jovanovich, n. d.), pp. 122, 123, 124.

46. The Tantric tradition of India provides a close parallel to this Hebraic understanding, for which see Madhu Khanna, *Yantra: The Tantric Symbol of Cosmic Unity* (London: Thames and Hudson, 1979): "The yantra-mantra complex is basically an equation that unites space (ākāsa), which in its gross form appears as shapes, and vibrations, which in their finite forms occur as the spoken or written word" (p. 34). See also pp. 11, 36, 38, 44.

47. Husserl, *Origin of Geometry*, p. 170.

48. Ibid., p. 171.

49. Carlo Suares, *The Sepher Yetsira*, trans. Micheline & Vincent Stuart (Boulder, Colo.: Shambhala, 1976), p. 39.
50. Ibid., p. 41.
51. From the "Fragments of Philolaus," Diels-Krans 1, 4, 11, 21, in *The Pythagorean Sourcebook and Library*, comp. and trans. by Kenneth Sylvan Guthrie (Grand Rapids, Mich.: Phanes Press, 1987), pp. 168, 171, 174.

Chapter 4

1. For this association of the geometric mean with the concept of divine mediation, I am indebted to Simone Weil's brilliant essay, "The Pythagorean Doctrine." See chap. 3 n. 9.
2. See de Santillana and von Dechend, *Hamlet's Mill*, p. 340.
3. Ibid., p. 59.
4. See John Noble Wilford, "Search for 'Nemesis' Intensifies Debate Over Extinction,"*New York Times*, 18 December 1984, p. C1.
5. *The American Heritage Dictionary of the English Language*, ed. William Morris (New York and Boston: American Heritage Publishing Co. and Houghton Mifflin, 1969), p. 1548.
6. *Sepher Yetsira*, trans. David R. Blumenthal, in his *Understanding Jewish Mysticism: A Source Reader* (New York: Ktav, 1978), p. 23.
7. Ibid., pp. 22–30.
8. See Martin Brennan, *The Stars and the Stones: Ancient Art and Astronomy in Ireland* (London: Thames & Hudson, 1984).
9. *The American Heritage Dictionary*, p. 690.
10. To quote a reference to this theory: "the clay theory proposes that the first duplicating systems had neither nucleic systems nor proteins but, rather, were made of inorganic minerals. This theory has generated one of the sharpest debates in this field, between what some call 'mud versus soup' as the birthplace of life. The idea, proposed by A. Graham Cairns-Smith of Glasgow University, is that clay crystals forming and expanding in a repetitive manner were the first replicating, hence 'genetic,' organisms. Defects in crystal structures are a form of information that could also result, through selection, in the evolution of varieties of those best able to fill available space, such as the interstices of sandstone in which clay often forms. . . . scientists at the NASA-Ames Research Center in Mountain View, Calif., have shown that clays can stimulate chemical reactions and also have the ability to store and transfer solar energy to organic molecules. Dr. Cairns-Smith and others suggest that some nucleic acid precursor associated with a successful clay 'organism' might gradually, as its traits were shaped through natural selection, have taken on more and more of the information and replication duties, eventually supplanting the crystal altogether." Quoted from Erik Eckholm, "Search for the Origin of Life Enters a Dynamic New Phase," *New York Times*, 29 July 1986, p. C4.

11. John Noble Wilford, "Peering Back in Time, Astronomers Glimpse Galaxies Aborning," *New York Times*, 20 October 1998, p. F1.

12. For extensive information on the history of the divine feminine in Hebrew culture and its mystical tradition see Raphael Patai, *The Hebrew Goddess*, 3rd enlarged ed. (Detroit: Wayne State Univ. Press, 1990); and Elliot Wolfson, *The Circle in the Square* (Albany, N.Y.: SUNY Press, 1995).

13. *Shiur Qoma*, trans. The Work of the Chariot, in D. Meltzer, *The Secret Garden*, p. 32.

14. R. A. Schwaller de Lubicz, *Sacred Science: The King of Pharaonic Theocracy*, trans. André and Goldian VandenBroeck (New York: Inner Traditions International, 1982), pp. 214, 217.

15. See ibid., pp. 208–25. Another interesting cross-cultural correspondence can be seen with regard to the Egyptian Nun: "Pharaonic theology speaks of the origin through the Heliopolitan mystery: There is *Nun*, the primordial ocean; within *Nun* there is a fire which acts and produces *Tum*, the first earth or hillock which emerges from *Nun*. This fire is *Nun* itself" (p. 17). Now the Hebrew alphabet also has a letter pronounced *nun* that has been kabbalistically associated with the feminine creative force, most particularly with the Shekhinah and the Sefirah Malkhut with which she is associated. In a work attributed to the first known Kabbalist, Isaac the Blind, there are references to "Diadem, which is the nun" and "the final *H* is a sign for Diadem," the final Hey of the Tetragrammaton, here referred to, also being identified with Malkhut. In his anthology containing this work, the editor Joseph Dan comments: "The letter *nun*, in both its regular and final forms, is linked in classical Kabbalah with the tenth and lowest *sefirah*, Kingdom. For a summary of the kabbalistic associations, see R. Moses Cordovero, *Pardes Rimmonim* (Munkacs, 1906), 26:17." All quotations from *The Early Kabbalah*, ed. Joseph Dan, pp. 82, 84, 86. In addition to the historical evidence for an association between the letter Nun and Malkhut (Kingdom), a logical case may be made for its association with the upper feminine Sefirah of Binah (Understanding) since the Gematria equivalent of the letter Nun is the number fifty, and fifty is a number associated with Binah in the standard kabbalistic reference to the "Fifty Gates of Understanding." It is also from Binah or Imma, the Partzuf form of this Sefirah, that the sea of creation is thought to flow in seven streams to the seven lower Sefirot. Because of the numerical correspondence between the letter Nun and Binah, I would suggest that this was the original basis for the association of this letter with a feminine Sefirah and that it was later transferred to the tenth Sefirah identified with the more central feminine personality of the Shekhinah. As with the earlier association between the Greek Gaia and the Hebrew letter-numbers for 13, discussed in chapter 4, so here there would seem to be an association between the Egyptian Nun and the Hebrew letter-number Nun=50 that also involves the feminine elements in the creation myths of these cultures.

16. *The Ethiopic Book of Enoch*, 2.187, 188, 243–44 (82:2, 4, 5, 6; 105:1–2).

17. This is clearly shown in the commentary of Ogden Goelet, Jr., appearing in *The Egyptian Book of the Dead*, trans. Raymond O. Faulkner (San Francisco: Chronicle Books, 1994), p. 143: ". . . underneath the earth were located the regions of Nun, the primordial waters. . . . The name 'Nun' itself seems to mean something like 'The Watery One.' . . . Every evening the aged sun entered the underworld and travelled through it, immersed in Nun, only to emerge at dawn as Khepri, the newborn sun. Thus, the waters of Nun had a rejuvenating, baptismal quality essential to rebirth. Perhaps the most frequent and important of all the components of the afterworld is the *Duat*, the Underworld, a vast region lying under the earth. . . . this was the realm of Osiris and the place through which Re travelled every night in his journey beneath the earth. . . . It is to some extent connected with the waters of Nun. . . ." Nicolas Grimal, in *A History of Ancient Egypt*, trans. Ian Shaw (Oxford: Blackwell, 1992), p. 127, also shows, in speaking of the "Dwat, the underworld," that the "Dwat was presented as an equivalent of Nun, the first waters from which the creator had evolved." For my further treatment of the Egyptian Nun in relation to the Hebrew letter *nun*, see note 15 above and *Renewing the Covenant*, p. 252n.

18. Linda Schele and David Freidel, *A Forest of Kings: The Untold Story of the Ancient Maya* (New York: William Morrow, 1990), p. 78. See also their full discussion of the Mayan calendar with excellent illustrations, pp. 77–84, on which my analysis is largely based.

19. Theon of Smyrna, *Mathematics Useful for Understanding Plato*, p. 68.

20. Ibid..

21. Ron Schultz, "Interview: Murray Gell-Mann," *Omni* 7 (May 1985): 92.

22. An interesting association can be made between this view of the Mosaic Covenant and the cognitive development of the child as charted by Jean Piaget. For it is at the average age of seven, a number of particular significance with respect to the counting of weeks with which we have been concerned, that the child is shown to move from a subjective perception of the world as undifferentiated from its ego to that objectification of the world as separate from its ego that is correlated with its new capacity for numerical counting. See, for instance, Jean Piaget with Barbel Inhelder and Alina Szeminska, *The Child's Conception of Geometry*, trans. E. A. Lunzer (New York: Basic Books, 1960), pp. 6, 149, passim. See also Joseph Chilton Pearce, *Magical Child Matures* (New York: E.P. Dutton, 1985), pp. 76–78, for an analysis of this Piagetian stage of "concrete operational thinking" that relates it to the myth of separation from the Garden and its attendant psychological dangers. Seen in this context, the Sinai Covenant can be understood to provide exactly the means required to avoid these dangers.

23. As quoted in Kaplan, *Meditation and Kabbalah*, p. 238.

24. The Tetragrammaton expansion Ab = 72 must be distinguished from the Name of seventy-two letters derived from Exod. 14:19–21, three verses with exactly seventy-two letters each of which are formed into seventy-two unpronounceable triplets by taking first the first, then the last, then the first letters of these

words. This Name was associated by Abulafia and others with the complementary Name of forty-two letters, comprised of the first letters of the prayer Ana
Bekhoach, a prayer that, because it is composed of seven lines of six words
each, provided me with the original understanding that the meaning of these
Names was contained in the process of multiplication. I have discussed these
two additional Names in chapter 2 of *Renewing the Covenant*, pp. 57–62, where
they were also coordinated with the Sefirot, the seventy-two-lettered Name
with the same Sefirot of Chokhmah and Binah so associated by Chayyim Vital.

25. See Scholem, *Kabbalah*, p. 130.

26. As quoted in Ben Zion Bokser, *The Jewish Mystical Tradition* (New York: Pilgrim
Press, 1981), pp. 98–99.

27. Ibid., p. 98.

28. For my full treatment of the prayer service, with suggestions of how it may be
effectively performed as well as an extended discussion of its cosmological purpose, see chapter 4 of *Renewing the Covenant*.

29. Barfield, *Saving the Appearances*, p. 124.

30. William Chomsky, *Hebrew: The Eternal Language* (Philadelphia: Jewish Publication Society, 1957), p. 108.

31. Research cited by Marks in *The Unity of the Senses* supports this view of the
affective nature of elemental speech sounds, particularly of the vowels, his further analysis giving added weight to the theory of natural language, at least
with respect to the original linguistic roots, which was advanced in chapter 3:
"Elemental speech sounds, both individually and in combination, sometimes
serve in and by themselves to evoke meanings—as if the sounds that constitute
a word form part of the semantic content. . . . Here may be found the power of
sound *qua* sound, the power to evoke or suggest meanings in ways that are not
arbitrary. . . . Vowel sounds have a peculiarly great potency in arousing visual
images synesthetically. . . . That sounds can generate meanings wholly apart
from what they pick up in the immediate semantic context is supported by a
number of experimental findings that used nonsense material. . . . One way that
sounds symbolize meaning is by means of affect. . . . Pseudoverse containing
'light, open, thin vowels'. . . was consistently judged more serene, playful, deli-
cate and happy than pseudoverse containing 'dark, full rounded vowels' . . .
judged more dignified, exciting, and vigorous. Interestingly, differences among
consonants, and among combinations of consonants, yielded only small varia-
tions in affective responses" [pp. 76, 77, 86, 199].

32. J. Weingreen, *A Practical Grammar for Classical Hebrew* (Oxford: Clarendon
Press, 1939), pp. 6–7. See also E. Kautzsch, *Genenius' Hebrew Grammar*, trans.
A. E. Crowley (Oxford: Clarendon Press, 1910), pp. 35–49; and William R.
Harper, *Elements of Hebrew*, revised by J. M. Powis Smith (Chicago: University
of Chicago Press, 1959), pp. 8–9.

33. *Zohar*, 2:216a, as quoted in Kaplan, *Meditation and Kabbalah*, pp. 33–34.

34. In Chayyim Vital's *Etz Chayyim*, chap. 5; 1:11, this understanding is expressed
as follows: "And know that when reference is sometimes made to the Malkhut

of Abba . . . the meaning is that [of] the glans of the Yesod [and this] is the mystery of circumcision and the uncovering, the Yesod and the glans. This glans we call the Malkhut of Abba." My translation.

35. Jacob Koppel, *Sha'arei Gan Eden* (Jerusalem: Yeshiva Torat Chayyim, 1977), p. 38. My translation.

36. Rudolf Steiner, *The Inner Nature of Music and the Experience of Tone* (Hudson, N.Y.: Anthroposophic Press, 1983), pp. 37–38.

37. William Wordsworth, "Tintern Abbey," ll. 95–96.

Chapter 5

1. For my full development of a simplified method of performing the Sh'ma as an introduction to a kabbalistic meditation, see chapter 2 of *Renewing the Covenant*. See also chapter 4 of that book for my treatment of the Sh'ma in the context of the prayer service.

2. For a full treatment of the prayer service, see chapter 4 of *Renewing the Covenant*.

3. On this "prophetic position," see Kaplan, *Meditation and the Bible*, pp. 70–74.

4. Gershom Scholem, *Kabbalah*, p. 107.

5. For my fuller treatment of Ana Bekhoach in relation to the Name of forty-two letters, see chapter 2 of *Renewing the Covenant*, and for my musical setting and treatment of this prayer in the context of the prayer service, see chapter 4 of that book.

6. In Kaplan's edition and translation of the *Sefer Yetzirah* this appears in his collated main text of chap. 1, v. 13, as follows: "He chose three letters from among the Elementals [in the mystery of the three Mothers Aleph Mem Shin (אמש)] and He set them in His great Name and with them, He sealed six extremities" (p. 80).

7. As those interested in harmonic music might appreciate some further definition of the scales produced by the higher harmonics, I will introduce it here as this information is not readily available. The scale beginning on the seventh harmonic continues with ever diminishing seconds or whole tones, though the intervals surrounding the twelfth harmonic of Sol_3—produced by a flat Fi and sharp Si (or to maintain the *descending* names of the chromatic solfeggio scale, by Say and Lay)—approach the half tone that tradition has defined as the interval between the fifteenth and sixteenth harmonics, that between Ti_1 and Do_5. What might be called the "Septimal Harmonic Scale" concludes with the fourteenth harmonic, Tay_{-2}. Similarly, that which might be called the "Octaval Harmonic Scale" begins at the eighth rather than seventh harmonic and continues past the septimal scale to the major seventh, Ti_1, and the octave, Do_5. Using the rather crude approximations of the chromatic solfeggio scale names, and maintaining a stationary rather than a movable Do, these scales may be charted as follows, the intervals for each tone from the fundamental tone being given in parentheses after the names of these tones, while the constant intervals from harmonic to harmonic are given in the last column, the septimal scale tones are given with their descending solfeggio names, and those of the Octaval scale with their ascending solfeggio names.

Septimal Scale			Octaval Scale			Constant Intervals		
7:	Tay–$_1$	(1.0)	8:	Do$_4$	(1.0)	8/7	=	1.142
8:	Do$_4$	(1.142)	9:	Re$_1$	(1.125)	9/8	=	1.125
9:	Re$_1$	(1.285)	10:	Mi$_2$	(1.25)	10/9	=	1.111
10:	Mi$_2$	(1.42)	11:	Fi–$_1$	(1.375)	11/10	=	1.100
11:	Say–$_1$	(1.57)	12:	Sol$_3$	(1.5)	12/11	=	1.091
12:	Sol$_3$	(1.70)	13:	Si+	(1.625)	13/12	=	1.083
13:	Lay+$_1$	(1.85)	14:	Li–$_2$	(1.75)	14/13	=	1.076
14:	Tay–$_2$	(2.0)	15:	Ti$_1$	(1.875)	15/14	=	1.071
			16:	Do$_5$	(2.0)	16/15	=	1.060

Table of Harmonic Scales

The octaval scale is certainly the more familiar, having a recognizable Do, Re, Mi, Sol, Ti, and Do, and it may be sung like the regular minor scale, ascending with the major seventh (Ti) and descending with the minor seventh (Tay or Li) so as to maintain the eight tones of the normal scale despite its unusual nine harmonics.

8. *Īśa Upaniṣad*, in *A Source Book in Indian Philosophy*, ed. Sarvepalli Radhakrishnan and Charles A. Moore (Princeton: Princeton University Press, 1973), pp. 39–41.

9. *The Bhagavad Gita*, trans. Antonio T. de Nicolas, in his *Avatara: The Humanization of Philosophy Through the Bhagavad Gita* (New York: Nicolas-Hays, 1976), pp. 129–35.

10. For further background on Īśa and devotional Hindu religion, see the various introductions in Radhakrishnan and Moore, *A Source Book*, particularly to the two works cited above. For a lucid treatment of this devotional strand in Hindu religion, see also Santosh Kumari N. Desai, "Our Understanding of Hindu Religion," *Explorations* 6 (Winter 1987–88), 53–68. I am greatly indebted to my colleague Dr. Desai for her help in directing me to the major references to Īśa in the Hindu tradition and especially for providing me with the definitions in the Sanskrit dictionary.

11. *Principal Shivaram Apte's Sanskrit-English Dictionary*, ed. P. K. Gode and C. G. Karve (Poona, India: Prasad Prakashan, 1957), 1:393.

12. *Sanskrit-English Dictionary*, 1:393. This quotation has been somewhat abbreviated in form.

13. J. H. Hertz, *The Pentateuch and Haftorahs*, 2nd ed. (London: Soncino Press, 1972), p. 13.

14. I employed a similar technique in my extended study of the Hebrew word *vehayah* in the appendix to *Renewing the Covenant*. Translated in the King James Version as "and it shall come to pass," I show it rather to be consistently used as a biblical power word, a use that culminates in levels of spiritual mastery similar to what will be seen to be the highest uses of the word *ish*. Both verbal studies, plus that on the *shofar*, the ram's horn, in chapter 1 of that book, pp. 10–19, provide special means of access to the deeper levels of biblical meaning deriving from such linguistic usage and reflective of its spiritual culture.

15. Ibid., p. 26.

Chapter 6

1. John Michell, *City of Revelation* (New York: David McKay, 1972), pp. 23, 25.
2. Thorleif Boman, *Hebrew Thought Compared with Greek* (Philadelphia: The Westminster Press, 1960), pp. 200, 201, 202, 204, 205.
3. Susan A. Handelman, *The Slayers of Moses: The Emergence of Rabbinic Interpretation in Modern Literary Theory* (Albany: State University of New York Press, 1982), p. 21.
4. E. D. Hirsch, Jr., *Validity in Interpretation* (New Haven: Yale University Press, 1967), pp. 170, 204, 205.
5. Max Black, *Models and Metaphors: Studies in Language and Philosophy* (Ithaca, N.Y.: Cornell University Press, 1962), pp. 219, 238.
6. Ibid., pp. 222, 229.
7. Ibid., pp. 233, 237.
8. Ibid., p. 238.
9. Edmund Husserl, *The Origin of Geometry*, appendix to Jacques Derrida, *Edmond Husserl's Origin of Geometry: An Introduction*, trans. with preface by John P. Leavey, Jr. (Stony Brook, N.Y.: Nicolas-Hays, 1978), p. 171.
10. Handelman, *The Slayers of Moses*, p. 56.
11. Michell, *City of Revelation*, p. 55.
12. See Scholem, *Kabbalah*, pp. 362–68, and his article "Magen David" in *Encyclopaedia Judaica* (New York: Macmillan, 1971), vol. II, pp. 68–97.
13. See Scholem, *Kabbalah*, p. 363.
14. Gershom Scholem, "The Star of David: History of a Symbol," *The Messianic Idea in Judaism and Other Essays on Jewish Spirituality* (New York: Schocken Books, 1978), pp. 259, 264, 266, 271.
15. Raphael Patai, *The Jewish Alchemists* (Princeton: Princeton University Press, 1995), p. 60.
16. Ibid., pp. 66, 67, 68, 69.
17. Ibid., p. 66.
18. Ibid., p. 140.
19. Ibid., p. 127.
20. Ibid., p. 28. See also Scholem, "The Star of David," p. 271.
21. Ibid., pp. 323, 324.
22. Scholem, *Kabbalah*, pp. 27–28.

23. See Kaplan, *Sefer Yetzirah*, pp. xvi–xix.
24. In the poem entitled "A Valediction Forbidding Mourning."
25. *Zohar*, 1:13, (1:3b Mantua text).
26. In Meltzer, *The Secret Garden*, p. 4.
27. *Zohar*, 1:13 (1:3b).
28. Ibid., 1:63 (1:15a).
29. Jenny, *Cymatics*, 2:96, 100.
30. Robert Lawlor, "Ancient Temple Architecture," *Lindisfarne Letter 10: Geometry and Architecture* (W. Stockbridge, Mass.: Lindisfarne Press, 1980), p. 43.
31. In private correspondence, Stanley Krippner, who has done much research in shamanism, replied as follows to my query concerning a hexagram model for the shamanic worlds: "there is abundant evidence linking the *Fire* to the top of the vertical axis and *Water* to the bottom." For additional sources, see Michael Harner, *The Way of the Shaman* (Toronto: Bantam Books, 1982), pp. 3, 13, 30, 45-46, 49-50 (associations of water with the Lower World); Mircea Eliade, *Shamanism*, trans. Willard R. Trask, Bollingen Series 76 (Princeton: Princeton University Press, 1964), pp. 5, 205, 335, 363 (associations of fire with the Upper World), pp. 266–68 (associations of mountains with the Upper World), and 39 (association of water with the Lower World); and Joan Halifax, *Shaman: The Wounded Healer* (New York: Crossroads/Continuum, 1982), pp. 84, 93 (associations of mountains with the Upper World).
32. The hexagram basis for characterizing the directional orientations of the two forms of "higher" consciousness identified in this Genesis context with the fifth and sixth "days" will be further corroborated by the different geometric modeling presented in my forthcoming two-volume work, *The Star and the Tree*.
33. *Zohar*, 1:127 (34a).
34. In Eruvin 18a and Berakhot 61a, the Talmud resolves the contradictions between the creation accounts in Genesis 1 and 2 through the understanding that the first refers to the creation "in thought" while the second refers to the creation "in deed." This understanding is reflected in various other talmudic and later sources, for which see Aryeh Kaplan's essay on the age of the universe, in his *Immortality, Resurrection and the Age of the Universe: A Kabbalistic View* (New York: Ktav, 1993), and Luria's treatment of the double conception of Ze'ir Anpin in chapter 7.
35. See Mathers, *The Kabbalah Unveiled*, chapter 28, *Idra Rabba*, p. 180.
36. Particularly in the Lurianic system presented in the sixteenth-century *Etz Chayyim* of Chayyim Vital, the Genesis story of Adam is understood to occur in the spiritual realm of Yetzirah and to be the precipitating cause of the final manifestation of the fourth material world of Assiyah, our world, an understanding that complements Luria's cosmological concept of the Shevirah, the shattering of the orignal Sefirot. In the alternative cosmology of the *shemitot* presented in the fourteenth-century *Temunah*, the myth of Eden is similarly placed in the prior cosmic *shemitah* of Chesed, while our present condition is located in the *shemitah* of the next lower Sefirah, that of Gevurah. In both cases the metaphor of the Fall would seem to be the most apt description for the catastrophic cosmic descent that the Jewish esoteric tradition, in concert with Christian theology, has

attributed to the events in the Garden of Eden recounted in Genesis.

37. *Zohar*, 1:6 (1:1b–2a).

38. Ibid., 1:20–21 (1:5a).

Chapter 7

1. A. E. Waite, *The Holy Kabbalah* (New Hyde Park, N.Y.: University Books, 1969), p. 383.

2. Kaplan, *Sefer Yetzirah*, pp. 261–62. All chapter and verse references will be given in the text and are from the "Shorter Version" of the *Sefer Yetzirah* appearing on pp. 261–67. In the single case of 1:13, the bracketed phrase I have inserted is from the Lurianic-Gra version, found on p. 80 of this edition. Use of the Shorter Version is particularly pertinent in this chapter because its imperative mode makes possible the meditative use of this text that is here being developed. I am most pleased that the long delayed publication of this Kaplan edition has enabled me to incorporate into my text the version used in my personal study of the text with Kaplan that gave me my initial deep knowledge of this seminal kabbalistic text.

3. Ibid. pp. 261.

4. Ibid., p. 262.

5. For my earlier treatment of the meditative technique I have decoded in the *Sefer Yetzirah* in the context of a full treatment of kabbalistic meditation, see chapter 2 of *Renewing the Covenant*.

6. Ibid., p. 265.

7. *The Bahir*, trans. and commentary by Aryeh Kaplan (New York: Samuel Weiser, 1979), p. 34 (v. 95).

8. See, for instance, Kaplan, *Sefer Yetzirah*, p. 203: "These correspond to the twelve edges of a cube."

9. *Zohar*, 1:13, (1:3b Mantua text).

10. *Book of Formation (Sefer Yetzirah): The Letters of our Father Abraham* (Hollywood, Calif.: Work of the Chariot, 1971). This interesting volume can be ordered from P.O. Box 2226, Hollywood, Calif. 90028.

11. Vital, *Etz Chayyim*, chap. 1, vol. 1, p. 2. My translation.

12. Ibid., chap. 2, vol. 1, pp. 3–4.

13. Ibid., chap. 1, vol. 1, p. 3.

14. Ibid., chap. 4, vol. 1, p. 8.

15. Ibid., chap. 2, vol. 1, p. 5.

16. Ibid., chap. 4, vol. 1, p. 8.

17. Ibid., chap. 4, vol. 1, p. 9.

18. Ibid., chap. 11, vol. 1, p. 16.

19. Ibid., chap. 2, vol. 1, pp. 3–4.

20. Ibid., chap. 4, vol. 1, p. 8.

21. The cross-sexual relationship of the children to the parental Partzufim, so similar to Sophocles' classic treatment of his charcters Oedipus and Electra, can

receive further support from the completely different correspondence of the Partzufim with the Hebrew vowels discussed in chapter 4.

22. *Etz Chayyim*, chap. 4, vol. 1, p. 9.
23. Ibid., chap. 2, vol. 1, p. 5.
24. Ibid., chap. 7, vol. 1, p. 13.
25. Mathers, *The Kabbalah Unveiled*, p. 227.
26. Jalandris (Joseph Jochmans), *Earthfire 1: Exploring the Energies of the Ancients* (San Francisco: n. p., 1981), pp. 23–27. See also David D. Zink, *The Ancient Stones Speak* (New York: E. P. Dutton, 1979).
27. *Etz Chayyim*, chap. 7, vol. 1, p. 13.
28. See David Bohm, *Wholeness and the Implicate Order* (London: Ark Paperbacks/ Routledge and Kegan Paul, 1983), pp. 172f.

Chapter 8

1. *Zohar*, 1:65 (1:15b); 1:130 (1:34b);1:147 (1:47a).
2. Vital, *Etz Chayyim*, chap. 9, vol. 1, p. 13. My translation.
3. Ibid., chap. 2, vol. 1, p. 4 and chap. 3, vol. 1, p. 6.
4. For Luria's development of this concept of the cosmological exile of the Shekhinah, see Scholem, *Major Trends in Jewish Mysticism*, pp. 250, 275, 286.
5. *Sefer Yetzirah*, p. 261 (5:1).
6. The tripling progression for the *Sefer Yetzirah* Tree can be demonstrated in the following table if the cubic edge can be identified with the point hexagon of a tonally named hexagram and the diagonal of such a cube with a line of this hexagram, this table also giving the measurement in inches of all the hexagrams that can be projected through to the octave:

TONE	SIDE	DIAGONAL	SIDE	DIAGONAL
Do	1	$\sqrt{3}$		
Di			2/3	2
Re	$\sqrt{3}$	3		
Ri			2	$2\sqrt{3}$
Mi	3	$3\sqrt{3}$		
Fa			$2\sqrt{3}$	6
Fi	$3\sqrt{3}$	9		
Sol			6	$6\sqrt{3}$
Si	9	$9\sqrt{3}$		

TONE	SIDE	DIAGONAL	SIDE	DIAGONAL
La			6√3	18
Li	9√3	27		
Ti			18	18√3
Do	27	27√3		
Di			18√3	54

TABLE OF CONSTRUCTION-ELEMENT LENGTHS

As can be seen, in this table the basic proportion deriving from expansion through the whole-step or double-point progression is 1:√3::√3:3 rather than that which in a three-dimensional cubic construction would lead to the proportion 1:√2::√2:2. This tripling proportion is also true of the double-point progression that for convenience can be considered to be built upon the initial single-point construction of the half step of Ri, whose point-hexagon length is 2. Now if the interpretation of the *Sefer Yetzirah* Tree was correct in identifying the whole-step progression beginning with 1 with the cube-octahedra, and the half-step progression beginning with 2 with the dodeca-icosahedra, then there is clearly no way of getting from 1 to 2, for these not only belong to different continuous proportions but signify different solids.

7. See Theon of Smyrna, *Mathematics Useful for Understanding Plato*, pp. 1–2. For a good history of the duplication problem, see also Howard Eves, *An Introduction to the History of Mathematics*, 5th ed. (New York: CBS College Publishing, 1983), pp. 79–80, 91–94.

8. For the 10-cubit, or 15-foot, size of this cube's dimensions, see Aryeh Kaplan, ed. and trans., *The Living Torah* (New York: Maznaim, 1981), p. 233n.

9. What is interesting in this regard is the contrast provided between the kabbalistic suppression of the full ascending triangle of the underlying hexagram and the Pythagorean suppression of the descending triangle in its great Tetractys symbol. As shown in chapter 3, the Tetractys is composed of ten points forming an ascending equilateral triangle in descending levels of one, two, three, and four points. But if the Tetractys is perceived as composed of three sides of four points each with one point in the center, then it should be clear that the only way the two midpoints on these sides can be determined by geometric means, as opposed to arithmetic measurement, is through construction of its suppressed inverse aspect, the missing triangle of the hexagram whose invisible presence is betrayed by the six points at which it intersects the visible Tetractys triangle. Although it was earlier argued that the cosmology of the Jewish esoteric tradition is associated with a larger esoteric tradition that, in part, had its roots in Pythagorean geometry, this symbolic difference suggests a greater difference of

spirit between the Jewish form of this tradition and its Gentile counterparts. For in the basic forms of Neoplatonic philosophy derived from Pythagorean thought, the spiritual movement is primarily away from the world and toward the One, whereas Jewish mysticism remains firmly rooted to this world; its visionaries always return to community.

10. Cordovero, *Pardes Rimmonim*, ed. Shapiro, 7:32a–b, p. 316. My translation.

11. An analogue to this mystery of generation would also seem to be encoded in the three elements of Plato's creation myth in the *Timaeus*: Sameness, Difference, and Existence. Though these three elements are normally understood to be equal constituents of the world soul, Plato's numerological associations of Sameness with the feminine and Difference with the masculine suggests what is always mythologically true of the union of feminine and masculine entities, the generation of new life, and the third element of Existence should thus be understood not as either an equal counterpart or the source of Sameness and Difference but as their product. For similar interpretations of the relationship of these three Platonic entities, see A. E. Taylor, *The Mind of Plato* (Ann Arbor: University of Michigan Press, 1960, orig. pub. 1922): "The 'soul' of the world is constructed from three elements, Sameness, Otherness, and an entity which is described as produced by a preliminary union of the first two" (p. 139); and John Michell, *City of Revelation*, who refers to "the hierogamous union described by Plato as the fusion of the Same and the Other" (p. 91).

It is Plato's harmonic numerology that forms the basis of such an interpretation of cosmic generation. As shown by Ernest G. McClain, *The Myth of Invariance* (New York: Nicolas-Hays, 1976): "*even* numbers which *define* the octave matrix are 'female,' *odd* numbers which *fill* that matrix with 'tone-children' 'are male'" (p. 4). The association of the harmonic even numbers with Sameness and of the harmonic odd numbers with Difference arises from the fact, which was fully developed in chapter 3, that each new tone is defined by a unique odd number while the even numbers represent the infinitely extended octave resonances of those original tones. Thus the fundamental Do tone is the first harmonic while its octave resonances are the second, fourth, eighth, sixteenth, etc., harmonics. Similarly the next odd number, three, defines the Sol tone while its octave resonances are the even sixth, twelfth, twenty-fourth, etc., harmonics.

There is a difference, however, between the Platonic and kabbalistic gender associations of the even and odd numbers, particularly those of the numbers two and three. In the Pythagorean-Platonic tradition, the infinite extension of the harmonic even numbers is associated with the feminine and the finite particularity of the harmonic odd numbers with the masculine while the reverse is true of the kabbalistic Tree, the second Sefirah Chokhmah being identified with the paternal Partzuf Abba and the third Sefirah Binah with the maternal Partzuf Imma. This kabbalistic association of the principle of Sameness with the masculine Abba and of Difference with the feminine Imma can be further supported by the Tetragrammaton correlations with the Partzufim, Abba being represented by the *same* letter Yod as that of the source Partzuf Arikh Anpin and Imma by the *different* letter Hey, and it is an essential element of the traditional view of the Tree, the right column of Abba being identified with the expansive, right-brained qualities normally ascribed to the feminine and the left column of Imma with the contractive, left-brained qualities normally ascribed to the masculine. This represents a kabbalistic inversion of gender associations, which attributes the more mystical qualities to the male and the more concretizing qualities to the female. There is a final association of the Platonic and Hebraic traditions that can be made if Sameness can be related to that which is similar to its source, Difference to that which is different from it, and Existence to that which follows from these prior two conditions. This is the creation account in Genesis in which the light of the first day can be considered a direct emanation from the source, and so the same as it, the firmament of the second day that which puts difference between the source and the creation, and the life generated on the third day their existential product.

12. *The Bahir*, pp. 11–12.
13. See ibid.,144, 145, 168; pp. 53, 64.
14. I am personally indebted for this reference to Aryeh Kaplan.

Chapter 9

1. For further information on general systems theory, see Ludwig von Bertalanffy, "The History and Status of General Systems Theory," in *Trends in General Systems Theory*, ed. George J. Kirr (New York: Wiley-Interscience, 1972); Paul A. Weiss, *The Science of Life* (Mt. Kisco, N. Y.: Futura, 1973); Ervin Laszlo, *The Systems View of the World* (New York: George Braziller, 1972); and Erich Jantsch, *The Self-Organizing Universe* (Oxford: Pergamon Press, 1980).
2. Fritjof Capra, *The Tao of Physics* (Boulder: Shambhala, 1975), p. 255.
3. See Bohm, *Wholeness and the Implicate Order*, pp. 140–213.
4. Heinz R. Pagels, *The Cosmic Code: Quantum Physics as the Language of Nature* (Toronto: Bantam Books, 1983), pp. 213, 214.
5. Sir James Jeans, *Physics and Philosophy* (New York: Dover Publications, 1981, orig. pub. 1943), p. 172.
6. Paul Davies, *Superforce: The Search for a Grand Unified Theory of Nature* (New York: Simon & Schuster, 1985), pp. 144, 145.
7. As quoted in Pagels, *Cosmic Code*, p. 239.
8. I should note that this same counterpoint of three with two is also a distinguishing characteristic in the Kabbalah between the three upper and two lower Partzufim, as discussed in chapter 7, and so indicates another correlation between sacred and secular science.
9. A problem of charge differential develops, however, between the separated proton and neutron fields, whether in their own geometric space or in the vacuum, that needs to be addressed. If we can accept the charge constraints that must be operative in the nucleus, then we can say that real particles cannot be electrically neutralized either by virtual particles or by those of antimatter; for if this were possible, all the protons would be neutralized either by the virtual negative pions or the negatively charged antiprotons, and the nucleus would not

have the positive charge necessary to attract or be coupled with the negatively charged electrons. Extending these constraints to the separate baryon fields means that the virtual pions can either neutralize each other or the virtual baryons and antibaryons. To reach the resultant charge attributed to such fields, neutral for the neutron field and positive for the proton field, we would have to add the special qualification that the electrical mate of choice for a virtual pion would be an oppositely charged virtual baryon or antibaryon, namely, a proton or antiproton, and that only in the absence of such a mate will it couple with an oppositely charged virtual pion. Thus within the proton macrohexagons of either field, the protons will be neutralized by the negative pions and the antiprotons by the positive pions, while within the neutron macrohexagons of either field the negative and positive pions will neutralize each other. In this way both fields beyond the central macrohexagons will become neutral. The difference in charge between these fields is a product, then, only of the central macrohexagons in which is situated the one real particle of the field. In the case of the central neutron macrohexagon there is no difference from the rest of the field since the virtual pions simply neutralize each other. But the case of the central proton macrohexagon is different since, unlike the surrounding virtual proton macrohexagons, this contains a real proton that cannot be neutralized by a virtual pion. Thus in the central proton macrohexagram, the negative pions will be neutralized by the positive pions and what will be left are one positively charged real proton and two positively charged virtual protons, the immediate field of the proton reinforcing its own real positive charge.

The best solution to the problem of the charge of these virtual quantum fields would seem to be the one just offered. But if the special qualification with respect to the preferred electrical coupling of the virtual pions is not enforced, then both fields will develop powerful, though still virtual, positive charges. Such a result, though unlikely, is interesting since it might explain another difference between protons and neutrons when taken artificially out of the nucleus, as in particle accelerators or in these matrix models of the baryon fields. This is the difference that protons have thus far proved to be stable while neutrons "decay" into a proton and two other particles, an electron and an antineutrino, which may be a product of the electroweak force thought to be responsible for such neutron decay. But the theory does not explain how the weak force can change a down quark into an up quark, thus transmuting a neutron into a proton. If we grant, however, that both the proton and neutron virtual fields have virtual positive charges, then this very fact would help to explain the charge stability of the proton and the charge instability of the neutron. If sufficient energy were added to the neutron field as could transmute a virtual positive pion into a real positive pion, then an exchange of quarks could be postulated between them that could leave a proton and a neutral pion as the particle product of a sufficiently powerful collision between the original neutron and the energized positive pion of its field, this in addition to the lepton particles that may be explained as a by-product of the electroweak energy used to energize the virtual field. An experimental confirmation of the presence of a positive pion transformed into a negative pion during the process of neutron decay would support the second interpretation of the mechanism of charged pion neutralization in the virtual baryon fields. But a lack of such confirmation would not discredit the matrix modeling, only this second interpretation, and it would thus permit only the first interpretation here offered and preferred because of its consistency with the accepted charges of the baryon fields.

10. Jeans, *Physics and Philosophy*, p. 163.
11. Pagels, *Cosmic Code*, pp. 62, 63.
12. Jeans, *Physics and Philosophy*, p. 169.
13. Davies, *Superforce*, pp. 108, 109.
14. Georg Cantor, *Gesammelte Abhandlungen*, as quoted in Rudy Rucker, *Infinity and the Mind: The Science and Philosophy of the Infinite* (Toronto: Bantam Books, 1983), p. 10.
15. Jeans, *Physics and Philosophy*, pp. 178, 179.
16. Ibid., p. 166.
17. Ibid., p. 170.
18. *Sefer Yetzirah*, p. 265.
19. James Gleick, "Rethinking Clumps and Voids in the Universe," *New York Times*, 9 November 1986, pp. A1, 40.
20. John Noble Wilford, "Galactic Evenness Gives Astronomers Pause," *New York Times*, 25 February 1990, p. A25.
21. David Finkelstein, "Beneath Time: Explorations in Quantum Topology," unpublished paper based on a lecture to the International Society for the Study of Time III, Alpbach, Austria, July, 1976, pp. 4–5. For further treatment of Finkelstein's contribution, see Gary Zukov, *The Dancing Wu Li Masters: An Overview of the New Physics* (New York: William Morrow, 1979), pp. 270–96.
22. Finkelstein, "Beneath Time," p. 4.
23. For this interpretation of the vow of the Pythagorean initiate to keep the incommensurability of the diagonal an "unutterable" secret, see Simone Weil, "The Pythagorean Doctrine," p. 162.
24. See Jeans, *Physics and Philosophy*, pp. 176–217.
25. See *Sefer Yetzirah*, 1.5, p. 261, and also Kaplan's commentary on this same page and my extended analysis of this quoted verse in chapter 10.

Chapter 10

1. Pagels, *Cosmic Code*, p. 280.
2. Ibid., pp. 283, 284.
3. Ibid., pp. 243, 259–60.
4. Scholem, *Kabbalah*, p. 130.
5. Ibid., p. 130.
6. Ibid.
7. Ibid.
8. Steven Weinberg, *The First Three Minutes: A Modern View of the Origin of the Universe* (New York: Basic Books, 1977), p. 76.

9. Ibid., p. 76.

10. Ibid., p. 64.

11. Ibid., p. 131.

12. Ibid., p. 56.

13. Pagels, *Cosmic Code*, p. 276.

14. Vital, *Etz Chayyim*, 11b, as quoted in David S. Ariel, *The Mystic Quest: An Introduction to Jewish Mysticism* (New York: Schocken Books, 1988), pp. 165, 167, 168.

15. Pagels, *Cosmic Code*, p. 284.

16. Weinberg, *First Three Minutes*, pp. 31–32.

17. Ibid., p. 32.

18. Ibid., pp. 36–37.

19. For Sholem's final acceptance of this late dating, see his *Origins of the Kabbalah*, pp. xiv, 460–61n.

20. See note 32 in chapter 6.

21. For further information on the *shemitot*, see Scholem, *Kabbalah*, pp. 120–22, 336.

22. *Sefer Yetzirah*, p. 261. See also Kaplan's illuminating commentary on this verse, p. 44.

23. For his original definition of the term "synchronicity," see C. G. Jung, "Foreword," *The I Ching*, trans. Richard Wilhelm/Cary F. Baynes, Bollingen Series 19 (Princeton: Princeton University Press, 1978), p. xxiv.

24. Davies, *Superforce*, pp. 160, 164-65, 237.

25. Pagels, *Cosmic Code*, p. 257.

26. As quoted in Michael Talbot, *Mysticism and the New Physics* (New York: Bantam Books, 1981), p. 77.

27. Davies, *Superforce*, p. 133.

28. As quoted in Pagels, *Cosmic Code*, p. 239.

29. Ibid., p. 161.

30. Ibid., p. 270.

31. Ibid., p. 273.

32. See ibid., pp. 202, 209, 220.

33. For a full treatment of this power of life in the context of information theory, see Jeremy Campbell, *Grammatical Man* (New York: Simon and Schuster, 1982).

34. For the full modeling of this Sabbatical cosmos by the Sabbath Star Diagram, see my forthcoming *The Star and the Tree*.

35. Pagels, *Cosmic Code*, p. 287.

36. For a similar view of the vitality implicit in matter, see Pierre Teilhard de Chardin, *The Phenomenon of Man* (New York: Harper & Row, 1975), pp. 54-9.

37. As quoted in Pagels, *Cosmic Code*, p. 137.

38. For my full analysis of this association of the Lurianic *Reshimu* with the residual background radiation and its implications for the constituents of the higher soul bodies generated through prayer, see the section entitled, "The Heart of the Matter," in chapter 4 of my book *Renewing the Covenant*, pp. 184–99.

39. Weinberg, *First Three Minutes*, p. 155.

40. Albert Einstein, *Cosmic Religion and other Opinions and Aphorisms* (New York: Covici, Friede, 1931), p. 98.

Bibliography

Primary Sources:

Aristotle. "Poetics," *The Basic Works of Aristotle*, ed. Richard McKeon. New York: Random House. 1941.

Bahir, The. Ed. and trans. Aryeh Kaplan. New York: Samuel Weiser, 1979.

Bhagavad Gita, The. Trans. Antonio T. de Nicolas, in his *Avatara: The Humanization of Philosophy Through the Bhagavad Gita*. New York: Nicolas-Hays, 1976.

Complete Dead Sea Scrolls in English, The. Ed. and trans. Geza Vermes. New York: Penguin Putnam, 1997.

Cordovero, Moses. *Pardes Rimmonim*, ed. Yisrael Yehudah Shapiro. Jerusalem: Rabbi Atiah, 1969. Hebrew.

Dead Sea Scrolls, The. Ed. and trans. Millar Burrows. New York: Viking Press, 1956.

Egyptian Book of the Dead, The. Trans. Raymond O. Faulkner, commentary Ogden Goelet, Jr. San Francisco: Chronicle Books, 1994.

Enoch, The Book of or 1 Enoch. Ed. and trans. R. H. Charles. Oxford: Clarendon Press, 1912.

Enoch, The Ethiopic Book of. Ed. and trans. Michael A. Knibb. Oxford: Clarendon Press, 1978.

Enoch, 3 or The Hebrew Book of Enoch. Ed. and trans. Hugo Odeberg. New York: Ktav Pub., 1973, orig. pub. 1928.

"Īśa Upanisad," *A Source Book in Indian Philosophy*. Ed. and trans. Sarvepalli Radhakrishnan and Charles A. Moore. Princeton: Princeton University Press, 1973.

Josephus, *Jewish Antiquites*. Trans. Ralph Marcus. 9 vols. Loeb Classical Library. Cambridge: Harvard University Press, 1963.

Kabbalah Unveiled, The. Trans. S. L. MacGregor Mathers. London: Kegan Paul, Trench, Trubner, 1926.

Koppel, Jacob. *Sha'arei Gan Eden*. Jerusalem: Yeshiva Torat Chayyim, 1977. Hebrew.

Philolaus. "Fragments of Philolaus," *The Pythagorean Sourcebook and Library*. Ed. and trans. Kenneth Sylvan Guthrie. Grand Rapids, Mich.: Phanes Press, 1987.

Plato. "Cratylus," *The Dialogues of Plato*. Trans. B. Jowett. Oxford: Clarendon Press, 1953.

Sefer Yetzirah: The Book of Creation in Theory and Practice. Ed. and trans. Aryeh Kaplan. York Beach, Maine: Samuel Weiser, 1990.

Sefer Yetzirah, Book of Formation: The Letters of our Father Abraham. Trans. The Work of the Chariot. Hollywood, Ca.: The Work of the Chariot, 1971.

Sepher Yetsira. In *Understanding Jewish Mysticism: A Source Reader*. Ed. and trans. David R. Blumenthal. New York: Ktav, 1978.

Shi'ur Qomah: Liturgy and Theurgy in Pre-Kabbalistic Jewish Mysticism. Ed. and trans. Martin Samuel Cohen. Lanham, Md.: University Press of America, 1983.

Shiur Qoma. Trans. The Work of the Chariot. In *The Secret Garden: An Anthology in the Kabbalah*, ed. David Meltzer. New York: Seabury Press, 1976.

Siddur Tillat Hashem. Ed. and trans. Nissen Mangel. Brooklyn: Merkos L'Inyonei Chinoch, 1982.

Theon of Smyrna. *Mathematics Useful for Understanding Plato*. Trans. from the Greek/French ed. of J. Dupuis by Robert and Deborah Lawlor, ed. Christos Toulis. San Diego: Wizards Bookshelf, 1979.

Torah, The Living: A New Translation Based on Traditional Jewish Sources. Ed. and trans. Aryeh Kaplan. New York: Maznaim, 1981.

Vital, Chayyim. *Etz Chayyim*. Tel Aviv: Kitve Rabbeinu ha-Ari, 1959. Hebrew.

Zohar, The. Trans. Harry Sperling, Maurice Simon, & Dr. Paul P. Levertoff. 5 vols. London: Soncino Press, 1978.

Secondary Sources:

American Heritage Dictionary of the English Language, The. Ed. William Morris. New York and Boston: American Heritage Publishing Co. and Houghton Mifflin, 1969.

Barfield, Owen. *Saving the Appearances*. New York: Harcourt Brace Jovanovich, n.d.

Benveniste, Emile. "The Nature of the Linguistic Sign," *Problems in General Linguistics*. Trans. Mary Elizabeth Meek. Coral Gables, Fla.: University of Miami Press, 1971.

Bertalanffy, Ludwig von. "The History and Status of General Systems Theory." *Trends in General Systems Theory*, ed. George J. Kirr. New York: Wiley-Interscience, 1972.

Birnbaum, Philip, ed. and trans. *Prayer Book for Sabbaths and Festivals*. New York: Hebrew Publishing Company, 1978.

Black, Max. *Models and Metaphors: Studies in Language and Philosophy*. Ithaca: Cornell University Press, 1962.

Blau, Joseph Leon. *The Christian Interpretation of the Cabala in the Renaissance*. Port Washington, N.Y.: Kennikat Press, 1965; orig. pub. 1944.

Boccaccini, Gabriele. *The Parting of the Ways between Qumran and Enochic Judaism*. Grand Rapids, Mich.: Wm. B. Eerdmans, 1998.

Bohm, David. *Wholeness and the Implicate Order*. London: Ark Paperbacks/ Routledge and Kegan Paul, 1983.

Bokser, Ben Zion. *The Jewish Mystical Tradition*. New York: Pilgrim Press, 1981.

Boman, Thorlief. *Hebrew Thought Compared with Greek*. Philadelphia: Westminster Press, 1960.

Brennan, Martin. *The Stars and the Stones: Ancient Art and Astronomy in Ireland*. London: Thames & Hudson, 1984.

Buber, Martin. *I and Thou*. Trans. Ronald Gregor Smith. New York: Charles Scribner's Sons, 1953.

———. *The Legend of the Bael-Shem*. Trans. Maurice Friedman. New York: Schocken Books, 1969.

Campbell, Jeremy. *Grammatical Man: Information, Entropy, Language, and Life*. New York: Simon & Schuster, 1982.

Capra, Fritjof. *The Tao of Physics*. Boulder, Colo.: Shambhala, 1975.

Chomsky, William. *Hebrew: The Eternal Language*. Philadephia: Jewish Publication Society, 1957.

Cytowic, Richard E. *The Man Who Tasted Shapes: A Bizarre Medical Mystery Offers Revolutionary Insights into Emotions, Reasoning, and Consciousness*. New York: Putnam, 1993.

Dan, Joseph. *Jewish Mysticism*. 4 vols. Northvale, N. J. and Jerusalem: Jason Aronson, 1998.

———, ed. *The Early Kabbalah*. Trans. Ronald C. Kiener. New York: Paulist Press, 1986.

Davies, Paul. *Superforce: The Search for a Grand Unified Theory of Nature*. New York: Simon & Schuster, 1985.

Desai, Santosh Kumari N. "Our Understanding of Hindu Religion." *Explorations* 6 (Winter, 1987–88), 53–68.

de Santillana, Giorgio and Hertha von Dechend. *Hamlet's Mill: An Essay on Myth and the Frame of Time*. Boston: Gambit, 1969.

de Saussure, Ferdinand. *Course in General Linguistics*. Trans. Wade Baskin. New York: Philosophical Library, 1959.

Eckholm, Eric. "Search for the Origin of Life Enters a Dynamic New Phase." *New York Times*, 29 July 1986, p. C4.

Einstein, Albert. *Cosmic Religion and other Opinions and Aphorisms*. New York: Covici, Friede, 1931.

Eliade, Mircea. *Shamanism*. Trans. Willard R. Trask. Bollingen Series 76. Princeton: Princeton University Press, 1964.

Elior, Rachel. "From Earthly Temple to Heavenly Shrines: Prayer and Sacred Liturgy in the *Hekhalot* Literature and its Relation to Temple Traditions."

Tarbiz 64, April–June 1995.

Finkelstein, David. "Beneath Time: Explorations in Quantum Topology." Unpublished form of a paper based on a lecture to the International Society for the Study of Time, III, in Alpbach, Austria, July 1976.

Freud, Sigmund. *The Interpretation of Dreams*. Trans. James Strachey. New York: Basic Books, n.d.

Gleick, James. "Rethinking Clumps and Voids in the Universe." *New York Times*, 9 November 1986, pp. A1, 40.

Goode, Erica. "When People See a Sound and Hear a Color." *New York Times*, 23 February 1999, p. F3.

Green, Arthur E. "The Role of Jewish Mysticism in a Contemporary Theology of Judaism." *Shefa Quarterly: A Journal of Jewish Thought and Study* 1, September 1978.

———. *New York Times Book Review*, 30 October 1988, pp. 32–33.

Grimal, Nicolas. *A History of Ancient Egypt*. Trans. Ian Shaw. Oxford: Blackwell, 1992.

Gruenwald, Ithamar. *From Apocalypticism to Gnosticism*. Frankfurt am Main: Peter Lang, 1988.

Halifax, Joan. *Shaman: The Wounded Healer*. New York: Crossroads/Continuum, 1982.

Handelman, Susan A. *The Slayers of Moses: The Emergence of Rabbinic Interpretation in Modern Literary Theory*. Albany: State University of New York Press, 1982.

Harner, Michael. *The Way of the Shaman*. Toronto: Bantam Books, 1982.

Harper, William R. *Elements of Hebrew*. Rev. J. M. Powis Smith. Chicago: University of Chicago Press, 1959.

Heninger, S. K. Jr. *Touches of Sweet Harmony: Pythagorean Cosmology and Renaissance Poetics*. San Marino, Ca.: Huntington Library, 1974.

Hertz, J. H., ed. and trans. *Pentateuch and Haftorahs, The*. 2nd ed. London: Soncino Press, 1972.

Hirsch, E. D. Jr. *Validity in Interpretation*. New Haven: Yale University Press, 1967.

Husserl, Edmond. *The Origin of Geometry*. Appendix to Jacques Derrida, *Edmond Husserl's Origin of Geometry: An Introduction*. Trans. with Preface John P. Leavey, Jr. Stony Brook, N.Y.: Nicolas-Hays, 1978.

Idel, Moshe. *Kabbalah: New Perspectives*. New Haven: Yale University Press, 1988.

———. *The Mystical Experience in Abraham Abulafia*. Trans. Jonathan Chipman. Albany: State Unversity of New York Press, 1988.

Jacobs, Lewis. *Hasidic Prayer*. New York: Schocken Books, 1978.

Jalandris (Joseph Jochmans). *Earthfire 1: Exploring the Energies of the Ancients*. San Francisco: n. p., 1981.

Jantsch, Erich. *The Self-Organizing Universe*. Oxford: Pergamon Press, 1980.

Jaynes, Julian. *The Origin of Consciousness in the Breakdown of the Bicameral Mind*. Boston: Houghton Mifflin, 1976.

Jeans, James, Sir. *Physics and Philosophy*. New York: Dover, 1981; orig. pub. 1943.

Jenny, Hans. *Cymatics*. 2 vols. Basil: Basilius Presse, 1974.

Jung, C. G. "Forward." *The I Ching*. Trans. Richard Wilhelm/Cary F. Baynes. Bollingen Series 19. Princeton: Princeton University Press, 1978.

Kaplan, Aryeh. *Meditation and the Bible*. New York: Samuel Weiser, 1978.

———. *Meditation and Kabbalah*. York Beach, Maine: Samuel Weiser, 1982.

Kautzsch, E. *Genenius' Hebrew Grammar*. Trans. A. E. Crowley. Oxford: Clarendon Press, 1910.

Khanna, Madhu. *Yantra: The Tantric Symbol of Cosmic Unity*. London: Thames & Hudson, 1979.

Kook, Abraham Isaac. *The Lights of Penitence*. Trans. and intro. Ben Zion Bokser. New York: Paulist Press, 1978.

Lawlor, Robert. "Ancient Temple Architecture." *Lindisfarne Letter 10: Geometry and Architecture*. West Stockbridge, Mass.: Lindisfarne Press, 1980.

———. "Pythagorean Number as Form, Color and Light." *Lindisfarne Letter 14: Homage to Pythagoras*. West Stockbridge, Mass.: Lindisfarne Press, 1982.

———. *Sacred Geometry*. New York: Crossroad, 1982.

Leet, Leonora. *Renewing the Covenant: A Kabbalistic Guide to Jewish Spirituality*. Rochester, Vt.: Inner Traditions, 1999.

Marks, Lawrence E. *The Unity of the Senses: Interrelations Among the Modalities*. New York: Academic Press, 1978.

McClain, Ernest G. *The Myth of Invariance*. Stony Brook, N.Y.: Nicolas-Hays, 1976.

Michell, John. *City of Revelation*. New York: David McKay, 1972.

Neusner, Jacob. "Varieties of Judaism in the Formative Age." *Jewish Spirituality From the Bible Through the Middle Ages*. Ed. Arthur Green. New York: Crossroad, 1988.

Pagels, Heinz R. *The Cosmic Code: Quantum Physics as the Language of Nature*. Toronto: Bantam Books, 1983.

Patai, Raphael. *Man and Temple in Ancient Jewish Myth and Ritual*. 2nd ed. New York: Ktav, 1967.

———. *The Jewish Alchemists*. Princeton: Princeton University Press, 1995.

———. *The Hebrew Goddess*. 3rd enlarged ed. Detroit: Wayne State University Press, 1990.

Pearce, Joseph Chilton. *Magical Child Matures*. New York: E. P. Dutton, 1985.

Piaget, Jean with Barbel Inhelder and Alina Szeminska. *The Child's Conception of Geometry*. Trans. E. A. Lunzer. New York: Basic Books, 1960.

Principal Shivaram Apte's Sanskrit-English Dictionary. Ed. P. K. Gode and C. G. Karve. Poona, India: Prasad Prakashan, 1957.

Quispel, Gilles. "The Birth of the Child: Some Gnostic and Jewish Aspects." *Eranos Lectures 3: Jewish and Gnostic Man*. Dallas, Tx.: Spring Pub., 1973.

Ricoeur, Paul. *The Rule of Metaphor; Multi-Disciplinary Studies of the Creation of Meaning in Language*. Trans. Robert Czerny. Toronto: University of Toronto Press, 1977.

Rosenzweig, Franz. *The Star of Redemption*. Trans. William W. Hallo. Boston: Beacon Press, 1971.

Rudhyar, Dane. *The Magic of Tone and the Art of Music*. Boulder: Shambhala, 1982.

Rucker, Rudy. *Infinity and the Mind: The Science and Philosophy of the Infinite*. Toronto: Bantam Books, 1983.

Schele, Linda and David Freidel. *A Forest of Kings: The Untold Story of the Ancient Maya*. New York: William Morrow, 1990.

Schiffman, Lawrence H. *Reclaiming the Dead Sea Scrolls*. Philadelphia: Jewish Publication Society, 1994.

Scholem, Gershom. "A Candid Letter About My True Intentions in Studying Kabbalah." *On the Possibility of Jewish Mysticism in Our Time & Other Essays*. Ed. Avraham Shapira, trans. Jonathan Chipman. Philadelphia: Jewish Publication Society, 1997.

———. "Magen David." *Encyclopaedia Judaica*. Jerusalem: Keter; New York: Macmillan, 1971. Vol. XI.

———. *Kabbalah*. New York: New American Library, 1978.

———. *Major Trends in Jewish Mysticism*. New York: Schocken Books, 1961.

———. *On the Kabbalah and Its Symbolism*. Trans. Ralph Manheim. New York: Schocken Books, 1969.

———. *On the Mystical Shape of the Godhead: Basic Concepts in the Kabbalah*. Trans. Joachim Neugroschel, ed. Jonathan Chipman. New York: Schocken Books, 1991.

———. *Origins of the Kabbalah*. Trans. Allan Arkush, ed. R. J. Zwi Werblowsky. Princeton: Jewish Publication Society and Princeton University Press, 1987.

———. *Sabbatai S'evi: The Mystical Messiah*. Trans. R. J. Zwi Werblowsky. Bollingen Series 93. Princeton: Princeton University Press, 1973.

———. "The Star of David: History of a Symbol." *The Messianic Idea in Judaism and Other Essays on Jewish Spirituality*. New York: Schocken Books, 1978.

Schultz, Ron. "Interview: Murray Gell-Mann," *Omni* 7 (May, 1985): 92.

Schwaller de Lubicz, R. A. *The Temple of Man*. Trans. Deborah Lawlor and Robert Lawlor. 2 vols. Rochester, Vt.: Inner Traditions, 1998.

———. *Sacred Science: The King of Pharaonic Theocracy*. Trans. Andre and Goldian VandenBroeck. New York: Inner Traditions, 1982.

Steiner, Rudolf. *The Inner Nature of Music and the Experience of Tone*. Hudson, N. Y.: Anthroposophic Press, 1983.

Suares, Carlo. *The Sepher Yetsira*. Trans. Micheline & Vincent Stuart. Boulder: Shambhala, 1976.

Talbot, Michael. *Mysticism and the New Physics*. New York: Bantam Books, 1981.

Taylor, A. E. *The Mind of Plato*. Ann Arbor: University of Michigan Press, 1960; orig pub. 1922.

Teilhard de Chardin, Pierre. *The Phenomenon of Man*. New York: Harper & Row, 1975.

VandenBroeck, Andre. *Philosophical Geometry*. Rochester, Vt.: Inner Traditions, 1987.

Waite, A. E. *The Holy Kabbalah*. New Hyde Park, N. Y.: University Books, 1969.

Weil, Simone. "The Pythagorean Doctrine." *Intimations of Christianity*. Trans. Elisabeth Chase Geissbuhler. London: Routledge and Kegan Paul, 1957.

Weinberg, Steven. *The First Three Minutes: A Modern View of the Origin of the Universe*. New York: Basic Books, 1977.

Weingreen, J. *A Practical Grammar for Classical Hebrew*. Oxford: Clarendon Press, 1939.

Weiss, Paul A. *The Secret of Life*. Mt. Kisco, N.Y.: Futura, 1973.

Werblowsky, R. J. Zwi and Geoffrey Wigoder, eds. *The Encyclopedia of the Jewish*

Religion. New York: Holt, Rinehart and Winston, 1965.

Wilford, John Noble. "Galactic Evenness Gives Astronomers Pause." *New York Times,* 25 February 1990, p. A25.

———— "Peering Back in Time, Astronomers Glimpse Galaxies Aborning." *New York Times,* 20 October 1998, p. F1.

———— "Search for 'Nemesis' Intensifies Debate Over Extinction." *New York Times,* 18 December 1984, p. C1.

Wolfson, Elliot R. *Along the Path: Studies in Kabbalistic Myth, Symbolism, and Hermeneutics.* Albany, N.Y.: State University of New York Press, 1995.

———— *Circle in the Square: Studies in the Use of Gender in Kabbalistic Symbolism.* Albany: State University of New York Press, 1995.

Yates, Frances A. *The Occult Philosophy in the Elizabethan Age.* London: Routledge and Kegan Paul, 1979.

Yerushalmi, Hayim. *Zakhor: Jewish History and Jewish Memory.* Seattle: Washington University Press, 1982.

Zink, David D. *The Ancient Stones Speak.* New York: E. P. Dutton, 1979.

Zoller, Robert. *Lost Keys to Prediction.* New York: Inner Traditions, 1980.

Zukov, Gary. *The Dancing Wu Li Masters: An Overview of the New Physics.* New York: William Morrow, 1979.

Index of Persons

Abraham ben David of Posquieres, the Rabad. 53–54, 57
Abulafia, Abraham. 36, 62, 90, 146–47, 256, 429n
Akiba, Rabbi. 6, 7, 49, 217
Alshekh, Moses. 67
Altman, Alexander. 50
Aristotle. 98, 101, 102, 338, 374, 397

Baal Shem Tov. 64
Barfield, Owen. 107–08, 150
Beardsley, Monroe C. 102
Benveniste, Emile. 101, 103, 110
Birkoff, Garrett. 373
Black, Max. 102, 209–10
Blau, Joseph Leon. 414n
Blumenthal, David. 123
Boccaccini, Gabriele. 415–16n
Bohm, David. 292, 344, 438n
Bohr, Niels. 365, 374

Boman, Thorlief. 99, 103, 206–07
Born, Max. 357, 368, 376
Brennan, Martin. 123
Buber, Martin. 10
Burrows, Millar. 43

Cairns-Smith, A. Graham. 426n
Campbell, Jeremy. 441n
Cantor, Georg. 359, 395
Capra, Fritjof. 334, 340
Charles. R. H. 38
Cohen, Martin Samuel. xii, 50, 55, 416–17n, 418n
Cordovero, Moses Ben Jacob. 13–20, 233, 245, 316–17, 391, 427n
Cytowic, Richard E. 105, 425n

Dan, Joseph. 46, 55–56, 415n, 419–20n, 427n
Davies, Paul. 346, 358–59, 396–97

Davis, Marc. 122
de Broglie, Louis. 357
Desai, Santosh Kumari N. xii, 431n
de Santillana, Giorgio. 92–94, 112
de Saussure, Ferdinand. 100–01
Dirac, Paul. 345, 371
Donne, John. 218, 433n

Eckholm, Eric. 426n
Einstein, Albert. 138, 388, 394, 406, 412
Eleazar of Worms, 327, 417–18n, 420n
Eliade, Mircea. 433n
Elior, Rachel. 46
Epstein, Abraham. 217
Eratosthenes. 309
Euclid. 109, 207, 309
Eves, Howard. 436n

Feynman, Richard. 338, 365
Finkelstein, David. xii, 374–75, 440n
Frazer, Sir James. 120
Freud, Sigmund. 96–97, 104, 107, 208, 284
Friedmann, Alexandre. 388

Gell-Mann, Murray. 138, 403
Georgi, Howard. 399
Gikatilla, Joseph. 13, 66
Ginzberg, Louis. 217
Glashow, Sheldon. 399, 403
Godwin, Joscelyn. 423n
Goelet, Ogden, Jr. 428n
Goode, Erica. 425n
Graetz, Heinrich. 217
Green, Arthur. 28
Grimal, Nicolas. 428n
Gruenwald, Ithamar. 41, 415n

Halevi, Judah. 90
Halifax, Joan. 433n
Handelman, Susan A. 103, 218
Harner, Michael. 433n
Hayyot, Judah. 65
Heisenberg, Werner. 347, 373, 377

Helmholtz, Hermann. 224
Heninger, S. K. 422n
Hertz, J. H. 193, 195
Hirsch, E. D. Jr. 208–10
Hubble, Edwin. 381
Husserl, Edmund. 109, 210
Hut, Piet. 122
Hykes, David. 179–80

Ibn Umail. 214
Idel, Moshe. **62**, 421n
Isaac ben Abraham, the Blind. 420n, 427n
Isserles, Moses of Cracow. 65

Jacob ha-Kohan. 417n
Jacobs, Lewis. 64
Jantsch, Erich. 438n
Jaynes, Julian. 101
Jeans, Sir James. 345, 357–58, 360, 368–69, 376
Jenny, Hans. 107, 223–24
Jesus. 9, 40
Josephus. 5, 41, 75
Jung, C. G. 441n

Kalonymous Family. 419n
Kaluza, Theodor. 396
Kaplan, Aryeh. xi–xii, 72, 89, 217, 253–57, 414n, 415n, 424n, 430n, 433n, 434n, 436, 438n, 440n, 441n
Karo, Joseph. 7
Keats, John. 95, 100
Kepler, Johannes. 232
Khanna, Madhu. 425n
Kierkegaard, Soren. 144
Klein, Oscar. 396
Kook, Abraham Isaac. 10
Koppel, Jacob. 155
Krippner, Stanley. xii, 433n
Kubrick, Stanley. 410

Laszlo, Ervin. 438b
Lawlor, Robert. x, xii, 82–83, 98–99, 224, 423n

Lieberman, Saul. 46
Longinus. 144
Luria, Isaac. 10, 12–15, 19–20, 28, 63,
    72–73, 141, 145, 153, 156, 164, 178,
    231, 233, 272, 296, 316, 319, 322,
    381–82, 384, 391, 435n

MacLeish, Archibald. 95
Macrobius. 82
Maius, J. H. 47
Mani. 40, 415n
Maria Hebraea. 213–17, 326
Marks, Lawrence E. 97–98, 429n
Mathieu, W. A. 423n
McClain, Ernest G. 437n
Meltzer, David. 416n
Michell, John. 206, 437n
Milton, John. 16, 218, 414n
Moore, Charles A. 431n
Moses ben Jacob of Kiev. 65
Moshe of Narbonne. 36

Nechunya ben ha-kana. 174
Neusner, Jacob. 5, 41
Newton, Sir Isaac. 372, 387

Odeberg, Hugo. 47, 50

Pagels, Heins R. 345, 357, 381–82, 386,
    387, 397–99, 403–04
Patai, Raphael. **213–16**, 420n, 427n
Pauli, Wolfgang. 346
Pearce, Joseph Chilton. 428n
Penzias, Arno. 381
Philo Judaeus. 75
Philolaus. 26, 112–13
Piaget, Jean. 428n
Plato. 26, 82–82, 99, 104–05, 108, 137,
    204, 207, 265, 268, 277–86, 285,
    288–89, 293, 296, 304, 308–09,
    419n, 437–38n
Pythagoras. *See* Pythagorean
Quispel, Gilles. 40

Rabinowitz, I. 103

Radhakrishnan, Sarvepalli. 431n
Raup, David M. 122
Richards, I. A. 102
Ricoeur, Paul. 102, 208
Rincius, Paulus. 14
Rosenzweig, Franz. 10
Rudhyar, Dane. 423n

Sabbatai Tz'vi. 391
Salam, Abdus. 399–400
Scholem, Gershom. 7, 10, 25, 40–41,
    46, 54, 55, 56–57, **65–67**, 75, 86,
    171, 213, 383, 413n, 414n, 415n,
    416n, 418n, 419n, 421n, 422n,
    432n, 441n
Schrodinger, Erwin. 357, 368, 386
Schwaller de Lubicz, R. A. 131–32,
    424n
Sepkoski, J. John. 122
Shiffman, Lawrence H. 5, 41, 43, 413n
Simeon ben Yohai. 58–61
Smith, Huston. 179
Sophocles. 284, 434n
Steiner, Rudolf. 158, 232
Suares, Carlo. 110–11

Taylor, A. E. 437n
Teilhard de Chardin, Pierre. 441n
Theon of Smyrna. 137, 309, 436n

Urbach, Ephrayim E. 46

VandenBroeck, Andre. 423n
Vermes, Geza. 5, 41
Vital, Chayyim. xii, 15, 19, 26, 63, 64,
    66, 129, 140–41, 253, 270, 272–73,
    280–89, 293, 301–04, 319, 386,
    418n, 421n, 429–30n, 433n
Von Bertalanffy, Ludwig. 338, 428n
Von Dechend, Hertha. 92–94, 112
Von Dobschutz, E. 206
Von Newmann, John. 373
Wacholder, Ben Zion. 415n
Waite, A. E. 253
Weil, Simone. 423n, 426n, 440n

Weinberg, Steven. 351, 381, 385, 387, 388, 398–400, 411

Weiss, Paul A. 438n

Werblowsky, R. J. Zwi. 418n

Wheeler, John A. 397

Wigoder, Geoffrey. 418n

Wilson, Robert W. 381

Wittgenstein, Ludwig. 102

Wolfson, Elliot R. **417–18n**, 427n

Wordsworth, William. 27, 204–05, 414n

Work of the Chariot, 261–62, 416n

Yates, Frances A. 414n

Yeats, William Butler. 76, 423n

Yerushalmi, Joseph Hayim. 415n

Zoller, Robert. xii, 424n

Zosimus the Panopolitan. 213

Zukov, Gary. 440n

Index of Primary Sources

Bible, The. 2, 4, 9, 27, 30–38, 44, 51–52, 69, **193–97**, 218–19, 221, 327–28

Bahir, Sefer ha-. 13, 53, 56, 57, 86, 203, 253, 256, 257, 266, 293, 307, 318–20, 324–25, 414n

Baraita de Ma'aseh Bereshit. 220

Bhagavad-Gita. 191–92, 197

Chokhmah, Sefer ha-, by Eleazar of Worms. 420n

Cratylus, by Plato. 104–05

Dead Sea Scrolls. 5, 41, 214

Enoch, The Ethiopic Book of or 1 Enoch. 38, 44, 45, 47, 48, 56, 132–33

Enoch, The Hebrew Book of or 3 Enoch. 46–47, 48, 51, 56, 65, 71

Esh M'Saref. 215–16

Etz Chayyim, by Vital. xii, 15, 19, 26, 63, 66, 129, 140–41, 203, 253, 270, 272–73, 280, 288–89, 293, 301–04, 319, 386, 418n, 429–30n, 433n

Hekhalot Rabbatai. 45

Îśa Upanishad. 190–91, 197

Massekhut Atzilut. 86, 391

Midrash. 8, 90, 193

Mishnah. 7, 44, 217, 419n

Pardes Rimmonim, by Cordovero. 14–19, 316–17, 427n

Portae Lucis, by Rincius. 14

Raza Rabbah. 53–54, 56, 57

Seder Eliyyahu Zuta. 54–55

Sefer Yetzirah. xi, 3, 5, 6, 7, 11, 13, 15, 20, 26–27, 52–53, 57, 75, 85, 86, 87–95, 105, 110, 117–21, 123, 127–28, 133, 136, 137, 148, 166, 175, 177, 178, 203, 216–17, 228, 253–56, 296, 304–08, 310, 317–24, 370, 378, 393–94, 410, 420n, 422n, 430n, 434n

Sha'arei Gan Eden, by Koppel. 155

Sha'arei Orah, by Gikatilla. 13

Shem, Sefer ha-, by Eleazar of Worms. 327

Shi'ur Komah. 45–51, 53, 54, 55, 56, 57, 126, 145, 256, 416n, 418n, 424n

Shulchan Arukh, by Karo. 7

Shushan Sodoth, by Moses ben Jacob of Kiev. 65

Talmud. 8, 20, **32**, 37, 39, 47, 54, 55, 67, 208, 212, 231, 297, 391, 417n, 418n, **433n**

Temunah, Sefer ha-. xii, 187, 231, 391, 433n

Tikkunei Zohar. 86, 391

Timaeus, by Plato. 204, 437–38n

Zohar. 8, 13, 15, 20, 22, 55, **57–66**, 69–71, 72, 85–86, 110, 154, 203, 204, 218, 220–222, 229, 247, 249–51, 258, 270, 280, 283, 296, 299–300, 307, 317, 324, 326, 386, 416n, 421–22n

  Idra Rabba. 58–59, 129, 236, 285, 300, 418n

  Idra Zuta. 59–60, 64, 273, 418n

Index of Subjects

Alchemy. **212–17**, 228, 256, 319, 405

Adam Kadmon, primeval man, cosmic man, anthropocosmos. 52, 57, 92–93, 121, 145, 253, 256, 290, **322**, 410, 424n

Antimatter. 345–46, 353, 362–63, 371–73

Astronomy, solar and lunar cycles and calendars. 27, 36–37, 88, 90, 92–93, 118–19, 121–23, 126, 128–30, 132–37, 371–73

Biblical Figures:
    Aaron. 5, 32
    Abraham. 30–31, 35, 51, 52, 94, 130, 196, 197, 296
    Adam. 108–09, 124–25, 193–94, 240, 285, 289, 322, 327, 410
    Bezaleel, 249

Daniel. **37–38**, 43, 44, 45, 47, 56, 417n

David. 5, 212

Eliezer. 5, 196

Elijah. **34–35**, 54–55, 249, 419n

Elisha. **34–35**

Enoch. 417n

Essau. 51, 195

Eve. 193–94, 285, 327

Ezekiel. 4, 10, **34–38**, 40, 44, 45, 52, 56, 57, 65, 256, 417n, 419n

Isaac. 31, 195

Isaiah. 36

Jacob. 23, **51–52**, 71–72, 195, **417–18n**

Joseph. 195–96

Laban. 51, 196

Lot. 195

Methuselah. 132

Michah. 34

Moses. 4, 5, 7, 8, 32, 53, 129, 249, 327, 416n, 418n

Noah. 195

Samson. 197

Sarah. 30–31, 51–52, 130

Solomon. 4, 91, 212, 215

Zechariah. 70

Biblical Quotations:

Gen. 1:9; 216. Gen. 1:14; 137. Gen. 2:23; 193. Gen. 2:24; 193. Gen. 4:1; 193.   Gen. 3:6, 16; 194. Gen. 6:9; 195. Gen. 7:2; 194. Gen. 9:5; 194. Gen. 9:20; 194. Gen. 10:5; 195. Gen. 11:3; 194. Gen. 11:7; 194. Gen. 13:11; 194. Gen. 13:16; 196.   Gen. 15:10; 194. Gen. 16:3; 194. Gen. 17:1–19; 9. Gen. 18:1–2; 196. Gen. 19:8; 194. Gen. 19:9; 195. Gen. 20:7; 194. Gen. 22:13; 31. Gen. 22:18; 31. Gen. 23:6; 195. Gen. 24:16; 194. Gen. 24:21, 22, 24, 26, 29, 30, 32, 58, 61; 196. Gen. 24:40; 196. Gen. 24:65; 195. Gen. 25:27; 195. Gen. 26:10; 194. Gen. 26:13; 195. Gen. 26:31; 194. Gen. 29:19; 194. Gen. 29:32, 34; 194. Gen. 30:15, 20; 194. Gen. 30:43; 195. Gen. 31:49; 194. Gen. 31:50; 196. Gen. 32:7; 1945. Gen. 32:24; 196. Gen. 32:28; 417n. Gen. 32:30; 196. Gen. 33:1; 194. Gen. 34:14; 194. Gen. 34:20; 194. Gen. 37:15, 17; 195. Gen. 37:19; 194. Gen. 38:1–2; 195. Gen. 38:25; 194. Gen.   39:2; 195. Gen. 39:11; 194. Gen. 39:14; 194, 195. Gen. 38:25; 194. Gen. 39:11, 14; 194. Gen. 40:5; 194. Gen. 41:2, 33, 38; 196. Gen. 41:44; 194. Gen. 42:11, 13. Gen. 42:25, 35; 194. Gen. 42:30, 33; 196. Gen. 43:3, 5, 6, 7, 11, 13; 196. Gen. 43: 17, 19; 195. Gen. 44:11, 13; 194. Gen. 44:15, 26; 196.

Gen. 44:17; 195. Gen. 45:1, 22; 194. Gen. 47:20; 194. Gen. 49:6, 28; 194. Exod. 4:22; 9, 130, 310, 417n. Exod. 6:6–7; 327. Exod. 7:5; 327. Exod. 9:1; 327. Exod. 16:23; 131. Exod. 19; 6; 33. Exod. 25:40; 249. Exod. 29:1; 32. Exod. 29:20; 32. Exod. 29:31–33; 33. Exod. 29:44–46; 33, 416n. Exod. 31:13, 16; 131. Exod. 33:11, 14–15, 20; 416n. Exod. 34:20; 32. Exod. 35:10; 91. Exod. 36:2; 249. Lev. 11:44; 39. Deut. 6:4,5; 69, 413n. Deut. 16:9–10; 131. Deut. 29:28; 326. Jud. 13:6; 197. 1 Kings 19:22; 34. 2 Kings 2:11–12; 34–35. Job 26:7, 13; 90. Ps. 133:3; 60. Isa. 6:1; 36. Ezek. 1:26, 28; 36. Ezek. 2:1–2; 35. Mic. 6: 6, 8; 34. Dan. 7:9, 13–14, 18; 37. Dan. 8:15, 17; 37

Big Bang. 126, 243, 245, 372, 380–82, 384–89, 401

Chabad Tradition. 236

Chakras. 169–75, 181

Chaos. 124–25, 338

Christianity, Christian. 15, 41, 45, 47–48, 126, 178, 415n, 418n, 433n

Chariot. *See* Merkabah

Circumcision. 31, 154

Creation Accounts:

In Genesis 1. 3, 4, 26, 28, 75, 124, 138, 163, 185, 202–03, 206, 214, **220–31**, 241, 285, 438n

In *Zohar.* 220–22, 258

Cube, significance of. 255–56, 265, 298–300, 322

Da'at (Knowledge). 22, 27, 119, 139, 203, 236, 246–47, 295, 303, 316, 326–28, 334

Diadems. 59, 427n

Diatonic Scale. 80–81, 135, 241–42

Dimensions, geometric. 138, 337, 393–412

Double Heart. **163–65, 169–75**, 183–

84

Duplication of the Cube. 27, 203, 296, **308–10**, 315, 324, 436n

Egypt (Mitzraim). 8–10, 129, 131, 134, 213, 216–17, 427n

Ein Sof. 221, 277, 383, 386, 388

Essenes. 5–8, 41, **43–45**, 47, 75, 214, 217, 419n

Faces. 58, 67, 188, 416n

Feminine Divine Aspects. 27, 57–62, 64, 67–72, 122–26, 176–78, 270–75, 280–88, 388, 390, 421–22n, 427n

Four Worlds of Kabbalah. 8, 22, 36, 62, 86, 203, 229, 231, 240–43, 245, 252, 258, 265, 267,   285, 296, 325, 334, 388–95, 400–02

Garden of Eden. 108–11, 124, 240, 246, 285, 392, 428n, 433–34n

Gematria. 3, **11–12**, 25–27, 87–88, 110–11, **118–129**, 141–49, 186

General Systems Theory. 338, 356, 365, 397–99, 438n

Glory (Kavod). 36, 39, 48–49, 53, 57, 256, 417n

Gnosticism. 40–41, 62, 75, 419n

Golem. 256

Greece, Greek. 9, 27, 74–75, 204, 206–08, 217, 265, 296, 308–09, 332, 393

GUT (Grand Unification Theory). 396–99

Harmonic Series. 3, 24, 75–77, **80–81**, 167, 178–90, 222–23, 230, 254, 423n, 430n, 437n

In conjunction with geometry and number. 3, 11, 26, 36, 75, 87, 202, 214, 241

Hasidism (modern). 9, 10, 44, 63–64

Medieval Ashkenazi. 53, 55–57, 417–18n

Heart. 89, **91–94**, 105, 110, 113, 121,

132, 138, 149, 163–64

Hekhalot. See Merkabah

Hermetic Tradition. 8, 204, 216

Hexagram (Star of David, Shield of David/Magen David, Solomon's Seal). 3, 6, 8, 9, 26, 93–   9 4 , 1 1 3 , 172, 177, 202, **212–17**, **218–32**, **260–89**, 321, 326, 433n, 436n

Symbol of Heart Chakra. 94, 172, 212

Hinduism (Yoga, India). 8–9, 169, 176, 178, 189–92, 223, 254

Holy of Holies (in the Temple). 4, 60, 158, 265, 297, 300, 307, **309**, 315, 420n, 436n

Ish (Man). 26, 169, 177–78, 185, **189–97**, 432n

Islam. 41, 212–13, 215–16

Kedushah (Prayer). 49–50, 71, 157

Language. 11, 24–26, 75, **94–113**, 117, 136, 188

Levites. 41, 51, 55

Lurianic Cosmology. xii, 12, 22, 28, 60–64, 72–73, 129, 140–41, 150, 153, 154, 203, 253,   270, 381, 385, 387, 389, 399, 400, 410, 441n

Tzimtzum. 15, 19, 63, 145, 146, 150, 277, 288, 383, **385–409**, 414n

Shevirah. 19, 63, 289, 293–94, 399, 433n

Tikkun. 19, 63, 72, 94, 145, 153, 229, 231, 247, 273, 287–88, 293, 298, 300, 390–91

Mayan Calendar. 135–36

Measure of the Body. 49, 145, 256

Meditative Practices. 6, 167–68, 175–81, 189–90, 253–55, 434n

Menorah. 9, 248–49

Merkabah (Chariot) Texts. 7, 9, 34–37, 41, **45–57**, 62, 63, 145, 231, 256,

391, 416n, 418n, 419n, 424n

Messiah, Messianic. 34, 40, 113, 135, 227, 231, 273, 390–92

Metatron, angel. 47–53, 57, 65, 71, 417n, 418n, 422n

Microwave Background Radiation. 381, 384–85, 441n

Mother Letters (in the *Sefer Yetzirah*). 89, 133, 166–67, 175, 216, 228, 267

Name of Forty-Two Letters (in the prayer "Ana Bekhoach"). 174–75, 430n

Name of Seventy-Two Letters. 428–29n

Neolithic. 9, 94, 136

Nun (Hebrew letter). 427n, 428n

Pagan deities:
    Amitabha, Buddhist. 9
    Apollo, Greek. 76, 308–09, 315
    Gaia, Greek. 27, 123–25, 186, 427n
    Horus, Egyptian. 9, 131–32, 134
    Krishna, Hindu. 9, 191
    Shiva, Hindu. 191
    Vishnu, Hindu. 191

Partzufim (divine personalities). 19, 22–23, 28–29, 63, 66–68, 72, 129–30, 152–56, 163, 166, 184–85, 188, 214, 268–94, 300–04

Pharisees. 5, 41, 45

Platonic (regular) Solids. 257–69, 277–86, 288–89, 293, 296, 304, 328

Prayer. 6, 44, 50–52, 58, 63–64, 68–73, 149–50, 157, 164, 167, 168, 174–75, 415n, 418n, 419n, 429n, 430n, 441n

Presence (Shekhinah). 48, 49, 60, 70–71, 157, 176, 309, 322, 388, 390, 416n, 417n, 435n

Priesthood, Hebraic, Temple. 2–11, 23, 24, 25, 30, 32–39, 41, 43, 44, 46, 52, 55, 58, 60, 61, 62, 67, 70, 71, 74, 167–68, 203, 213, 214, 216–17, 252, 265, 296, 315, 326, 416n, 417n, 419n

Zadokite priestly family. 5–7, 35, 41–42, 45, 214, 415–16n

Probability. 356–57, 363, 376–79

Provencal Kabbalists. 53–54, 55–57

Providence. 393, 395, 406

Pythagoras, Pythagorean. xi, 5, 6, 8, 11, 26, **74–87**, 94, 99, 108, 112–13, 117–19, 128, 137, 202, 204, 206–07, 217, 229, 245, 293, 374–75, 392, 410, 436–37n, 440n

Quantum Physics. xii, 28, **332–98**, **402–12**

Quantum Cosmology. 28, **380–412**

Qumran. *See* Essenes

Rabbinical, talmudic. 4–7, 37, 45–46, 56, 131, 208, 211, 217, 392, 419n

Sabbath. 130–31, 133, 136–38, 143, 227, 230–31

Sabbatical Cosmic Structure. 20, 28, 138, **228–30**, 241, **390–412**, 433n, 441n

Sabbath Star Diagram. **232–52**, 267, 271, 274, 278, 287–89, 295, 301–03, 306, 325, 328, 400–02, 441n

Sacrifice (priestly practice of). 2, 5–6, **30–34**, 43, 50–52, 135, 174

Sadducees. 5, 6, 41, 43, 45

Science of Expressive Form, the. xi, 24, 96, **204–12**

Secret Nature of the Priestly Legacy. 7, 9, 38–39, 42, 43, 45, 55, 418n

Sefirot. 6, 17–23, 53, 56, 57, 63, 138, 140–08, **169–188**, 239–40, 256, **300–04**, 319–22, 392

Semiotics. 100–03

Shamanic Tradition. 227–28, 433n

Shemitot. 187, 231, 391–93, 395

Sh'ma (Prayer). 6, 26, 30, 44, 50, **68–73**, 111, 149–50, 154, 157, 160, 167–68, 179, 189, 223, 413n, **421n**, 430n

Siddur. 54–55, 418n

Sinai Covenant. 118, 131, 134–35, 139,

143, 428n

Mount Sinai. 4, 227, 249

Son, Hebraic Secret Doctrine of. **9–10**, 22, 24, 25–26, **30–73**, 74–75, **113**, 118, 128, 142, 177, 185, 197–98, 214, 216, 253, 296, 328, 395, 408, 411, 417n

  Israel as the divine son (Ex. 4:22). 9, 12, 26, 32, 39, 43, 44, 61, 71–72, 131, 143, 309–10, **322**, 417n

  Son (*ben*). 27, 118, **121–29**, 132, 140–46, 156

  Son of man (*ben adam*). 35, 37–39, 43, 47, 48, 55, 58, 132, 417–18n

  Son of the world to come (*ben olam ha-ba*). 49–50, 52, 53, 54, 55, 68, 126, 139, 142, 145, 147, 186, 424n

  Ze'ir Anpin, the Partzuf of the son. 28–29, 58, 63, 65, 66, 72–73, 129–30, 152, 164, 172, 253, 277–94, 304, 408, 417–18n, 422n

Soul Levels. 22, 89, 170–73, 176, 181–84, 187, 230, 253, 395, **404–12**

Superstring Theory. 138, 402

Supersymmetry Theory. 396–97

Synchronicity. 395, 406, 407

Synesthesia. 91–92, 105–06

Taoism. 173, 375

Temple, First and Second, Desert Sanctuary. 4–7, 25, 34, 36, 41, 43, 44, 45, 46, 50, 52, 55, 56, 265, 315, **326**, 415n, 416n, 419n

Tetractys (Pythagorean symbol). 8, **84–87**, 148, 375, 436n

Tetragrammaton. 12, 24, 26–27, 58, 60, 65, 75, **117–164**, 165–67, 175, 177–78, 186, 190, 228, 291–92, 309, 383, 408, 437–38n

  Expansions. 12, 126–27, **140–47**, 428n

  Pronunciation. 158–64

  Vertical Form. 22–23

Throne of Glory. 35, 39, 47–49, 65, 69, 71, 132, 254–56, 391, 416n

Tiferet (Sefirah signifying the divine son, Jacob, the heart of Adam Kadmon, and the Tetragrammaton). 23, 60, 72, 121, 130, 163, 166, 171, 184, 187–88, 408, 410, 417n

Tree of Life Diagram. x, xi, 3, 6, 8, 9, **12–24**, 26, 56, 57, 62, 63, 66–67, 70, 75, 87, 110, 121, 138, 140–49, 163, 165, 168, 181, 198, 202–07, 228, 232–51, 316–328, 334, 380, 401, 437n

  Adam Kadmon Tree. 21–22, 57, 166, 169, 171, 183, 240

  Sefer Yetzirah Tree, 27, 91, 155, **257–94**, 380, 435–36n

  Sixfold Tree of Knowledge. 27, 228, 252, **304–18**

Uncertainty Principle. 347, 373, 377

Unification (Yichud). 3, 60–61, 64, 69–70, 153–55, 163, 270–77, 307, 390, 408, 422n

Vehayah, Veyehi. 12, 414n, 432n

Other Titles of Interest

The Universal Kabbalah

Leonora Leet, Ph.D.

This landmark work by an innovative modern Kabbalist develops a scientific model for kabbalistic cosmology and soul psychology derived from the kabbalistic diagram of the Tree of Life and the author's own Sabbath Star diagram—a configuration of seven Star of David hexagrams. This geometric model begins with the four worlds of the classical Kabbalah, which bring us to the present time and birthright level of the soul, and is then expanded to three higher enclosing worlds or levels of evolving consciousness. The Sabbath Star diagram therefore accommodates both the emanationist cosmology of the earlier Zoharic Kabbalah and the future orientation of the later Kabbalah of Isaac Luria. The hexagram elements that construct each expansion of the Sabbath Star diagram configure the cosmic stages of each of its "worlds." The matrix that is produced by these construction elements configures the level of the multi-dimensional soul that is correlated with each cosmic world. In its final stage, this model unites the finite and infinite halves of the Sabbatical world in a way that exemplifies the secret doctrine of the Kabbalah.

Not only does this work offer a new, inclusive model for the Kabbalah but it also provides a basis for complexity theory, with its final extrapolation to infinity. The universality of this model is further shown by its applicability to such other domains as physics, sociology, linguistics, and human history. This universal model encodes the laws of all cosmic manifestation in terms that are particularly coherent with the formulations of the Kabbalah, giving a mathematical basis to many aspects of this mystical tradition and providing a new synthesis of science and spirituality for our time that may well write a new chapter to the Kabbalah.

528 PAGES, 8.5 X 11 HARDCOVER • ISBN-13: 978-0-89281-189-2
16-PAGE COLOR INSERT AND 79 BLACK-AND-WHITE ILLUSTRATIONS

The Kabbalah of the Soul

The Transformative Psychology and Practices of Jewish Mysticism

Leonora Leet, Ph.D.

Working from an original synthesis of the major kabbalistic traditions of cosmology derived from the Bible, the *Zohar*, and the school of Isaac Luria, Leonora Leet has erected a new framework for understanding the mechanism of the transformative spiritual work that enables the human soul to reach increasingly higher dimensions of consciousness. She develops a powerful meditative technique called "the Transformative Moment," whose workings are exemplified by Jacob and Joseph and that allow the individual to progress through all the higher levels of the soul, even possibly to attain the miraculous powers of the legendary spiritual masters. She correlates the hierarchy of soul levels with Ezekiel's Throne vision to show the various paths the soul may travel toward self-realization: sex, love, power, knowledge, holiness, and unification. The first four paths relate to the four-faced living creatures—the bull-ox, lion, eagle, and man. The final two paths correlate to the prophet and the envisioned man on the throne whom he recognizes to be his divine higher self, the knowledge that defines the secret doctrine of the whole of the Jewish mystical tradition culminating in the Kabbalah.

384 PAGES, 6 X 9 • ISBN-13: 978-0-89281-957-7

Renewing the Covenant

A Kabbalistic Guide to Jewish Spirituality

Leonora Leet, Ph.D.

The covenant that bound God to the Patriarchs in a special relationship of obligation and empowerment was renewed by God with Israel at Sinai and Moab. Each of these three Jewish covenants can be associated with a particular spiritual practice: the Patriarchal Covenant with Father Isaac's practice of meditation; The Sinai Covenant of Holiness with the observance of the Sabbath required in its Ten Commandments, and the Moab Covenant of Love, comprising the entire Mosaic Torah, with the practice of prayer instituted there. In *Renewing the Covenant*, Leonora Leet shows how this ladder of increasingly demanding and potent covenantal practices can enable one to ascend to ever higher levels of mystical Judaism.

At this threshold of a new millennium, increasing numbers of people are seeking a more direct connection with the Divine. To aid such a process, *Renewing the Covenant* provides new paths for entering the treasurehouse of Jewish spirituality and achieving higher consciousness, paths that can deepen the devotions of both nonobservant and traditionally observant Jews. This process of covenant renewal begins with effective kabbalistic techniques of meditation combining mantra with visualization, proceeds through the return to a reconstructed Sinai Sabbath, and arrives at the culminating practice of ritual prayer whose performance can fulfill the kabbalistic purpose of creation. When undertaken in the steps laid out by Dr. Leet, this process can help many to discover forms of spiritual practice precisely tailored for the modern world, as well as a new appreciation for the rich spiritual heritage of Judaism.

272 PAGES, 6 X 9 • ISBN-13: 978-0-89281-713-9

Inner Traditions • Bear & Company
P.O. Box 388
Rochester, VT 05767
1-800-246-8648
www.InnerTraditions.com
Or contact your local bookseller

Leonora Leet (1929–2004) received her Ph.D. from Yale University and was a professor of English at St. John's University who specialized in Renaissance literature, a field in which she published widely. She pursued her study of the Kabbalah and Jewish spirituality under noted kabbalist Aryeh Kaplan and Zalman Schachter-Shalomi and found support for her work in scholars such as Stanley Krippner, Martin Samuel Cohen, Robert Zoller, Santosh Desai, John Anthony West, Joscelyn Godwin, and Robert Lawlor, with whom she studied Pytharoean geometry at Lindisfarne Institute.

Leet's previous books on the Kabbalah are *Renewing the Covenant*, *The Universal Kabbalah*, and *The Kabbalah of the Soul*.